THE ARMED FORCES OF WORLD WAR II

Andrew Mollo

THE ARMED FORCES OF WORLD WAR II

Uniforms, insignia and organization

GREENWICH EDITIONS

This edition published in 2000 by
Greenwich Editions
10 Blenheim Court
Brewery Road
London N7 9NT

First published in 1981 by Macdonald & Co

A CIP catalogue record for this book is available from the British Library

ISBN 0-86288-350-4

Production by Omnipress
Printed in The Slovak Republic
60373

Little, Brown and Company (UK)
Brettenham House
Lancaster Place
London WC2E 7EN

Andrew Mollo would like to thank Philip Buss whose advice and consultancy have been invaluable. Grateful thanks are due to Christopher Barbarski, Eric Lefèvre, David Littlejohn, Laurie Milner, E. W. Jørgensen, Guido Rossignoli, D. M. Sekulich, P. Simonsen, René Smeets, Kari Stenman, Glen Sweeting, Thorkild Tønnesen, François Vauvillier, Paul Verheye and Ernesto Vitetti.

Malcolm McGregor would like to express his sincere gratitude to the individuals and institutions listed below for help and information generously provided during the preparation of the figure drawings and in the course of his researches into material for the rank insignia charts. While giving credit to those whose contributions have helped in the effort to make the illustrations in this book as accurate as possible, he owns that any errors or omissions are his alone.

The staff of the Photographic Department of the Imperial War Museum, London, without whom it would surely have been impossible to carry out the work in this particular fashion; Reading Room of the Imperial War Museum, London; Belgian Embassy, London; Musée Royal de l'Armée, Brussels; Royal Norwegian Embassy, London; Norwegian Naval Museum, Horten, Norway; Greek Embassy, London; General Air Staff, Athens; Dept. of Army History, Hellenic Army Headquarters, Athens; Royal Danish Embassy, London; Mariners Bibliotek, Copenhagen; Inga Fl. Rasmussen, Tøjhusmuseet, Copenhagen; Chief of Defence, Denmark; South African Embassy, London; Chief of the SADF, Republic of South Africa; Finnish Embassy, London; General Headquarters Finnish Defence Forces, Helsinki; New Zealand High Commission, London; Ministry of Defence, Wellington, New Zealand; Ministry of National Defence, Taiwan, Republic of China; Sikorski Institute, London; Museums of the Royal Corps of Transport, Aldershot; Lieut-Col Howard Cole; Marshal of the Royal Air Force Sir Neil Cameron GCB CBE DSO DFC past Chief of the Defence Staff, London; Major A. J. Donald RM, Royal Marines Museum, Southsea, Hants; Royal Naval Museum, Portsmouth; Royal Air Force Museum, London; National Maritime Museum, London; Gurkha Museum, Aldershot; Black Watch Museum, Perth, Scotland; Museum of the Corps of Royal Military Police, Chichester, Sussex; Ian V. Hogg; Commander Maitland-Thornton OBE RNVR, Mons; Frank Steff; Brian L. Davis; Mrs R. A. Rigg; Christopher Barbarski; Royal Netherlands Embassy, London; Stephen Bosley of Coldstream Military Antiques, Amersham, England.

Picture acknowledgements
The uniforms of the Allied forces were painted by Malcolm McGregor, who also painted the plates of rank insignia. Pierre Turner painted the uniforms of the Axis forces.

The organisational diagrams were drawn up by Adrian Gilbert and Michael Hodson.

The largest single source of photographs for the book has been the collection of Andrew Mollo himself (Historical Research Unit), and we were also fortunate in being able to use the resources of the Robert Hunt Library. These apart, the photographs came from the following organisations and individuals:
Associated Press; Australian War Memorial; Bibliothèque Nationale, Paris; Bundesarchiv, Koblenz; Communist Party Picture Library; Etablissement Cinématographique et Photographique des Armées, Paris; Imperial War Museum; Musée de la Guerre, Vincennes; National Maritime Museum; Novosti; PAV; J. Piekalkiewicz; Signal; Sikorski Institute, London; US Air Force; US Army; US Coast Guard; US Marine Corps and US Navy.

For their help in drawing up the table of ranks, Orbis Publishing would like to thank the embassies of the following nations: Belgium, Bulgaria, Denmark, Finland, France, Hungary, Japan, Netherlands, Norway, Poland, Soviet Union, West Germany, Yugoslavia.

CONTENTS

INTRODUCTION

With the publication of this volume I have at last produced the sort of book about which I dreamed as a boy of five, when I first became interested in military uniform at the end of World War II. Living as I did near Aldershot – home of the British Army – I saw so many men and women in uniform that my childish curiosity led me to ask what a particular uniform or badge signified. The postwar period when men and women all over Europe were gratefully shedding their uniforms, was a pretty bleak one for anybody trying to satisfy such an unusual interest. There were no lavishly stocked model shops, no book shops offering rows of titles ranging from the armies of Byzantium to those of NATO. The only military books available were the Times and Hamilton illustrated histories of World Wars I and II, and the dreary old regimental histories. So bit by bit I assembled my own scrap books from cuttings and the odd coloured postcard or photograph. Any representation of a soldier, however inaccurate, was gratefully pasted in. While other children were preoccupied with football and cricket I used to demolish the Illustrated London News.

This book has been divided into five main sections, each of which deals with a major theatre of operations. The armed forces engaged in a particular theatre are described under three sub-headings – background, organisation and uniform. The coverage given to a nation is not necessarily in proportion to its size or contribution to the war. The major nations are already well covered in numerous books, but there is very little readily available in the English language on the smaller nations.

The uniform text is perforce brief, but the running text is complemented by Malcolm McGregor's and Pierre Turner's superb artwork, the detailed captions to the figure drawings, and the 165 black and white photographs. Obviously one has not been able to go into the minutiae so beloved by the expert, but in no other book will be found 365 figure drawings based on contemporary photographs, 53 coloured charts of badges of rank and other insignia, and 14 organisational diagrams.

THE WAR IN EUROPE 1939-40

On 1 September 1939 the armed forces of Nazi Germany began World War II by invading Poland. Within a year, Denmark, Norway, Holland, Belgium and France had also been defeated by the German armies and Great Britain was preparing to resist invasion. Meanwhile, the Soviet Union had attacked Finland and, during the winter of 1939–40, the 'Winter War' was fought. With the notable exception of Nazi Germany, the organisation of the armed forces which fought these early campaigns was dominated by memories of the past (most particularly by memories of World War I) and this was also the case in the design of uniforms. Most nations began the war with many formations equipped with clothing of an earlier epoch; some were in a process of transition (the British Army, for example) and some wore World War I uniforms designed for other nations' armies.

Germany

Army

On 16 March 1935 Adolf Hitler re-introduced conscription and announced to the world the formation of a German air force. Needless to say this brought the restrictions imposed on the size and the strength of the German armed forces to an abrupt end. The next four years saw the rapid expansion of the German Army; a transformation from General Seeckt's *Reichswehr* into Hitler's *Wehrmacht*.

In September 1939 the German Army went to war with forces which, although well trained in the latest concepts of mechanised warfare, had gained little combat experience except in the Spanish Civil War; and that had been very limited. Much of the specialised motorised equipment had yet to reach the field armies and so all the non-panzer and non-motorised divisions still travelled on foot and relied mainly on horses to haul their equipment and artillery.

Whatever the shortcomings in quantity and quality of equipment, German human material was of the best. The Versailles Treaty, which had limited the *Reichswehr* to one hundred thousand men, was turned to advantage, in that only the best personnel were retained in a completely professional army. There was even a surplus of soldiers to man the armed police forces of the various German states (*Landespolizei*), and these were later to be incorporated in the Army when conscription was re-introduced. There was, in addition, a vast pool of semi-trained manpower in the para-military formations of the Nazi Party.

Apart from the conscripts the German Army needed to attract volunteers who would make a career in the Army. To achieve this, terms of service were made more attractive, smart new uniforms introduced and well-equipped modern barracks constructed. At the same time attempts were made to break down much of the traditional petty authoritarianism of the Army, while retaining and even elevating the privileged position of the German soldier in society. The soldiers of the *Wehrmacht* set themselves very high professional standards so that when they went to war in 1939, they did so with enthusiasm and the strong conviction that they were the finest soldiers in the world.

Hitler's main problem with the Army came from certain senior officers who opposed his aggressive foreign policy and held conservative views on the conduct of war, but these men had little influence. Their opposition was always hesitant, and affected by their approval of Hitler's modernisation programme, while they would always be bypassed or replaced if they proved too troublesome. The German Army of World War II was in general a loyal, obedient and confident instrument of the Nazi dictator.

Organisation In March 1939 the operational control of the Armed Forces was unified under the *Oberkommando der Wehrmacht* (OKW) whose chief was *Generaloberst* (Colonel-General) Keitel.

1

2

3

The management of the Army was the responsibility of the Army High Command, the *Oberkommando des Heeres* (OKH), which included the General Staff, although it was the Supreme Commander, Adolf Hitler, who was increasingly to take over the day-to-day running of the war.

In 1939 Germany was divided into 13 geographical districts known as *Wehrkreise*, each of which was a depot for a number of divisions and formed a 'home-base' for their regiments. On mobilisation there were 51 active divisions:

39 infantry divisions (including four motorised);
5 panzer divisions (plus a panzer brigade);
4 light divisions;
3 mountain divisions.

When Germany mobilised, the system was rapidly expanded to include 16 reserve, 21 territorial (*Landwehr*) and 14 so-called *Ergänzangsdivisionen* divisions. During 1939–40 the number of panzer divisions was doubled (mainly by 'converting' light divisions) so that there were 10 such divisions by the spring of 1940.

For the Polish Campaign the OKW created two army groups: Army Group North (divided into 2 armies each of 3 corps) consisted of 1 panzer division, 1 mixed Army/SS panzer division, 2 motorised divisions, 16 infantry divisions and a cavalry brigade. Army Group South (10 corps in 3 armies) consisted of 4 panzer divisions, 4 light, 21 infantry and

Left: Staff officers of the 7th Panzer Division (commanded by Erwin Rommel) discuss their plans during the campaign of the spring of 1940. The officer in the centre, holding the map, is wearing the older pattern field cap, without chinstrap, and the badge on his left breast pocket is the tank badge for the Spanish Civil War. The officer on the left wears the side cap.

Below: Typically well-equipped German infantry of the first year of the war. The helmets were still shiny at this early period, and displayed the national colours. The sergeant (on the right) carries an MP28 sub-machine gun, and the two soldiers have sacks of grenades slung round their shoulders.

1 Captain, General Staff, German Army, 1939

As an officer on the General Staff this captain wears crimson stripes (Lampassen) *on his breeches and crimson piping on his shoulder straps and cap. A particular feature of the staff officers' uniform was the collar patches* (Litzen) *where the bars were given a quite distinctive pattern of embroidery. Those officers permanently attached to OKW wore gold embroidered collar patches. In the German Army staff officers were held in high regard and played an important part in the conduct of operations.*

2 Colonel-General, German Army

Eduard Dietl, an Austrian, became a legend in his lifetime when his leadership helped save the German Army from disaster during the Norwegian campaign. Shown here in the uniform of a mountain-troop commander, he wears a piped service tunic (without mountain troop insignia) and a mountain cap with the silver national emblem and the 'edelweiss' on the left side of the cap. At this time there was no piping around the crown. On his right breast pocket is the highly prized and rarely awarded Army mountain guide badge. Other decorations are the Knight's Cross of the Iron Cross awarded to him in May 1940, the bar to the Iron Cross 1st Class, and a wound badge. Befitting a commander of mountain troops, Dietl wears mountain boots and puttees.

3 NCO, German Army, 1939-40

This German infantryman wears a combat uniform typical of the early period of the war. The field-grey blouse with dark blue collar and stone grey trousers were soon to be discontinued, while the collar and trousers of uniforms being manufactured were of field-grey cloth. His non-commissioned officer rank is indicated by the aluminium lace around the collar and on the shoulder straps, and as a section leader, (Gruppenführer) *in charge of ten men he is armed with an MP38 sub-machine gun.*

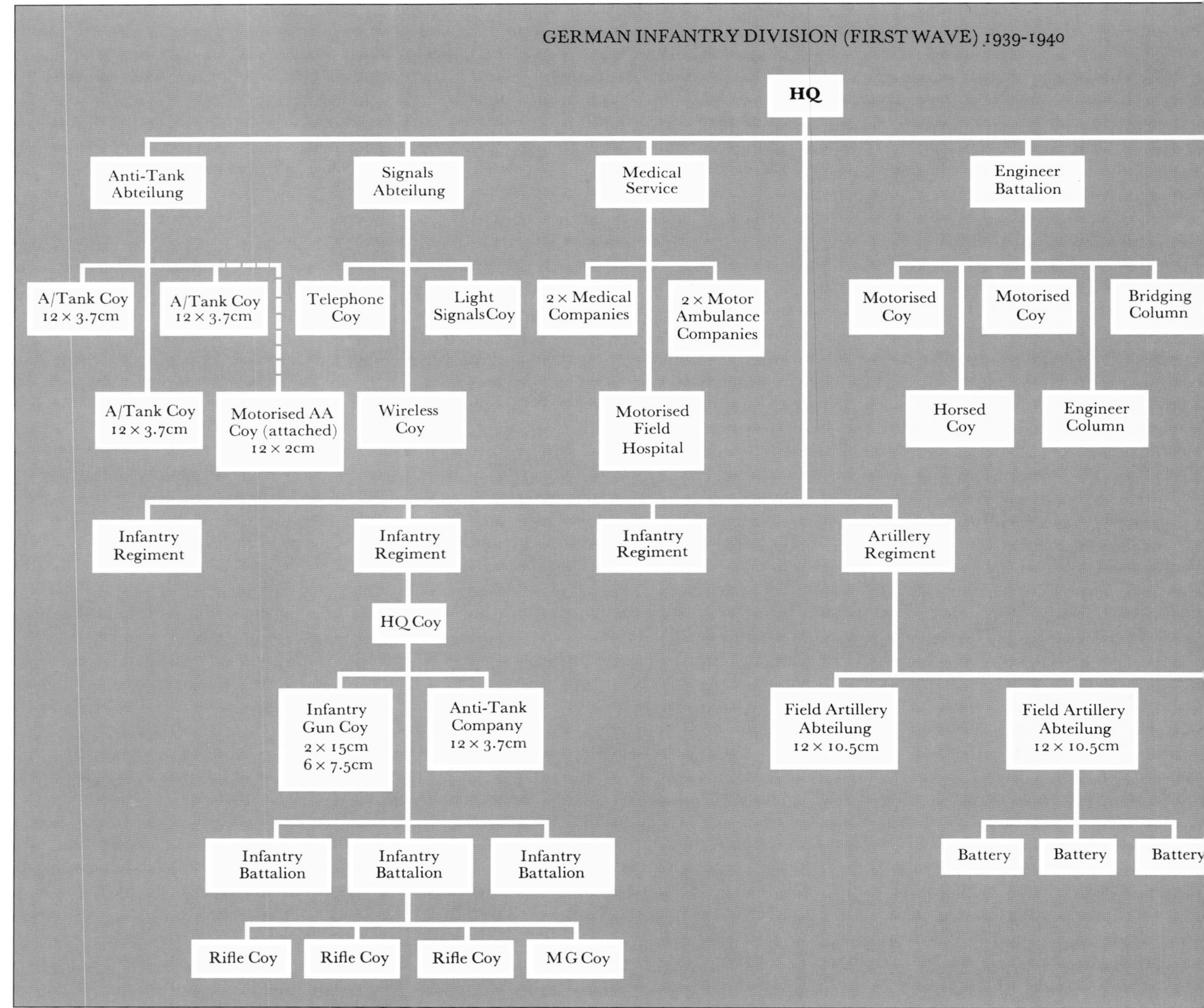

3 mountain divisions. Two of XVII Army Corp's infantry divisions were Slovak, while attached to XIII Army Corps was the motorised SS infantry regiment *Leibstandarte* (Bodyguard Regiment) *Adolf Hitler*.

The most important formation in the German Army was the division which could be one of five basic types: infantry, motorised infantry, panzer (armoured), light and mountain. Infantry divisions had been raised in *Wellen* (waves) and the divisions of each wave varied to some extent in size, organisation and equipment carried, depending upon their purpose and the availability of men and materials. The 35 divisions formed as part of the original 'wave' had a total strength of nearly 18,000 men each while those of the next wave were about 15,000 men strong. Divisions formed in the third and fourth waves had considerably less artillery support than the earlier formations. The infantry division comprised three infantry regiments (each of approximately 3,000 men) and one artillery regiment plus supporting divisional units as illustrated in the diagram. Contrary to the practice in most armies, the engineer battalion and the reconnaissance *Abteilung* (the *Abteilung* was a unit of varying size, between the regiment and the company, battery or squadron. It approximated to the British battalion, artillery regiment or tank regiment) were combat units, and, being equipped with flamethrowers and anti-tank guns, often led assaults on enemy positions. Another feature of the German Army was the decentralisation of heavy weapons within the division so that each regiment had its own anti-tank and infantry gun company.

The infantry regiment possessed its own headquarters with a staff company and signals, bicycle and engineer platoon. In the infantry battalion there were three rifle companies (about 180 men with an anti-tank rifle squad); a machine-gun company with three machine-gun platoons (12 men and two heavy machine guns each), and a heavy mortar platoon of three sections each with 19 men and two 8.1cm mortars. The division of the battalion into one machine-gun and three rifle companies was the pattern in the first wave divisions while in later waves there were four 'mixed' rifle

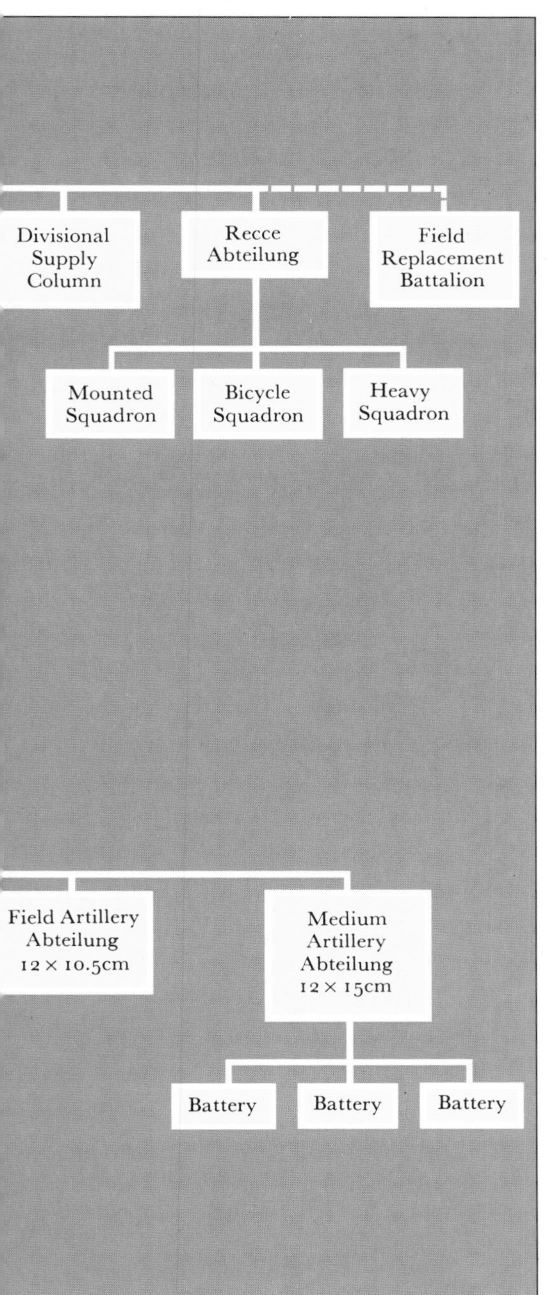

Above: These tankmen are wearing the black tank crew uniform. A padded helmet was worn under the beret. The white cross was used as identification during the Polish campaign, and the tank is one of the few Mk IVs to see service in 1939.

companies. The firepower of a regiment was as follows:
26 heavy machine guns;
85 light machine guns;
18 × 8.1cm mortars;
27 × 5cm mortars;
12 × 3.7cm anti-tank guns;
6 × 7.5cm infantry guns;
2 × 15cm infantry howitzers.

The artillery regiment was divided into three field artillery *Abteilungen* each with three four-gun batteries of 10.5cm gun-howitzers. The medium artillery *Abteilung* was originally a non-divisional unit attached to the artillery regiment, but later became an integral part of first wave divisions.

In addition to the divisional artillery which could vary in type and organisation from one division to another, both armies and corps had at their disposal additional batteries of medium and heavy artillery. These batteries could range in size of calibre from the dual-purpose 8.8cm gun to the massive 60cm self-propelled howitzer known as a *Karl Mörser*. Most of the heavy anti-aircraft batteries were under Luftwaffe control but could be allocated to the Army for specific operations.

Motorised infantry divisions were intended to keep up with fast-moving panzer divisions, and so they were completely equipped with motor vehicles. For the Polish campaign there were four motorised infantry divisions, each of three infantry and one motorised artillery regiment, but after this campaign they lost their third infantry regiment as more panzer divisions were formed.

The panzer division during the Polish and French campaigns consisted of two tank regiments of two battalions each of four companies with 32 tanks each. This gave a total of 561 tanks including reserves and staff vehicles, although on mobilisation tank strength was usually below establishment with an average of about 320 vehicles. The division was equipped with a combination of Mark I and II light tanks (armed only with machine guns and 2cm cannon), Czech 38(t) tanks and a few heavier Mark III and IV tanks. Each division had two fully motorised infantry regiments which were later to be redesignated as *Panzergrenadiere*. The reconnaissance battalion was equipped with armoured cars and motorcycles, and the division also had its own motorised signals battalion and other services. The success of the German armoured formations lay not in the quality of their vehicles (which were in some respects inferior to those of their opponents during the campaigns of 1940) but in a superiority of organisation and tactical ability which enabled them to be the cutting-edge of the Army.

The original light divisions, formed in 1937–8, were motorised cavalry formations which varied in organisation but usually comprised a light tank battalion, one or two cavalry rifle regiments (each of two or three battalions) a motorised artillery regiment (24 × 10.5cm gun howitzers); an anti-tank battalion (36 × 3.7cm, 12 × 2cm guns) and a motorised reconnaissance battalion or regiment equipped with armoured cars. As a divisional organisation they were undergunned and underarmoured and following the Polish campaign the light divisions were uprated to panzer divisions. In late 1940 four infantry divisions were redesignated as 'light' divisions although their organisation was still basically that of an infantry division.

The three mountain divisions were organised on lines similar to those of the standard infantry division although in the field organisation varied according to circumstances. A typical establishment would be two infantry regiments, each divided into three battalions; the battalion comprising five companies. In keeping with their ostensible role they had a high proportion of lightweight and easily manageable equipment. The artillery regiment had two *Abteilungen* of eight 7.5cm guns each, one *Abteilung* of eight 10.5cm guns and one *Abteilung* of eight 15cm guns. The anti-tank *Abteilung* comprised 24 motorised 3.7cm guns and was strengthened by the two regimental anti-tank companies which each had a strength of nine 3.7cm and three 4.7cm guns. In mountainous or rough country the mountain divisions proved a success; their flexible structure (based upon the battalion as opposed to the regiment) as well as first class training made them formidable opponents and provided them with an élite status within the German Army. In open terrain, when faced by conventionally armed formations, their lack of heavy firepower told against them, however.

By 1939 there was only one cavalry formation left in the German Army, the 1st Cavalry Brigade (although it should be emphasised that the employment of horses for a variety of duties was widespread and remained so throughout the war). The brigade was composed of two mounted cavalry regiments and a battalion of mounted artillery. The regiments were divided into four cavalry squadrons and one 'heavy' squadron (6 × 8cm mortars, 4 × 7.5cm guns) with a combined strength of about 1400 men each. Even in blitzkrieg warfare there was still a place for cavalry: on 25 October 1939 the Brigade was redesignated the 1st Cavalry Division and reinforced in December with the 2nd Cavalry Brigade.

The decisive but hard fought victory over Poland (losses were 10,600 killed, 30,000 wounded and 3400 missing) surprised the world, and Hitler was able to brush aside the few remaining voices of caution within the German military establishment. Germany transferred her forces to the West in preparation for the invasion of France. By May 1940, the number of divisions in the German army was as follows:

129 infantry divisions;
4 motorised infantry divisions;
4 light motorised infantry divisions;
10 panzer divisions;
3 mountain divisions;
1 cavalry division.

In addition the *SS-Verfügungstruppe* (from April 1940, known as the Waffen-SS) provided three motorised infantry divisions and a brigade. There were now over two-and-a-half million men under arms in the German Army, of which the Waffen-SS contributed about 100,000.

Above right: Mountain troops in 1940. Skis were not standard issue, but were used when appropriate. The NCO in front has tinted goggles, and wears non-regulation ski boots.

Below: A group of motorcyclists, about to listen to a gramophone they have found. The man on the left and the soldier kneeling have waterproof coats; the others wear standard greatcoats.

For the invasion of France the German Army was organised into three army groups: Army Group A (von Rundstedt) with 45½ divisions including 7 panzer; Army Group B (von Bock) with 29½ divisions including 3 panzer, and Army Group C (von Leeb) with 19 divisions. Army Group C held a defensive position against the Maginot Line while the main offensive was launched by Rundstedt's Army Group A in the Ardennes with a subsidiary invasion of Holland and Belgium undertaken by Army Group B.

From 9 April (when German troops invaded Denmark and Norway) to the armistice with France on 25 June, the German Army confirmed the superiority of its organisation and tactics. Losses in Norway were 5636 men; the invasion of France and the Low Countries cost 27,074 killed, 111,034 wounded and 18,348 missing.

UNIFORM The field-grey uniform of the German Army was a development of that worn during World War I. The final version was introduced in stages from 1935 onwards.

In the Army there were two kinds of uniform: that issued by the state, and that provided by the wearer either at his own expense or at the expense of the state. During peacetime and in the first year of the war, officers often continued to wear tailor-made uniforms in the field, but since these were impractical, uncomfortable and costly to replace, they increasingly wore issue uniforms with officers' badges of rank.

The basic field-grey uniform was standardised throughout the Army and its principal components were the steel helmet, side cap, field-blouse, greatcoat, trousers and marching boots. Mountain troops received the same uniform but the side cap was replaced by a mountain cap, and the trousers and boots by long baggy trousers gathered at the ankle, elasticated puttees and mountain boots. Mounted personnel were not only to be found in the cavalry, but in the many units which still relied on horses for transport or reconnaissance. They were given breeches lined with leather and heavy riding boots.

A special black uniform for crews of enclosed armoured vehicles was also introduced in 1935. It consisted of a black padded beret which served as a crash helmet, short double-breasted jacket and long baggy trousers. This uniform, which was at first only to be worn when on duty with the vehicle, was both practical and popular. Its black colour, offset by a silver death's head badge, was dramatic and contributed in no small way to the *esprit* of this young arm; and so it was extended to crews of self-propelled guns who received a field-grey version at the beginning of 1940.

Generally speaking the German clothing industry had achieved miracles in keeping pace with the expansion of the Army and the German uniform was a rare combination of tradition and modernity, comfort and smartness. Even so there were not enough uniforms to go round and the vast stocks of uniforms found by the Germans in Austria, Czechoslovakia, and Poland were sorted, stored, stripped of national emblems and issued to German conscripts to compensate for shortages.

INSIGNIA The primary method of identifying rank in the German Army was by means of the system of shoulder straps which not only showed the wearer's rank, but his arm of service, formation and status. In addition, officers were distinguished by their head-dress (peaked cap with silver chin cords and side cap with silver piping) and brown leather equipment. All non-commissioned officers wore the basic soldiers' uniform (unlike many European armies modelled on the French system where NCOs wore the officers' uniform), but were identified by silver lace on their tunic collar and shoulder straps. Soldiers wore their badges of rank on the left sleeve.

The arm of service was indicated by various colours (golden yellow in the cavalry, for example, as illustrated in the insignia chart) which appeared as piping on the peaked cap, chevrons on the front of the side cap, stripes on the collar patches, and as piping and underlay on the shoulder straps.

Medals and decorations were comparatively rare at the beginning of the war, being restricted to World War I awards, long service awards, political awards, and decorations awarded for service in the Spanish Civil War. It was, however, characteristic that the Germans continued to wear decorations in action, although this singled them out as targets for snipers.

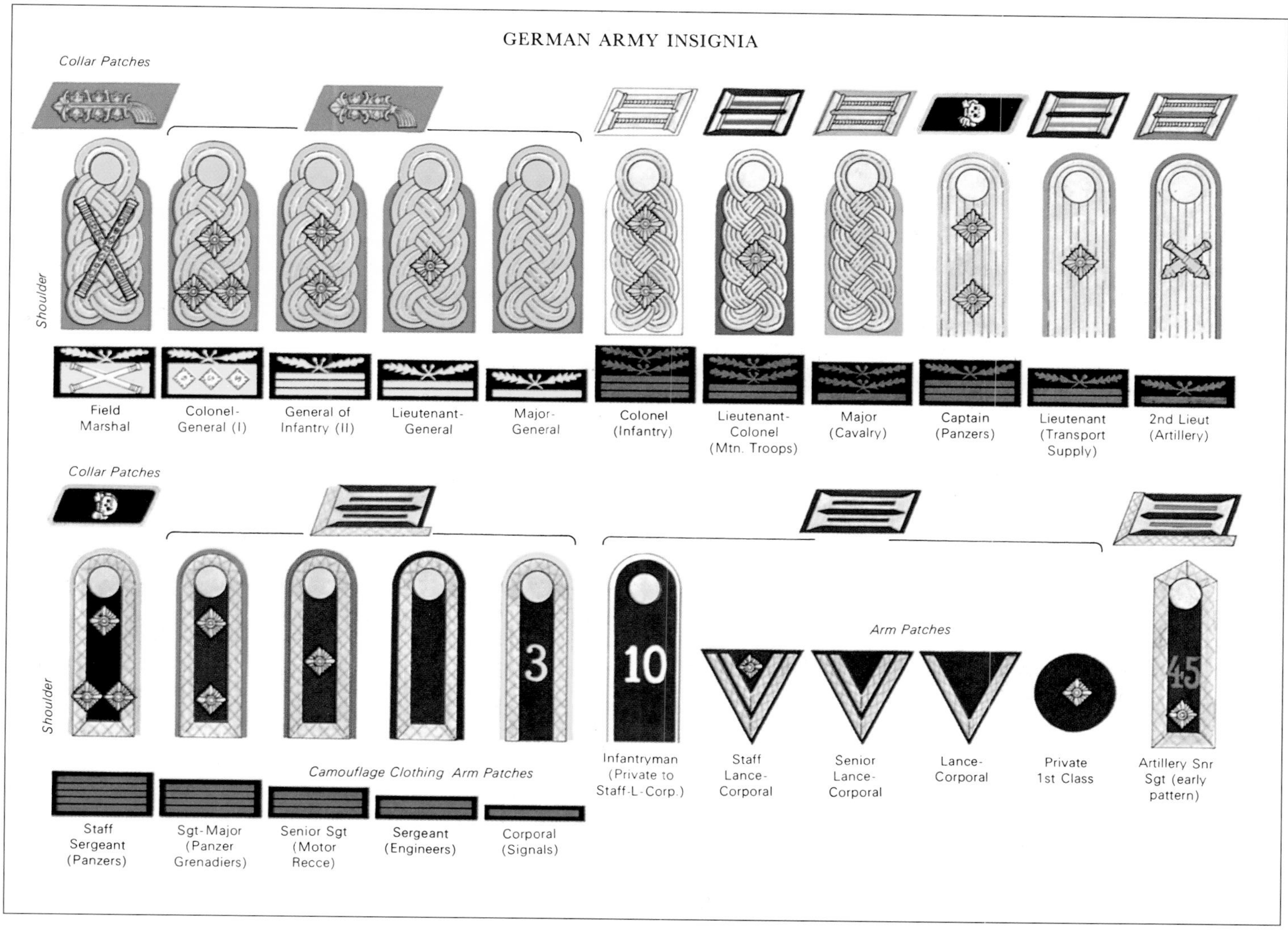

4

5

4 Lieutenant, German Police, 1939

Shown here is the standard service dress for officers of the so-called order police (Ordnungspolizei). *During the war police battalions were used as garrison troops in occupied territories, while others were conscripted into the Army to act as military policemen. Rank is indicated by the Army-pattern shoulder straps for commissioned ranks. The usual weapon with this order of dress was an automatic pistol although swords were still worn for ceremonial occasions.*

5 Private, SS Police, 1940

The combination of Army collar patches and SS national emblem on the left sleeve is rather unusual, but this rifleman is from the SS Polizei-Division *whose personnel were drawn from the German police. The uniform is basically that of the German Army (field-grey tunic, boots and trousers) while the helmet is the 1935 model as issued to the barracked units of the police All ranks continued to bear police rank titles and used the military salute. The rifle is the Mauser 98K, a five-shot weapon which was becoming obsolete by 1939; the grenade is the* Stielgranate *24. The rifleman also carries a gas mask and camouflage cape.*

PARA-MILITARY UNITS

Para-military units played an important part in the campaign of 1939, and in the creation of those tensions which the Germans used to justify their invasion of Poland. Despite its status as a Free City, German 'tourists' were introduced into Danzig during the summer of 1939, and on 18 August came the public announcement of the formation of the German-sponsored *SS-Heimwehr Danzig* (Danzig Home Defence SS). It was organised like a German infantry battalion but with four rifle companies as well as a machine-gun and infantry-gun company, a signals and engineer platoon and two anti-tank platoons. Its strength was 42 officers and 1,500 men and it was fully motorised.

In September the Danzig *Heimwehr*, together with the Danzig Police, took part in the attack on the Polish controlled Post Office, and in the assault on the Westerplatte fortress. After the Polish campaign the battalion was disbanded with its personnel going as cadres to other SS units.

In addition to the Danzig *Heimwehr* other units and formations of the embryonic Waffen-SS participated in the Polish Campaign alongside German Army units, thereby gaining valuable experience. Immediately behind the advancing armies came units of the German Labour Service (*Reichsarbeitsdienst*) which repaired bridges and roads under the supervision of Army engineers. Electricity, gas and telecommunications were restored by the Technical Emergency Service (*Technische Nothilfe*), while in the newly-occupied towns and villages traffic was controlled and roads kept clear for the armed forces by the special Traffic Regulating Service (*Verkehrs-Erziehungsdienst*) of the National Socialist Motor Transport Corps (NSKK).

Internal security and the full horror of the Nazi regime were ruthlessly imposed by special mobile units of the German Police (*Einsatzkommandos*) who arrested or executed a long list of people considered too dangerous or unworthy to live under the 'new order'.

As German regular troops were withdrawn from Poland, garrison duties were taken over by SS *Tokenkopf* (Death's Head) Infantry Regiments and battalions of German Security Police (*Schutzpolizei*).

UNIFORM The *SS-Heimwehr Danzig* had field-grey Waffen-SS uniform with the death's head on the right collar patch and a black cuff-band on the left cuff with *SS-Heimwehr Danzig* in silver letters. The Danzig *Landespolizei* wore a police green uniform, but instead of the German national emblem, they wore a death's head on the peaked cap and on the right side of the steel helmet. Both the NSKK and the *Reichsarbeitsdienst* had khaki uniforms and wore the NSDAP armlet on the left sleeve. The Technical Emergency Service had a black uniform but men attached to Army units were issued with field-grey uniforms.

AIR FORCE

The creation of the first German Air Force (Luftwaffe) as an independent branch of the German armed forces was announced in March 1935, although, in fact, a semi-clandestine build-up had taken place before this under the cover of the German Air Sports Association (*Deutsche Luftsportverband* or DLV). Soon after Hitler's seizure of power, Hermann Göring was appointed first postwar Air Minister. By the time the existence of an Air Force was made public it already had about 1000 aircraft and 20,000 officers and men. Expansion and the replacement of obsolete aircraft with the very latest models took place very rapidly and by 1937 the Luftwaffe was able to test its modern aircraft and tactical theories in the Spanish Civil War.

In March 1938 German aircraft were used to transport troops during the annexation of Austria (which resulted in the incorporation of the Austrian Air Force into the Luftwaffe), and in September German airborne troops took part in the occupation of the Sudetenland. When the Luftwaffe went to war in September 1939 it was a well equipped and highly trained force, which had been created to perform a specific role as conceived by the *Wehrmacht* strategists, who saw it as an adjunct to land warfare. To perform its tactical role, the Luftwaffe had pioneered Army/Air Force co-operation, developed effective dive-bombing techniques in support of ground forces, and perfected the transport of troops and supplies by air. In addition it had taken over from the Army its experimental parachute troops and had radically improved the techniques by which troops could be landed in the combat zone by parachute and glider. But when Germany's lightning and unexpected successes took on larger implications, the Luftwaffe, so well adapted to a close-support role, was unable to provide the long-range bomber force necessary to strike effectively at British and Soviet industry and communications.

6

7

Below: The fighter ace Adolf Galland climbs out of his Bf 109. He is wearing the fighter pilot version of the 'Mae West' life-jacket.

ORGANISATION Control of the Luftwaffe was exercised by the Luftwaffe High Command (*Oberkommando der Luftwaffe* or OKL) which had under its command four Air Fleets (*Luftflotten*) with their headquarters in Berlin (No.1), Brunswick (No.2), Munich (No.3), and Vienna (No.4). The administration of the Air Fleets was carried out by the Air Region (*Luftgau*) headquarters which were based on various airfields. The fighting forces were formed into flying corps (*Fliegerkorps*) which were made up of a number of different types of flying unit according to the role that they had to play. The main unit within a *Fliegerkorps* was the *Geschwader* (no exact British equivalent existed). Each *Geschwader* had a staff unit and three or four groups (*Gruppen*) of three or four squadrons (*Staffeln*) of 10 to 12 aircraft each. The three types of *Geschwader* were *Jagdgeschwader* (single-seater fighters), *Kampfgeschwader* (bombers) and *Stukageschwader* (dive bombers).

The aircraft strength of a *Geschwader* was 90 to 120 aircraft, which included a

6 General, German Air Force, 1939

This air force general wears parade dress, which is basically the service dress with an aiguillette and full-dress belt. The primary means of identifying rank are the collar patches and shoulder straps, and in common with all general officers he wears gold buttons and badges and white stripes (Lampassen) *on his breeches. During the war the wearing of the aiguillette and full-dress belt was discontinued, while the sword was usually replaced by a pistol.*

7 Senior Sergeant, German Air Force, 1939

During the summer months (30 April to 30 September) before the war, officers and non-commissioned officers could wear a cap with white top and white trousers and shoes, while officers could also wear a white tunic. After war broke out, the white-topped cap continued to be worn in Italy, the Mediterranean, southern Russia, and occasionally in Germany. On the figure shown here, rank is identified by the lace on the collar and shoulder straps and the metal wings on the collar patch. The scarlet arm-of-service colour identifies him as an anti-aircraft artilleryman and the badge on the left cuff shows that its wearer is a qualified armourer.

staff flight of four aircraft for the commander (*Kommodore*) and his adjutant, the staff major and the operations officer or '1a' as he was known.

Luftwaffe personnel numbered about 1,500,000 men at the beginning of the war: this included the large figure of 900,000 in the anti-aircraft artillery, 25,000 headquarters and administration staff, 50,000 aircrew and other flying personnel, 100,000 in air signals, 60,000 construction personnel and 80,000 in maintenance and supply, while the remainder were undergoing training.

The Luftwaffe forces ranged against Poland on 1 September 1939 were divided into two air fleets. *Luftflotte* 1 was based in Pomerania, and *Luftflotte* 4 in Silesia. There were also two independent commands, the 2nd Air Division and the Air Command for Special Purposes (*Fliegerfuhrer z.b.V.*). Aircraft strength was about 850 bombers and dive-bombers and 400 fighters. In the first two days of the campaign these forces completely destroyed the Polish Air Force. When the campaign came to an end the Germans had lost 285 aircraft and 734 airmen killed, wounded and missing. It had been a striking demonstration of air power.

The X *Fliegerkorps* played a vital role in the invasion of Norway and Denmark. Its three principal tasks, which had to be carried out in close co-operation with the Army and Navy, were to secure air superiority, capture airfields so that transport aircraft could land troops and supplies, and lastly to prevent the Royal Navy from interfering with German naval operations. These tasks were reflected in the make-up of the forces used. Over half the available thousand aircraft were transports, while over one quarter were bombers.

For the campaign in the West the Luftwaffe deployed 3,902 aircraft. Colonel-General Kesselring commanded *Luftflotte* 2 with I, IV and IX *Fliegerkorps* in support of General von Bock's Army Group B. Colonel-General Sperrle commanded *Luftflotte* 3 with II, V and VIII *Fliegerkorps* in support of General von Rundstedt's Army Group A. For the Battle of Britain which followed the

8

9

10

8 Major, German Air Force, 1940

This Luftwaffe officer wears a beige canvas one-piece flying suit (issued for summer use), over which is worn a life jacket, coloured yellow for air-sea rescue. Rank is denoted by the special flying uniform badge which was worn on the upper sleeve of flying uniforms and overalls. A bomber commander, this major is kitted out in a flying uniform typical of those worn during the Battle of Britain.

9 NCO, German Air Force, 1940

The teamwork which existed between the ground crew and the pilots who flew the aircraft contributed much to German success in the air. This non-commissioned officer wears a black twill side cap and black cotton drill overall. His rank group is indicated by the grey lace on the overall collar.

10 Senior Sergeant, German Air Force, 1940

This NCO of flying troops wears the side cap (Fliegermütze) *and flying blouse* (Fliegerbluse) *which was a garment originally introduced for wear under flying suits. The first pattern had no national emblem nor pockets, but had twisted cord in the arm-of-service colour around the collar. Originally the* Fliegerbluse *was issued to flying personnel only but it became popular throughout the Luftwaffe.*

Above: Mountain troops who have just made an emergency drop clamber out of their parachute clothing at Narvik in 1940. The NCO removing his 'bone sack' and the two soldiers in the foreground wear mountain troop caps, but probably wore paratroop helmets (one of which is in the picture) for the drop itself.

defeat of France, the two air fleets mentioned above were joined by Colonel-General Stumpff's *Luftflotte* 5 in Norway.

The strength of the two air fleets based in France was as follows (with the numbers of aircraft serviceable and ready to fly in parenthesis):
809 (650) Bf 109 fighters;
250 (170) Bf 110 fighter-bombers;
316 (250) Ju 87 (Stuka) dive-bombers;
1130 (770) bombers.

The air fleet in Norway played a minor part in the Battle of Britain deploying these serviceable aircraft: 70 Bf 109 fighters, 30 Bf 110 fighter-bombers and 95 bombers.

Despite poor strategic handling of the Air Force by Göring during the Battle of Britain, the Luftwaffe aircrews conducted a gallant and skilfull campaign against their British opponents. Indeed, in terms of tactical skill the British had much to learn and copied a number of German flying techniques and formations most notably the *Schwarm* formation (four planes flying as two pairs) instead of the 'Vic-3' (three planes in a 'V' formation).

Losses during the Battle of Britain are difficult to calculate, but were probably about 1700 fighters and bombers.

AIRBORNE FORCES

The formation of parachute troops began almost simultaneously in both the German Army and Air Force. On 1 October 1935, General Göring's personal guard regiment, which originally had belonged to the Prussian Police, was transferred to the Luftwaffe as the General Göring Regiment. At the same time volunteers from the regiment were sent to Altengrabow training ground where the formation of the Luftwaffe's parachute rifle regiment was taking place.

In Spring 1936 the Army established an experimental staff with 15 officers and 80 other ranks, which was to become the Army's parachute rifle battalion. During the occupation of the Sudetenland the battalion came under the tactical command of the Luftwaffe, and on 1 January 1939, the battalion was transferred to the Air Force. From then on the Luftwaffe assumed total responsibility for the recruitment, training, equipment and operational control of parachute troops, and Germany became the only country in which parachute troops were exclusively part of the Air Force. Although paratroops were part of the Luftwaffe, the other component element of Germany's airborne forces, the air landing troops, remained as part of the Army. Air landing troops were infantry soldiers trained in the skills of rapid airborne landings (as indeed their name suggested) and equipped with a number of specialised lightweight weapons.

11 Paratroop NCO, German Air Force, 1940

This uniform was originally developed in the German Army which organised the first unit of parachute troops. The cut-down helmet had a thick sorbo-rubber lining and could be worn with a cloth cover. The overall or 'bone sack' was made of cotton duck material and was worn over the field equipment. The trousers were field-grey (not grey-blue as often shown in postwar illustrations) and had special pockets on the side of the thighs to hold a knife, field-dressing and other necessities. Elbow pads (not shown), knee pads and padded gloves were all necessary to help avoid injury during landing as the RZ1 parachute was rather primitive.

In July 1938 Major-General Student was transferred to the Luftwaffe from the Army, to undertake the development of the parachute troops, but by the time the Germans went to war in September 1939, the 7th Airborne (*Flieger*) Division was still in the process of formation.

After a winter spent in further specialist training an air landing corps was formed from the 7th Airborne Division and the 22nd Infantry Division.

Germany's parachute troops played a small, though successful, role in the Norwegian campaign which included the relief of General Dietl's beleagured command at Narvik. Some of the 'paratroopers' dropped during this operation were mountain soldiers who had undergone a seven-day parachuting course. The invasion of Holland and Belgium in 1940 saw the most spectacular triumph of this new arm when paratroops under the command of Major-General Student captured the modern Belgian fortress of Eben Emael and the bridges over the Albert Canal, the key points in the line of Belgian fortifications.

The parachute division was similar in organisation to the infantry division with two or three parachute rifle regiments each of three battalions; an artillery regiment of two *abteilungen* equipped with 10.5cm recoilless guns and an anti-tank battalion armed with airborne 5cm guns or lightweight 7.5cm guns.

UNIFORM Members of the German Air Sport Association began to wear a blue-grey uniform in 1933, and since this organisation was to provide much of the cadre for the new German Air Force, it was both logical and economical that this existing uniform should form the basis of the new Luftwaffe uniform, which appeared in public for the first time in March 1935.

The blue-grey uniform resembled that of the British Royal Air Force. Headgear consisted of a peaked cap with artificial mohair band, and a side cap; the tunic was worn open with shirt and tie, with either matching long trousers and black shoes or breeches with high boots; the greatcoat was also worn open and was double-breasted. The basic cut of the uniform was the same for all ranks, but whereas officers' uniforms were made of smooth cloth, issue uniforms were made of a coarser wool.

One of the most comfortable and popular items of clothing was the so-called *Fliegerbluse*, which was a short jacket with concealed buttons and no breast pockets. It was designed to be worn under the flying suit, but was also often worn by aircrew instead of a flying suit or flying jacket.

Working dress was either the natural-coloured cotton drill uniform, or black working overalls. Officers also had a lightweight version of their service tunic or

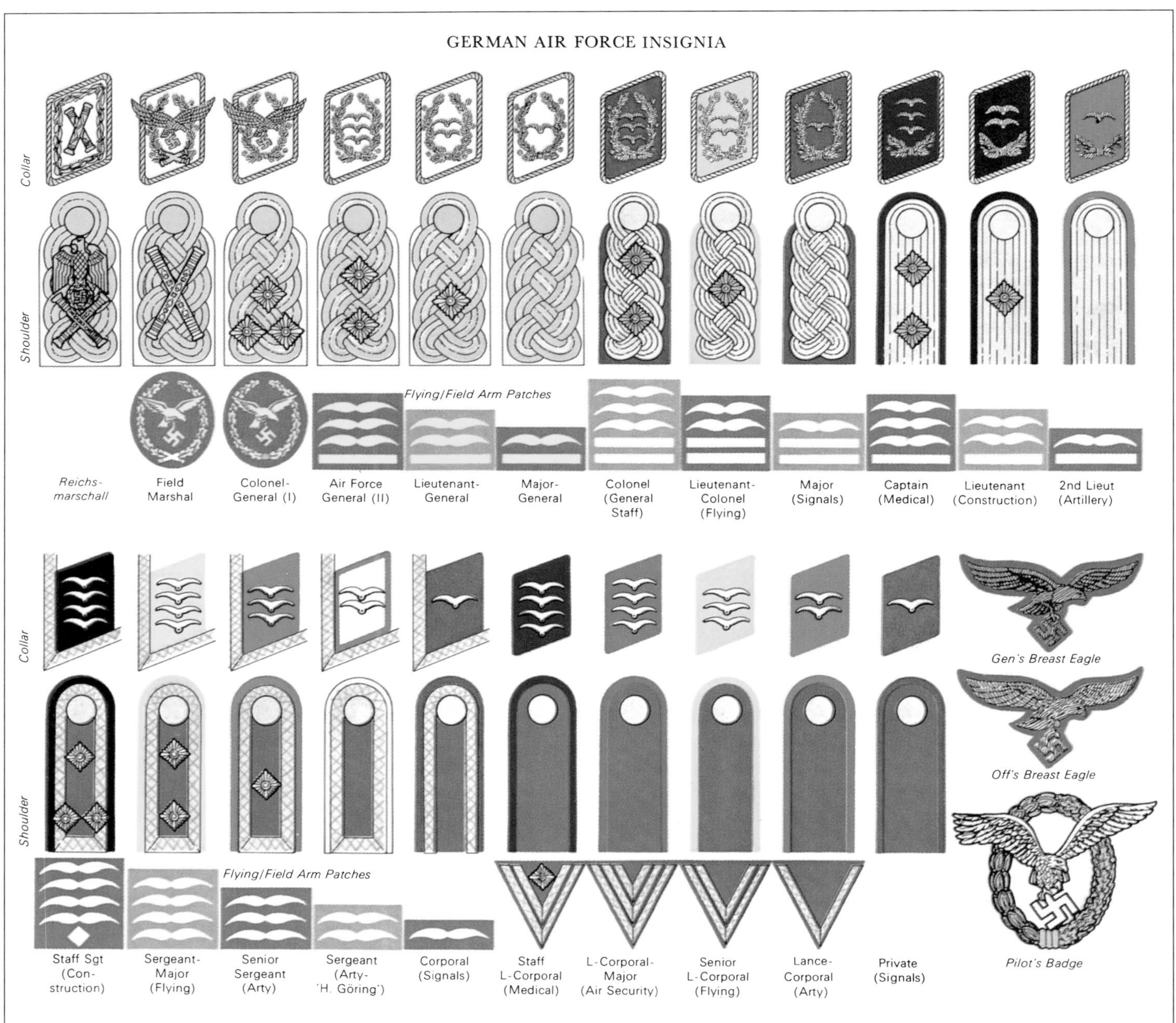

flying blouse, designed for everyday wear in warm weather, or for wear when working in an office.

At the beginning of the war flight clothing consisted of a beige linen flying helmet and one-piece overall, while in cold weather there were both lined and unlined leather flying helmets and suits. Flying boots were made of black leather and suede and were lined with lambswool.

Paratroops wore standard Luftwaffe uniform with a yellow arm-of-service colour since they were classified as flying troops. But as the first parachute troops had been formed by the Army, it was the Army that developed the special jump uniform. The first type included a cut-down version of the standard M1935 steel helmet, a loose-fitting olive-green smock which was designed to be worn over the equipment, and long field-grey trousers which were tucked into soft leather rubber-soled lace-up boots. When the Army parachute rifle battalion was transferred to the Luftwaffe this experimental uniform underwent further development in the Luftwaffe, and was to become the model for the uniform of the British airborne forces.

INSIGNIA While the Luftwaffe retained Army rank titles and rank badges in the form of Army shoulder straps, it also introduced two new systems of badges for wear on the collar patches and on the flying suit. Luftwaffe general officers were further distinguished by white lapels on the undress jacket and greatcoat, and white stripes (*Lampassen*) on the breeches and trousers.

Arm of service was indicated by the colours (*Waffenfarben*) which appeared on the head-dress, on the collar patches and shoulder straps, and on the collar piping.

A large percentage of Luftwaffe personnel were skilled tradesmen and they wore a badge on the lower left sleeve with an emblem which indicated their particular skill. Aircrew specialists wore a winged badge whereas ground crew wore circular ones.

12 Admiral, German Navy, 1940
Admiral Rolf Carls was Commanding Admiral of the Baltic Sea Fleet. As shown here, he wears a peaked cap with double row of embroidered oak leaves, and a greatcoat with blue lapels. Rank is indicated by the two pips of the shoulder straps. He was awarded the Knight's Cross of the Iron Cross on 14 June 1940.

13 Lt.-Commander, German Navy, 1940
This Korvettenkapitän *wears the standard naval officers' service dress: a peaked cap with single row of gold embroidered oak leaves on the peak and a reefer jacket with rank distinction lace on the cuffs. Decorations are the ribbon to the Iron Cross 2nd Class, Iron Cross 1st Class and below that a wound badge in black.*

NAVY

The Treaty of Versailles strictly limited the size of the German Navy and forbade the design or construction of submarines, aircraft carriers, naval aircraft or heavy coastal artillery. The displacement of new vessels was limited to 10,000 tons.

Hitler chose to ignore the restrictive terms of the treaty, but was also anxious to remain on good terms with England. On 18 June 1935 the Anglo-German Naval Treaty was signed and while this limited the strength of the German Navy to 35 per cent of that of the Royal Navy, it permitted Germany to have submarines and all the other types of ships forbidden her under the Treaty of Versailles. An ambitious programme of ship-building (the 'Z' plan) was set under way in 1937, and by September 1939 the German Navy comprised:
2 old battleships;
2 battlecruisers;
3 pocket battleships;
3 heavy cruisers;
6 light cruisers;
22 destroyers;
20 torpedo boats;
59 U-boats.

ORGANISATION The German Navy was divided into three basic arms under the command of a leader (*Führer*) or flag officer. The capital ships came under the direct control of the *Oberkommando der Kriegsmarine* (OKM) and then the group commands (*Gruppenkommandos*). The flotillas of minesweepers, patrol boats, coastal defence ships and auxiliaries of all types and sizes came under the naval security section. The third arm, which was to pose the greatest threat to the Allies at sea, was the submarine command.

Volunteers and conscripts underwent their basic training in regiments (*Schiffsstammregimenter*), while petty officers

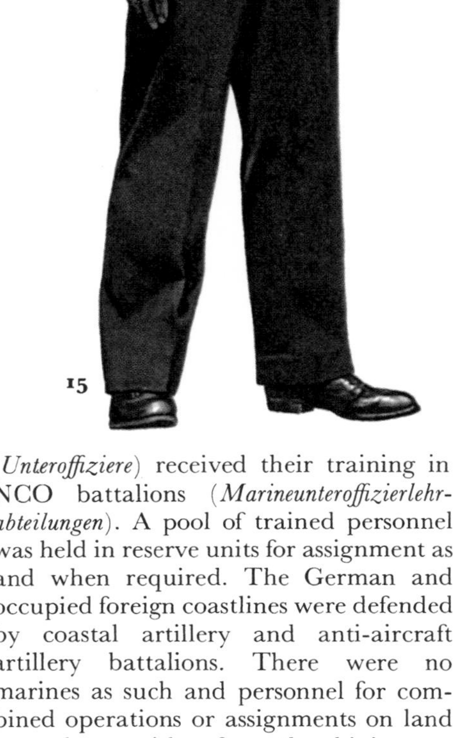

14

15

16

14 Petty Officer, German Navy, 1939
This sailor wears pre-war walking-out dress, which fell into disuse after the first two years of the war. For security reasons, the cap tally with the name of the ship (Panzerschiff Deutschland) *was soon replaced by a standardised model, bearing only the word* Kriegsmarine. *Petty officer rank is indicated by the gilt metal badge on the left sleeve and the rank distinction lace on the cuff. The lanyard shows that the wearer is a marksman.*

15 Seaman, German Navy, 1939
Illustrated is the pre-war summer parade dress as worn between 30 April and 30 September. The white cap cover, the tally with the name of the ship and white shirt (Bluse) *were not officially worn during the war, although sailors on leave in Germany did sometimes ignore regulations. With this and other orders of dress the trousers were usually worn rolled-up (as in illustration number 16).*

16 Seaman, German Navy, 1940
This rating in landing rig wears the 1935 pattern steel helmet, a pea-coat, and standard German Army field equipment. Sailors equipped like this took part in the capture of the Westerplatte fortress during the Polish campaign and fought in Norway. The rifle is the Mauser 98K.

(*Unteroffiziere*) received their training in NCO battalions (*Marineunteroffizierlehrabteilungen*). A pool of trained personnel was held in reserve units for assignment as and when required. The German and occupied foreign coastlines were defended by coastal artillery and anti-aircraft artillery battalions. There were no marines as such and personnel for combined operations or assignments on land were drawn either from the ship's company, or from the training and reserve units. By May 1941 the strength of the Navy had reached 404,000 in all ranks.

Unlike most of the other great navies, the *Kriegsmarine* did not have its own aircraft. An Air Force general was attached to OKM and was responsible for providing the Navy with its requirements in the air. The *Führer der Marineluftstreitkräfte* was Major-General Geissler and both his aircraft and men were carefully selected for the special tasks they had to carry out.

The war began with both remarkable success and significant failures. U-boats gained their first important victories (sinking the British vessels *Courageous* and *Royal Oak*), and magnetic mines presented the British with a nasty if only temporary shock. Naval units played an important part in the capture of the Polish coastal fortress at Westerplatte near Danzig; German ships safely transported German forces to Norway and German submarines threatened Britain's maritime life-lines. But in doing so the Germans lost three valuable capital ships and ten destroyers. The decisive battles of the sea war were still to come.

UNIFORM The German uniform of World War II was basically the uniform introduced in 1848 for the Prussian Navy, and was based on that of the British Royal Navy. There were three main types of uniform: navy-blue, white for summer and tropical wear, and field-grey for land-based personnel. There was a whole range of protective clothing for extreme conditions ranging from the severe cold of the Arctic to the heat of the Mediterranean.

The basic uniform for officers, petty officers and cadets is illustrated by figure

Left: Günther Prien, the U-boat commander whose sinking of the Royal Oak *was an early success for the* Kriegsmarine. *He wears the white cap cover typical of U-boat commanders and, again in keeping with U-boat tradition, his reefer jacket is battered and old.*

13 while the regulation greatcoat is shown by figure 12, although it shows the pattern with blue lapels which was worn only by flag officers. Ratings wore the cap with blue or white top; the white top was discontinued at the beginning of the war. This cap fell into general disuse except as walking-out and full-dress head-gear. During the war the most common type of head-dress for all ranks was the side or boarding cap. The basic uniform for ratings in wartime is shown in figure 15. Petty officers wore a cap with black peak and chin strap, a double-breasted reefer jacket with shoulder straps, white shirt, black tie and long trousers with black shoes.

Sailors serving in land-based units or in landing parties wore standard Navy uniform depending on the season or climate but with a steel helmet and Army personal equipment, as well as trousers rolled up to mid calf and worn outside the marching boots. From 1938 personnel in naval artillery units, NCO training battalions and, later on, members of the Naval Air Spotting Company were issued with a field-grey uniform which closely resembled that of the German Army except that all buttons, badges and lace were in gilt or yellow, as opposed to grey and silver.

INSIGNIA Officers were identified by the pattern of embroidery on the cap peak, the number and width of the gold lace rings on the reefer cuffs, or by the shoulder straps on the greatcoat and field-grey uniform. Petty officers and cadets wore their rank badges in the form of shoulder straps on the reefer, while ratings wore chevrons on the upper left sleeve of the jumper and pea-jacket. (See rank insignia chart.)

There was no arm-of-service designation as such in the Navy, but the special skills and trades held by ratings were identified by the badges worn on the upper left sleeve. Administrative officials wore silver buttons, badges and lace. On the field-grey uniform, officers displayed their branch-of-service colour and badge on the Army-pattern shoulder straps.

GERMAN NAVY INSIGNIA

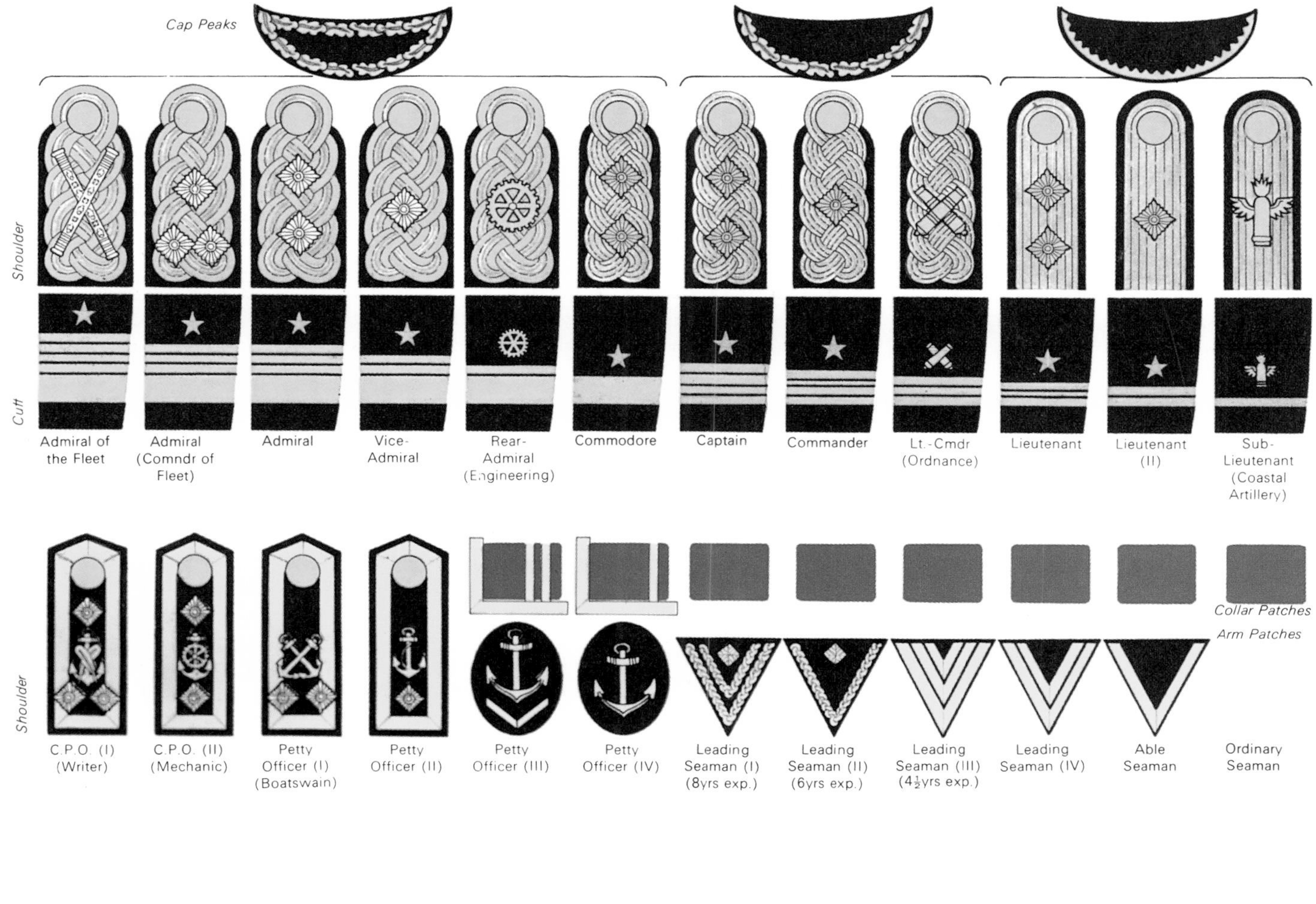

Cap Peaks

Shoulder

Cuff

Admiral of the Fleet
Admiral (Comndr of Fleet)
Admiral
Vice-Admiral
Rear-Admiral (Engineering)
Commodore
Captain
Commander
Lt.-Cmdr (Ordnance)
Lieutenant
Lieutenant (II)
Sub-Lieutenant (Coastal Artillery)

Shoulder

Collar Patches

Arm Patches

C.P.O. (I) (Writer)
C.P.O. (II) (Mechanic)
Petty Officer (I) (Boatswain)
Petty Officer (II)
Petty Officer (III)
Petty Officer (IV)
Leading Seaman (I) (8yrs exp.)
Leading Seaman (II) (6yrs exp.)
Leading Seaman (III) (4½yrs exp.)
Leading Seaman (IV)
Able Seaman
Ordinary Seaman

POLAND
ARMY

The Polish national Army came into existence after World War I, and, like all the armies of the newly-independent states which emerged at this time, it was equipped from the dumps of the vanquished. Not until 1937 was a programme of modernisation undertaken, and when war came two years later, the Polish Army was still basically obsolete; but although lacking in modern equipment and under poor strategic direction, the Polish Army fought bravely.

In 1939, as Europe moved towards war, the Polish government ordered partial mobilisation in March and August, and then, on 30 August 1939, general mobilisation was declared. Along her western frontiers Poland deployed seven armies and a tactical group which accounted for over half her infantry divisions and nearly three-quarters of her cavalry brigades. The remainder of the Army was in the process of formation and was to be used as reinforcements and operational reserves.

At dawn on 1 September 1939 German forces swept into Poland in the first blitzkrieg of the war. For 36 days the Polish armed forces put up a bitter resistance, despite their lack of modern weapons and equipment, and yet the lack of any real understanding of modern warfare (from grand strategy to minor tactics) by the Polish Army made defeat inevitable. Casualties were high: 66,300 killed, 130,000 wounded and over 400,000 prisoners-of-war.

ORGANISATION The President of the Republic was the Commander-in-Chief of an army of 1,500,000 soldiers. Its frontline strength of 1,000,000 men was organised in:
39 infantry divisions (including 9 reserve divisions);
11 cavalry brigades;
2 motorised brigades;
a variable number of infantry brigades.

Armament comprised 4500 guns and mortars, 2000 anti-tank and 3000 anti-aircraft guns.

The infantry division comprised three regiments of infantry and a regiment of light or field artillery plus the usual divisional services which included a reconnaissance unit with a company of TKS tankettes. In a small number of active divisions a heavy artillery group (of 105mm guns and 155mm howitzers) was included.

Line infantry and mountain rifle regiments had a regimental staff, three

17 18

infantry battalions, an administrative company, a pioneer platoon, and a signals company. They had an establishment strength of 1900 officers and men armed with Mauser M29 rifles or 9mm M38 pistols. Support weapons were:
90 light machine guns (Browning M28);
36 heavy machine guns (Browning M30);
27 light mortars;
6 heavy mortars;
2 field guns;
9 anti-tank guns.

Polish infantry regiments were poorly equipped, both in quality and quantity of artillery support weapons, compared to their German counterparts. The Polish reliance on offensive tactics only exposed more cruelly this weakness.

The various types of artillery were field, mountain, horse, heavy, extra heavy, and anti-aircraft. A field artillery regiment had a staff, a signals troop and three batteries each of three troops of four guns (24 × 75mm M1897/17 and 12 × 100mm Austrian M14 howitzers).

Artillery was mostly horsedrawn with the exception of the anti-aircraft guns which were motorised. Mountain artillery had the same basic organisation except that a regiment had no signals section. The 65mm and 75mm mountain guns were carried on horseback, while the 100mm howitzer was drawn by a two-wheeled cart and two horses. At all levels, the Polish army was short of artillery, a weakness particularly marked in the larger formations which rarely possessed a full complement of heavy guns.

The Polish Army had a small tank force but the Polish High Command had little experience in the handling of tanks with the result that in 1939 Polish armoured units were soon overwhelmed by the German panzers. In 1939 the Polish armoured forces consisted of:
170 11-ton 7TP light tanks (armed with a 37mm Bofors gun);
50 Vickers six-ton tanks;
67 Renault FT-17 light tanks (of World War I vintage);
about 700 TK/TKS tankettes and 100 armoured cars.

In addition there were 53 Renault R-35 light tanks which did not take part in the fighting and were withdrawn to Romania.

Characteristic of the Polish army was the size and prestige of the cavalry. There were 210 squadrons, consisting of three regiments of light cavalry, 27 regiments of lancers and 10 regiments of mounted rifles. The 11 cavalry brigades were intended to play an important strategic role, although in fact they were unable to do so (partly because they were badly positioned at the outbreak of hostilities) and they proved extremely vulnerable. Pride in the cavalry tradition (many troopers continued to carry lances) and personal bravery were unavailing against the apparatus of modern war.

The organisation of the cavalry brigades varied somewhat but normally conformed to the pattern given in the diagram overleaf. There were either three or four cavalry regiments; a large battery of horse artillery and a rifle battalion as

Left: Polish cadets at a pre-war torchlit review. This photograph shows particularly well the 'zig-zag' collar embroidery on Polish uniform, (which had its origin in the collar markings of the Polish troops of the Napoleonic armies) and the design of the Polish helmet. The leather equipment is of the German pattern.

17 Colonel, Polish Army, 1939
The commander of the 7th 'Wielkopolski' Mounted Rifles wears the standard officers khaki service dress with the traditional square-topped czapka. *The regiment is identified by the colour of the cap band and the pennant-shaped collar patches. On the left breast pocket he wears the regimental badge of the 7th Mounted Rifles above that of his former reigment, the 1st Mounted Rifles. The medal is the* Virtuti Militari, *an award for gallantry.*

18 Trooper, Polish Army, 1939
This trooper wears the French 1915 model Adrian *steel helmet which was standard issue in mounted units, and a sheepskin coat which was designed to be worn instead of the long double-breasted greatcoat in very cold weather. The rifle is the German Mauser 98K.*

19 Private, Polish Army, 1939
This modern-looking uniform was standard throughout the infantry, although it had not always reached the other arms. The arm-of-service colour (dark blue for infantry) appears on the collar patch, and the badges of rank on the shoulder straps. Equipment is similar to the German pattern but made greater use of cheaper webbing equipment. The rifle is the Polish version (the M29) of the German Mauser.

20 Tank crewman, Polish Army, 1939
Crews of armoured vehicles wore special clothing originating in France which consisted of a cut-away helmet for motorised troops and the three-quarter-length leather coat. They also wore a one-piece khaki overall. The distinctive insignia of armoured troops were the orange and black triangular collar patches. The helmet is the French pattern for motorised troops, which existed in many variations and was used in many countries.

19

20

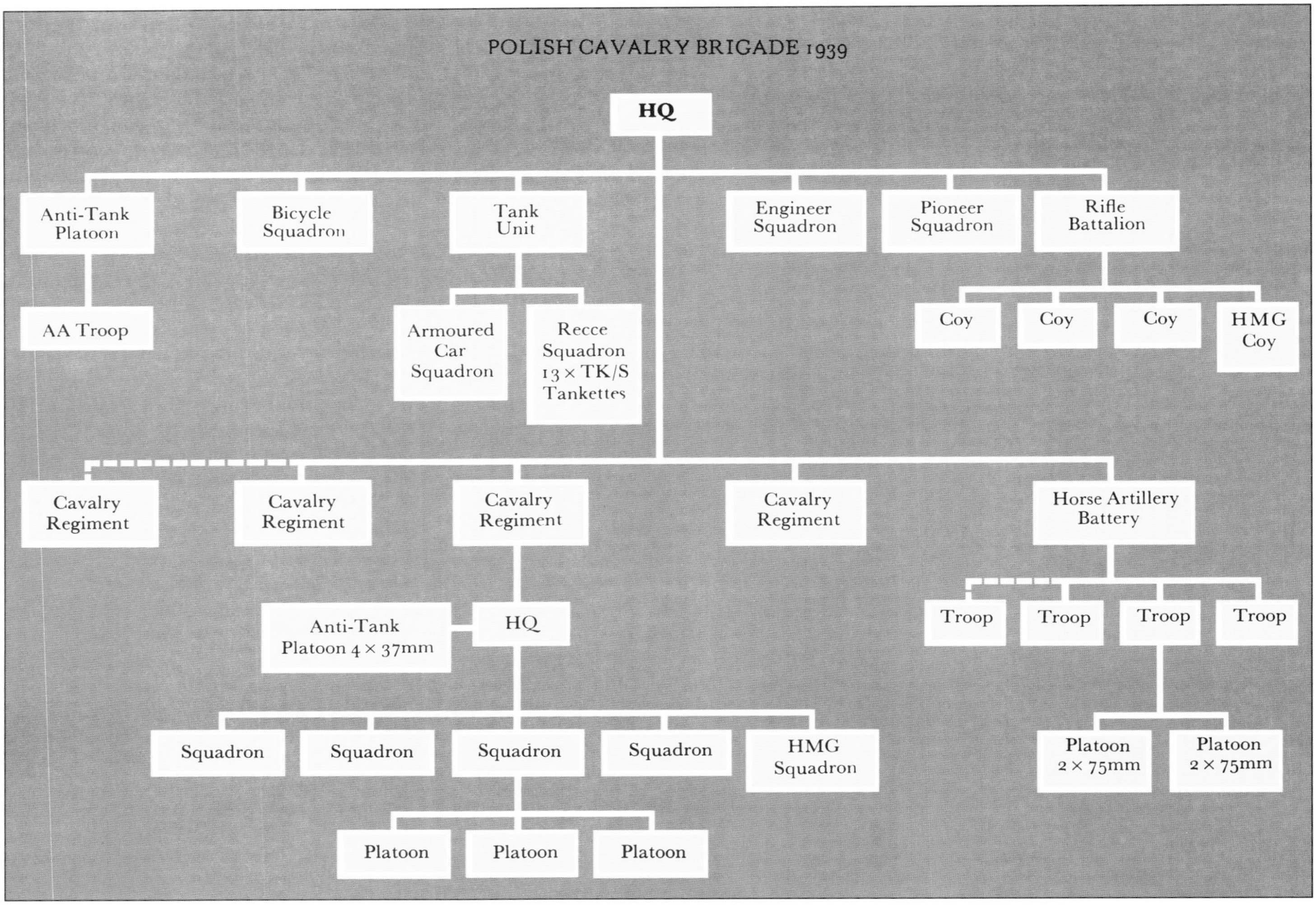

POLISH CAVALRY BRIGADE 1939

- **HQ**
  - Anti-Tank Platoon
    - AA Troop
  - Bicycle Squadron
  - Tank Unit
    - Armoured Car Squadron
    - Recce Squadron 13 × TK/S Tankettes
  - Engineer Squadron
  - Pioneer Squadron
  - Rifle Battalion
    - Coy
    - Coy
    - Coy
    - HMG Coy
  - Cavalry Regiment
  - Cavalry Regiment
  - Cavalry Regiment
    - HQ
      - Anti-Tank Platoon 4 × 37mm
    - Squadron
    - Squadron
    - Squadron
      - Platoon
      - Platoon
      - Platoon
    - Squadron
    - HMG Squadron
  - Cavalry Regiment
  - Horse Artillery Battery
    - Troop
    - Troop
    - Troop
      - Platoon 2 × 75mm
      - Platoon 2 × 75mm
    - Troop

well as the normal brigade services, including a small tank unit. At full strength a four-regiment brigade had 6911 men and 273 officers. Support weapons were:
16 × 75mm guns;
18 × 37mm anti-tank guns;
2 × 40mm anti-aircraft guns;
2 × 81mm mortars;
9 × 50mm mortars.

UNIFORM The uniform of the Polish Army was originally introduced in 1919, gradually improved and standardised in the 1920s and modified again in 1935; it was this uniform that was worn in the brief 1939 campaign. The uniform was highly standardised and existed in five basic patterns: for officers, dismounted personnel, mounted personnel, mountain troops and armoured vehicle crews.

The basic service dress for officers is illustrated by figure 17. For undress occasions the breeches and boots were replaced by long khaki trousers with stripes and black leather undress ankle boots. The greatcoat for all ranks was khaki, single-breasted with a large pointed fall collar, and had matching pointed shoulder straps and turn-back cuffs with tab and two buttons. Cavalry wore very long greatcoats which almost touched the ground.

Infantrymen and all dismounted personnel wore the uniform illustrated by figure 19. With orders of dress not requiring the steel helmet, soldiers normally wore a khaki side cap, or a soft version of the square-topped *czapka*. Personal equipment was based on the German pattern. Mounted personnel wore the basic khaki uniform but retained the French *Adrian*-pattern steel helmet, and were issued with riding breeches and high boots. The units forming the 11th Carpathian Mountain Division had two distinctive items of

Right: The band of the 7th Lubelski Lancers mounted on greys. The troopers are unmistakably Polish in their long greatcoats and czapkas.

uniform. The first was a circular khaki felt hat, not unlike the British steel helmet in shape, and the second a long khaki cape which was worn over the left shoulder.

Personnel in armoured units wore the basic khaki uniform but when serving with their armoured vehicles they wore either a black beret or the French-pattern tank helmet (as in figure 20) and a one-piece khaki overall and brown leather gauntlets. Officers had a three-quarter-length black leather coat with black cloth collar and shoulder straps.

INSIGNIA Rank badges were worn on the head-dress and on the shoulder straps (see insignia chart). General officers were distinguished by silver zigzag embroidery on the cap band, collar patches, shoulder straps and cuffs, and by dark blue stripes on the breeches and long trousers.

Arm-of-service and regimental colours appeared on the cap band and collar patches, which were in the form of lance pennants for all cavalry and armoured units, while those for all other units followed the shape of the collar points in the French manner. These were sometimes adorned by a small white metal badge which identified special appointments, trades, or units.

AIR FORCE

The Polish Air Force dated in embryonic form from the end of World War I; from even before Poland gained her independence. In December 1918 Polish airmen who had served in the French, Austrian and Imperial Russian air forces swore allegiance to the Polish Republic. In September 1919 a Commander-in-Chief was appointed and a re-organisation undertaken which established the Air Force as a part of the Army, and not an independent service.

Between 1 and 6 September 1939 the Air Force was able to put up a coherent air defence, but was soon completely overwhelmed by both the quantity and quality of German aircraft, and disorganised by the surprise strafing of the airfields at the onset of offensive operations. Further re-organisations and change of bases only added to the breakdown of organisation and supply, and lack of fuel and liaison made further resistance virtually impossible, although isolated units continued to attack German ground forces whenever they could.

When Poland capitulated on 5th October she had lost 327 machines, while 98 were evacuated to Romania.

ORGANISATION The Air Force was commanded by the Aviation Commander with the rank of general, who was directly subordinate to the Ministry of Military Affairs. At the end of 1937 an Air Staff was formed within the General Staff, but it was to act independently of the Aviation Commander.

In the Spring of 1939 an operational plan was undertaken which entailed a re-grouping of aircraft into two formations. The bulk of the aircraft were distributed amongst the individual armies along the German border and formed the Army Air Force while a central reserve

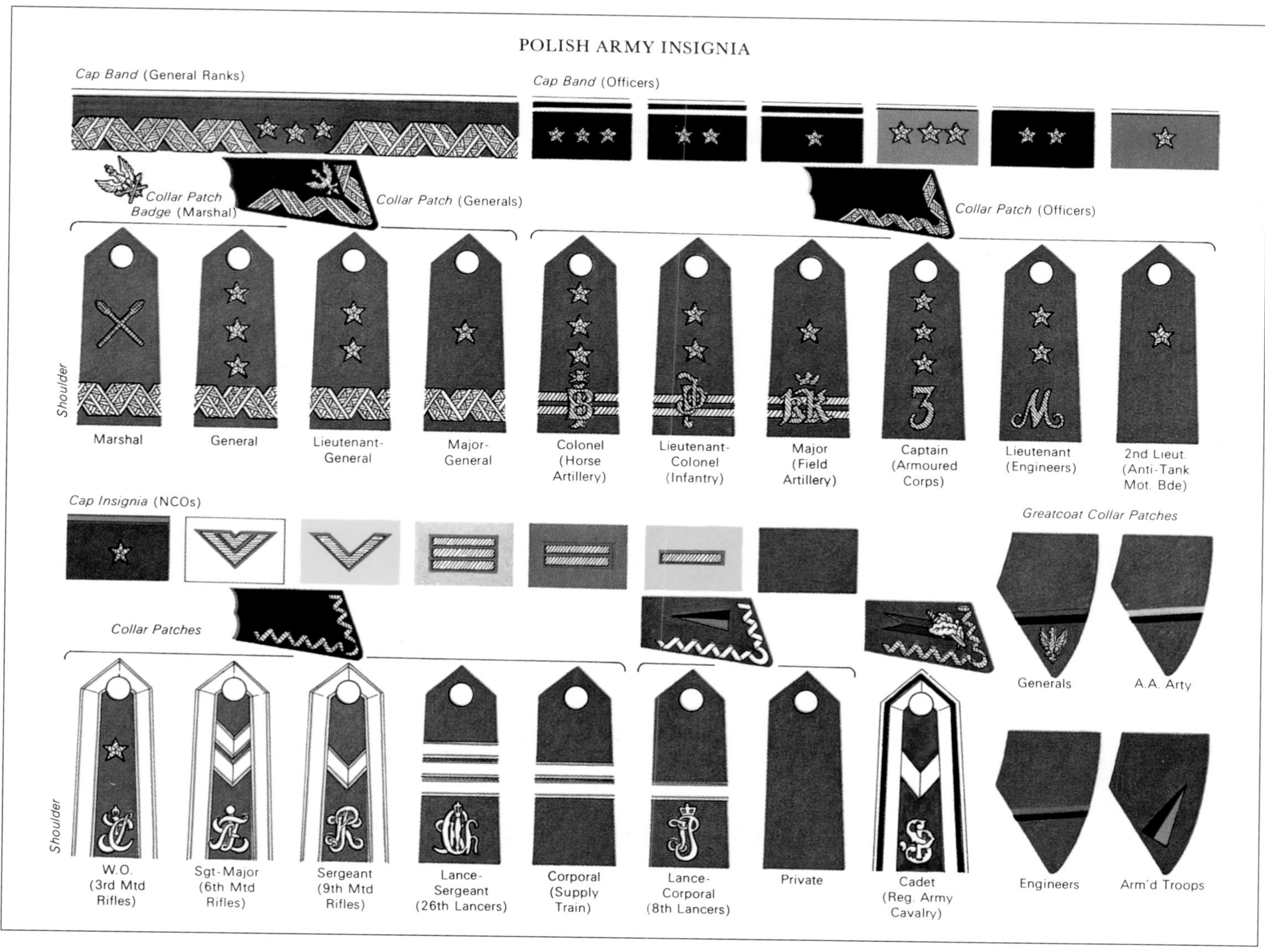

21 Captain, Polish Air Force, 1939

This captain wears the 1936 pattern service dress with rank badges on the front of the cap and on the shoulder straps. The Air Force version of the national eagle is displayed on the cap. On his left breast he wears the Pilot Observer (combat) badge which was issued in 1928 for aviators with dual qualifications although in 1933 the badge was superseded by two separate qualification badges. The dagger, which was identical to the pattern worn by tank officers, was worn with most orders of dress.

22 Lieutenant, Polish Air Force, 1939

In the summer months, crews of enclosed aircraft wore this one-piece overall which was made of undyed linen. A special version of the badges of rank was worn on the left sleeve; the two-star badge illustrated is that of a lieutenant. In common with the flying crew of many nations, this officer wears his own scarf, to prevent his neck chafing against the rough overall cloth. He wears the standard leather flying helmet with goggles.

23 Sergeant-Major, Polish Air Force, 1939

As working dress this staff sergeant wears a sensible and practical working uniform. The only insignia to be worn on this dress were the badges of rank which appear on the beret and shoulder straps.

was held back under the control of the Commander-in-Chief and was known as the Dispositional Air Force. Each army had from three to seven squadrons of reconnaissance, light-bomber and fighter planes acting in a localised ground-support role. The Dispositional Air Force comprised 145 aircraft, organised in:
1 pursuit brigade of 5 fighter squadrons;
one bomber/reconnaissance brigade of 8 squadrons;
1 observation squadron;
4 liaison squadrons.

On 1 September 1939 the frontline strength of the Polish Air Force was 433 aircraft: 59 fighters, 154 bombers, 84 observation machines with negligible armament, and 36 liaison aircraft.

UNIFORM The military aviation of the Polish Army began to replace its Army uniforms with a blue-grey design in 1936. The new uniform was to be worn by all officers and regular NCOs by 1 April 1938.

The service dress for officers is illustrated by figure 21; the greatcoat was grey, double-breasted and with two rows of three white metal buttons. Generals, staff officers and cadets wore the same badges on the greatcoat collar as on the tunic collar. The tunic for other ranks was worn with closed collar and matching pantaloons or long trousers.

Working dress was officially as shown in figure 23, although more typical working dress was probably a crumpled pair of overalls. In warm weather an unlined beige flying suit as illustrated by figure 22 was worn, and in colder weather both a lined and unlined leather flying suit, or a three-quarter-length black leather French-pattern flying coat.

INSIGNIA Rank badges were worn on the head-dress (peaked cap and beret), on the shoulder straps of the tunic and greatcoat, and on the upper left sleeve of the flying suit.

Certain categories of officers wore white metal badges on the tunic and greatcoat collar. Medical officials wore cherry coloured cloth as backing to their rank distinction braid on the peaked cap, and as lace on the tunic cuffs and trousers. Administrative officials wore royal blue as their arm-of-service colour.

21

22

23

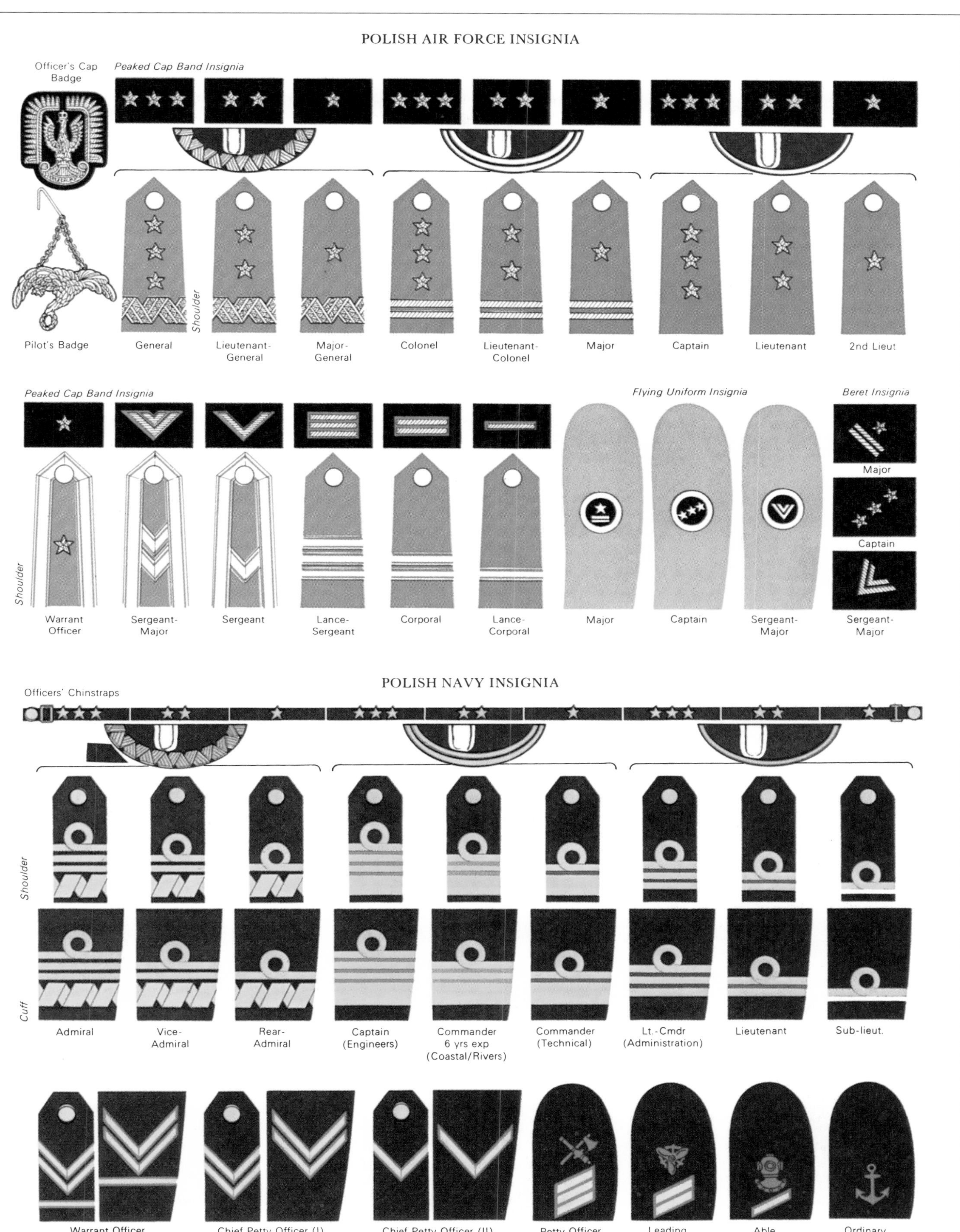
POLISH AIR FORCE INSIGNIA
Officer's Cap Badge
Peaked Cap Band Insignia
Shoulder
Pilot's Badge
General
Lieutenant-General
Major-General
Colonel
Lieutenant-Colonel
Major
Captain
Lieutenant
2nd Lieut
Peaked Cap Band Insignia
Flying Uniform Insignia
Beret Insignia
Major
Captain
Shoulder
Warrant Officer
Sergeant-Major
Sergeant
Lance-Sergeant
Corporal
Lance-Corporal
Major
Captain
Sergeant-Major
Sergeant-Major
POLISH NAVY INSIGNIA
Officers' Chinstraps
Shoulder
Cuff
Admiral
Vice-Admiral
Rear-Admiral
Captain (Engineers)
Commander 6 yrs exp (Coastal/Rivers)
Commander (Technical)
Lt.-Cmdr (Administration)
Lieutenant
Sub-lieut.
Warrant Officer
Chief Petty Officer (I)
Chief Petty Officer (II)
Petty Officer (Ordnance Artificer)
Leading Seaman (I) (Stoker)
Able Seaman (Diver)
Ordinary Seaman (Unqualified)

NAVY

At the Treaty of Versailles Poland was granted some ninety miles of Baltic coastline. The great port of Danzig (Gdansk) was declared a Free City, so the Poles had to construct a large modern naval complex at Gdynia to the west of Danzig. Fortifications with coastal artillery were built at Westerplatte and Hel.

The 180-man garrison of the naval fortress at Westerplatte resisted German air and sea bombardment and attacks from German naval landing parties until forced to surrender on 13 September. The defence of the Hel Peninsula continued until 1 October when ammunition ran out; 3200 soldiers and sailors were taken prisoner, and they left behind over 200 dead and wounded.

24 Able Seaman, Polish Navy, 1939
This able seaman wears the standard 'square rig' of the Polish Navy. The cap tally reads: Marynarka Wojenna. *Rank is indicated by the stripe on his sleeve under the non-substantive badge (RT for* Radio Technik). *The equipment, rifle (Polish 7.92mm Wz29) and gaiters were worn by guards of honour.*

24

Above: A Polish seaman with white-topped summer cap surrenders at Westerplatte.

At sea the Polish Navy had four destroyers, five submarines, one minelayer, six minesweepers and two gunboats. On the eve of the German invasion three of the destroyers and the submarines were ordered to sail to England. After a difficult and dangerous voyage the destroyers and two submarines reached Leith in Scotland on 1 September 1939. The three remaining submarines were unable to break out of the Baltic Sea, and were interned in Sweden.

ORGANISATION The flag officer commanding the Polish Fleet was Vice Admiral J. Unrug. The main naval ports were Gdynia, Oksyvie and Rozewie. In 1939 the strength of the navy was about 400 officers and 4000 ratings. There were no marines as such in the Polish Navy, but there was one naval infantry regiment.

UNIFORM Polish Navy uniforms were very similar to those worn in most other navies, and were based on regulations issued in 1920, 1922, 1927 and 1930.

The uniform for officers is illustrated in the photograph, while cadets and chief petty officers wore the same basic uniform with special rank distinctions (see insignia chart). In hot weather these ranks could wear a white cap cover, white tunic with stand collar, long white trousers and white canvas shoes.

Ratings wore the uniform illustrated by figure 24, although personal equipment and white gaiters were only worn by landing parties or on ceremonial occasions. In cold weather sailors and petty officers had a three-quarter-length pea-coat, while they also received a white uniform for summer and tropical wear. Working dress was a white American-pattern hat and off-white linen jumper and trousers. Petty officers wore a peaked cap and a single-breasted blue tunic with stand collar, patch pockets and five buttons on the front of the tunic.

INSIGNIA Rank was indicated by the number and width of the gold lace stripes on the cuffs and shoulder straps of officers, chief petty officers and petty officers. Officers also had rows of gold braid on the cap peak (gold zigzag embroidery for admirals), and tiny five-pointed gold stars on the chin strap so that it was possible to tell the rank of an officer by looking at his cap. This was useful since Navy personnel often wore protective clothing which did not display badges of rank.

From 30 November 1938 corps and branch colours appeared as backing or 'lights' (the coloured cloth which appeared between the rows of rank distinction lace on the cuffs and shoulder straps). Seamen wore trade and speciality badges in red on the upper left sleeve, while petty officers had yellow badges.

Below: Serving with the Royal Navy after the defeat of Poland, the ratings in this photograph are still wearing Polish caps under their duffle coats.

FINLAND

ARMY

During the autumn of 1939, fearful of the eastward expansion of Nazi Germany, the Soviet government made overtures to Finland for an exchange of territory which would push back the border in the Karelian Isthmus (to make Leningrad more secure) and demanded a long-term lease on the Baltic port of Hanko. The Finns refused, and on 30 November 1939 the Red Army crossed the Finnish border.

The Finnish army was one of the smallest in Europe and the Red Army expected little opposition. But the Soviet invasion found the Finns well prepared; and they turned to their advantage the sub-zero temperatures and deep snow which in any case favoured a defensive. The main Finnish defence, the Mannerheim Line, held until 12 February 1940, although once it was breached there was no alternative but to sue for peace. For an army which never exceeded 200,000 men, Finnish losses were very high: 25,000 killed and 45,000 wounded.

There was talk of Allied intervention since the Soviet Union had signed a non-aggression pact with Hitler's Germany, but the only country to make a sizeable contribution was Sweden which provided weapons, a squadron of aircraft and two battalions of infantry. Volunteers from a number of countries including Norway, Italy, Britain and the United States of America were formed into a volunteer battalion, but it was not ready in time to take part in the fighting.

ORGANISATION Although capable of forming 12 divisions, Finland only had nine at the outbreak of war, and these were sadly lacking in motor transport, communications equipment, anti-tank guns, and automatic weapons. The armed forces were maintained by a small regular cadre which relied on an annual intake of conscripts to complete its numbers. In peacetime, conscripts served for one or one-and-a-half years depending on the arm of service. On completion of conscription the Finnish soldier passed into the reserve in which he remained until the age of 60, when he joined the ranks of the militia.

The country was divided into nine Military Districts, each of which was expected to field a division as well as to provide depots, installations, and facilities to enable the Army to mobilise rapidly.

The organisation of a division consisted of a divisional staff, three infantry regiments, an artillery regiment and companies of signals and pioneers. The artillery regiment comprised 36 guns of various calibres, all of them pre-1918 models and many unsuitable for modern warfare. Although a number of 120mm mortars had been ordered, none had been delivered by the outbreak of war and so the division had only eighteen 81mm mortars, clearly insufficient when compared to the hundred or so mortars of a Soviet division. The supply of automatic weapons was rather better, there being 250 Suomi sub-machine guns and 116 machine guns per division. At full strength a division had 14,200 men.

In addition to the nine divisions of infantry there was an independent cavalry brigade which was made up of a staff, two cavalry regiments, a rifle battalion (mounted on bicycles) and a horse artillery battery.

There was little reserve artillery and the whole field Army possessed only 100 Bofors 37mm anti-tank guns and no anti-aircraft guns at all. The Army had had only minimal experience of tank warfare; but the densely wooded terrain of southern Finland reduced the role of the

25

26

25 Marshal, Finnish Army, 1940

As the only person of that rank in the Finnish Army Marshal Mannerheim's uniform was by definition unique. The badges on the shoulder straps are the Finnish lion in silver and above that the regimental badge of the Uusimaa Dragoons, Mannerheim's old regiment. Rank is not indicated on the collar in this illustration but would otherwise consist of crossed batons and three lions in gold on a silver background (see insignia chart). Suspended from his neck is the Mannerheim Cross of the Cross of Liberty, an award for outstanding gallantry and merit in wartime. On the left sleeve is a Civil Guard badge.

26 Captain, Finnish Army, 1939

Germany had played a leading role in the development of the Finnish Army after World War I and the field-grey M1936 uniform illustrated here has a distinctly German cut. The officer's sheepskin coat and other forms of protective clothing were normal winter issue to the Finnish Army. His winter field cap has a fur-lined peak and flaps which could be turned back; the peak being fastened by the blue and white national cockade and the gilt Finnish lion, the badge of regular Army officers. Arm of service and rank are denoted by the collar patch: a deep green patch with grey frame for the infantry and three brass roses for a captain.

tank to that of infantry support. Some 30 Vickers light tanks had been supplied but they played only a minor part in this infantry war.

There were few medical supplies and communication was at best rudimentary: there was no wireless system and the Army had to rely on field telephones and when that failed a system of runners. This deficiency was particularly serious given the great distances that had to be covered by the beleaguered Finnish Army and, in addition, effective artillery support for the infantry was impossible without radio.

Despite these problems the Finnish Army had two great advantages: firstly, a thorough knowledge of the land in winter weather conditions; and secondly, vastly superior human material which expressed a fierce determination to resist the foreign aggressor. These two qualities came together in the crack battalions of ski troops – men experienced in cross-country skiing and able to cover long distances silently and more quickly than troops equipped with any other form of transport. In particular, the *Sissi-Joukkeet* (guerrilla ski troops) operated behind enemy lines, and proved a considerable thorn in the side of the Red Army.

Below: This Finnish sniper in the Karelian forest wears a snow-camouflage suit and is armed with a rifle with telescopic sights. Snow suits such as the one shown here were merely a thin cloth smock (with hood) and loose over-trousers worn on top of normal winter clothing.

UNIFORM The Finnish Army uniform which was worn throughout World War II was introduced in 1936, and was basically the same for all ranks.

Head-dress consisted of a peaked field cap, although senior officers still continued to wear the old stiff cap with embroidered peak. The tunic was single-breasted with stand-and-fall collar, matching shoulder straps, and six buttons in front. The pleated breast patch pockets had a flap and button, while the side pockets had a flap only. All ranks wore matching breeches and high black leather boots.

To operate in the severe winter, troops received sheepskin caps and coats, white snow camouflage clothing and various types of special footwear which included felt boots. During the Winter War the Finns made use of clothing and equipment captured from the Red Army, but the importation of military equipment from all over the world meant that the Finnish Army suffered from a lack of standardisation which was only partially remedied by the Germans in 1940–41.

INSIGNIA Rank was indicated on the tunic collar patches, and by the rank distinction lace on the greatcoat cuffs. On the raincoat and other types of winter and protective clothing, rank distinction lace appeared on a patch which was buttoned onto the cuffs. Other ranks wore chevrons on the shoulder straps.

The principal methods of indicating arm of service were the colour of the collar patches and the yellow metal badges which were worn on the shoulder straps. In the Imperial Russian tradition (Finland had been part of the Russian Empire until 1917) most formations, units, staffs and establishments had a distinctive metal badge which was worn on the left breast pocket.

AIR FORCE

The Finnish Air Force was not an independent arm but formed part of the Army under its own commander. The Air Force was based on the British model with many instructors and some aircraft being supplied by Great Britain. At the beginning of the war, however, the Air Force was much below establishment and had practically no reserve. The front-line strength was 200 aircraft, but only 108 were operational. Personnel consisted of some 2500 men.

The Air Force was organised as follows:
1st Flying Regiment (ground support, dive bombing and reconnaissance): 4 squadrons each with 3 flights of 4 aircraft (a total of 48 aircraft);

27

27 2nd Lieutenant, Finnish Air Force, 1940
During the war Air Force officers wore a combination of the blue and the grey service uniform; as does this lieutenant. Apart from his blue cap he can be identified as an Air Force officer by the colour of his collar patches and the winged propeller badge on the shoulder straps. Rank is shown by the single rosette on the collar patch. This officer does not wear the white metal flying badge on his left breast pocket, and so he is not a qualified pilot. Breeches tucked into high boots were a very common item of Air Force clothing.

2nd Flying Regiment (fighter defence): 2 squadrons each with 3 flights (a total of 46 aircraft);
3rd Flying Regiment (bombing and long-range reconnaissance): 2 squadrons each with 3 flights (a total of 16 aircraft).

In addition, 2 squadrons for naval reconnaissance, the Air Combat School, and 3 Operational Training Regiments functioned as independent units.

Despite its inherent weaknesses, the Finnish Air Force fought hard and

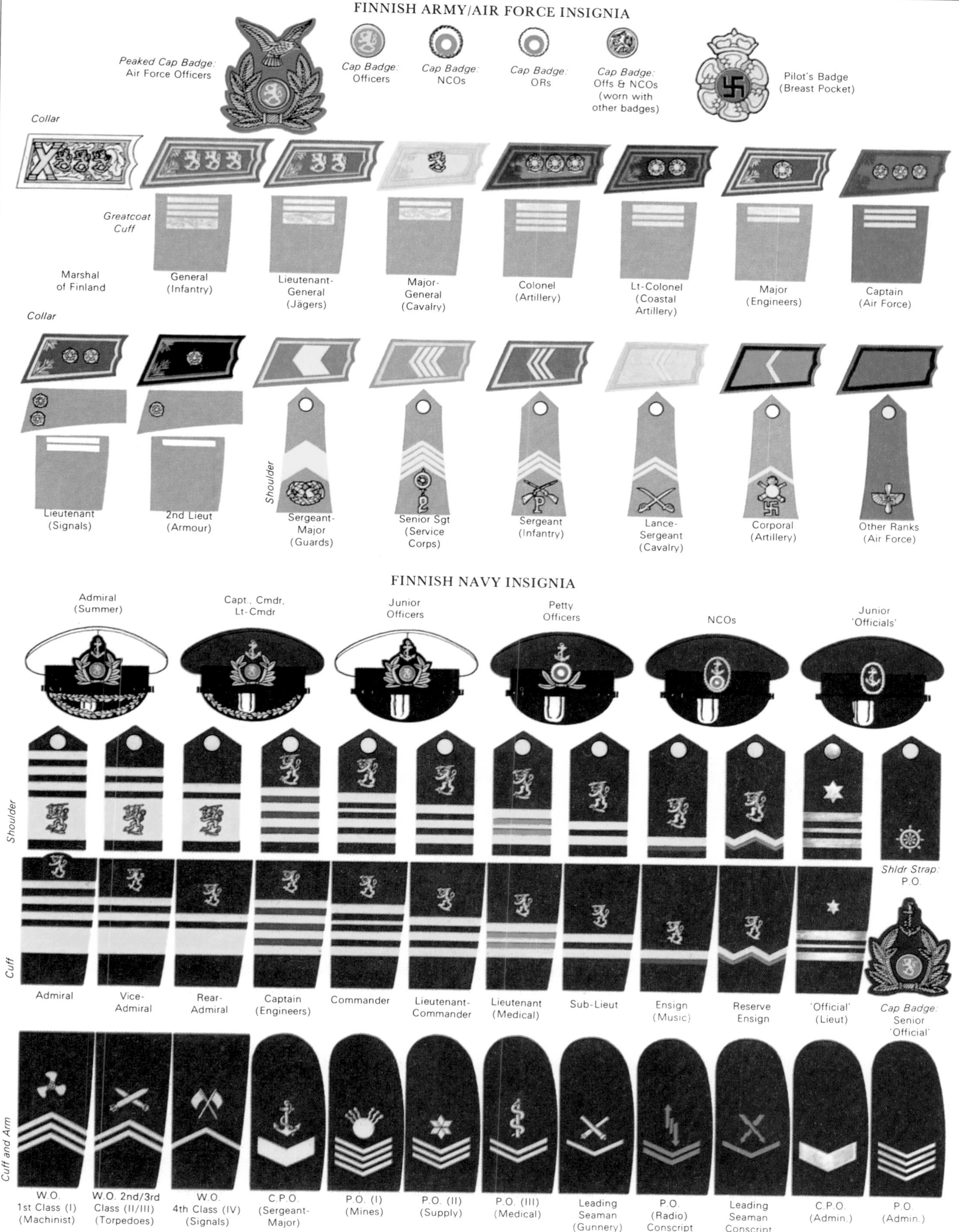
FINNISH ARMY/AIR FORCE INSIGNIA
Peaked Cap Badge: Air Force Officers
Cap Badge: Officers
Cap Badge: NCOs
Cap Badge: ORs
Cap Badge: Offs & NCOs (worn with other badges)
Pilot's Badge (Breast Pocket)
Collar
Greatcoat Cuff
Marshal of Finland
General (Infantry)
Lieutenant-General (Jägers)
Major-General (Cavalry)
Colonel (Artillery)
Lt-Colonel (Coastal Artillery)
Major (Engineers)
Captain (Air Force)
Collar
Shoulder
Lieutenant (Signals)
2nd Lieut (Armour)
Sergeant-Major (Guards)
Senior Sgt (Service Corps)
Sergeant (Infantry)
Lance-Sergeant (Cavalry)
Corporal (Artillery)
Other Ranks (Air Force)
FINNISH NAVY INSIGNIA
Admiral (Summer)
Capt., Cmdr, Lt-Cmdr
Junior Officers
Petty Officers
NCOs
Junior 'Officials'
Shoulder
Cuff
Shldr Strap: P.O.
Admiral
Vice-Admiral
Rear-Admiral
Captain (Engineers)
Commander
Lieutenant-Commander
Lieutenant (Medical)
Sub-Lieut
Ensign (Music)
Reserve Ensign
'Official' (Lieut)
Cap Badge: Senior 'Official'
Cuff and Arm
W.O. 1st Class (I) (Machinist)
W.O. 2nd/3rd Class (II/III) (Torpedoes)
W.O. 4th Class (IV) (Signals)
C.P.O. (Sergeant-Major)
P.O. (I) (Mines)
P.O. (II) (Supply)
P.O. (III) (Medical)
Leading Seaman (Gunnery)
P.O. (Radio) Conscript
Leading Seaman Conscript
C.P.O. (Admin.)
P.O. (Admin.)

inflicted heavy losses on the Red Air Force, claiming 208 victories. Its own losses were 62 combat aircraft and 72 men.

UNIFORM A branch of the Army, the Finnish Air Force did not originally have a special uniform. Eventually a dark blue service dress was introduced for officers, but during the war the most common uniform was that worn by the Army, although items of the blue and grey uniform were sometimes worn together.

Flying clothing consisted of a one-piece unlined overall and leather flying helmet and gloves. Crews of open aircraft and bombers were equipped with fur-lined flying suits and boots, and with fur mittens.

INSIGNIA Army badges of rank were worn on Army uniforms and a special pattern of gold lace stripes was worn on the lower sleeves of the blue (Air Force) uniform.

The Air Force arm-of-service colour was blue and this appeared on the collar patches of Army uniforms. The Air Force emblem was the winged propeller which was worn on the shoulder straps. Qualified pilots wore a white metal badge on the left breast pocket.

Below: Wearing a winter flying-suit and fur mittens, this Finnish aircrewman is better equipped than were many of his colleagues. But the cold was such that very few sorties could be flown and action was rare for the flyers.

NAVY

The President of Finland was Commander-in-Chief of the armed forces, while one of his deputies was chief of the Navy. Under him was the chief of the Coastal Defence Fleet, who, in time of war, came under the operational command of the Army. The strength of the Navy in 1939 consisted of 396 officers and 3613 other ranks.

The greatest problem faced by the Finnish Navy was the shortage of ice-free ports. Apart from three ports on the Murmansk coast, in winter all other ports were seldom ice-free and often completely frozen.

To carry out its principal task of coastal defence, the Finnish Navy had at its disposal 3 gunboats, 30 minelayers and minesweepers, and a number of motor launches and auxiliaries. There were also seven motor torpedo boats of British and Italian design, and five modern submarines. The largest units of the fleet were two heavily armed and armoured coastal defence ships each with a crew of 300 men. The Lake Ladoga Flotilla comprised 20 vessels of various types, but most of these were scuttled or handed over to the Soviet Union in 1940. The Naval Air Force comprised four squadrons including one torpedo bomber squadron.

Severe winter conditions hampered naval activity during the Winter War, although some Finnish submarines operated in the approaches to the Gulf of Bothnia. Coastal batteries (there were two regiments of coastal artillery) did, however, play a significant role in the defence of Finnish territory.

28 Seaman, Finnish Navy, 1939
Over his standard 'square rig' this sailor wears one of the various types of protective clothing issued to members of the Finnish Navy. This outfit is made of water-repellent canvas and is lined with fleece. He is also equipped with a rudimentary radio-telephone apparatus.

UNIFORM The Finnish Navy uniform was very similar to that of the British Navy. Officers and chief petty officers wore a peaked cap, reefer jacket with white shirt and black tie, long trousers and black shoes. The greatcoat was double-breasted with two rows of six buttons.

Petty officers and ratings wore a square rig and a blue cap with long tally on which appeared the name of the vessel or installation in gold lettering, a jumper with blue denim collar, bell-bottomed trousers and black shoes. In cold weather sailors wore a double-breasted pea-coat.

In very cold weather officers wore a black astrakhan cap and all ranks received special cold- and foul-weather clothing. In hot weather officers wore a white uniform while petty officers and ratings wore the white cap cover.

Personnel serving on shore installations or in the coastal artillery wore Army uniforms – often the obsolete 1922 pattern – with Navy head-dress and rank badges.

INSIGNIA Officers wore rank distinction lace on the cuffs and on the greatcoat and white tunic shoulder straps. Other ranks wore chevrons on the upper left sleeve.

The branch or corps of officers was identified by the colour which appeared as 'lights' between the rank distinction lace. Petty officers had gold while conscripts had red branch of service badges above their rank chevrons.

Soviet Union
Army

During 1939–40, the Soviet armed forces were undergoing a period of transition. New weapons and tactical ideas were being developed, but misguided and often stultifying central control meant that there was little sense of initiative or responsibility, and important advances in any sphere were often left in isolation. The excellent progress made in tank construction, for instance, was counterbalanced by the absence of an effective radio-communication system, without which tanks were severely restricted.

The baleful influence of Stalin over the Soviet armed forces during the 1930s culminated in the purges of 1938 which decimated the officer corps. Almost inevitably, the most able and outspoken officers were destroyed by the purges and this was a significant factor in the poor performance of the Red Army in the Winter War against Finland in 1939. It has been estimated that Soviet casualties were about 200,000 men during this short campaign.

At the time little or nothing was known in the West about the Red Army of Workers and Peasants. Some twenty

Below: General T. F. Shtykov inspects the weapons of his troops on the Leningrad Front. The men are all well furnished with winter clothing.

29

30

29 Marshal of the Soviet Union, Red Army, 1940

Marshal S. K. Timoshenko was commander of the Kiev Military District and Commander-in-Chief of the Soviet forces during the war against Finland. He wears the new grey parade uniform which had been introduced in July 1940 for generals and marshals as part of a gradual process of enhancing the status of senior Red Army officers. Rank is denoted by the cap badge, collar patches and sleeve insignia. Timoshenko's decorations are (from top to bottom): the Gold Star of a Hero of the Soviet Union; two Orders of Lenin; three Orders of the Red Banner, and the Red Army 20th anniversary medal.

30 Private, Red Army, 1939

The private is wearing a cloth helmet (the budionovka *or* shlem*) named after the Russian Civil War cavalry commander Budenny, which was found to be unsatisfactory and during the Winter War against Finland began to be replaced by the fur cap with earflaps. The colour of the cloth star and the raspberry red collar patches identify his arm of service as the infantry. Rank badges appeared on the collar patches only. Equipment is rudimentary but effective and (apart from the gasmask in its canvas bag) was the same as that worn during World War I. The rifle is the Moisin-Nagant 7.62mm M1930.*

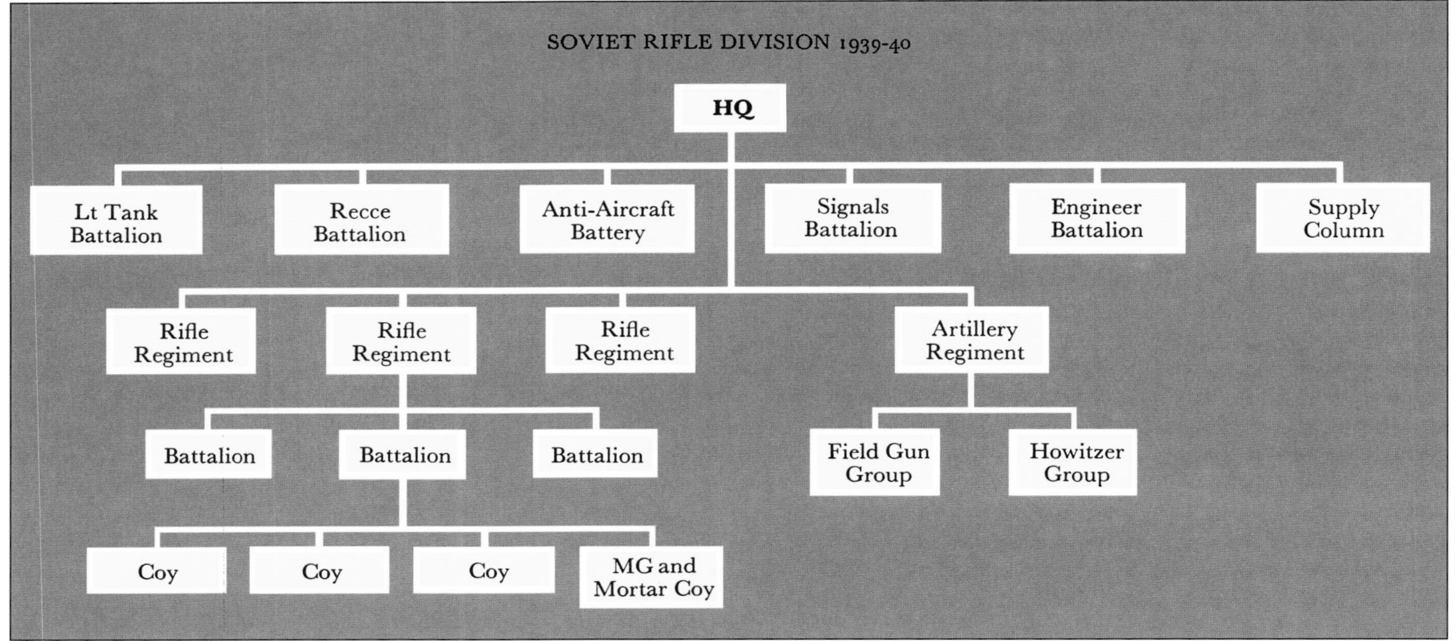

years of isolation had veiled much of what went on in the Soviet Union.

ORGANISATION Overall control of the Red Army was exercised by the People's Commissariat for Defence and the Commander-in-Chief, First Marshal of the Soviet Union K. E. Voroshilov. Decisions were reached in consultation with the Council for Work and Defence, and the eighty-member War Council. Directly subordinate to Voroshilov's Commissariat was the General Staff which was divided into seven departments: operations, organisation, railways, intelligence, mobilisation, anti-aircraft defence and topography. Four deputies were responsible for armaments, land, air and sea forces.

The Army was essentially a standing army which was run by a professional cadre, but it relied on conscription for the mass of its personnel. Men were liable for military service for a period of 22 years from the age of 20 to 41. A conscript served three to four years, depending on his arm of service, in the active or cadre troops, after which he entered the active reserve. From the age of 27 to 35 he was part of the 1st Reserve, and from 35 to 41 part of the 2nd Reserve. The peacetime strength of the army was estimated at 1,800,000 men, while mobilised strength could be as high as 11,000,000.

The Soviet Union was divided into 13 military districts and 2 military commissariats. Each had under its command separate heavy artillery, motorised mechanical corps, aviation, engineer and technical troops as well as all the Field Army units and installations under its jurisdiction. The Field Army consisted of:

35 rifle (infantry) corps (about 100 rifle divisions including 23 Territorial divisions);
7 cavalry corps (32 cavalry divisions);
12 independent cavalry divisions;
5 tank corps (10 tank brigades);
1 motorised rifle brigade.

A rifle corps comprised three to four rifle divisions, a regiment of corps artillery, pioneer, bridging and signals battalions and a squadron of aircraft.

The Soviet rifle division of 1939 had an establishment strength of nearly 19,000 men and was in theory well equipped with supporting arms. As can be seen in the diagram, the Soviet division was a 'combined arms' force capable of undertaking most tasks at divisional level. In practice, however, a chronic shortage of trained manpower prevented the technical and mechanical elements working effectively with the result that the division was little more than a formation of riflemen with artillery support.

The division was, in theory at least, lavishly supplied with artillery, with 12 × 152mm and 28 × 122mm howitzers, 42 × 76mm and 54 × 45mm guns, and over 100 mortars of various calibres ranging from 50 to 120mm. A novel feature was the inclusion of a battalion of T-26 light tanks and armoured cars but they proved ineffective during the fighting in Finland and were withdrawn.

A rifle regiment had a strength of about 2900 officers and men, armed with 7.62mm Moisin-Nagant rifles and M1933 Tokarev pistols. Support weapons were:

81 light machine guns (7.62mm Degtyarev);
58 heavy machine guns (7.62mm Maxim);
6 infantry guns;
6 anti-tank guns.

Great importance was attached to artillery and the Red Army experimented with large groups capable of delivering massive barrages on given targets, a method which was to be fully exploited during the later stages of World War II.

Artillery was organised in 140 light artillery regiments each with a regimental staff, staff battery, anti-aircraft battery and three to four battalions each with three to four batteries of three or four guns each. There were 35 heavy corps artillery regiments with tractor-drawn 150mm guns and howitzers, and 20 artillery regiments held in reserve for use by the Supreme Commander. Anti-aircraft artillery battalions were also motorised and equipped with guns ranging from 40mm Vickers M18s to the 105mm Leningrad M1934.

During the inter-war years Soviet industry began to deliver increasing numbers of armoured fighting vehicles which the Red Army, partly under British influence, had decided to concentrate into large independent armoured formations.

These tank formations (which became an independent arm of the Red Army) were based around either the mechanised brigade (three battalions of 32 T-28 tanks, a battalion of reconnaissance – BT-7 and BT-8 – tanks, and a motorised machine-gun battalion) or the tank brigade (four battalions of T-28 tanks). This was in addition to the battalion of T-26 tanks which formed part of some infantry divisions, the BT-7 tanks which were issued to mechanised units in cavalry formations, and the T-35 tanks which made up the strength of the heavy tank brigades held as Army reserve troops. But experience during the Spanish Civil War and the disastrous showing of armoured formations in unsuitable and sub-zero conditions in Finland led to the abandonment of this progressive development in favour of the French practice of splitting-up tanks amongst the infantry as mobile gun platforms.

Another new concept developed by Soviet military planners was the use of troops and equipment transported by air and dropped by parachute. During large-scale manoeuvres in the Kiev military district in 1935–6 a complete rifle division with all its supporting arms was dropped by parachute. Even light tanks, slung underneath heavy bombers, were dropped from tree-top level without parachutes. But this was merely an exercise, and in the politically unstable days of the late 1930s the techniques of airborne warfare were not developed further by the Red Army. Although the Germans were impressed few others seem to have seen the significance of this novel form of warfare.

The Soviet Union placed great reliance on cavalry because of vast distances, poor road and rail communications and the inability of Soviet industry to provide vehicles for all of such a huge army. In 1937–38, for example, large-scale cavalry formations, able to operate as independent forces, had been created as a 'strategic cavalry'.

A cavalry corps consisted of a corps staff, three cavalry divisions, and corps troops. The cavalry division comprised:
divisional staff;
2 brigades (each of 2 regiments);
2 motorised rifle battalions;
1 horse artillery regiment;
1 armoured car (or tank) battalion;
pioneer and signals squadron;
supply unit.

The cavalry regiment comprised:
regimental staff;
5 squadrons of sabres;
1 machine gun squadron (mounted in carts);
1 artillery battery (76mm guns);
pioneers, signals and chemical troops;
baggage train.

Below: A Soviet machine-gun team training on the M1910 Maxim, an old but reliable weapon which was in widespread use. They are wearing the shlem *and standard-issue greatcoat.*

Uniform The Soviet Union maintained the largest Army in Europe, and in order to keep it supplied with uniforms and personal equipment, Soviet industry could only produce tried and tested designs. Many of the basic patterns of clothing had been designed at the beginning of the century at the time of the Russo-Japanese War, and had proved themselves during World War I. Westerners often describe Russian uniform as cheap and shabby, and refer to a lack of standardisation. In fact, the traditional Russian uniform had a certain rugged smartness when well worn, and since everything was manufactured in state factories the degree of standardisation achieved was never equalled in any other Army.

The basic uniform consisted of a flat 'Japanese-style' peaked cap, a khaki shirt in traditional cut but with stand-and-fall collar, which was worn outside the trousers. Breeches were either of a matching colour or dark blue. High boots were increasingly replaced by ankle boots (often of American manufacture) and puttees. This basic uniform was worn throughout the year, but in winter all ranks wore a long grey greatcoat (*shinel*) and grey cloth pointed helmet (*shlem*).

In addition to the basic items described above officers had a superior quality shirt, with piping, which was made of cotton for summer and wool for winter wear. The greatcoat was made of good quality cloth with piping and brass buttons. At the end of 1935 officers had received a new single-breasted tunic which could be worn with either breeches and boots or long trousers and shoes.

31 Colonel, Red Army, 1939
As part of a general smartening-up process, and to enhance the importance of the tank arm within the Red Army, a new steel-grey service dress was introduced in December 1935. During the war tank troops wore the standard khaki uniforms but occasionally an officer continued to wear his grey peaked cap. There is no confirmation that other ranks received steel-grey service uniforms.

In the 1930s the armoured troops became one of the most prestigious arms of the Red Army, and this status was reflected in a new steel-grey uniform which was introduced in 1935 as an undress and full-dress uniform. In the field officers wore the standard Army uniform or the special protective clothing issued to crews of armoured vehicles. This clothing consisted of a leather helmet fitted with padded ribs, a one-piece black overall and leather driving gauntlets.

Soviet insignia is examined in the section on the Eastern Front.

AIR FORCE

Throughout the 1920's and 1930's the Soviet Government made enormous efforts to build up a large modern air force, but the difficulties in finding suitable designs and the machines and materials to mass produce aircraft were enormous.

To overcome the lack of pilots and mechanics the government poured money into the voluntary organisation *Osoaviakhim* (Society for the Support of Defence, Aviation and Chemical Defence). Soon after its formation in 1927 it had a membership of three million which had grown to 13 million by 1936. Aero clubs were set up to provide pilots, mechanics and parachutists, and until 1940 all Red Air Force volunteers came from this source. Shortages of instructors, training aids and aircraft meant that the standard attained was very low, however, and it was finally decided to select Air Force recruits from the annual military draft.

Between 1935 and 1937, 3576 aircraft, including a large proportion of four-engined bombers, were produced, but as the numbers increased so effectiveness decreased because the technical standard of the aircraft industry was falling behind developments in more advanced industrial nations.

The Red Air Force had its first practical experience in the Spanish Civil War and this resulted in certain organisational and operational changes, but it was the traumatic experience of the Winter War against Finland (in which some 1000 Soviet aircraft were lost) that really showed up the alarming shortcomings in training, tactics and equipment. Red Air Force commanders were not ignorant of these defects but the purges of 1937–1938, which removed many senior commanders, meant that the remedies undertaken were not necessarily the most effective.

ORGANISATION The Soviet government not only had to overcome technical and manpower problems in the construction of an air force, it also encountered difficulties in its organisation. Soviet military doctrine considered air power as an adjunct to land warfare and so the Air Force continued to be part of the Army. But by 1937 the Air Force had grown in size and importance to such an extent that it was decided that an Air Force representative should be admitted to the State Commissariat for Defence.

The Air Force of the Red Army (VVS-RKKA) was, however, divided into two basic components. The first was the Air Force of the Red Army which consisted of fighter and ground attack regiments under the direct control of a Military District (later Front). The second component was the Long-Range Bomber Force which was at the disposal of the State Commissariat of Defence for tactical deployment on any front when necessary.

Above: A group of Soviet pilots, preparing for take-off. They are wearing leather flying coats, fur-lined helmets and goggles.

In April 1939 a thorough re-organisation within the Air Force took place. The largest formation was now the air division, which comprised between four and six air regiments (formerly brigades). Each regiment consisted of about 60 aircraft with additional reserve planes (usually about 40 aircraft).

There were three types of Air Regiment:

bomber regiments with four squadrons of 12 aircraft each;

fighter regiments with four squadrons of 15 aircraft each;

ground attack regiments with four squadrons of 15 aircraft each.

The squadron was divided into wings (*Zven 'ya*) of three aircraft.

The Air Force attached to a Military District or Front included a number of fighter and bomber regiments, while mixed regiments with both bomber and fighter components were attached to army corps, which also retained their own reconnaissance squadrons.

UNIFORM As members of the Red Army, Air Force personnel wore Army uniforms. Following the French custom, however, a dark blue uniform was introduced in 1935 for wear as a dress and undress uniform. Items of the blue uniform continued to be worn with khaki clothing during the war, because of the shortage of uniforms in the wartime Soviet Union.

The basic pre-war flight clothing for fighter pilots was a fur-lined leather flying helmet and double-breasted brown leather coat. In warm weather pilots of enclosed aircraft wore their service uniforms. Bomber crews wore either an unlined one-piece black overall or a fur-lined one-piece flying suit, with soft fur-lined flying boots which could cover the thighs, but were often worn with the tops folded down to give the appearance of fur leggings (as in figure 32).

NAVY

As a land power the Soviet Union did not look upon the Red Navy's role as a strategic one. Its main tasks, therefore, were the patrolling of territorial waters, the protection of shore installations, the support of land forces, and the provision of vessels and personnel for amphibious operations.

ORGANISATION The head of the Red Navy, the Chief of Naval Forces, was directly subordinate to the People's Commissar for Defence, and acted as the latter's deputy and adviser on all naval matters. The Navy was divided into the Fleet, including the Underwater (submarine) Fleet, the Naval Air Force, and Coastal Defence.

Conscripts in the Navy usually served for five years in one of the four fleets (Baltic, Northern, Black Sea and Pacific), or in one of the flotillas which operated in the seas and lakes of the Soviet Union. The Red Navy did not have a special force of marines, but used its ratings – who had all undergone basic infantry training in the fleet depots – for combined operations when necessary. The strength of the whole Soviet Navy in 1939 was estimated at 40,000 men of whom 22,000 were serving at sea.

The fleet involved in the war against Finland was the Baltic Fleet. At the beginning of the war the fleet was operationally subordinated to the Leningrad Military District, and comprised the following:
2 battleships;
2 cruisers;
21 destroyers and torpedo boats;
52 submarines;
41 motor torpedo boats;
13 minelayers, minesweepers and auxiliaries;
2 escort and patrol boats.
Added to this were the small craft of the Lake Ladoga Flotilla.

32 Pilot, Red Air Force, 1939
Over his service uniform this pilot of a Tupolev SB-2 bomber wears a one-piece fur-lined flying suit, on which he carries his equipment: including pistol, map case and parachute harness. The thigh-length fur-lined flying boots were often worn turned down as illustrated. The extreme cold of the Russian winter made such warm clothing a vital necessity.

33 Seaman, Red Navy, 1939
This Red Fleetsman on guard duty wears the standard naval cap and the greatcoat which had replaced the pea-coat (bushlat) *in cold weather. The cap tally translates as 'Northern Fleet'. Over his right shoulder he carries a gas mask in a canvas bag. The rifle is the Moisin-Nagant M1930 rifle with bayonet fixed in reserve position.*

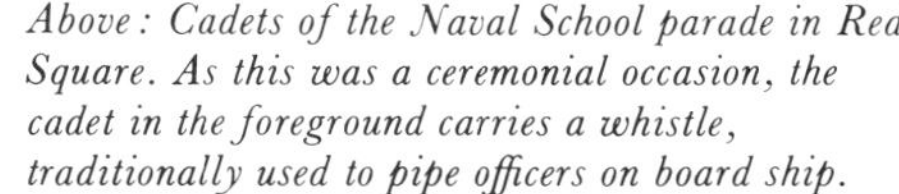
Above: Cadets of the Naval School parade in Red Square. As this was a ceremonial occasion, the cadet in the foreground carries a whistle, traditionally used to pipe officers on board ship.

32

33

The extreme winter weather restricted naval operations and activities were limited to providing artillery support for land operations, and providing personnel for landing operations in the Gulf of Finland and on the Karelian Isthmus.

Uniform Uniform in the 'Muscovy Fleet', as the Red Navy was sometimes called, followed the standard international naval pattern, but incorporated two unusual features: it was the only navy in which the sailor's traditional square rig was worn with the petty officer's peaked cap, and in which the sailor's uniform combined both the colours blue and black.

The officers' black uniform consisted of peaked cap, reefer jacket with white shirt and black tie, black trousers and black leather shoes. The black greatcoat was double-breasted with two rows of six gilt metal buttons. Ratings wore a dark blue jumper (*flanelevka*) and black bell-bottom trousers. The cap had a long ribbon or 'tally' on which appeared the name of the ship in gilt cyrillic letters.

Warrant officers (*mishman* from the English midshipman) and chief petty officers wore the officer's uniform with a special cap badge, while petty officers with more than five years' service wore the peaked cap with sailor's uniform.

DENMARK
ARMY

The German pretext for the occupation of Denmark, was to protect her from attack by Britain, and so German troops were ordered to make the take-over as peaceful and friendly as possible. In fact Danish casualties were only 12 airmen, 11 soldiers and 3 frontier guards killed.

The German authorities allowed the King and government to exercise limited power, while all questions relating to the occupying power were the subject of negotiation between the two parties. The Danish forces were to continue to exist, but in much reduced circumstances, with a total strength not exceeding 3300 men. These consisted of the Royal Life Guards, trained conscripts and conscripts required for maintenance and repair work. In addition there were a number of reserve officers and NCOs undergoing training in the Army Officers' School.

Relations between the two countries deteriorated, however, and the Germans imposed restrictions which in November 1942 banned Danish soldiers and the wearing of military uniform from Jutland. The Danish Army was then concentrated in Sjaelland and the Island of Funen. The final act came in August 1943 when the Germans took the Danish garrison by surprise and disarmed it after a short fight. Thereafter all Danish military personnel were made prisoners-of-war, and the armed forces disbanded.

ORGANISATION The Danish Defence Act of 1937 set up a peacetime establishment of two divisions, an independent anti-aircraft and engineer regiment, an army air force, the Bornholm garrison, a transport battalion and a general headquarters.

In peacetime the regiments and battalions were no more than a small administrative staff responsible for the training of the annual intake of 6599 conscripts who were allocated as follows: 4340 to the infantry, 465 to the Life Guards, 374 to the cavalry, 1120 to the artillery, and 300 men to the engineers. On 8 April 1940 there were 6600 conscripts with eleven month's training service with the colours, as well as a further 2050 non-combatants. During the German invasion part of this force was on leave, while a further seven per cent were unfit for duty.

The Sjaelland Division had its headquarters in Copenhagen and consisted of the Life Guards, the 1st, 4th and 5th Infantry Regiments, the Guards Hussars, the 1st and 2nd Field Artillery Regiments, the 13th Anti-Aircraft Battalion and an engineer battalion.

The Jutland Division had its headquarters in Viborg with the 2nd, 3rd, 6th and 7th Infantry Regiments the infantry pioneer regiment, the Jutland Dragoon Regiment, the 3rd Field Artillery Regiment, the 14th Anti-Aircraft Battalion, and the 2nd Engineer Battalion.

The establishment strength of an infantry regiment was 3000 all ranks who were armed with Krag-Jørgensen M84/24 rifles and Bayard M1910 pistols.

34

35

34 Staff Officiant, Danish Army, 1940

This warrant officer has been issued with the old 1864 model black greatcoat, which was the same for other ranks but without the turn-ups on the cuffs. As well as the M1923 steel helmet, he carries a khaki field cap (with the national cockade just visible on the front) tucked into his Sam Browne belt. The two gold rosettes on the brown silk shoulder straps indicate his rank. Below his old-style black greatcoat, the warrant officer is probably wearing the new khaki uniform. Although most other ranks had not been issued with the new colour, many NCOs and officers had purchased khaki uniforms privately.

35 Private, Danish Army, 1940

Although the 1915 pattern grey wool clothing was outmoded by 1940 it was still worn by the rank and file, and trousers turned over the boots were a characteristic feature of Danish uniform. This private is equipped with a haversack and below that the 1926 gas mask; an entrenching tool with a knife bayonet attached, and the Danish M1923 steel helmet. Armament consists of a Danish M1889/10 8mm rifle with ammunition pouches strapped onto the belt.

36 First Lieutenant, Danish Air Force, 1940

Apart from the pilot's wings, this uniform was worn by both Army and Air Force officers. On the officer's pattern cap is the national cockade and below that the badge for junior officers. The uniform is the khaki M1923 pattern worn with a Sam Browne belt. Rank is denoted by the gold star (of an officer) on the collar and the two five-pointed stars (of a first lieutenant) on the grey silk shoulder straps. The breeches are tucked into the standard pattern high polished boots.

Above: The crew of a Danish anti-aircraft gun undergoing training. This photograph shows the shape of the Danish helmet extremely well.

The supporting arms of the regiment consisted of:
256 light machine guns (Madsen M24);
32 heavy machine guns (Madsen M29);
24 horse drawn machine guns (Madsen M29);
24 heavy mortars;
6 horse-drawn anti-tank guns (37mm Bofors).

An artillery regiment consisted of a staff, and four battalions each of three batteries. Artillery pieces used were Krupp 75mm field guns, Schneider 105mm guns and Schneider 50mm howitzers.

UNIFORM In 1940 Danish Army uniform was in the process of change, and a new khaki uniform with brown leather equipment and footwear was replacing the old uniform with its black leather equipment and footwear. Denmark's neutrality and peacetime economies meant that the changeover only took place slowly, and when the Germans invaded in April 1940, they encountered soldiers dressed in both grey and khaki uniforms with a mixture of brown and black equipment. Generally speaking officers and regular NCOs wore khaki, but the bulk of the Army and in particular conscripts wore grey tunics and greatcoats, light blue trousers, and black leather equipment.

The khaki uniform consisted of a single-breasted tunic with stand-and-fall collar fastened with six bronzed buttons and pleated patch pockets. The greatcoat was double-breasted with two rows of six buttons and a large fall collar. Trousers were worn rolled half way up the calf outside the leather lace-up field boots. The new M1923 (1937) pattern steel helmet had a distinctive shape and had the Danish coat of arms on the front. When the helmet was not needed all ranks wore a khaki side cap.

The Royal Danish Life Guards had a field uniform in the same cut, but it was made in a grey-green cloth, not dissimilar to the German field-grey, and later in the war this uniform was adopted by the German-sponsored Schalburg Corps.

INSIGNIA Rank was indicated by the number, width and colour of the lace and braid on the side cap, and the shoulder straps. Corporals wore yellow lace chevrons on the sleeves.

For arm-of-service identification, certain categories of commissioned ranks wore gilt metal badges on the tunic collar, while other ranks wore an enamelled badge above the right breast pocket.

AIR FORCE

The Air Force, which formed part of the Army, consisted of two battalions, one of which was based on Jutland, and the other on Sjaelland. On the morning of 9 April 1940 the Air Force order-of-battle was as follows:
1 squadron with 13 interceptor aircraft;
1 squadron with 8 interceptors and 2 reconnaissance aircraft;
1 squadron with 11 reconnaissance and 1 training aircraft;
1 squadron with 14 reconnaissance aircraft and an autogiro;
the Air Force School with 18 training aircraft.

Following the German disbandment of the remaining Danish armed forces in August 1943, a number of Danish pilots made their way to Sweden where they began to train on Swedish aircraft (Saab B-17s). It was planned to form an air support unit for the Danish Brigade in Sweden, but this plan was not completed before the end of the war.

UNIFORM Air Force personnel wore Army uniform, although officers do appear to have preferred an open version of the khaki service tunic. Qualified flying personnel wore embroidered 'wings' on the right breast.

36

NAVY

The King of Denmark was Commander-in-Chief of the armed forces while actual command of the Navy was exercised by the Naval Minister, Vice-Admiral H. Rechnitzer, who was also responsible for all coastal defences. The personnel of the Navy in 1940 was about 1500 men, and the main base was at Copenhagen. The Navy comprised:
12 coastal defence ships;
17 motor torpedo boats;
9 submarines;
14 minesweepers;
6 minelayers;
several fishery control vessels.

The Naval Air Service had at its disposal sixty-four aircraft, but only two of these were shipborne.

Despite warnings of an imminent German attack on 4 April 1940, no warlike preparations were made for fear of providing provocation. When it was reported that large numbers of German warships and transports were sailing in Danish waters through the 'Great Belt', Danish ships were ordered not to open fire unless fired upon. As the German ships were not resisted there was no fighting and no ships were sunk at sea.

The Danish Navy continued to exist under the German occupation and even undertook some local minesweeping, but it was not long before relations between the two countries deteriorated to such an extent that the Danes prepared to sail their ships to Sweden, or scuttle them. On 29 August 1943, following the failure of German attempts to negotiate the surrender of the sovereignty of the Danish Navy, 31 vessels were scuttled.

UNIFORM Danish Navy uniform, as worn during World War II, was originally introduced in the 1870s and amended in 1909 and 1932.

Officers, chief petty officers and petty officers wore a peaked cap, reefer jacket with white shirt and black tie, matching navy-blue trousers, and black shoes and socks. The navy-blue greatcoat was double-breasted, and here the Royal Danish Navy departed from the established practice and officers wore rank distinction lace on the greatcoat cuffs, instead of on the shoulder straps.

Right: A Danish rating in square rig, the basic uniform of the Navy.

Below: A Danish Navy flyer wearing basic uniform under his harness. His rank (sub-lieutenant) is shown on the cuffs.

Ratings in square rig wore the standard sailor's cap with a circular cockade in the national colours on the right side, and a blue jumper worn outside bell-bottomed trousers. Under the jumper was worn a white shirt with blue denim collar edged with three white lines, and a black scarf. In summer all ranks wore a white cap cover and there were white versions of both officers' and ratings' uniforms.

INSIGNIA The rank group was indicated by the cap badge, and the rank by the number of bands and width of the rank distinction lace on the cuffs of officers and chief petty officers. Ratings and petty officers wore their rank badges on the upper sleeve.

For arm-of-service distinction, officers serving in special branches such as the reserve or coastal artillery wore a letter ('R' with anchor or 'K') inside the 'curl' of the rank distinction lace, while other branches were identified by coloured backing or 'lights' which appeared between the rank distinction lace. Naval aviators wore the letter 'F' (*Flyver*) in the 'curl' and gold-embroidered wings on the breast.

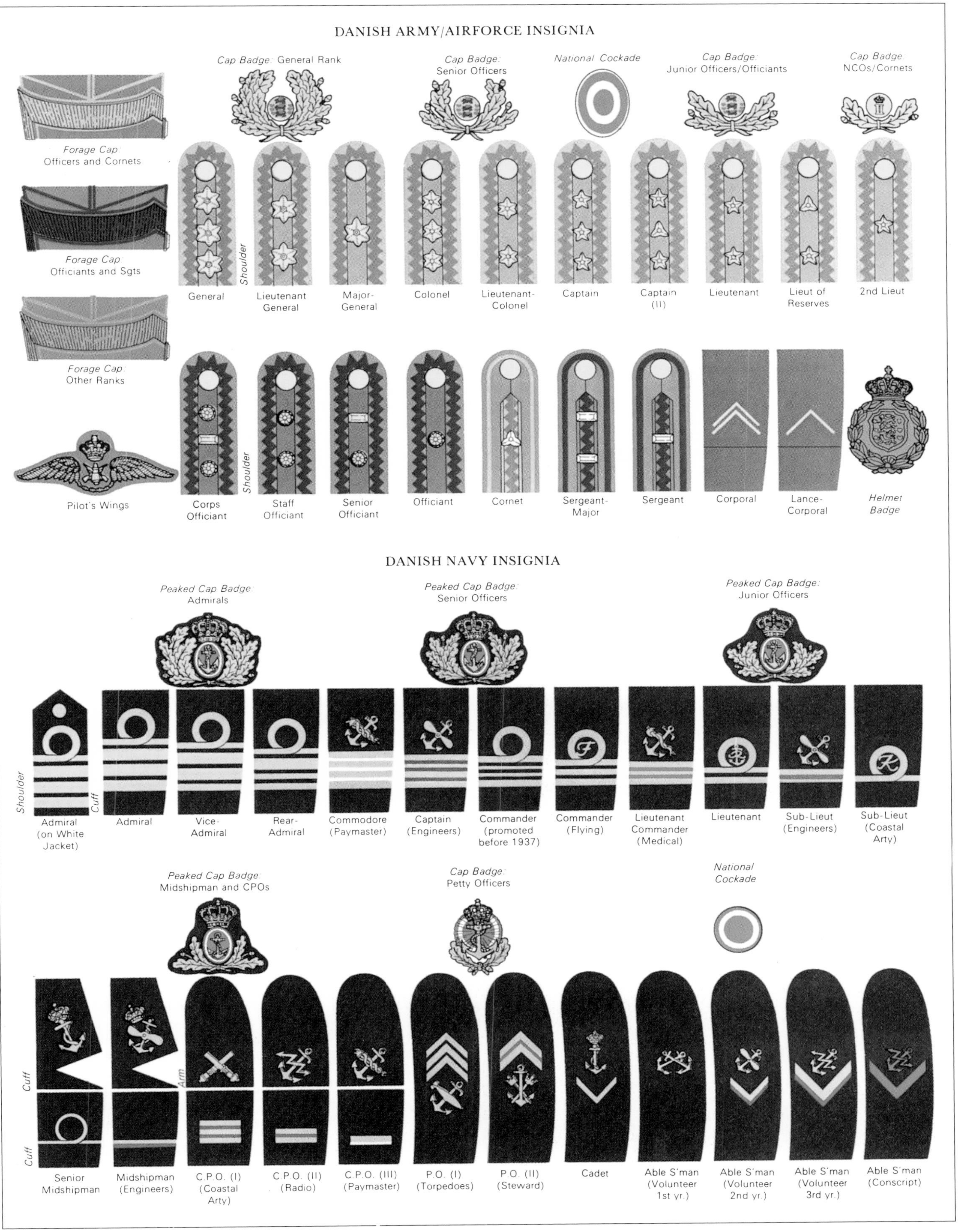
DANISH ARMY/AIRFORCE INSIGNIA
Cap Badge: General Rank
Cap Badge: Senior Officers
National Cockade
Cap Badge: Junior Officers/Officiants
Cap Badge: NCOs/Cornets
Forage Cap: Officers and Cornets
Forage Cap: Officiants and Sgts
Forage Cap: Other Ranks
Shoulder
General
Lieutenant General
Major-General
Colonel
Lieutenant-Colonel
Captain
Captain (II)
Lieutenant
Lieut of Reserves
2nd Lieut
Pilot's Wings
Shoulder
Corps Officiant
Staff Officiant
Senior Officiant
Officiant
Cornet
Sergeant-Major
Sergeant
Corporal
Lance-Corporal
Helmet Badge
DANISH NAVY INSIGNIA
Peaked Cap Badge: Admirals
Peaked Cap Badge: Senior Officers
Peaked Cap Badge: Junior Officers
Shoulder
Cuff
Admiral (on White Jacket)
Admiral
Vice-Admiral
Rear-Admiral
Commodore (Paymaster)
Captain (Engineers)
Commander (promoted before 1937)
Commander (Flying)
Lieutenant Commander (Medical)
Lieutenant
Sub-Lieut (Engineers)
Sub-Lieut (Coastal Arty)
Peaked Cap Badge: Midshipman and CPOs
Cap Badge: Petty Officers
National Cockade
Cuff
Cuff
Arm
Senior Midshipman
Midshipman (Engineers)
C.P.O. (I) (Coastal Arty)
C.P.O. (II) (Radio)
C.P.O. (III) (Paymaster)
P.O. (I) (Torpedoes)
P.O. (II) (Steward)
Cadet
Able S'man (Volunteer 1st yr.)
Able S'man (Volunteer 2nd yr.)
Able S'man (Volunteer 3rd yr.)
Able S'man (Conscript)

NORWAY
ARMY

In 1939, after more than a hundred years of peace, Norway did not possess a large standing army and her government considered that effective national defence against a major power was impossible. The Soviet Union's invasion of Finland in 1939 was a severe shock, and during the winter a sizeable Norwegian force was established in northern Norway. After the Soviet Union signed an armistice with the Finns in March 1940, however, the force was disbanded. When the Germans invaded on 8 April, the Norwegian Army was only partially mobilised and in the process of training new recruits. But despite these disadvantages, Norway put up a stubborn fight and it was two months before the country was completely overrun and the British, French and Polish contingents evicted. The government finally capitulated on 9 June 1940. Despite bitter fighting casualties had been light; the Norwegians lost just 1335 killed and wounded. Small contingents of Norwegians managed to escape to England, while others crossed into Sweden.

ORGANISATION King Haakon VII was Commander-in-Chief of a basically territorial army, which when fully mobilised, was to have had a strength of about 100,000 men. A small cadre of regular officers and NCOs was responsible for running the Army and for the training of conscripts.

The country was divided into six Military Districts or Commands with their headquarters in Halden, Oslo, Kristiansand, Bergen, Trondheim and Harstad. Each Command was initially expected to field a brigade, later to be expanded to a division and garrison and ancillary troops.

An infantry division comprised a staff, two or three infantry regiments, and either a field artillery regiment, or a mountain artillery battalion. The 2nd Infantry Division in Oslo included the Royal Guard and a cavalry regiment. The 5th and 6th infantry divisions had, in addition, a pioneer and flying battalion.

An infantry regiment had a strength of 3750 men armed with Krag-Jorgensen M1894 rifles. Some regiments had a bicycle company for reconnaissance duties, which in winter became a ski troop. Support weapons consisted of:
96 light machine guns (6.5 mm Madsen);
36 heavy machine guns (Colt-Browning M29);
8 heavy mortars.

37 Lieutenant, Norwegian Army, 1940
This infantry officer wears the basic 1934 pattern service dress with rank distinctions appearing on the kepi and on the collar, while arm of service is identified by the design of the buttons and the colour of the piping on the kepi, tunic collar, cuffs and trousers. In very cold weather officers and men often wore various kinds of sheepskin coats and other types of protective clothing over this uniform. In his holster he carries the M1914 service pistol, and the pouch on the left holds three magazines for the same weapon.

38 Corporal, Norwegian Army, 1940
The soldier depicted here wears the winter version of the service dress tunic, which was sufficiently baggy to allow plenty of warm clothing to be worn underneath. His soft cap with earflaps was known as a 'Finnmark' cap. The trousers are worn tucked into thick knitted socks over which he wears canvas gaiters (both these items proved popular with the inadequately equipped German soldiers). On his pack is the obsolete dark-blue overcoat which was still worn in 1940. The rifle is the 6.5mm Krag-Jorgensen M 1894. The old-pattern red piping is worn.

37

38

Field artillery regiments had three battalions of two or three batteries of four guns. The first and second battalions were equipped with Kongsberg 120mm field howitzers, while the third battalion acted as a reserve with three batteries of Ehrhardt 75mm M1901 field guns. All artillery pieces were horsedrawn.

The anti-aircraft regiment was motorised and equipped with Madsen 20mm heavy machine guns, and Kongsberg 75mm M1932 anti-aircraft guns.

UNIFORM The grey-green uniform of the Norwegian Army was originally introduced in 1912. The uniform was highly standardised and the same for all ranks. The basic uniform for officers and other ranks is illustrated in figure 37, but additionally there was a side cap with piped flap and two patterns of steel helmet. The first helmet was the British Mark I which was being replaced by the Swedish civil defence helmet (designated M1931 by the Norwegians). In 1935 an oval stamped badge bearing the Norwegian lion was issued for wear on the front of the helmet.

Over the tunic, which existed in three patterns, a double-breasted water-repellent grey-green cotton-duck jacket

Left: Three Allied soldiers evacuated from Norway: from left, a French chasseur alpin, *a British infantryman and a Norwegian officer.*

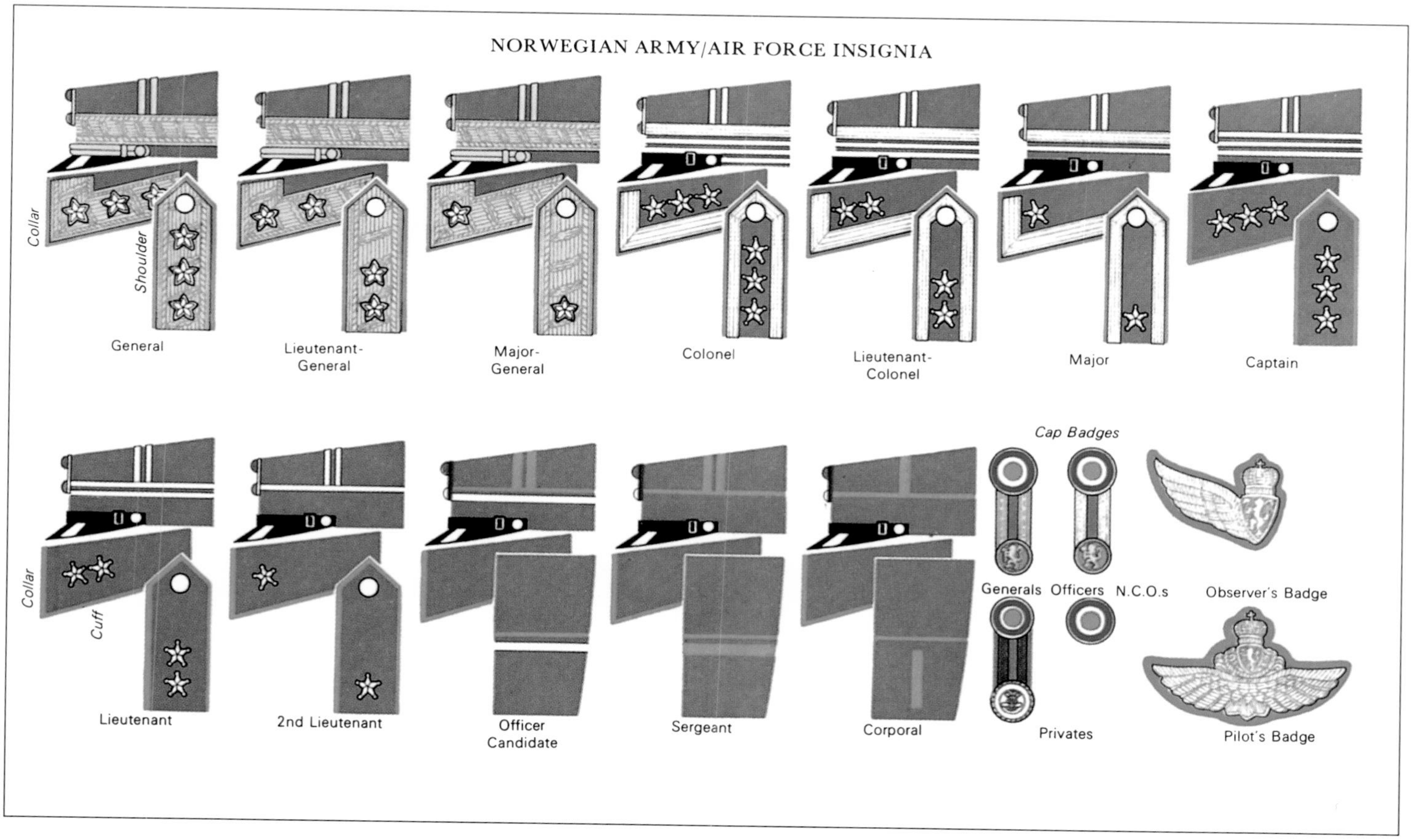

NORWEGIAN ARMY/AIR FORCE INSIGNIA

Collar
Shoulder
General
Lieutenant-General
Major-General
Colonel
Lieutenant-Colonel
Major
Captain

Collar
Cuff
Lieutenant
2nd Lieutenant
Officer Candidate
Sergeant
Corporal

Cap Badges
Generals
Officers
N.C.O.s
Privates
Observer's Badge
Pilot's Badge

without insignia was often worn. Norwegian officers and men also wore sheepskin coats and other items of civilian winter clothing.

INSIGNIA Rank distinction lace appeared on the kepi, tunic collar and greatcoat shoulder straps, while NCOs had rank distinctions on the cuffs.

Arm of service was indicated by the colour and design of the uniform buttons.

AIR FORCE

By midday on 9 April 1940, the German armed forces had occupied nearly all the airfields and seaplane bases south of Narvik, and most of Norway's semi-modern fighters (Gloster Gladiators) had been destroyed in the defence of Oslo on the opening day of the German invasion. Thereafter, the Air Force took little part in the fighting.

The Air Force was organised in three flights (one each of fighters, bombers and reconnaissance aircraft) with a total of 76 aircraft and 940 men, and was intended to play a ground-support role.

UNIFORM Air Service personnel wore Army uniforms with a bright green arm-of-service colour as piping on the kepi, side-cap, tunic, greatcoat and trousers. The silver buttons bore a horizontal propeller and a crown.

INSIGNIA Rank distinction lace appeared on the kepi, tunic collar and greatcoat shoulder straps. NCOs wore their rank badges on the cuffs. There were also distinctive patterns of cap badge for NCOs, officers and generals.

There were no branch or arm-of-service badges as such, but pilots and observers wore silver-embroidered wings on the right breast.

NAVY

On 8 April 1940, the day before the German invasion, 5200 officers and men were serving in the Navy and its Air Service. Despite the fact that the bulk of the vessels of the Norwegian Navy were obsolete, they gave a good account of themselves, during the hostilities with Germany. Indeed, during the fighting most of them were put out of action or sunk. There were initially 113 vessels, comprising:

2 small armoured cruisers;
10 minelayers;
7 destroyers;
3 large 'Trygg' class torpedo boats;
14 torpedo boats;
9 submarines;
8 minesweepers;
9 patrol boats;
49 vessels converted to patrol boats.

Only 13 of these made British ports after capitulation.

NORWEGIAN NAVY INSIGNIA

Peaked Cap Badge: Admirals

Peaked Cap Badge: Officers

Cuff

Admiral · Vice-Admiral · Rear-Admiral · Commodore · Captain · Commander (Engineering Speciality) · Lieutenant-Commander · Lieutenant (Special Service) · Sub-Lieutenant · Commander (Medical) · *Reserve Officers* Lt-Comdr (Supply) · Sub-Lt (Engineers)

Cadet (Collar Anchor) · Cuff · Cadet (3rd Grade) · Cadet (2nd Grade) · Cadet (1st Grade) · P.O. 1st Class (I) (Gunnery) · P.O. 2nd Class (II) (Radio) · P.O. 3rd Class (III) (Reserve) · Leading Seaman · Able Seaman · Ordinary Seaman

Cockade: O.R.s

Peaked Cap Badge: P.O.s

39

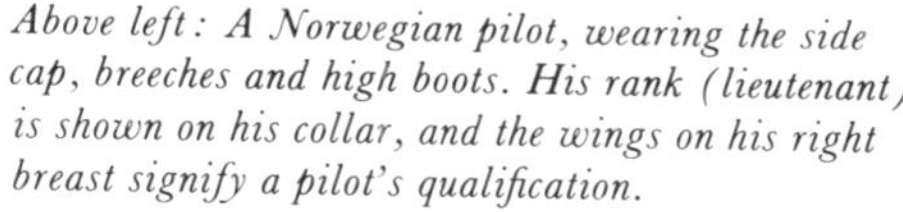

Above left: A Norwegian pilot, wearing the side cap, breeches and high boots. His rank (lieutenant) is shown on his collar, and the wings on his right breast signify a pilot's qualification.

Above: Norwegian sailors in exile in Britain. This photograph is particularly interesting in that it shows the national differences in the standard naval uniform. The sailor in the right foreground is wearing Norwegian uniform; the others have British clothing. The inspection is by King Haakon.

39 Seaman, Norwegian Navy, 1940
This Dekksmann *wears Norwegian Navy 'square rig' with his rank badge on the left sleeve. On the cap tally appears the legend,* Den KGL Norske Marine *('Royal Norwegian Navy'). He carries a 6.5mm Krag-Jørgensen M1894 rifle and ammunition pouches.*

On 22 April 1940, while fighting was still in progress, the Norwegian Government decided to requisition the whole Norwegian merchant fleet still under its control. 1000 ships (totalling 4,000,000 tons) manned by 30,000 seamen were saved for the Allied cause, and played an indispensable part in the Battle of the Atlantic.

In addition to the fleet there were coastal fortifications armed with guns of various calibres at Oscarborg, Oslofjord, Kristiansand, Bergen and Agdenes, which were manned by 308 officers and 2095 other ranks.

The Norwegian Naval Air Service had been formed as early as 1915, and because of its small size necessarily played only a limited role in the war against Germany. Some Navy aircraft did, however, fly to northern Norway after the initial German attack, and they continued to operate from there until fighting ceased on 7 June 1940.

UNIFORM The uniform worn during the 1940 campaign was based on the regulations of 1907, and in most respects conformed to the standard international pattern.

Officers, cadets and petty officers (quartermasters) wore a peaked cap, double-breasted reefer jacket with white shirt and black tie, matching blue trousers and black shoes. The greatcoat was double-breasted. Ratings wore the uniform illustrated in figure 39, over which, in cold weather, they wore a double-breasted pea-coat. The winter head-dress for officers was a black astrakhan cap on which was a special pattern of cap badge.

INSIGNIA Rank was indicated by the pattern of cap badge for admirals, officers, chief petty officers, quartermasters, cadets and petty officers. As in other Scandinavian navies, conscripts had special insignia. Rank distinction lace appeared on the reefer cuffs and on the greatcoat shoulder straps. Ratings wore their rank badges on the upper left sleeve.

As arm-of-service distinctions, officers in certain branches were identified by the shape of the 'curl' on the rank distinction lace, or the absence of a 'curl', and the colour of the 'lights' between the rank distinction lace. Chief petty officers had gold badges while other petty officers and ratings wore red branch badges above their rank badges.

Naval Air Service personnel wore naval uniform while qualified flying personnel wore gold-embroidered wings on the right breast. Ratings wore their uniform with special branch and trade badges incorporating wings and the letter 'A' on the upper left sleeve.

NETHERLANDS
ARMY

During World War I Holland's neutrality had been respected and during the inter-war years her government saw fit to reduce spending to an absolute minimum.

Germany's warlike stance, and warnings from well-informed sources failed to alert the Dutch government to the strong possibility that this time her neutrality would be violated. Thus it was not until April 1940 that the Dutch armed forces were mobilised. Some German officers who had misgivings about invading a neutral country informed the Dutch of the exact date of the invasion, and Dutch forces were placed on an alert from early morning on 10 May 1940. Despite the warning and many valiant acts of self-sacrifice, the German invasion was over in five days and Holland was forced to capitulate. After the war the Dutch command was blamed for this poor performance, but in fact there was little the Dutch could have done in the circumstances. The German High Command was impressed by the tenacity of the Dutch Army but it had neither the equipment, nor the appropriate training and experience to put up much more than a token resistance against the invading forces.

Many Dutchmen avoided German capture and eventually reached England, where they continued their struggle.

40 Lieutenant-Colonel, Dutch Army, 1940

An officer of infantry cyclists, this lieutenant-colonel wears standard service dress with the side cap which was introduced in 1937 to replace the kepi (finally abolished in the spring of 1940). Badges of rank based on the Austrian pattern are worn on the collar (two stars and a bar for a lieutenant-colonel) and his arm of service is shown by the blue (infantry) piping and the bicycle wheel on the collar. On the 'Sam Browne' belt he wears a Belgian 9mm FN pistol with two extra magazines in the pouch.

41 Corporal, Dutch Army, 1940

This infantryman wears the 1912 pattern 'grey' uniform and the standard Dutch steel helmet with the 'Lion of Nassau' badge. Just before the war a more comfortable pattern of tunic was introduced with stand-and-fall collar and no piping, but it was not issued in any great numbers before the German invasion. Rank is indicated by the chevron on the sleeve and arm of service by the green piping and the horn badge on the collar. The trade badge on the left sleeve is that of a pistol marksman. The rifle is the 6.5mm Mannlicher M1895 model. The Dutch uniform, as shown here, was quite distinctive, mainly because of its combination of a unique helmet (the only equivalent was in the Romanian Army), an old-fashioned cut and the green colour.

ORGANISATION The Army consisted of a small professional cadre of 1500 officers and 6500 other ranks which was responsible for maintaining the military establishment, and for the training of the annual intake of 60,000 conscripts, who were eligible for eleven months military service between the ages of 20 and 40. The field army on mobilisation numbered 114,000 men, or, including reserves, 270,000 all ranks.

The country was divided into four army corps based on Amsterdam, Arnhem, Breda and Amersfoort. An army corps comprised a corps staff, two infantry divisions, one or two heavy artillery regiments, one independent artillery battalion, and a signals and reconnaissance battalion. In addition, there was a light brigade (consisting of a staff, signals battalion, armoured car squadron, cyclist regiment, two hussar regiments and one horse artillery regiment) and an anti-aircraft brigade with staff and two anti-aircraft regiments.

An infantry regiment had a strength of 2691 all ranks armed with Mannlicher M9 rifles and FN 9mm pistols. Support weapons consisted of:

72 light machine guns (Lewis M20);
36 heavy machine guns (Schwarzlose MO8/15);
6 heavy mortars;
4 anti-tank guns.

UNIFORM A grey-green uniform was introduced in 1912, but the colour soon underwent a change, so that by the outbreak of war in 1940 the colour was almost identical to German field-grey. The issue uniform was simple, but outdated in the sense that the cut was still tight and restricting, and the full lining made it hot in summer and difficult to dry when wet. In 1937 the uniform underwent certain modifications which made it more practical. The stiff stand collar became a softer stand-and-fall pattern, exterior pockets were added, breeches were introduced for mounted personnel, and a new comfortable side cap became the basic form of head-dress. Before the outbreak of war the regulars wore a black dress uniform when not on active duty, while cavalry and horse artillery retained vestiges of their former full-dress uniforms.

The Dutch issue tunic had a stand or stand-and-fall collar, seven matt bronzed buttons in front, two slash breast pockets with pointed flap and button, and round cuffs. The shoulder straps, which were stitched down, ended in a roll which prevented the equipment from slipping off the shoulders.

The greatcoat was double-breasted with a large fall collar, two rows of five metal buttons, turn-back cuffs, slanting slash side pockets with rectangular flaps, and a half-belt at the back fastened with three buttons. There were no shoulder straps or piping on the greatcoat.

In 1940 head-dress consisted of the side cap or steel helmet. The stiff shako fell into disuse in spring 1940, although some officers continued to wear it. The side cap was introduced in 1937 and was piped in arm-of-service colour for other ranks, or metallic braid for officers.

All unmounted other ranks wore matching knickerbockers and puttees, while officers, warrant officers and NCOs wore matching breeches (sometimes piped) and black riding boots or ankle boots and leather gaiters. Gloves were of brown leather or grey-green wool.

Crews of enclosed armoured vehicles wore a brimless helmet and a one-piece grey overall.

Officers and warrant officers wore a brown leather waistbelt with a brass two-pronged buckle and leather cross-strap. On the right they usually carried the Belgian 9mm FN short automatic pistol in a brown leather holster.

Below: A Dutch mortar team in action. The photographer has managed to capture the bomb leaving the weapon. The equipment of the nearest infantryman includes gas-mask, knapsack, bedding-roll and an old-fashioned sword-bayonet.

INSIGNIA General officers were distinguished by a special peaked cap, gold-embroidered oak leaves on the tunic collar and two rows of crimson piping on the breeches. All officers had gold braid piping on the side cap, and badges of rank on the tunic and greatcoat collar. Other ranks wore sleeve badges of rank.

Arm of service was identified by the colour of the piping on the side cap, tunic collar and cuffs and breeches of officers and warrant officers. The rank distinction lace worn on the sleeves by NCOs and men was edged in arm-of-service colour. Some units and formations wore a metal badge on the left of the side cap.

AIR FORCE

In 1937 the Dutch government, alarmed by Germany's warlike stance, embarked on a programme of limited expansion and re-organisation of the Army Air Force. The Air Force remained part of the Army but became a semi-independent arm to which was added, in November 1938, anti-aircraft artillery, searchlight sections and air observer corps; and the whole was designated Air Defence Command.

In May 1940 the active element of the Army Air Force was divided into two air regiments; the first consisting of four fighter squadrons, one bomber and one reconnaissance squadron, and the second consisting of four reconnaissance wings and two fighter squadrons.

It was decided to replace the obsolete aircraft then in service (Fokker DVII fighters and Fokker CL and CV two-seater reconnaissance planes), and orders were sent out for 36 Fokker DXXI single-seater fighters, 36 Fokker GIA twin-engined fighters, 16 Fokker TV bombers and (from the United States) 18 Douglas DB-8A-3N attack bombers. A further 23 Curtiss Hawk 75A single-seat fighters were also ordered but these were not delivered by the invasion.

On 10 May 1940 the Army Air Service had 139 operational aircraft at its disposal, although not all of them were the newer types. Nearly all of these were destroyed as a result of the German surprise attacks on Dutch airfields. Personnel losses were about 8000 which included 500 men taken prisoner.

42

42 2nd Lieutenant, Dutch Air Force, 1940

This 2nd Lieutenant wears an Army officers' uniform, privately purchased and made out of whipcord, as opposed to the coarse and darker cloth of the issue uniform. He also wears the obsolete but handsome kepi which was occasionally still worn in 1940. The colour of the piping and the badge on the collar identify him as an airman, while the metal 'wings' on his left breast show he is a qualified pilot. Fighter pilots usually wore a leather flying helmet and a three-quarter-length double-breasted leather coat, with rank badges on the collar.

UNIFORM AND INSIGNIA Air Force personnel wore Army uniforms with blue piping and an embroidered badge consisting of a radial engine and twin-bladed propeller on their collars. Qualified pilots and observers had a gilt metal badge which was worn on the left breast of the tunic and greatcoat.

Flying clothing was of the French pattern and consisted of a leather flying helmet or a steel helmet and double-breasted leather jacket. The rank stars in metal were affixed to the collar.

43 Leading Seaman, Dutch Navy, 1940
This leading seaman wears the standard 'square rig' of the Royal Netherlands Navy. The cap tally with the legend Koninklijke Marine *('Royal Navy') in Gothic lettering began to be replaced by one in block lettering at the beginning of the war. He wears infantry equipment and carries a 6.5mm Mannlicher M1895 rifle.*

NAVY

Before the War the Dutch Navy in European waters was intended primarily for local coastal defence and mine-laying work in the North Sea; its most powerful units were stationed in the Dutch East Indies. By 1939, however, new warships were being constructed which were suitable for both the Far East and Europe.

In May 1940 the Chief of Naval Staff and Commander-in-Chief of Naval Forces was Vice-Admiral J. Th. Furstner. Personnel was about 11,750 men including Marines. The vessels consisted of:
4 cruisers;
8 destroyers;
23 submarines;
7 escort and patrol vessels;
5 motor torpedo-boats;
28 mine-sweepers.

The Navy played a limited if courageous role in the battle for Holland. Ships patrolled the coastline giving supporting fire to land forces, and in one unique instance a Dutch ship shelled a beach on which German troop-carrying aircraft were landing. Small craft assisted by transporting troops and supplies.

When defeat became inevitable, Dutch ships ferried troops across the sea, and 20,000 men reached Britain.

The bulk of the Dutch Navy's aircraft were stationed in the Dutch East Indies, although in May 1940 it disposed of 44 seaplanes and 30 training aircraft in Holland. The Naval Air Service carried out a number of reconnaissance missions and shot down one modern German fighter, but by 13 May there was hardly a serviceable aircraft left.

On Tuesday 14 May, the day of the Dutch capitulation, the last six seaplanes at Veere left for France, and during the course of the day were followed by any machines able to fly. During the campaign in Holland the Naval Air Service had lost 18 seaplanes at their moorings, and all the trainers on the ground.

UNIFORM The uniform worn during World War II was governed by regulations which came into force in April 1933.

The uniform for officers followed the standard pattern, although instead of a greatcoat issue wear was a frock coat with rank distinction lace on the cuffs. The uniform for ratings is illustrated by figure 43, although the illustration shows the old-pattern cap tally, which was replaced at the beginning of the war by one with block lettering. The Dutch sailor also had a double-breasted peacoat with brass buttons.

For all ranks there were white uniforms for summer and tropical wear which included white covers for the standard head-dress, and a white sun helmet or straw panama hat.

INSIGNIA Officers and warrant officers wore rank distinction lace on the cuffs and on the shoulder straps of the white tunic. Senior petty officers wore their rank badges on the cuffs of the blue uniform, and on the collar patches of the Marine Corps (grey-green) and tropical uniforms. Ratings wore cuff rank badges.

Officers wore their arm-of-service emblem in the centre of the cap badge and on the reefer jacket collar. Speciality insignia was worn on the upper left sleeve. Naval aircrew wore gilt metal 'wings' on the left breast.

MARINES

On 10 May 1940, the *Korpsmariniers* (originally formed in 1665 and in action against the English in 1667) was stationed in Rotterdam.

The Rotterdam garrison included one hundred trained conscripts 1st Class, one hundred 3rd Class, and one hundred with only three months' service. At the naval depot there were a further 150 Marines, 90 conscripts and 600 new recruits. Despite their small number and lack of training, the Marines fought stubbornly against German parachute troops both on the Zuider Zee and in defence of the Maas bridges at Rotterdam, until, on 14 May 1940, they surrendered together with all other forces in Holland.

UNIFORM AND INSIGNIA The field-dress of the Dutch Marine Corps was that of the Army, but during the German invasion in May 1940 the Marines wore the M1928 steel helmet painted black with a white metal foul-anchor on the front and a navy-blue double-breasted greatcoat with brass buttons. Rank badges were worn as on the Navy uniform.

Below: Marines of the Rotterdam garrison marching through the town, wearing their double-breasted greatcoats. The man on the right is wearing both sword and pistol.

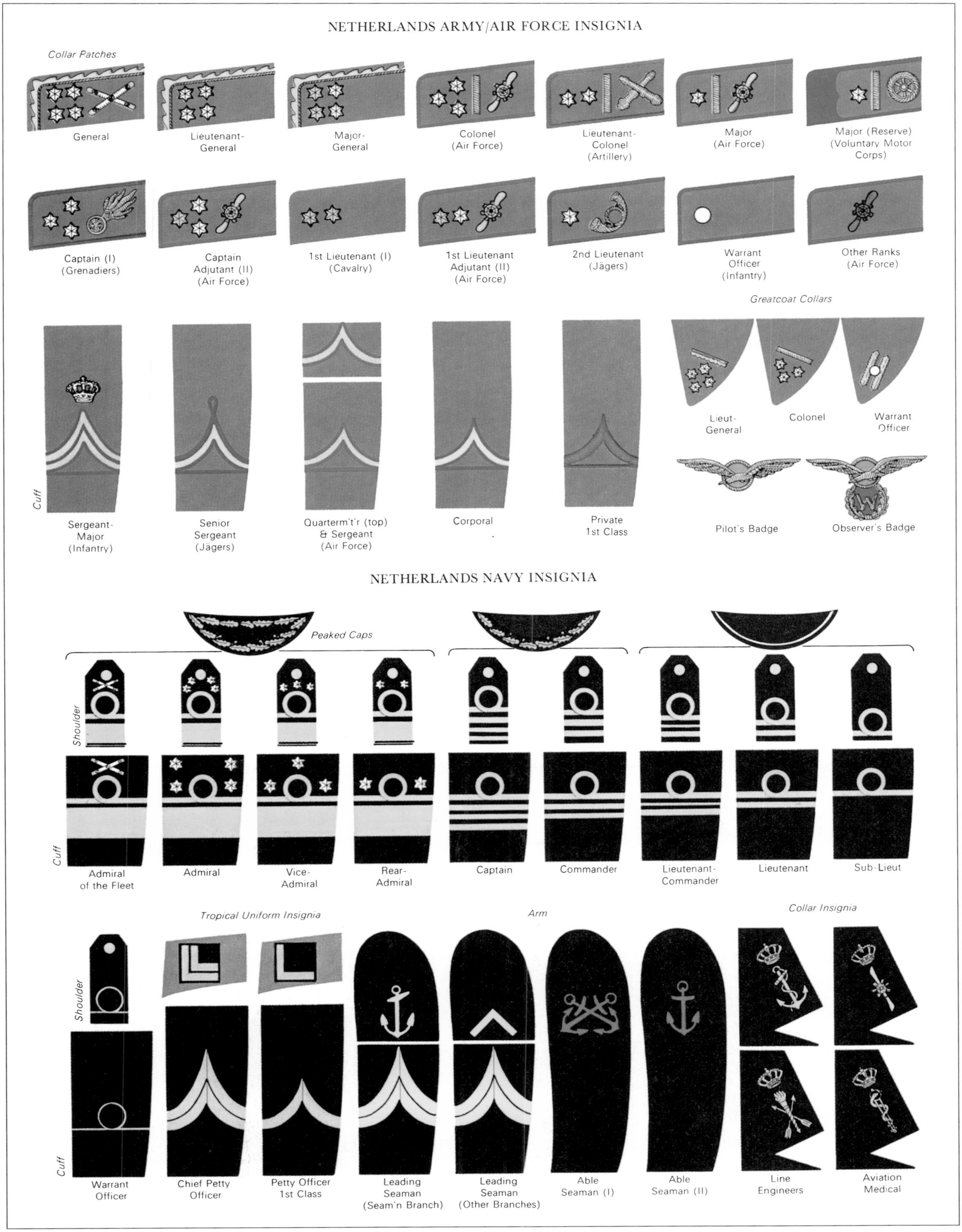

NETHERLANDS ARMY/AIR FORCE INSIGNIA

Collar Patches

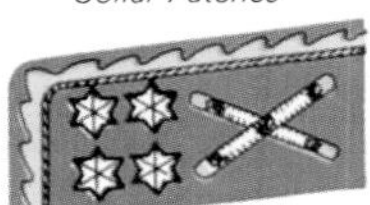
General

Lieutenant-General

Major-General

Colonel (Air Force)

Lieutenant-Colonel (Artillery)

Major (Air Force)

Major (Reserve) (Voluntary Motor Corps)

Captain (I) (Grenadiers)

Captain Adjutant (II) (Air Force)

1st Lieutenant (I) (Cavalry)

1st Lieutenant Adjutant (II) (Air Force)

2nd Lieutenant (Jägers)

Warrant Officer (Infantry)

Other Ranks (Air Force)

Cuff

Sergeant-Major (Infantry)

Senior Sergeant (Jägers)

Quarterm't'r (top) & Sergeant (Air Force)

Corporal

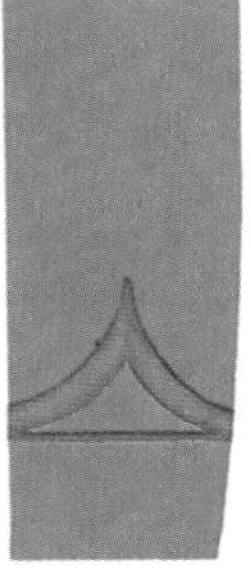
Private 1st Class

Greatcoat Collars

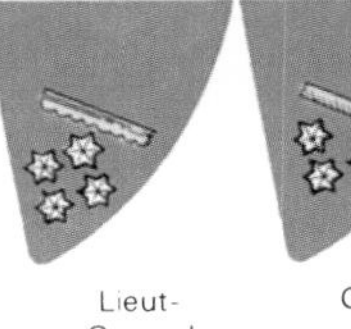
Lieut-General

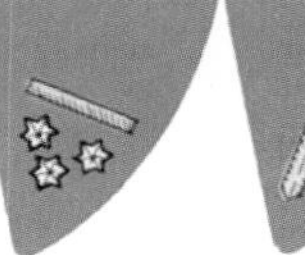
Colonel

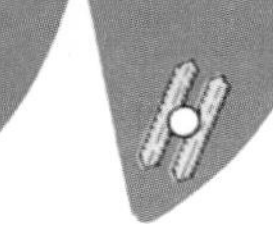

Warrant Officer

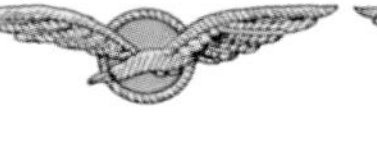
Pilot's Badge

Observer's Badge

NETHERLANDS NAVY INSIGNIA

Peaked Caps

Shoulder

Cuff

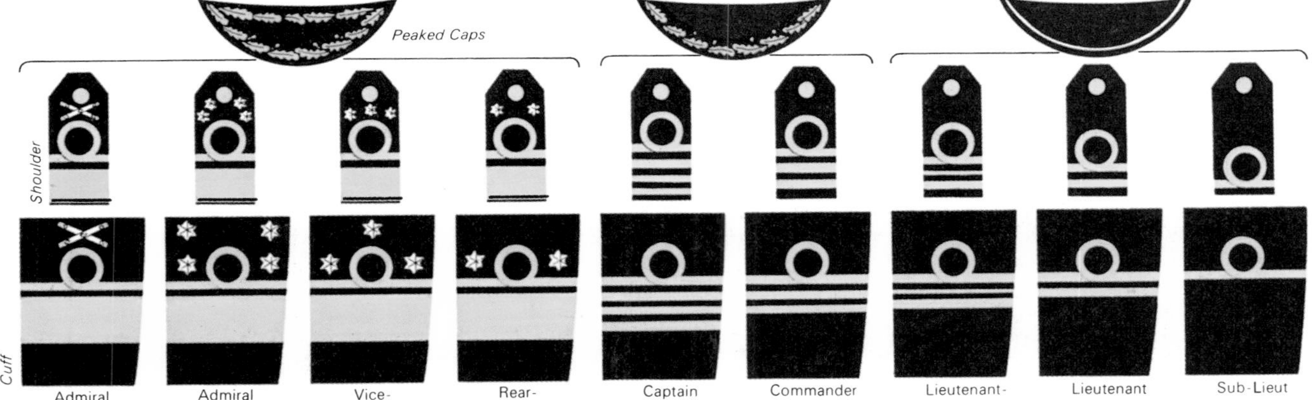
Admiral of the Fleet | Admiral | Vice-Admiral | Rear-Admiral | Captain | Commander | Lieutenant-Commander | Lieutenant | Sub-Lieut

Tropical Uniform Insignia

Arm

Collar Insignia

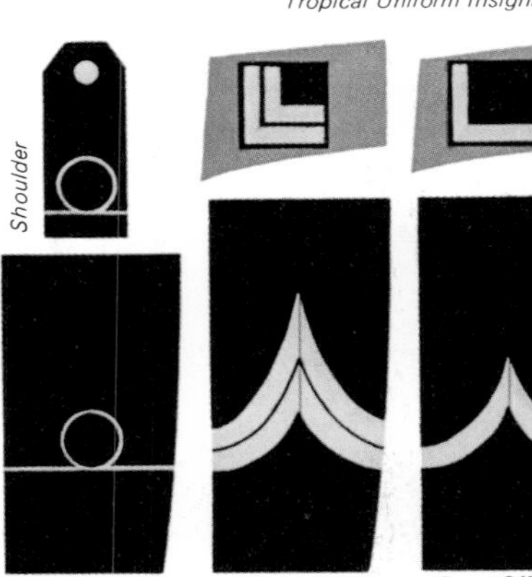
Warrant Officer

Chief Petty Officer

Petty Officer 1st Class

Leading Seaman (Seam'n Branch)

Leading Seaman (Other Branches)

Able Seaman (I)

Able Seaman (II)

Line Engineers

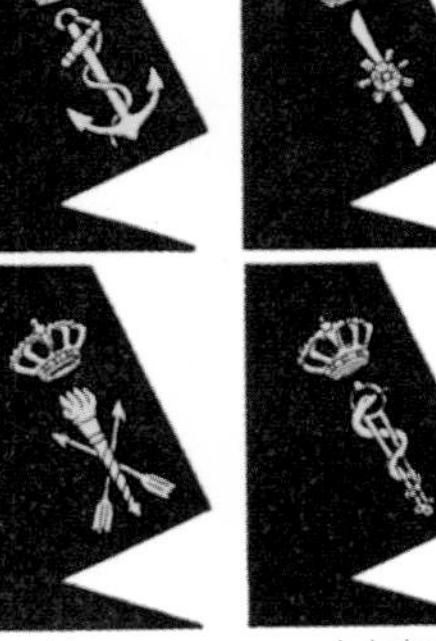
Aviation Medical

BELGIUM

ARMY

In 1914 neutral Belgium had been suddenly attacked by the German Army and had experienced four years of trench warfare. After the German occupation of the Rhineland in 1936 the country was again jolted into awareness of impending danger. National service was extended from 8 to 12 months, the military budget increased by 15 per cent, and new fortifications were constructed. But this could not conceal the fact that military thinking had not progressed beyond the trenches of World War I. Armour, for example, was only considered an offensive weapon, and Belgium, whose Army had a purely defensive role, had no tank units. Belgium fielded 22 divisions against the invading forces of Army Group B in 1940, and the tenacity of the Belgian infantry at first surprised the Germans. Nonetheless, the Belgian army was on the point of collapse within two weeks of the invasion, and on 28 May the last units surrendered. After 18 days of fighting, casualties were 23,350 killed and wounded.

ORGANISATION The 100,000-strong Belgian Army under its Commander-in-Chief, King Leopold, was basically a standing army but one which relied on conscription for its annual intake of recruits. Its strength on mobilisation was in the region of 550,000 men, which for a small country of eight million people was a remarkable feat.

The country was divided into three army corps areas based on Brussels,

44 Colonel, Belgian Army, 1940
This colonel of the 1st Infantry Regiment is wearing typical service dress and boots with leggings. The regimental number appears on the shoulder straps. The uniform is very similar to that worn by British field officers of the same period and was introduced in 1915 (the original officers' tunic had a stand collar). The arm of service is shown by the crown on the cap (surmounted by the Belgian national cockade) and the red collar patches with blue piping. The swagger stick and jodhpurs add a final British flourish to this typical Belgian colonel.

45 Sergeant, Belgian Army, 1940
This sergeant, identified by the diagonal silver bar on his sleeve, wears the 1915 model French Adrian *steel helmet with the Belgian lion on the front. His arm of service (the infantry) is indicated by the colour of the collar patches and the crown on his shoulder straps. The regimental number is worn on the left sleeve, but this was often removed before going into action for security reasons. The spray of flowers, the* petites cloches de Mai *indicates that it is Labour Day: 1 May 1940. The rifle is a Belgian 7.65mm Mauser M1889, a copy of the more famous German model, a reliable bolt-action weapon which was used in both World Wars.*

Below: Belgian soldiers take a rest by the roadside as a British lorry passes on 13 May 1940. The troops are carrying all the personal equipment they will need in action.

Antwerp and Liège, a cavalry corps in Brussels, an army artillery brigade in Antwerp, the Ardennes Rifle Corps in Namur, as well as three independent frontier bicycle battalions, six infantry divisions, and two cavalry divisions.

The army corps comprised a staff, two infantry divisions, one corps artillery regiment, and one pioneer regiment.

An infantry division had a staff, and three infantry regiments. Each regiment had 3000 men armed with Mauser M35 rifles. The support weapons of a regiment were:
108 light machine guns (Browning M30);
52 heavy machine guns (Maxim M08);
108 light mortars;
9 heavy mortars or infantry guns;
6 anti-tank guns.

The corps artillery regiment had four battalions each with two batteries. Transport was partly horsedrawn and partly motorised. The corps' guns were 16 Schneider 155mm M17 field howitzers, 8 Schneider 105mm M13 guns and 8 Cockerill 120mm M32 field guns.

Just before the war there was a rapid attempt to improve mobility and one of the two divisions in the Ardennes Rifle Corps and the two cavalry divisions received motor vehicles. The Motorised Cavalry Corps had a staff, two cavalry divisions, one corps artillery regiment and a bicycle pioneer battalion. A cavalry division had three mixed regiments each with a battalion of cavalry, a battalion of motorcyclists, an armoured car squadron, and a training squadron.

UNIFORM During World War I, the Belgian Army adopted khaki uniforms mainly because Britain was the only country providing sufficient new uniforms to replace the obsolete coloured ones then in use.

The Belgian soldier of 1939, however, had a predominantly French appearance which was emphasised by the *Adrian* steel helmet and the habit of wearing the greatcoat skirts folded back. In complete contrast, the officers looked British, especially after 1935 when an open tunic for wear with collar and tie was introduced.

The Ardennes Rifles Corps wore a variation on this basic style: a green beret with boar's head badge, a shortened version of the greatcoat and long leather leggings. Mechanised troops received either a fibre helmet of Belgian design, or the French steel helmet for motorised troops, both of which were adorned in front with a lion's head. In addition mechanised troops received a leather jacket and breeches with long leggings, or a one-piece khaki overall.

INSIGNIA Rank distinctions appeared on the peaked cap, side cap, and on the collar patches and shoulder straps. Other ranks also wore their rank badges on the cuffs.

The primary means of identifying the arm of service was the colour of the collar patches and the collar patch piping. In addition there was an extensive range of yellow metal badges which appeared on the head-gear, collar patches and on the shoulder straps. Finally, a number of staff and administrative functions were identified by embroidered badges on the collar patches and also sometimes on the front of the peaked cap.

AIR FORCE

On 1 March 1920 an air force was formed as part of the Belgian Army. From its beginning until the outbreak of war the Air Force was plagued by a shortage of modern aircraft. While developing its own fighter (the Renard R-36), Belgium imported aircraft from England and the USA.

When the Germans invaded only 180 of the 234 aircraft were operational, and most of these were obsolete. All but one of the few modern Hurricanes were destroyed on the ground at Schaffen before the Belgian aircraft could disperse.

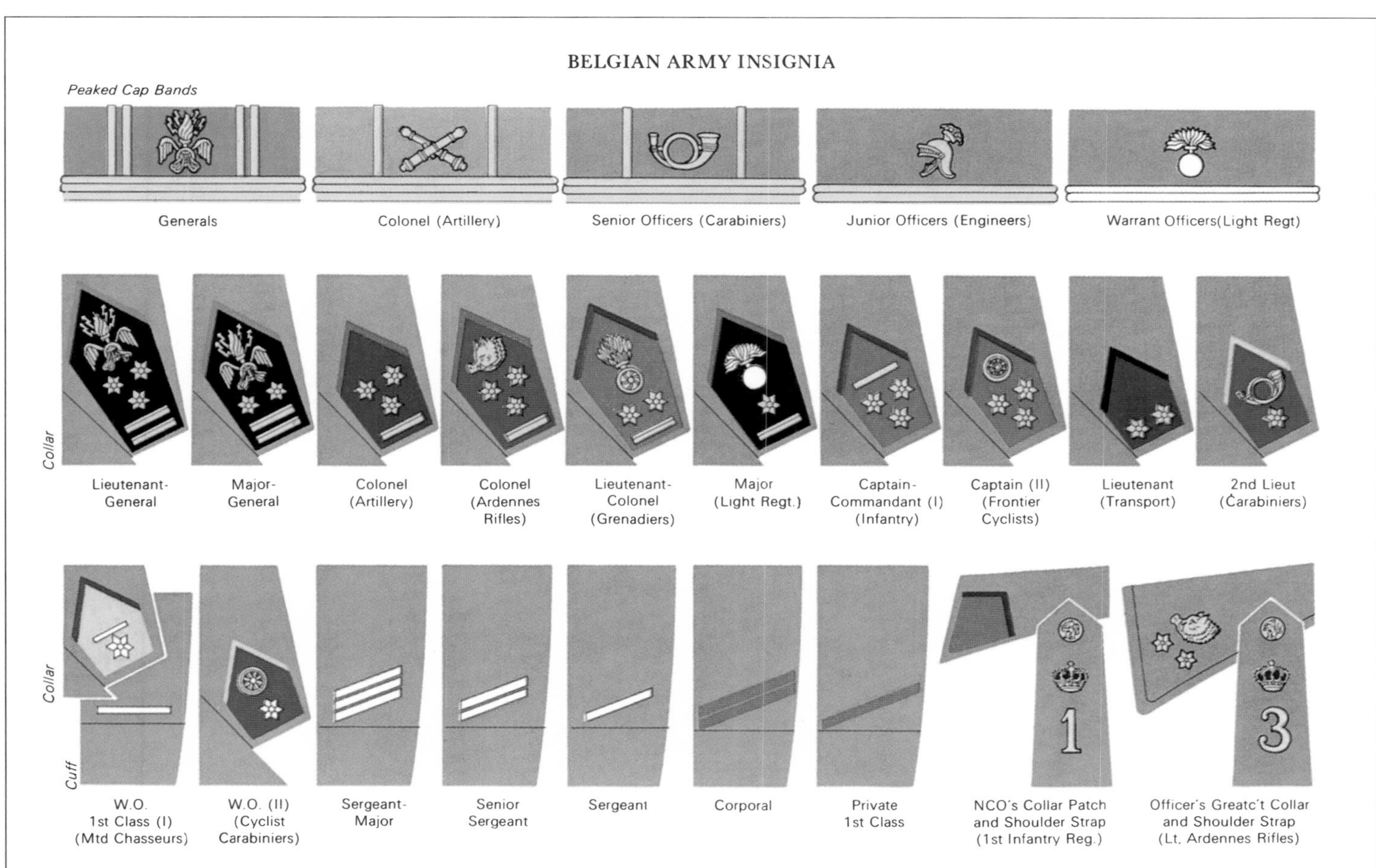

ORGANISATION In May 1940 the *Aéronautique Militaire* was grouped together with the Observer Service and Anti-Aircraft Artillery to form the Territorial Air Defence (*Défense Aéronautique du Territoire* or DAT).

The Belgian Air Force consisted of three regiments: the 1st an observation and Army co-operation unit; the 2nd a fighter regiment, and the 3rd a reconnaissance and bombing regiment. In addition there was one auxiliary regiment with ancillary and refuelling companies.

The 1st Air Regiment comprised six squadrons, with a total of 62 serviceable machines. The 2nd air regiment also had six squadrons and totalled 79 aircraft. The 3rd Air Regiment totalled 41 aircraft in four squadrons. Each flying squadron had a complementary anti-aircraft squadron (*Escadrille de Parc*).

UNIFORM There were two basic uniforms in the Air Force. The first was that of the Army of which the Air Force was a branch. The second was a blue-grey air force uniform which was introduced for wear by the regular cadre of flying personnel. This situation was further complicated by the continued wearing of regimental uniform by a number of Air Force officers.

The blue-grey uniform is illustrated by figure 46. In addition there was a peaked cap with black band and black peak and a double-breasted, blue-grey greatcoat. More common than the breeches and boots were long blue-grey trousers with black shoes.

INSIGNIA Rank badges on the blue-grey uniform were the same as those worn on the khaki uniform.

The arm-of-service colour which appeared on the collar patches of khaki uniforms was bright blue with red piping. Enamelled squadron badges were worn on the right breast pocket.

NAVY

By the end of the 19th century, the Belgian Navy had virtually ceased to exist, and it was not until the end of World War I that attempts were made to re-form it. During the inter-war years this tiny force was once again disbanded because of lack of funds, and it was only on 15 September 1939 that the *Marine Korps* (later *Corps de Marine*) was again established.

In November 1939 conscripts with previous naval experience were transferred from the Army to the *Corps de Marine* which then had a theoretical

46

47

46 Major, Belgian Air Force, 1940
As a pilot in the 2nd Air Regiment the major wears the blue-grey service uniform of the regular flying branch. All other officers in non-flying branches and reserve pilots serving in the Army continued to wear Army uniform. Rank badges appear on the collar patches, 'wings' on the left sleeve, and the squadron badge on the right breast pocket.

47 Pilot, Belgian Air Force, 1940
Typical of all flying clothing was the one-piece overall which was issued in a number of different colours, including white. The tartan silk scarf was to protect the neck from chafing against the overall collar when scanning the sky for enemy aircraft, and the parachute is that of a fighter pilot.

Right: Belgian sailors in 1940. On the left is a lieutenant (his rank shown by the two stars on the greatcoat collar and the two bands on the cap) and on the right a petty officer second class (recognisable as such by the two bars on the cuff and the cap). The seaman's cap is of the French pattern, with pompom on the top and cord fastened around the cap rather than under the chin. He is heavily laden, a sign that the German victory was by now inevitable, and he is about to be evacuated.

strength of 30 officers (mainly Army reservists with merchant marine experience), 98 petty officers, and 513 petty officers second class and ratings. These were to provide the personnel for a headquarters and 1st Squadron at Ostende, 2nd Squadron at Zeebrugge, 3rd Squadron at Antwerp, and a replacement and training squadron.

Vessels consisted of small coastal craft armed with one 47mm gun and two machine guns, while other vessels were requisitioned from their civilian owners. Some large wooden trawlers were used as minesweepers. There were two coastal guns – one in Antwerp and the other in Zeebrugge – which were manned by Army crews.

During the German invasion, the Navy lost about a quarter of its personnel, while a number of survivors found their way to England. By May 1943 the Belgian section of the British Royal Navy had seven ships and about 350 men.

UNIFORM New regulations for Belgian Navy uniform were published in January 1940, and so any alterations to existing uniforms were only beginning to percolate through the Navy when Germany invaded.

The Belgian uniform followed the 'international' model, but also bore marked similarities to that of the French Navy. Officers and petty officers wore a peaked cap, reefer jacket with white shirt and black tie, long trousers with black shoes and a double-breasted greatcoat. Quartermasters and ratings wore a blue cap with light blue woollen pompom on top and cap tally with *Marinekorps* in gold. The blue jumper had a blue denim collar edged with three white lines. The pea-coat was double-breasted with two rows of five brass buttons.

INSIGNIA Here the Belgian Navy departed from convention in two respects. Because the Naval Corps was basically a branch of the Army, officers and chief petty officers wore black collar patches piped in light blue on which they wore Army rank badges. Officers and chief petty officers also wore rank distinction lace on the peaked cap in the French manner. In 1940 the seaman's cap legend was changed to read just *Marine*.

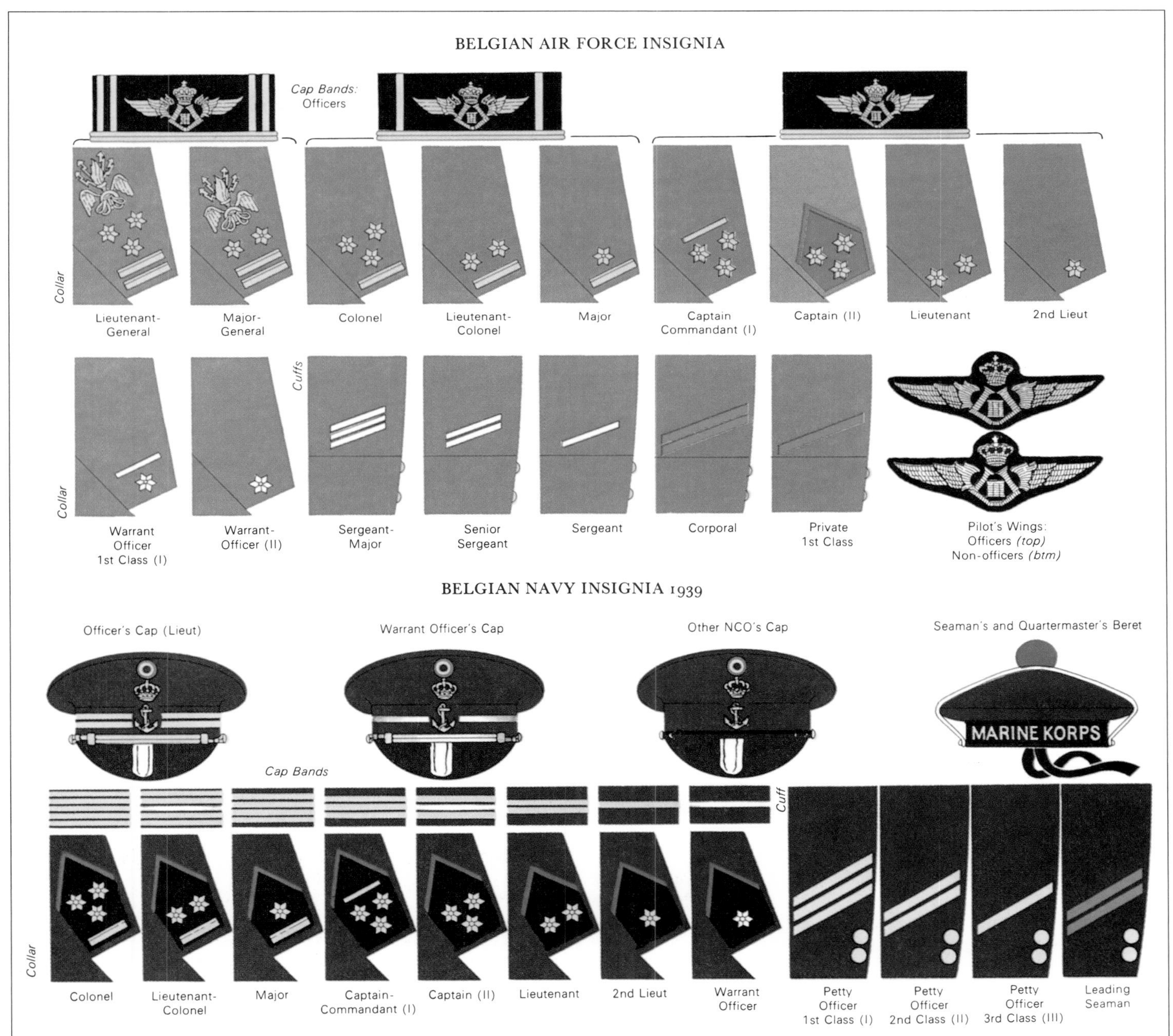

FRANCE

ARMY

France emerged from World War I with considerable military prestige, but the Army and indeed the whole nation were exhausted. After the experiences of World War I, there was considerable weight of opinion and political pressure behind the view that a strategy based upon a solid defensive line accorded best with the demands of modern warfare and the needs of the country. The result was the construction of the fortress complexes of the Maginot Line, which absorbed a great deal of the defence budget. The French military establishment had its critics, and there was a small but vociferous school of thought which condemned the reliance on static fortifications. The French Army, based on conscription, was of variable quality; reserve divisions especially were often considered a liability, and observers, including the British General Brooke, were shaken by their insubordination and slovenly appearance.

The French Army was mobilised on 1 September 1939: about 5,000,000 reservists were to be added to the standing army of 900,000 men. The *drôle de guerre* (Phoney War) and bitter winter, however, added to the low morale of the armed forces. On 10 May 1940 the German offensive began by outflanking the Maginot Line in an advance through the Ardennes region, a move totally unexpected by the Allies. Once knocked off balance France never recovered and despite brave and sometimes effective counter-attacks, German tactics, troop training, morale and much military equipment proved decisively superior. After a campaign lasting less than two months France was forced to sue for peace and an armistice was signed on 22 June 1940.

Under the terms of the armistice, in the unoccupied zone of France those forces that remained intact were rapidly demobilised except 100,000 men who were to maintain order (*l'armee de l'armistice*). The French fleet and colonial forces were to remain intact for the time being. Total casualties amounted to 290,000 men killed or wounded and 1,900,000 taken prisoner.

A large number of men had succeeded in escaping to the colonies, however, and many had been evacuated to England.

There was one redeeming feature in this massive defeat: the performance of the French forces on the Italian border, where 185,000 men (in three divisions and various garrison forces) under

Above: The crew of a French Char B1 *tank pose for the camera above the 75mm gun which was the tank's main armament. They are wearing the typical helmets and leather clothing of armoured troops.*

Below: A French soldier prepares to fire a Hotchkiss M1914 machine gun. This is a good close-up of the standard-pattern helmet. The letters 'RF' on the grenade stand for République française.

48 Major, French Army, 1940

The old-style closed tunic with badges of rank appearing on the front of the side cap (bonnet de police) *and on the cuffs is worn here by a battalion commander. The arm-of-service colour and his corps number appear on the collar patches, while each regiment (here the 46th Infantry) also had a metal badge which was worn on the right breast pocket. As a field officer who traditionally rode a horse, he wears breeches and boots with spurs. The medal ribbons are for the* Croix de Guerre *1914–1918 (red and green), and the Dardanelles campaign (white and green).*

49 Private First Class, French Army, 1940

This artilleryman is wearing walking-out dress with a blue-black kepi and a tunic (the vareuse*) which came in a number of different patterns, with seven, six and finally five buttons. An alternative tunic in gabardine was designed for summer wear. In 1938 the old breeches were beginning to be replaced by knickerbockers for dismounted personnel. The gas mask is the ANP 1931 model. The artillery arm is identified by the colour of the kepi and collar patches on which the regimental number of the 182nd Artillery Regiment also appears. The badge on the left sleeve is as worn by armourers.*

50 Sergeant, French Army, 1940

This sergeant of motorised troops wears the protective clothing typical of the tank arm. He carries the padded M35 helmet under his arm, and is wearing the tank beret, which bore the tank badge (crossed cannon and a medieval helmet). The leather coat and trousers gathered at the ankles (pantalon cachou) *were standard issue. His rank badge is on the jacket front, and his unit markings, on the collar (for the 2nd BCC), are green; grey was more normal.*

General Olry completely halted the Italian attack of 20–25 June at a cost of 37 killed, 42 wounded and 150 missing.

ORGANISATION In May 1940, the French Army on the north-east front, which stretched from Switzerland to the North Sea, was divided into the 1st and 2nd Army Groups and the 7th Army. These forces comprised:
63 infantry divisions (of which 30 were regular);
7 motorised infantry divisions;
3 armoured divisions;
3 light mechanised divisions;
5 cavalry divisions;
13 fortress divisions.

The general reserve comprised a further 17 infantry, 2 motorised and 3 armoured divisions.

The backbone of the French Army was the infantry which, apart from increased firepower, was in organisation and training, very similar to that of World War I, and still relied on horse transport to a great extent. The basic French infantry division had provided a model for those of many other countries, and consisted of a divisional headquarters, three infantry regiments, two artillery regiments, and a reconnaissance group of four squadrons: headquarters, motorcycle, horse and weapons. The support elements of the division included two companies of engineers, a telegraph and a radio company, two baggage trains (one horsedrawn, one motorised), an artillery park and a medical group. The divisional anti-tank unit comprised a company of twelve 25mm anti-tank guns and a battery of 47mm guns, and was attached to one of the Infantry Regiments. The full complement of a division was 17,000 men and 500 officers.

Each regiment possessed a headquarters company, a weapons company (six 25mm guns, two 81mm mortars and three gun carriers), a supply company and three infantry battalions making a total of about 3000 men and 80 officers armed with Ruby or Starr 7.65mm pistols and Lebel rifles of various models. The battalion comprised a headquarters section, three rifle companies (190 men divided into a headquarters and four rifle sections) and a machine-gun company made up of one gun section (two 25mm guns and two 81mm mortars) and four machine-gun sections each with four heavy (Hotchkiss M14) machine guns. The smallest unit in the Army was the group of 11 men equipped with a light (Châtellerault M24/29) machine gun; three groups making a rifle section. Total support weapons of a regiment comprised:
112 light machine guns;
48 heavy machine guns;
9 light mortars;
8 heavy mortars;
9 infantry and anti-tank guns.

In May 1940 France had over 3000 tanks, and in terms of numbers, quality and firepower they were generally superior to those employed by the Germans. Tactically, however, the French were definitely inferior, and with one or two exceptions the handling of this valuable force was uninspired and wasteful. The basic armoured unit was the tank battalion, comprising a staff, three tank companies and a reserve company (in all, some 45 to 60 tanks). There were 39 tank battalions in 1940 and for tactical

48

49

50

purposes they were twinned to form tank battalion groups. At the outbreak of war only five battalions had received the latest tanks (the D-2 and B-1 models) while the rest still retained a variety of modern and semi-obsolete types. In addition to the battalion groups there were also 11 independent tank companies.

Between January and May 1940, four reserve armoured divisions were formed and placed at the disposal of the General Headquarters. Each division was formed from a *demi-brigade* (two battalions) of Char B tanks, two battalions of Hotchkiss light tanks, a battalion of motorised rifles, a regiment of tractor-drawn artillery (two groups of 105mm guns), and engineer, aviation and service units. These divisions absorbed a number of the above-mentioned tank battalions and companies.

Armoured fighting vehicles were also to be found in the cavalry divisions undergoing mechanisation, in five light cavalry divisions which were also still not completely mechanised, and in the reconnaissance groups. All these formations combined horsed cavalry, motorcycle troops, armoured cars, tanks, and infantry mounted in cross-country vehicles. Finally there were the three light mechanised divisions each of which had two regiments of tanks, a squadron of armoured cars and motorcycles and a regiment of motorised infantry (*Dragons portés*). However, it should be pointed out that not all of these formations had received all their equipment by May 1940, and many were still being formed.

French cavalry, although in the process of motorisation, still represented a large mounted force. Apart from the cavalry in the mechanised brigades and light mechanised divisions, there were also regiments of *Cuirassiers, Dragons, Dragons portés, Chasseurs à Cheval* and *Hussards.* In May 1940 the three remaining cavalry divisions were partially motorised and formed into light mechanised divisions and light cavalry divisions.

Troops from Algeria, Morocco and Tunisia counted as part of the metropolitan army, and North Africans made a large contribution to the French Army. The 12 North African infantry divisions were each composed of three infantry regiments and one artillery regiment. They included regiments of the French Foreign Legion, *zouaves*, and Moroccan, Algerian and Tunisian *tirailleurs* (light infantry).

Three Brigades of *spahis* from Algeria and Morocco fought with distinction before retreating to the unoccupied zone of France. A *spahi* brigade had a strength of some 80 officers, 2200 other ranks (of whom 930 were French), 2000 horses and 150 motor vehicles.

French colonial troops came under the control of a special directorate of the Ministry of War, and were stationed partly in the colonies and partly in France. Their commandant had the status of regional commander and was appointed Senior Commandant of Colonial Troops in France. The designation of formations as 'colonial' meant either that it had been raised in France to serve in the colonies, or that it was composed of native troops from the French Empire.

In May 1940 there were nine divisions of colonial infantry, while in the 102nd Fortress Division there was a *demi-brigade* each of Indochinese and Malagasy machine gunners helping to man the Maginot Line. In addition a number of metropolitan divisions had been brought up to strength by the addition of non-metropolitan regiments.

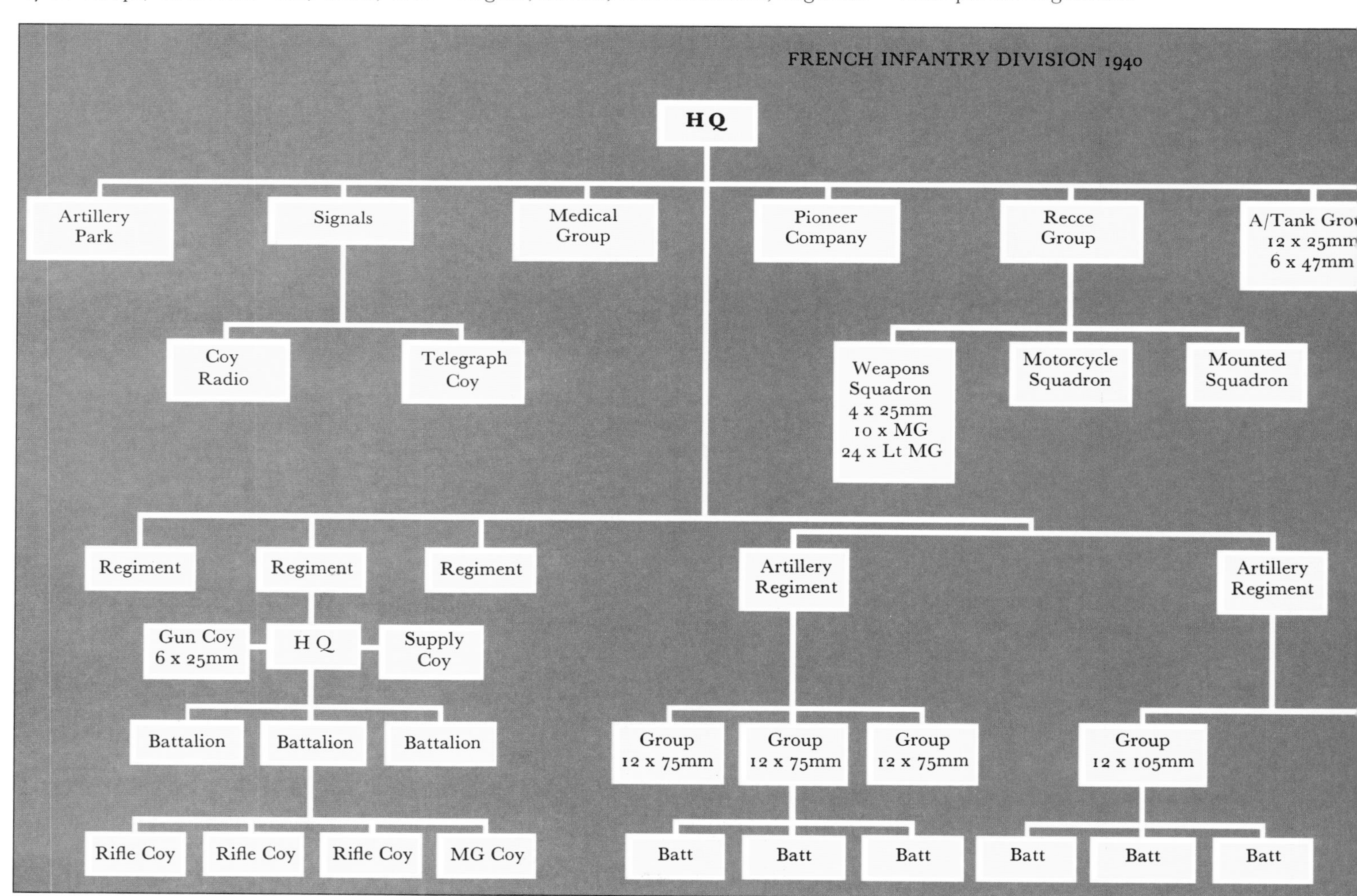

UNIFORM Twenty years after its introduction, the old 'horizon blue' gave way to khaki when in 1935 this became the standard colour of French Army uniforms. Previously only the colonial and African troops had worn khaki. In the years leading up to World War II, a number of modifications to existing uniforms were made, and completely new items of clothing and equipment were introduced, but these had not reached all troops by the summer of 1940.

Officers either continued to wear the old closed tunic, or the new open pattern illustrated by figure 52. In the field, generals wore a plain khaki kepi with metal rank stars on the front. The greatcoat was single-breasted, with five or six buttons in front and low fall collar with pronounced points, and turnback greatcoat was single breasted, with five cuffs. In undress uniforms officers could wear long khaki trousers with brown piping and stripes.

The basic field uniform for other ranks is illustrated by figure 51. Other forms of head-dress were the khaki side cap and the khaki beret for fortress troops. One of the main variations on the field

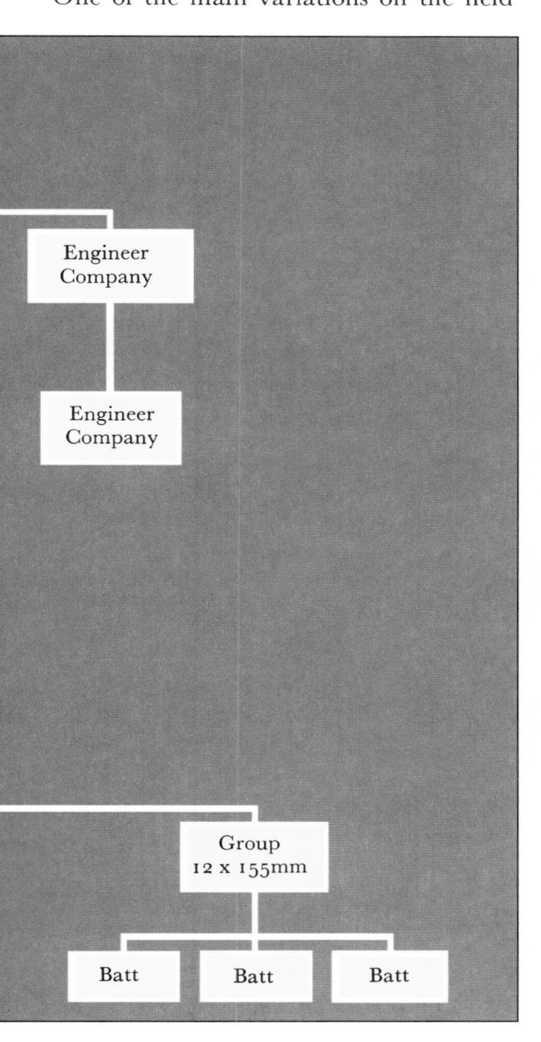

51

52

51 Corporal, French Army, 1940

This corporal of the 24th Infantry Regiment wears the 1926 model of the Adrian *helmet (which had its shell stamped from one piece of manganese steel), the 1938 model single-breasted greatcoat, and the ANP 1931 model gas mask. The rest of his equipment, including the Lebel ammunition pouches, waterbottle, haversack and pack are the standard issue originally introduced in World War I. The carbine is the 8mm* mousqueton *M92/16. This carbine was not a very good weapon, with its difficult bolt action and a tendency to jam.*

52 Lieutenant-General, French Army, 1940

This divisional general wears service dress with the new open tunic which replaced the closed model worn by the infantry officer, figure 48. On active service generals usually wore a plain khaki kepi with metal stars on the front according to rank. Rank is identified by the embroidery and braid on the kepi and the stars on the cuffs. All officers, including generals, were entitled to wear five different types of uniform, and the kepi was worn with all except the field clothing.

Left: One of the North Africans serving in France – a Moroccan tirailleur *with an impressive array of medals and decorations.*

uniform was worn by mounted personnel in cavalry, horse artillery and horse-drawn supply trains. They received a single-breasted greatcoat and riding breeches, while their footwear consisted of ankle boots, spurs and leggings.

Rifles (*chasseurs à pied*) and mountain rifles (*chasseurs alpins*) wore a distinctive dark-blue uniform, although they retained the khaki infantry greatcoat for winter field wear. The head-dress was a dark blue beret.

The winter of 1939–1940 was particularly severe and the French soldier found his uniform inadequate for the temperature which sometimes reached minus 20 degrees centigrade. Winter clothing had to be improvised by the unit or individual and consisted in the main of additional underwear and pullovers. The most common forms of external winter clothing were sleeveless sheepskin coats and gauntlets, rubber boots, and winter camouflage dress.

Members of motorised and armoured formations received the standard uniform but when on duty with their vehicles they wore a special helmet or a black beret, and either the obsolete double-breasted black leather coat or the new single-breasted brown model. Over khaki trousers and puttees they wore khaki drill trousers which fastened around the ankle. In warm weather tank crews usually wore their two-piece working overalls. Motorcycle troops also wore the motorised troops' helmet and a leather coat, or the new 1938 model double-breasted cotton duck jacket, or a waterproof canvas raincoat.

The colonial and African troops serving in France during the 1940 campaign wore standard French Army uniform with certain distinctive features; the Foreign Legion, for example, had the right to wear the white kepi (although it was seldom worn in action) while the *zouaves, tirailleurs* and *spahis* wore *chechias* or turbans of different colours. In addition, the Foreign Legion and the *zouaves* wore a blue sash, *tirailleurs* a red sash, and *spahis* a white and red burnous.

INSIGNIA Officers' rank was denoted by the insignia on the sleeves of the tunic and greatcoat and on the kepi and forage cap. On the coat and other overgarments rank insignia was shown by a series of stripes on tabs which were affixed to a coat button. Officers of general rank had gold oak leaves embroidered on the kepi while other officers wore gold and silver lace on the kepi to denote rank. The regimental badge or number was shown on the front of the kepi.

Insignia for warrant officers and NCOs was worn as chevrons and stripes on the arm. Ranks from corporal upwards were entitled to wear a gold or silver chinstrap on the kepi. The colour of the chevrons and numerals and the colour of the collar patch itself identified the unit of the wearer. Infantry and tank troops, for example, had khaki patches; but while infantry had blue chevrons and red numerals, the tank troops usually had grey chevrons and numerals. Artillery had red collar patches with blue chevrons.

AIR FORCE

The French Air Force (*Armée de l'Air*) was formed as an independent service on 1 April 1933. Head of the service was the Air Minister who was also president of the Supreme Air Council which dealt with organisation, co-operation with land and sea forces, supply, training, tactics and equipment.

The air defence of France and her overseas Empire was the responsibility of five Air Regions (Dijon, Paris, Tours,

53

Left: *French aircrew about to leave on a mission. They are wearing full leather protective clothing, helmets and gauntlets.*

Aix-en-Provence and North Africa) each of which was sub-divided into two Air Districts. The largest flying formations were the air divisions and independent brigades. An air division had two or three brigades each with two or three squadrons. Frontline strength on the eve of World War II was 1200 fighters, 1300 bombers and 800 reconnaissance aircraft, and in August 1939 there were 110,000 personnel of all ranks, a figure which had risen to 150,000 by March 1940.

The Air Force had suffered considerable neglect between the wars, and its performance in 1940, with machines which were in general much inferior to those of the enemy, was not impressive. Indeed, according to French sources, only 420 modern fighters and 31 heavy bombers were serviceable when the Germans struck in May.

Anti-aircraft artillery, except that forming part of the field army, came under the commander of anti-aircraft artillery in the Air Ministry. On mobilisation a reorganisation took place which divided the anti-aircraft defence of France into the interior and coastal regions. The latter came under the control of the Naval Minister, while the former was organised into five battalions each with three batteries of 75mm guns and a sixth battalion equipped with searchlights. In wartime anti-aircraft artillery also assumed responsibility for barrage balloons.

UNIFORM In July 1934 the Air Force adopted a dark 'Louise-blue' uniform whose origin was to be found in the dark blue uniform worn by the army engineers who had pioneered military aviation before World War I.

The service dress for officers and regular NCOs is illustrated by figure 55. A double-breasted greatcoat with two rows of three gilt metal buttons was often worn over this. Other ranks had a dark steel-grey blouse with a round fall collar which was worn closed but left exposed a blue shirt and black tie. It was worn with matching long trousers

54

55

53 Private, French Army, 1940
The French and Polish mountain troops who fought as part of the Allied Expeditionary Force in Norway were dressed and equipped as the figure shown here. This chasseur alpin *of the French 5th* demi-brigade *wears the blue* chasseur *beret and waterproof cotton duck anorak, but for additional warmth he has been issued with a sheepskin jacket which is carried rolled on the rucksack. Armament consists of a pistol and a 7.5mm MAS 36 carbine. Gaiters and skis were standard issue for French mountain troops, although in fact these soldiers had little opportunity to use their skis during the fighting in Norway. Mountain troops of all nations during the war tended to carry more equipment than the average infantryman and this somewhat overburdened figure is no exception.*

54 Pilot, French Air Force, 1940
This pilot of a Potez 63/II reconnaissance aircraft wears the standard padded chrome leather flying helmet, one-piece overall, and Chanole *parachute with a quick release harness.*

55 Sergeant-Major, French Air Force, 1940
Sergeant Duval, air gunner in the GAO (groupe aerienne d'observation) *502, wears the 'Louise-blue' Air Force service dress with badges of rank on the cap and cuffs. The wings on the right breast were worn by all flying personnel, whereas the metal badge on the right breast was worn only by crews of aeroplanes and airships. The badge on the left breast pocket flap is a squadron emblem. This non-commissioned officer wears medal ribbons for the* Médaille Militaire *(yellow and green), an award for soldiers who had distinguished themselves in war, and the* Croix de Guerre *(red and green).*

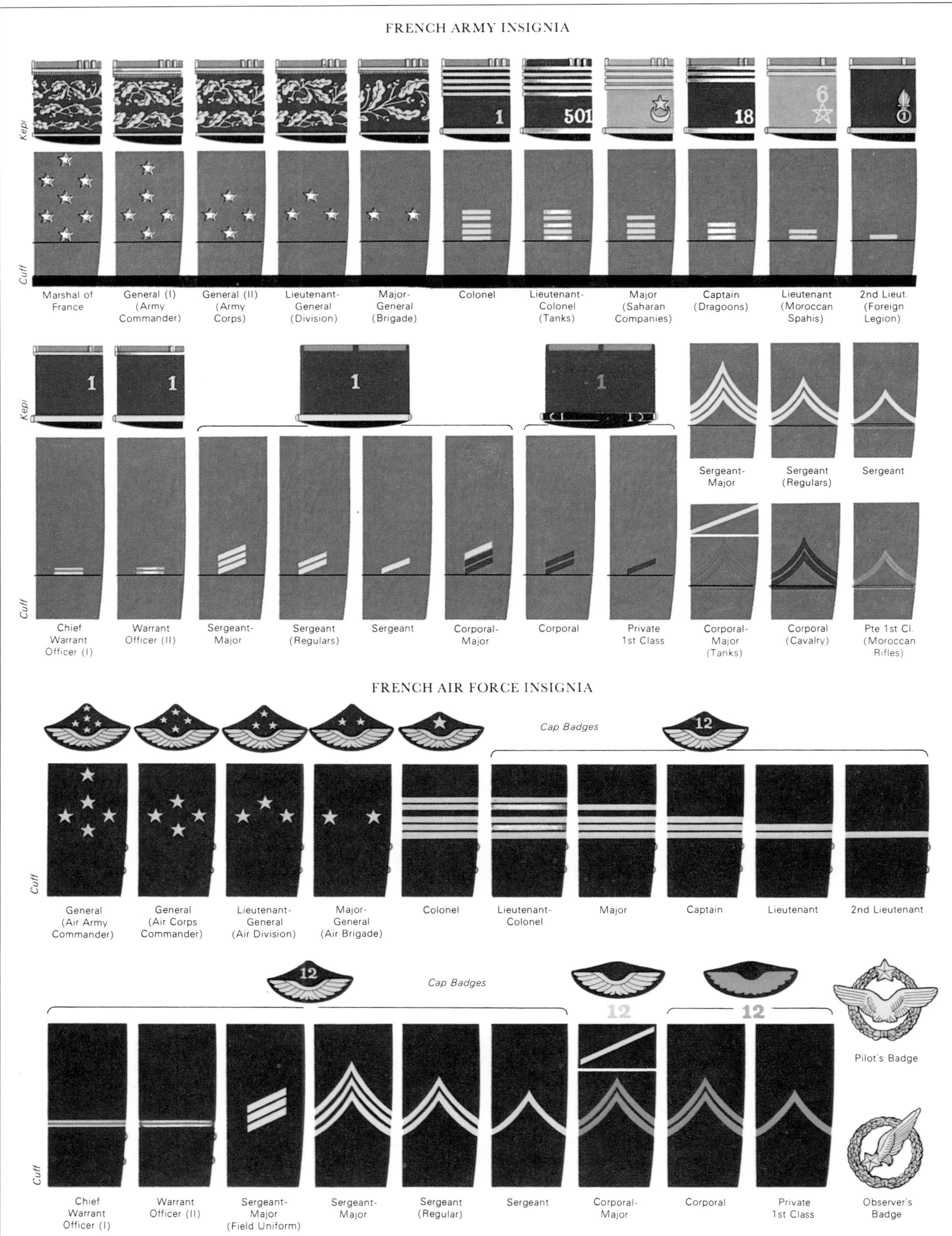
FRENCH ARMY INSIGNIA
Kepi
Cuff
1
501
18
6
Marshal of France
General (I) (Army Commander)
General (II) (Army Corps)
Lieutenant-General (Division)
Major-General (Brigade)
Colonel
Lieutenant-Colonel (Tanks)
Major (Saharan Companies)
Captain (Dragoons)
Lieutenant (Moroccan Spahis)
2nd Lieut. (Foreign Legion)
Kepi
Cuff
1
1
1
1
Sergeant-Major
Sergeant (Regulars)
Sergeant
Chief Warrant Officer (I)
Warrant Officer (II)
Sergeant-Major
Sergeant (Regulars)
Sergeant
Corporal-Major
Corporal
Private 1st Class
Corporal-Major (Tanks)
Corporal (Cavalry)
Pte 1st Cl. (Moroccan Rifles)
FRENCH AIR FORCE INSIGNIA
Cap Badges
12
Cuff
General (Air Army Commander)
General (Air Corps Commander)
Lieutenant-General (Air Division)
Major-General (Air Brigade)
Colonel
Lieutenant-Colonel
Major
Captain
Lieutenant
2nd Lieutenant
12
Cap Badges
12
12
Pilot's Badge
Cuff
Chief Warrant Officer (I)
Warrant Officer (II)
Sergeant-Major (Field Uniform)
Sergeant-Major
Sergeant (Regular)
Sergeant
Corporal-Major
Corporal
Private 1st Class
Observer's Badge

and a 'horizon-blue' greatcoat. This obsolete infantry greatcoat began to be replaced in 1937 by the cavalry pattern coat but in 'Louise blue'.

Head-dress consisted of a peaked cap with white cover for summer wear, a black beret for everyday and working wear, and the two patterns of French Army steel helmet (the *Adrian* model of the infantry and the version worn by motorised troops).

The standard canvas flying suit is illustrated in figure 54, but many pilots of single-seater aircraft wore a double-breasted leather jacket.

INSIGNIA Rank was indicated by the embroidery or rank distinction lace on the peaked cap and on the cuffs of officers and warrant officers. On the working cap the rank distinction lace was restricted to an oval patch on the front of the cap, rather than around the circumference of the cap band. Other ranks also wore their rank badges on their head-dress and cuffs. On flying clothing and working dress, rank distinction lace was worn on a cloth patch which was buttoned to the front of the garment.

For arm-of-service distinction, certain branches and sometimes units themselves were identified by an emblem or number which was incorporated in the winged badge which was worn on the front of the peaked cap and on the right breast. Other ranks wore their branch colour in the form of chevrons on the collar patches, while the formation number or emblem was embroidered in orange for other ranks or gold for NCOs.

Pilots of aircraft and balloons and cadet pilots, mechanics and observers wore a distinctive circular white metal badge on the right breast pocket.

NAVY

The Ministry of National Defence co-ordinated the activities of the three ministries representing the armed forces. The most important office of the Ministry of Marine was the Chief of the Admiralty, Vice-Admiral F. X. Darlan. He controlled all operations at sea and was also responsible for coastal defence. His immediate subordinates were the squadron and base commanders.

In January 1937 France began a programme of modernisation and expansion which elevated the French Fleet to fourth largest in the world, although it was considerably smaller than that of her ally, Great Britain.

On 23 August 1939 Navy reservists were called up, anti-aircraft defences manned, and liaison officers were exchanged with the Royal Navy. By 1 September 1939 the strength of the French Navy was 160,000 personnel of all ranks.

The deployment of the French Navy on the outbreak of war was as follows:
Indo-China: 2 cruisers, 5 destroyers, 2 submarines, and a number of sloops and river gunboats;
Casablanca: 2 destroyers and 4 submarines to cover the routes between France, Dakar and the West Indies;
Channel: 7 destroyers, plus the equivalent of an Army division for coastal defence;
Bay of Biscay: 3 destroyers;
Mediterranean: In agreement with the British Admiralty the strongest concentration of French vessels was in the Mediterranean where the powerful Italian fleet posed a threat to the vitally important sea routes from France to North Africa and the British routes via the Suez Canal to Gibraltar. The Mediterranean Squadron was commanded by Vice-Admiral R. E. Godfroy and was based at Toulon and Mers-el-Kébir. It comprised 3 battleships, 1 seaplane carrier, 10 cruisers, 48 destroyers and 53 submarines. The submarine strength reflected France's emphasis on underwater warfare both for fleet work and for the destruction of commercial vessels. The giant *Surcouf* was actually officially designated a 'corsair' submarine;
Atlantic: established at Brest was an independent *Force de Raid* under Vice-Admiral M. B. Gensoul. It was to operate against German surface warships which might try and break out into the Atlantic and was composed of 2 battlecruisers, 1 aircraft carrier, 3 cruisers and 10 destroyers. By concentrating their most modern warships – specially designed to counter the latest enemy vessels – the French Navy had produced the first task force of World War II.

The early war strength of the Fleet Air Arm (*Aéronavale*) was four squadrons of dive-bombers, two of seaplanes and one of flying boats. They were all intended to be shipborne, although the employment of the two rather slow carriers on ferrying duties meant that the aircraft had to be shore-based, apart from those planes mounted on capital ship and cruiser catapults. In 1939, naval aircraft strength was 350 planes.

The Battle of France was fought and lost on land, but the French Navy proved itself a brave and capable force during the combined operations in Norway and during the evacuation of Allied forces from France. As the German Army approached the Channel coast French ships were ordered to leave the

56 Petty officer, French Navy, 1940

Shown here is summer parade dress as worn by a petty officer, second class. He is wearing the white cap cover and white trousers; his status as a petty officer is shown by the officers' uniform and the two diagonal yellow stripes on the sleeve (these were sewn to the uniform, whereas on white summer working dress, they were often detachable). He wears a fourragere *of the* Croix de Guerre *on his left shoulder, and the badge of a master gunner or machine gunner on his left sleeve. His medal ribbon is the* Medaille d'Orient, *awarded to troops who had fought in the French Army of the East during World War I. The rifle, infantry equipment and gaiters were worn by ratings and petty officers with full dress uniform. The rifle is the M92/16 carbine a widely-used although unpopular weapon.*

57

58

Channel and Biscay ports. Some set sail for England, while the majority headed for the Mediterranean ports of Oran and Mers-el-Kébir, others to Alexandria and some to Dakar in French West Africa.

According to the terms of the Armistice of 22 June, the new (Vichy) French government could retain its warships (which had not been defeated at sea), provided they placed themselves under German or Italian control. This meant in harbours within the Axis sphere of influence rather than under Axis control. Accordingly some 70 to 80 seagoing capital ships, cruisers, destroyers and submarines were berthed at Toulon under Admiral Jean de Laborde (Commander-in-Chief of the French Navy). Most of these ships were scuttled on 27 November 1942.

Meanwhile, following the Armistice, there were two French battleships, ten destroyers, 12 sloops, seven submarines and a number of smaller vessels sheltering in Plymouth, Falmouth, Portsmouth and Sheerness.

At dawn on 3 July 1940, in Operation 'Catapult', British boarding parties wearing carpet slippers stole on board the French ships in British ports and disarmed the surprised French crews, but not without bloodshed.

On 3 July the French Fleet lying in Mers-el-Kébir received the British ultimatum to place itself at the disposal of the British and continue the war against Germany and Italy, agree to be disarmed under British supervision, sink itself, or be sunk. Bad communications with the newly-established Pétain government and the unyielding atmosphere of the

57 Leading Seaman, French Navy, 1940

This leading seaman presenting arms wears parade dress: the standard 'square rig' cap with distinctive red pompom, striped vest and blue collar. (In fact, sailors were often called 'blue collars'.) The cap legend is Maritime Nationale. *White gaiters were only worn with parade dress. The carbine (a modified 8mm M92/16) has an M92 knife bayonet.*

58 Lieutenant, French Navy, 1940

Lieutenant H. L. G. Rousselot of the submarine Rubis *wears the standard French naval officer's uniform. Rank is indicated by the lace rings on the cap and cuffs. The embroidered* passants *on the shoulders were originally intended to hold the full-dress epaulettes, but in fact they were never worn on the reefer jacket.*

Left: French ratings on board the Jaguar, *the flagship of the 2nd Torpedo Flotilla, in Gravesend in 1939. They are wearing working rig of natural coloured cotton drill.*

negotiations led to the understandable French rejection of British demands. At 5.54 pm the British Fleet opened fire and in sixteen minutes three French capital ships had been disabled while one capital ship and a number of smaller vessels managed to slip away to Toulon. In this and a subsequent attack the French lost 1297 killed and 351 wounded. At Alexandria, the French agreed to disarm their ships and no lives were lost.

It is now clear that the French had no intention of letting their Fleet fall into German hands, and all British policy succeeded in doing was antagonising the bulk of the French Navy, which resulted in the refusal of most of the French sailors in England to join the FNFL (Free French Naval Forces), and the strengthening of the Vichy French resolve to resist the anti-German Free French landings in Dakar two months later. Ironically the Vichy government continued to pay allowances to the relatives of men serving with the FNFL.

UNIFORM The French Navy uniform of World War II was the result of regulations issued in 1922 (for petty officers) and 1931 (for officers) although the traditional 'square-rig' for ratings originated in 1858.

Service dress for officers is illustrated by figure 58. The greatcoat was double-breasted with two rows of five buttons in front. There was also a double-breasted raincoat which was worn without insignia.

Officers could wear the blue reefer jacket with cap with white cover, white trousers and white canvas shoes, or they could wear the special white summer jacket. There was also a khaki drill uniform for wear on duty in hot climates.

Warrant officers (*officiers mariniers*) and petty officers wore officers' uniform as a full-dress or for walking-out, but on board they usually wore a blue linen working jacket.

Ratings wore the uniform illustrated by figure 57, over which they could wear the double-breasted pea-coat in cold weather. Working dress was either blue or undyed denim, and for summer and wear in hot climates there was both a white version of the 'square-rig', or a special white uniform with shorts and sun helmet. There was no special corps of marines, and so sailors serving on land or in disembarkation companies were issued with the Army-pattern steel helmet and navy-blue greatcoat, infantry equipment, and canvas leggings.

INSIGNIA Officers, warrant officers, petty officers and all other ranks entitled to officers' uniform wore their badges of rank on the peaked cap, shoulder straps and cuffs. Ratings wore their badges of rank on the cuffs of the jumper, pea-coat and greatcoat.

Arm-of-service colours appeared on the cuffs and as 'lights' between the rank distinction lace on the cuffs and shoulder straps. Specialist badges were nearly always worn on the upper left sleeve, and on the pea-coat and greatcoat collar.

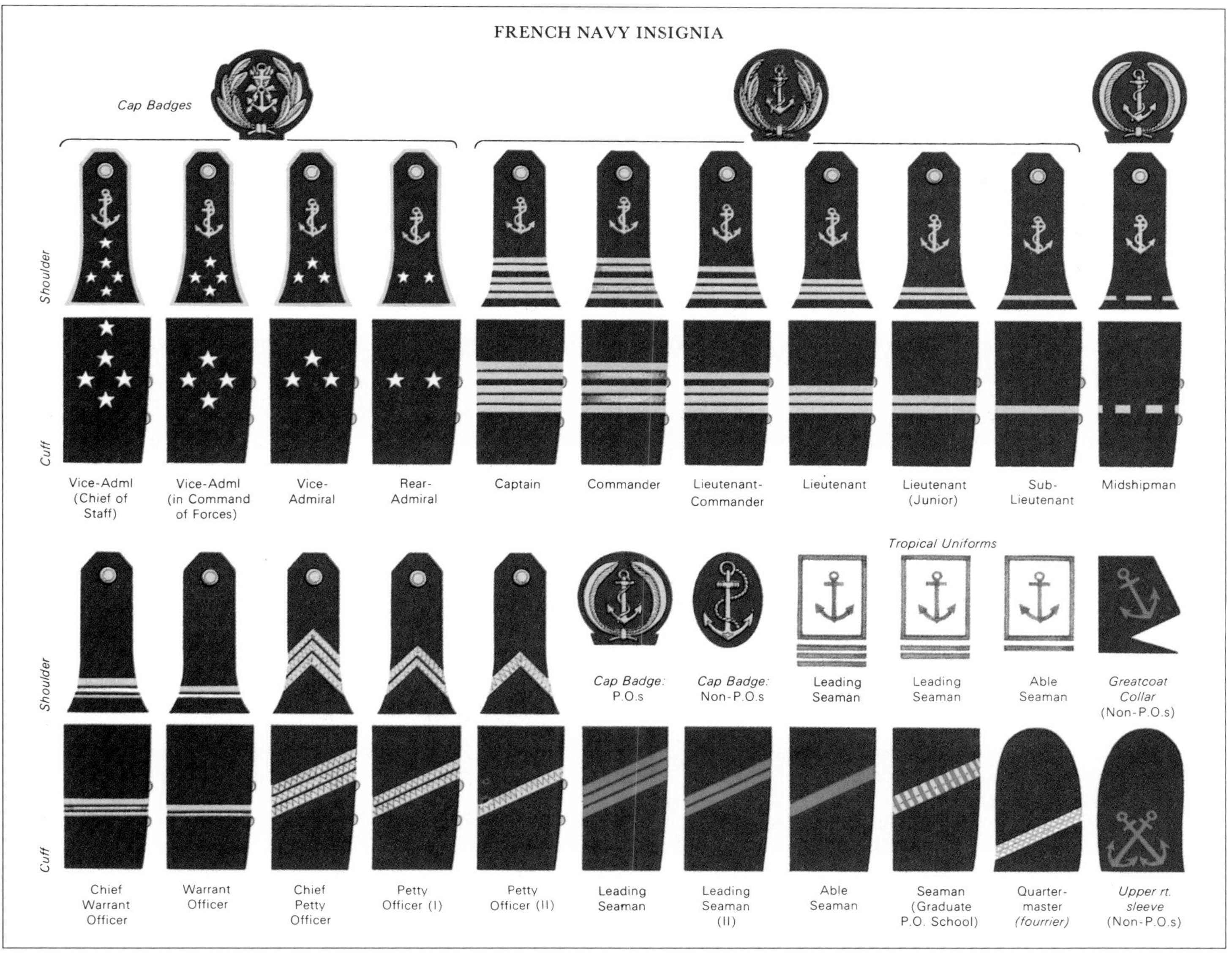

ARMED FORCES IN EXILE, FRANCE 1939–40

POLISH ARMY

Many Polish soldiers, singly or in small groups, had evaded capture or escaped internment after the defeat in 1939, and made their way to France through the Baltic countries in the north, and through Hungary, Romania, Yugoslavia and Italy in the south. The formation of a Polish Army in France had begun in November, 1939, and a large camp was set aside for the Poles in Coetquidan in Brittany. Polish volunteers arrived in a steady stream until they filled camps in no less than three French *départements*.

Gradually an army began to take shape. It was to comprise a headquarters, training establishments, two infantry divisions with a further two in the process of formation, an independent Highland Brigade, and an armoured cavalry brigade: a total strength of some 72,000 men. When the German invasion took place, the Polish Army was only half ready. The 3rd and 4th Infantry Divisions were called upon to provide 12 anti-tank companies to reinforce French divisions, while the 10th Armoured Cavalry Brigade, after only a few days in which to get used to its new equipment was split into two, and a combat group was sent straight into action. The Independent Highland Brigade which had been modelled on the French *chasseurs alpins* – although few of its men knew much about mountains – was shipped off to Norway. In France the 1st Grenadier and 2nd Rifle Divisions sustained heavy casualties before being driven across the border into Switzerland and internment.

From a total of 83,000 men serving in the Polish Forces abroad on 15 June 1940, 24,000 were evacuated to England where they joined 3700 Poles already serving with the Royal Navy and the Royal Air Force, 5000 were in the Middle East, and 50,000 were casualties, prisoners of war, or internees.

ORGANISATION The 1st Grenadier Division and the 2nd Rifle Division had three infantry regiments each, a regiment of field and a regiment of medium artillery, an engineer battalion, pioneer company, reconnaissance unit, signals battalion, radio telegraph company, divisional anti-tank company, two transport companies, a platoon of military police and various services: a total of 16,000 men in each division. The 3rd and 4th Infantry Divisions had only two infantry regiments, although it was planned to add a third at some later date.

The Independent Highland Brigade consisted of two demi-brigades of two battalions each with three rifle and one support company armed with rifles and pistols, supported by fifteen 60mm and fifteen 81mm mortars and 25 anti-tank guns. Its strength was 182 officers, 45 officer cadets (*aspirants*), 742 NCOs and 3809 other ranks.

The 10th Armoured Brigade had been formed from troops of the former Polish Armoured Brigade which, following the Polish defeat, had been interned in Hungary. The men had then filtered through to France in small groups. By June 1940 its strength was 3323 all ranks. It was organised as a tank regiment of two battalions with a total of 90 R-35 tanks, a motorised cavalry regiment of two battalions, an artillery battery of two troops of 105mm guns, and an anti-tank gun troop with 25mm guns, a signals squadron, engineer company and services. In addition there was a detached 'Combat Group' which consisted of 102 officers and 1607 other ranks.

UNIFORM Polish troops in France at first received obsolete French 'horizon-blue' uniforms left over from World War I, but these were gradually replaced by the standard khaki pattern. Those officers who still possessed pre-1939 Polish uniforms tended to wear them off duty. The standard uniform for officers was a side cap, an open single-breasted khaki tunic with khaki shirt and tie, and matching breeches with either brown lace-up boots or high black boots. Equipment was in brown leather, as for French officers.

Other ranks also received a standard khaki field uniform and the Highland Brigade which was sent to Norway was issued with additional mountain troop clothing and equipment. Other forms of head-dress for other ranks were a khaki beret for mountain troops, black beret for armoured troops and the two patterns of the French steel helmet on the front of which were painted the Polish eagle in white.

INSIGNIA Rank badges appeared on the side cap and beret and on the shoulder straps for all ranks. Cloth collar patches in arm-of-service or regimental colours appear to have been rarely worn by anybody other than commissioned officers.

59 Sergeant, Polish Army, France 1940
This sergeant waiting to embark at Brest for Norway wears the new pattern French Army uniform complete with knickerbockers (pantalons golfs). *Polish rank badges are worn on the shoulder straps, and the Polish national emblem is painted on the front of the 1926-model steel helmet. The leather equipment is of World War I pattern while the rifle is the French Lebel M86/93.*

POLISH AIR FORCE

The crews of the 84 Polish aircraft which had been evacuated to Romania in October 1939 were interned, but one by one they managed to reach France, where, by April 1940, 8678 Polish airmen assembled. This number represented almost the complete trained flying and ground personnel of the pre-war Polish Air Force.

Despite shortages of equipment and machines and poor morale it was decided to form one fighter group and one bomber group. On 4 January 1940 the Franco-Polish Air Agreement was concluded: this recommended the formation of two fighter groups, a reconnaissance group and a personnel pool. On 22 February 1940 General Sikorski, Commander-in-Chief of Polish Forces, detached the Air Force from Army control and made it an independent branch of the armed forces. When the Germans invaded France in May 1940 only the Polish fighter groups had become operational, while the other formations were being equipped and undergoing training.

On 19 June General Sikorski appealed to his Polish troops to make their way to England where Polish forces would again be re-formed. Some pilots flew their aircraft to England, while others escaped by ship. By July 1940 some 550 Polish airmen had reached England. During the fighting in France Polish airmen claimed 56 enemy aircraft destroyed for the loss of 11 pilots and 40 aircraft.

UNIFORM Polish Air Force personnel were (after a delay) equipped with the 'Louise-blue' uniform of the French Air Force. On their head-dress (peaked cap or beret) they wore the Polish eagle and their badges of rank. Polish qualification, school, establishment and regimental badges were worn on the French uniform, and rank badges were attached to the shoulder straps.

CZECHOSLOVAK ARMY

Before 1938, the 1,500,000 strong Czech Army was one of the largest in Europe. After the Munich Agreement, Czech soldiers began to leave their homeland, and the first Czech units abroad were formed in Poland. The nucleus of a Czech Army was constituted from about 1000 soldiers and 150 airmen, but it was not long before Poland herself was crushed, and the Czechs were forced to leave Poland; some travelling to the Soviet Union, some to the Middle East and some to France.

At first, the French had insisted that all Czechs serve in the French Foreign Legion, but after France's own entry into the war an agreement was negotiated by the Czech National Committee in Paris to cancel the Foreign Legion obligation.

At the Foreign Legion base at Agde in southern France, the Czechs were formed into the 1st Czech Division, made up of the 1st and 2nd Infantry Regiments. The organisation, equipment and armaments were French, although many of the weapons were leftovers from World War I. During the Battle of France the 1st Regiment (at Coulommiers) and the 2nd (on the Marne) tried to halt the 16th Panzer Division, but had their flanks

Above: Polish pilots wearing French leather equipment, but with Polish badges on the front of their peaked caps.

Below: Polish troops in French uniforms at a camp in England in 1940. They bear the Polish eagle on the French Adrian *helmet.*

Right: Czech and French airmen in 1940, soon after their evacuation to the United Kingdom. The Czechs are wearing French Air Force uniform with Czech caps and rank badges, and both Czech and French wings on the right breast. The French officer in the right foreground wears French wings, a French formation sign on his left breast and a French cap badge, whereas the man on the far left wears the Czech pilot's badge on his right breast.

60 Lance-Sergeant, Czechoslovak Army, France 1940

This sergeant of the 1st Infantry Regiment wears French Army uniform with Czech badges of rank on the shoulder straps. Both the tunic (vareuse) *and knickerbockers are of the new pattern. He is equipped with a French World War I helmet and an 8mm M1892 revolver.*

61 Staff-Captain, Czechoslovak Air Force, France 1940

On the French 'Louise-blue' uniform this Czech pilot wears a Czech cap badge and Czech rank insignia on the shoulder straps. On his left breast pocket is the Czech pilots' badge; on the right the French aircraft pilots' badge with French aviation wings above. The medal ribbon indicates an award of the Croix de Guerre *for World War II.*

60

61

turned and had to fight a rearguard action back across France: they were eventually re-grouped at Narbonne before being evacuated from Selte.

UNIFORM AND INSIGNIA The Czech soldiers serving in Czech units with the French Army wore French Army uniform with Czech badges of rank on the shoulder straps. Graduates of the Officers' Academy wore their graduation badge on the right breast pocket.

CZECHOSLOVAK AIR FORCE

A number of Czech airmen made their way to France, but it was not until France declared war on Germany that it was agreed that the Czechs should serve in the French Air Force. They were distributed between 15 squadrons of fighter and bomber aircraft. On 1 June 1940 a treaty was signed establishing Czech Air Force units to operate in conjunction with the Czech Army in France, and two Czech squadrons began formation. After the fall of France, the airmen were evacuated to Britain.

UNIFORM AND INSIGNIA The Czech airmen with the French Air Force wore the French 'Louise-blue' uniform with a Czech cap badge, rank insignia on the shoulder straps and various flying badges of the former Czech Air Force on the left or right breast pocket.

GREAT BRITAIN

ARMY

On 2 September 1939, the day before England declared war on Germany, a small military advance party was flown to France, and soon after this the British Expeditionary Force began crossing the Channel. By 27 September, 152,031 soldiers, 21,424 vehicles and all the necessary weapons and stores had arrived in France.

A general headquarters was established near Arras while the British I Corps (1st and 2nd Divisions) took their places in the line along the Franco-Belgian frontier east of Lille. As agreed between the British and French governments the BEF came under overall command of the French Commander-in-Chief of the North East Theatre of Operations (General Georges), but the British commander, General Gort, reserved the right to appeal to the British Government if he thought any order given to him might imperil the BEF.

For the next six months little military action took place except a minor, half-hearted French offensive in the Saar region. The BEF trained, consolidated its position, and built up its depots and dumps. From November, by arrangement with the French, one British division at a time served for a short spell under French command on the Saar front to get experience. By the end of April 1940, the strength of the BEF was 394,165 men.

When war did begin in earnest on 10 May 1940 the small British contingent was unable to stem the rapid German advance: within two weeks the BEF was forced back towards the Channel coast and Operation 'Dynamo' – the evacuation from Dunkirk – was put into effect. Largely through the efforts of the French Army in holding back German forces (as well as Hitler's controversial order to halt the Panzers outside Dunkirk) 224,320 British (including 15,850 wounded) and 141,842 Allied soldiers were evacuated. Although Dunkirk was the last act of a major British defeat, the escape from France of over a third of a million trained soldiers was a great achievement and a considerable boost to sagging British morale.

3457 members of the BEF were killed during the campaign in France, and although the British role in the fighting was only a minor one many German soldiers had been impressed by the disciplined performance of the British troops. Adolf Hitler, made this comment on the British Army:

> The British soldier has retained the characteristics which he had in World War I. Very brave and tenacious in defence, unskilful in attack, wretchedly commanded. Weapons and equipment are of the highest order, but the overall organisation is bad.

ORGANISATION The King, with the rank of Field Marshal, was the titular head of the Army but actual control of Britain's military strength was exercised by the Army Council, a body established in February 1904. The Council had both civil and military members under its president the Secretary of State for War. The members, whose task was collectively to advise the Secretary of State, were the Parliamentary Under-Secretary, the Financial Secretary of the War Office, the Chief of the Imperial General Staff, the Adjutant-General to the Forces, the Quarter-Master General to the Forces, and one Civil Service member, the Permanent Under-Secretary of State

62 Captain, British Army, 1940

Shown here is a captain of the Grenadier Guards in the BEF. Officers of the five regiments of Foot Guards retained a number of regimental distinctions on their khaki service dress. For instance, instead of the standard 'pips' which denoted rank, the Guards used a system either of miniature stars of the Orders of the Garter (Grenadiers, Coldstream and Welsh Guards), Thistle (Scots Guards) or Shamrock (Irish Guards). This captain still wears the old-fashioned service dress which had largely been replaced by battledress in 1940. The combined belt, cross strap and sword frog was called a 'Sam Browne' after its inventor. The medal ribbon is the British War Medal 1914–1920.

63 Sergeant, British Army, 1940

This Welsh Guards sergeant wears the old khaki service dress with knickerbockers and long puttees, which was in the process of being replaced by the battledress at the beginning of the war. Over the jacket he wears a leather jerkin lined with thick khaki cloth. This item had first been worn during World War I and had proved both popular and practical. The equipment is the 1937 pattern web equipment with the gas mask (on chest) in the 'ready' position. The rifle is the .303 rifle No. 1 SMLE (Short Magazine Lee Enfield), Mk 3.

62

63

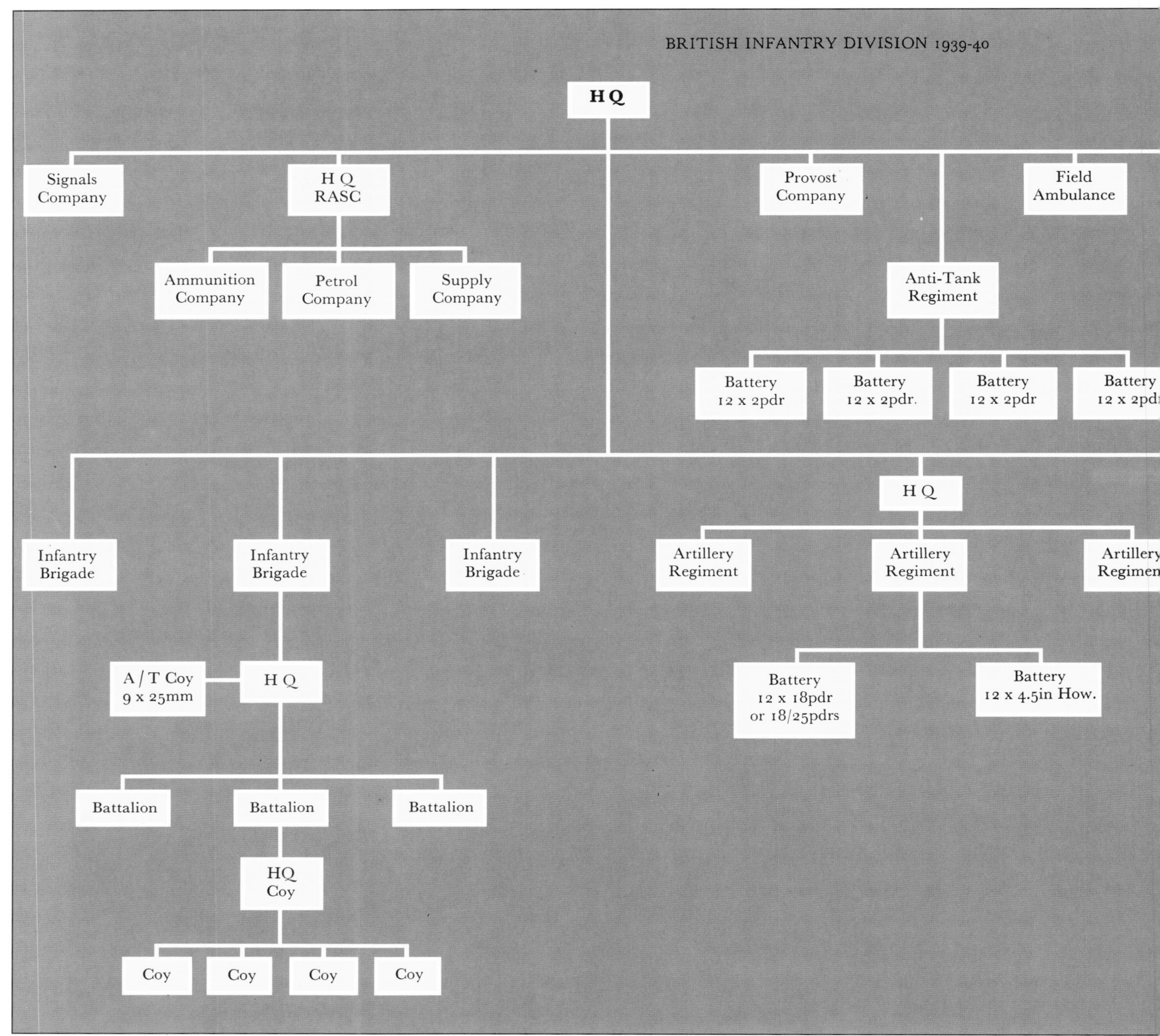

for War. In addition to their collective responsibility the members of the Army Council were also responsible individually for the operation of their respective departments within the War Office. The Department of the Chief of the Imperial General Staff, for example, contained the Directorates of Military Operations, Military Intelligence, and Military Training, while the Adjutant-General's Department housed the Directorates of Recruiting and Organisation, Mobilisation, and Personal Services. The Chief of the Imperial General Staff as the senior military officer represented the Army on the Chiefs of Staff Committee which reported to the three Service Ministers and the Defence Committee.

In 1939 the regular British Army had a strength of 227,000 men, inclusive of British troops in India and Burma, and was organised in:

2 regiments of the Household Cavalry;
20 regiments of cavalry of the line;
5 regiments of foot guards;
64 regiments of infantry of the line;
the Royal Artillery;
the Royal Tank Regiment;
auxiliary units and services.

This force was supported by the Territorial Army which had a strength of 204,000 officers and men organised in a field force of nine infantry divisions, one mobile division, two cavalry brigades, and an anti-aircraft corps of five divisions. During 1939, there was a massive increase in the size of the Territorial Army as it was put on a war footing and by August it numbered 428,000 men. This rapid growth was the result of a surge in volunteer recruitment, the recall of reservists and the imposition in May of compulsory service.

The United Kingdom was divided into six geographical Army Commands, two Independent Districts, and one functional command responsible for anti-aircraft defence. The geographical commands were the Aldershot, Southern, Eastern, Northern, Western, and Scottish Commands, with the London District and

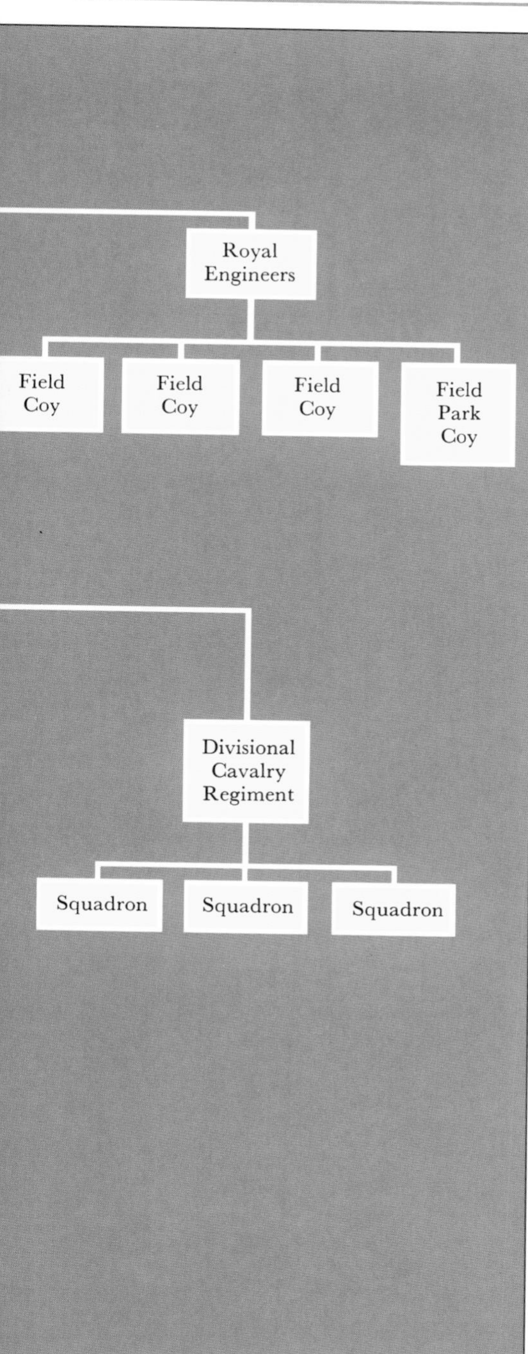

the Northern Ireland District. The Commands were divided into a series of areas and zones depending upon the importance and number of troops stationed within them. A General Officer Commanding-in-Chief was responsible for each Command and the overall framework was controlled by the General Headquarters of the Commander-in-Chief, Home Forces.

The troops within each command were organised in corps, divisions, and brigades or as depots and training establishments. In peacetime, Aldershot was the premier Army Command with two regular divisions stationed there, while Southern, Eastern, and Northern commands each had one regular division. Each Command also contained three or four Territorial Army Divisions which were administered to a large extent by the Territorial County Associations. When hostilities began the Territorial Army merged with the regular Army but all subsequent expansion was based on the Territorials and all recruits whether volunteers or conscripts were deemed to have enlisted in the Territorial Army.

As in all other armies the infantry division was the basic formation of the British Army. Divided into three infantry brigades with three regiments of field artillery and supporting units the division totalled 13,600 men. Despite its relatively small size the British division was exceptionally well equipped, particularly in artillery with 36 × 18 pounders, 36 × 4.5 inch howitzers (or converted 18/25 pounders), and 48 × 2 pounders (or 25mm) anti-tank guns as well as the three brigade anti-tank companies. The divisional cavalry regiment had under its command 28 light tanks and 44 Universal (Bren) carriers. The infantry battalion (33 officers and 780 men) was divided into four rifle companies (each with a headquarters and three platoons) and a headquarters company of six platoons (signals, anti-aircraft, mortar, carrier, pioneer and administration). In wartime the battalion and the brigade were the basic tactical formations; the infantry regiment being an administrative unit.

Below: British troops in training, using Thompson sub-machine guns and wearing the standard gas-mask which (in spite of fears that gas would be used by the Germans) never saw action.

Besides the field artillery regiments, there were the larger calibre medium and heavy artillery regiments. The medium artillery regiment had a strength of 650 men and two batteries each of eight guns, either 6 inch howitzers or 60 pounders. The heavy artillery regiment (700 men) had one four-gun battery of 6 inch howitzers and three four-gun batteries of 8 inch or 9.2 inch howitzers.

The largest tank formation in the British Army was the armoured division which comprised two armoured brigades, an artillery support group and two motorised infantry battalions. A typical armoured brigade would be made up of three armoured regiments each consisting of a headquarters squadron and three tank squadrons adding up to a total of 52 cruiser tanks, 10 scout cars and 575 men.

Uniform At the beginning of the war the uniform of the British Army was undergoing a major change. In 1937 a new field uniform consisting of a baggy waist-length 'blouse' and long baggy trousers gathered at the ankle began to be introduced under the name of 'battle-dress'. Although impractical and difficult to wear smartly, it was both easy to manufacture and required comparatively little cloth. At the same time a light-weight version made of denim was introduced as a working dress and summer battledress.

64 Lance-Corporal, British Military Police, 1940
'MPs' were well known for the standard of their turn-out and were expected to set an example to their fellow soldiers. The most distinctive features are the arm brassard and the peaked service cap with traditional red top. This lance-corporal (there were no privates in the military police) wears one chevron on the sleeves of his greatcoat, which is the pattern for mounted personnel. He carries a Webley .455 No. 1 Mk 6 revolver.

65 Lance-Corporal, British Army, 1940
As a member of a Highland regiment, this lance-corporal of the Black Watch wears the cut-away version of the service dress tunic which was called a doublet. The head-dress or 'Tam o'Shanter' had a khaki pompom or touri, and instead of a badge the Black Watch wore a red hackle. On the left sleeve is the formation sign of the 4th Infantry Division (evacuated at Dunkirk), lance-corporal's chevron, and proficiency badges of a driver and a rifle marksman. At the bottom of the sleeve are two good conduct chevrons. The kilt is in 'government' or Black Watch tartan. The lance-corporal is armed with a .303 rifle No. 1 Mk 3 with a 1907 Mk 1 bayonet.

While the battledress was being issued soldiers continued to wear the old khaki service dress, illustrated by figure 63. Officers wore their own version which had an open tunic for wear with collar and tie, and pantaloons which tended to look like golfers' knickerbockers. Mounted officers continued to wear beige cord breeches and brown leather field boots with spurs.

With the introduction of battledress for all ranks the officers' service dress was reserved for more formal occasions. The greatcoat for all ranks was double-breasted, although the old single-breasted pattern for other ranks continued in use. There were no variations of the battledress as such, but the blouse could be worn with tartan kilt or trews in those regiments which traditionally wore them.

Officers wore the peaked, service dress cap, the side or field service cap in regimental or corps colours with the badge on the left front, or any other form of head-dress prescribed by individual units, such as the glengarry, Tam o'Shanter or coloured beret. The standard head-dress for other ranks was the khaki field service cap, or stiff khaki peaked cap for those in the Guards or Military Police.

Crews of armoured fighting vehicles wore the black beret and overalls of the Royal Tank Corps, but as more and more cavalry regiments were mechanised an increasing number of colourful and distinctive head-dresses began to adorn the heads of armoured car crews.

INSIGNIA Rank was indicated by the pattern of embroidery on the cap badge for general and staff officers, and by the metal or cloth rank badges which were worn on the shoulder straps by all commissioned ranks. Warrant officers wore their rank badges on the lower sleeves, while other ranks wore theirs on both upper sleeves.

The primary means of identifying corps, regiment, or arm of service in the British Army was the badge which appeared on the front of the peaked cap or beret and on the left front of the field service cap. A reduced version of the same badge was worn on the collar of the service dress jacket. On the service dress tunic for other ranks, the regiment or corps was identified by the buttons and metal shoulder titles. On the battledress all ranks wore cloth formation signs and shoulder flashes below which appeared a strip of cloth in the arm-of-service colour.

THE HOME GUARD

The German invasion of Holland and Belgium focused attention upon the use of paratroops to occupy areas behind the enemy's main defence lines and it seemed highly probable that this form of attack would be employed against Britain. As a precaution Anthony Eden, the Secretary of State for War, broadcast an appeal on 14 May 1940 for fit men between the ages of 16 and 65 to enrol in a military organisation which would be known as the Local Defence Volunteers (LDV). By 20 May nearly 250,000 volunteers had come forward and by the end of the month the figure had reached 300,000. The force was to be organised in conjunction with the Territorial County Associations and came under the operational command of the C-in-C, Home Forces. On 31 July 1940 the title

64

65

Right: Troops of the 13/18th Royal Hussars are briefied by a lieutenant (two pips on his shoulder strap) during an exercise near Arras in October 1939. The men are wearing armoured-vehicle overalls and are armed with the regulation issue Enfield Mk 1 revolver which was worn with the low-slung holster of the tank crewman.*

66  67 68

66 Corporal, British Army, 1940

This corporal of the Hampshire Regiment has the new battledress and a Mk 1 steel helmet with elasticated chin strap. He wears 1937-pattern web equipment with binocular case on his left. As in figure 68 the service respirator is carried on the chest in the 'ready' or 'alert' position. The rubber 'Wellington' boots were not standard issue but were made available in very wet weather to soldiers in the trenches. Below the basic ammunition pouch is a pleated hip pocket which held a field dressing. The rifle is the standard .303 rifle No. 1 Mk 3.

67 Private, British Army, 1940

Over khaki battle dress this private in the 2nd battalion of the East Yorkshire Regiment on duty on the Maginot Line at St Francois wears a specially manufactured snow suit. Ammunition is carried in a cloth bandolier. The rifle is the .303 No. 1 Mk 3.

68 Other Ranks, British Army, 1940

During the Norwegian Campaign British soldiers were issued with this heavy and uncomfortable 'Tropal' coat which was lined with kapok. For added warmth, the soldier is also wearing a 'balaclava helmet'. His gas mask is in the 'ready' position and the two pouches contain magazines for a Bren gun.

Above: *King George VI inspects Local Defence Volunteers being given Bren gun instruction in July 1940. The men kneeling have LDV armlets just visible on their right arms.*

69 Lance-Corporal, Home Guard, 1943
The first volunteers who offered their services in the defence of the British Isles from German invasion had no uniforms and precious little armament. Eventually the light working version of the battle dress – known as demims – was issued together with various patterns and combinations of patterns of equipment. On his side (field-service) cap this lance-corporal wears the badge of the Hertfordshire Regiment, and on the left sleeve the 'Home Guard' shoulder title above HTS (which stands for Hertfordshire) and the battalion number. The medal ribbons are World War I awards including the British War Medal 1914–20 (far left). The web ammunition pouches were specially produced for the Home Guard. On his US Enfield .30 M1917 rifle is painted a red band which indicated that the rifle took non-standard (that is, .30 instead of .303 inch calibre) ammunition.

70 Lance-Corporal, British ATS, 1940
This lance-corporal of the ATS (Auxiliary Territorial Service) wears a privately purchased coloured field service cap; the issue pattern was khaki. The formation sign is that of 1st Anti-Aircraft Division which was heavily engaged in 1940–41 defending London from aerial attack. Since she is attached to the Royal Artillery she wears the RA badge on her left breast.

of the force was changed to the Home Guard.

The immediate problem faced by The Home Guard was an acute shortage of arms, uniform and equipment. There were military rifles for only one-third of the Guard and the remainder had to make do for many months with shotguns, sporting rifles, and even golf clubs and home-made pikes. The Home Guard were unpaid and were required for duty and training only after working hours. They were organised as battalions, companies, and platoons but there was no fixed size for these units and a company could be 300 or 400 men strong. Commanders of units were not commissioned officers but holders of appointments and every man whatever his rank was subject to Military Law as a private soldier. The Home Guard was dispersed through the country and each city, town and village had its contingent. Their duties consisted of guarding important buildings, road junctions, railways and factories, and patrolling coastal areas where enemy landings might be made. By the end of July 1940 the Home Guard numbered 500,000 all ranks and during the invasion months of that year its presence and enthusiasm not only helped to inspire the population of Britain but

69

70

also relieved large numbers of regular troops from the distraction of guard and garrison duties.

Some of the American residents of London volunteered for service in the Local Defence Volunteers. They then formed themselves into the 1st American Squadron of the Home Guard which became known as the 'Red Eagles'. Some 128 Americans served in this unit during the whole of World War II, and not only provided their own motor vehicles, but purchased their own 'Tommy Guns'.

UNIFORM At first, Local Defence Volunteers wore their everyday clothes and a khaki armlet on the upper right arm, with the letters LDV in black. Former soldiers, particularly officers, wore their old uniforms although this practice, together with the wearing of insignia of former regiments or corps on Home Guard uniform, was actively discouraged.

As soon as was possible, Home Guard members began to be issued with denims and, later, battledress so that gradually they received the same kit as a serving soldier. Equipment was at first of the so-called Home Guard Pattern with leather waistbelt and straps, web pouches and special pattern water bottle and haversack.

INSIGNIA The first insignia proper to be issued was the 'Home Guard' armlet, and large letters cut from coloured cloth to denote the zone ('S' for South for instance), but these were soon changed to a regional patch above another which bore the battalion number. Home Guard staff attached to district commands wore the formation sign of the command.

A few Home Guard units in coastal areas adopted naval rig on which they wore their Home Guard insignia.

THE AUXILIARY TERRITORIAL SERVICE

Women in uniform, first in the Women's Legion and later in the Women's Army Auxiliary Corps (formed in 1917), had made a significant contribution to Britain's military performance during World War I. As the possibility of war with Germany became more certain in the late 1930s consideration was once again given to the employment of women in the Army. The formation of the Auxiliary Territorial Service received Royal Assent on 9 September 1938 and it was planned to raise 20,000 women volunteers between the ages of 18 and 50 who would be attached in companies to Territorial Army units. Although they wore uniform the women of the ATS were not at this stage subject to military law and they were employed as orderlies, cooks, drivers, and clerks with the official status of camp followers. On general mobilisation the recruitment limit of 20,000 was raised to 40,000 but the only additional tasks entrusted to the ATS were those of signal duties, and all officers and other ranks remained civilians.

In Spring 1940 a number of ATS telephonists and drivers arrived in France for service with the BEF's lines of communication. After Dunkirk the acute manpower shortage brought home to the Army the importance of the role women could play. The establishment of the ATS was raised to 200,000 and in April 1941 its members were given full military status although only a modified form of the Army Act was applied to women.

The area of employment in which women could be used within the Army was expanded to over one hundred occupations including many of the more skilled trades such as service at searchlight, radar and artillery stations. The ATS was not, however, integrated into the Army and it developed its own organisation and administrative system based on platoons, companies, and groups. Platoons contained from 23 to 75 women, two to five platoons made up a company, and groups were formed of varying numbers of companies with the proviso that each group must have a minimum strength of 250 women. Groups were usually formed geographically to conform as far as possible to the boundaries of the military area in which they operated. By the end of December 1941 the overall strength of the Service stood at 2468 officers and 81,965 other ranks.

ROYAL AIR FORCE

During the inter-war years the British Government tried to maintain an Air Force with a merely defensive capacity, but when, in October 1938, a re-armament programme was initiated it provided for a large expansion of the Royal Air Force, so that it could not only continue to defend Great Britain, but also carry offensive operations into Germany should the need arise. Since the British Government did not wish to get involved in land warfare on the Continent, no consideration was given to providing air support, or for the dispatch of large air forces overseas.

The initial establishment of the BEF, however, included a so-called Air Component of two bomber-reconnaissance

Below: At the cockpit of his Spitfire is the fighter pilot 'Ginger' Lacey who, with a score of 18 aircraft shot down, 6 damaged and 4 probables was Britain's top ace during the Battle of Britain.

71 Airman, RAF, 1939
This airman is kitted out with a thermally insulated jacket and trousers made from glazed sheepskin by the Irvin Parachute Company. A number of these suits were wired for electrically-heated gloves and socks.

72 Aircrew, Royal Air Force, 1939
This member of a Whitley bomber crew wears an 'Irvin Harnisuit' over his service dress. The 'Harnisuit' had an inflatable life-belt and three attachment points for the parachute. He is equipped with a type B helmet and an oxygen mask with a fitted microphone and oxygen tube. The boots are of the 1936 pattern – polished black leather with a sheepskin lining.

73 Officer, Royal Air Force, 1940
Rather unusually this fighter pilot wears his parachute over his officer's service dress. The prized 'wings' are on his left breast. The parachute harness has a quick release device (metal disc) with the parachute release handle to its right. The parachute is the 'seat-type' used by pilots of single-seater aircraft..

74 Sergeant, Royal Air Force, 1940
Sergeant G. W. Garton wears RAF service dress with silk scarf to prevent his neck from getting sore from continuous scanning of the sky for intruders. The 'Mae West' life jacket is the 1932 pattern which had to be inflated by the wearer and was sometimes painted yellow as an aid to identification by air-sea rescue. He carries a type B helmet with a type D face mask with microphone and wears 1940-pattern flying boots with canvas calves. Sergeant Garton, a Hurricane fighter pilot, commanded 'A' Flight, No. 43 Squadron in 1940 and later became Wing Commander, DSO, DFC.

squadrons, four fighter squadrons, six Army co-operation squadrons, and two flights of an HQ communication squadron. In addition it was agreed with the French government that an Advanced Air Striking Force of medium bombers from Bomber Command would operate from France, but would not be under the operational command of the BEF. By 27 September 1939 RAF personnel in France numbered some 9392 men.

In January 1940 it was decided to unite the Air Component and the Advanced Air Striking Force under the command of the Air Officer Commanding-in-Chief British Air Forces in France, Air Marshal Barratt.

As soon as possible after its arrival in France, the RAF took part in operations which brought it in contact with German aircraft. Although a number of German machines were shot down, RAF losses were heavy as many of their planes (the Fairey Battles and Blenheims for example) were found to be inadequately armed and ill-suited to combat with modern fighter planes like the Messerschmitt Bf 109.

Britain was anxious not to squander its precious aircraft by using them as a sort of fire brigade at the beck and call of the Allied land forces. The RAF wanted to ensure that its bombers were only used to cause maximum destruction to the enemy, although strategic bombing of targets in Germany was only authorised on 15 May 1940. Fighters based in France and England were to be deployed against the enemy as long as it did not impair Britain's ability to defend herself. On 10 May 1940, 416 of Britain's total number of 1873 first-line aircraft were stationed in France, but on 20 May it was decided to bring back to England the remaining 66 fighters so that they could continue the war from English airfields.

The first phase of the German plan for the invasion of England was to gain control of the air and so during the months of July and August 1940 the RAF prepared its forces for the inevitable battle against the Luftwaffe.

Right: These fighter pilots off duty by a Spitfire can be seen wearing a variety of aircrew clothing including the 1940-pattern flying boots and a sheepskin-lined leather jacket.

73

74

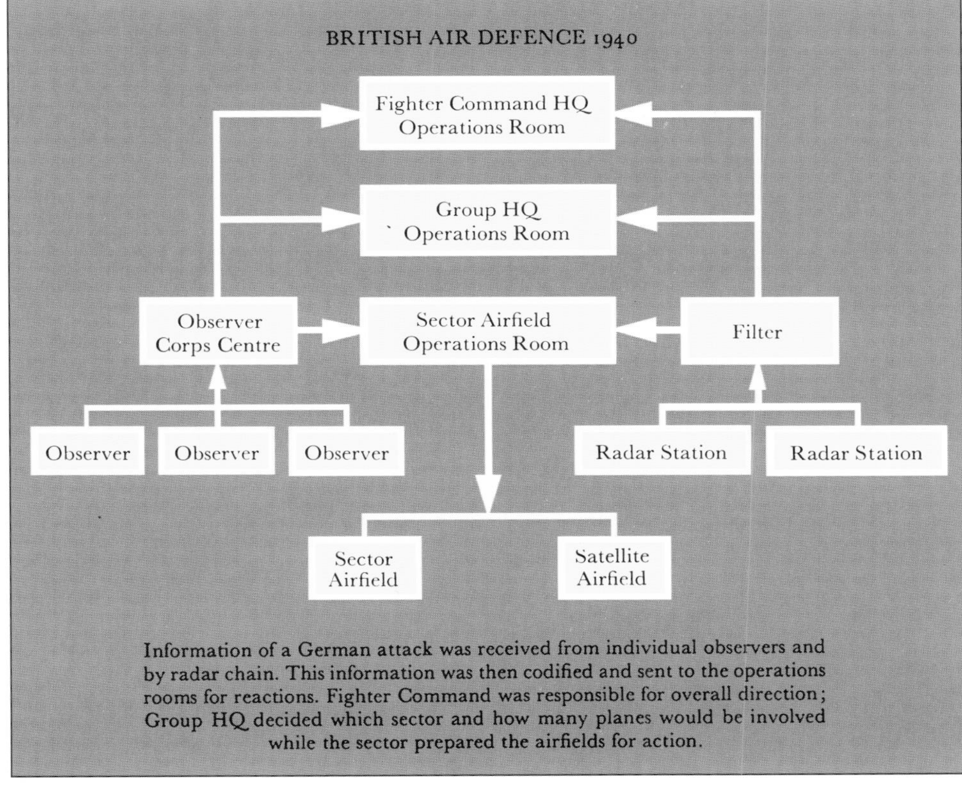

Information of a German attack was received from individual observers and by radar chain. This information was then codified and sent to the operations rooms for reactions. Fighter Command was responsible for overall direction; Group HQ decided which sector and how many planes would be involved while the sector prepared the airfields for action.

The main defence possessed by the British was RAF Fighter Command which was under the inspired leadership of Air Chief Marshal Sir Hugh Dowding. The country was divided into four large areas to be defended by fighter Groups, the most important being 11 Group under the command of Air Vice-Marshal Keith Park. This Group covered London, the Home Counties and south-east England, the fighting areas of the Battle of Britain. Underneath the Group was the sector (nine in 11 Group) which would control anything from two to five squadrons. In some sectors all the squadrons would be based on the one airfield, in others they would be spread out over as many as four airfields. A typical sector was Northolt which was organised as follows:

No. 1 Sqdn – 10 Hurricanes;
No. 275 Sqdn – 13 Hurricanes;
No. 604 Sqdn – 10 Blenheims;
No. 609 Sqdn – 15 Spitfires.

By the end of July the RAF had 530 fighter aircraft ready for combat out of a total of just over 600, with another 289 fighters in reserve.

The RAF had considerable advantages over the Luftwaffe, the chief of these being a flexible command structure which ensured resources were not wasted; an integrated radar system which usually enabled RAF fighter pilots to intercept the German bomber squadrons; and the advantage of fighting over home territory. The margin of the RAF's victory over the German Air Force was slim but it was sufficient to deter the *Wehrmacht* from seriously contemplating an invasion of Britain.

UNIFORM Before the war the RAF uniform was basically the same as that of the Army but in blue-grey, although unlike the Army, all ranks in the RAF had an open tunic which was worn with collar and tie. In 1940 a blue-grey version of the battle-dress began to be issued.

Officers wore the service dress consisting of peaked or field service cap with cloth covered peak, black mohair band and gold-embroidered badge. The tunic was worn open with blue shirt and black tie and long matching trousers with black socks and shoes. The greatcoat was double-breasted with matching cloth belt, and in addition there was both a mackintosh and raincoat.

Other ranks wore the uniform illustrated by figure 75, although the most typical form of head-dress was the field service cap, or stiff peaked cap with metal cap badge. In wartime, RAF personnel were issued with the Mk 1 steel helmet and 1937 pattern webbing in blue-grey. The

75 76

working dress of ground crews was a field service cap and dark blue or black overalls. Flying clothing is illustrated by figures 71 to 74.

INSIGNIA The RAF was unique in introducing not only a new system of rank insignia, but also a range of special rank titles. Officers wore rank distinction lace on the cuffs of the tunic and on the greatcoat shoulder straps. NCOs wore chevrons on both sleeves of the tunic and greatcoat. Contrary to the practice in most other Air Forces there were no special rank badges for wear on flight clothing.

There were no arm-of-service or branch badges as such, but a number of specialists were identified by special insignia, some of which appear in the illustrations.

ROYAL NAVY

From the outbreak of war the Royal Navy was engaged in action throughout the world. The hunt for the *Graf Spee*, for example, tied up large numbers of British naval forces in the South Atlantic, until the German battlecruiser was scuttled in the River Plate on 19 December 1939. In home waters, the Navy played an important role in the defence of Norway, inflicting heavy casualties on the German forces. The major work of the Navy, however, was the protection of British merchant vessels from the ever-present threat of the German U-boats which, even in the first months of the war, were causing heavy losses.

At the beginning of the War, the Royal Navy was the most powerful in the world. It had the largest number of ships and a network of naval bases and coaling stations around the globe. This massive organisation was directed from offices in Whitehall by the Board of Admiralty. The chairman of the board was officially titled First Lord of the Admiralty and was a political appointee responsible to the cabinet and to Parliament.

Professional expertise was provided by the five Sea Lords, all serving officers in the Royal Navy. The First Sea Lord, Admiral of the Fleet Sir Dudley Pound was responsible for running the Navy's operations throughout the world, and was assisted in this by a naval staff. He was also the Royal Navy's representative on the Joint Chiefs of Staff Committee together with the heads of the Army and Air Force.

Before mobilisation the strength of the Navy was 9762 officers and 109,170 ratings. In January 1939 there were in addition 51,485 men in the Royal Fleet Reserve, 10,038 in the Royal Naval

75 Sergeant, Royal Air Force, 1940
The issue service dress for other ranks in the RAF was identical in cut to that worn by officers, but was made of serge. On the sleeves this sergeant wears three chevrons beneath the eagle badge which was worn by all ranks below warrant officer first class.

76 Leading Aircraftwoman, Royal Air Force, 1940
This leading aircraftwoman wears the women's version of the standard RAF service dress as worn by members of the Women's Auxiliary Air Force (or WAAFs as they were known). The badges on her left sleeve are the RAF eagle above the letter 'A' for auxiliary, the flash for a wireless operator, and the horizontal propeller which was the badge of rank of a leading aircraftman/woman.

77 Chief Petty Officer, Royal Navy, 1940
As this figure is wearing working rig his jacket is single-breasted whereas a double-breasted jacket would be worn on all other occasions. On the jacket collar is the non-substantive trade badge which denotes this CPO as a gunner's mate.

78 Petty Officer, Royal Navy, 1940
The 'square rig' illustrated was the basic uniform for Royal Navy ratings and had provided the model for the uniforms of many of the world's navies. At the outbreak of war the cap tally with name of the ship was officially replaced by one bearing only the letters HMS (His Majesty's Ship) without the ship's name. On his right sleeve is the non-substantive badge which identified the wearer's trade (two stars and crossed guns for gunlayer first class), while on the left sleeve is the substantive or rank badge for petty officer.

77 78

Reserve (mainly serving in the Merchant Navy), 2049 in the Royal Navy Auxiliary Sick Berth and Wireless Auxiliary reserves, and 6180 in the Royal Naval Volunteer Reserve.

Royal Navy dispositions in European waters in September 1939 were as follows: Home Fleet (Admiral Sir Charles Forbes) based at Scapa Flow;
7 battleships and battlecruisers;
2 aircraft carriers;
15 cruisers;
17 destroyers;
7 minesweepers and sloops;
21 submarines.

Left: A group of British sailors just recently returned to port illustrate the various types of working dress worn by the Royal Navy during the war.

Right: The commanding Officer (Commander J. G. W. Deneys, DSO) and a group of the crew of the destroyer HMS Vanoc. *The various ranks of the ship are clearly shown in this photograph. Seated are the officers and behind them are the confirmed petty officers – wearing peaked cap and single-breasted jacket – and petty officers, while the back row is composed of the ship's ratings.*

North Atlantic Command (Rear-Admiral N. A. Wodehouse) – responsible for waters west of Gibraltar:
2 cruisers;
9 destroyers;
2 submarines;
2 minesweepers.
Concentrated in home waters for patrol, escort and striking purposes were:
2 battleships;
5 cruisers;
2 aircraft carriers;
65 destroyers;
12 minesweepers.

Escort vessels served worldwide, while a number of ships of all types were undergoing refit, were in reserve, or being used on miscellaneous duties such as training.

Captains commanded battleships, battlecruisers, cruisers and aircraft carriers, which were organised in squadrons of between two and nine ships under a rear-admiral. Eight destroyers, each in the charge of a commander, plus a specially fitted leader commanded by a captain, usually comprised a flotilla. All smaller warships were grouped in flotillas, usually under a captain or commander with subordinate officers commanding individual ships.

Since 1937 (although in practice only since May 1939) the Royal Navy had maintained its own Naval Air Branch under its chief, Vice-Admiral Sir Alexander Ramsey.

The Fleet Air Arm as it was known went to war with 190 aeroplanes in aircraft and seaplane carriers; plus spotter floatplanes mounted on catapults in capital ships and cruisers.

Throughout the war, RAF Coastal Command operated reconnaissance, escort and strike squadrons. From April 1941, they came under the operational control of the Admiralty while remaining part of the RAF.

Below: A British sailor on guard duty ashore. He is armed with a rifle and fixed bayonet and equipped with gaiters and standard issue ammunition pouches. Of interest is the cap tally which displays HMS without the ship's name – a wartime security measure.

UNIFORM Royal Navy uniform, which had evolved over many years, became the model for the uniforms of most of the world's navies during the nineteenth century.

The basic uniform for officers consisted of a peaked cap which could be worn with a white cover; double-breasted 'reefer' jacket which was worn with white shirt and black tie; matching long trousers and black socks and shoes. The greatcoat was double-breasted and was worn with brown leather gloves. The uniform for chief petty officers was similar to that of commissioned officers, while the so-called 'fore and aft' rig was also worn by petty officers and other junior ratings who were not members of the seaman branch.

Ratings wore the 'square rig' illustrated by figure 78, but instead of the short winter coat found in some navies, ratings received a single-breasted greatcoat. For everyday work ratings wore a blue boiler-suit, or one of the many other different types of protective clothing. In cold weather ratings received a thick white woollen pullover and sea socks for wear inside rubber boots, a knitted woollen cap comforter and the famous duffle coat. In rough seas sailors wore waterproof clothing, notably the oilskin 'sou'wester' and coat.

INSIGNIA Both flag and senior officers were identified by gold embroidery on the cap peak, while all officers wore rank distinction lace on the cuffs of the reefer jacket or on the greatcoat shoulder straps. Officers in the Royal Naval Volunteer Reserve had 'wavy' rank distinction lace, while Royal Naval Reserve officers had plaited rank distinction lace in which the 'curl' formed a six-pointed star. Seamen and petty officers wore their rank badges on the upper left sleeve, while chief petty officers had three buttons on each cuff and a special cap badge.

For arm-of-service distinction, non-executive officers in civil branches wore 'lights' which appeared between the rank distinction lace. Specialists wore distinguishing badges on the collar if chief petty officers, or otherwise on the right arm.

79 Captain, Royal Navy, 1940
This officer wears the traditional double-breasted 'monkey jacket', or reefer, as part of his temperate-climate uniform. Rank is denoted by the four gold rings on the sleeve and by the single row of oak leaves on the cap's peak (the latter piece of insignia was common to the ranks of commander and commodore 2nd class). The captain's arm-of-service colour (the purple 'lights' in between the gold rings) indicates that he is an engineer.

ARMED FORCES IN EXILE GREAT BRITAIN 1940–45

After the fall of France, Great Britain was the only unconquered European country still fighting Hitler. Naturally, the governments of many of the countries which the Germans had overrun set up forces in exile in Great Britain, and many Frenchmen, who were in an anomalous position because Pétain's Vichy régime had concluded a treaty with the Germans, also wished to continue fighting. These forces varied in size and importance.

FREE FRENCH ARMY

In the middle of June 1940 French military personnel in England consisted mainly of those who had been evacuated at Dunkirk, or who managed to escape soon after. The largest single group, however, were the 15,000 men of the Light Mountain Division which had been evacuated from Norway. Following the fiasco in Norway and the capitulation of France, morale was at a low ebb and over half the Light Division demanded to be repatriated, in spite of appeals from General de Gaulle.

Finally, on 1 July 1940, those who had volunteered to continue the fight were assembled at Olympia in London where they were formed into the *Légion de Gaulle*, or, as the British preferred to call it, the Fighting French.

In the late summer of 1940 there were two groups of French military personnel in England: those who had declared themselves for de Gaulle and those who wanted to continue in the service of the legitimate government of France under Marshal Pétain. The Pétainists retained their French uniforms in their entirety, while the Gaullists began to sew blue, white and red ribbons on their side caps and shoulder straps.

This distinction became unnecessary when British battle-dress was eventually issued to the Free French, but as with all the other Allied contingents the wearer's nationality was identified by the nationality shoulder title, which for the French was the word 'France' in white on a khaki ground.

FREE FRENCH AIR FORCE

Twelve French pilots were ready in time to take part in the Battle of Britain and five lost their lives. The first Free French Squadron in the RAF was No 340 'Ile de France' which was formed at Turnhouse on 16 November 1941. Other Frenchmen followed this lead and were sent to serve in RAF squadrons while some joined the main French depot at Old Dean near Camberley or were sent as reinforcements to existing Free French units in Africa.

Meanwhile on 29 September 1940 the 1st Company of Air Force Infantry (*Infanterie de l'Air*) was formed, and at Christmas 1940 it had completed its parachute training. It took part in special operations in occupied France, before the company was transferred to the Army as the 1st Company Free French Parachute Troops.

French airmen in Great Britain continued to wear their 'Louise-blue' uniform, but since it was difficult to acquire replacements in wartime England, most tended to wear RAF blue battle-dress with French insignia as an everyday uniform. Instead of the black beret, which was worn as an informal working head-dress, French airmen began to wear the side (field-service) cap in English cut but with French rank distinction lace in the form of a chevron in front, and a gilt metal winged badge on the left side.

Above the right breast pocket those entitled to wore the metal wings of the *Forces Françaises Aériennes Libres* (FFAL) as well as the RAF or Royal Canadian Air Force 'wings' which were worn above the left breast pocket.

FREE FRENCH NAVY

At the time of the French capitulation a considerable number of French ships were sheltering in British ports and on 1 July 1940 the Free French Naval Forces were officially formed.

Following the British action against French vessels in British ports (Operation 'Catapult'), French sailors were treated as prisoners of war and interned. Under these circumstances it was not surprising that General de Gaulle's appeal to Frenchmen everywhere to continue the struggle against Germany fell on deaf ears, and nearly all the French sailors in England demanded to be repatriated. Eventually they were sent by ship to Casablanca.

Despite this, sufficient volunteers came from abroad and the slow process of building up the *Forces Françaises Navales Libres* (FFNL) in Great Britain began.

The largest vessel was the old battleship *Courbet* (22,000 tons) which served as a floating battery in Portsmouth Harbour. In addition there was an auxiliary cruiser, four frigates, nine corvettes, two minesweepers, four submarines and from October 1942, eight motor torpedo-boats. There were at least another 34 small

80 Private, Free French Forces, Great Britain 1940

This 'Fighting Frenchman' as they were then called, wears British battle dress with the M1915 helmet and French boots and equipment. By September 1940 when this uniform was being worn the only insignia to have been introduced were the nationality title, and a strip of red, white and blue ribbon on the shoulder strap which signified adherence to General de Gaulle. The private carries a French gasmask case, and the rifle is a French Berthier M07/15, a slight improvement on the obsolete Lebel rifle which was standard issue to French troops in 1940.

vessels of various types and three training ships moored in Portsmouth Harbour. By 1943 the strength of the French Navy in Great Britain was about 8000 men – a figure considerably higher than might have been expected after Mers-el-Kébir.

Three battalions of naval infantry (each of three companies of three sections) were also raised. The 3rd Battalion, formed from Basques and Spaniards who had been exiled in South America following the Spanish Civil War, was soon disbanded on political grounds. In July 1941, the 1st Company of Naval Infantry (1ere Compagnie de Fusiliers Marins) was formed, and joined No. 2 Commando.

Members of the FFNL continued to wear French Navy uniform, but from July 1940, they wore on the right breast the badge of the Cross of Lorraine. Since French weapons and equipment were often difficult to procure, sailors were issued with British web equipment and weapons.

Naval infantry (*fusiliers marins*) who were trained as commandos in the United Kingdom, wore British battle-dress with French Navy head-dress and French insignia together with the 'commando' shoulder flash.

POLISH ARMY

Polish troops began arriving in the United Kingdom on 24 June 1940. September 1940 saw the formation of the Polish Corps which was to have a headquarters, two rifle brigades and a cadre for a third, as well as the various supporting arms and corps services. The continuing shortage of other ranks and specialists and the overall lack of equipment which prevailed at this time ensured, however, that there were delays in completing the formation.

Towards the end of 1940 the strength of the Corps was 3498 officers and 10,884 other ranks making the Polish contribution to the British armed forces by far the most significant of the exile armies. The shortage of artillery was remedied by the attachment of a regiment of British medium field artillery. Since there were no armoured fighting vehicles, armoured personnel formed rifle units.

The Polish troops who arrived in England after the fall of France wore French uniforms and these were retained until British uniforms could be issued in July 1940. For some months the French *Adrian* helmet continued to be worn with British uniform until it was replaced, but the French motorised troop helmet, which had proved both popular and practical, continued in use during the training in the United Kingdom until a suitable British alternative could be found. Those officers who possessed their pre-war Polish Army khaki service dress continued to wear it.

On the head-dress which included the square-topped Polish *czapka* and the side (field-service) cap, the Polish eagle appeared in white metal. On the beret it was in cloth, and on the various patterns of helmet it was painted in yellow anti-gas paint. On the upper sleeves Poles wore a red cloth nationality title with 'Poland' in white. Polish rank badges continued to be worn on the shoulder straps and on the head-dress and a small cloth collar patch denoted regiment or arm of service.

POLISH AIR FORCE

The status of Polish airmen in Great Britain was subject to extensive negotiation between the British and Polish governments, but on 5 August 1940, when there were over 8000 Poles ready to enlist in the Royal Air Force Volunteer Reserve, a new agreement between the Polish and British authorities was concluded. Legally the Polish Air Force was now part of the independent Polish armed forces; its personnel were to swear allegiance only to Poland, and the Polish flag was to fly side by side with the Union Jack on airfields

81

Above left: Sailors of the Free French Navy at a memorial service in London. French uniform is worn with the addition of the letters FFNL (Forces Françaises Navales Libres) *on the cap tally. The three stripes on the left arm of the sailor in the centre of the picture denote him as a leading seaman.*

Below left: Polish troops march through an English town during the summer of 1940. British battledress is worn with the addition of Polish insignia on the side cap and on the collar. Polish soldiers were well-known for their smart military bearing which has been well captured in this photograph.

Above: A Polish pilot is helped into his plane by a Polish Air Force corporal just after the Battle of Britain. The corporal has the Polish eagle insignia on his cap band and on his collar he has the three bars of a lance-sergeant, his old Polish rank. Polish aircrew made a valuable contribution to the successful outcome of the Battle of Britain, inflicting heavy casualties on the German Luftwaffe, especially during September.

used by the Polish Air Force. In all matters concerning organisation, training, supplies and discipline the Polish Air Force was subordinate to the RAF.

The first Poles to go into action with the RAF in July 1940, served in RAF squadrons, but by the end of August Nos. 302 (*Poznanski*) and 303 (*Kościuszko*) Squadrons were operational and making a vital contribution to the outcome of the Battle of Britain. By the time the fighting was over at the end of October 1940, the Poles had claimed 203 enemy aircraft destroyed or just over seven and a half per cent of the total number destroyed during the whole battle. The cost was 29 Polish pilots killed. Poles also made their contribution in No. 1 Bomber Group which flew operational sorties against the German invasion fleet which was being assembled in the Channel ports.

Early on, as members of the RAFVR, Polish airmen wore RAF uniform with no national identification, although some officers wore their Polish cap badge on the left breast pocket of the tunic. Then nationality titles with 'Poland' in light blue lettering on grey-blue for officers and light blue on dark blue for other ranks, were introduced for wear on the upper sleeves. With the establishment of an independent Polish Air Force (PAF) in August 1940, Poles continued to wear RAF uniform.

On the head-dress Polish airmen wore the PAF cap badge, and on the collar they could wear a small patch which was a reduced version of their Polish shoulder straps on which they used to wear their badges of rank. All ranks wore their former Polish rank badges on these collar patches, and wore their British rank badges in the usual RAF manner. Although the PAF retained Army rank titles, equivalents were found for all RAF ranks except Air Commodore which did not exist in the pre-war Polish Air Force.

Qualified flying personnel wore a special badge on the left breast, while officers continued to wear the metal badges of their former schools, establishments or regiments or a smaller enamelled PAF squadron badge on the left breast pocket.

81 Captain, Polish Air Force, Great Britain 1940

This Polish Air Force captain (equivalent to RAF flight lieutenant) had RAF officers' service dress with nationality flashes on the upper sleeve; a squadron badge (No. 302 Squadron) a ribbon for the Virtuti Militari *award, and above that the Polish pilot's badge. On the RAF cap is the new style (1940) Polish Air Force cap badge. Members of No. 302 Squadron traditionally wore a light chocolate-brown scarf, a non-regulation addition to their official uniform.*

POLISH NAVY

The crews of the Polish ships which arrived in Leith in Scotland on 1 September 1939 were the first Polish servicemen to arrive in Britain, but they were quickly put to sea again to take part in patrol and convoy work.

On 18 November 1939 the Anglo-Polish Naval Agreement was signed in London and it established the terms under which the Polish detachment of the Royal Navy would operate. Ships of the Polish Navy would be crewed and commanded by Poles wearing Polish uniforms; ships

Top: Dutch soldiers undergoing street-fighting training in England. Although Dutch helmets have been retained their uniform and equipment is British-supplied. The sergeant in the centre of the picture carries a Thompson sub-machine gun which was first introduced in the British Army in 1940.

Above: Personnel of the Polish submarine Sokol *parade on their vessel. A variety of ranks are shown wearing their Polish uniforms. The figure on the far right of the photograph is a leading seaman.*

would fly the Polish ensign, but in all operational matters the Polish detachment would be subordinate to the British Admiralty.

In the first year of the war Polish units carried out convoy duties on the vital Atlantic routes, and two vessels participated in the Dunkirk evacuation. As there was a surplus of trained Polish crews the British Government began to lease additional destroyers, submarines, and motor torpedo boats to the Polish Navy.

NETHERLANDS ARMED FORCES

Following the Dutch capitulation on 14 May 1940, a considerable number of Dutch soldiers left Holland for England. As soon as possible after their arrival in Britain, Dutch personnel were formed into the Royal Dutch Brigade, which was renamed the Princess Irene Brigade on 27 August 1941.

At first British uniforms were worn but with Dutch helmets and equipment which were withdrawn when British kit became available. On British uniforms Dutch officer's badges of rank were worn on coloured collar patches, and the Dutch Lion appeared on the head-dress shoulder straps, and on the upper left sleeve of both the battle dress and service dress. To prevent infiltration by German agents, the cloth under the badge was removed.

In 1944 new dress regulations for the Royal Netherlands Land Forces were prepared for publication in October 1945. The uniform was basically British on which officers wore Dutch-pattern rank badges, while other ranks had British-type chevrons.

Members of the Dutch Army Air Service who managed to reach England after the fall of France, were, from August 1942, gathered together in 'A' Flight No. 167 Squadron, RAF.

From August 1942 'A' Flight took part in the day-to-day operations of a typical home-based fighter squadron. In June 1943 it was decided to make the squadron an all-Dutch one, whereupon it was re-numbered No. 322 Squadron.

Dutch airmen serving with the RAFVR received British uniforms on which they wore the 'Netherlands' nationality title which was later changed to the Dutch spelling 'Nederland'. Officers and warrant officers wore on the upper left sleeve the Dutch lion above the nationality title which was machine-embroidered in light blue on grey-blue cloth.

During the course of the war blue collar patches were introduced on which Dutch metal rank badges were fixed for officers and warrant officers, while NCOs were given British-type rank chevrons for wear on the sleeve.

The Dutch ships which reached English ports were equipped with radar and asdic and formed the nucleus of the Royal Netherlands Navy-in-exile (sometimes called the Dutch Naval Squadron). More ships were made available by the Royal Navy, and later by the USA. Altogether 51 major seagoing warships served the

Allied cause, and 21 were lost, one ending its days as part of a Mulberry Harbour. Personnel strength was about 6500 officers and men in the active Navy and Dutch equivalents of the Royal Naval Reserve and Royal Navy Volunteer Reserve. Officer cadets continued training in the Dutch East Indies and then at Dartmouth. A group of 40 Dutch marines joined No. 10 (Inter-Allied) Commandos and began training.

In 1939 the Dutch merchant marine comprised 1532 vessels totalling 2,972,871 tons, and most of these were able to join the Allies. The tankers were particularly valuable, and so too was the huge troopship *Nieuw Amsterdam*. Her defensive armament included two quadruple 40mm anti-aircraft gun mountings, remotely controlled.

The Royal Netherlands Naval Air Service had comprised 44 seaplanes and 30 trainers. The best aircraft were the ten Fokker T.VIII-W/G seaplanes, eight of which survived the German invasion and reached France. After anti-submarine patrols along the Channel coast, they flew to Calshot on 20 May 1940.

In the United Kingdom, the remains of the Royal Netherlands Naval Air Service, consisting of 26 seaplanes and 80 airmen was attached to Coastal Command. The Fokker T.VIII-W/G seaplanes formed No. 320 Squadron at Pembroke Dock, while other airmen served in No. 321 Squadron. The two squadrons were later merged as part of the 2nd Tactical Air Force. They still remained part of the Royal Netherlands Navy, however, as did the Fairey Swordfish crews who flew from two merchant aircraft carriers.

Dutch sailors serving with the Royal Netherlands Navy in the United Kingdom continued to wear Dutch uniform as long as it was procurable, but very often Royal Navy issue uniform was issued and modified to conform to the Dutch pattern. On Royal Navy uniform Dutchmen wore the 'Netherland' nationality title, and sometimes painted the Dutch national colours on the side of the British steel helmet.

NORWEGIAN ARMED FORCES

The Norwegian Army High Command arrived in England in July 1940 and began to draw up a 'Military Agreement' between the Norwegian and British Governments. This called upon the Norwegian Government to establish combat forces as quickly as possible so that she could take an active part in the war.

In the meantime a Norwegian company, named after its commander Lieutenant (later Captain) Linge, was established to operate with the Special Operations Executive (SOE) in German-occupied Norway. At the end of 1940, following transfers of personnel to the Navy and Air Force, the strength of the Norwegian Army was 110 officers and 1090 other ranks.

In March 1941 the Norwegian Brigade was formed with a headquarters, infantry battalion and a field artillery battery.

The commando raid on the Lofoten Isles in March and the evacuation of Spitsbergen in July 1941, resulted in a welcome influx of Norwegian recruits, and by the spring of 1942 the Norwegian Army had a strength of 250 officers and 2300 other ranks. The Army's strength remained so small, however, that its operational uses were severely limited. When liberation came on 13 May 1945 the Norwegian Army (numbering about 2500 men) was mainly attached to British formations and headquarters.

Norwegian troops serving with the British Army wore British uniform with 'Norge' or 'Norway' nationality titles on the upper left sleeve and the Norwegian flag in miniature on the upper right sleeve. All ranks wore Norwegian cap badges and Norwegian badges of rank on the collar of battle-dress, service dress, and on other types of field uniform, and on the shoulder straps of the greatcoat.

By the time the fighting in Norway came to an end, about 120 airmen and three aircraft had reached Britain. In 1940, training facilities were established in Canada, and soon 120 officers and men began training at the 'Little Norway' camp near Toronto. The first Norwegian air squadron (No. 330) became operational on 25 April 1941 and served with RAF Coastal Command. Later that year – while plans were proceeding for the formation of a united Royal Norwegian Air Force – the first Norwegian fighter squadron (No. 331) was formed, on 21 July. In January 1942 it was joined by a second Norwegian fighter squadron (No. 332). At about this time there were 200 Norwegian officers and 1400 other ranks serving with the RAF.

From 1941 steps were being taken to unify the Norwegian Army and Naval Air Services into the Royal Norwegian Air Force, and this officially took place in August 1944. By January 1945 the RNAF was operating 80 aircraft in five squadrons with 483 officers and 2099 other ranks.

As early as 1941 Norwegians serving with the RAF as a nucleus of the Royal Norwegian Air Force (RNAF) began wearing RAF uniform with Norwegian insignia. As in the Army the nationality of the wearer was identified by the 'Norway' nationality title on the upper left, and the Norwegian flag on the upper right sleeve.

Rank was indicated by the pattern of the cap badge on the head-dress, and by

Above left: A pilot and chief petty officer of the Dutch Naval Air Service just after their arrival in England in 1940.

Above: A Norwegian Army colonel in Britain. Rank is indicated by the three stars and braid on the collar and the nationality badge is visible.

82 Lieutenant, Norwegian Air Force, Great Britain 1941
This officer wears the new grey-blue uniform recently introduced for the combined Royal Norwegian Air Force. The uniform was closely modelled on that of the RAF, while officers badges of rank followed the Norwegian Army pattern (two silver stars for Lieutenant), and those for other ranks the British model.

the colour of the chin strap on the peaked cap. Rank distinction lace and five-pointed stars were worn on the collar by officers, while NCOs wore chevrons on both sleeves. Pilots, observers, wireless operators and air gunners wore embroidered 'wings' on the right breast.

At the end of the Norwegian Campaign two old destroyers, one submarine, ten fishing protection vessels and a number of auxiliary craft reached British ports. Steps were immediately taken to re-build the Norwegian Navy and many Norwegians serving in other branches of the armed forces were transferred to the Navy.

By January 1943 the Royal Norwegian Navy had almost reached its pre-war strength with 4906 men, including 484 officers, 121 cadets, 434 quartermasters, 3860 ratings and seven pilots. At the end of the war it had exceeded its pre-war strength with 7366 officers and ratings, and 58 vessels, which included:
6 destroyers;
4 corvettes;
10 motor torpedo-boats;
3 motor launches;
2 submarines;
1 submarine chaser;
19 minesweepers;
11 patrol craft;
1 depot ship.

Top: The Norwegian submarine HNMS Ula *returns to port after a mission at sea; the crew displaying their combat record in a somewhat unorthodox manner. The two crewmen with peaked caps are petty officers.*

Above: Norwegian fighter pilots relax in their dispersal hut. Uniform and equipment is mainly British RAF while the insignia remains Norwegian. Above the pilot's wings of the figure second left is the star and braid of the rank of major in the Norwegian Air Force.

Right: Armed with a Bren light machine gun, this Czech soldier is on an exercise in Britain. Visible on his British uniform is the 'Czechoslovakia' nationality title and on his side cap is the Czech lion badge.

83 General, Czechoslovak Army, Great Britain 1940

Shown here is General Sergej Ingr, Czech Minister of Defence-in-exile. He wears a mixture of Czech and French uniform: the tunic is French, while the insignia and cap with embroidered peak are Czech. His rank as a general is defined by the shoulder straps and lime leaf emblem on the collar patches; the three cuff stars show that he is a divisional commander.

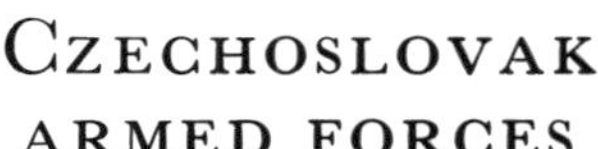

Czechoslovak Armed Forces

The first Czech army camp in England was established at Cholmondeley Castle near Chester, where the various units were re-grouped into battalions of motorised infantry. After further technical training with British weapons they moved to new bases and rendered assistance to bombed cities, being particularly commended for their quick action following the devastating raid on Coventry in November 1940.

Czech military personnel arrived in England wearing their French uniforms and these continued to be in use until British Army uniforms could be procured. For a short period British battle-dress was worn with the French *Adrian* steel helmet. On British uniforms Czechs retained their cap badges and rank insignia on the shoulder straps, and wore the 'Czechoslovakia' nationality title on the upper left sleeve. Officers also wore their Officer's Academy graduation badge on the right breast pocket, as does the general in figure 83.

The first Czech fighter squadron (No. 310) was formed on 10 July 1940 and its sister squadron (No. 312) on 29 August 1940. Also in July a Czech bomber squadron became part of No. 3 Group. No. 310 Squadron was soon involved in the Battle of Britain while No. 312 Squadron fought over Liverpool. Josef František, a Czech pilot, was the top Allied ace; in all, 87 Czech pilots participated in the Battle and eight were killed. By this date a Czech Inspectorate General was established to co-ordinate the activities of the Czech Air Force, which now formed a semi-independent section of the Royal Air Force Volunteer Reserve.

Czech personnel serving with the RAF wore RAF uniform with RAFVR insignia. On the upper left sleeve they wore the 'Czechoslovakia' nationality title, and on the right breast pocket they wore the various flying badges of the former Czechoslovak Air Force.

Danish armed forces

A total of 774 Danish men and women joined the British forces and 43 of them were killed in action. About 110 Danes also served with the American forces in Greenland and elsewhere. Because of the great difficulty in escaping from Denmark and getting to England, only a few selected officers were smuggled out of the country to serve in special units and in headquarters.

About 20 Danish naval officers found their way to England, where they served in the Royal Navy. In 1943 a Danish unit was formed within the Royal Navy, and by the end of the war a number of minesweepers had Danish crews and flew both the 'Danebrog' and the Royal Ensign. In May 1945 these ships arrived in Copenhagen and together with the Danish Naval Flotilla from Sweden formed the nucleus of the postwar Royal Danish Navy.

Above: Belgian aircrew wearing a mixture of Army and Air Force uniform and insignia examine a life jacket for the benefit of the camera.

Left: General van Strydonck inspects his British-equipped Belgian troops.

Belgian armed forces

Between 28 May 1940 and the fall of France no member of the Belgian Armed Forces was officially evacuated or ordered to make his way to England. The Belgian nationals who reached England, Gibraltar or the French colonies did so on their personal responsibility, and technically faced charges of treason which were only annulled in 1948.

On 21 June Lieutenant-General van Strydonck began to form the hundred or so Belgians into one combattant and one non-combattant company. Eventually the 1st Battalion of Fusiliers was expanded into the 1st Independent Belgian Brigade Group while other soldiers served with the SOE and the Special Air Service.

On 1 September 1940, the Belgian troops who had reached England were issued with British battle-dress at their camp in Tenby.

The first regulations for the Belgian Forces in Great Britain – *Forces Belges Au Royaume-Uni* – was dated 24 April 1941. All ranks were to wear British rank badges and buttons. On the upper left sleeve the nationality title 'Belgium' appeared in red embroidery, and on the right sleeve the Belgian national colours of black, yellow and red. These were also painted on the left side of the steel helmet. The Belgian lion in bronzed metal was worn on the left side of the side cap, while officers wore a gilt metal crown above an enamel cockade in the national colours on the front of their peaked cap.

Arm-of-service colours appeared as backing to the cloth pips for officers and as strips of cloth which were worn underneath the nationality title. The colours corresponded to those in use in the British Army.

Between 28 May 1940 and the fall of France, the situation in Belgium was so uncertain that no systematic attempt was made to evacuate Belgian airmen to England. About 120 Belgian airmen reached England, by various routes, in time to participate in the Battle of Britain.

On 12 February 1942 the Belgian Air Force was reconstituted on British soil, on which occasion it was ceremonially presented with a colour which had been buried in non-occupied France, and then smuggled to England by the Belgian *Capitaine d'Aviation* Vandermies when he returned from a secret mission. While Belgians served in, and even commanded, RAF squadrons, the majority served in Nos. 349 and 350 (Belgian) Squadrons of the RAF.

Belgian airmen serving in the Royal Air Force Volunteer Reserve wore RAF uniform which had only the 'Belgium' nationality title to distinguish them.

American volunteers

Even before the United States entered the war, Americans were actively engaged in the war against Germany. Individually or in groups some 20,000 Americans travelled to either Canada or Britain to offer their services to the British or Canadian Armed Forces.

As a result of the Commonwealth Air Training Plan, 400 American technicians arrived in secret in Northern Ireland, where they underwent training as aircrew or worked on technical installations.

During the Battle of Britain seven American volunteers were serving in Fighter Command, and in August another group of Americans arrived in Southampton. In September they were formed into No. 71 Squadron RAF, which was soon to become better-known as the 'Eagle Squadron'. Two other squadrons (Nos. 121 and 133) were formed, but in September 1942 it was decided to transfer the three squadrons to the United States Army Air Force (USAAF).

THE WAR IN THE MEDITERRANEAN

From June 1940, when Italy declared war on France and Great Britain, to April 1945, when the German Army in Italy surrendered, the Mediterranean Sea was the centre of a series of campaigns, which involved fighting in North Africa, Ethiopia, Syria, Iraq, Greece, Yugoslavia, Italy and southern France; not to speak of the air and sea wars. These campaigns demanded great flexibility, both in organisation and uniform. Formations suited to mobile desert warfare were unlikely to feel at home in the mountains of Greece and Italy, for example. The same went for uniform, with the added problem that many nations sent their troops to this theatre wearing quite unsuitable clothing, which was modified as the war progressed. And a final complication was the large number of irregular units – either outright partisans or *ad hoc* formations within the regular forces – which had their own distinctive clothing and organisation.

Italy
Army

The Italian Army had suffered heavy losses for only limited gains during World War I and in common with the other combatant nations the Army was drastically reduced in size and influence following the 1918 armistice. But the development of the fascist corporate state in the 1920s saw a revival of the influence of the Army. The new leader of Italy, Benito Mussolini, combined an authoritarian approach to domestic affairs with an aggressive foreign policy. The Army was expanded to become the instrument of Mussolini's territorial ambitions. In 1935 Italy invaded Ethiopia, and in April 1939 took over Albania.

Despite Mussolini's grandiose claims, Italy did not possess the capability to wage effective war. The population was apathetic, there was a severe shortage of strategic raw materials and the Army, woefully lacking in the necessary arms and equipment, was insufficiently prepared in the techniques of modern warfare.

Italy's entry into the war – the campaign against France from 10 to 25 June 1940 – was a humiliating fiasco, partly because strategic planning was centred on the Mediterranean, and the General Staff was caught off balance by the directives for an Alpine campaign. The Army suffered over 4,000 casualties in this brief campaign (the French lost just over 200 men).

A further military setback occurred a few months later when an Italian Army of around 160,000 men invaded Greece from the new territorial acquisition of Albania. Much to the surprise of the Italians and, indeed, to the world in general, the Greek Army repulsed the poorly-organised invasion.

East Africa was the scene of further disasters. The Italian Army in East Africa (*Africa Orientale Italiana* or AOI) was impressive on paper with 88,000 Italian and 200,000 colonial troops but there were many weaknesses. The artillery was antiquated and reserves of equipment, supplies and ammunition were so low that the Viceroy and Commander-in-Chief, the Duke of Aosta estimated that in the event of war he could only hold out for six or seven months at the most.

On 19 January 1941 the first British forces invaded Ethiopia and within the space of four months the Duke of Aosta was forced to surrender all his troops to the victorious British.

In Libya, Italy suffered another disaster: eight divisions were destroyed and 130,000 men taken prisoner in Wavell's offensive of 1941. The arrival of the Africa Corps in February 1941 prevented a total collapse but after that the Italian Army played a subordinate role in Axis operations.

Right: Pictured at a review, these Italian troops exhibit the old-style black velvet collar on their uniforms. The officers' lighter uniforms are clearly visible, while the regimental badge is carried on the steel helmets.

84

85

86

84 Private, Italian Army, 1940
The Italian infantryman was as inadequately dressed for the bitter winter campaign of 1940–41 as his Greek adversary, and both sides suffered from exposure. The Italian Army greatcoat was cheaply made of coarse cloth and was not even double-breasted. No special winter clothing was issued and the only soldiers to have even adequate clothing were the mountain troops. Characteristic of the Italian Army were the two ammunition pouches carried at the front of the belt.

85 Colonel, Italian Army, 1940
This colonel commanding the 36th Infantry Regiment in France in 1940 continues to wear the old cordellino *uniform with gold wire and rank badges. On the field service uniform the cap badge was usually embroidered in black thread, but this officer continues to wear the gold-embroidered pattern. The madder red backing to the cap and rank badges was only worn by colonels commanding a regiment. The crown and swords on the breast is the badge for promotion due to meritorious service in the field, while above the medal ribbon the metal eagle denotes the colonel as a graduate of a war academy.*

86 Private, Italian Army, 1940
The standard field service uniform remained virtually unchanged throughout the war. The knickerbockers were either worn with the woollen socks illustrated or with leather leggings by motorised personnel. The steel helmet is the model 933 which often had a regimental badge in black paint on the front. The green collar patch was worn by the two regiments in the Alpi Brigade (51st and 52nd regiments) whose members sometimes also wore a red tie in memory of Garibaldi. The rifle is the Mannlicher-Carcano M1891. This weapon was obsolete by 1940; even in 1934, during the Abysinnian campaign, there had been complaints about its performance.

Some 99,000 Italians were captured when the Axis forces surrendered in 1943; the North African campaigns had cost Italy the equivalent of 25 divisions.

During the course of the war 20 new divisions were raised but they could not replace the massive losses suffered by the Italian Army. Mussolini's 'crusade against Bolshevism' cost Italy dear; of the 229,000 despatched to the Eastern Front over half became casualties. In Africa as a whole, 27 divisions were destroyed between December 1940 and May 1943. Another 36 divisions were immobilised outside Italy, occupying France or suppressing guerrilla activities in the Balkans. A number of divisions were undergoing retraining and there were only 20 divisions to face the Allied invasion of 1943.

On 25 July 1943, Mussolini was deposed. When Badoglio, the new head of government, agreed to surrender terms with the Allies, the Germans moved swiftly in Operation *Achse*. The Italian Army was ruthlessly disarmed by the Germans (who meted out severe reprisals for the slightest Italian resistance) and ceased to exist as a coherent force.

ORGANISATION The nominal Commander-in-Chief of the Italian Army was His Majesty King Emmanuel III, although most of his responsibilities had been taken over by the Chief of State, Benito Mussolini. Under Mussolini came the supreme command (*Commando Supremo*), an organic staff which functioned through the respective defence ministries (War, Admiralty and Air) via the various high commands (Army Group West, Albania, East Africa, the Aegean and Libya).

All Italian citizens from the ages of 18 to 54 years were liable for military service. The first stage was that of conscript service where the recruit served 18 months with the colours, followed by post-military training which ran from the completion of service until the 33rd birthday. After that date the citizen went into the reserve and could be liable to call-up in time of war until the age of 54. Until 1943 Italy did not suffer from a shortage of manpower; the problem lay in training and equipping her soldiers.

In 1940 over 2,000,000 Italians were under arms, the 73 divisions of the Army being organised as follows:

59 infantry divisions;
6 Alpine divisions;
3 mobile (*celere*) divisions;
2 motorised divisions;
3 armoured divisions.

In addition there were frontier guard troops whose number was estimated to be equivalent to nine divisions. Although an impressive total on paper, few of the divisions had their full complement of men and equipment.

While the division was the basic formation in the Italian Army a number of troops were organised at corps or army level essentially to act as higher formation reserve units.

The Italian infantry division was known as a 'binary' division (*divisione binaria*) because it was based around two infantry regiments. From 1 March 1940 an MVSN Legion of two battalions was attached to most of the divisions, partly to increase the manpower of the division but also to include fascist troops within regular army formations. The infantry division comprised:

divisional headquarters (336 men);
two infantry regiments (3279 men each);
mortar battalion (435 men);
pack gun company (241 men);
divisional artillery regiment (2769 men);
engineer battalion (440 men);
Blackshirt legion (1693 men).

This was in addition to the divisional services and in some instances a reserve infantry battalion. The division totalled about 13,500 men at full strength.

The infantry regiment was normally composed of three rifle battalions, although a few regiments had as many as five battalions. The armament of the regiment included:

24 heavy machine guns;
108 light machine guns;
6 × 81 mm mortars;
54 × 45 mm mortars;
8 × 47 mm guns.

The infantry battalion with an establishment strength of 876 men was divided into a headquarters company, three rifle companies (156 men sub-divided into a headquarters platoon and three rifle platoons each of two sections) and a support arms company of two machine gun platoons (four heavy machine guns each) and two 45mm mortar platoons (nine mortars each).

The two Blackshirt battalions were organised on the same lines as the regular battalions but with less men (700 each). The legion had a support arms company comprising two machine-gun platoons (each with three guns) and two 81mm mortar platoons (each with three mortars).

The artillery regiment consisted of a regimental headquarters; a horsedrawn 100mm howitzer battery; a horsedrawn 75mm gun battery; a 75mm park howitzer battery and a mechanised 20mm anti-aircraft troop. Each battery comprised three troops of four guns each; the anti-aircraft troop being divided into four two-gun sections.

The mortar battalion consisted of three 81mm mortar companies (six mortars each) and the gun company had eight 47mm guns divided into four platoons.

The engineer battalion consisted of a pioneer company and a telegraph and radio-telephone company.

Although each division had direct control of most of the heavy support weapons it would need, the armament and equipment of the Italian division compared unfavourably with its British counterpart. Whereas the Italian divisional artillery regiment could only muster 36 antiquated medium-calibred guns, the British division possessed 72 modern, mixed-calibre guns and howitzers. Another weakness (especially in North Africa) was the heavy reliance on horse transport.

A number of infantry divisions were designated mountain infantry divisions, being partially adapted for conditions in rough and mountainous country. The only organisational difference compared to the standard division was in the artillery regiment, which comprised three

Right: Prisoners wearing the uniform of the fascist MVSN militia queue for daily rations near Addis Ababa. Their uniform is standard Italian Army issue, with the exceptions of the silver fascio *on each collar patch and sleeve rank chevrons in black.*

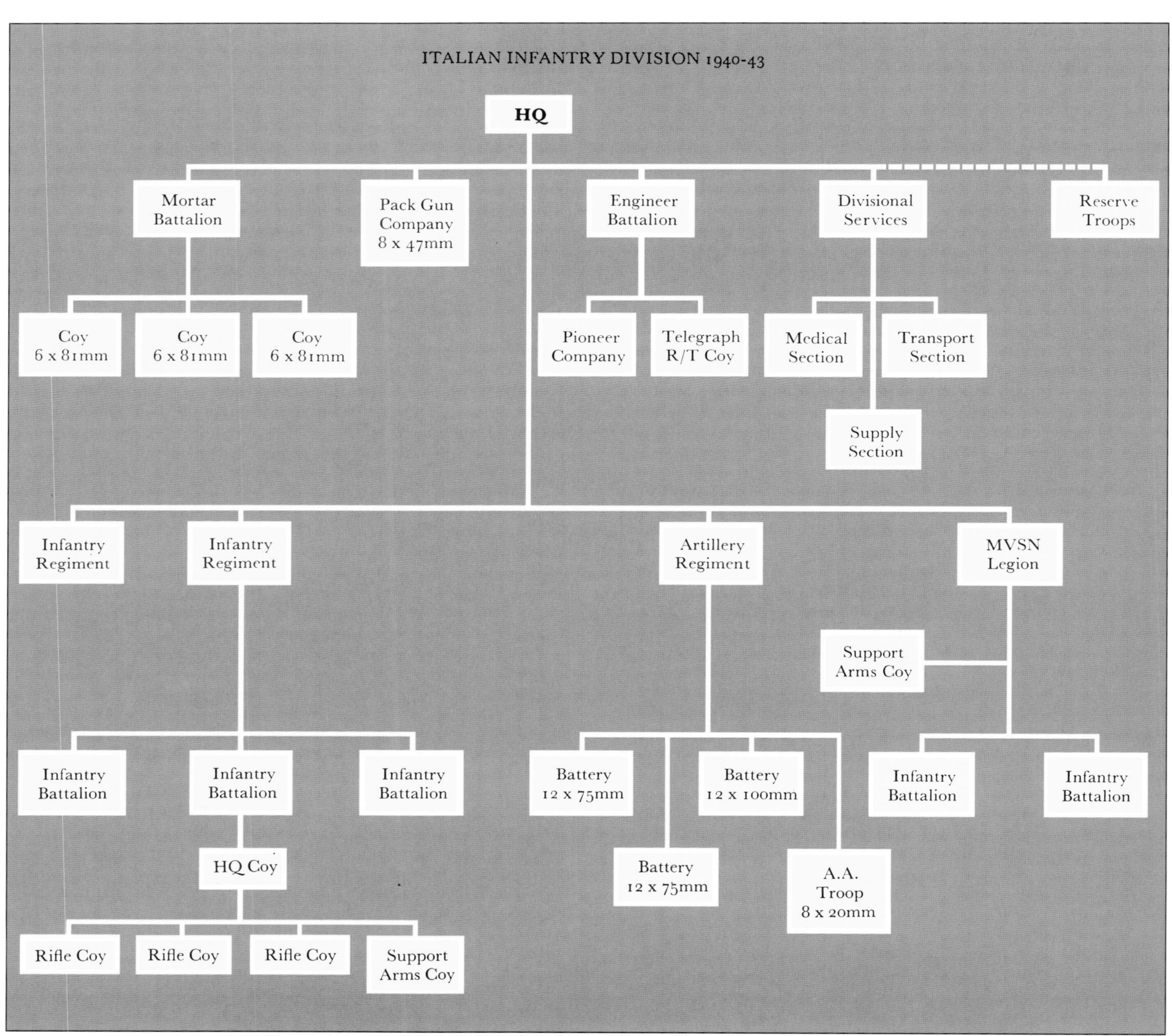

87 Sergeant, Italian African Police, 1942

This sergeant of the Polizia Africa Italiana *wears standard Italian Army tropical uniform consisting of side cap* (bustina), *jacket or* sahariana, *breeches and leather leggings for motorised personnel. Distinctive insignia are the cap badge and blue aiguillette. He carries a 9mm Beretta M38A sub-machine gun.*

88 Lieutenant, Italian Army, 1940

This infantry lieutenant in Sidi Azeis in August 1940 wears typical tropical dress. On the front of his side cap (the bustina*) is the infantry cap badge with the regimental number in the centre of the grenade. The shoulder straps bore two stars for a lieutenant, while the collar star was common to all arms and ranks.*

89 Carabinieri Private, Italian Army, 1942

The Royal Carabinieri *was the senior arm of the regular Army with fine traditions and hand-picked men. In addition to their military tasks* Carabinieri *also carried out military police duties. Distinctive insignia was the exploding grenade cap badge over a tricolour in national colours and special collar patches. The bandolier was only issued to mounted or motorised personnel.*

87

88

89

75mm howitzer batteries each of three troops, the guns of which could all be transported in horse-drawn wagons or on pack animals. Despite the high proportion of pack animals the personnel of these divisions were not specially trained in mountain warfare.

The real mountain troops were the Alpini divisions whose personnel – drawn from Italy's Alpine regions – was of superior quality; well trained in mountain warfare they were expert in the handling of pack artillery.

The Alpine divisions differed in organisation from the regular infantry formations in that the regiments had their own detachments of artillery, engineers and ancillary services which were affiliated to them on a permanent basis from the divisional organisation. This made the regiment reasonably self-supporting and capable of independent action for considerable periods of time; often an essential requirement in mountainous terrain. If necessary, battalions and even companies could be detached from their parent units to be combined with units of artillery to form semi-independent *raggruppamenti.* The division consisted of:

divisional headquarters (388 men including an anti-tank platoon);
two Alpine regiments (4757 men each);
divisional artillery regiment (1710 men);
mixed engineer battalion (341 men);
chemical warfare company (234 men);
two reserve battalions (766 men each);
divisional services (medical and supply sections and a transport column, a total of 1500 men).

The Alpine regiment was composed of headquarters company, which included a platoon of flamethrowers, three Alpine battalions and regimental services (consisting of a medical platoon, field hospital, supply platoon and transport unit). Each Alpine battalion (1267 men at full strength) was formed from three Alpine companies (340 men divided into three rifle platoons and a machine gun platoon) and a headquarters company. The fire-power of the regiment was as follows:

27 heavy machine guns;
81 light machine guns;
17 40mm mortars;
12 81mm mortars;
27 flamethrowers.

The artillery of the Alpine division consisted of two 75mm howitzer batteries, each of three four-gun troops, which were all transported on pack animals. The two batteries were split between the two Alpine regiments, with the three troops of the battery being allotted to each of the Alpine battalions. The reserve or complement battalions were similarly divided between the Alpine regiments.

During 1942 attempts were made to increase fire-power and mechanisation within the Army. Additionally a new, more flexible organisational structure was introduced. The 'North Africa 1942' division was made up of two infantry regiments, an artillery regiment, a mixed engineer battalion and medical and supply sections. The infantry regiment could vary considerably in size being based around the company which was organised as follows:

headquarters section (15 all ranks);
rifle platoon (35 all ranks, six LMGs);
machine gun platoon (23 all ranks, three HMGs);
light gun platoon (24 all ranks, three 20mm guns);
anti-tank platoon (36 all ranks, three 47mm guns).

Two to four of these companies formed a battalion and two or three battalions (plus a regimental headquarters company and a 81mm mortar company) formed a regiment. A regiment of three battalions

90 Sergeant, Italian Army, 1941

The bersaglieri *were an élite corps of riflemen formed by Luciano Lamarmora during the Italian* Risorgimento. *The traditional cockerel feathers usually adorned the round black hat worn by the* bersaglieri *but during the war they were equally proudly worn on the steel helmet and solar topee. This sergeant of the 6th Regiment wears standard tropical clothing with leather leggings for motorised personnel. The carbine is the 7.35mm M91 with folding bayonet.*

91 Alpine 2nd Lieutenant, Italian Army, 1943

This officer wears a mixture of uniform and equipment typical of wartime. The distinctive head-dress was a felt hat with eagle feather and a woollen pompon on the left side. The colour of the pompom identified the battalion. The cap badge is a black eagle over crossed rifles and hunting horns. The tunic is the pre-1940 pattern with detachable shoulder straps. In addition to his pistol he carries a Moschetto M38/42 sub-machine gun with folding bayonet, and so he also has to wear other ranks' equipment with ammunition pouches to hold the clips.

of four companies would have a strength of just over 2000 men.

The artillery regiment was composed of one or two 12-gun 100mm batteries, two 12-gun 75mm batteries and an 8-gun 20mm troop. Some regiments were equipped with a battery of German 8.8cm guns. The regiment was mechanised to a higher degree than previously, although few units had their full complement of motor vehicles.

In order to increase mobility a number of infantry divisions were in theory fully mechanised although they retained a good proportion of animal transport. Known as lorry-borne or motor transportable divisions they were organised as a normal infantry division except that they had a larger complement of mortars and were without the Blackshirt Legion.

Those motor transportable divisions in Africa were upgraded to become motorised divisions 'North Africa' type. In spite of their name they were not fully motorised, relying on other non-divisional sources for transportation. They had a strength of 6800 men and were organised as follows: two infantry regiments each with two infantry battalions (580 men each) and a support and anti-tank battalion (anti-aircraft company, anti-tank company, mortar company and machine gun company); a standard artillery regiment; a light tank battalion (an HQ section of seven tanks, and three companies of 13 tanks each); a divisional support and anti-tank battalion; and a mixed engineer battalion.

The motorised division proper was similar in organisation to the 'North Africa' type but it included a regiment of *bersaglieri* – a unit of élite riflemen – which brought up the divisional strength to 9216 soldiers. The *bersaglieri* regiment had 1827 men and was constituted as follows:

headquarters company;
motor cycle company;
two lorry-borne *bersaglieri* battalions;
support and anti-aircraft battalion.

Each *bersaglieri* battalion had a headquarters company, two rifle companies and a support and anti-tank company.

The mobile (*celere*) divisions were old cavalry formations that had undergone some degree of mechanisation. They were designed to operate in a reconnaissance or support role; fire-power being sacrificed for mobility. The division, with an overall strength of 7739 men, comprised:

two cavalry regiments (878 men each);
a *bersaglieri* regiment (2727 men);
bersaglieri motor cycle company (178 men);
anti-tank company (155 men, 8 × 47mm guns);
divisional artillery regiment (1523 men);
light tank group (312 men);
mixed engineer company (366 men).

Divisional services were provided by a medical and a supply section and a motor transport group with 218 vehicles.

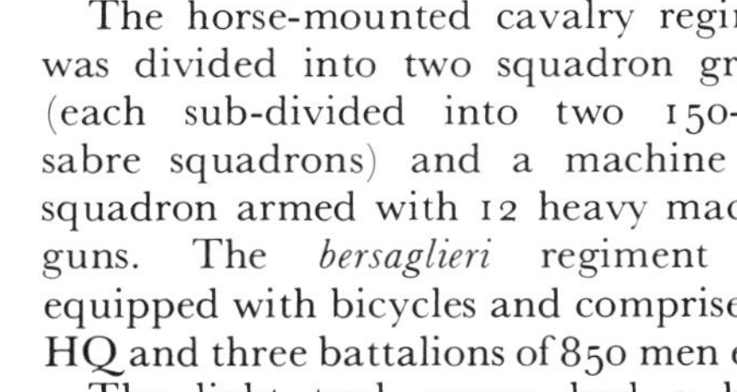

The horse-mounted cavalry regiment was divided into two squadron groups (each sub-divided into two 150-man sabre squadrons) and a machine gun squadron armed with 12 heavy machine guns. The *bersaglieri* regiment was equipped with bicycles and comprised an HQ and three battalions of 850 men each.

The light tank group had a headquarters of nine tanks and four squadrons each with a tank for the squadron commander and three platoons of four tanks.

The vulnerability of the mobile division was quickly exposed and attempts were made to mechanise the formations fully, but shortages of trained personnel and equipment prevented this.

Pre-war the armoured divisions were armed only with light tanks and were incapable of providing the armoured spearhead that the panzer formations did for the German Army.

During the course of the war the armoured divisions were reorganised with the introduction of a better medium tank (*Carro Armato* M13/40), self-propelled guns and heavier divisional support weapons. Nevertheless the Italian armoured division could not compare equipment-wise with its British counterpart. The division comprised:

tank regiment;
artillery regiment;
divisional support and anti-tank battalion;
mixed engineer company;
bersaglieri regiment.

The tank regiment normally had three, although sometimes there could be as many as five, tank battalions. Each battalion had a strength of 457 men and 55 tanks armed with 47mm guns and was divided into a headquarters company, a reserve company of six to eight tanks and three tank companies.

The mechanised artillery regiment was organised as follows:

2 twelve-gun 75mm batteries;
1 eighteen-gun 105mm battery;
1 eight-gun 90mm battery;
2 ten-gun armoured batteries of self-propelled guns mounted on M13/40 tank chassis.

In addition there was a troop of 47mm anti-tank guns and three anti-aircraft troops armed with 20mm guns.

The divisional support and anti-tank battalion had the same organisation as the motorised division, 'North Africa' type and the *bersaglieri* regiment had the standard motorised division organisation.

Although the Italian Army did not employ airborne troops in the spectacular manner of their Axis partner two parachute divisions were raised. The organisation of these formations was broadly

Below: Italian Alpini, *pictured during a break in operations, wearing white snow camouflage. The soldier on the right displays the eagle feather and pompom on his helmet; the former identifies him as a member of the crack Alpine divisions, while the colour of the latter would identify the battalion to which he belongs.*

similar to that of the Alpine division, the parachute regiments including units of all divisional supporting arms and services enabling them to act in an independent role.

The division was divided into two parachute regiments, each of four battalions, and an artillery regiment of two batteries which was split up amongst the parachute regiments. The parachute battalion (comprising a headquarters unit and three parachute companies) had a strength of 326 men and was well-armed with 54 light machine guns and 62 semi-automatic rifles. At divisional level there was a motor cycle company, an 81 mm mortar company and in addition an engineer company.

The Alpine and *bersaglieri* regiments were often of the highest quality but most of the infantry formations were poorly-equipped, and badly supplied. The Italians tended to subordinate the infantry to other arms; and Italian soldiers were never convinced of the necessity or righteousness of their involvement in the war.

Italian military doctrine stressed the primacy of the offensive, the defensive being considered as a temporary expedient prior to launching a rapid counter-offensive. In reality, however, Italian attacks were seldom pressed home with much conviction: in 1940 the Greek Army considered that Italian assaults would grind to a halt if contained for only 20 minutes. Despite popular myth the Italian soldier did not lack bravery, what he lacked were the arms and equipment necessary for modern warfare.

92

92 Paratroop Captain, Italian Army, 1942
This captain wears the special helmet and camouflage smock introduced in 1942. The badge of rank is worn on the front of the camouflage smock, as well as on the front of other types of leather, camouflage and waterproof clothing. The sub-machine gun is the Beretta M38A, which was usually only issued to special troops.

93 Tankman, Italian Army, 1941
The special clothing worn by Italian tank crews was based on the French model and consisted of overalls, crash helmet and threequarter-length leather coat. The distinctive insignia of Italian armoured troops were the blue collar patches with red double flame for tank troops, and white double flame for units equipped with tankettes.

94 Corporal, Italian Colonial Army, 1942
This corporal of the Gruppi Sahariana *wears the white full-dress jacket with sirical trousers. The coloured sash indicated the service group (the 3rd), while the rank badge on the right sleeve is the pattern introduced in 1939 when Libyans were granted Italian nationality. The equipment is the standard pattern adopted in 1920 by all desert troops.*

95 Corporal, Italian Colonial Army, 1940
This corporal from Italian East Africa wears the uniform prescribed by the 1929 regulations. The head-dress was called a tarbusc *and its tassel identified the battalion (VI Eritrea) as did the coloured sash. The rank chevrons were worn on the left sleeve above three stars which indicated ten years' service. The rifle is the Mannlicher-Carcano M91/38.*

COLONIAL TROOPS

As an imperial power Italy employed colonial troops in a number of capacities. The best troops for desert warfare were the *Sahariani* who were completely mechanised, having their own complement of motorised artillery. Most of Italy's colonial troops were poorly armed and untrained for modern warfare.

In Libya the Royal Corps of Libyan Troops was raised consisting of infantry and cavalry units. The two infantry divisions were destroyed in the fighting of 1940–41 and were only partially re-formed, existing only as administrative depots. The cavalry was organised in groups of squadrons consisting of a headquarters and four squadrons of 150 men each.

The motorised saharan troops (*Compagnia Sahariana*) consisted of six companies organised as follows:
a headquarters platoon;
two or three machine gun platoons;
an anti-tank platoon;
a reconnaissance section of two to three *Ghibli* aircraft.
The strength of the company comprised 147 men, 20 motor transport vehicles, eight heavy machine guns and two 47 mm anti-tank guns.

Camel-mounted troops were employed by the Saharan Command for desert patrol purposes and consisted of two companies, each of 280 men, four machine guns and 12 automatic rifles.

UNIFORM Despite the fact that the Italian Army had developed a comfortable and practical uniform as far back as the wars of the *Risorgimento*, the first grey-green uniform introduced in 1909 included two very uncomfortable and impractical features – a stiff high collar and puttees.

The 1934 amendments to the 1931 dress regulations introduced a tunic with open collar for wear with shirt and tie. This fashion had been adopted during World War I by the *Arditi* (commandos) and then taken over by the Fascist Militia. As soon as war came the trend was towards simplification and removal of the difference between the uniforms of officers and men.

The standard uniform for other ranks was made of a coarse dark grey-green cloth, while officers continued to wear uniforms made of a much lighter shade of twill (*cordellino*). The issue tunic had four patch pockets and a cloth belt fastened with two grey-green buttons. The old collar in black or facing colour was replaced by one in grey-green. The shirt and tie were also grey-green but some regiments wore a red or blue tie, and the *Carabinieri* retained their black tie on certain occasions. The greatcoat was single-breasted although a double-breasted version for officers and mounted personnel continued to be worn. Dismounted personnel wore baggy trousers with either puttees or black leather leggings if serving in motorised or tank units. Mounted personnel wore breeches with leather leggings.

Head-dress included the side cap or

93 94 95

bustina which was supposed to have replaced the peaked cap on active service, the 1933 model steel helmet, the grey-green felt hat with feather for *Alpini* (see figure 91), and the dark crimson fez with light blue tassel which was worn by the *bersaglieri*. In 1942 a new *bustina* with peak, like that worn by the Africa Corps, was introduced and found particularly suitable for wear in hot climates.

Special clothing was issued to personnel in motorised and tank units (see figure 93) which consisted of a black leather helmet with neck flap and a double-breasted black leather jacket. Parachute troops received a very practical collarless grey-green jacket cut like a *sahariana* and long baggy trousers worn gathered at the ankle. At first the *bustina* was to have been worn with this uniform but it was soon replaced by a grey-green beret. Parachute troops were also the first to wear camouflage clothing.

Italian soldiers in the colonies had two uniforms in the same basic cut as the grey-green ones, but in khaki cloth or khaki drill depending on the season. Also in use was the bush jacket or *sahariana* which was equally popular in the German and Italian forces. Also popular were shirts and shorts worn with sandals. The basic head-dress was the sun helmet with arm-of-service badge in brass mounted on a circular cockade in the national colours on the front.

Officers had two basic uniforms. Service dress was a khaki version of the grey-green uniform, which with few additions could be worn as a full-dress. Head-dress was a khaki or white *bustina* which later was manufactured with a peak. Officers serving with colonial battalions in East Africa were permitted to continue wearing their arm-of-service badge of origin on their head-dress. The sun helmet was also made in khaki and white versions.

The field service dress was basically a shirt, *sahariana*, shorts with woollen socks and ankle boots or sandals, or breeches and brown leather boots. Officers serving in *meharisti* (units mounted on dromedaries) or saharan units also wore a white *sahariana* and loose baggy trousers: a practical and comfortable outfit.

INSIGNIA In the Italian Army rank badges appeared on the head-dress, shoulder straps, sleeves, cuffs, and on the front of various kinds of protective clothing. Officers and warrant officers wore rank distinction lace on their peaked cap band and on the left side of the *bustina*, and in the form of chevrons on the left side of the *Alpini* hat. On the temperate weather greatcoat and on the tunic rank badges were worn on the cuffs, but on the tropical jacket, *sahariana* and shirt they appeared on detachable shoulder straps. Other ranks wore small rank chevrons on the upper left sleeve of the tunic and greatcoat.

The rank badges of indigenous non-commissioned officers and men in colonial units consisted of red chevrons on a black cloth ground which were combined with stars according to length of service. On certain types of head-dress each rank chevron was represented by a star. (As illustrated in figure 95.) Those officers serving in the Army's colonial units wore the standard pattern rank badges. A badge worn on the front of most kinds of head-dress, including the steel helmet, identified the wearer's unit or arm of service. During the war this form of distinction became less common.

Collar patches appeared in regimental or arm-of-service colours, while certain arms had so-called 'flames' with one, two or three points. Other units had an emblem. The five-pointed star was common to all soldiers.

The colour of the bolero and sash of North African troops varied according to battalion, squadron or arm of service, whereas the sash worn by East African troops identified the arm of service. The *Penne di Falco* (colonial cavalry of the AOI) wore a wide sash of a tartan pattern in their squadron group colour around their *tarbusc*.

On the upper left sleeve was also worn a metal or cloth divisional shield on which appeared the number and name of the division, while the colour of the shield identified the type of division (red for motorised, blue for infantry and green for Alpine).

FASCIST MILITIA 1939–43

Roughly equivalent to the German Waffen-SS was the Italian Fascist Militia (*Milizia Volontaria Per La Sicurezza Nationale* or MVSN) more popularly known as the 'Black Shirts'. This fascist para-military organisation was formed in 1922 by Mussolini from the bands of ex-servicemen known as *Squadristi*.

The Commanding General of the MVSN was Mussolini himself while executive command was exercised by a chief-of-staff, who, during wartime, came under the command of the Italian Army. In imitation of the old Roman Army the MSVN adopted antiquated designations for its organisation:
Zona (Division);
Gruppo (Brigade);
Legion (Regiment);
Coorte (Battalion);
Centuria (Company);
Manipolo (Platoon);
Squadra (Section).

Ranks were similarly arranged: a *Console* commanded a regiment, and a *Centurione* a company. A Legion was composed of 3 cohorts and a cohort had 3 centuries.

The Militia was organised into 14 Zonal Commands (roughly equivalent to Army Corps areas), and there were 133 Legions each with two battalions (one of men aged between 21 and 36 and a second territorial battalion with men up to the age of 55). The average strength of a legion was intended to be 1300 men, but legions were usually understrength for one reason or another. Total strength at the outbreak of war was estimated at 340,000 men.

At the beginning of the war three Black Shirt divisions were formed, while a number of battalions went to reinforce infantry divisions. Black shirts had served in Abyssinia and Spain, and fought on all the World War II fronts Italy engaged in. The remaining Militiamen served as Army auxiliaries or in the special Militias: these were the Railways, Port, Post and Telegraph, Forestry, Anti-Aircraft and Coastal Defence, Frontier and University Militias. With the collapse of the Fascist regime the MVSN was disbanded.

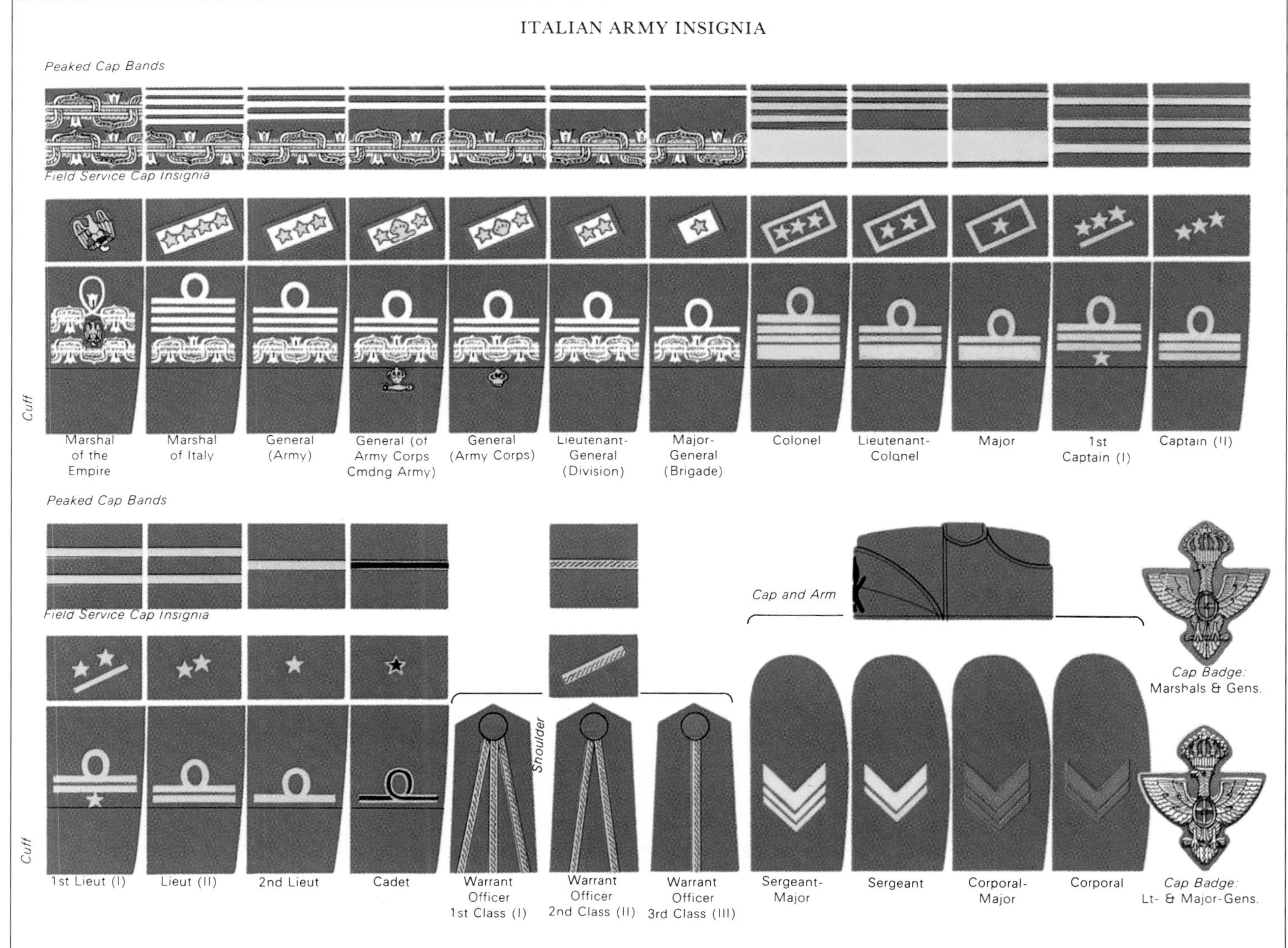

UNIFORM From June 1940 members of the MVSN Legion serving with the Italian Army wore standard grey-green uniform and its variations such as the khaki drill worn in the tropics. However, the Fascists retained the black shirt, black collar patches with the silver *fascio* and the black fez with tassel. Badges of rank were also basically the same as those worn in the Army except that a lozenge-shaped loop replaced the Army oval loop on the uppermost bar. Titles were different and echoed those of the legions of ancient Rome. Each of the three Black Shirt divisions had a distinctive black armshield which was worn on the upper left sleeve.

96 Corporal, MVSN
The fascist militia uniform was basically that of the Italian Army although MVSN men were distinguished by black shirts and black ties (hence the name Blackshirts). This corporal wears medal ribbons of the Crown of War Merit, Ethiopian Campaign, Volunteer in Spain, and ten years' service in the MVSN. The special dagger was a distinctive part of Blackshirt uniform.

96

AIR FORCE

On 24 January 1923 the Italian Royal Air Force (*Regia Aeronautica*) was formed as an independent arm, separate from the air services of the Army and Navy and in 1925 the establishment of an Air Ministry put the new service on a secure footing. During the inter-war years the Italian Air Force was held in high regard: Italian planes were technically advanced, and her Air Force commanders, who included the aerial theorist Giulio Douhet, were considered to be amongst the most progressive and imaginative in Europe. And yet by 1940 the Air Force was in decline.

Having built up a modern air force in the 'twenties and 'thirties, Italy did not develop it further with the result that at the outbreak of war Italy's front-line planes were largely obsolescent. During the course of the war attempts were made to replace the Fiat CR-32 and CR-42, the mainstay of Italy's fighter arm, but the industrial and technical weakness of the country failed to produce a plane in sufficient quantities that remedied the Italian problem of poor armament and a weak power-plant.

A further serious problem facing the Air Force was the defence of Italy's colonial possessions and its over-commitment in fulfilling Mussolini's grandiose designs.

Following the declaration of war on 10 June 1940, the Italian Air Force engaged with its French and British counterparts throughout the Mediterranean. Initially the Italian Air Force did reasonably well but with the introduction of the RAF's Hawker Hurricane towards the end of 1940 the balance of forces was tipped to the Allies' advantage.

During the October of 1940 Mussolini despatched an expeditionary force to Belgium in order to take part in the Battle of Britain. But once pitted against RAF Fighter Command on its home ground, the mixed Italian fighter/bomber force was badly mauled and was retired to defensive duties. A further expeditionary force was sent against the Soviet Union in the August of 1941 as part of the 'Crusade against Bolshevism'; the net result of which was to stretch Italian resources and to deny desperately needed aircraft to the Mediterranean Fronts.

In the Mediterranean the Air Force was engaged in the aerial assault on Malta and in supporting the Army in Libya. The failure to knock out Malta and prevent British convoys from traversing the Mediterranean made possible the build-up of British forces in North Africa and ultimately ensured the defeat of the out-numbered Axis forces in the autumn of 1942.

In Italian East Africa the Air Force provided the Army with reconnaissance and ground support services. The sides were fairly evenly matched, but the Italian Air Force was worn down in a battle of attrition. Italian pilots fought on to the bitter end until the last aircraft was shot down on 24 October 1941.

Mounting aircraft losses during 1941 and 1942 were not met by increased aircraft production, and Germany eventually took over the brunt of the aerial war in North Africa, the Italian Air Force concentrating on reconnaissance and supply duties as well as the defence of the homeland from the increasing attacks of Allied bomber forces.

The collapse of the Axis forces in North Africa in May 1943 and the massive build-up of Allied aircraft put the Italian Air Force on the defensive. Despite valiant efforts the Air Force was unable to stem the tide of Allied material supremacy. On 8 September, with the signing of the armistice, the *Regia Aeronautica* was no more.

The Italian Air Force had begun the war with nearly 2000 operational aircraft ready for combat and with almost the same number in reserve. By the September of 1943 the Air Force numbered 1200 aircraft of which about half were serviceable.

ORGANISATION In 1940 the Italian Air Force was divided into four Territorial Air Zones which covered metropolitan Italy and five overseas Commands. While the Air Force was an independent service within the Italian armed forces there was an Army air force of 37 squadrons which was attached directly to the ground forces as well as a Navy air service of 20 squadrons of sea-planes and flying-boats and ten squadrons of transport aircraft.

There were 12,000 pilots and aircrew, 6100 non-flying officers and 185,000 other ranks in the Air Force in 1940.

The basic tactical unit was the squadron (*squadriglia*) which had a strength of around nine aircraft with another three in reserve, although bomber squadrons usually had only six front-line planes. Occasionally the squadron might be broken down into two sections (*sezzione*) which could act in a semi-independent role.

Two or three squadrons formed an air group (*gruppo*) and two or more groups would form a wing or *stormo*, the basic tactical formation within the Air Force. Two or three wings would on occasion combine to form an air brigade which in turn with another brigade would form an air division. The largest formation in the

97 Air Marshal, Italian Air Force, 1940
Air Marshal Italo Balbo wears a combination of tropical and temperate uniform. On the cap is the elaborately embroidered greca *which was the distinctive mark of general officers and marshals. Badges of rank also appear on the shoulder straps of the* sahariana. *One of the most popular figures in the Fascist movement, Balbo was accidentally shot down and killed by Italian anti-aircraft fire near Tobruk shortly after the declaration of war in the summer of 1940.*

98 Major, Italian Air Force, 1940
The one-piece white flying suit was typical of the war in East and North Africa, although the white jacket of the two-piece flying suit was often worn with khaki drill shorts or other types of trousers. Badges of rank appear on the cuffs and the squadron badge on the left breast.

99 Major, Italian Air Force, 1942
This torpedo-bomber pilot wears a leather flying helmet and a flying jacket over his service dress. His rank badges are worn on the cuffs of the flying jacket and on the left breast is the metal badge of the torpedo bombardiers.

Air Force was the air fleet which consisted of two or more homogeneous fighter or bomber air divisions.

The forces within the Territorial Air Zones based in Italy were organised as follows:
Northern Zone – seven wings of bombers and three wings (plus one group) of CR-42 fighters;
Central Zone – three wings of bombers and two wings and a group of fighter planes;
Southern Zone – five bomber wings and one fighter wing as well as an autonomous fighter group and dive-bomber group;
South-Eastern Zone – one wing of night-bombers and float-planes and a group of obsolescent CR-32 fighters.

The largest of the overseas commands was that based in Libya and comprised four bomber wings; a fighter wing and three other fighter groups; and two groups plus two squadrons of colonial reconnaissance aircraft. The heavy losses incurred by the British offensive in January-February 1941 entailed a full-scale reinforcement of the Italian Air Force in North Africa.

Italian air strength in North Africa reached its peak in October 1942 with the following operational groups:
seven groups of MC-202 fighters;
five groups of CR-42 fighters;
one group of Ju 87 Stuka dive-bombers;
one group of Z-1007 bombers;
two groups of SM-79 bombers.
The shortage of spare parts and aviation fuel severely reduced the efficiency of the Italian Air Force in North Africa which by early 1942 had, in effect, become subordinate to the Luftwaffe.

The Air Force in Italian East Africa was divided into three Commands:
Eritrea – ten bomber squadrons and three fighter squadrons;
Central Ethiopia – nine bomber squadrons, two fighter squadrons and one ground-attack squadron;
Southern Ethiopia – three bomber squadrons.

All told there were 338 aircraft spread throughout East Africa, of which 187 were with operational units.

97

98

99

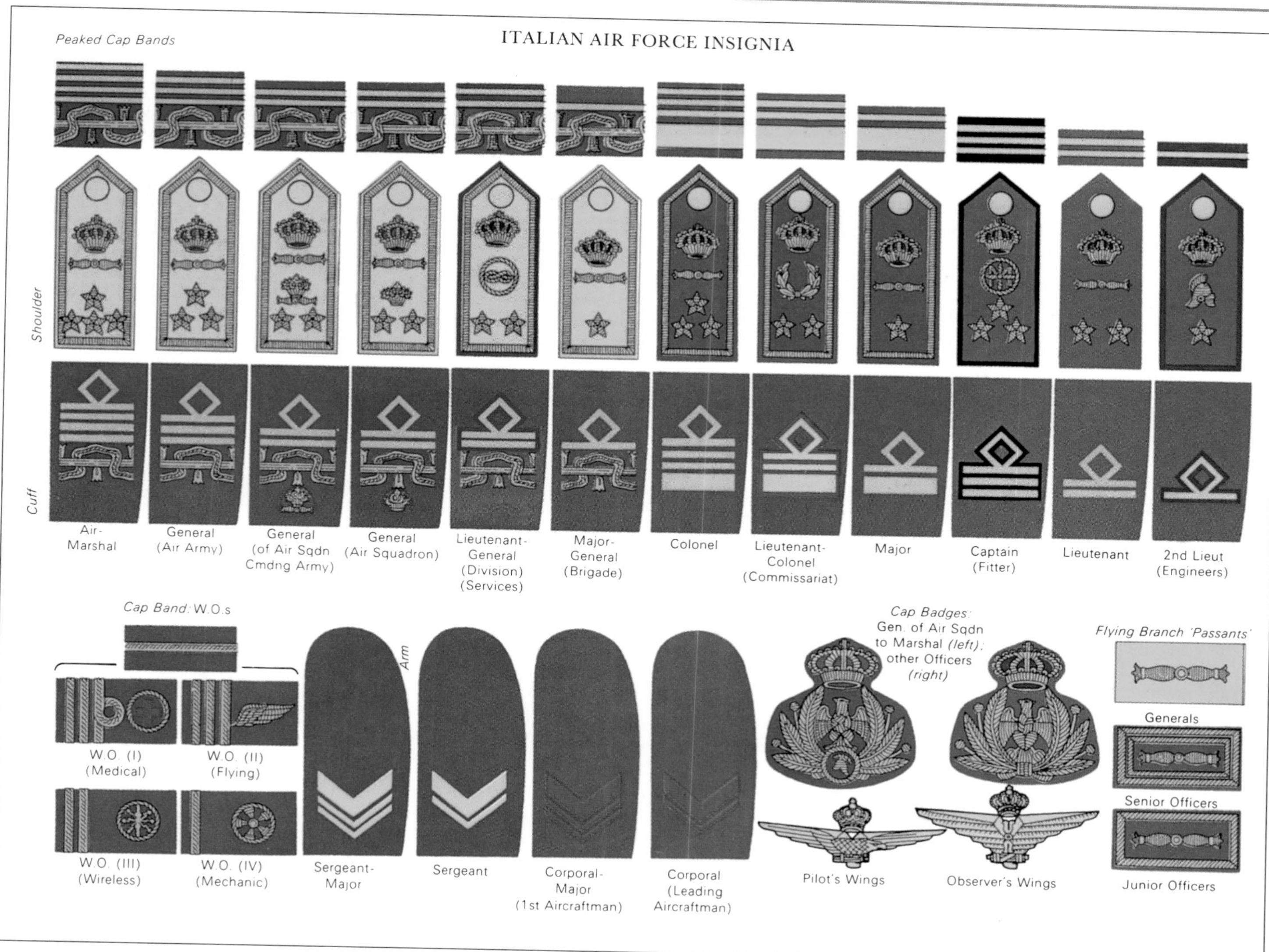

The Italian Army's invasion of Greece was supported by the Albanian Air Command (one bomber and one float-plane wing; plus one SM-79 bomber group, a group of ground-attack planes and two fighter squadrons) and the Italian South-Eastern Zone. With reinforcements this brought Italian strength to 380 planes against 149 Greek aircraft, although the Greek Air Force was itself being reinforced by RAF fighter and bomber aircraft. Throughout the early months of 1941 there was a constant battle between the Italian Air Force and the RAF and Greek Air Force to gain control of the skies; the conflict only being resolved by the German invasion of Yugoslavia and Greece in April 1941. Units of Italian aircraft remained in Greece until 1943 with the responsibility of attacking Allied shipping in the Aegean and eastern Mediterranean.

Although there had been occasional bombing raids on Italy by RAF Bomber Command, it was only in 1942, with the development of the successful long-range four-engined bomber, that the industrial centres of northern Italy came under any sustained attack from aircraft based in England.

Three groups of night-fighters were formed and a number of radar-equipped Messerschmitt Bf 110 and Dornier Do 217J aircraft were supplied from Germany but without a proper ground control system, an effective defence proved impossible. Fortunately for Italy, the main brunt of the Allied strategic air offensive was directed against Germany.

The loss of North Africa brought most of the Air Force back to Italy in order to defend the homeland against the expected Allied invasion. On 10 July 1942 – the date of the Allied invasion of Sicily – there were 165 aircraft on the island itself as well as units from the Italian Southern Zone. Although a transport ship was sunk on the first day of the invasion Italian losses were heavy. Allied air superiority over the battle-ground wore the Italian Air Force down. Many aircraft were destroyed on the ground by the Allies while the remaining serviceable aircraft were overwhelmed.

UNIFORM The uniform of the Italian Air Force was basically the same as that of the Army, but it was manufactured in grey-blue cloth. There were minor differences in cut, such as the pocket flaps which were three-pointed as opposed to straight. The side cap was a special model with a pleat in the crown, while airmen wore narrower pantaloons and puttees. Officers tended to wear long trousers and black shoes more often than their colleagues in the Army.

At the beginning of the war some of the frills disappeared: the shoulder straps and full-dress belt were abandoned, as was the coloured backing to the rank distinction lace which indicated the branch of the wearer.

The flying helmet was made of brown leather and there were two types of flying suit in general use. The winter model was lined and made of brownish olive-green material, whereas the summer one was made of white linen. Both types were manufactured in a one- or two-piece version. The Air Force parachute unit, *Arditi dell Aria*, had a grey-blue version of the Army parachute uniform on which was worn Air Force rank badges.

INSIGNIA Non-commissioned officers and men wore the same rank badges as their counterparts in the Army. Officers wore Army rank distinctions on the peaked cap and on the cuffs, but on the cuffs the loop was replaced by a diamond. The embroidered *greca* for general officers was in gold. On tropical jackets and shirts rank badges were worn on grey cloth shoulder straps.

During the war, the branch of service was identified by a small circular badge at the bottom of the cap badge. Other ranks wore a metal version of the same badge on their shoulder straps. This badge was also embroidered in gold wire on the grey cloth passants worn on both shoulders of the tunic and greatcoat by officers.

Pilots and observers wore gilt metal wings on the left breast above the medal ribbons, while aircrew wore a number of different badges on the left breast pocket. These badges were awarded in three classes for exceptional performance of duty.

NAVY

Mussolini hoped that the *Regia Navale* would play an important part in any Mediterranean war. He saw control of the sea (*Mare Nostrum* – Our Sea – was how he described the Mediterranean) as an essential prerequisite for expanding his empire into Nice, Corsica, Tunis and the Balkans. Italian naval building accelerated during his tenure of power, and by June 1940, the Navy comprised:
4 battleships;
8 heavy cruisers;
14 light cruisers;
128 destroyers;
115 submarines;
62 motor-torpedo boats.

There were also 4 battleships fitting out. The personnel of 4180 officers and 70,500 ratings was expanded rapidly on mobilisation, until there were, on average, 190,000 men serving at any time between 1940 and 1942.

The surrender of the French fleet in June 1940 seemed to offer a great opportunity to the *Regia Navale*; one of its main rivals had been removed at a stroke. But although the main Italian vessels were modern, fast and well-armed, and (in spite of graceful lines) had considerable armoured protection, the Italian vessels were overborne by the might of the British Royal Navy. Early defeats at Taranto and Matapan, although not crippling in themselves, confirmed British superiority; the absence of both radar and a proper fleet air arm were considerable handicaps; and a shortage of fuel proved a progressively crippling brake on operations. Only the small attack craft lived up to expectations, in many brave and successful actions.

From June 1940 to September 1943, the Navy lost one battleship and 13 cruisers, out of total losses of 339 ships of all types, and 24,660 men.

ORGANISATION The supreme commander of the Italian armed forces and Minister of Marine was Benito Mussolini, but executive control was exercised by the Under-Secretary and Chief of Naval Staff (*Supermarina*) Admiral Domenico Cavagnari. Commander-in-Chief of the Fleet was Admiral Campioni. Departments of the Ministry of Marine and the Naval Staff undertook the customary responsibilities of the admiralty, with one exception. The Ministry of Marine submitted design requirements to a separate department which catered for the needs of all three services. Examples of this were the battleships *Littorio* and *Vittorio Veneto*, projected by General Umberto Pugliese, whose team supervised the arrangements for their construction by Ansaldo at Genoa and CRDA at Trieste.

The Navy was organised in two squadrons with torpedo-boats, submarines, training and reserves forming four main sub-divisions.

When Italy entered the war on 10 June 1940, the *Regia Navale* was disposed as follows.

The Taranto Command, which included Messina and Augusta, comprised:
2 battleships in divisions of 2 to 4 vessels, each commanded by a divisional rear-admiral. Several divisions were grouped together under a vice-admiral;
44 destroyers and torpedo-boats in divisions of 2 to 4 vessels;
22 submarines;
16 motor torpedo-boats in flotillas;
2 minelayers;
4 escort and patrol boats.

The Venice (Adriatic) Command including Brindisi and Bari comprised:
8 destroyers and torpedo-boats;
4 submarines;
16 motor-torpedo boats;
1 escort and patrol boat.

La Spezia Command including Cagliari consisted of:
21 destroyers and torpedo-boats;
36 submarines;
26 motor-torpedo boats;
1 minelayer;
3 escort and patrol boats.

The Naples Command consisted of:
4 cruisers;
18 destroyers and torpedo-boats;

Above: The wartime grey-green working rig of the sailor on the left contrasts with his companion's more formal square rig.

11 submarines;
6 motor torpedo-boats;
3 minelayers;
1 escort and patrol boat.

The Sicily-Libya Command, which included Syracuse, Palermo, Tripoli and Tobruk, consisted of:
1 cruiser;
24 destroyers and torpedo-boats;
26 submarines;
12 motor torpedo-boats;
2 minelayers;
3 escort and patrol boats.

The Dodecanese (Leros) Command comprised:
6 destroyers and torpedo-boats;
8 submarines;
20 motor torpedo-boats;
1 minelayer.

The Red Sea (Massawa) Command (which was destroyed in April 1941) comprised:
9 destroyers and torpedo-boats;
8 submarines;
5 motor torpedo-boats;
4 escort and patrol boats.

There were 1235 Italian merchant ships, totalling 3,448,453 tons.

The Navy lacked aircraft, and was dependent on the Air Force for protection and reconnaissance. This was an unsatisfactory state of affairs; co-operation was poor, and although the torpedo-bombers and reconnaissance aircraft of the *Regia Aeronautica* were effective, high-level bombers did not have much success against ships at sea.

The Navy did possess a small, antiquated air arm, the *Aviazione per la Regia Marina*, which was dispersed among the various commands, and it was clear that a fast aircraft carrier was required. *Aquila* was converted from a liner, but she was not ready by the time the armistice was signed.

This lack of close air support was particularly serious because of Italy's problem of supplying her forces in North Africa. Land-based fighters, including the deadly Stukas, could not prevent aerial, surface and submarine harassment of Axis Mediterranean convoys. Each handful of German and Italian merchantmen had to be escorted by two or three destroyers and torpedo boats, which suffered grievous losses: 85 of the escorts were sunk while only 33 were built from dwindling stocks of raw materials, or captured from defeated navies.

There were few specialist escort vessels. It had been hoped that a combination of minefields (most warships except the very largest were equipped for minelaying) and defensive patrols by major surface units and submarines would seal off the Adriatic and Tyrhennian Seas, forming two corridors of sea power from Italy to North Africa and the Dodecanese. Meanwhile a smaller number of warships was to be employed against French and British communications.

The construction of smaller corvette-size escorts was begun and 32 were completed but, five had been lost by 8 September 1943. As the war progressed, however, experience and the installation of German detection equipment accounted for the loss of at least another 19 British submarines.

The Italian Navy did have one great advantage: it was the only fleet with continuous peacetime experience of fast attack craft. The MAS-boats (torpedo-armed motor boats or anti-submarine motor boats) were equipped with non-tumbling gyros which enabled their torpedoes to be dropped from light racks, and were driven by Isotta Fraschini petrol engines.

The tradition of attack in small craft was the basis of the most successful of all formations in the Royal Italian Navy: *Decima Flotiglia MAS* (10th MAS Flotilla) formed in August 1940 under *Capitano di Fregata* Vittorio Moccagatta. There was a Surface Division, commanded by *Capitano di Corvetta* Giorgio Giobbe and an Underwater Division under the leaderships of *Capitano di Corvetta* Prince Junio Valerio Borghese: under the Republic he ran the whole flotilla. Their weapons were explosive motor boats (delivered by destroyers), guided two-man torpedoes (launched from submarines) and small charges (carried by free-swimming frogmen).

Overcoming early misfortunes and, on occasion, suffering high casualties, they wrecked the cruiser HMS *York* in Suda Bay, disabled the two battleships HMS *Queen Elizabeth* and *Valiant* at Alexandria, and conducted a two-year campaign against shipping at Gibraltar. This last was undertaken secretly, operating from Spanish territory, with the assistance of the Italian Naval Consul. Threat of such attacks added to the strain on the defenders of all Mediterranean anchorages.

Italian submarines and MAS boats also operated outside the Mediterranean. From January 1941 onwards a total of 32 submarines joined Admiral Dönitz's U-boats in the Atlantic. Although they accounted for the loss of about a million tons of Allied shipping, their large conning towers and slow surface speed made them unsuitable for wolf-pack attacks on convoys. Several were later converted for use as undersea blockade runners between the Far East and Europe.

Meanwhile six midget submarines had been transported overland to the Black Sea, becoming operational on 19 June 1942. They lay in wait off the Crimean coast for Soviet vessels attempting to supply the besieged town of Sevastopol or

100 Submarine Commander, Italian Navy, 1943

In contrast to the formally dressed Naval Officer in figure 101, this submarine commander wears a very unorthodox outfit, the only regulation part of which is the peaked cap. The windcheater is worn with sports shorts and seaboots and sea socks.

101 Ranking Lieutenant, Italian Navy, 1942

This officer wears standard officers service dress with peaked cap and 'reefer' jacket. Rank is indicated by the bands around the cap, the bars and 'curl' on the cuff and by the 'passants' on the shoulder (these are shown in more detail in the rank insignia chart).

100 101

102

103

104

102 Seaman, Italian Navy, 1941
This rating wears the basic 'square rig' of the Italian Navy in the correct manner. On the cap tally appears the legend, Regia Marina *in gold letters. On the back of his blue denim collar are two five-pointed white stars.*

103 Seaman, Italian Navy, 1942
This seaman operating out of Bordeaux is serving on a submarine, hence the dolphin badge on his left breast. This practical uniform in Army grey-green with black beret was introduced for submarine crews during the course of the war and was only to be worn on board ship.

104 Sergeant-Major Italian Marine Infantry, 1942
This is basically the same uniform as worn by the submariner but in the version for marines with pantaloons and puttees. The distinctive badge of the marines was the Lion of St. Mark which was worn on the cuffs, while the badges of rank appear as inverted chevrons on the sleeve. The web equipment was made under contract in Britain by the Mills company. The dagger is similar to the pattern worn by the Fascist Militia. Although only of ceremonial value the wearing of these weapons was widespread in the Italian armed forces.

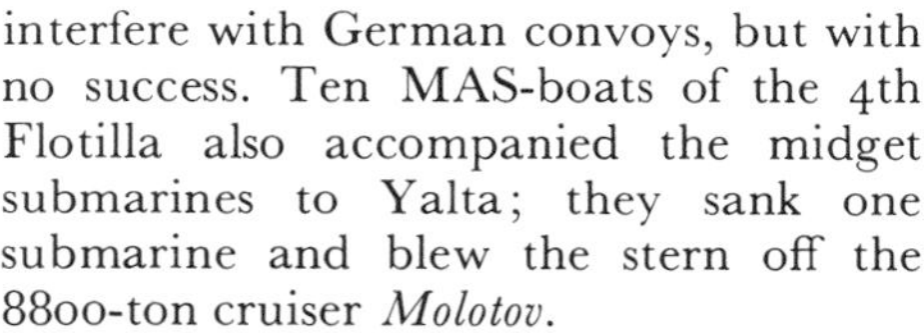

interfere with German convoys, but with no success. Ten MAS-boats of the 4th Flotilla also accompanied the midget submarines to Yalta; they sank one submarine and blew the stern off the 8800-ton cruiser *Molotov*.

Another four MAS-boats served on Lake Ladoga in northern Russia from the summer of 1942 to June 1943, and were subsequently handed over to the Finnish Navy. In September 1943, all surviving Italian vessels in the Black Sea, at Bordeaux, and in the Far East, were seized by the Romanians, Germans and Japanese.

At the time of the Italian Armistice in September 1943, all *Regia Navale* warships were ordered to make their way to Allied ports. Some were already at sea, but others had to fight their way out of German control. Only a small number preferred to remain in the service of Mussolini and the newly-declared Italian Socialist Republic: the Navy had strong Royalist traditions and felt no loyalty to the Fascist regime. Its personnel braved the Luftwaffe dive-bombers rather than surrender to the Germans.

UNIFORM The uniforms of the Royal Italian Navy were based on the regulations published in February 1936. Typical officers' service dress is illustrated in figure 101. In the summer months or in tropical waters officers wore a white cap cover and single-breasted white tunic trimmed with white lace.

Petty officers wore the same blue uniform as officers but the white tunic was simpler having open patch pockets and no lace trimming.

Ratings wore the square rig illustrated in figure 102 and were also issued with a three-quarter-length pea-coat. In the summer they also wore a white cap cover and shirt with blue denim collar and cuffs.

During the war, and particularly in small vessels such as submarines dress was varied and informal. Officers continued to wear their peaked cap or a peaked field cap, on the left side of which there was a reduced version of the rank badge. Overalls, windcheaters, shirts of various colours and pullovers were worn in conjunction with items of regulation uniform. A simpler version of the working rig in grey-green is illustrated in figure 103.

Marine officers wore grey-green Army uniform with Naval rank distinctions on the cap and cuffs. Other ranks wore the uniform illustrated in figure 104. In North Africa Marines wore a khaki drill uniform which was similar in cut to the grey-green version.

INSIGNIA Officers wore rank distinction lace on the peaked cap and on the cuffs. On the greatcoat, white tunic and tropical jackets officers and petty officers wore rank badges on shoulder straps. Commissioned warrant officers wore officers' uniforms with rank distinction lace on the cuffs surmounted by a small metal branch badge. Petty officers and ratings wore the same rank badges as Army non-commissioned officers on the sleeves.

Only line officers were entitled to wear a curl on the rank distinction lace on the cuffs, while those in other branches had a branch colour appearing in the centre of the cap badge, as backing to the rank lace on the cap and cuffs, and as piping on the passants and shoulder straps. Ratings wore their branch badges above their rank chevrons on the sleeves.

ITALIAN SOCIAL REPUBLIC 1943–1945

ARMY

On 12 September 1943 German paratroopers liberated Mussolini and six days later the Italian Social Republic was formed on the side of the Germans against the Allies and the Kingdom of the South.

The formation of an army in a war zone was not easy. The Germans refused to release the 600,000 men they had taken into captivity on 8 September, but did allow the recruitment of 13,000 volunteers from amongst the prisoners. By March 1944 the Fascists had 60,000 men.

Between September and November 1944 the first four divisions which had been sent to Germany for equipping and training, returned to Italy. They fought alongside the Germans throughout the rest of the Italian Campaign.

UNIFORM In the beginning the uniforms of the Army of the RSI were basically the same as those worn prior to 8 September 1943. However, all monarchistic symbols were removed from the insignia and the five-pointed star was replaced by a Roman sword within a wreath of laurel which became the symbol of the RSI.

At the end of 1944 new dress regulations were issued which attempted to Germanise Italian uniform, but the general situation and lack of supplies meant that these regulations never really came into force, and only a few senior officers ever actually wore them. The RSI was far too busy fighting for survival against the Allies and the internal threat posed by the partisans to worry too much about new uniforms.

Uniform became a very mixed combination of the classic *sahariana* with anoraks, camouflage clothing, and the new collarless parachutist's jacket. The old grey-green tunic was often rebuttoned in the German style. Typical were the long baggy trousers fastened at the ankle and worn with ankle boots and rolled woollen socks, or pantaloons with puttees or leggings. Both officers and men contributed to the confusion by adopting the

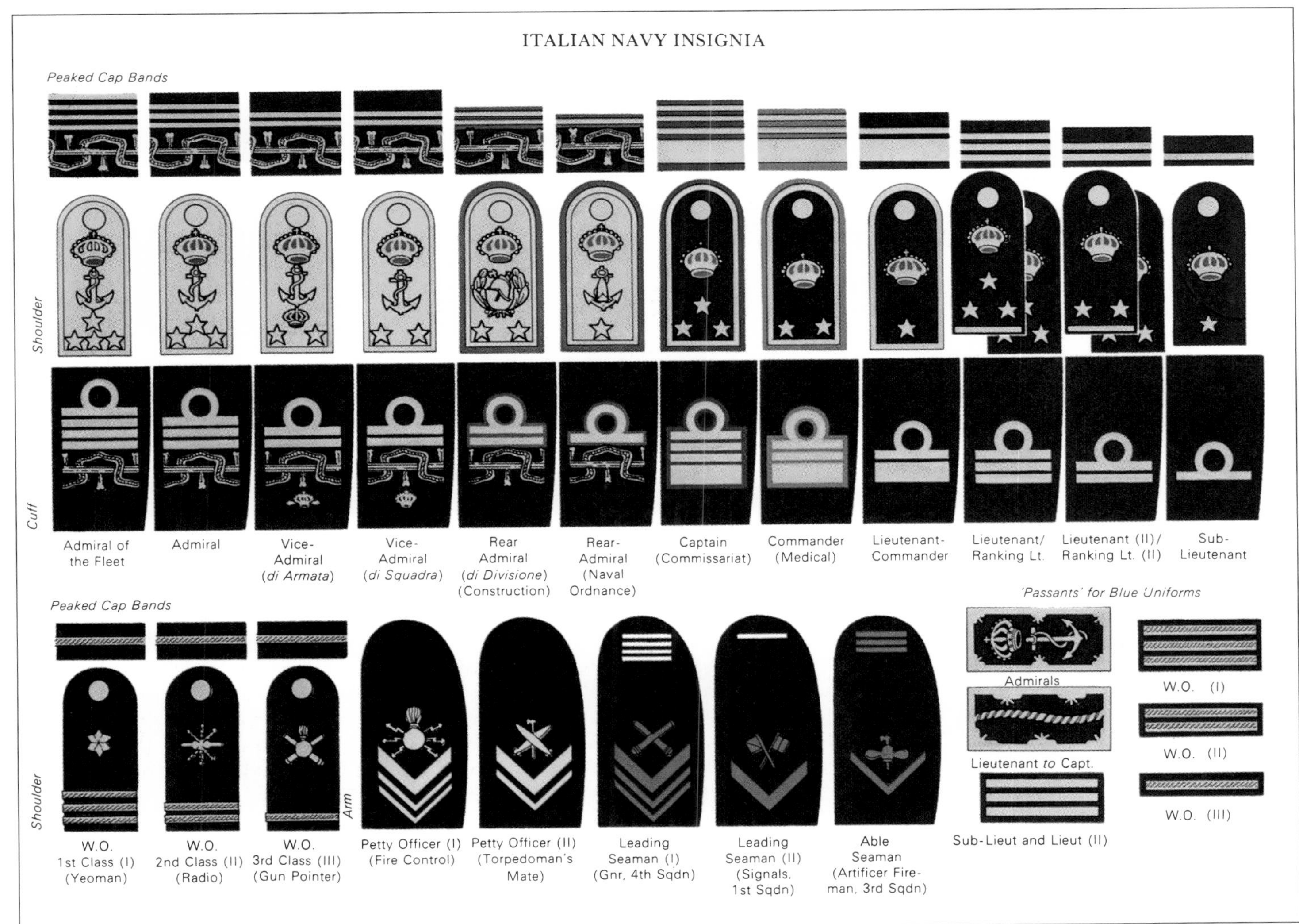

105 Militiaman, Legion Tagliamento, Italian Social Republic, 1944

Typical of the type of para-military uniform to be seen on the Fascist side at the end of the war was this outfit worn by a Legionary 'M' (Mussolini) of the Republican National Guard (GNR). The black head-dress was similar to the pattern worn in dark red by the bersaglieri. *The Legion badge, a silver* fascio *on a red letter 'M', was worn on the collar of the black shirt or on black collar patches. Equipment is a mixture of Italian and German. The belt is Luftwaffe, the grenades German, the dagger is the standard MVSN pattern, and the sub-machine gun is the Beretta M38. This weapon had been widely used before 1943, and proved very popular with RSI para-military forces and partisans alike, because it was well made and reliable.*

106 Major-General, Italian Social Republic Air Force, 1944

The service dress is still that which was in use before September 1943, but with new-pattern peaked cap. The gladi *have replaced the stars on the collar. In his button-hole is the ribbon of the Iron Cross 2nd Class; German decorations were still being worn by Fascist troops.*

Above: Italian troops loyal to Mussolini celebrate the fact with some Germans in October 1943. A variety of uniforms are on show: the German on the right in peaked cap, for example, is in tropical uniform, with the distinctive badge on the cap front. In the centre, an Italian officer is standing next to another German in tropical gear. The Italian soldiers are wearing various elements of the standard uniform, including the shirt, jacket, shorts, trousers and cap.

most disparate and eccentric styles of dress. The peaked *bustina* was widely worn alongside the *alpini* hat and the *bersaglieri* fez.

Insignia Rank insignia was moved from the cuffs to the shoulder straps, but the new pattern of rank insignia prescribed in the September 1944 regulations was never introduced. The original divisions which were equipped and trained in Germany adopted German rank insignia for other ranks as a practical measure to enable German training personnel to recognise the rank of Italian non-commissioned officers and men, but on their return to Italy German rank badges were usually removed. New coloured badges and collar patches were also introduced to identify arm of service.

Para-military forces

The *Guardia Nazionale Repubblicana* was formed on 24 November 1943 to replace the MVSN which had been found to be unreliable. The GNR, composed of ex-members of the *Carabinieri* Militia (which had also been disbanded for having shown

105

106

**107 Major,
Italian Social Republic Air Force, 1944**
The badge on the cap is the new pattern and the lace around the cap band denotes his rank. The jacket is the sahariana, *on the collar of which are worn the* gladi *of the Social Republic armed forces. On his left breast he wears pilot's 'wings' and Italian medal ribbons as well as the Iron Cross and the ribbon for the Iron Cross 2nd Class.*

**108 Private,
Italian Social Republic Marine, 1944**
This bearded marine wears the special grey-green uniform originally introduced for Army parachutists. The Lion of St. Mark is no longer worn on the cuffs but on the collar patches which also bear the gladio. *He is armed with a Beretta M38 sub-machine gun.*

**109 Seaman,
Italian Social Republic Navy, 1944**
This seaman wears Naval square rig with web equipment (originally manufactured in England for RIN) and steel helmet with the second pattern anchor painted on the front. On the back of the blue collar the star was replaced by a white gladio.

allegiance to the King) and former members of the Italian African Police, was called upon to carry out both military and civil police duties.

With the constitution of the Social Republic ex-members of the old Fascist squads (*Squadristi*) reappeared and began to scour the country looking for 'traitors'. Pavolini, secretary of the National Fascist Party, wanted to use the squads in the war against both the resistance and the partisans, and so on the 26 July 1944 the Black Brigades were formed as the armed force of the Fascist Party. Notorious for their ferocity in the service of the German security forces (SS and Police), the Black Brigades represented all the best and worst elements of the Social Republic – decorated heroes, child mascots, common criminals, opportunists and idealists.

UNIFORM The National Guard retained the collar patches and black shirt of the former Militia (MVSN), but adopted a pair of red letter 'M's (Mussolini) instead of the *gladio*.

The Black Brigades (*Brigate Nera*) had in theory the simplest of uniforms consisting of black beret, black shirt and grey-green tunic or woollen sweater. Trousers were grey-green or khaki depending on season. In reality they appeared in an amazing array of extravagant and irregular uniforms and insignia of personal invention whose common denominator was the skull and crossed bones and mottoes involving death.

AIR FORCE

The Air Force of the RSI was formed on 27 October 1943. Its creation was due to the efforts of Lieutenant-Colonel 'Iron Leg' Botto, a man noted for his great organisational talents and firmness in respect of both restless pilots and the Germans. Following the armistice, the Germans had requisitioned aircraft and equipment as well as pilots and technicians. Botto managed to get most back, but his clashes with General Wolfram von

107

108

109

110

110 Major-General, Italian Co-Belligerent Forces, 1944
This officer, commanding the Gruppi di Combattimento 'Folgore' *(Combat Group 'Lightning') wears British battle dress with khaki beret, but all insignia is Italian. Rank badges are worn on the cuffs and on the left side of the beret. On the collar are the light blue collar patches of the parachute troops, while high on the left sleeve he wears the combat group's formation sign – the Italian Tricolor with a black bolt of lightning.*

Richthofen and German attempts to incorporate the RSI Air Force into the Luftwaffe meant that the Air Force did not become operational until October 1944. In the period January 1944 to April 1945 it succeeded in shooting down 240 Allied aircraft, mostly B-17 and B-24 bombers.

The main strength of the RSI Air Force was in fighter and torpedo aircraft. There was a bomber squadron but for political reasons it was sent to the Eastern Front. Torpedo aircraft operated against the Allied Fleet in the Mediterranean from March 1944, and in June of that year took part in the bombing of Gibraltar.

After September 1943 the uniform of the Air Force of the Italian Social Republic remained virtually unchanged except that the star was replaced by the *gladio*.

NAVY

Few Navy personnel joined Mussolini's MAS Flotilla instructed German K-men in the employment of small battle units and worked with them in attacks on Allied shipping (which by then had prepared routine precautions against them). There were about a dozen MAS-boats and midget submarines in Fascist service: most ex-Italian vessels were manned by the *Kriegsmarine*, however. The Fascist Navy only reached a twentieth the size of the Co-Belligerent Fleet.

The uniforms of the Navy of the Italian Social Republic underwent few changes. The crown was removed from the cap badge and replaced by a winged bird and the stars were replaced by the *gladio* on the collar of both the reefer and sailor's blue jean collar. Rank distinction lace on the cap band was replaced by different patterns of chin cords which were blue and gold for junior and gold for senior officers. The traditional sailors' cap fell into disuse and was replaced by a blue beret with a small gilt metal anchor on the front, and from 1943 Republican Marines began to receive the grey-green parachute troop uniform as illustrated in figure 108.

ITALIAN CO-BELLIGERENT FORCES

On 28 September 1943 the first military unit of the Kingdom of the South was constituted as the First Motorised Combat Group (*1. Raggruppamento Motorizzato*) with a strength of 295 officers and 5387 men. Its first action was in the Cassino sector at Monte Lungo, and did much to remove Allied distrust of Italian soldiers fighting on their side.

Following service with the American 5th Army and re-organisation the *Raggruppamento* was transferred to the Polish Army on the extreme left of the British 8th Army.

On 17 April 1944 the formation, now 22,000-men strong, assumed the name Italian Liberation Corps (*Corpo Italiano di Liberazione*). The continuous influx of volunteers made it necessary to form further formations, but for political reasons what had now become divisions were still called combat groups. Each *Gruppi di Combattimento* had two infantry and one artillery regiment, a mixed battalion of engineers, two sections of *Carabinieri* and services totalling 400 officers and 9000 men.

The first six of these groups entered the line at the beginning of 1945, but political considerations still meant that the Allies underscored the part played by Royalist troops in the victory in Italy.

The Italian Navy played an important role once the armistice was signed. Altogether five battleships, eight cruisers, 33 destroyers, 39 submarines, 12 motor torpedo-boats, 22 escorts and three minelayers of the *Regia Navale* formed a Co-Belligerent Force. There were an additional four squadrons of seaplanes from the *Regia Aeronautica*. The Italian C-in-C established his headquarters at Taranto, but three cruisers were soon detached to help hunt blockade runners in the South Atlantic. Other vessels were assigned to various tasks in the Mediterranean after undergoing refits and repairs. One of the force's most significant contributions during this period was its cooperation in the rehabilitation of Italian harbours. At the same time, Italian frogmen joined British human-torpedo teams in sinking two cruisers and the aircraft carrier *Aquila* lying disabled in German-occupied ports.

The other major element of the Italian forces on the Allied side was, of course, the partisans; but they were unstandardised in organisation and uniform.

UNIFORM At the beginning the grey-green or khaki Italian uniforms continued to be worn with the insignia of the House of Savoy on the breast. The lack of supplies of all sorts, partly due to Allied bombing and partly as a result of German requisitioning forced the Italians to adopt Allied uniform and equipment. The choice was for English uniforms on which the Italian insignia was to remain unchanged. Even the *Bersaglieri* and the *Alpini* attached their respective feathers to the British Mk. 1 steel helmet. Since it was necessary to differentiate the Italians from the rest of the Allied troops, a rectangular badge in the Italian national colours was introduced for wear high on the left sleeve. The emblem of the combat group was printed in black on the white of the Italian *Tricolore*. Officers moved their rank badges from the cuff to the shoulder straps.

The uniforms of the Royalist Air Force and Navy did not undergo any great changes.

GREECE

ARMY

From 1935 until the German invasion, Greece was a constitutional monarchy under King George II, but the actual power was in the hands of her dictator-President General Metaxas.

The Greek armed forces, like most of those of the smaller nations, suffered from a shortage of modern weapons and motor transport. However, the mountainous frontier with Albania was ideal for defensive fighting, and the natural sturdiness of her soldiers proved too much for the Italian forces which invaded on 28 October 1940. The outnumbered Greek forces were able not only to contain the Italian attack, but force the invaders back into Albania, where, with the British aid in men and *matériel*, they were able to hold them until the Germans invaded from Yugoslavia on 6 April 1941. This attack, by the best army in Europe, overwhelmed the Greek defences, and despite bitter resistance the Germans forced the Greek Army in eastern Macedonia to capitulate and the Allies to retreat. On 20 April the Greek Epirus Army surrendered and on 22 April the Allies began their evacuation of Greece.

ORGANISATION The Commander-in-Chief of the Greek Armed Forces was General Papagos and the control of the Army was exercised by a General Headquarters and five Army Corps areas.

In 1940, just before the Italian attack, Greece mobilised her armed forces. The field army was organised in two Army Groups, six general headquarters, six infantry and nine mountain divisions, four mountain brigades and one cavalry division. At the outbreak of war the Army numbered 430,000 men, but losses were heavy and some 60,000 men were killed, wounded or missing after the winter fighting.

In March 1941, shortly before the German invasion, the Greek Army, under four army high commands and three general headquarters, comprised:
5 infantry divisions;
14 mountain divisions;
1 infantry brigade;
1 motorised division;
1 cavalry division.

In March 1941, total strength was 540,000 men, but this included 50,000 recruits with only one month's training. The German invasion cost the Greeks 15,700 battle casualties; about 220,000 Greek soldiers were taken prisoner, but released soon after.

The army corps each consisted of two to four infantry or mountain divisions. I, II, III, IV Corps were each supported by a heavy artillery regiment of 7 batteries (8×85mm, 8×105mm and 12×155mm guns) while V Corps had 4×85mm guns, 4×105mm guns and 4 static six-inch guns. Each corps also had its own anti-aircraft support of 88mm, 37mm and 20mm guns.

An infantry division consisted of three infantry regiments, a regiment of divisional artillery and ancillary units. The mountains divisions were particularly important given that the Greek Army, woefully deficient in modern equipment, preferred to fight in the mountains. The mountain divisions were organised on the same basis as the infantry divisions, but with rather less artillery. Mountain and infantry divisions were 12,000-strong.

The 56 regiments of infantry each consisted of a regimental staff, reconnaissance platoon, HQ platoon, staff company, and two battalions each with battalion staff, three rifle companies and one machine-gun company. Regimental strength was about 58 officers and 1100 men. The main weapon was the Mannlicher-Schönauer M1903/14 rifle. Support weapons comprised:
36 light machine guns (Hotchkiss 8mm);
8 heavy machine guns (St Etienne M07);
4×81mm mortars;
2×65mm mountain guns.

The crack infantry of the Greek Army were the *Evzones*. Originally formed as light infantry during the war for independence at the beginning of the 19th century, these highlanders became part of the regular army in 1833. In 1940 they served in light regiments and in the Royal Guard.

Divisional artillery for the mountain divisions consisted of four batteries (in the Greek Army a battery consisted of four guns) of 75mm mountain guns, and two batteries of 105mm guns. Infantry divisions had nine batteries of 75mm field guns. Each Army Corps had its own allocation of heavy artillery (see above) and there were, in addition, 12 batteries of heavy artillery for use with the field army.

Since the artillery was equipped with either French, German or Czech guns Britain was unable to supply ammunition, and stocks in America were soon exhausted, so all the British could do was supply the Greeks with Italian *matériel* captured in Libya.

In addition to the line infantry and mountain regiments there were a number of battalions and companies for island and land frontier defence, as well as a number of mobile and static machine gun units. When the British landed in Greece

111 Sergeant, Greek Army, 1940
Under the British Mk 1 steel helmet can just be seen the badges on the side cap which he wears underneath. Arm-of-service colour (for infantry) appears on the collar although this was often omitted during the war, and his sergeants' chevrons are on the left sleeve. The rifle is the 6.5 Mannlicher M1903/14.

in March 1940 they were dismayed to find that many divisions existed in name only. One division of recently-assembled troops had a strength of just six battalions, and its transport was limited to the commander's motor car and five trucks, while the 'motorised' division had been formed from 2000 recently conscripted garage hands. It had only 24 light Italian and Dutch tankettes, some Italian lorries, a few British Bren Gun Carriers, and some motor cycles and motor cars.

There were two regiments of cavalry each with four sabre squadrons, a machine gun troop with 12 machine guns and a squadron with four 81mm mortars. A third regiment, in the process of motorisation, consisted of four squadrons equipped

112 Lieutenant, Greek Army, 1941
The kepi is the pre-war model with rank distinction lace. Rank badges were worn on the shoulder straps, while the black collar patches indicate artillery. As a mounted officer this lieutenant wears riding breeches and boots. In addition to his 'Sam Browne' belt he carries binoculars and a map case.

113 Lieutenant-Colonel, Greek Army, 1941
The service dress worn by this officer was almost identical to the British model with metal rank badges on the shoulder straps. The Greek Crown above an enamel cockade in the Greek national colours was worn on most head-dresses. The arm of service was denoted by the dark red gorget patch with yellow grenade for infantry officers.

114 Private, Greek Army, 1941
This Evzone *wears the Greek steel helmet over his side cap and a coarse compressed goat-fleece cape over his service dress. Instead of the more typical pantaloons and puttees this stalwart wears the tight pantaloons, stockings and footwear, which were the military version of the native dress of the Greek mountain dwellers. Again, the enamel cockade is clearly visible on the cap.*

with armoured cars, one machine-gun troop, one squadron with 81 mm mortars and a mounted machine-gun troop with three machine-gun companies each with 12 machine guns, and a sabre troop. These three regiments together with a battery of mountain artillery, a pioneer squadron and a radio squadron were formed into an independent brigade and played an important role in the defeat of the Italian invasion.

Apart from this large formation, there were mounted forces serving as reconnaissance units with the Army Corps and infantry divisions; these reconnaissance battalions consisted of two squadrons, a machine-gun company or section, and (for the corps units) a mortar section.

The Greek Army had put up a stout resistance to the forces of the Axis, and Greek partisans were to prove a redoubtable foe for the Germans.

Uniform Greek Army uniform had developed along British lines and the service dress for officers illustrated in figure 113 differed only in so far as officers wore collar patches, and on the khaki peaked cap general and field officers had gold embroidery on the peak. The greatcoat for officers was double breasted and was also worn with collar patches and shoulder strap rank badges.

Other ranks' uniforms were made of coarse khaki cloth and were also similar in cut to the British khaki service dress. In fact uniforms supplied by Britain were worn complete with buttons bearing the British coat of arms. The uniform consisted of side cap, tunic, single-breasted greatcoat, and pantaloons worn with puttees and ankle boots. Mounted personnel wore breeches and riding boots or leather leggings.

A distinctive uniform based on Greek national dress was worn by the crack *Evzones* who formed the Royal Guard. On active service the more extreme features such as the pleated kilt and shoes with woollen pompoms were, of course, replaced by the more practical uniform worn by the other dismounted soldiers.

There were two steel helmets in general use in the Greek Army. The first was the

112

113

114

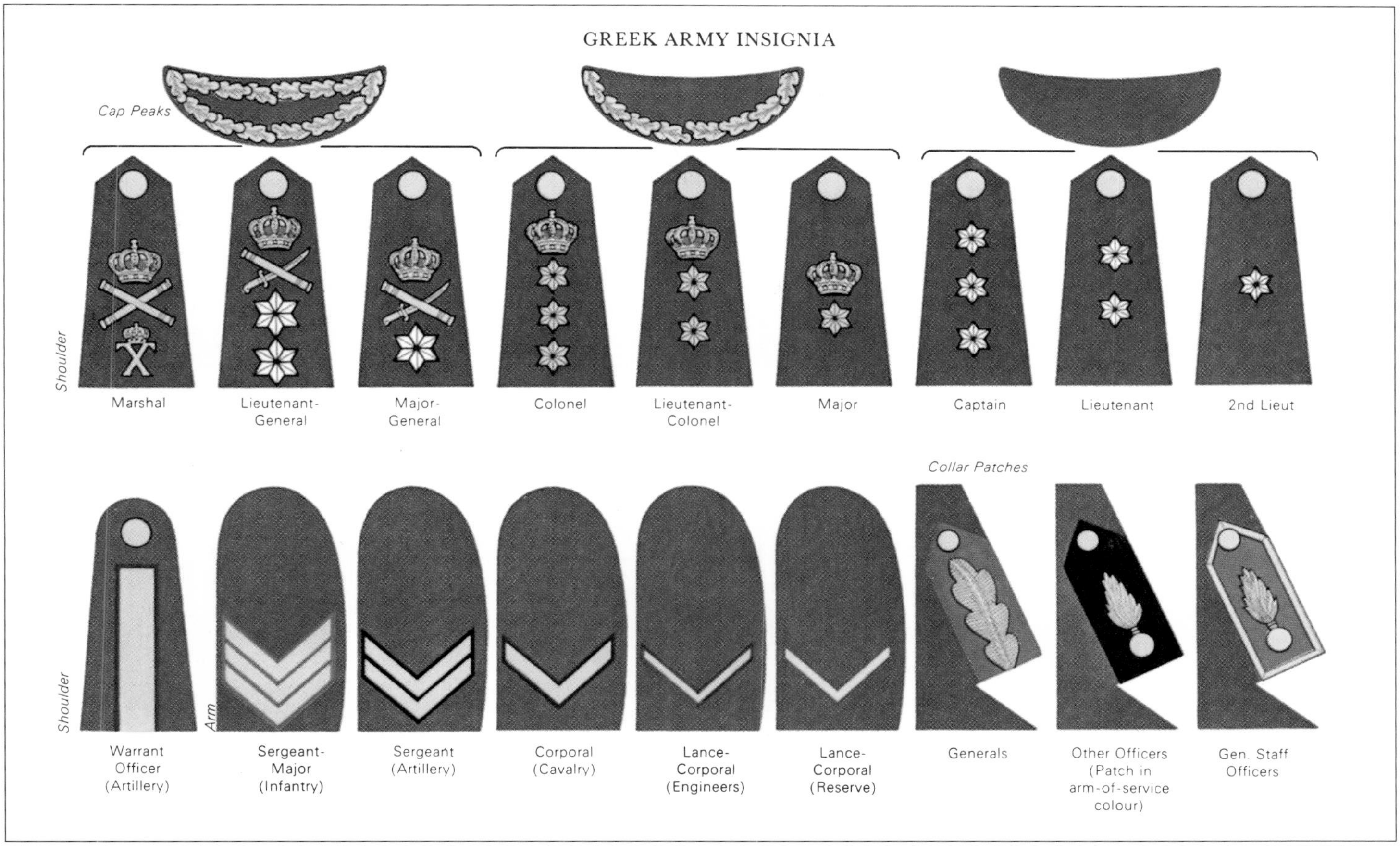

GREEK ARMY INSIGNIA

Cap Peaks

Shoulder

Marshal · Lieutenant-General · Major-General · Colonel · Lieutenant-Colonel · Major · Captain · Lieutenant · 2nd Lieut

Collar Patches

Shoulder · Arm

Warrant Officer (Artillery) · Sergeant-Major (Infantry) · Sergeant (Artillery) · Corporal (Cavalry) · Lance-Corporal (Engineers) · Lance-Corporal (Reserve) · Generals · Other Officers (Patch in arm-of-service colour) · Gen. Staff Officers

British Mk. 1 pattern, which was in the process of being replaced by a Greek model similar to the Italian helmet.

INSIGNIA Officers wore rank badges on the shoulder straps of the tunic and greatcoat, while non-commissioned officers wore chevrons on the sleeves. Those for regulars were in gold or yellow lace and were edged in the arm-of-service colour, while the chevrons for conscripts were silver and unedged.

The arm-of-service colour appeared on the collar patches and as edging to the rank chevrons of regular non-commissioned officers.

AIR FORCE

The Greek Air Ministry was responsible for the air services maintained by the Greek Army and Navy. There was no independent Air Force as such. The Army air service was small with just 250 officers and 3000 men. Many of the pilots had undergone their training in England, and although outnumbered first by the Italians and then by the Germans, the air service put up a stubborn resistance in the campaigns of 1941.

In 1940 the combined strength of the Army and Navy air services was as follows:
44 fighters (including Polish P.Z.L.24s, Gloster Gladiators and a few Hurricanes);
46 bombers and reconnaissance planes;
16 general purpose aircraft;
20 flying boats (Fairey IIIs and German Do 22s).

When the Germans invaded in April 1941 only 41 combat aircraft were still operational.

The Army air service was organised in three flying regiments each of two squadrons, based on rather primitive airfields in Athens, Candia, Drama, Joannina Larissa, Salonica, Tanagra and Thebes. Its primary role was to provide air support for ground operations, but by

Right: Greek Air Force groundcrew in service dress talk to an RAF pilot. Both the side and peaked caps are being worn.

January 1941 casualties and lack of spares had practically grounded it, and so the Greek command had to appeal to the RAF to switch its emphasis from bombing Italian lines of communication to providing air support to ground forces.

UNIFORM The grey-blue service dress for officers is illustrated in figure 115, although on active service officers appear to have preferred wearing breeches and high boots. The side cap and the greatcoat were, like the rest of the uniform, modelled on the British RAF pattern. Other ranks wore a grey-blue version of the khaki uniform with side cap, single-breasted tunic, pantaloons and puttees and ankle boots.

Flying clothing consisted of the usual leather flying helmet, goggles, and fleece-lined leather flying jacket which was worn over the service dress or overall.

INSIGNIA Officers wore rank distinction lace on the cuffs, while general officers had two and field officers one row of gold embroidered oak leaves on the cap peak. Other ranks wore Army-pattern rank badges on the sleeves. There were no arm-of-service colours as such, but qualified pilots wore embroidered 'wings' over medal ribbons on the left breast.

NAVY

The executive commander of the Navy was the Chief of the Admiralty, Admiral A. Sakellariou. Under him were 6300 regular naval officers and men and 11,000 reservists and the following vessels:

1 old armoured cruiser built in 1905/06;
2 old light cruisers;
4 old destroyers;
4 Hidra Class (Italian) destroyers;
13 old torpedo boats;
2 motor torpedo-boats;
6 submarines.

The Greek Navy suffered its first loss on 15 August 1940, before the opening of hostilities, when the minelaying cruiser *Helli* was alleged to have been sunk by an Italian submarine. On the outbreak of the war two months later the Navy's first task was to ensure the safe passage of thousands of Army reservists recalled to the colours from the numerous Greek isles. At the same time the Navy patrolled the coast of Albania and provided artillery support.

German entry into the Greco-Italian war was heralded by aerial attacks which destroyed a number of Greek warships. On 21 April 1941 the Greek government decided to evacuate the mainland, and the port of Salamis was blown up as the last ship carrying Allied troops left. 29 warships and auxiliary vessels were sunk – a very high proportion of the pre-war Navy.

115 Wing Commander, Greek Air Force, 1941
Air Force officers with the rank of Squadron Leader and above wore a row of gold-embroidered oakleaves on the cap peak. Rank distinction lace on the cuffs followed the Navy pattern and had a diamond shaped 'curl' on the upper row. The embroidered wings are worn on the left breast above the ribbons.

116 Able Seaman, Greek Navy, 1941
This seaman in parade dress is dressed like a 'matelot' in the British Royal Navy. The inscription on the cap tally reads, B. Naytikon. *The red chevron on his arm indicates his rank and the torpedo badge his speciality. He is armed with an M1903/14 rifle.*

UNIFORM Greek naval uniform followed the international pattern, and like the uniforms of the other branches of the armed forces, followed closely the British style.

Officers wore the peaked cap with or without white cover and a gold-embroidered cap badge on the front. The reefer jacket had rank distinction lace on the cuffs and was worn with long trousers and black shoes. In the summer months or in tropical waters officers wore a white tunic with stand collar, white trousers and the standard-issue white canvas shoes.

Petty officers wore a similar uniform to that worn by officers, but had a special cap badge.

Ratings wore the uniform illustrated in figure 116, and a white version in tropical waters. The leggings were the same webbing pattern as worn in the British Royal Navy but the waistbelt and leather ammunition pouches were as issued to the Greek Army.

Officers wore rank distinction lace on the cuffs and on the shoulder straps of the greatcoat and white tunic. Petty officers and ratings wore their rank badges on the upper sleeve.

GREEK AIR FORCE INSIGNIA

GREEK NAVY INSIGNIA

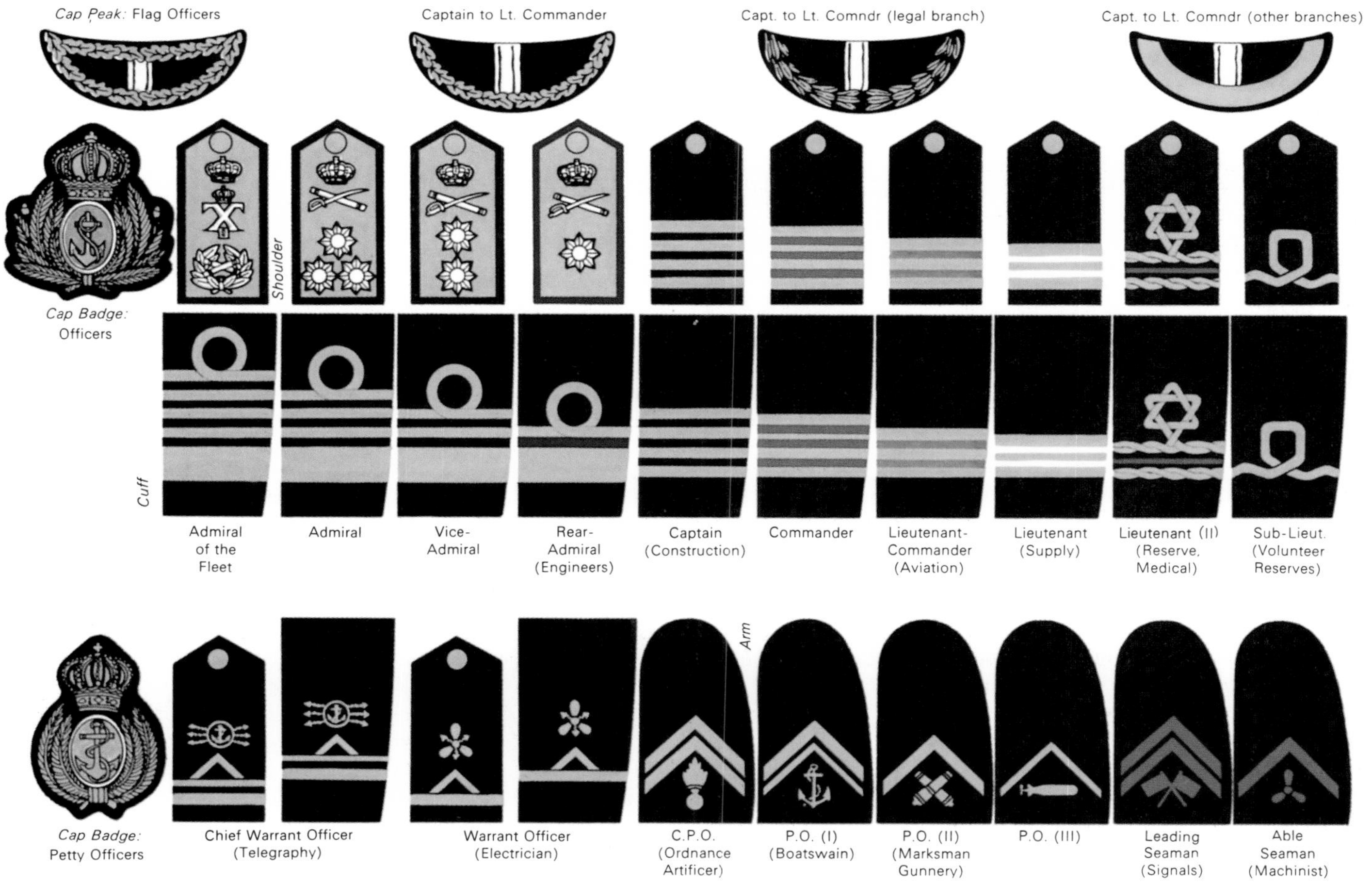

YUGOSLAVIA

ARMY

The titular head of the armed forces was the King. At the end of March 1941 a group of Army officers overthrew the Regent Prince Paul and declared Crown Prince Peter King, although technically he was under age. This coup was seen abroad as a spontaneous patriotic rejection of the unpopular alliance with Germany although the coup had been planned long before negotiations for the alliance began. The Germans immediately prepared to invade.

When the Germans attacked at 5.15 am on 6 April 1941, from bases in Bulgaria, the Yugoslav Army (including some 400,000 recent draftees) was spread out along 1800 miles of border. The front soon crumbled and on 9 April further massive attacks were launched from Austria and Hungary. Two days later the Italians and Hungarians joined in the fray. By 13 April organised resistance was coming to an end and on 17 April 1941 Yugoslavia capitulated. 6028 officers and 337,684 other ranks were captured by the Germans.

ORGANISATION Yugoslavia had a standing army and the male population was liable for military service from the age of 20. The first one and a half years was done in the active army, followed by 18 years in the reserve, and a final ten years in the reserve of the reserve army. The peacetime strength of the Army was 148,000 and mobilised strength approximately 1,400,000 men.

The Army was divided into five army corps with headquarters in Neusatz, Sarajevo, Üskup, Agram and Nis. They comprised:

16 infantry divisions;
1 independent guards division;
2 cavalry divisions;
32 regiments of artillery (a total of 90 battalions and 213 batteries);
6 regiments of engineers;
various supporting arms.

An army corps consisted of a headquarters and three or four infantry divisions; an infantry division had a headquarters, two to four infantry regiments, one or two artillery regiments or an independent artillery battalion and technical troops. Two infantry divisions were organised slightly differently and were classified as mountain divisions. The infantry regiments were 2400 men strong, and their support weapons were 168 machine guns and four infantry guns.

The guards division had a headquarters, one infantry regiment and one

117 118

117 1st Captain, Yugoslav Army, 1941
This officer wears the standard service dress of the Royal Yugoslav Army. The rank badges take the form of Imperial Russian shoulder boards. On the front of the side cap is an oval enamel cockade in the national colours over which is superimposed the gilt metal cypher of King Peter I. The arm-of-service colour appears on the collar and as piping on the tunic cuffs. Shoulder boards indicated not only the rank of the wearer, but his arm-of-service (infantry) and in this case his regimental number. The aiguillette was the badge of an ADC. The breeches were also striped in arm-of-service colour.

118 Senior Sergeant, Yugoslav Army, 1941
This non-commissioned officer in the Yugoslav artillery wears the issue version of the uniform worn by the officer in figure 117. Unlike the officers' uniform, the shoulder straps for other ranks did not follow the Russian pattern. Arm-of-service colour appears as collar patches and as piping to the shoulder straps. The wearing of the officers' belt by senior non-commissioned officers and warrant officers was a custom copied from the French. Non-commissioned officers did not, however, have the metal cypher of King Peter over the national cockade on the cap front.

119 Private, Yugoslav Army, 1941
This soldier wears the old Serbian World War I uniform which was in the process of being replaced by a new single-breasted tunic. The steel helmet is the French Adrian pattern with Yugoslav coat of arms on the front. He is armed with a Yugoslav 7.9mm M1924 rifle which was actually the Czech ZB made under licence in Yugoslavia. The ZB was widely used by central European armies.

119

cavalry brigade and one field artillery regiment; cavalry division had a headquarters, two cavalry brigades, one bicycle battalion, one battalion of horse artillery, and an engineer unit.

The invasion of Yugoslavia had obliged Hitler to postpone the invasion of the Soviet Union by one vital month. The Germans were so anxious to redeploy that the task of rounding-up, disarming and demobilising the Yugoslav Army was incompletely carried out. Thousands of Yugoslav soldiers, perhaps as many as 300,000, retained their arms and either went home or joined bands of soldiers in the mountains. It was these men and their officers who, as the Yugoslav Army in the Homeland, were the first to raise the banner of resistance in German-occupied Europe.

UNIFORM In 1941 the uniform of the Royal Yugoslav Army was basically that of the Serbian Army in World War I. Although new uniforms were being gradually introduced, many soldiers still wore the obsolete pattern. The colour of the issue uniform was a brownish grey, while officer's uniform, made of superior quality cloth, were a greener, lighter colour.

The typical service dress for officers is illustrated in figure 117. The greatcoat was double-breasted with two rows of six buttons, matching collar, turn-back cuffs. The uniform worn by all other Army ranks consisted of a French *Adrian* steel helmet with stamped metal Yugoslav coat of arms on the front, side cap with cockade in the national colours on the front, tunic, greatcoat and pantaloons worn with puttees and ankle boots. There was a more comfortable and practical uniform for mountain troops which included a loosely cut tunic and long baggy trousers gathered at the ankle. Crews of armoured fighting vehicles wore the French helmet for motorised troops and a brown leather double-breasted jacket.

INSIGNIA All ranks wore their rank badges on the shoulder straps. The shoulder straps for officers were based on the Russian Tsarist model, although the stars were similar to those used on German shoulder straps. Another unusual feature was the imitation gold and silver lace

Far left: Men of the Belgrade 'Iron Regiment' on the march. Uniform consists of the double-breasted tunic, French-pattern helmet, trousers and puttees. The officer saluting is distinguishable as a 2nd lieutenant by the single pip on his shoulder board.

Left: A Yugoslav tank commander wearing the early version of the French helmet for motorised troops which was standard issue.

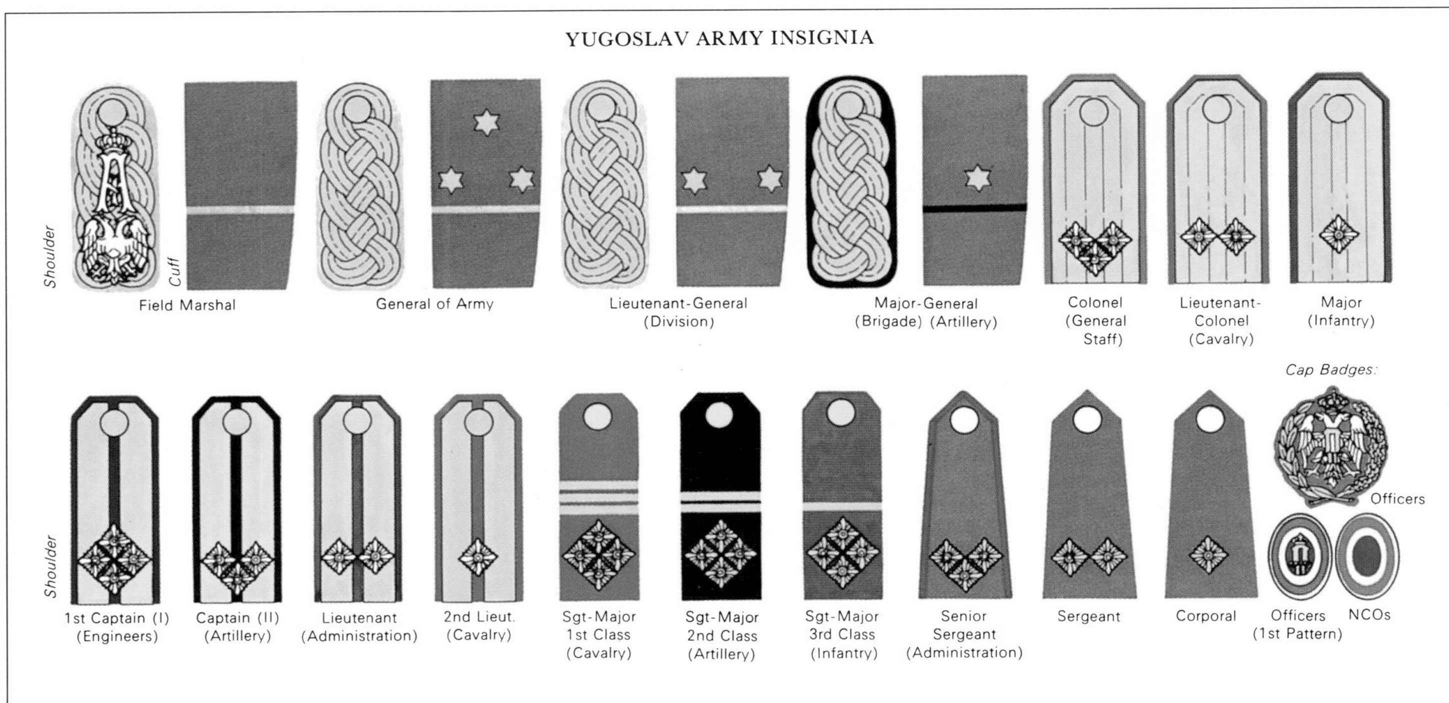

stamped out of metal. There was also a special system of rank badges for wear on raincoats, anoraks and other kinds of protective clothing.

Arm-of-service colours in the form of piping appeared on the head-dress, tunic, greatcoat and trousers and on the shoulder straps and collar patches on the greatcoats. Regimental and academic badges in metal were worn on the breast pockets of the tunic.

Uniform The grey-blue uniform of the Royal Yugoslav Air Force was introduced in 1938 and consisted of peaked cap, side cap, open tunic with patch pockets which was either worn with long matching trousers and black shoes, or matching breeches and black high boots. In the summer months officers and senior regular non-commissioned officers could wear a cap with white cover and white version of the service dress tunic.

The other ranks' version of the uniform was similar to that worn by officers but was of poorer quality and cut, with trousers or pantaloons and puttees.

The Corps of Anti-Aircraft Artillery had slightly different uniforms although technically belonging to the Air Force. The colour was grey blue but the officer's tunic was in black velvet and the cuffs were piped in black. Badges of rank were only worn on the shoulder straps.

Air force

The Army Air Service, which included balloon companies and the anti-aircraft artillery, came under the Minister of War. In 1938 the Air Force was organised in three brigades with a total of 14 bomber, eight fighter and 21 reconnaissance flights. Aircraft strength was estimated at 500 with a further 300 reserve and training aircraft. These totals included 30 Italian Savoia-Marchetti bombers, 70 Dornier Do17Ks and 50 Bristol Blenheims. 73 fighters were German Bf 109Es (although only 46 were serviceable when war broke out) and 40 were Hurricanes.

Pitted against the might of the Luftwaffe the Yugoslav Air Force had little chance and by 13 April 1941 had almost ceased to exist.

Personnel strength in the flying branch was 980 officers, 1600 non-commissioned officers, 720 air gunners and 7500 other ranks.

Right: King Peter of Yugoslavia, in exile with some of his officers. They are mainly from the Air Force, with pilots' badges on the right breast.

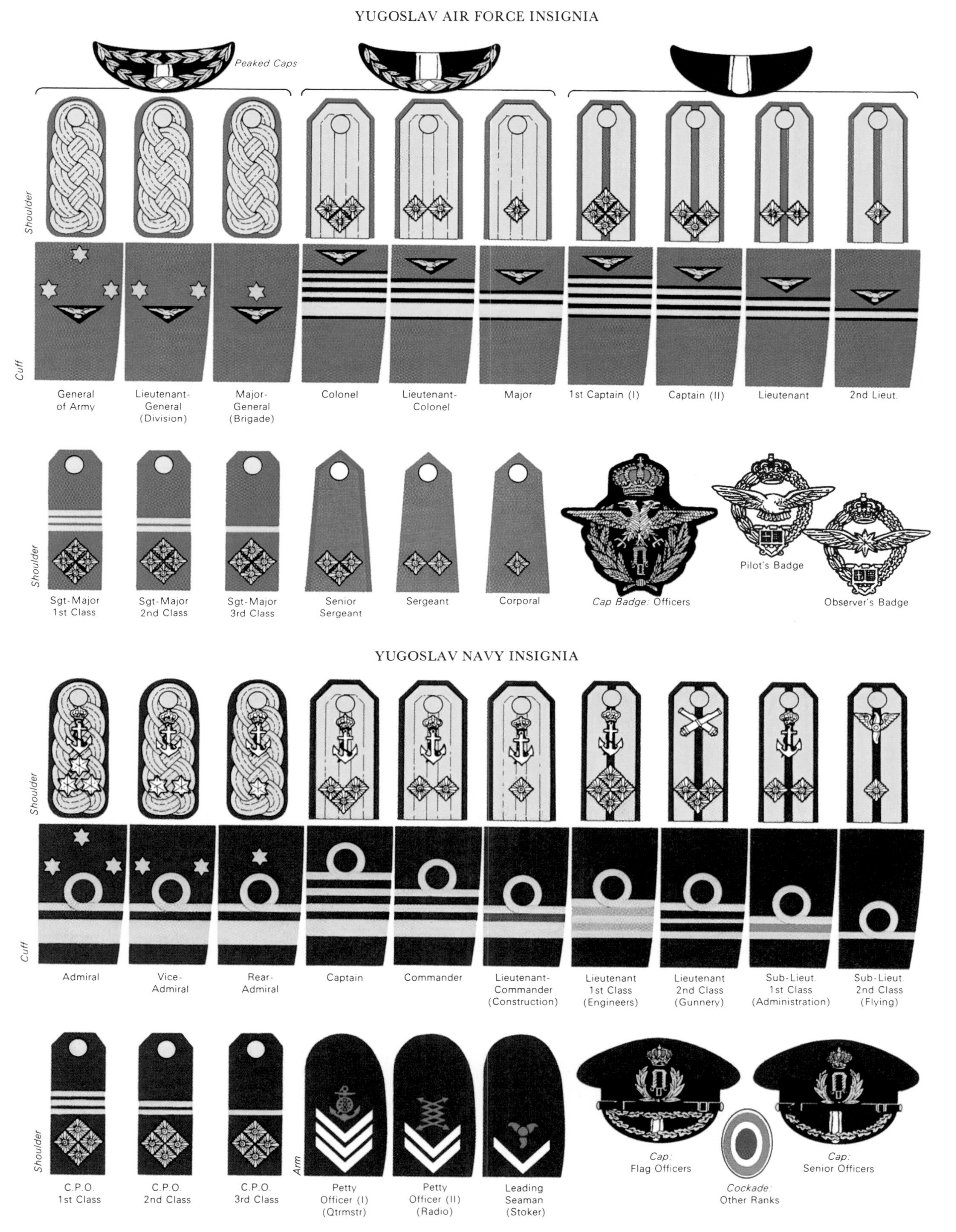
YUGOSLAV AIR FORCE INSIGNIA
Peaked Caps
Shoulder
Cuff
General of Army
Lieutenant-General (Division)
Major-General (Brigade)
Colonel
Lieutenant-Colonel
Major
1st Captain (I)
Captain (II)
Lieutenant
2nd Lieut.
Shoulder
Sgt-Major 1st Class
Sgt-Major 2nd Class
Sgt-Major 3rd Class
Senior Sergeant
Sergeant
Corporal
Cap Badge: Officers
Pilot's Badge
Observer's Badge
YUGOSLAV NAVY INSIGNIA
Shoulder
Cuff
Admiral
Vice-Admiral
Rear-Admiral
Captain
Commander
Lieutenant-Commander (Construction)
Lieutenant 1st Class (Engineers)
Lieutenant 2nd Class (Gunnery)
Sub-Lieut. 1st Class (Administration)
Sub-Lieut. 2nd Class (Flying)
Shoulder
Arm
C.P.O. 1st Class
C.P.O. 2nd Class
C.P.O. 3rd Class
Petty Officer (I) (Qtrmstr)
Petty Officer (II) (Radio)
Leading Seaman (Stoker)
Cap: Flag Officers
Cockade: Other Ranks
Cap: Senior Officers

120 Captain, Yugoslav Air Force, 1941
The service dress followed the usual pattern although badges of rank appeared in both the traditional Army manner on the shoulder boards, and on the cuffs. Flying personnel were distinguished by an eagle worn above the lace on the cuffs, while qualified pilots wore a metal badge on the right breast. The decoration is the Yugoslav Order of the White Eagle.

Insignia All ranks wore their rank badges on the shoulder straps, while officers also wore rank distinction lace on the cuffs. Field officers had one and general officers two rows of gold embroidery on the cap peak. General officers also wore five-pointed stars in the French manner on the cuffs of the tunic and greatcoat.

The Air Force was divided, as far as arm-of-service distinction was concerned, into four branches. Flying personnel wore a gold-embroidered bird with outstretched wings above their rank distinction lace on the cuffs and qualified aircrew wore a metal badge above the right breast pocket. Ground personnel did not have the bird emblem on the cuffs. Engineering officers had red lights to the rank distinction lace on the cuffs and on the shoulder straps, and instead of the bird they had a triangle within a circle on the cuffs. Anti-aircraft officers had crossed cannon barrels surmounted by a bird on the cuffs and a black arm-of-service colour.

Yugoslav cap badges and qualification badges continued to be worn on British Royal Air Force uniform by members of the Royal Yugoslav Air Force serving with the Allies in the Middle East.

Navy

The Yugoslav Navy, under the command of Vice Admiral Marjan Polić, had an active strength at the beginning of the war of 625 active officers and 5700 men with a further 400 reserve officers and 900 men. Because of its small size the Navy was not expected to carry out offensive operations, but to provide support for land operations. It comprised:
1 training cruiser;
1 Yarrow Class destroyer;
5 destroyers;
6 old torpedo boats;
2 submarines;
6 mine sweepers;
2 old motor torpedo-boats.

The Navy was quickly overwhelmed in the Balkan Campaign with only one submarine and a few smaller craft escaping to join the Allies, while those craft still afloat in or near harbours were taken over by the Italians.

Uniform Navy uniform corresponded to the international pattern. Officers wore the peaked cap, double-breasted reefer, long trousers with black shoes and double-breasted greatcoat. In the summer months officers wore a white cap cover and open single-breasted jacket.

Ratings had the standard square-rig with soft cap bearing a cap tally with '*Ratna Mornarica*' in Cyrillic letters below an oval cockade in the national colours. In winter, ratings wore a double-breasted pea-coat.

Insignia Ratings wore inverted white tape chevrons on the left sleeve, while petty officers had blue cloth shoulder straps on which they wore their rank badges. Officers wore both shoulder boards and rank distinction lace on the reefer cuffs, while shoulder boards only were worn on white jacket and greatcoat.

Ratings wore red trade badges above their rank chevrons. Officers wore small white metal branch badges on the shoulder boards, while branch colours appeared both there and as lights between the rank lace on the cuffs.

Yugoslav personnel serving with the British Royal Navy wore Royal Naval uniform with the Yugoslav cap badge where applicable and sometimes 'Yugoslavia' on both sleeves at shoulder height. Shoulder boards were worn only on the greatcoat and white jacket.

Below: Yugoslav cadets on the bowsprit of the training vessel Jadran. *Although rather posed (the ship is entering Portsmouth in 1939) the photograph shows standard 'square rig' well.*

GERMANY

ARMY

German involvement in the Mediterranean theatre began early in 1941 with the arrival of the Luftwaffe and Rommel's Africa Corps in North Africa, and was to continue until the final surrender in 1945. The Germans fought campaigns in three major areas: in Yugoslavia and Greece in 1941; in North Africa, 1941–43, and in Sicily and Italy, 1943–45.

YUGOSLAVIA AND GREECE, 1941

In order to secure his southern flank for the invasion of the Soviet Union Hitler forced Yugoslavia's Prince Regent Paul into the Axis alliance, but when he was overthrown by anti-German patriots in Belgrade, Hitler ordered the invasion of Yugoslavia and the expulsion of the British from Greece.

Operation *Marita*, the invasion of Yugoslavia, was launched on 6 April 1941 (after a mere ten days of preparation) and was a complete success; for the loss of 558 men the Yugoslav Army was completely destroyed, and over 300,000 men taken prisoner. Simultaneously, five divisions of List's 12th Army invaded Greece and by the end of April the country lay in German hands, although losses here were rather higher, at just over 5,000. The Wehrmacht's victory in the Balkans was due to the imaginative handling of armoured and airborne forces against the armies of a disorganised enemy.

ORGANISATION The German forces stationed in the Balkans were organised in two armies and a panzer group: 2nd Army (von Weichs) based in Hungary consisted of four corps:
LII Corps – two infantry divisions;
LI Corps – two infantry divisions;
XXXXIX Corps – one light infantry and one mountain division;
XXXXVI Motorised Corps – one motorised division and two panzer divisions.

12th Army (List) and 1st Panzer Group (von Kleist) based in Romania and Bulgaria were deployed as follows:
XXX Corps – three infantry divisions;
XVIII Corps – two mountain and one panzer division;
XXXX Motorised Corps – one infantry division, one motorised brigade (SS *Leibstandarte Adolf Hitler*) and one panzer division;
XI Corps – one infantry and one mountain division;
XIV Motorised Corps – one motorised and two panzer divisions;
XXXXI Motorised Corps – one motorised infantry regiment (*Grossdeutschland*), one motorised brigade (Hermann Göring) and one motorised division (SS *Das Reich*).

One corps of three infantry and one panzer division was held in reserve while a further three panzer divisions were under the direct control of OKH.

It can be seen from the list above that the corps was a very flexible structure, which could be composed of a variety of different formations to suit local needs: XVIII Corps, for example, was composed of two mountain divisions and one panzer division, specifically for operating in difficult terrain.

The divisional organisation of the German Army was much the same as it had been in 1940 with the exception of the panzer formations which were reorganised to include a better balanced infantry element, to avoid the problem encountered in France in 1940 when unsupported tank units raced on ahead of the foot-slogging infantry. The panzer division now had one tank regiment, two motorised infantry regiments and stronger supporting units which included self-propelled anti-tank guns and artillery. It was 15,600 men strong and had an establishment strength of 211 tanks. The Mark III and IV tanks now formed the striking force of the panzer division.

NORTH AFRICA, 1941–43

General Rommel arrived in Tripoli on 12 February 1941 and two days later the first units of what was to become the celebrated Africa Corps (*Deutsches Afrikakorps* or DAK) began to disembark.

The German commander launched an offensive against the British almost immediately with the newly-constituted 5th Light Division and two Italian divisions. Despite initial success the Axis forces were held by the British: this offensive was the prelude to a series of attacks and counter-attacks launched by both the British and Axis over the following eighteen months.

The Africa Corps built up a fearsome reputation in mobile warfare because its flexible combination of tanks, anti-tank guns and infantry proved too sophisticated for its British opponents. Compared to the Eastern Front, however, the battles in the desert were small-scale affairs: in January 1942, Rommel attacked from El Agheila with just 84 German medium and heavy tanks, and in May 1942 he had just 40 of the main battle tank, the Mark IV. The build-up of British strength and Rommel's failure to secure a decisive victory led to the defeat of the Axis forces at El Alamein in October 1942 and their retreat from the desert.

After the landing of Allied forces in French North Africa (Operation 'Torch') the German High Command began to pump men and materials into Tunisia but this strategically mistaken move came too late to effect the outcome of the campaign, the net result being to ensure the capture of over 100,000 unwounded veteran German soldiers. Total Axis losses in the North African campaigns were around 620,000 men, over a third of whom were Germans.

121

121 Major-General, German Army, 1942
Generalmajor Freiherr von Esebeck was commander of the 15th Panzer Division from 1940 to 1943. As shown here, he wears issue tropical uniform with the peaked cap from his temperate uniform; a typical mix. His decorations are the Knight's Cross, 1939, bar to the Iron Cross 1st Class, Iron Cross 1st Class 1914 and Tank Assault Badge in silver. The collar patches were common to all general officers, and the specific rank was only displayed on the shoulder straps.

122

123

122 Infantryman, German Army, 1943
This machine gunner wears the tropical uniform issued to German troops serving in the so-called Adriatic Coast Line which stretched from Trieste to the Greek Isles. As a machine gunner he carries on his belt a pouch containing tools and an anti-aircraft sight for his MG43 machine gun, and an automatic pistol.

123 Officer, German Army, 1942
This officer wears the tropical field cap, bleached almost white by the sun, and goggles to protect his eyes from the clouds of dust thrown up by vehicles moving in the desert. The greatcoat is the standard pattern which was usually worn with shoulder straps to identify the wearer's rank. The web belt is the special pattern for officers, with round buckle.

124 Sergeant-Major, German Army, 1942
This NCO in the Military Police (Feldgendarmerie) *wears standard Africa Corps uniform with the duty gorget and cuff-band which were the distinctive badges of the military police. The gorget with its luminous national emblem and chain led its wearers to be known as 'chained dogs'* (Kettenhunde). *The arm-of-service colour was orange which appeared as a chevron on the field cap and on the shoulder straps.*

125 2nd Lieutenant, German Army, 1942
This tropical version of the side cap was issued to crews of armoured fighting vehicles since it was more convenient than the field cap, which had a large peak and tended to get in the way inside a tank. On the tropical field blouse he wears the insignia from his temperate uniform, while as a quasi-official distinction he wears the death's heads from his black panzer jacket on the lapels. Shorts and high-laced tropical field boots formed part of the basic tropical uniform. Badges are the Iron Cross 2nd Class ribbon and badge on the left breast pocket, above the silver Tank Assault Badge.

ORGANISATION The Africa Corps was originally formed from the 5th Light Division which was later redesignated the 21st Panzer Division and consisted of:
5th Panzer Regiment – two strong tank battalions totalling 150 Mk II, III and IV tanks;
104th (Motorised) Infantry Regiment – two battalions of panzer grenadiers;
3rd (Motorised) Reconnaissance Battalion;
two strong anti-tank battalions;
one artillery battalion.

This division was soon reinforced by the 15th Panzer Division, the two formations becoming the nucleus of the Africa Corps.

In August 1941 the Africa Corps was further reinforced by the German 90th Light Division, the Italian XX and XXI Corps and the Italian Savona Division and was upgraded to become Panzer Group Africa. The 90th Light Division was organised from units already in

Right: Captured Panzer Grenadiers in tropical uniform. Note the badges on the issue caps, the web equipment and the infantry assault badges.

124

125

Africa and comprised a motorised panzer grenadier regiment and three motorised infantry regiments, one of which included Germans from the French Foreign Legion.

Panzer Group Africa developed into Panzer Army Africa in January 1942, being supplemented with 164th Infantry Division (three motorised panzer grenadier regiments) in July 1942 and by the Ramcke Parachute Brigade. Also known as the German/Italian Panzer Army the title of this formation was changed to the 1st Italian Army on 23 February 1943 and was combined with the 5th Panzer Army to form Army Group Africa, the last grouping of Axis forces in North Africa.

The 5th Panzer Army had evolved from the German 90th Corps, which arrived in Tunisia in 1942 after Operation 'Torch', and in March 1943 comprised:
10th Panzer Division (7th Panzer and two infantry regiments);
21st Panzer Division;
334th Infantry Division (three motorised infantry regiments);
999th Infantry Division;
Division von Manteuffel (a mixed parachute and panzer grenadier formation).

In addition there were two Luftwaffe AA divisions and units of Italian infantry.

The strength of the Army Group in March 1943 was about a third of a million men, and although the Germans accounted for only a third of this number their superior equipment, training and organisation ensured that they had the major role in the last battles for North Africa.

ITALY, 1943–45

The loss of North Africa, the imminent collapse of the fascist government in Italy and the Allied invasion of Sicily placed the Germans in a difficult position. In order to secure Italy as a buffer against the Allies, German divisions were dispatched over the Alps ready to take over the country when the new Italian government made peace with the Allies, which they duly did on 8 September 1943.

Through dogged rear-guard actions combined with Allied indecision the German Army gained time for the construction of a series of defensive lines along the Italian peninsula which successfully delayed the Allied advance until April 1945. The outstanding feature of the war it Italy was the skilful defensive fighting of the German Army under the leadership of Field Marshal Kesselring, culminating in the battle for Monte Cassino which brought the American and British armies to a standstill for over six months.

German strength in Italy in 1944 reached 26 divisions (including six panzer and panzer grenadier divisions) and six fascist Italian divisions, but, lacking effective air support, the German Army was forced into a defensive role. Although the Allied forces were starved of men in preference to the main European theatre in France, superiority in equipment and air power ensured the defeat of the German Army Group C which surrendered on 2 May 1945.

ORGANISATION Italian defences in Sicily had been strengthened by the 15th Panzer Grenadier Division and the 'Hermann Göring' Panzer Division. After the Allied landings, two paratroop regiments and the 29th Panzer Grenadier Division were brought in. General Hube took command of these forces and managed to transport most of them back to Italy when Allied victory became inevitable. 4325 Germans died in the short campaign.

Following the successful takeover of Italy through Operation *Achse*, the German High Command reorganised its defence system. Italy had been divided into two army groups each of eight divisions: Army Group C covering the southern half of the country under Field Marshal Kesselring and Army Group B responsible for northern Italy and France under Field Marshal Rommel.

In late 1943, however, Army Group B was reassigned to prepare for the invasion of France from England, and the whole of Italy came under Kesselring's Army Group C. Reinforcements during the autumn of 1943 brought up the German Army in Italy to a strength of 25 divisions which were organised into two armies: Vietinghoff's 10th Army and von Mackensen's newly-formed 14th Army.

This strength stayed fairly constant: in March 1945 there were still 23 divisions, containing 491,000 men when Kesselring moved to north-western Europe and Vietinghoff took overall command.

Given the German Army's defensive role and the mountainous nature of many of the battlefields, the infantry rather than the armoured formations bore the brunt of the fighting, and specialised forces – such as the mountain troops – came into their own. In particular, the ability of small infantry units to operate independently in difficult climatic and geographic conditions was essential.

The company was the basic tactical unit in the German Army, as it was in all other armies, and its organisation varied according to its function.

The infantry company was divided into three or four platoons each of which would be sub-divided into three or four sections, each section consisting of about eight to twelve men grouped around the general purpose MG34 or MG42 machine gun. In keeping with the German principle of decentralisation each company would have its own heavy weapons section which could include mortars, *Nebelwerferen* and machine guns in a heavy support role. During the course of the war the establishment strength of the company decreased (from around 180 to 200 men in the early 1940s to about 140 men in 1944–45) but its firepower increased, through the widespread introduction of good quality short-range (MP38/40) and long-range (MG42) automatic weapons.

UNIFORM Unlike Britain, France and Italy, Germany had no colonial empire and so when it became apparent that she would soon become involved in a desert war, Germany had to design and manufacture a whole range of tropical clothing and equipment over night. With no practical experience nor time for development it was natural that Germany should copy the uniform of those nations with a colonial empire.

When in February 1942 the first German troops landed in Tripoli they exchanged their field-grey uniforms for tropical versions. With their sun helmets, well-cut tunics and breeches and laced field boots they could not fail to look like pre-war British soldiers in India. The Germans soon found their pseudo-functional outfit looked very smart by European standards, but had little in common with the loose and sloppy clothing developed by the native inhabitants of those parts.

It was not long before the Germans realised the functional limitations of their restrictive clothing and the sun helmet, laced field-boots, tight-fitting field-blouse and breeches were relegated to the baggage. The soldiers in the field developed their own style of clothing which they found to be the most comfortable and practical. The typical outfit of the German desert fighter consisted of a field cap with large peak which shaded the eyes from the fierce desert sun, a shirt, long trousers gathered at the ankles, or shorts, woollen socks, and canvas and leather ankle boots. The German field-blouse continued to be widely worn, but it was not as comfortable as the Italian *sahariana*, which Germans soon 'procured' for themselves. Armoured fighting vehicle crews received a tropical version of the side cap which was more suited for wear inside a tank than the peaked cap.

With the rapid drop in temperature at night, personnel wore a knitted woollen waist protector next to their skin, and a woollen greatcoat over their other clothing. German supply officers tried to make good shortages of steel helmets and woollen pullovers, both of which were found to be essential in desert warfare.

126 Lieutenant, German Infantry, 1944
The well-patched breeches, worn-out boots and general shabbiness of this infantry officer taken prisoner in Italy in July 1944 draw attention to the poor level of supply of German troops in Italy. He wears an old-style field cap or peaked service cap with chin cords removed and a rush-green drill tunic, in the button-hole of which appears the ribbon of the medal for the Winter Campaign in Russia. Equipment is the standard officers' belt and issue map case. The rank of this officer is denoted by the single pip on the shoulder strap.

127 2nd Lieutenant, German Army, 1944
The combination of tropical and temperate clothing worn by this mountain troop officer was quite typical of the Italian Campaign. On the left side of the field cap and on the right sleeve appears the Edelweiss badge of the mountain soldier (Gebirgsjäger). *Trousers tapering to the ankle and ankle boots were also a distinctive feature of mountain troop uniform. The badges worn on the left breast pocket are the Infantry Assault Badge (in white metal) and the World War II Wound Badge. Wound badges were issued in black metal for the first two wounds; in silver for the third and fourth; and in gold for the fifth and subsequent wounds.*

126

127

Above: German infantry in 1944 in Italy. The right breast eagle of the leading man identifies them as Luftwaffe personnel.

Below right: A Luftwaffe major in tropical dress. His rank is shown by the shoulder straps – interwoven braid without pips.

In Italy tropical uniforms continued to be worn by German troops combined with items of temperate uniform, which sometimes gave a rather mixed appearance, as in figure 127.

INSIGNIA Rank badges were the same as those worn on the temperate uniform, although the aluminium NCO lace was replaced by yellow-brown silk lace. Officially all ranks were to wear a standardised collar patch, although many officers and all general officers wore the collar patches from their temperate uniform.

Arm-of-service colour (*Waffenfarbe*) appeared in the form of a chevron on the front of the field and side cap, and as piping or underlay on the shoulder straps.

AIR FORCE

The Mediterranean theatre was never a top priority for the Luftwaffe and its units there were generally deprived of resources relative to the forces engaged on the Eastern Front and in the defence of the *Reich*.

There were four major areas of Luftwaffe involvement. Firstly, in the Balkans during 1941, close support of the Army was essential for the conquest of Yugoslavia and Greece and the invasion of Crete. Secondly, there was the central Mediterranean, where the security of Axis supply routes to North Africa and the defeat of the British fleet were the objectives. Neither of these aims was achieved, mainly because the key stronghold of Malta was never reduced. Thirdly, there was the close-support of land operations in North Africa, which gradually became impossible as Allied material superiority eventually told. Finally, the Luftwaffe played a minor role in the Italian campaign (where it was very short of aircraft), although attacks on shipping – particularly at Bari in November 1943 and during the Anzio landings – were sometimes successful.

While the over-stretched Luftwaffe in North Africa was desperately fighting in the air to obtain superiority and to provide close support for the Africa Corps, it also played an important part in the fighting on the ground. Rommel soon realised that in the vast flatness of the desert his existing anti-tank artillery was far too weak, and began to attach motorised batteries of Luftwaffe anti-aircraft guns to his field formations. Time and time again the great accuracy and velocity of the 8.8cm gun resulted in the decimation of Allied tank attacks.

ORGANISATION The first deployment of the German Air Force in the Mediterranean was the arrival of the X *Fliergerkorps* from Norway in December 1940 to provide support for the ground forces in North Africa and cut off the British supply routes in the Mediterranean. For a time the German Air Force had control of the skies, its Messerschmitt Bf 109s proving more than a match for the RAF's Hurricanes.

In the Balkans the 4th Air Fleet of 1200 aircraft supported the German Blitzkrieg with great success and contributed to the hard-fought victory over Crete. Large numbers of aircraft from both the X *Fliegerkorps* and the 4th Air Fleet were withdrawn for the invasion of the Soviet Union, however, leaving the Luftwaffe desperately short of aircraft in the Mediterranean.

German aerial forces in Africa during the summer of 1941 were disposed thus:
Tripoli – one Ju 87 dive-bomber *Gruppe*;
Sirte – one Ju 87 dive-bomber *Gruppe*;
Gazala – one Bf 109 fighter *Gruppe* and one Bf 110 fighter-bomber *Gruppe*;
Benghazi – one Ju 88 bomber *Geschwader*.

The appointment of Field Marshal Kesselring as overall commander in the Mediterranean theatre in December 1941 ensured a better allocation of aircraft, and II *Fliegerkorps* was brought in from the Eastern Front as a reinforcement. In the late spring of 1942, there were 660 aircraft available for use in the attack on Malta, but strength declined from then on, accentuated by fuel shortages.

128

129

130

128 Sergeant, German Air Force, 1941
This Stuka pilot, just shot down over the Libyan Desert, wears the summer flying helmet in canvas, Luftwaffe tropical shirt and trousers. In his right hand he carries a metal container for a thermos flask.

129 Lieutenant-General, German Air Force, 1942
This general officer wears the standard Air Force tropical uniform with the peaked service cap of his temperate uniform. His rank is displayed on both his collar patches and on the shoulder straps. Decorations are the 1939 Bar to the Iron Cross 1st Class, Iron Cross 1st Class 1914, Pilot's Badge and a Wound Badge.

130 Lieutenant-Colonel, German Air Force, 1943
With the Luftwaffe tropical uniform this officer wears the tropical version of the peaked cap which was unique to the Air Force and was equipped with a neck flap à la French Foreign Legion. His shoulder straps combine both his arm-of-service colour and badges of rank. Above the left breast pocket he wears a Front Flight Bar with pendant which bore the number of missions flown, Iron Cross 1st Class, Pilot's Badge and Wound Badge.

In 1941 the Luftwaffe had formed a special staff (*Luftgaustab z.b.V Afrika*) to control and co-ordinate the ground organisation of the Air Force and its supply channels. This staff also controlled the static flak artillery which guarded harbours, airfields and supply depots. By August 1941, Panzer Army Africa had at its disposal six batteries of motorised anti-aircraft artillery.

In September 1942 Luftwaffe ground strength in North Africa was 12,000 men, 3400 vehicles and 70 guns over 4cm.

The material build-up of the British and newly-arrived American forces during late 1942 gave them a general air superiority that the Luftwaffe was never able to challenge, although the German planes regularly scored tactical victories over their opponents. A considerable proportion of the Luftwaffe began to be devoted towards intercepting the African-based Allied bomber raids against southern and central Europe. When deprived of fighter support the Allies suffered heavy losses from the experienced German interceptors.

A further role for the Luftwaffe in the spring of 1943 was the supply of Axis forces in Tunisia. Although desperately vulnerable to Allied fighter attacks the German (and Italian) transport planes kept up a regular supply of men and materials (some 19,000 men and 4500 tons of stores were carried across to North Africa during the December and January of 1942/43).

Desperately outnumbered in the air over Italy during 1943–45, the Luftwaffe could only provide occasional support for the Army in field, most of its resources being devoted to air defence against Allied bomber raids.

Luftwaffe units were withdrawn from Italy in June 1944 following the Normandy landings leaving only one night ground-attack *Gruppe* and a few reconnaissance units: a total of 170 aircraft of various types.

The defence of Italy was left to newly formed units of the fascist Social Republic, which were clearly unable to take on the combined power of the Allied Air Forces (by March 1945, there were over 4000 Allied aircraft in the Italian theatre).

131

132

133

AIRBORNE FORCES

Germany's airborne forces were engaged on all the major fronts during the war but it was in the Mediterranean that they achieved lasting fame, fighting in Greece and Crete, North Africa and Italy. Their major employment was, however, as conventional infantry rather than parachute troops.

ORGANISATION After the success of the paratroopers in Holland and Belgium the XI Air Corps was officially formed in the summer of 1940 under the command of General Kurt Student. The new formation was first employed in action during the German invasion of Greece when the 2nd Parachute Regiment was air-dropped over the Corinth canal in an attempt – unsuccessful as it turned out – to secure the single bridge over the canal.

Control of Greece was not control of the Mediterranean, however, and plans were drawn up for the invasion of the strategically important island of Crete. The XI Air Corps would be the spearhead of the assault: the invasion by some 22,000 men and over 500 transport planes as well as seaborne forces began on 20 May 1941 and after 11 days of bitter fighting, in which the Germans suffered 3250 dead or missing and 3400 wounded, the Allied forces evacuated the island, leaving over 10,000 men as prisoners. The capture of Crete was one of the greatest triumphs of the airborne forces but the very high casualties of this parachute operation so shocked Hitler that from then on these élite troops fought mainly in an infantry role.

The assault on Crete was carried out by the 7th Air Division supported by the 5th Mountain Division. The 7th Air Division was organised as follows:

three parachute regiments each of three battalions;
air signals company;
transport company;
medical company;
light anti-aircraft battery;
anti-tank gun company;
pak gun battery;
motorcycle platoon.

After the invasion, the 7th Air Division

131 Corporal, German Air Force, 1943
This Corporal of the 'Hermann Göring' Division in Tunisia wears the camouflage shelter quarter as a poncho over his Luftwaffe tropical uniform. Members of the 'Hermann Göring' division wore a blue cuff-band on the right cuff which bore in white letters the name 'Hermann Göring'. On his belt he has two pouches for magazines for his sub-machine gun.

132 Sergeant-Major, German Air Force, 1943
For the rescue of Mussolini, members of the parachute unit under the command of Major Mors wore the special helmet with German camouflage net, smock in geometric camouflage pattern and Luftwaffe tropical trousers. The cloth bandolier holds spare magazines for the Fallschirmgewehr *(a special assault rifle for paratroopers). The four white cloth wings on the sleeve identify the wearer as a sergeant-major.*

133 Private, German Air Force, 1941
This rifleman (Jäger) *in Crete wears the parachutist's 'bone sack' in plain olive green cotton duck. The helmet is fitted with a cover which had tapes to hold foliage. The trousers are also standard paratroop issue in field-grey with fastenings on the outside leg for the knee bandages to be removed once on the ground.*

was withdrawn and re-posted to the Eastern Front, being replaced by the 22nd Infantry Air Landing Division, an otherwise normal infantry division trained and equipped for air transport, which had been unable to participate in the assault.

In Africa the parachute arm was represented by a mixed parachute brigade of 2300 men under Major-General Ramcke, originally trained for the abortive Malta operations, but dispatched in October 1942 to help Rommel in the desert. The brigade consisted of four battle groups of approximately battalion strength with units of artillery, anti-tank guns and engineers. The brigade fought on throughout the North African campaign until the surrender in Tunis in May 1943.

As the Allies prepared to invade Sicily and Italy the parachute formations were gathered together and formed a highly mobile strategic reserve. Based in the south of France the force, still known as XI Air Corps, consisted of the old 7th Air Division (newly designated the 1st Parachute Division) and the recently-formed 2nd Parachute Division – in all, six regiments which with corps troops totalled 30,000 men.

The success of the paratroops in Sicily and southern Italy led to their further expansion, ten divisions plus other parachute units being formed before the end of the war. In central Italy the I Parachute Corps was formed in January 1944, comprising the 4th Parachute Division and 3rd Panzer Grenadier Division and later incorporating the 1st and 4th Parachute Divisions. (The organisational structure of the 1st Parachute Division is shown in the accompanying chart.) The I Parachute Corps earned the admiration of the Allied troops during its long defence of Monte Cassino, where its soldiers (nicknamed the 'Green Devils' by the Americans) endured immense aerial and artillery bombardment. The corps was also engaged continuously in the defensive battles north of Florence during 1945, surrendering to the Allies in the April of that year.

UNIFORM As in other branches of the Armed Forces, Luftwaffe personnel received a special tropical dress which in many respects was much more comfortable and practical than that issued to the Army.

The standard tropical uniform is illustrated by figure 130. Certainly the most distinctive feature of this uniform was the tropical peaked cap with neck flap à la French Foreign Legion. There was no special tropical greatcoat and so Luftwaffe personnel continued to wear the blue-grey temperate model.

This basic uniform was also worn by personnel serving in the ground combat formations of the Luftwaffe, but members of the 'Hermann Göring' Division also received Waffen-SS camouflage smocks

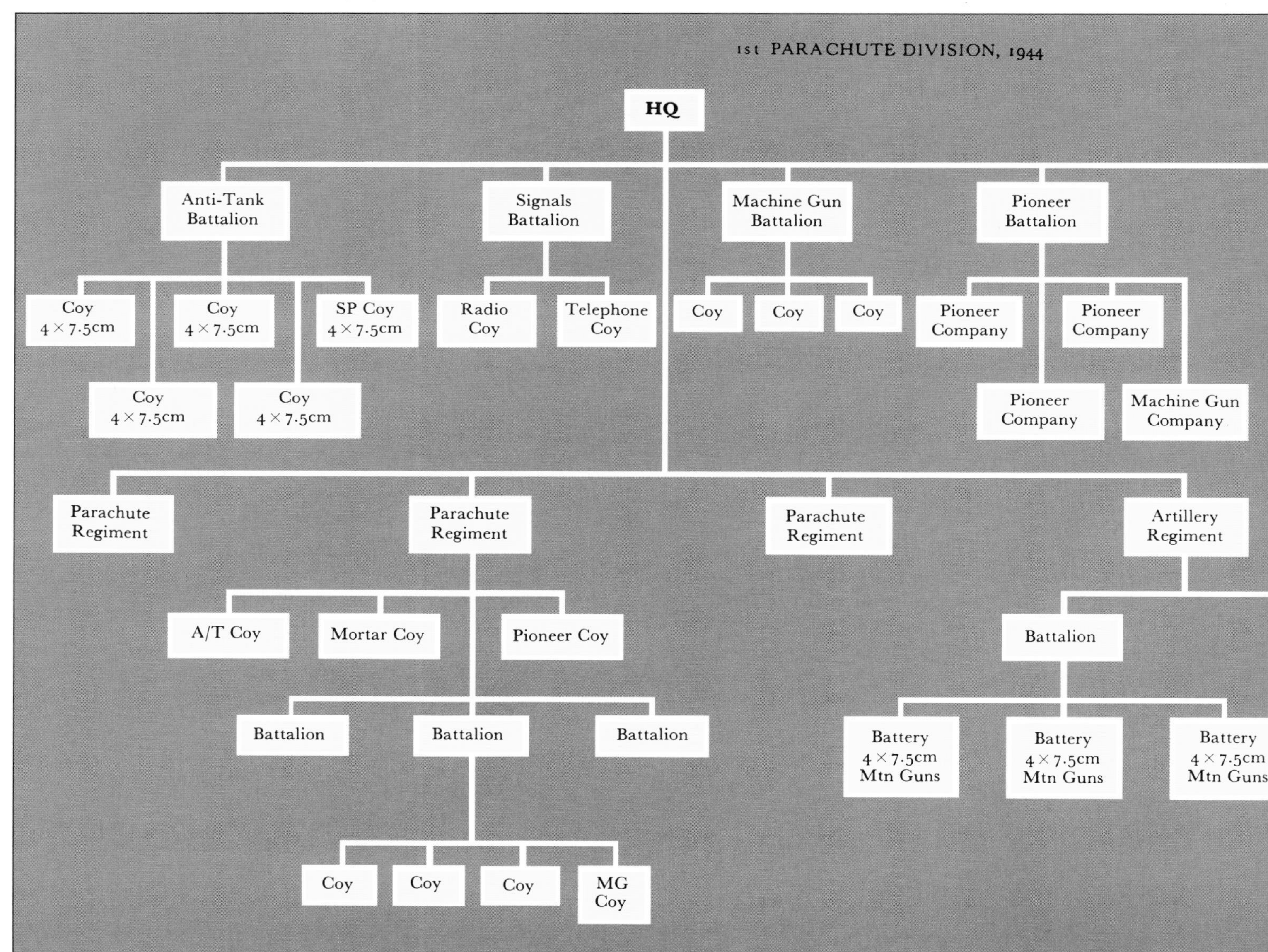

and helmet covers, and Ramcke's parachutists had a tropical version of their jump smock.

Badges of rank and arm-of-service badges were as for the temperate uniform, although Luftwaffe collar patches do not appear to have been worn very often by troops in the field.

NAVY

In anticipation of the necessity for very close Italo-German naval co-operation in the Mediterranean a German naval liaison staff was established in Rome in June 1940 under Rear-Admiral Weichhold. The principal task of this staff was to keep open the supply lines which served the German troops fighting in North Africa. Losses from Allied air, surface and submarine attacks reached a peak in April and May 1941, and the German Navy was obliged to transfer submarines to the Mediterranean and X *Fliegerkorps* was ordered to concentrate on convoy defence. As long as Malta held out none of these measures had any decisive effect and sinkings of Axis transports went on unabated, resulting in a German supply crisis in November 1941.

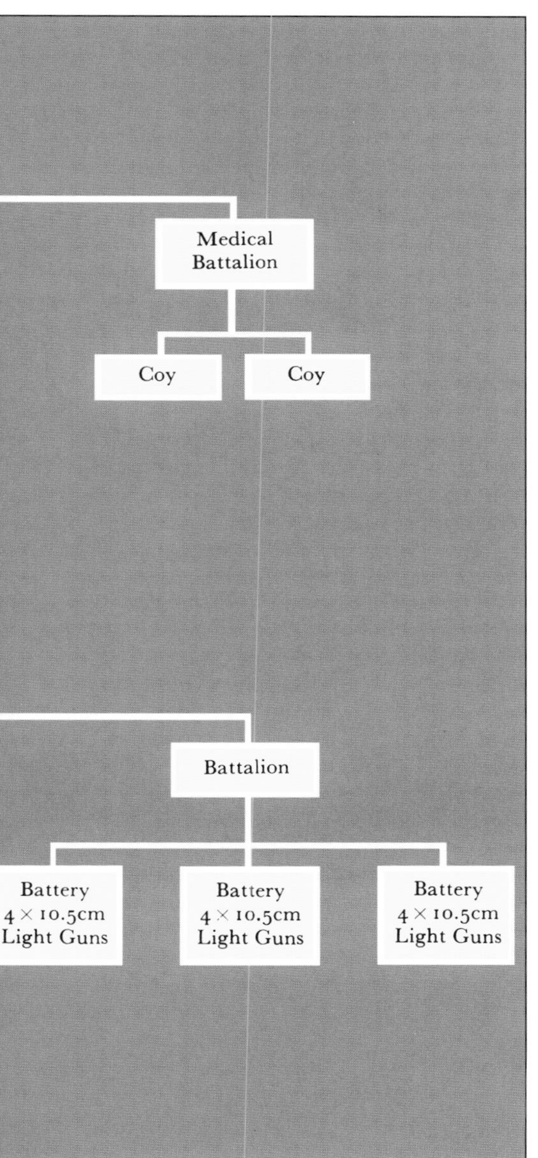

After the beginning of the attack on Tobruk in the spring of 1942, the German Navy established Command Post North Africa on 23 May 1942. This staff conducted naval operations including the deployment of submarines, motor-torpedo boats and mine-sweeping flotillas, and was also responsible for delivering supplies and reinforcements to the German fighting forces in the coastal areas. At the beginning of 1942 there were 24 submarines active in the Mediterranean which, with small vessels and shore establishments, gave a combined strength of about 15,000 men.

Following the collapse of Italy in 1942 there was little the German Navy could do to contest the naval superiority of the British in the Mediterranean, although valuable work was carried out transporting troops in the Aegean.

UNIFORM The German Navy had long experience of the tropics, having raised and equipped expeditionary forces for service in China and German East Africa at the turn of the century.

Before the outbreak of war the German Navy wore a white uniform in Germany and her territorial waters between 20 April and 30 September, or as and when required in foreign waters. Officers and chief petty officers wore a cap with detachable white cover, single-breasted white tunic with stand collar (which in 1938 was altered to an open pattern for wear with white shirt and black tie), long white trousers and white canvas shoes.

Ratings also wore a cap with white cover, or from 1938 with all informal orders of dress, a white side cap with a blue national emblem. The white cotton shirt had pointed blue cuffs and could be worn with either a plain white exercise collar, or with a blue denim collar and the black silk. The white shirt could be worn with either blue or white bell-bottomed trousers, dark blue socks and black shoes or black marching boots.

After considerable experimentation a white sun helmet was introduced in 1938, only to be replaced in 1940 by a light khaki model, which, however, proved to be an unpopular item of head-dress.

On small ships and submarines dress was so informal that it bordered on the slovenly. Officers usually wore a peaked cap with white cover (for the commander only) or a side cap, various types and colours of shirt worn open at the neck with shoulder straps. Some ratings wore their white sports vest with or without the blue national emblem on the breast. The rest of this 'uniform' consisted of shorts or swimming trunks, canvas shoes with rope soles or sandals.

134

134 Chief Petty Officer, German Navy, 1944

This sailor, depicted in the later stages of the war, wears khaki battledress similar in pattern to that of the British model. The three pips on the shoulder strap edged with yellow lace denote the wearer's rank as a chief petty officer. An Iron Cross First Class has been awarded; this medal was reinstituted by Hitler on 2 September 1939; it was traditionally only awarded during wartime and was by far the most common award for valour.

INSIGNIA Rank badges were of little importance when crews of motor torpedo-boats and submarines knew each other so well. The commander was identified by his white cap cover, and officers and chief petty officers wore shoulder straps, while ratings wore their chevrons on long-sleeved garments.

GREAT BRITAIN

ARMY

The Mediterranean theatre was an area of prime importance to Britain. She had many interests there and the Suez canal was the most important artery of the Empire. British and Empire forces were engaged continuously from the Italian attack in 1940 to the defeat of Germany in 1945, fighting in North and East Africa, Syria, Iraq, Greece, Sicily, Italy and Yugoslavia and garrisoning areas as far apart as Gibraltar and Persia.

After two years of inconclusive fighting, Allied forces took an irreverisble offensive from October 1942, but tenacious defence and the decision of the Allies to give north-west Europe priority meant that the fighting in Italy was prolonged and difficult.

ORGANISATION In August 1939 the land forces in Egypt under Lieutenant-General Sir Henry Maitland Wilson consisted in the main of an armoured division (7th) still in the process of formation, three British infantry brigades, plus a small number of artillery and engineer units. Additional forces scattered through the Middle East Theatre comprised the Headquarters of the 7th and 8th Infantry Divisions and three infantry brigades in Palestine; two British infantry battalions in the Sudan; lightly-equipped locally raised forces in Iraq, Uganda, Kenya and British Somaliland, and small British garrisons in Malta, Gibraltar, Cyprus and Aden. The first reinforcement from India, the 11th Indian Brigade Group, had also recently arrived.

The desert was to be a theatre of war in which an army's success depended primarily upon the quality and quantity of its armoured forces. The British had begun to prepare in earnest in 1938 with the formation of the Matruh Mobile Force from the units of the Cairo Cavalry Brigade. By October 1939 the force had been transformed into a Mobile Division by its commander Major-General P. C. S. Hobart, and the light Mark III, VIA, and VIB tanks and 3.7 inch mountain howitzers were being replaced by A9 cruiser tanks and 25 pounder howitzers. The division's order of battle was:

Light Armoured Brigade: 7th, 8th, and 11th Hussars;

Heavy Armoured Brigade: 1st and 6th Royal Tank Regiments;

plus units of the Royal Horse Artillery and infantry in what was known as Pivot Group.

135

136

In April 1940 the armoured formations were reorganised into two homogeneous brigades, the Light Armoured Brigade becoming the 7th Armoured Brigade and the Heavy Brigade becoming the 4th Armoured Brigade. The resulting formation was renamed the 7th Armoured Division and it took over control in May of all troops in the Western Desert until the establishment of Headquarters Western Desert Force on 17 June 1940. In Egypt General Wavell could call on a force of approximately 36,000 men including Indian and New Zealand units, while in Palestine there were 27,500 troops including a horse cavalry division. In essence the fighting troops under Western Desert Force consisted of an armoured division with only two armoured regiments in each brigade, and a British infantry brigade. All units were short of equipment, transport, and artillery, and the 7th Armoured had only 65 cruiser tanks against a requirement of 220. Despite these deficiencies, however, Western Desert Force soon established its superiority over the Italians during operations on the Egyptian-Libyan frontier.

135 Sergeant, British Army, 1942

The black beret with its silver badge was the distinctive head-dress of the Royal Tank Regiment, and was to be made famous by General Montgomery who wore one as commander of the 8th Army. In fact, the beret that Montgomery wore was 'donated' by this tankman, Sergeant James Fraser, a crewman in Montgomery's command tank. The shirt, shorts, socks or hose tops and short puttees were standard desert wear. The coloured slides or flashes on his shoulder straps and the black lanyard were worn by those soldiers serving in the 6th Royal Tank Regiment. On the 1937-pattern web belt he carries a .38 Enfield No. 2 Mk I revolver in the special holster issued to tank crews, although it was usually worn lower and strapped to the thigh.

136 Captain, British Army, 1940

Cavalry officers in the Western Desert often wore brightly coloured field service caps with embroidered badges as does this Captain in the 3rd Kings Own Hussars. Metal rank 'pips' were fastened to detachable khaki drill shoulder straps. The trousers made of beige corduroy and suede 'chukka' boots with rubber soles were unofficial but often worn. The 1937-pattern web equipment includes a pouch for a compass on the right, and another for ammunition on the left side.

In spring 1941, British forces in North Africa were reduced by the dispatch of a number of units to aid Greece. There were over 50,000 British and Empire forces in Greece, as well as 100 tanks. They were organised as follows:
1st Armoured Brigade;
6th Australian Division;
2nd New Zealand Division;
two medium artillery regiments.

Nevertheless they were soon overrun by the invading Germans, suffering some 11,000 casualties in the process; the remainder were evacuated to Crete and North Africa. The troops in Crete (about 28,000 men) were themselves forced to evacuate by the German airborne invasion, the British Army contingent suffering 612 killed, 224 wounded and 5315 taken prisoner.

The British operations in Italian East Africa were a complete success, however. Two columns of British and Empire troops launched a pincer offensive against the Italians. On 19 January 1941, the first column of two Indian divisions and native troops advanced from the Sudan. The second column, striking north from Kenya on 24 January, had three South African divisions. The two columns totalled around 70,000 men. In the three-month campaign the British and Empire forces captured 50,000 prisoners and the whole of Italian East Africa for a cost of under 500 casualties.

The British faced further trouble in the Middle East from a German inspired uprising in Iraq (soon put down however) and from Syria, under the control of Vichy France. British possessions in the Middle East were threatened by the Vichy forces, some 35,000 men strong, and so a scratch force of 20,000 soldiers was gathered together to invade Syria on 8 June 1941. The Allied forces consisted of:
7th Australian Division;
5th Indian Infantry Brigade Group (plus attached groups including the Transjordanian Frontier Force);
a Free French division.

Damascus was quickly captured but the Vichy French continued a bitter struggle only surrendering to the British and Allied forces on 12 July.

In the late summer and autumn of 1941 the British forces in Egypt prepared for their next offensive. There were changes in both organisation and command, with General Sir Claude Auchinleck replacing General Wavell as Commander-in-Chief Middle East on 15th July. The flow of reinforcements to the theatre had reached 239,000 men (144,000 from the United Kingdom) between January and July, and had included the 50th British Division and Headquarters 10th Corps. On 9 September 1941 the Western Desert Force was reconstituted as the 8th Army with XIII and XXX Corps under its command. The units in Palestine and Syria were regrouped as the 9th Army with the 1st Australian and 10th Corps.

By November, the British armoured forces available to General Auchinleck had also grown in size and strength. The 7th Armoured Division had been re-equipped, the 22nd Armoured Brigade had arrived in Egypt, the 32nd Army Tank Brigade was operational in Tobruk and the 1st Army Tank Brigade was in the process of formation in XIII Corps.

From late 1941 until the summer of 1942, the 8th Army fought a series of engagements which revealed serious deficiencies in its preparedness for desert warfare when compared with the best German units. The fighting during the 'Crusader' battles in November 1941, for example, had convinced General Auchinleck that the British armoured division

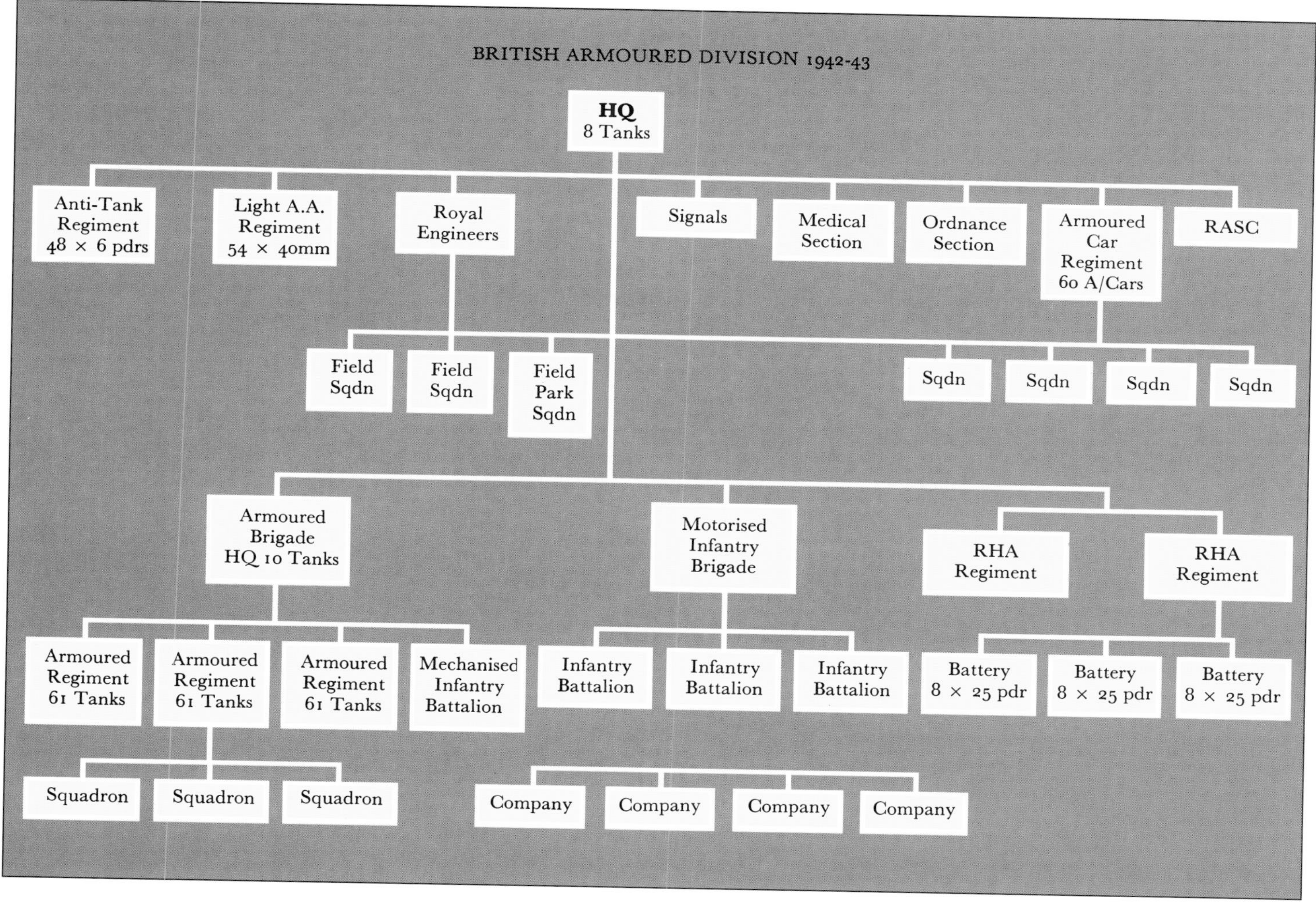

was an unbalanced formation containing too much armour and too little infantry. He therefore reorganised the armoured divisions so that in future they would essentially consist of one armoured brigade group (totalling just under 200 tanks) and one motor brigade group equipped with armoured cars, supported by artillery, engineers and administrative units. The Army tank brigades, each containing three regiments of about 60 tanks, would continue to be independent formations allocated to larger groupings as the need arose. Auchinleck also reorganised the infantry brigade to achieve a more permanent combination of the constituent arms. Infantry divisions were to consist of three brigade groups each with three battalions, a regiment of field artillery (24 25-pounders), an anti-tank regiment (48 6-pounders), an allocation of anti-aircraft artillery, engineers, and administrative units. Unfortunately these changes had not been fully implemented when Rommel attacked on 26 May, pushed the 8th Army back and captured Tobruk on 21 June.

During the period from November 1941 to August 1942 the British 8th Army had suffered 102,000 battle casualties (of which 49,000 were British) but reinforcements continued to arrive and the Army's

Below: Men of the Queen's Regiment marching into Tobruk in November 1942.

Below Left: Sappers at work mine-detecting, wearing the typical clothes of the desert soldier.

137

137 Soldier, Abyssinian Patriot Army, 1941

A number of Abyssinian soldiers fought with the British Army against the Italians in Ethiopia and were equipped in a European fashion but the figure illustrated here has arms and equipment taken from any source available. In addition to his ammunition belt and revolver he is armed with a German 7.92mm 98K rifle.

138 Guardsman, British Army, 1943

In sharp contrast to the Guard's splendid reputation for smartness, this battered survivor of Monte Camino wears a steel helmet over the woollen cap comforter, and a khaki woollen scarf and standard double-breasted greatcoat. In addition to the basic 1937-pattern web equipment he has a cotton bandolier containing additional ammunition.

139 Lieutenant, British Army, 1943

This officer is from the 2nd Cameronians, forming part of the 5th Infantry Division of the 8th Army in Italy. The head-dress is the Tam o'Shanter which was worn by Scottish regiments with the badge mounted on a piece of tartan cloth. The issue battledress for officers was identical to that issued to the men, but during the war officers were allowed to wear the blouse open at the neck with shirt and tie. His rank badges are the two cloth 'pips' on the shoulder straps while on his sleeve he wears the formation sign of the 5th (Y for Yorkshire) Division above a dark green strip of cloth which indicates his arm of service, namely that of a rifle regiment.

140 Private, British Army, 1944

Of particular interest here is the way in which the typical 'Tommy' in the Italian Campaign carried his personal equipment. On his back is the small pack of the 1937-pattern web equipment. Under its flap he has stowed his 'BD' blouse and a pick head.

138

139

140

strength rose from 88,000 in January 1942 to 126,000 by May. Amongst the 149,800 reinforcements that had arrived in the Middle East between January and August were the British 8th Armoured Division, and the 44th and 51st Infantry Divisions. For the El Alamein offensive General Montgomery, the new commander of the 8th Army, was able to deploy three corps: XXX Corps (five infantry divisions, one armoured brigade group); XII Corps (two infantry, one armoured division); and X Corps (three armoured divisions).

The fighting strength of the 8th Army during the battle was approximately 195,000 men and it suffered a total of 13,560 casualties of which 58 per cent were United Kingdom troops.

As the Axis forces broke away from El Alamein with the 8th Army in pursuit, Allied assault forces were landing in French North Africa. The Eastern Assault Force included the 11th and 36th British Brigade Groups (9000 men) and the mixed Anglo-American 1st and 6th Commandos (2000 men). The British contingent was thereafter expanded to form the 1st Army, which by 20 December 1942 totalled 189,000 personnel and fielded the 6th Armoured and 78th Infantry Divisions. On 11 April 1943 the 1st and 8th Armies linked up in Tunisia and several of the latter's formations were placed temporarily under the command of the former. By the end of April the 1st Army contained two British corps and one American and one French corps.

It has been estimated that the three years of battle in the Middle East from June 1940 to May 1943 cost the forces of the British Empire 220,000 casualties.

With the surrender of the German and Italian forces in North Africa on 13 May 1943 Allied reserves of manpower and equipment became available for deployment elsewhere in the Mediterranean theatre – in Sicily, for example.

The war establishments of the British formations in North Africa and the Middle East differed significantly from those in the United Kingdom. The scale of movement was considerable, the 51st Division with auxiliary troops totalling 40,000 men with 8000 vehicles.

For the invasion of Sicily on 9 July 1943 the British troops in the 8th Army were organised in two corps:

XIII Corps:
5th Division;
50th Division;
231st Brigade;

XXX Corps:
51st Division;
1st Canadian Division.

On 25 July they were reinforced by the 78th Division, bringing up the total number of British and Commonwealth troops to 115,000 men. After a skilfully fought campaign the Anglo-American forces had control of the island on 17 August, the British suffering 9353 casualties.

The invasion of the Italian mainland commenced on 3 September 1943, with assault landings mounted from Sicily via the straits of Messina by the troops of XIII Corps. On 9 September the 1st Airborne Division was put ashore at Taranto with the task of securing the 'heel' of Italy. By 16 September the 8th Army's strength in Italy had grown to 63,600 men with 15,270 vehicles; only 635 casualties had been suffered.

The US 5th Army, which landed at Salerno on 9 September, was composed of both American and British formations, the latter consisting of the British X Corps comprising the 7th Armoured Division, 46th and 56th Infantry Divisions and the 23rd Armoured Brigade. During the battle at Salerno, British units lost 725 officers and men killed, 2739 wounded and 1800 missing. Naples fell on 1 October and on the 12th the long advance on Rome began.

The major problem once the Allies had established themselves in Italy was the need to increase their forces as quickly as possible in the face of German superiority in numbers. In the last week of September 1943 the 8th Army had been reinforced by the 78th Infantry Division (11th, 36th, and 38th Brigades), the 4th Armoured Brigade, the Special Service Brigade (3rd Commando, 40th Royal Marine Commando, and 1st Special Raiding Squadron) and the 8th Indian Infantry Division.

On 9 October 1943 the 8th Army comprised two corps, each of two infantry divisions, one armoured brigade and one army artillery group.

By the end of November British land forces in Italy totalled 351,000 officers and men. The average size of a British infantry division including its supporting units was by now 40,000 men. The problem of finding infantry reinforcements for Italy was thus often acute, particularly in view of the fact that 58 per cent of the 46,000 battle casualties suffered by British Army units between September 1943 and March 1944 were incurred by the infantry. By February 1944 the infantry battalions of the 1st and 56th Divisions were fighting with only 72 and 68 per cent respectively of their establishment of other ranks, and in March the official establishment of infantry battalions in the Mediterranean had to be reduced from 844 all ranks to 726.

By the end of December the British element of 5th US Army had lost the 7th Armoured Division, which had been withdrawn in preparation for the invasion of Normandy, but was in the process of receiving the 1st Infantry Division as reinforcement. Since its arrival in Italy X Corps had suffered casualties of 1669 killed, 7023 wounded, and 2869 missing. The 8th Army had also changed its complexion and consisted of two British infantry divisions (the 5th and 78th), two Indian infantry divisions (the 4th and 8th), the New Zealand Division, one Canadian infantry and one Canadian armoured division. In the New Year a policy of reinforcing the US 5th Army from 8th Army and of filling the subsequent gaps with formations newly-arrived in Italy was set in motion, and in preparation for the landings at Anzio the US 3rd and British 1st Divisions formed the US 6th Corps.

For the landing on 22 January 1944 the 1st Division deployed the 2nd and 3rd Infantry Brigades and 24th Guards Brigade, the 46th Royal Tank Regiment and the 2nd Special Service Brigade (9th and 43rd Royal Marine Commandos). By 9th February the Division had been reduced by battle casualties to little more than half its established strength and six weeks after the landing British casualties had mounted to 10,168. When the Allied Armies entered Rome on 4 June 1944 British and Commonwealth casualty figures since the crossing from Sicily had reached 73,122: 14,331 killed, 47,966 wounded and 10,825 missing.

On 30 December 1943 General Sir Oliver Leese had assumed command of 8th Army on the departure of Montgomery for 21st Army Group, and Sir Henry Maitland Wilson replaced Eisenhower as Supreme Allied Commander, Mediterranean Theatre. General Sir Harold Alexander who had been Eisenhower's Deputy became Commander-in-Chief, Allied Armies in Italy.

When Alexander had launched his final drive for Rome, the 8th Army had entered battle with three British and Commonwealth Corps and the Polish Corps. XXX Corps had left for the United Kingdom on 5 November 1943 and X Corps had returned from the 5th US Army on 31 March 1944. 8th Army's

Above: Soldiers trudge up a rocky hillside. The caps are the Tam o' Shanter.

141 Lance-corporal, Royal Military Police, 1943

This military policeman serving with the 46th (North Midland and West Riding) Division in the Plain of Naples wears a steel helmet with painted band and letters 'MP'. On the right sleeve he wears a blue armlet which also bore the red letters 'MP'. The coat is the special pattern issued to motorcyclists.

141

order of battle in addition to the Poles was therefore:

V Corps:
10th Indian Infantry Division;
4th Indian Infantry Division;
7th Armoured Brigade;

X Corps:
2nd New Zealand Division.

XIII Corps:
4th Infantry Division;
8th Indian Division;
1st Canadian Tank Brigade;
78th Infantry Division;
6th Armoured Division.

Army Reserve:
1st Canadian Corps;
25th Army Tank Brigade;
6th South African Armoured Division.

By August 1944 8th Army was disconcertingly well-supplied with armoured units for a campaign in which it was almost impossible to employ armour to its full effect. By May 1944 the 8th Army possessed some 1200 tanks, but what it still lacked was sufficient infantry to break rapidly through German defensive lines which used every available advantage of terrain. The V Corps, spearhead of the offensive, did employ four infantry divisions (the British 4th, 46th and 56th and the Indian 4th) but casualties were heavy: in the three months since July the 8th Army had suffered nearly 20,000 battle casualties with the result that every infantry battalion had to be reorganised. The offensive ground to a halt in the autumn of 1944.

Meanwhile in the Balkans a British force comprising a parachute and an armoured brigade were dispatched to aid the Greek nationalist troops gain control of Greece following the German departure in 1944.

During the winter of 1944–45 the British forces prepared for the forthcoming assault on the German lines. The British Army, supported by a massive aerial bombardment, launched its offensive on 9 April which was a complete success; within three weeks the German Army was at the point of collapse and surrender terms were agreed on 2 May. British casualties during the Italian campaign amounted to 88,790 men.

UNIFORM The regulation tropical dress of the British Army at the beginning of the war in the Middle East was quite a formal affair which required liberal applications of starch and much ironing. As soon as fighting started in earnest a more comfortable and practical outfit was evolved which became increasingly standardised and the differences between officers and men became less pronounced.

Officers wore a tropical version of the khaki service dress which was made of khaki-drill, gabardine or barathea consisting of tunic, shirt and tie, shorts or long trousers which were worn with either khaki socks and shoes or puttees and ankle boots. Mounted personnel wore breeches with either puttees or field boots. The Wolseley-pattern sun helmet was gradually replaced by the steel helmet, peaked cap or field service cap.

On active service all ranks wore the khaki-drill shirt, pullover, shorts or long trousers, while officers in North Africa began to find corduroy trousers and rubber-soled suede 'chukka' boots better suited for wear in the desert.

The rapid changes in temperature which were encountered in the Middle East meant that all ranks had to be equipped with a greatcoat.

INSIGNIA Badges of rank were worn on the shoulder straps by officers, and a slit in the pullover enabled the shoulder straps of the shirt underneath to be worn outside the pullover. Non-commissioned officers wore their rank chevrons in white tape on the shirt and pullover. Formation signs and other corps or regimental insignia were either worn on the shoulder straps or sewn to the sleeves of both the khaki cloth and drill uniforms.

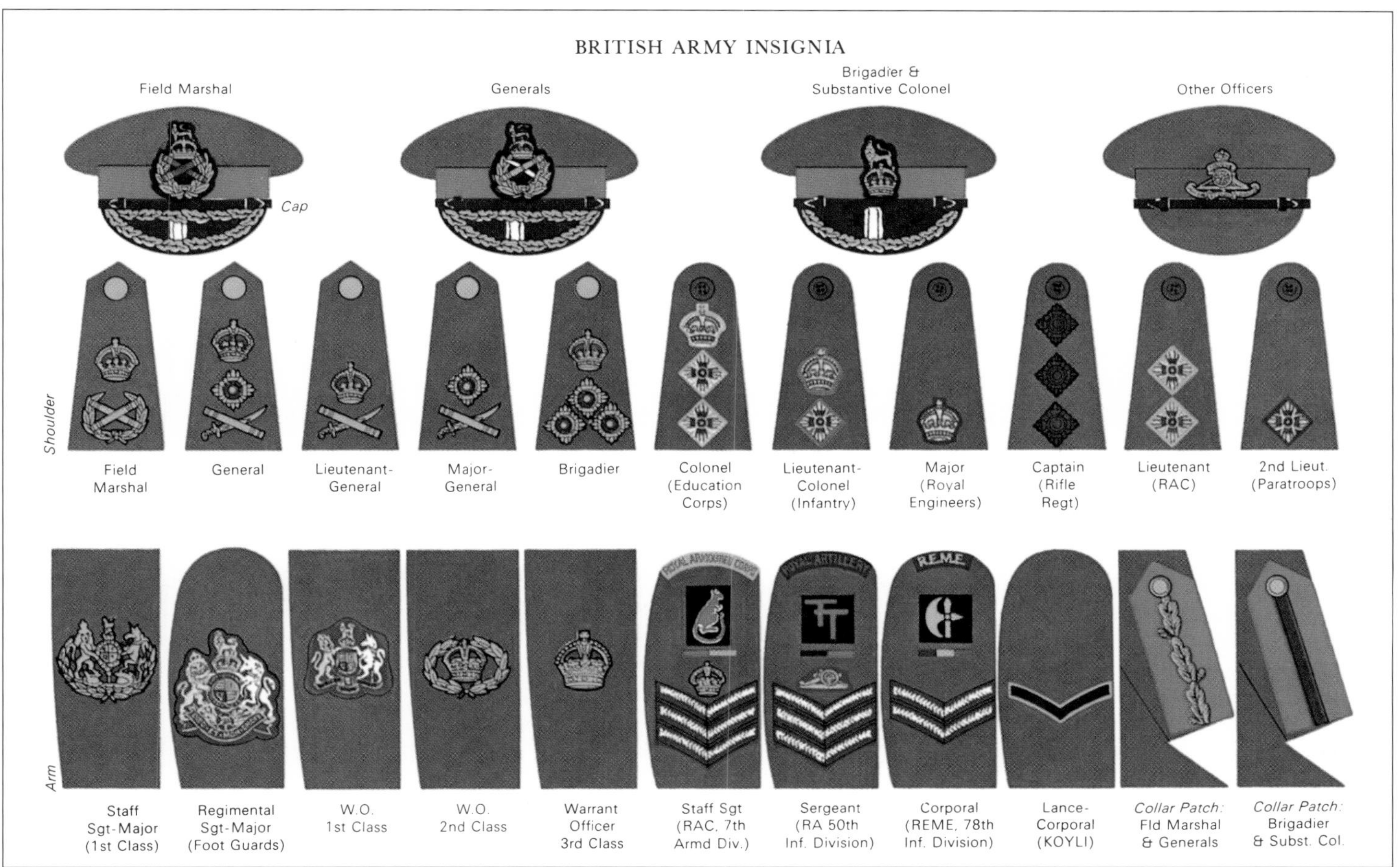

142 Flying Officer, Royal Air Force, 1941
Over his khaki-drill shirt with rank badges on the shoulder straps, this flying officer wears typical flying equipment consisting of flying helmet and goggles while in his hand he holds a radio-telephone jack plug. In front hang the oxygen mask and radio-telephone microphones while behind is the seat-type parachute which was worn by RAF fighter pilots.

AIR FORCE

The responsibilities of the RAF in the Mediterranean theatre were complex and wide-ranging, covering a vast geographical area and calling for action in a variety of different roles ranging from ground support work to strategic bombing. Until 1942 the RAF was often short of aircraft and equipment but following the Axis defeat at El Alamein and the arrival of American forces in North Africa the RAF was able to build up a material superiority that was to play a decisive part in securing victory in the Mediterranean.

ORGANISATION The peacetime responsibilities of the Air Officer Commanding, Middle East, encompassed the air forces in Egypt, Palestine, the Sudan, and Kenya, but in the event of war he was also to control the air element in Aden, Malta and Iraq. This vast Command was subsequently expanded to include Persia and the remainder of the Mediterranean theatre up to 100 miles west of Malta. The period between September 1939 and the Italian declaration of war in June 1940 was used to build up the RAF's capabilities in the Middle East within the limitations imposed by the maintenance of the air defence of Great Britain and by operations in France. Yet when Italy declared war the RAF was still greatly outnumbered by the Regia Aeronautica, with the Middle East Air Force comprising only 29 squadrons many of which were equipped with aircraft approaching obsolescence.

The Middle East Air Force was to operate against the Italians in two main theatres, the Mediterranean, and East Africa and the Red Sea; the first attacks being launched on 11 June 1940. By the end of the year a considerable measure of air superiority had been achieved but a further battlefront was created by the Italian invasion of Greece on 28 October, to which the RAF responded by sending nine squadrons to support the Greek Army.

When the German invasion began in the first week of April 1941 the RAF presence in Greece amounted to two detachments of Wellingtons and nine squadrons, a total of nearly 200 aircraft of which 80 were serviceable. During the campaign these squadrons bombed German communications and troop concentrations in Bulgaria and Yugoslavia, provided fighter protection for Allied units, and defended Athens. In the process they lost 209 aircraft and suffered casualties in pilots and ground crew of 163 men.

After the defeat in Greece a new threat was developing in Syria where German aircraft were using Vichy French airfields as a means of subverting British control of the Middle East. In the bitter campaign which developed as Allied troops advanced into Syria the RAF deployed four understrength or re-equipping squadrons and one flight of Gladiators; a total of approximately 50 front-line aircraft. Support was also provided by the Fleet Air Arm from Cyprus and a squadron from Iraq, and subsequently by seven more squadrons of fighters and bombers.

In the Western Desert the first German aircraft appeared at the close of 1940 and when the Africa Corps launched its offensive at the end of March 1941 the RAF had only four squadrons available for the defence of Cyrenaica. The position improved during April and by the middle of the month the units deployed in the desert under No. 204 Group amounted to six squadrons and two squadron detachments. In addition No. 257 Wing of Wellingtons based in the Canal Zone was available for operations in the desert.

The lull in operations in the Western Desert in the summer and autumn of 1941 was used to reorganise, re-equip, and reinforce RAF Middle East. By July 13,000 additional personnel had arrived, and replacement aircraft brought the number of serviceable aircraft in the Middle East to 520. Free French, Greek, and Yugoslav squadrons were also formed alongside the British and Dominion units, and the tenure of a new Air Officer Commanding-in-Chief began with the appointment of Air Marshal A. W. Tedder on 1 June 1941. By the middle of October Tedder had under his command 52 squadrons with 846 aircraft of which 780 could be classified as modern. Tedder created three new subordinate RAF commands in the Middle East: Air Headquarters Egypt replaced No. 202 Group; Air Headquarters Western Desert was formed from No. 204 Group;

Below: Wing Commander Duncan Smith and (left) Group Captain Bryan Kingcombe after a successful day's operations in Italy in November 1943.

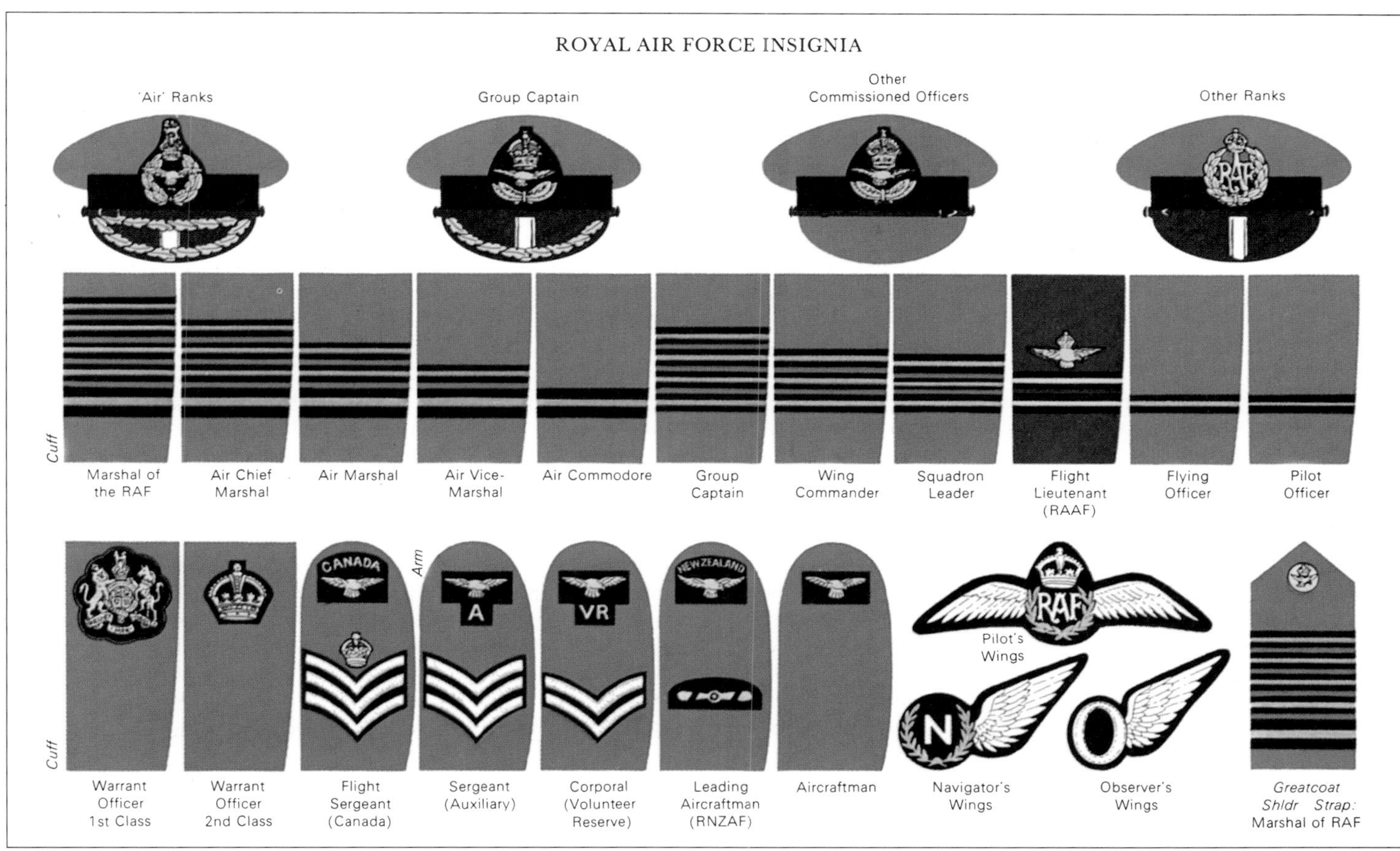

and Headquarters Palestine and Trans-jordan was elevated to control the Levant. The total RAF strength in the Middle East was 57,000 officers and men of whom 7000 were committed to the reinforcement routes and 6500 to signal communications.

By November 1941 the squadron strength of the Western Desert Air Force was just in excess of 27, made up as follows:

14 squadrons of short-range fighters;
2 squadrons of long-range fighters;
8 squadrons of medium bombers;
3 squadrons of tactical reconnaissance aircraft;
1 flight of survey reconnaissance aircraft;
1 flight of strategical reconnaissance aircraft.

Of these squadrons, six were South African, two were Australian, one was Rhodesian, and one Free French. During Operation 'Crusader' the Middle East Air Force fought for and gained air superiority, disrupted the Axis supply network, and assisted in the land battle.

Between February and May 1942 the Axis Air Forces made a determined effort to render Malta useless as an air and sea base. Although a squadron of Spitfires flew in from carriers as reinforcements, the number of serviceable Hurricanes had been reduced to 30 by mid-March, and the majority of the Wellington force was withdrawn from the island. On 20 April 47 Spitfires flew in from the USS *Wasp* but by the evening of the following day only 17 remained in action. A further reinforcement of 62 Spitfires, flown off the *Wasp* and HMS *Eagle* on 9 May, together with the dispersal of German bomber strength to Cyrenaica, Russia, and France, finally marked a turning point in the battle of Malta and the RAF was able to resume offensive operations against Rommel's supply lines.

The RAF was heavily committed during the Battle of Gazala in May and June 1942, and by the middle of July eleven fighter squadrons were at half strength, seven squadrons were still equipped with obsolescent aircraft, and nine squadrons were without any operational aircraft at all.

When the Battle of Alam El Halfa began at the end of August the RAF had 565 aircraft in the Western Desert plus the 165 heavy and medium bombers of No. 205 Group in support. For the loss of 68 aircraft this force harried and bombed the Africa Corps at every opportunity during the week's fighting and their effort contributed significantly to the failure of the German offensive.

The deployment of the US Army Middle East Air Force in October 1942 led to some reorganisation within the Desert Air Force; the 25 British and American fighter squadrons, for example, being divided between two fighter groups, Nos. 211 and 212. The most modern fighters were allocated to No. 211 Group which was known as Force 'A'. Operational control of the American medium day-bombers was also placed in the hands of the Western Desert Air Force. Altogether 96 squadrons totalling 1500 front-line aircraft were assembled in support of the 8th Army for the Battle of El Alamein.

The RAF participation in operation 'Torch' was numerically smaller than that of the USAAF and it was allotted its own sphere of activity, known as Eastern Air Command, to the east of Cape Tenes. To co-ordinate the Allied air effort in North Africa a unified command structure was adopted on 17 February 1943, combining the three major Anglo-American commands – RAF Middle East, RAF Malta, and North-west African Air Forces – as the Mediterranean Air Command.

Mediterranean Air Command disposed of 267 squadrons, of which 121 were British and Commonwealth and 146 American, and for the invasion of Sicily 2510 of the Command's 3462 aircraft were serviceable. During the campaign the Allied Air Forces destroyed 740 enemy aircraft in the air.

On 10 December 1943 the Headquarters of Mediterranean Air Command absorbed that of Northwest African Air Force to become Mediterranean Allied Air Forces. The Tactical, Strategic, and Coastal Air Forces previously under Northwest African command re-emerged as the Mediterranean Allied Tactical Strategic and Coastal Air Forces.

The pattern of air activity which quickly established itself as the remaining Luftwaffe strength was diverted to France and the Eastern Front became almost a routine for the rest of the campaign. Fighters and fighter bombers provided tactical support and reconnaissance, and interdicted secondary road and rail communications. Medium and light bombers attacked supply dumps and primary communication systems while the strategic bombers ranged into Austria, Germany and Romania. By the close of the campaign in Italy the number of aircraft lost by the Mediterranean and Middle East Commands between June 1940 and May 1945 stood at 5735.

Throughout, the Royal Air Force gave assistance to the Partisan groups operating against the Axis in the Balkans.

In March 1944 responsibility for air operations in the Balkans had been transferred from RAF Middle East to the Mediterranean Allied Air Force and in June 1944 the Balkan Air Force was formed. By January 1945 the Air Force consisted of three fighter wings, a bomber wing and a special operations wing.

Royal air force regiment

The possibility of a German invasion of the United Kingdom in 1940 posed a serious threat to the security of the RAF's home airfields. The shortage of manpower had meant that the defence of airfields rested partly with the Army and partly with RAF personnel. This arrangement presented problems of training, fitness, and continuity since Army detachments were frequently changed at short notice. The campaign on Crete in the Spring of 1941 reinforced the need for an adequate local defence of airfields and in February 1942 the Royal Air Force Regiment was formed from the 66,000 personnel serving with airfield defence squadrons.

The normal field squadron consisted of 7 officers and 178 airmen organised as three rifle flights plus support, armoured car, and anti-aircraft flights.

Uniform Tropical dress for Air Force officers at the beginning of the war was similar to that worn in the Army with the exception of a black tie and black leather shoes.

The khaki Wolseley sun helmet had a khaki puggree and a flash in RAF colours on the left side. The tunic was single-breasted and worn open with a khaki shirt and had a matching cloth belt with brass open-frame buckle. Both long and short trousers were worn, the latter with khaki socks. In shirt-sleeve order a light khaki shirt with either long or short sleeves could be worn with an open collar. In the desert campaign a considerable mixture of khaki-drill and grey-blue clothing was worn.

Other ranks also had a formal khaki-drill tunic with brass buttons (later changed to black plastic) khaki shirt, long or short trousers and khaki socks. Sometimes the grey-blue field service cap was worn with RAF badge on the left side, but this was replaced later in the war by a grey-blue beret, particularly in the RAF Regiment. The RAF Regiment served in both the Middle East and in Italy where it received khaki battledress. Badges of rank were worn on the shoulder straps by officers and on the sleeves by non-commissioned officers and airmen. On the khaki-drill uniform the propeller badge for leading aircraftmen was in red, although it soon bleached to almost white.

Below: Officers and ratings of the Fleet Air Arm pose in front of a Swordfish. The distinction between the officers' and ratings' uniform in this order of dress is clearly shown.

Royal navy

The Mediterranean was a traditional focus of British maritime power. In World War II this importance was accentuated after the fall of France in the summer of 1940, because the Mediterranean Sea was now the only theatre left in which British naval and military forces could strike back at the overwhelming strength of the two Axis powers, Germany and Italy.

In 1939 the responsibility for the Mediterranean had been divided between Britain and France but the collapse of France and the loss of her powerful fleet, and Italy's declaration of war on 10 June 1940 placed the Royal Navy in a difficult position.

Out-numbered by the Italian Navy, the British plan was to hold the three decisive strategic points of Gibraltar, Malta and Suez and through them hold open the vital Mediterranean supply routes. Although untennable as a major naval base because of its proximity to Italy, Malta was the linch-pin of the system; a stopping-off point for the convoys and a base from which to attack the Axis supply routes to North Africa.

British planning was expressed on the tactical level by a series of aggressive raids against the Italian Navy. On 11 November 1940, aircraft of the Fleet Air Arm attacked the Italian Fleet at Taranto, crippling three of the five battleships moored there. This success was followed by the Battle of Cape Matapan, a British victory which denied the Axis naval forces control of the central Mediterranean in 1941.

143 144 145

The surrender of the Italian Navy in September 1943 brought in 700 warships and merchantmen and confirmed Allied naval domination of the Mediterranean. Until the end of the war the Royal Navy carried out routine supply duties as well as providing invaluable artillery support to the Allied invasion forces in Italy (especially the hard-pressed beach-head at Anzio) and to the invasion of southern France in August 1944.

ORGANISATION The Mediterranean Fleet in 1939 was under the command of Sir Andrew Cunningham and comprised:
three battleships (*Warspite, Barham, Malaya*);
one aircraft carrier (*Glorious*);
two cruiser squadrons, each of three ships;
four destroyer flotillas, a total of 31 ships;
four escort vessels;
one submarine flotilla of ten submarines;
one motor torpedo-boat flotilla of ten vessels;
one minesweeper flotilla of five ships.

In addition there was a netlayer, a minelayer and a repair ship plus other, smaller auxiliary vessels.

The fleet was based at Alexandria although the facilities there for repair and maintenance were far from satisfactory. Two subsidiary bases at Haifa and Port Said were occasionally used to spread the risk of attack from the air but these were too distant from the central Mediterranean to be of very much use.

In the first year of the war the Mediterranean Fleet suffered a number of reductions including the despatch of the 2nd Destroyer Flotilla (five destroyers) to home waters. Following the Italian declaration of war, however, attempts were made to reinforce the Fleet and in June 1940 Force 'H' was formed, based at Gibraltar and comprising the aircraft carrier *Ark Royal*, two battleships and a small number of cruisers and destroyers.

During the fighting in the Mediterranean in 1941–42, Royal Navy losses were heavy but nonetheless the Mediterranean theatre received regular reinforcements so that by the autumn of 1943 the

143 Lieutenant, Royal Navy, 1943
This submarine commander wears the Navy peaked cap with Army battledress and rank badges on the shoulder straps. Under the battledress blouse (which could be worn open by officers) he wears a typical naval roll neck pullover.

144 Lieutenant, Royal Navy, 1943
This officer wears the rig for land operations in the tropics. His rank and Royal Naval Volunteer Reserve status are displayed on the shoulder straps. Over his khaki-drill jacket he wears the 1937-pattern web equipment. The leather leggings were standard issue for officers wearing landing rig. Royal Navy officers played an important part in supervising amphibious operations.

145 Admiral, Royal Navy, 1943
Admiral Sir John Cunningham, Naval Commander-in-Chief Levant, wears regulation Navy whites. The cap was either made with a white top, or a washable white cover was put over the blue cloth cap. Badges of rank were worn on the shoulder straps. On his left side he wears the Order of the Bath, and below that the Norwegian Royal Order of St Olaf, and the Royal Greek Order of George I. The sword is the regulation M1891 naval officers' sword.

Royal Navy had attained an overwhelming material superiority over the Axis Navies. The Mediterranean Station, which included the old Levant Command, was organised as follows:
1st Battle Squadron – six battleships and two aircraft carriers;
12th Cruiser Squadron – five cruisers;
15th Cruiser Squadron – five cruisers;
six anti-aircraft ships;
four escort carriers;
99 escort vessels (destroyers, sloops, frigates and corvettes);
five destroyer flotillas (27 ships);
Levant Command destroyers (11 ships);
two submarine flotillas (24 vessels);
90 minesweepers;
six motor torpedo-boat flotillas (39 MTBs).
This force was supplemented by an armada of auxiliary vessels and a sizeable detachment of French ships which included two cruisers and seven destroyers.

During the war in the Mediterranean 167 British and Commonwealth warships were lost including one battleship (*Barham*), the two aircraft carriers *Ark Royal* and *Eagle*, 14 cruisers and 50 destroyers.

UNIFORM Before and during the war officers wore the white uniform illustrated by figure 145, although this uniform also included a white sun helmet which was only rarely worn during the war. A similar white uniform was also worn by chief petty officers and petty officers, while miscellaneous junior ratings had the same tunic with black plastic buttons. Ratings wore a white uniform consisting of a hat, shirt, jumper with blue denim collar and long navy-blue trousers with black shoes.

In February 1938 another simpler white uniform for everyday wear had been introduced for all ranks. Officers, chief petty officers and petty officers wore a cap with white cover or sun helmet, white shirt worn open at the neck, white shorts, white socks and canvas shoes. Miscellaneous junior ratings wore this uniform with black socks and shoes, while seamen wore a white shirt with blue dungaree binding around the collar which was usually worn under a jumper.

During the war the Royal Navy also adopted khaki-drill, and in 1941 khaki battledress which was worn with naval head-dress. Royal Marines also had a khaki-drill uniform which was basically the same as that worn in the Army, although long trousers were worn with long puttees. A distinctive feature of Royal Marine uniform was the fabric belt in the corps colours.

INSIGNIA Badges of rank were worn on the shoulder straps and sometimes painted on the steel helmet. Chief petty officers and petty officers wore their particular cap badge, and chief petty officers retained the three buttons on the cuffs of the white tunic. Other ratings wore their rank badges on the left sleeve. Royal Marines wore their rank badges in the Army style on the shoulder straps. Officers in the civil branches of the Royal Navy wore coloured backing or 'lights' to the rank lace on the shoulder straps, while cadets and midshipmen had a strip of the same coloured cloth on their shoulder straps. Chief petty officers and petty officers and seamen wore their branch badges on the collar or on the right sleeve.

Officers in the Fleet Air Arm wore the letter 'A' within the curl on the shoulder straps.

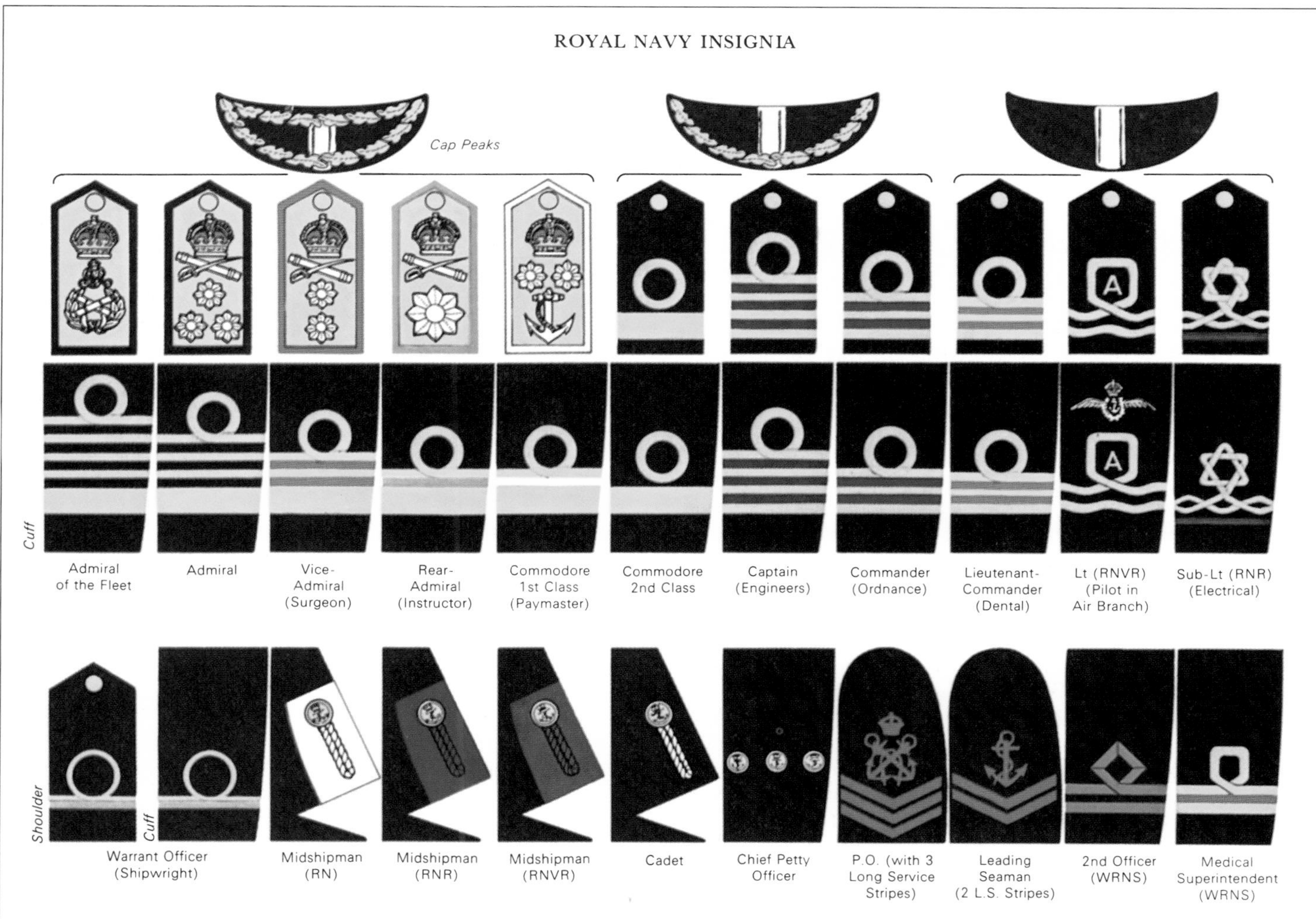

146 Sergeant, Indian Army, 1940
The helmet of this sergeant is covered in sacking which acted both as camouflage and as a cloth which could be used to shield the face from sand storms. The shirt and shorts in khaki-drill are the standard British pattern but the equipment is a combination of the 1908-pattern web and Indian leather. In his right hand the sergeant carries two 'Molotov cocktails' and in his left two No. 36 grenades.

147 Corporal, Indian Army, 1940
This Naik *of the 6th Rajputana Rifles in North Africa wears standard Indian Army dress with distinctive puggree bearing the regimental badge. Under the pullover he wears the typical collarless shirt which was usually manufactured in grey material. The belt and pouches are Indian pattern as is the bayonet which had a shorter blade than its English counterpart.*

146

147

British Empire Forces

The forces of the British Empire were, of course, mobilised as part of the British war effort. They represented a significant part of Britain's strength – especially the Indian Army.

Indian Army

The Indian Army had rather an anomalous position in that it could not be considered a colonial force, but it had a position very different to that of the Dominion armies. This unique status was reflected in the composition of the Indian brigades, in which one British battalion served alongside two Indian battalions. Brigade field artillery was normally British, but signals, service and ordnance units were Indian. Although the senior officers were British, the lower officers were a mix of Indians and British.

Units of the Army had begun to move to strategic points of the Empire before war was declared. On 3 August 1939 the 11th Indian Infantry Brigade (2nd Battalion Queen's Own Cameron Highlanders, 1st Battalion 6th Rajputana Rifles, and 4th Battalion 7th Rajput Regiment) left India for Egypt. It was followed on 23 September by the 5th Indian Brigade and a Divisional Headquarters and both brigades became part of the 4th Indian Infantry Division. The 1st Battalion 2nd Punjab Regiment and the 3rd Battalion 15th Punjab Regiment went to Aden while a mountain battery was sent to East Africa.

In August 1940 the Government of India offered to provide an additional four infantry divisions and one armoured division for overseas service if the United Kingdom was able to supply the necessary equipment. The infantry divisions were accepted but the shortage of available tanks prevented the use of the armoured division at this stage.

On 25 August 1941 the 8th Indian Division (18th and 24th Brigades) and the 10th Division (21st and 25th Brigades) together with the 2nd Indian Armoured Brigade moved into Persia to forestall the considerable German fifth column in that country. The advance involved only minimal casualties for the participants, Persian, British and Indian, and on 30 August contact was made with the 'co-operating' Russian forces at Senna. By the end of August there were seven Indian infantry brigades, a machine-gun battalion, and an armoured brigade deployed in Iraq, Syria and Persia. The 4th and 5th Divisions were in the Near East, and in September and October the 6th Indian Division arrived at Basra from where it relieved the 8th and 10th Divisions in Persia. The 5th Division then went to Cyprus, the 8th went to Kirkuk and the 10th to Habbaniya. The 6th Division was to remain in garrison in Persia for the remainder of the war.

At the beginning of April 1942 the Brigades of the 4th Division were redeployed, the 7th going to Cyprus, the 11th to the Canal Zone, and the 5th to the Syrian frontier. Their place in the Western Desert was taken by the 5th and 10th Indian Divisions the latter arriving at Halfaya Pass early in June. Both divisions had little desert experience but their troops fought effective rearguard actions at El Adem, Sollum-Halfaya, and Mersa Matruh as the British and Empire forces fell back to Alamein. In the fighting which brought the Axis forces to a standstill in July the 5th Indian Division suffered 3000 casualties but took 7000 enemy prisoners.

The casualties suffered by the Indian divisions in North Africa numbered 15,248 of whom 1299 were killed, 3738 wounded, 419 posted missing, and 9792 were prisoners of war.

The 4th and 10th Indian Divisions were involved in the fighting during the campaigns in Italy, and soldiers of the 4th played a prominent part in the battle of Monte Cassino, where it suffered 3000 casualties.

Uniform During the late 1930s Indian officers began to replace the old service dress tunic (with its stiff high collar and five buttons) with the new open pattern as worn in the British Army. Both patterns were worn by dismounted officers with plus-fours, puttees and brown ankle boots, or by mounted officers with cord breeches and either ankle boots and leather gaiters or brown leather field boots. Head-dress for Indians was the puggree which in peacetime had been an elaborate and colourful affair, but which in wartime was usually khaki. It was possible to tell from the shape of the puggree the wearer's religion and caste.

The first Indian troops to arrive in England were the animal companies of the Royal Indian Army Service Corps whose personnel wore either the puggree or the field service cap. Some soldiers wore the service dress tunic while others retained the long khaki *kurta*.

In the Middle East the Indians wore the same simple and practical uniform as worn in India. Head-dress was the puggree, British Mk 1 steel helmet, or field service cap. Over the collarless silver grey or cellular khaki shirt was worn a pullover together with either khaki drill shorts or long trousers. This uniform is illustrated in figure 147.

In Italy in the winter Indian troops received British uniform in its entirety. The uniforms worn by the 6th Duke of Connaught's Own Lancers (Watson's Horse) are a fairly typical example. At first khaki dungarees were worn with web belt, holster for .38 pistol and braces which crossed at the back; these were useful for hauling wounded crewmen out of armoured vehicles. In winter, British battle dress with the divisional sign on both sleeves, leather jerkin, woollen gloves and gum boots were the most usual wear.

Equipment was generally worn under the jerkin although the cloth ammunition bandolier was worn over it. In summer berets with the badge over the left eye, shirts, shorts, hose tops and anklets and ankle boots were general. The regimental shoulder title was often removed for security reasons and its place was taken by a strip of cloth in regimental colours.

British officers wore British Army rank badges while Indian officers commissioned by the Viceroy wore the same rank badges on the shoulder straps but with a piece of braid running across the shoulder strap under each pip and crown.

Africa

African Colonial troops had proved their value to the defence of Britain's overseas possessions during the First World War, being responsible for the conquest of the German West African Colonies of the Cameroons and Togoland and playing a large part in the campaign against Tanganyika. In 1939 the major African units, comprising native troops with European officers and a number of European NCOs, were the King's African Rifles, the Royal West African Frontier Force and the Somaliland Camel Corps.

148 Lance-corporal, Indian Army, 1944
*By the time winter came to Italy in 1943 most Indian troops had received British uniform and protective clothing. This Lance-*Naik *of the Royal Gurkha Rifles wears battledress with dark rifle-green rank chevrons under the formation sign of the 8th Indian Division. The sub-machine gun is the US M1928 Thompson. Hanging at the back of the belt is the* kukri, *a traditional Gurkha close-combat weapon.*

149 Private, Royal West African Frontier Force, 1943
The uniform is typical of that worn by African troops such as those serving in the King's African Rifles. The regimental title is worn on a slide on the shoulder straps. Equipment is the British 1937-pattern web equipment and the rifle is the British .303 rifle.

Left Above: An officer of the 6th Rajputana Rifles scans the horizon. The Indian forces were noted for their smartness and efficiency – very obvious here.

Left Below: Two different styles of puggree, as worn by a Sikh of the 13th Frontier Force Regiment and a Dogra (left) of the 12th Frontier Force Regiment.

THE KING'S AFRICAN RIFLES

In peace the King's African Rifles comprised two infantry brigades recruited in Kenya, Uganda, Tanganyika, Zanzibar and Nyasaland. The officers and senior NCOs were seconded for service from their British regiments and the proportion of Africans to Europeans in a battalion was approximately 16:1. Just before the war in 1938 the strength of its two brigades (Northern and Southern) amounted to a combined total of only 94 officers, 60 British NCOs and 2821 African other ranks. After the outbreak of war, however, this force provided the trained nucleus for a rapid expansion of the KAR and there was no shortage of potential recruits. On 9 October 1939 the Regimental strength had increased to 517 officers 1020 British other ranks, and 11,091 Africans, and by March 1940 the totals had reached 883, 1374 and 20,026 respectively. The establishment of a KAR battalion was 36 officers, 44 British NCOs and other ranks, and 1050 African other ranks.

Initially the regiment deployed as 1st East African Infantry Brigade and 2nd Infantry Brigade, the former being responsible for coastal defence and the latter for the defence of the interior. At the end of July 1940 two further brigades, the 5th and 6th were formed, and the establishment of two divisions was planned; a Coastal Division and a Northern Frontier District Division. The divisions were redesignated as the 11th and 12th (African) Divisions and during operations against the Italian Empire in East Africa they were reinforced by South African infantry and supporting units.

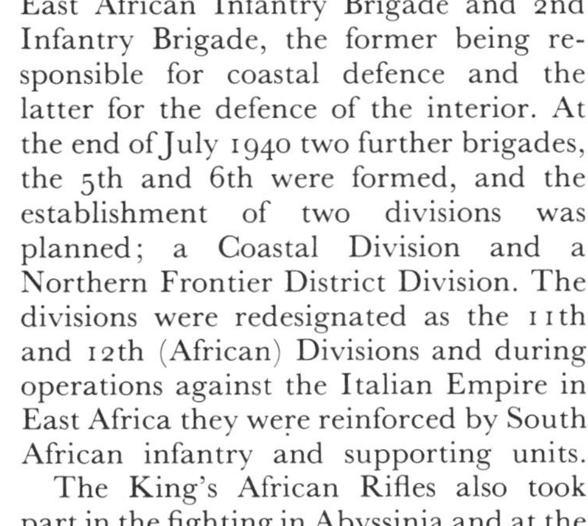

The King's African Rifles also took part in the fighting in Abyssinia and at the conclusion of operations in East Africa the Regiment's strength stood at 28 battalions.

THE ROYAL WEST AFRICAN FRONTIER FORCE

In 1939 the West African Frontier Force, originally raised in 1901, comprised the Nigerian Regiment, the Sierra Leone Battalion, the Gambia Company, and the Gold Coast Regiment. Under the terms of war contingency plans both Nigeria and the Gold Coast were to provide brigade groups for service in East Africa. The brigades were established in Kenya by July 1940 and together with East African brigades they formed the 11th and 12th (African) Divisions. They served in the campaign in East Africa until the completion of operations in Galla-Sidamo, the Nigerian Brigade returning to West Africa in August 1941 and the Gold Coast Brigade in October. On their return the formations were re-designated as the 1st and 2nd (West African) Brigade Groups as part of the expansion of West African forces to a strength of three brigade groups in Nigeria, one brigade group in the Gold Coast, and one battalion in both Sierra Leone and Gambia.

THE SOMALILAND CAMEL CORPS

In September 1939 the Somaliland Camel Corps comprised a Headquarters Company, two camel companies, one infantry company, and a company of reservists. Their total strength was 14 British officers, 1 British NCO and 554 Non-European other ranks, and initially they came under the command of the garrison of French Somaliland. The corps fought alongside units of the King's African Rifles and the Northern Rhodesia Regiment in the defence of British Somaliland, but with the final withdrawal most of the Somali troops were disbanded. Two Somali infantry battalions were, however, raised in September 1942 and January 1943 and

148

149

in May they were formed as 71st (Som) KAR and 72nd (Som) KAR.

UNIFORM The KAR gave up their smart red fezzes and *zouave* jackets for the slouch hat and standard khaki-drill uniform. The various battalions were identified by a colour which appeared as backing to the rank chevrons, proficiency badges and in the sash or cummerbund which was worn around the waist, although this was worn less during the war. All ranks wore the shoulder title KAR.

Just before the outbreak of war the uniform of the RWAFF was simplified and the old Kilmarnock cap was replaced by the slouch hat, and the native *chaplis* or sandals by British Army ammunition boots. The rest of the uniform for other ranks is as illustrated in figure 149. Officers wore khaki-drill with either slouch hat or sun helmet.

The Somaliland Camel Corps also had a distinctive dress which was based on the standard British Army khaki drill but which included a knitted woollen pullover with drill patches on the shoulders. Shorts were worn with woollen socks or puttees and *chaplis*, boots or bare feet. Equipment consisted of a leather ammunition bandolier and leather waist belt. Officers wore the sun helmet and khaki-drill uniform. Other ranks wore a *kullah* with puggree which ended in a long tail which hung down the back.

SOUTHERN RHODESIA

In 1939 the Permanent Staff Corps of the Rhodesian armed forces numbered only 47 officers and men but the nation's police force, the British South Africa Police, had long served as a first line of defence and it was thoroughly trained for a military role. During the Second World War Rhodesia provided more troops per capita than any other Commonwealth country and of the 10,000 white Rhodesians available for active service 6500 served overseas. 1730 black Rhodesians also served outside Rhodesia and total enlistments during the war stood at 15,000 African troops and 11,000 Europeans and mixed race personnel.

Rhodesian artillery units served throughout the Middle East and in May 1940 the decision was taken to raise the Rhodesian African rifles as an *askari* regiment with white officers. The 2409 Rhodesians who joined the Southern Rhodesia Air Force were absorbed into the RAF and three squadrons carried the designation 'Rhodesia': No. 44 of Bomber Command, and Nos. 237 and 266 of Fighter Command.

TRANSJORDAN FORCES

In 1921 Emir Abdulla, the ruler of the newly created territory of Transjordan, raised an armed force of 1000 men which from 1923 became known as 'The Arab Legion'. By the start of the Second World War half the Legion's total strength of 1600 officers and men could be designated as combat units, and at General Wavell's request this element was expanded to seven permanent battalions of about 350 men each. These battalions were then used throughout the Middle East as garrison units protecting vital installations. The Desert Force was also expanded from one mechanised regiment to a brigade of three regiments.

150 Corporal, Transjordanian Frontier Force, 1940
The traditional Arab head-dress of this corporal is in two parts: the cloth itself was called a kafiyeh *and the cord which held it on the head a* jagal. *The grey shirt and black puttees underline the basic 'police' function of this* gendarmerie *type unit. The weapon is the British Bren gun, with its spare magazines carried in special pouches.*

150

Whereas the Arab Legion was responsible to its own Government, the Transjordan Frontier Force was controlled by the High Commission for Palestine and ultimately came under the command of the British War Office. It was raised at the end of March 1926 as four mounted squadrons. Units of the force served against Vichy troops in Syria.

UNIFORM The basic uniform of the Arab Legion was British battledress in serge for winter or khaki-drill for summer wear. Officers had both a khaki cloth and light khaki-drill service dress with which they wore a blue field service cap piped in scarlet and black leather Sam Browne and shoes.

Bedu serving in the Desert Police and later Desert Mechanised Force wore a military version of their national dress. On the head was worn the red and white *shemagh* which was held in place by a black *jagal* on which was pinned the Arab Legion badge in white metal. The main garment was a long khaki *jelabiyah* or *dishdash* which came in serge for winter and khaki drill for summer wear. Around the waist a narrow belt was worn from which was hung a personal dagger and regulation pistol in holster. Ammunition was carried in red leather bandoliers worn over both shoulders so that they crossed and were fastened to another ammunition belt worn around the waist. Another distinctive feature of this colourful uniform was a complicated red cord combined with a pistol lanyard.

Officers wore their rank badges in white metal on the shoulder straps in the British manner while non-commissioned officers wore white tape chevrons. On leaving cadet school subalterns served a three year probationary period during which time they wore a silver bar on the shoulder straps.

Within the Legion battalions and, later, regiments were identified by coloured cloth slides on the shoulder straps. Pinned to the slide was a metal shoulder title with the inscription *'Al Jeish el Arabi'* (Arab Army) in Arabic script.

MALTESE FORCES

Maltese regiments had been an integral part of the British Army since the nineteenth century and on the outbreak of hostilities in 1939 they again took their place in the Empire's order of battle. The traditional role of the Royal Malta Artillery was coast defence but in the years before the Second World War increasing emphasis had been placed upon anti-aircraft defence so that by 1942 the RMA had a strength of $5\frac{1}{2}$ regiments.

In 1931 the decision was taken to expand the cadre company of the King's Own Malta Regiment to battalion strength with an establishment of four infantry companies, each of four platoons of 30 other ranks, a headquarters wing and machine-gun platoon. By 1935 the Battalion had achieved its full strength of 22 British and Maltese officers and 610 other ranks and on 26 August 1939 it was mobilised for the defence of north-west Malta. The introduction of conscription on Malta meant that a further three battalions were raised. The Maltese land forces wore British uniform and equipment and made a valuable contribution to the defence of their island.

PALESTINIAN FORCES

In 1939 the Jewish Agency in Palestine requested the formation of Jewish units within the British Army and permission was given for enlistments in either the Pioneer Corps or the Royal Army Service Corps on a one to one basis with Palestinian Arab volunteers. As a result the 601st to 609th companies of the Pioneer Corps were formed and a total of 1200 men were provided to man a mule train of the RASC. With the exception of companies 601 and 609 the pioneers were captured or dispersed during the campaign in Greece, but seven new Jewish transport units were raised in the RASC, and nine companies were raised for prisoner of war guard duties as part of the East Kent Regiment. 3500 Jewesses joined the Auxiliary Territorial Service and 500 joined the Women's Auxiliary Air Force.

The Headquarters of the Jewish Infantry Brigade Group was formed in Egypt on 28 September 1944 and the 1st, 2nd, and 3rd Palestine Rifles together with the 1st Palestine Light Anti-Aircraft Battery came under its command.

The Brigade was attached to 15th Army Group in Italy on 5 November 1944 serving with the 8th Indian Infantry Division in March 1945 and with 10th Corps in April and May. It fought in the battle for Bologna between 14–21 April and remained in the Italian Theatre until 27 July when it was transferred to the 21st Army Group in North-West Europe. The Brigade remained in Europe serving on the lines of communication of 21st Army Group until the end of August 1945.

UNIFORM All units raised in Palestine were given a sky-blue nationality title with 'Palestine' in white. The Palestinian Regiment had a brass cap badge which was so similar to a coin then in current circulation that the regiment soon became known as the Five Piastre Regiment.

151 Private, Australian Army, 1941
This infantryman from the 7th Australian Division in Syria wears British khaki-drill with the famous slouch hat bearing the Australian general service badge. The canvas anklets were unique to Australian troops. The 1937 pattern web equipment is worn with 1897-pattern bayonet and the rifle is the standard British .303. The Australian Army was armed mainly from British and US sources.

152 Private, Australian Army, 1940
The tunic worn by this private in the 2nd Company of the 6th Infantry Battalion was cut like a bushjacket with sleeves which could be fastened at the cuffs like a shirt. On the side of the slouch hat and on the collar he wears the Australian general service badge in bronzed metal, while on the sleeves he wears a formation sign which was the same as that worn in World War I but with a grey frame. Equipment is the 1908 web with gas mask and 1907-pattern sword bayonet. The mess tin was originally introduced in the latter part of the last century for dismounted personnel but was still being issued during World War II.

DOMINION FORCES

The Dominions of Australia, New Zealand, South Africa and Canada all sent troops to the Mediterranean theatre, where they fought alongside the armed forces of Great Britain.

AUSTRALIAN ARMY

Australian servicemen fought in North Africa and the Mediterranean theatre throughout 1941 and 1942. They proved some of the toughest soldiers on the Allied side, and were greatly respected by the Germans.

Seven RAAF squadrons (although only three – Nos. 3, 450 and 451 – were totally Australian), one cruiser and some smaller naval units fought in the Mediterranean theatre, but the main formations involved were the 6th, 7th and 9th Divisions. The 6th Division took part in the Allied offensive of January-February

1941, and Australians of the 9th Division played a crucial role in the defence of Tobruk from February to October 1941. During the siege, this division suffered casualties of 749 killed, 1996 wounded and 604 prisoners. Meanwhile, the 7th Division took part in the occupation of Syria, suffering 1600 casualties. The 6th Division was in Greece during April 1941, and its 2nd Brigade was on Crete when the Germans landed. Losses were 594 killed, 1001 wounded and 5109 captured during the Greek and Cretan campaigns.

The 6th and 7th Divisions were moved to the Far East when Japan declared war, but the 9th remained in Egypt, and its infantry played an important role in the battle of attrition at Alamein in October 1942. In the Alamein operations the division lost 1225 dead, 3638 wounded and 946 taken prisoner. In February 1943 it returned to Australia.

ORGANISATION In September 1939 Australia's regular forces comprised 3000 men and a staff corps. The Volunteer Militia had been expanded to 80,000 partly trained men but they were committed only to service at home. In 1914 Great Britain's declaration of war had been binding upon the whole Empire. This was not the case in 1939 and Australia in common with the other Dominions was free to make its own decision for peace or war. Both New Zealand and Australia declared war on the 3rd September, but Australia's decision on her contribution to the Empire's war effort was complicated by doubts concerning Japan's intentions. Japanese hostility would prevent the dispatch of an expeditionary force overseas and limit Australia's military options to the defence of her own shores, the Western Pacific and Singapore. The Australian Government accepted the opinion of its Intelligence staff that Japan would not attack in the Pacific unless the Allies were defeated in Europe and ordered the raising of a 'special force' of 20,000 men for service at home or abroad. At the same time the Militia was mobilised for training in two drafts of 40,000 men.

The 'special force' was soon designated the 6th Division, there already being five infantry divisions in the process of formation in the Militia. Its recruits were largely untrained as only 5000 men had volunteered from the Militia, but they were fit, eager to learn and young (the age limits for enlisted men were 20 to 35). The division's initial infantry establishwas three brigades each of four battalions. Although the division's manpower establishment was soon complete the provision of equipment was a major problem. Each battalion, for example, required ten machine-gun carriers, the 18 pounders and 4.5 inch howitzers of the field artillery regiments were to be replaced by the new 25 pounder gun-howitzer, and a mechanised reconnaissance regiment was to be formed with 28 light tanks and 44 machine-gun carriers.

The defeat of the Allies in France led to a surge of recruits in Australia and although the Government had authorised

153

Below: Australian NCOs, unmistakeable in slouch hats. They are wearing unit signs on the arm.

153 Private, Australian Army, 1941
Looking much like his British counterparts, this Australian infantryman in Bardia in January 1941 is dressed and equipped as a British 'Tommy', except for the anklets which are Australian. The greatcoat is the old single-breasted model. Equipment is the 1937-pattern web with additional ammunition carried in cloth bandoliers. The rifle is the .303 SMLE No. 1 Mk III.

154 Private, New Zealand Army, 1940
This private in a Maori Infantry Battalion wears the old-pattern khaki service dress with 'lemon squeezer' hat, general service cap badge and red infantry puggree. The battalion is identified by a coloured flash on the sleeves. The equipment is the 1908-pattern web and the rifle the British .303.

155 Gunner, New Zealand Artillery, 1940
On arrival in Egypt, New Zealanders were issued with British khaki-drill uniforms but retained the slouch hat with coloured puggree. The equipment is the 1908-pattern web with gas mask in the ready position.

a corps of three divisions (6th, 7th, 8th) with an establishment of 65,000 men it already had well over 100,000 volunteers. Recruiting was discontinued in September 1940 and it was decided to form a further division (9th) using men under training and the Australian troops already in Britain. By spring 1941, there were three divisions in the Middle East: the 6th (16th, 17th and 19th Brigades); the 7th (18th, 21st and 25th Brigades), and the 9th (20th, 24th and 26th Brigades). In all, there were 108,156 Australians under arms.

Uniform The basic service dress for other ranks is illustrated in figure 151, while officers wore the same khaki service dress as British officers, with either the slouch (or 'wide awake') hat or the peaked cap. Buttons and badges were usually in bronzed metal.

Because the issue khaki uniform was made of a lighter quality cloth than the British model it tended to be more suitable for wear in the desert but even so it was soon replaced by both British khaki drill and serge uniforms. Badges of rank were the same as those worn in the British Army.

Arm-of-service badges as such did not exist although units could be identified by a flash in the arm-of-service colour on the sleeves. The geometric shape of the flash was different for headquarters, divisions, brigades and services.

154

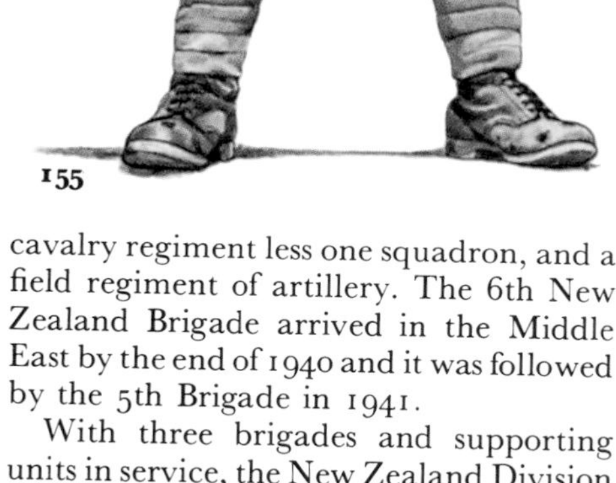

155

New Zealand army

New Zealand declared war on Germany on 3 September and by February 1940, the first New Zealand troops had reached the Middle East. New Zealand formations took part in Wavell's offensive, and the New Zealand Division came into being in Greece in 1941. The New Zealand Division proved well adapted to mobile desert warfare and its men played an important part in the 'Crusader' offensive of November 1941 and in the battles of 1942. By the end of the campaign in North Africa the division had suffered a total of 21,496 casualties, and out of a total (in February 1942) of 43,800 men sent to the Middle East, this was a very high proportion.

The New Zealanders came to Italy with a great reputation, and distinguished themselves in fighting across the Sangro and at Orsogna. After the hard, bloody struggle at Cassino they fought in the advance to Florence and in the battle for Rimini. When the war ended they had reached Trieste. During the war in Italy the New Zealand forces suffered 8668 casualties.

Organisation In 1930 compulsory military service had been suspended in New Zealand, and in 1939 the Army consisted of 10,364 voluntary territorials, 374 men in a Special Reserve and a Regular Force 578 strong. Conscription was introduced in 1940, and by May there were 19,423 troops under arms. These troops soon began to be deployed abroad.

The 4th New Zealand Infantry Brigade, the first echelon, 6529 strong, of the 2nd New Zealand Division bound for the Middle East, arrived at Suez on 12 February 1940. The Brigade was based on three infantry battalions, the 18th, 19th, and 20th, so numbered because 17 New Zealand battalions took part in the First World War. The Division's second echelon consisting of the 5th New Zealand Brigade and attached troops was diverted to Britain while en route for Egypt in June 1940. When hostilities began against Italy the New Zealand presence in the Middle East comprised an infantry brigade, a machine-gun battalion, a cavalry regiment less one squadron, and a field regiment of artillery. The 6th New Zealand Brigade arrived in the Middle East by the end of 1940 and it was followed by the 5th Brigade in 1941.

With three brigades and supporting units in service, the New Zealand Division was formed for the Greek campaign. At the end of the campaign the 4th and 5th Brigade Groups were evacuated to Crete while the 6th Brigade was landed at Alexandria. Approximately 7700 New Zealand troops took part in the defence of Crete organised in the 4th and 5th Brigades and an improvised formation, the 10th Brigade. They suffered casualties of 671 killed, 967 wounded, and 2180 taken prisoner.

During the fighting in 1941 and 1942 the division also suffered severly, and during the battles of the summer of 1942 it was reduced to two brigades.

In early summer 1943, the New Zealand Division began a four month period of rest and recovery aided by a home furlough scheme for its first echelons and the issue of new equipment. The 4th Infantry Brigade which had been withdrawn after suffering heavy casualties at Ruweisat Ridge in July 1942 now rejoined the Division as the 4th New Zealand Armoured Brigade (18th, 19th and 20th Armoured Regiments, 22nd Motorised Battalion). The 2nd Division thus comprised a divisional cavalry regiment, two infantry brigades (5th and 6th), one armoured brigade, plus artillery and supporting troops. After a period of re-training the New Zealanders sailed for Taranto, the first group of 5827 all ranks arriving on 9 October 1943, the second of 8707 nine days later.

During the first actions in Italy the established strength of the New Zealand Army units in Italy was over 19,000 and that of the seven infantry battalions (5th Brigade: 21st, 23rd, and 28th Battalions; 6th Brigade: 24th, 25th, and 26th Battalions; 4th Armoured Brigade: 22nd Motor Battalion) around 5200. Of this latter figure only about 3000 could be classified as assault troops so that in effect the fighting core of the Division comprised only one-sixth of its total strength. This was a not uncommon situation in both Allied and Axis divisions but during the Sangro-Orsogna fighting the New Zealanders suffered 1600 casualties of which 1200 were amongst the infantry battalions.

On 3 February 1944 a New Zealand Corps was formed consisting of 2nd New Zealand Division and 4th Indian Division with the addition of the 78th British Division on 18 February.

The battle order of the 2nd New Zealand Division, with one armoured and two infantry brigades, although suited to the open, fluid warfare of the Western Desert created difficulties of deployment in the slow, confined fighting experienced in Italy. There were just too few infantry to keep the cutting edge of the Division at full strength and efficiency. In most set-piece battles the 22nd Motor Battalion therefore found itself fighting in the line side by side with the infantry battalions. The problem was eased somewhat in the winter of 1944–45 by the expedient of increasing the number of infantry battalions in each brigade from three to four.

The total casualties incurred in the Middle East and Mediterranean between 1939 and 1946 by the New Zealand Expeditionary Force were 28,840: 5363 killed, 15,108 wounded and 8369 taken prisoner.

UNIFORM The first New Zealand troops to arrive in England in 1940 wore the khaki service dress illustrated in figure 154. The officers' version of the service dress tunic was worn open with a collar and tie.

On arrival in the Middle East, British Army tropical and temperate uniforms were introduced and gradually even the 'lemon squeezer' hat gave way to the beret or field service cap.

Badges of rank were identical to the British pattern, and arm-of-service badges included the cap badge and collar 'dogs' which identified corps or regiment, while the colour of the puggree on the slouch hat was in the arm-of-service colour.

Below: South Africans at Sollum in January 1942, equipped in the standard British manner.

SOUTH AFRICAN ARMY

South African forces campaigned in three major areas: East Africa, North Africa and Italy. They played a major role in the defeat of the Italian forces in Ethiopia and the 1st and 2nd South African Divisions, although understrength, fought during 1941 in North Africa. The surrender of Tobruk on 21 June 1942 was, however, a severe blow: 9780 South Africans of the 2nd Division – one-third of the South African forces in the field – were captured. On 12 November 1942 the 1st South African Division returned home, but from April 1944, the 6th South African Armoured Division fought in Italy.

ORGANISATION When South Africa declared war on Germany on 6 September 1939 the forces available for mobilisation included 3350 men of the Permanent Force, 14,631 volunteers of the Active Citizen Force, and the 122,000 citizens enrolled in the Commandos and Defence Rifle Associations. The Union had no armoured fighting units and there were only 71 field-guns and howitzers in service. The Government's objective was the creation of two main formations, a Home Defence Force, and a Mobile Field Force comprising a General Headquarters, two Active Citizen Force Divisions and supporting troops.

The first South African Army unit to reach Kenya arrived at Mombassa on 1 June 1940, to be followed by the 1st South African Infantry Brigade Group towards the end of July. On 13 August the 1st South African Division (1st, 2nd, and 5th Infantry Brigade Groups) was formed on the basis of an establishment of 37,593 men of whom 33,070 would be Europeans. By the end of the year 27,000 South Africans were serving in East Africa in the 1st Division or as part of the 11th and 12th African Divisions. Each South African Infantry Brigade Group consisted of three rifle battalions, an armoured car company, and supporting signal, engineer and medical units. The 1st Battalion of the South African Tank Corps had been established on 29 May 1940 using armoured cars.

As 1941 began South Africa could, on paper, call upon four divisions – the 1st in Kenya; the 2nd (3rd, 4th, and

156 Private, South African Army, 1940

This private of the Kimberley Regiment wears the 'polo-pattern' helmet with regimental flash on the side. The khaki drill jacket and long trousers were standard issue at the beginning of the war, while the short anklets replaced the long ones on mobilisation in 1940. The web equipment is the 1937-pattern and the rifle is the standard .303 SMLE No. 1 Mk. III.

157 Lieutenant, South African Air Force, 1942

This fighter pilot wears the characteristic South African sun helmet with SAAF cap badge and flash on the side. The rest of the uniform is basic khaki drill with 'wings' on the left breast and orange flash (for South African troops) on the shoulder straps, which bear the rank badges. Since the SAF formed part of the Army its personnel wore Army uniforms, although South Africans in the RAF wore the grey-blue uniform.

6th Infantry Brigades) and 3rd Divisions (7th, 8th, and 9th Infantry Brigades) which had been formed on 23 October 1940; and the 1st Mounted Commando Division.

The Headquarters of the 1st Division together with the 5th Infantry Brigade disembarked at Suez on 3 May 1941, and then moved to Mersa Matruh where they were joined on 12 June by the 2nd Infantry Brigade and at the beginning of July by the 1st Brigade. Manpower still posed a problem for the South African Divisions and the current Establishment Table of 24,108 officers and men, of whom only 13,073 were Europeans, reflected their growing dependence on non-European personnel in the service echelons. Of the 954 officers and men of each infantry battalion 249 were non-Europeans.

The 2nd Division (3rd, 4th and 6th Infantry Brigades) had begun to concentrate in Egypt at the end of June and it moved to El Alamein in the last week of July to construct defensive positions. The Division was short of half its transport and was also understrength; and when 2081 non-Europeans arrived as reinforcements they were re-routed to the equally undermanned 1st Division. On 5th October 1941 the 2nd Division came under the command of the 8th Army and units of both the 1st and 2nd Divisions took part in the Crusader offensive.

At the end of 1941 South Africa's land forces numbered, on paper, 198,036 other ranks of all races and 11,679 officers.

The troops serving in the two divisions represented less than half of the total of South African land forces in the Middle East which stood at 67,855. The 4th and 6th South African Armoured Car Regiments, for example, were serving with the British 7th Armoured and 50th Divisions.

After the Battle of Alam el Halfa the South Africans entered a period of re-fitting, reorganisation, and training.

On 1 February 1943 the 6th South African Armoured Division was formed. In April 1944 the division, comprising Headquarters, 11th Armoured Brigade, 12th Motorised Brigade, and divisional troops, began disembarkation at Taranto. The 12th Motorised Brigade served with the New Zealand Division during May and on the 20th of that month the 24th Guards Brigade (5th Grenadier Guards, 3rd Coldstream Guards, 1st Scots Guards) came under South African command. It was to fight with the South Africans until February 1945 and as a result of this addition of strength the 6th South African Armoured Division was probably the most powerful formation in Italy. The Division fought on in Italy until the German surrender in 1945, sustaining some 3543 casualties.

UNIFORM During the campaign in East Africa South African uniforms were in many respects similar to the British, but detailed differences such as the shape of the sun helmet and the high webbing gaiters gave the South African soldier a distinctive silhouhette.

The sun helmet had a narrow brim (see figure 156) and a khaki puggree on which was often worn a metal cap badge as well as a cloth flash in regimental or corps colours on the right side. South African Scottish regiments wore the Tam o' Shanter.

Badges of rank were, as in the British Army, worn on the shoulder straps across the base of which all South Africans serving abroad wore an orange strip.

The main methods of identifying arm of service, corps or regiment were the cap badge and collar 'dogs', and the flash on the side of the sun helmet. Unlike the British, South Africans also wore cloth shoulder titles on the khaki drill tunic and bush jacket.

Above: A captain of the SAAF displays the 'winged boot' badge given to those flyers who made their way back on foot after being shot down. The Army rank badges of the SAAF are clearly shown in this photograph.

SOUTH AFRICAN AIR FORCE

South African Air Force units first saw service in Kenya, where No. 1 Bomber Brigade, partly equipped with converted Ju 86 airliners and old Hartebeest bombers bombed enemy positions four hours before the official declaration of war. During the Abyssinian campaign South African planes accounted for 95 Italian machines. The main weight of the South African Air Force was then switched to the Desert. By October 1942 there were 13 South African squadrons operational during the battle of Alamein.

Air Force personnel wore Army uniforms with special bronzed cap badge and cloth wings on the left breast if entitled to them. South Africans serving with the RAF wore British uniform with the 'South Africa' shoulder title.

CANADIAN ARMY

The first extended campaign for the Canadian Army in Europe came when the 1st Infantry Division and the 1st Army Tank Brigade took part in the assault upon Sicily in July 1943.

As part of the 13th British Corps, the 1st Infantry Division and the 1st Army Tank Brigade made an assault landing across the Strait of Messina against minimal resistance on 3 September 1943. The Canadian casualty figures at the end of November after three months fighting in Italy were 316 officers and men killed and 879 wounded.

The first week in November saw the arrival of the 5th Canadian Armoured Division at Naples where they began to take over the much travelled heavy equipment of the British 7th Armoured Division which was returning to England.

In December 1943 the 1st Division relieved the British 78th Division on the Sangro Ridge. From there, after three weeks of bitter fighting culminating in a week-long battle for the town of Ortona, the Canadians forced the line of the River Moro. Their casualties in the December battles totalled 2339 with an additional 1600 on the sick list. The weather became an enemy to rival the Germans and for the next three months the Canadians maintained their salient from the sea to Villa Grande. At the beginning of February 1944 the 5th Canadian Armoured Division came into the line to relieve the 4th Indian Division and the 1st Canadian Corps was now operational. By the end of March the Canadian Army in the Mediterranean theatre was at a strength of 75,824 officers and men.

On 11 May the 1st Canadian Armoured Brigade serving with the 13th British Corps went into action against the Gustav Line in support of the 8th Indian Division. The 13th Corps broke through and the 1st Canadian Corps was brought in to continue the advance to the Hitler Line.

After operations on the Adriatic coast against the Gothic Line, during late 1944, the 1st and 5th Canadian Divisions together with the 1st Armoured Brigade left Italy for North-West Europe in February 1945. Since the landing in Sicily 91,579 Canadians had served in the Italian theatre of operations and 25,264 of them had become casualties with 5799 killed.

UNIFORM The uniform worn by Canadian soldiers, including the Scottish regiments, was modelled on the British pattern and any differences which existed at the beginning of the war were soon ironed out because replacements were difficult to obtain overseas. However, the Canadian battledress was made of a better quality cloth in a smarter shade of khaki and so it became much in demand with British officers.

Badges of rank conformed to the British pattern, while the cap badge and collar 'dogs' continued to be the principal way of identifying the corps or regiment. Canadian units also had cloth shoulder titles and formation signs.

Canadian Navy and Air Force uniforms were identical to the British pattern but with Canadian buttons. Canadians serving in the Royal Navy and Royal Air Force wore 'Canada' on the sleeves at shoulder height.

Below: Canadian soldiers on their way to Sicily in July 1943. They look very similar to British troops of the period, with the same uniforms, personal equipment and weapons.

ARMED FORCES IN EXILE, THE MEDITERRANEAN 1940–45

Exiled troops from the armed forces of various nations which had been overrun by the Axis powers fought in the Mediterranean on the Allied side. Some formed national contingents, while others entered the ranks of existing Allied forces. The national organisations formed were sometimes quite small, although others (such as the Polish Army Corps) were a significant addition to the Allied strength.

UNIFORM The soldiers from Poland, Greece, Yugoslavia and Czechoslovakia who fought alongside the Allied armies had either left their homelands before the war, or had found it impossible to live under enemy domination. These men who had neither language, customs or uniforms in common were only united in their fight against the common enemy. They arrived in the Middle East wearing civilian clothes or the uniforms of the armies in which they had served, and it was up to the British to provide quarters, rations, clothing, equipment and weapons.

Below: Troops of the Polish Corps in the mountains around Monte Cassino in the late Spring of 1944. They are wearing British uniforms.

The old national uniforms were hung up and only worn on special occasions. For everyday wear British uniforms, both tropical and temperate, were worn. National pride and the wish to continue the customs and traditions of armies which although beaten were not defeated led to the retention wherever possible of national insignia. Thus the Poles, who formed the largest contingent, wore the Polish eagle on their head-dresses including steel helmets, while Greeks, Yugoslavs and Czechs kept their cap badges.

POLISH ARMY

In April 1940 the formation began within the French Army of the Independent (Polish) Carpathian Rifle Brigade from amongst the 5,000 Poles who found themselves in the Middle East. The first base was at Homs near Beirut. With the fall of France the Brigade was ordered by the French authorities to lay down its arms, but between 27 and 30 June 1940, the Brigade crossed into Palestine and came under British command at Latrun Camp.

In October the Brigade, of 359 officers and 4573 men, moved to Egypt for the defence of Dikheila. It was planned to send the Brigade to Greece, but the German offensive in Libya intervened, and the Brigade moved to besieged Tobruk, and in December took part in the attack on Gazala before proceeding to central Cyrenaica, Egypt and finally Palestine,

158

158 Private, Polish Army, 1944
This uniform was originally developed for British mountain troops and was worn on such operations as the commando raid on the German Heavy Water plant at Telemark in Norway. In Italy this uniform was issued as winter clothing. Over the light snow suit the private wears special commando equipment which was made of canvas and was designed to be quickly jettisoned in water. He is armed with two No. 36 grenades, and the .303 SMLE No. 4 Mk 1 rifle.

where it was reorganised and reinforced by Poles recently arrived from the Soviet Union. On 3 May 1942 the Brigade became the 3rd Carpathian Rifle Division.

In December 1941 the Commander-in-Chief of Polish Forces in Great Britain General Sikorski visited the Soviet Union and obtained the consent of Marshal Stalin to the release of all Polish nationals held in Soviet prison camps and their transfer to Persia. This mass exodus took place in September 1942 and a total of 69,000 soldiers, 3600 women soldiers, and 4000 children arrived in Iraq where they joined the rest of the Polish forces in the Middle East. In Iraq the so-called Anders Army was re-organised, re-equipped and armed and trained by the British to become II Polish Army Corps.

The Polish Corps began to arrive in Italy late in 1943. A force about 50,000 men strong, consisting of the 3rd Carpathian Rifle Division, the 5th Kresowa Infantry Division and the 2nd Armoured Brigade, it was attached to the 8th Army and took part in the final assaults on Monte Cassino in May 1944, where its troops actually took the monastery, although at a cost of 4199 casualties. The corps remained in Italy and took part in the final offensive of April 1945 which led to the German surrender.

CZECHOSLOVAK ARMY

The first Czech units in the Middle East were established in Palestine under the command of Colonel Klapalek, and were formed into the 4th Infantry Regiment with over 1000 men. During October 1941 it was re-grouped and designated Czech Infantry Battalion No. 11/East. In 1941 the battalion completed its training with the British near Jericho and was then transported to Egypt where it was employed on guard duties.

Later the same year Colonel Klapalek requested a more active role and in August the battalion was moved to Tobruk where it joined the Polish Carpathian Rifle Brigade in defensive positions on the fortified perimeter of Tobruk. Early in 1942, however, it sustained very heavy losses as a result of air attacks. There was concern that the whole unit might be wiped out, and so it was pulled back and regrouped as No. 200 Light Anti-Aircraft Regiment East, and served at Haifa and Beriral.

GREEK ARMED FORCES

From amongst the Greeks who had been evacuated with the Allies from Greece, or who had managed to escape afterwards, Greek military units began to be formed in the Middle East. Gradually two units began to take shape. The first was the (3rd) Greek Mountain Brigade which took part in the battle of El Alamein after which it returned to Egypt fo further training.

In August 1944 the Brigade was sent to Italy where it fought well, capturing the town of Rimini until in November it returned to Greece and spent six weeks putting down the Communist uprising.

The second unit was formed in August 1942 in the Middle East from Greek soldiers, most of whom were officers – from the Royal Guard (*Evzones*). It was known as the Sacred Company and had a strength of some 500 men. It grew to battalion strength and fought in North Africa alongside the Free French and the New Zealanders and in Tunisia. It also provided parachutists and other personnel for Allied commando operations.

After the defeat of Greece both on the mainland and in Crete, the Air Force also began to be reformed in the Middle East.

On 10 October 1941 the first Greek squadron in the RAF, No. 361, was formed at Aqir. Following its almost immediate renumbering to No. 335, the squadron served in the western desert and in the Mediterranean. In September 1944 it moved to Italy and operated over Yugoslavia, Crete and the Greek mainland.

On 17 November the Royal Hellenic Air Force consisting of two squadrons of Hurricanes (Nos. 335 and 336) and one of Baltimores (a total of 36 aircraft) began to arrive on the Greek mainland.

The surviving units of the Greek Navy including 7 destroyers, 3 old motor torpedo-boats, 5 submarines, a repair ship and a large tanker, manned by 200 officers and 2700 ratings gathered at Alexandria, where the ships were repaired and equipped with modern anti-aircraft weapons.

By the end of 1941 the Greek Navy had been supplied, mostly by Britain, with 6 'Hunt' class destroyers, 4 corvettes, 6 mine sweepers and a number of other small craft. Personnel now stood at 240 officers and 3600 ratings, and by the end of 1942 had increased to 345 and 5800.

In March 1943, a severe crisis of morale in the Greek forces in the Middle East led to a mutiny on 5 Greek warships berthed in Alexandria which quickly spread to include 43 naval and merchant vessels. The mutiny was eventually put down by loyal Greek Marines, who suffered 50 casualties, and units of the Royal Navy. Throughout the rest of the war the Greek Navy operated in the eastern Mediterranean and Aegean and participated in the Sicily landings (6 ships) and in the Italian campaign.

YUGOSLAV ARMED FORCES

About 900 Yugoslav soldiers were evacuated to the Middle East to form an infantry battalion which was incorporated into the British King's Own Royal Regiment.

There was also a Yugoslav troop (2 officers and 14 men) in the 10th Inter-Allied Commando which carried out SOE-type operations in Yugoslavia.

A Free Yugoslav Air Force was formed in Amman in Jordan where some 700 airmen, 300 of whom were aircrew, had been assembled.

In 1944 two Yugoslav fighter squadrons were formed in the RAF. The first, No. 352, was formed on 22 April, and the second, No. 351, on 1 July 1944 at Benina. Then from their bases in Italy both squadrons fought in the skies above Yugoslavia before transferring to the Yugoslav Air Force in June 1945.

As the war came to an end, and Tito became the undisputed leader of Yugoslavia, many NCOs and men of the Royal Yugoslav Air Force requested to be allowed to join the partisans.

159 Sergeant, Belgian Colonial Army, 1943

Troops from the Belgian colonies were used as part of the Allied forces from June 1940. The tarbush *or fez, almost identical to that worn by British African troops, was equipped with a neck flap and had the corps badge on the front. On the sleeves of the khaki-drill tunic are rank badges. The equipment supplied by Britain is the 1939-pattern, a leather version of the 1937-pattern web equipment.*

FRANCE

ARMY

The Franco-German Armistice of 22 June 1940 divided France into two parts. The northern and western area of the country was to be under the direct control of the German armed forces while central and southern France was unoccupied and was given a limited degree of autonomy, being known as Vichy France after the town which became its new 'capital'.

Article IV of the Armistice allowed for a small French army to be kept in being in the unoccupied zone (*l'Armée de l'Armistice*) and for the military provision of the French Empire overseas. The function of these forces was to keep internal order and to defend French territories from any Allied assault while remaining, in theory at least, under the overall direction of the German armed forces.

Vichy forces in Syria, Madagascar and Dakar resisted fiercely Allied attempts to take them over, but the Vichy Army in North Africa hardly resisted the landings of Operation 'Torch'. The defeat of the Axis forces in North Africa and the American 'Torch' landings ensured the demise of Vichy France, and the German High Command set Operation '*Anton*' into action. On 11 November 1942 German armoured columns advanced over the demarcation line and overran the unoccupied zone. Following the German occupation, the *Armée de l'Armistice* was dissolved.

ORGANISATION The exact strength of the Vichy Metropolitan Army was set as 3768 officers, 15,072 NCOs and 75,360 men, all of whom were to be volunteers. In addition the size of the paramilitary Gendarmerie was fixed at 60,000 men plus an anti-aircraft force of 10,000 men. Despite the influx of trained soldiers from the colonial forces (reduced in size in accordance with the Armistice) there was a shortage of volunteers so that initially 50,000 men of the 'class of 1939' were retained until sufficient volunteers came forward to fulfill the quota. At the beginning of 1942 these conscripts were released, but still there was an insufficient number of men, a shortage that was to remain until the Army's dissolution despite Vichy appeals to the Germans for a regular form of conscription.

The Army was divided into two groups each of four military divisions and comprised:

18 infantry regiments;
11 cavalry regiments;
8 artillery regiments;
15 battalions of *chasseurs*.

The Army was deprived of tanks and other armoured vehicles and was desperately short of motorised transport especially in the cavalry units which were supposed to be motorised.

UNIFORM The uniform of the Vichy Army was as that of the Army in 1940.

MILICE

On 30 January 1943 the paramilitary organisation the *Milice* was established by Pierre Laval for the task of maintaining the 'new order' in occupied Vichy France. Inevitably this brought the *Milice* in direct confrontation with the Resistance, and it was to become the bitterest and most detested of collaborationist organisations.

The *Milice* was organised territorially in departments, regions and zones under the overall command of a secretary-general (Joseph Darnand) with his headquarters in Vichy. By Autumn 1943 the *Milice* had reached its maximum membership of 29,000 men, but only 10,000 were active, while the rest were either contributors or part-timers.

The military arm of the *Milice* was the *Francs-Garde*, which also had from June 1943 a regular and part-time branch. Regulars were paid, barracked and from October 1943 increasingly armed, but never exceeded a strength of 2000 men. Like the pre-war German paramilitary formations, the *Milice* adopted archaic terms for its sub-divisions. The basic unit was a five-man *main*, then came a *dizaine*, (ten men), *trentaine*, (30 men), *centaine* (100 men), and a *cohorte* (500 men), four of which formed a regimental-sized *centre* of about 2000 men.

If the military situation dictated, the part-time members were liable for call-up at short-notice and following the D-Day landings 3000 men were mobilised.

UNIFORM The dark blue uniform of the *Milice* was basically that of the French *Chasseurs Alpins* and consisted of black beret, open blue tunic and long trousers which were worn with shoes or ankle-boots and gaiters.

The emblem of the *Milice* was the gamma on the beret, steel helmet and on the right breast pocket. Members of the special units belonging to the *2e Service* (intelligence) wore a metal shield-shaped badge on the left breast pocket. It incorporated the unit's motto '*Devant*' (in front), the death's head and the gamma all in black on a white enamel ground. Equipment was that of the French Army while weapons were either French or came from stocks supplied by the British to the *Maquis* and captured by the security forces.

Rank badges were worn on the shoulder straps by all ranks but were based on those of the French Army.

Below: General Noguès (left, with five stars on his arm) and General Juin (with four stars) in Algiers in 1942. The loops on Noguès' pockets are to hold his orders and decorations.

PHALANGE AFRICAINE

Late in 1942, a unit of pro-Axis French volunteers began to be formed in Tunisia. Under the command of French officers about 300 volunteers (half of whom were Tunisian Arabs) were found for the *Phalange Africaine*. On 7 April 1943 the first contingent with the strength of a strong company arrived at the front at Medjez el Bab. After putting up a reasonably good showing in bitter defensive fighting against British troops the unit was practically annihilated on 29 April. On 8 May 1943 the survivors were paid-off and advised to disappear, while the officers were evacuated to Vichy where some continued to serve in the *Milice* and French Volunteer Legion.

UNIFORM French uniform was worn with the *francisque* on the right breast pocket, and the French national colours on the right side of the German steel helmet.

COLONIAL FORCES

The French territories in the Mediterranean consisted of the Algerian *département*, the protectorates of Tunisia and Morocco and the mandates of Syria and Lebanon. The Armistice called for the demilitarisation of Tunisia – in compliance with Italian wishes – and a general reduction of French colonial troops. Vichy France was permitted 55,000 men in Morocco, 50,000 in Algeria, the Army of the Levant in Syria and Lebanon being reduced from around 100,000 to just under 40,000 men.

The Vichy French Army of the Levant controlled the mandates of Syria and Lebanon and, although it did not mount offensive operations against the Allies, its very presence adjacent to the strategically vulnerable British oil and supply lines posed a constant threat. Syria was invaded by a mixed Allied force on 8 June 1941, the Vichy troops putting up a dogged resistance to the Allied advance, a resistance tinged with bitter ferocity with Frenchman fighting Frenchman.

When the fighting in Syria finally ended on 11 July 1941 the Vichy forces had lost 6000 men, 1000 of whom had been killed. A total of 37,736 soldiers were taken prisoner, but when given the choice of being repatriated or joining General de Gaulle only 5668 availed themselves of this opportunity, the remainder being transported to France.

ORGANISATION The Vichy Army in Syria was divided into the *troupes spéciales* (indigenous native soldiers) and the regular metropolitan and colonial troops. The *troupes spéciales* were formed by 11 battalions of infantry: 3 Lebanese (*bataillons de chasseurs Libanais*) and 8 Syrian (*bataillons du Levant*). In addition there were two artillery groups and supporting units as well as at least 5000 cavalry organised in squadrons of around 100 men each. Included in this cavalry force were 15 squadrons of Circassian cavalry of which three were motorised. The *troupes spéciales* were led by indigenous officers and NCOs although there was a small French officer cadre.

The regular French troops consisted of the four battalions of the 6th Foreign Legion – the best troops available to the Vichy commander, General Dentz – and the three battalions of the 24th Colonial Infantry Regiment who were brought up to strength by amalgamating them with two garrison battalions of Senegalese to become the 24th *Régiment Mixte Coloniale*.

The African troops were formed from six Algerian, three Tunisian, three Senegalese and one Moroccan rifle (*tirailleur*) battalion, the Moroccan troops being

160

161

160 Private, Vichy French Moroccan Spahis, 1941

The Adrian *helmet bears the crescent emblem worn by all Mohammedan troops. The collar patches bear the regimental number, and buttoned to the front of his* djellabah *is the rank badge of a* soldat de première classe. *Attached to the special leather equipment is the 1892 knife bayonet.*

161 Trumpeter, Vichy French Colonial Infantry, 1941

Viewed from the back one can clearly see the arrangement of equipment on this rifleman. The pack forms part of the 1935 equipment as does the two-litre water bottle. The haversack does not appear to be an issue item; nor does the coat hanger! His bugle hangs by the side of the pack with its red white and blue tasselled cord.

162 Colonel, Vichy French Colonial Infantry, 1942

This officer in Madagascar wears regulation tropical dress with sun helmet on the front of which is the gilt metal anchor, emblem of French colonial forces. The badges of rank are won on the shoulder straps, and the collar patches, which were rarely worn on the shirt, identify his unit.

162

considered troops of the first order.

The artillery available to the French consisted of 120 field and medium guns and numbered about 6700 men. There was also a mechanised element which was provided by the 6th and 7th *Chasseurs d'Afrique* whose forces totalled 90 tanks (Renault R-35s) and a similar number of armoured cars.

The contingent of North African cavalry consisted of the 4th Tunisian, 1st Moroccan and the 8th Algerian Spahis and amounted to about 7000 men, most of whom were either on horseback or in light lorries, with a few equipped with armoured cars.

UNIFORM The French standardised the uniforms of its colonial and African troops on the Metropolitan pattern while retaining certain national features which were only officially to be worn by indigenous personnel. However Europeans also wore them because not only did they go down well in France when on leave, but they were practical for wear in desert or *bled*.

Before the war officers had a light khaki working, and white undress uniform consisting of sun helmet, tunic and trousers. Other ranks serving in colonial forces had both a khaki drill uniform with shirt or tunic with stand collar, shorts or pantaloons, or a khaki cloth uniform consisting of a double-breasted khaki tunic, pantaloons, and greatcoat while both uniforms were worn with ankle boots and long khaki puttees. Head-dress for Europeans was basically the sun helmet, kepi, beret or side cap, while indigenous personnel wore a red *chechia* (fez) with khaki cover on active duty.

All ranks in all units wore the *Adrian* steel helmet on the front of which was a circular stamped metal badge bearing various devices. For example Mohammedans had the letters 'RF' above a crescent, colonial troops the anchor, and French Foreign Legion and *Chasseurs d'Afrique* (African Mounted Rifles) the same exploding grenade as French metropolitan troops.

Zouaves and *tirailleurs* (rifles) from Algeria, Morocco and Tunisia wore either tropical or temperate uniform with distinctive head-dress. The *chechia* was worn by Algerians and Tunisians, while Moroccans wore a turban which was rolled in a slightly different manner by each regiment. Since in wartime the turban was khaki the pre-war distinctive colours no longer applied.

Cavalry also wore the standard uniform but with baggy trousers and special leather leggings. Tunisian *spahis* wore the *chechia* with cover while Moroccan and Algerian *spahis* had their own distinctive turbans.

INSIGNIA Badges of rank were worn in the same manner on both temperate and tropical uniforms, although during the war it was more common to see officers wearing their rank badges on the shoulder straps. Other ranks wore their rank badges on a tab which was fixed to the front of their shirt, tunic, or special clothing.

Arm of service and unit was identified by the coloured kepi or by the colour or combination of colours on the collar patches. The regimental number appeared on the front of the kepi, on the collar patch, and later on the badge worn on the left sleeve of American uniforms.

AIR FORCE

As a result of British aerial assaults on the French fleet at Mers-el-Kébir and the fear of further bombardment against the French homeland the Axis armistice commission permitted the French to retain part of their Air Force. Similarly the French were allowed to keep Air Force detachments in their overseas colonies which were coming under attack from the Allies and, in the case of Indo-China, from the Japanese.

Below: Loading a Martin bomber of the Vichy Air Force. The men are wearing casual summer working clothes, with a variety of head-gear.

Organisation In the unoccupied zone of France the Vichy Air Force consisted of:
6 fighter groups;
2 night-fighter *escadrilles*;
6 bomber groups;
2 ground-attack groups;
3 reconnaissance groups.
A group was usually formed from two *escadrilles* which would normally consist of 12 aircraft. The group would consist only of planes of one type, e.g. fighter or bomber, but could be combined to form *groupements* which could be of various types.

Following the German occupation of Vichy France all the remaining aircraft were seized and the French air units disbanded.

In Syria many of the aircraft stationed there had been sent back to France in 1940, leaving only a number of obsolete models. Alarmed by the growing threat of a British invasion, a fighter group was dispatched from Algeria and once the fighting started three groups were flown in from France and three more from North Africa. This brought the Vichy strength up to 289 aircraft organised into:
3 fighter groups;
4 bomber groups;
1 bomber *escadrille*;
1 reconnaissance group;
6 army co-operation groups;
2 transport groups;
1 *flotille* of naval aircraft;
4 *escadrilles* of naval aircraft.

This gave them the edge over the Allied air units until British reinforcements arrived towards the latter part of the campaign. French losses were 179 planes, most of which had been destroyed on the ground.

While the Vichy land forces did little to resist the Anglo-American forces during the 'Torch' landings, the Air Force was hotly engaged. A determined resistance was carried out until 11 November 1942 when a cease-fire was called following which most of the French planes went over to the Allies to join with the Free French.

In Morocco there were two fighter, two reconnaissance and four bomber groups plus two *flotilles* of naval aircraft and two transport groups. In Algeria the Vichy Air Force consisted of three fighter, one reconnaissance and three bomber groups with one *flotille* of naval aircraft. In Tunisia a small presence was maintained by one fighter, two bomber and one reconnaissance group with one unit of naval flying boats.

Uniform Uniform and insignia were as before the fall of France.

Navy

Under the terms of the Franco-German Armistice the French Fleet was obliged to keep its ships under Axis control and be disarmed under German or Italian control. Little attempt to impose this clause of the Armistice was made, however, the Axis being content to leave the French ships in French hands so long as they were withdrawn from the British war effort.

Although the French Navy had no intention of allowing its ships to be used by the Axis, the British and Free French attacks against Mers-el-Kébir and Dakar, ensured that the Navy maintained a hostile attitude towards the Allied cause.

The Vichy Navy came to an abrupt end when the Germans occupied the 'free' zone in 1942. Initially the German Army made no attempt to gain control of the fleet in Toulon, but on 27 November the port was taken over, to which the French replied by scuttling their ships – more than 70 vessels – which included 3 battleships, 7 cruisers, 32 destroyers and 16 submarines.

The attempted German take-over of the Toulon fleet brought the remaining Vichy naval detachments in the colonies over to the Allies and the Free French. The Free French Navy was never an important force, consisting only of a few submarines and escort and auxiliary vessels, although the reinforcement of the colonial Vichy ships was able to provide the basis for a new French Fleet. Thus by the end of the war the Navy had a

163 Rear Admiral, French Navy, 1942
The cap for flag officers had an elaborately embroidered band on which also appeared the five-pointed white metal stars which denoted rank. On his white tropical jacket he wears detachable shoulder straps which also bore the badges of rank.

164 Leading Seaman, French Navy, 1941
The sun helmet and shirt formed part of the tropical uniform introduced in 1925, whereas the cotton duck trousers were part of the working rig. The two bars on the left breast denoted the rank of the wearer.

163

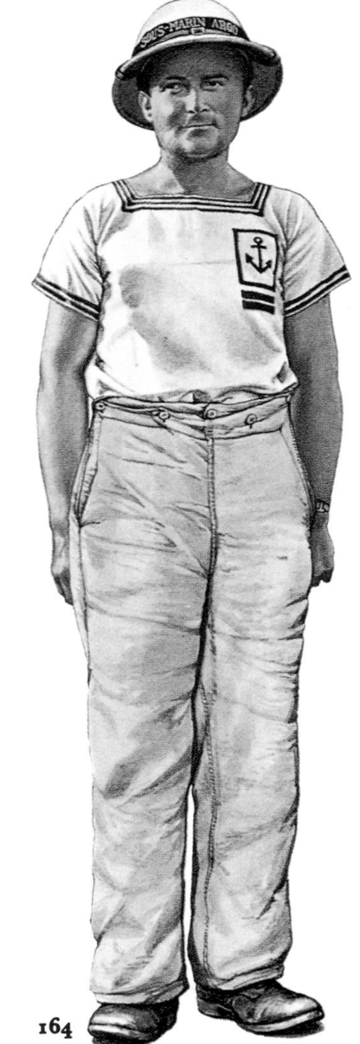
164

strength of 4 battleships, 9 cruisers and 11 destroyers, plus a number of smaller craft supplied by the British and Americans.

UNIFORM Uniform and insignia were as before the fall of France.

FREE FRENCH

ARMY

After the fall of France, various units of French troops in the Middle East preferred to join the Allies. Their position was difficult; many Frenchmen thought them a small group of dissidents, and considered their leader – de Gaulle – a traitor.

In May 1941, as the possibility of operations in Syria became apparent, the scattered Free French Forces were assembled at Quastina in Palestine and formed into the 1st Free French Light Division.

Although the Free French troops fought with traditional *élan* there were understandable problems of morale as former comrades-in-arms and fellow countrymen fought against each other. Altogether the Free French suffered 1300 casualties, a heavy total for such a small initial force.

After their victory in Syria the Free French troops were redeployed in North Africa being reinforced by other French units. Initially Free French forces played only a minor role in operations, their most notable success being at Bir Hakeim when the 1st Free French Light Division maintained a stubborn defence of the desert stronghold during the Gazala battle before breaking out of their surrounding position to rejoin the Allied lines.

The position of the Free French changed dramatically with the collapse of the Axis in North Africa and the refusal of the vast majority of Vichy forces to resist the Allied armies. The Free French commanders were able to persuade the Vichy troops to go over to the Allied cause, a conversion made easier by the German take-over of the unoccupied zone. Thus there was an enormous influx of numbers to the Free French who, with American help in armament and equipment, were now able to make a significant military contribution.

Free French troops fought in the final stages of the Tunisian campaign but it was the war in Italy where the newly reorganised forces were to make their mark. At the end of 1943 units of the French Expeditionary Corps began to arrive in Italy; at first two divisions, the Corps was reinforced by a further two divisions in the spring of 1944. The French Expeditionary Corps was heavily engaged in the battles of Cassino and it was its outflanking of the German mountain positions that made possible the Allied victory. After the capture of Rome in May 1944 the French troops were withdrawn from Italy in preparation for the liberation of France itself.

Above: A Free French captain of the 1st Moroccan Spahis *gives his men (in armoured crew helmets) instructions. The captain's kepi would be sky blue.*

ORGANISATION The 1st Free French Light Division which fought in Syria was divided into two small brigades, the first comprising a battalion of the 13th *Demi-Brigade* of the French Foreign Legion and two Senegalese battalions, the second, a naval infantry battalion (which included two motorised companies) and a further two Senegalese battalions. The division was supported by an artillery battery of six guns; a tank company (eight tanks and armoured cars) and a contingent of naval infantry. In addition there were two squadrons of Circassian cavalry and a squadron of *spahis* (mounted in trucks) under the command of Colonel Collet.

In North Africa, one of the first effective units was the Free French Fighting Column or 'L' Force, a small mixed force of armoured cars, tanks, infantry and anti-tank and anti-aircraft guns under the command of General Leclerc. 'L' Force fought through the desert campaigns until 1943 when it was withdrawn from the front line to be re-equipped and re-grouped with other French elements to become the French 2nd Armoured Division which then took part in the fighting in Normandy.

After the Syrian campaign the Free French could muster two brigade groups which were known as the 1st and 2nd French Light Divisions and were supported in the fighting in North Africa by a regiment of Moroccan *spahis* who were able to provide reconnaissance detachments for the Free French when necessary.

Following the defeat of the Africa Corps at El Alamein, the brigades were withdrawn from the front and in February 1943 began to be formed into the 1st Free French Division. Its two component brigades fought independently in Tunisia until the autumn of 1943 when they were moved to Tripolitania to be reorganised and re-equipped.

During the short lull in the fighting that followed the Axis surrender at Tunis in 1943 the French forces were reorganised from the old Vichy and Free French troops into the French Expeditionary Corps. Besides the Free French units, French troops consisted of the XIX Corps (three colonial divisions and an armoured group) and three battalions of the *Corps Franc d'Afrique* plus two Moroccan *tabors* which were grouped with the US 2nd Corps. A *tabor* was a unit of Moroccan irregular troops who were known as *goumiers*.

The four divisions of the French Expeditionary Corps under the command of General Juin comprised:
2 infantry regiments;
1 naval infantry regiment;
6 infantry battalions;
3 artillery regiments;
1 mountain artillery regiment;
3 *spahi* regiments;
3 Algerian rifle regiments;
5 Moroccan rifle regiments;
1 Tunisian rifle regiment;
1 *chasseur* battalion;
1 marine infantry battalion;
2 Foreign Legion battalions.

Besides the divisional troops there was a general reserve of three Moroccan *goumier tabors*, two armoured regiments and two regiments of artillery. The forces of the French Expeditionary Corps reached over 100,000 men, while casualties suffered in Italy totalled 7260 men.

UNIFORM Free French troops taking part in the abortive raid on Madagascar and in the campaign in Syria were equipped by Britain with British tropical uniforms and battledress which were worn with the Wolseley sun helmet. Officers and men in possession of French head-dress continued to wear it as long as possible. With battledress either the sun helmet or British steel helmets were worn.

At first insignia was limited to a flash in the French national colours which was worn on the front or left side of the sun helmet, and 'France' embroidered in white on khaki which was worn on the sleeves of the battle dress blouse. French

165

166

167

colonial infantry wore a metal anchor on the front of the sun helmet as illustrated in figure 162. French rank badges were usually worn on slides on the shoulder straps or in the shape of a tab on the front of the shirt or tunic.

French, African and Colonial troops continued to wear their existing uniforms as long as possible until they were replaced by either British or American uniforms and equipment. American uniform was supplied in vast quantities so that by the time the French Expeditionary Corps landed in Italy it was dressed in American uniforms with French head-dress (when available) and French insignia.

Left: Men of a North African unit of Juin's French corps (the most effective mountain fighters in the Allied armies) move up to the front during the Italian winter of 1944. They have American weapons and equipment, although some have retained the French Adrian *helmet. The camouflage netting over the helmets broke up the outline even when (as here) it would have been useless to insert any foliage as an aid to concealment.*

165 Private, Free French Senegalese Rifles, 1941
Serving in Syria, this colonial infantryman wears the chechia *with khaki cover, the double-breasted khaki cloth tunic with unit collar patches and lace on the cuffs. The equipment includes the French 1916-pattern ammunition pouches and what looks like a British respirator in its carrying bag.*

166 Sergeant-Major, Moroccan Spahis, 1943
This maréchal de logis-chef *of the 2nd* Spahis *stationed in Tunisia wears cavalry uniform with the Sam Browne belt of a warrant officer. Rank is shown by the three gold chevrons on the arm, and his formation by the collar patches with the Moroccan star.*

167 Private, Fighting French Foreign Legion, 1942
The defenders of Bir Hakeim wore British uniform with the famous white kepi. The collar patches were the same as those worn on French uniform, although the distinctive blue waist sash is not to be seen. Of note are the long shorts here worn folded back.

168 Goumier, French African Troops, 1943
This Goumier *serving with the French Expeditionary Corps in Italy wears a British steel helmet on top of his turban and a* djellabah *over his American combat uniform. It was possible to tell the tribe by the arrangement and colour of* djellabah.

169 Lieutenant, French Moroccan Spahis, 1943
Although the uniform is basically American, this officer still retains the French motorised troop helmet which he has adorned with an open five-pointed star and the two bars of his rank badge. On his shoulder straps he wears his badges of rank, and on the left sleeve a regimental badge.

AIR FORCE

While most members of the French Air Force accepted the terms of the 1940 Armistice a number escaped with their aircraft to British bases in the Mediterranean where they were re-formed and re-equipped in part with British aircraft. Free French air units fought in the Middle East, Eritrea and North Africa and with the incorporation of Vichy forces from North Africa were heavily engaged against Axis forces in Italy and southern Europe.

ORGANISATION In North Africa and the Middle East it took some time for the Free French units to re-form on a regular basis. By July 1941 there were two bomber groups operating in Africa and two fighter *escadrilles* were united in Syria to form the fighter group 'Alsace' which, equipped with Hurricanes, was actively engaged over the desert during the North African campaign.

The French air units which had gone over to the Allies following the 'Torch' landings were re-equipped with modern British and American aircraft, some groups being transferred to England to conduct bombing operations against Germany but other groups remaining in the Mediterranean to continue the air war against the Axis.

UNIFORM Members of the Free French Air Force cut off from their supplies of French uniforms had to make do as best they could. They tended only to wear French-made uniforms on ceremonial occasions or for walking out, while on duty they wore Australian Air Force blue battledress, or service dress with French insignia. Flying clothing was standard British.

From January 1943 selected personnel from the French Air Force in North Africa were sent to the United States of America for training. They wore French uniform with a 'France' badge on the upper sleeve, and special insignia incorporating three chicks in red, white and blue with the legend *'Ils Grandiront'* (they will grow). Flying clothing and the uniforms for everyday wear were soon supplied by America.

168

169

UNITED STATES
ARMY

Operation 'Torch' was the first great involvement of US troops in the Mediterranean theatre (and, indeed, the first successful large-scale campaign of the war by the Americans). The landings were followed by the defeat of the Axis forces in North Africa, and then the invasions of Sicily and Italy. The US 5th Army fought throughout the Italian campaign; its men were first to Rome, and were engaged in heavy fighting all the way up the peninsula. US ambitions for the Mediterranean were strictly limited, however (in contrast to the aspirations of their British ally). North-west Europe took precedence, and the 5th Army was weakened in 1944 to provide troops for the landings in southern France (Operation 'Dragoon'). Nevertheless, the 5th Army took a full part in the Italian fighting until the final German surrender there in May 1945. By the end of the war, the US Army had suffered 179,403 casualties in the Mediterranean: 38,741 dead, 107,617 wounded and 33,045 captured or missing.

ORGANISATION Although it is true that the United States mobilised its vast resources in a remarkably short time, American soldiers had ample warning of the coming crisis. In 1940 the Army was divided in three: the regulars, the National Guard and the Organised Reserve. The Regular Army numbered 243,095 and was scattered in 130 posts, camps and stations, the men serving short-term enlistments: the officers numbered 1400. The National Guard was 226,837 strong and was equipped by individual states and received two weeks' training each summer.

There was, in addition, a reserve of 104,228 officers in the organised reserve corps, composed of the Officer Training Camps. The Army received a standard institutionalised pattern of training: the service schools supervised training and the Service Boards tested and developed new equipment.

The continental United States, the Zone of the Interior, was administered by four armies and, in 1940, they only had skeleton staffs of 4400 troops each. There were nine infantry divisions; only three had a complement of regular formations, the other six were only 3000 strong. There was also a cavalry division and a mechanised brigade of 4000 and 2300 men respectively. Responsibility for speeding up mobilisation was given to General Headquarters (GHQ), and in 1941 it was given responsibility for the training of troops under the leadership of General Leslie McNair.

On 17 June 1941 the Army was expanded to 280,000 men and nine days later to 375,000. On 16 September the National Guard units were absorbed into the Army and Roosevelt persuaded Congress to pass the Selective Service Act; by July 1941, 606,915 men were inducted into the Army.

New units were usually formed around the regular or National Guard formations. At first there were 27 divisions, nine regular and 18 National Guard; there were also two armoured divisions and a further three completing their training.

American mobilisation proceeded fairly smoothly before the outbreak of war in December 1941. Thereafter the strain inflicted by the early disasters in the Pacific and the demand for continued

Right: American soldiers move cautiously forward in September 1943 during the Italian campaign. The sergeant in the foreground is carrying the baseplate of a mortar.

170

170 Staff-Sergeant, US Army, 1942
This GI (government issue) disembarking at Oran in November 1942 wears standard American Army combat uniform and equipment. The new steel helmet had a rough sandy finish, and officers sometimes painted their badges of rank on its front. Over an OD (olive drab) flannel shirt he wears a lightweight field jacket, OD trousers, canvas leggings and russet ankle boots. Under the woven equipment can be seen a life jacket and slung round the neck are cloth bandoliers holding extra rifle ammunition. Rank badges are worn on the sleeves and on the left the American flag is prominently displayed. Anglo-French relations in late 1942 were such that Americans were anxious that the French should not mistake them for British troops. The rifle is the US Calibre .30 M1 Garand semi-automatic rifle. This was an outstanding weapon: robust and reliable, it was the Army's standard rifle until 1958.

171 Officer, US Army, 1942
Much more popular than the double-breasted woollen greatcoat among infantry officers was the water-repellent cotton duck M1942 mackinaw lined with khaki cloth and fitted with its own belt as worn by the infantry officer here. Trousers are the standard OD woollen type worn with canvas leggings and ankle boots. On his pistol belt he carries a .45 pistol and a pouch containing two spare magazines. The sub-machine gun is the US Thompson .45 Model 1928 M1 sub-machine gun.

172 Private, US Army, 1942
This engineer clearing mines in North Africa wears the OD cotton fatigue cap, and two-piece fatigue uniform which was issued to all but crews of armoured fighting vehicles, who had a one-piece overall.

expansion proved too much. The War Department originally believed that it could mobilise three or four divisions per month after March 1942, but this rate could not be kept up; by the end of December 1942 only 42 of the planned 73 divisions had been mobilised. Indeed, by September the Army was short of 330,000 men and the ambitious plans laid in that month to create an army of 114 divisions were never realised.

The main factor which limited the size of the US Army, apart from the capacity of the American economy to equip such a large force quickly, was shipping. The shipping estimates showed that no more than 4,170,000 men could be shipped overseas by the end of 1944. In the event the number of divisions shipped abroad did not exceed 88. This fact was an important restraint on Allied strategy. Thus although expansion between December 1941 and December 1943 was unprecedented, with the Army growing from 1,657,157 to 5,400,888, a further increase in the number of units was not undertaken. By December 1944, 4,933,682 Americans were serving abroad in 80 divisions; these were supported by a mere three divisions in reserve.

In 1945 the US Army reached a total of 91 divisions, but three of these were broken up for reinforcements. The remaining 88 were maintained at full combat strength despite the fact that by the end of the Ardennes Campaign in January 1945, 47 regiments in 19 divisions had suffered between 100 and 200 per cent battle casualties.

The American unit organisation had finally been rationalised in 1940. The infantry divisions had adopted a triangular structure which eliminated the brigade, and comprised 15,500 men as a 'general purpose organisation intended for open warfare in theatres permitting the use of motor transport'. The division comprised three infantry regiments and an artillery regiment (four groups each of 12 howitzers), with the normal support of engineers, signals and supply units.

McNair was determined to strip the division of extraneous elements and keep it as lithe and mobile as possible. In 1942 he attempted to cut away the superfluous units and equipment and reduce the size of the division to 14,253 men. Mobility was increased by introducing $2\frac{1}{2}$-ton trucks, 'Jeeps' and $\frac{1}{4}$-ton trailers. The power of both offensive and defensive weapons was increased by introducing the 57mm anti-tank gun and replacing the 75mm howitzer with the 105mm. The infantryman was armed with the M-1 (Garand) rifle and the Rocket Launcher AT 236 (Bazooka) for use against tanks.

Headquarters special troops were set up to coordinate the divisional HQ, and a company each of ordnance, maintenance, quartermaster and signal troops were introduced. Despite a high degree of motorisation (1440 vehicles) a US infantry division did not, however, have the capacity to move all its equipment and personnel simultaneously.

The smallest unit in an American division was the squad of 14–16 men, the largest body of men that could be controlled by a single voice, usually that of a corporal or sergeant; in the artillery the smallest unit was the section. The platoon was composed of several squads or two sections of some 40–50 men commanded by a lieutenant who exercised his control through his squad leaders. The rest of the structure was triangular: three companies formed a battalion and three battalions a regiment.

The armament of the division during the early part of the war (August 1942) included the following:
147 × .30 machine guns;
133 × .50 machine guns;
81 × 60mm mortars;
57 × 81mm mortars;
109 × 37mm anti-tank guns;
18 × 75mm self-propelled howitzers;
36 × 105mm howitzers;
6 × 105mm self-propelled howitzers;
12 × 155mm howitzers.

The armoured division was basically composed of a reconnaissance battalion and four battalions of tanks. In 1942, there were 159 medium and 68 light

171

172

173

174

tanks. Accompanying them was an armoured infantry regiment of three battalions all mounted on half-tracks and three battalions each of 18 self-propelled 105mm howitzers. The service troops included an engineer battalion. With 68 armoured cars and over 1000 other wheeled vehicles, the establishment strength of 10,900 officers and men was fully mobile. The novel aspect of the American armoured division was that from March 1942 it was organised in two 'Combat Commands' (each of one tank, one infantry and one artillery battalion) and a general reserve. As all arms were fully motorised, this proved a flexible and very effective system, and in September 1943, three Combat Commands became the rule.

US Army units participating in Operation 'Torch', the invasion of French North Africa were:
Western Task Force of 35,000 men;
1 armoured division;
2 infantry divisions;
Central and Eastern Task forces,
1 armoured division;
3 infantry divisions.

While the Western Task Force was composed entirely of US personnel, the Central and Eastern forces also included British troops.

Activated on 10 July 1943 to carry out Operation 'Husky', the invasion of Sicily, the US 7th Army comprised:
4 infantry divisions;
1 airborne division;
2 armoured divisions.

At the end of the Sicilian Campaign the 7th Army was replaced by the 5th which had been training in North Africa. Elements of the 5th Army taking part in Operation 'Avalanche' the invasion of southern Italy were VI Corps consisting of:
4 infantry divisions;
1 airborne division;
rangers;
1 field artillery brigade and other units.

The 5th Army was an international force, consisting of British, French, Indian and even Brazilian troops, although the majority of its divisions were American. It provided troops for the Anzio landings, but after the fall of Rome was reduced to five divisions when four French and three US divisions were removed to invade southern France. For the final offensive of April 1945, however, its strength had grown to nine divisions in line with two in reserve. On May 2 there were seven US divisions in Italy: one mountain, one armoured and five infantry.

UNIFORM The Americans experience so many extremes of temperature and climatic conditions on their own continent, that it is not surprising that the American Quartermaster Department had to equip soldiers with a full range of uniforms ranging from lightweight khaki drill to clothing warm enough to wear in Alaska. However American combat clothing, which at the end of the war was the most advanced in the World, looked remarkably outdated in 1941. Figure 176 shows an American officer in a summer uniform worn until the war although it looked out of place anywhere but in Mexico in 1913.

There were three basic classes of uniform; Class A was the winter dress uniform, Class B was the intermediate season uniform with shirt, and Class C was the uniform worn in hot climates which was made of khaki drill or chino cloth as it was known in America.

By the time American soldiers set foot on African soil in November 1942, the uniform was still unproven, and yet it displayed many serious shortcomings. A major change had come in winter 1941 when the old British pattern Mk 1 steel helmet was replaced by a new two-piece American one, which was to prove so successful that it is still in use today. The rest of the uniform was highly standardised and the same for all ranks. The few items of tailor-made uniform reserved for officers were to be found in the service dress.

A new uniform had to be developed for crews of armoured fighting vehicles (figure 175) and the American solution to a problem which faced all designers of combat clothing was a fibre helmet, one-piece overall and olive drab field jacket with zip fasteners and knit collar, cuffs and waistband.

INSIGNIA Badges of rank for officers consisted of gold or silver metal badges which were worn on the shoulders or on the right side (generals both sides) of the shirt collar, on the left front of the overseas cap, and sometimes painted on the front and back of the steel helmet. Non-commissioned officers and men wore their chevrons on both sleeves.

Officers wore metal arm-of-service badges on both lapels, while other ranks wore them on the left side only as well as

173 Private, US Army, 1944

This buck private serving as an infantryman in the US 5th Army in central Italy wears the M1 helmet, M1941 OD field jacket and OD trousers with canvas leggings and boots. The equipment, consisting of haversack with entrenching tool and bayonet (M1942) with canteen suspended from the cartridge belt, is the standard pattern. The ground sheet is draped over the cartridge belt. The rifle is the US M1 Garand semi-automatic rifle.

174 Officer, US Army, 1945

By the last winter of the war in Italy American troops were beginning to receive suitable winter clothing, although soldiers continued to improvise as best they could to keep themselves warm and dry. This infantry officer wears a hooded snow smock over his field uniform with the special waterproofed M1943 trousers. Over his M1943 combat boots he wears rubber galoshes. On the cartridge belt are a pouch for spare magazines and the M4 knife bayonet. Additional carbine magazines are carried in a special pouch on the butt of the US Calibre .30 M1 carbine.

175 Corporal, US Army, 1942

The fibre helmet with ventilation holes was issued to crews of armoured fighting vehicles, as were the overalls he wears under the lined field jacket, which was so popular that every soldier tried to get his hands on one. Suspended from the woven pistol belt is a russet leather holster for the .45 Model 1911 A1 automatic pistol, a small pouch on the right for a field dressing and on the left a pouch for pistol ammunition.

176 Lieutenant-Colonel, US Army, 1941

This field officers wears the campaign hat with yellow cords for cavalry, 'chino', worsted or gaberdine shirt, cord breeches and russet field boots which were already a rarity by the time America entered the war.

175

176

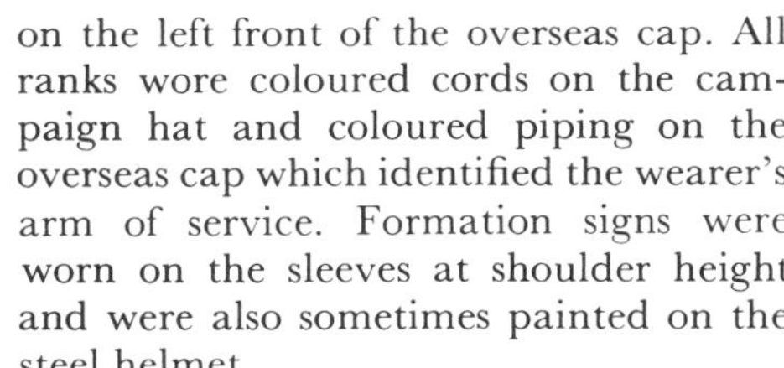

on the left front of the overseas cap. All ranks wore coloured cords on the campaign hat and coloured piping on the overseas cap which identified the wearer's arm of service. Formation signs were worn on the sleeves at shoulder height and were also sometimes painted on the steel helmet.

AIR FORCE

Prior to June 1941 the Air Force of the United States had comprised two elements, the GHQ Air Force and the Air Force, but through the work of General Marshall, and the Secretary of War, Henry L. Stimson, they were combined to form the USAAF.

For a nation as large as the United States its Air Force was relatively small, consisting in June 1941 of 9078 officers

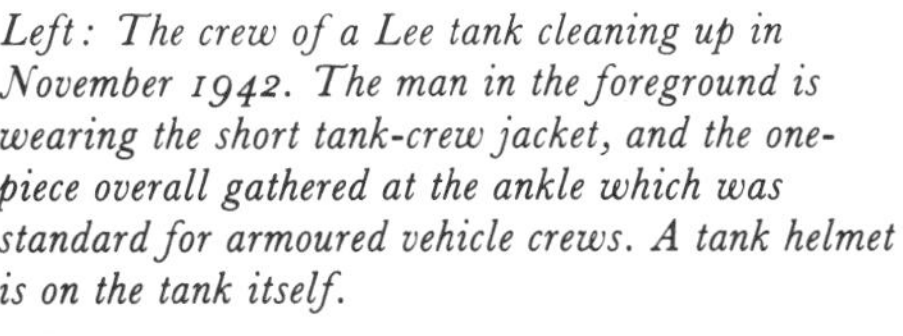

Left: The crew of a Lee tank cleaning up in November 1942. The man in the foreground is wearing the short tank-crew jacket, and the one-piece overall gathered at the ankle which was standard for armoured vehicle crews. A tank helmet is on the tank itself.

177 Technician 5th Grade, US Army Air Force, 1942
Here the Class A uniform is being worn with the steel helmet on a ceremonial occasion. Army Air Force insignia is worn on the collar and on the sleeves above the rank chevrons. The diagonal stripe on the cuff denotes three years' honourable service. The rifle is the US M1903 Springfield rifle.

and 143,563 enlisted men and about 6000 aircraft. But the next six months saw a rapid expansion of the USAAF, an expansion that was accelerated at a faster rate after the Japanese attack on Pearl Harbor on 7 December 1941. The USAAF reached the peak of its strength in March 1944 with 2,411,294 men while the number of planes used by the Air Force during the war was just over a quarter of a million – a reflection of American organisational and industrial strength.

As part of the reorganisation Major-General Henry H. Arnold was appointed Chief, Army Air Forces and was given a place on the Joint Chiefs of Staff, which greatly enhanced the prestige and newly-acquired independent status of the USAAF. Indeed, on 9 March 1942 the Army Air Force was made one of the three co-equal semi-autonomous branches of the War Department.

The USAAF was soon involved in the fighting over the Mediterranean in support of the Anglo-American landings in North Africa and once the Axis forces were cleared from Africa, air bases were set up for the aerial assault upon southern Europe. In combination with the British and other Allied air forces the American Army Air Force was able to gain an air superiority over the Mediterranean that was decisive in the successful conclusion of land operations. On the strategic level the industrial centres in northern Italy, Austria and southern Germany were heavily bombed, as were the Ploesti oil refineries in Romania but at the heavy cost of 350 aircraft. Tactically the USAAF played a vital part, acting in an interdiction role preventing supplies and men reaching the battlefronts as well as being engaged in direct battlefield operations.

ORGANISATION The USAAF in the Mediterranean consisted of the 12th and 15th Air Forces, both of which contained fighter and bomber units. The 12th Air Force was established on 20 August 1942 and was soon engaged in active operations in the support of the ground fighting in North Africa. Its initial strength was some 500 planes, a figure that was doubled by early 1943 when it was combined with RAF units to form the Northwest African Air Force under General Carl Spatz. The 12th Air Force acted in support of the Allied armies in Italy and in southern France after 1944 until the conclusion of fighting in May 1945.

The 12th Air Force, flying a total of 430, 681 sorties, dropped 217,136 tons of bombs and shot down 3565 enemy aircraft for the loss of 2843 planes.

The 15th Air Force was initially formed from the heavy bombardment units of the 12th Air Force on 1 November 1943, its role being to act as the strategic bomber force for the Mediterranean Allied Air Forces. From airfield in southern Italy this Air Force worked in tandem with the 8th Air Force based in Britain, attacking targets in German occupied Europe. During the winter of 1943–44, however, the 15th Air Force was mainly engaged in support of land operations in Italy and in Operation 'Strangle' (March–April 1944) it was involved in the interdiction campaign to isolate German forces in northern Italy.

Flying 242,377 sorties, the 15th Air Force dropped 309,278 tons of bombs, destroyed 6258 enemy aircraft and lost 3410 aircraft to enemy action.

Before its reorganisation in Great Britain on 16 October 1943 the US 9th Air Force had been stationed in the Mediterranean theatre. The 9th Air Force was officially formed on 12 November 1942 having formerly been known as the Middle East Air Force. The 9th Air Force concentrated on the disruption of enemy supply lines in the eastern part of the Mediterranean as well as acting in a ground-support role with the British 8th Army in the follow-up to El Alamein. During the period that the 9th was engaged in the Mediterranean 20,080 sorties were flown 20,127 tons of bombs were dropped and 610 enemy aircraft were shot down for the loss of 227 US planes.

UNIFORM As a branch of the Army the United States Air Force did not have its own distinctive uniforms, but continued to wear American Army uniforms throughout World War II. During the course of the war American airmen tried to develop their own particular style of dress, which made them instantly recognisable. For example they removed the stiffener from their peaked or 'vizor' cap which

Below: The basic warm clothing of the American Air Force: sheepskin-lined leather jackets, caps with ear flaps and the A-6 lined overshoes. These were all comfortable and practical items.

gave it a crushed look, they affected a less formal look, and of course the pilots and aircrew tended to have more decorations and 'wings' than ordinary soldiers.

On 21 June 1941 the air forces of the US Army became officially the United States Army Air Force, but this did not lead to new uniforms.

Flying clothing in Europe and North Africa included a one-piece beige flying suit, or a fleece-lined leather two-piece flying suit with helmet and a cap with peak and earflaps. Pilots of enclosed single-seater aircraft simply removed their tunic and donned a leather flying jacket over their shirt with rank badges on the collar.

INSIGNIA Badges of rank were identical to those worn by other branches of the American Army, although a new rank of Flight Officer was created in July 1942.

The arm-of-service badge was the winged propeller which was worn on both lapels by officers or on the left side of the collar and overseas cap by other ranks. Formation signs predominantly in ultramarine, white, red or yellow were worn on the upper left sleeve.

NAVY

The American contribution to the war in the Mediterranean was not enthusiastic and the decision to launch Operation 'Torch', the invasion of French North Africa, was not finally made until July 1942. The American Chiefs of Staff were opposed to it, claiming that the Mediterranean theatre represented a diversion from the vital theatre which lay in north-west Europe, and consequently the American naval contribution to the amphibious landings in the Mediterranean was not large. Another important factor limiting size was the reluctance of the Naval Staff to divert resources from the Pacific.

ORGANISATION US naval operations on the Mediterranean were organised around task forces for particular operations. For the North African landings in November 1942, Task Force 34 was assembled, which included 30 transports with the covering force provided by the Royal Navy. The most important US naval force was Western Naval Task Force whose objective was Casablanca. This was divided into four groups: the Covering Group of one battleship, two cruisers for fire support, covered by a screen of four destroyers. The second was the Northern Attack Group of one battleship, one cruiser, eight destroyers and eight transports. The Central Attack Group, the third, comprised one armoured and one light cruiser and four destroyers for fire support and fifteen transports. Protecting this force were one aircraft carrier, one auxiliary (later called an escort carrier) and five destroyers. The fourth group, the Southern Attack Group consisted of one battleship, one light cruiser and three destroyers for fire support, with six transports, two tankers, five destroyers and one submarine. Screening these were one auxiliary carrier and two destroyers. This Force totalled 102 vessels including auxiliary ships.

Once the final decision to attack Sicily had been taken at the Casablanca Conference, three task forces were assembled in the North African ports. Task Force 86 transported the 34th Infantry Division with two light cruisers and eight destroyers; Task Force 81 carried the 1st Infantry Division with two light cruisers and thirteen destroyers; and Task Force 85 transported the 45th Infantry Division escorted by one light cruiser and sixteen destroyers. The floating reserve carried two combat teams of the 2nd Armoured Division and one from the 1st. The whole force included 580 ships and landing craft with 1124 shipborne landing craft.

At Salerno, the American contingent formed the Southern Attack Force (Task Force 81). Its main convoy transported US 31st Infantry Division from Oran in thirteen transports, accompanied by three light cruisers and twelve destroyers. Task Force 81 was also called upon to mount the landing at Anzio. The American contribution called 'X-Ray' included four destroyers and one cruiser.

UNIFORM US Navy uniform as worn during World War II was introduced in 1862 and following various modifications and additions was subject to a complete review in 1941

The basic uniform for officers consisted of a peaked cap with both blue or white top, overseas cap, reefer jacket with white shirt and black tie and matching trousers with black shoes and socks. The greatcoat and raincoat were both double-breasted with two rows of four buttons in front. The same uniform with minor differences was worn by warrant officers and chief petty officers (see figure 180). There was also a white version of the basic uniform for officers, warrant officers and chief petty officers, which was sometimes dyed grey for wear as a working uniform. This was found unsatisfactory and a new Army-style light khaki working dress including both long and short sleeved shirts and overseas cap was introduced.

The square rig for ratings is shown in figure 179. In cold weather ratings wore a shortened overcoat or pea-coat with two rows of large plastic buttons bearing the American Eagle in front. Ratings also had plain whites with which the jumper was worn, without the blue denim collar but with the black silk.

Wartime working dress in warm climates was the white cap, blue shirt, and blue jeans, or a roll-neck pullover worn under a blue jean jacket. Winter or cold weather working dress included a padded blue cloth helmet, navy blue version of the Army tanker's jacket with knit collar and cuffs (see figure 178) and matching lined trousers. Foul weather clothing was made of black oilskin, or an olive drab

178 Seaman 2nd Class, US Navy, 1942

This rating wears the winter working head-dress to which a face mask could be attached in very cold weather. The lined jacket was worn without insignia, although sometimes improvised rank badges were worn on the head-dress. The trousers are the standard bell-bottoms which formed part of the 'square rig'.

179

180

181

rubberised material. These working rigs formed the basis for the battle rig with which was worn two patterns of steel helmets (often painted in battleship grey).

Probably the most famous American fighting men are the Marines or 'leather necks' who formed a special corps with its own traditions, uniforms and organisation. The basic service dress was green and the typical head-dress the felt campaign hat with red cords. Combat dress at the beginning of the war was the two-piece olive-drab (actually a pale grey-green) with open patch pockets and the letters USMC stencilled in black above the corps emblem on the left breast pocket. In cold weather a winter combat jacket was worn over the suit.

INSIGNIA The main means of identifying the rank of officers was the rank distinction lace worn on the cuffs and shoulder straps, but officers also wore Army rank badges in metal on the overseas cap (both blue and light khaki) and on the khaki shirt collar. Chief petty officers and petty officers wore their badges of rank on the sleeves, while the three classes of seamen had one to three white tape stripes on the cuffs of their dress jumper.

The Navy was divided into two basic branches which were the executive or line branch which was responsible for actually operating ships, and the other corps. Line officers had the five-pointed star above the rank distinction lace and rank badges on both sides of the shirt collar, while officers in other corps wore a corps badge above the rank lace, on the right collar only and on the left side of the overseas cap. For petty officers and ratings the system was simpler: they wore their rank badges on the left sleeve if in the corps or on the right if in the executive.

The USMC wore Army rank badges in metal for officers and in cloth for other ranks. The chevrons were in yellow upon red on the blue uniform, red upon green on the green uniform and khaki upon khaki on the khaki uniform. In 1942 it was ordered that chevrons would only be worn on the left sleeve. Certain officers (paymasters, quartermasters, aides-de-camp and band leaders) wore special Marine branch badges on the collar in place of the corps badge.

179 Petty Officer 1st Class, US Navy, 1942
Overseas the white fatigue cap replaced the unpopular 'Donald Duck' cap and was worn with all rigs. The three seaman grades were identified by the white tape stripes on the cuffs, while this petty officer's rank and radioman badges are worn on the left sleeve.

180 Chief Petty Officer, US Navy, 1941
The uniform is almost identical to that worn by officers except that the peaked cap has a special cap badge, and rank badges are worn on the sleeves of the so-called 'sack coat'. The fact that he wears his chevrons on the left sleeve and has the branch badge of a machinist identifies him as a member of the engineering corps. Each stripe on the cuff denoted four years' service.

181 Captain, US Marine Corps, 1942
With the green service dress, this officers wears the M1917 steel helmet which was originally the first British steel helmet with the A 1 modification – an American woven chin strap. The fouragère *is that of the French* Croix de Guerre *awarded to the 5th and 6th Marines for service in France during World War I, while the formation sign was originally that of the British 49th West Riding Division.*

THE EASTERN FRONT 1941-45

In terms of manpower, the Eastern Front was by far the largest theatre of war. Not only were enormous armies raised by Germany and the Soviet Union (in 1945 the Soviet field army totalled over six million men), but forces were raised from occupied and satellite nations. The countries of eastern Europe – Romania, Bulgaria, Hungary and Finland – also participated in the struggle, and Romania's army, for example, was almost a million men strong in 1941.

The problems of supplying such large numbers of men over vast distances and in extremes of climate meant that uniforms had to be extremely functional, and the Axis forces in particular often suffered severely from unsuitable clothing.

Soviet Union
Army

The Winter War against Finland had revealed many shortcomings in the Red Army and, in the following months, much work was done to improve the quality of the Army's personnel and equipment. On paper the Red Army of the summer of 1941 was a formidable force; in practice, there were still grave deficiencies which would be ruthlessly exposed by the German Army. The fighting on the Eastern Front dwarfed that in most other theatres, the numbers of men and vehicles involved were enormous, as were the casualties.

During the first German assaults, the Red Army almost collapsed. Units fell back, leaving behind them huge quantities of valuable supplies, ammunition and irreplaceable heavy equipment. Formations and units lost their coherence, and headquarters, often staffed by completely inexperienced staff officers, struggled with poor communications.

From June until the end of the year the Red Army withdrew eastwards, suffering grievous losses but also inflicting heavy losses on the enemy. In the autumn the front line ran from Leningrad in the north to Odessa in the south, but the Red Army had lost nearly one-third of its entire pre-war strength. Despite these colossal defeats the Germans had failed to annihilate the Red Army and had failed to take either Leningrad or Moscow.

Moscow now became the focal point of German efforts while Stalin, as Supreme Commander, decided to remain in Moscow and defend the capital to the bitter end.

On 5 December 1941, in temperatures of minus 30 degrees centigrade, the Red Army launched its counter-offensive with 720,000 men, 670 tanks (205 of which were heavy and medium models), 5900 guns and mortars and 415 rocket launchers. The offensive was the first success of the Red Army and was a tremendous boost to morale.

During the first months of the 1942 campaign, Stalin decreed an all-out offensive, but the operation ended in disaster as the Soviet armies were encircled and destroyed by the German Army Group South's own offensive. The Soviet forces were pushed back deep into the Caucasus. The bitterest fighting was concentrated around the key position of Stalingrad, and it was here that the German offensive foundered, unable to dislodge the Soviet defenders whose stubborn resistance during the autumn of 1942 was one of the turning points of the war.

On 19 November Marshal Zhukov launched Operation 'Uranus', the Soviet counter-offensive which surrounded the 22 divisions of the German 6th Army in Stalingrad and threatened to cut off the 1st Panzer Army in the Caucasus. The Soviet ring around Stalingrad tightened during the winter of 1942–43 and on 2 February all German resistance finally ceased. The Germans and Romanians suffered 150,000 killed and 91,000 men taken prisoner.

In the Spring of 1943 the Red Army pushed forwards as much as the weather and stiffening German resistance would allow. By the summer the front line had stabilised, the focus of strategic attention being the Kursk salient which jutted out

182

183

184

into the German line and which they were determined to eliminate.

The great German summer offensive against this salient, code-named 'Citadel', was intended to wrest the initiative from the Red Army, but it ground to a halt ten kilometres ahead of its start line. While the Germans battered at the Soviet defences, Red Army commanders moved powerful mobile reserves to one critical sector after another, thus robbing the enemy of local superiority. The scale and complexity of these movements showed just how far the Red Army command had progressed in its ability to wage mechanised warfare.

The Red Army was again on the offensive in the winter of 1943–44, putting further strain on the German defence. It was the summer offensive of 1944 that was decisive, however: 2,500,000 Soviet troops spearheaded by 5000 tanks and self-propelled guns crashed into Army Group Centre, destroying it and forcing back the German Army towards its own frontiers. The Red Army was by now clearly superior to the German Army, and its victory was only a matter of time. At the end of August 1944, the Red Army stood on the frontier of Eastern Prussia, and Berlin lay only 600 kilometres to the west.

Right: Red Army troops in Vyborg in 1944. They are wearing camouflage overalls (a black pattern on khaki) and carry PPSh sub-machine guns.

The honour of taking Berlin was bestowed on Marshal Zhukov's 1st Belorussian Front with four combined and two tank armies.

A massive artillery bombardment before dawn on 16 April 1945 heralded the beginning of the final offensive. German resistance was fierce, and it was not until the night of 30 April/1 May 1945 that soldiers of the 756th Infantry Regiment (3rd Strike Army) planted their colour on the top of the *Reichstag*.

Even prior to the victory in Europe, Soviet formations had been transferred eastwards in preparation for the invasion of Japanese-occupied Manchuria. On 9 August 1945 an invasion force of 11 combined-arms armies, one tank army and three air armies was launched against the Japanese. The total strength of the Soviet forces amounted to over one-and-a-half million men, 26,137 guns, 5556 armoured fighting vehicles and over 5000 aircraft. After a short and brilliantly-conducted campaign, the Red Army accepted the Japanese surrender on 24 August.

It has been estimated that 13,700,000 Soviet servicemen died during World War II.

Organisation Although it is hard to arrive at a completely accurate figure, there were about 170 million people in the Soviet Union in 1941, of whom all eligible adult males, totalling 25 million, were liable for military service. The length of service was two years, after which the recruit would go into the reserves, ready to be called to the colours when necessary.

The quality of peace-time training in the Red Army left much to be desired: instruction was by rote learning, so that recruits were taught to value obedience over initiative. The sluggish Soviet response to the German invasion reflected an inadequate level of technical competence.

The regular army consisted of some nine million men, of whom about a half were based in the European Soviet Union. On the western front the Soviet Union deployed 170 divisions in five major groups: Leningrad Military District (three armies); Baltic Special Military District (two armies); West Special Military District (three armies); Kiev Special Military District (four armies) and the Odessa Military District (two armies).

During the period leading up to Operation *Barbarossa*, the Soviet Army was undergoing the turmoils of reorganisation. This was a consequence of the salutary lessons imposed by the Finnish war and, more immediately, of the German *Blitzkrieg* in the west. Russian theorists now

182 Corporal, Red Army, 1941
The helmet is the 1940-pattern on the front of which the red star was sometimes painted. On the greatcoat (shinel) collar are the patches which identified both arm of service and the rank of the wearer, which is efreitor *(from the German* Gefreiter *or soldier freed from some menial tasks after having done his basic training). Equipment consists of gas mask worn on the left and entrenching tool on the right, waist belt with ammunition pouches, and the pack which was simply a khaki cloth sack. Armament consists of a 7.62mm Tokarev M1940 rifle. These light, self-loading rifles needed careful maintenance, and were normally only issued to NCOs, who were felt to be likely to look after them properly.*

183 Sergeant, Red Army, 1941
The cavalry arm-of-service colour (blue) appears on the cap band and collar patches, on which was worn the crossed swords and a horseshoe badge. The shirt is unusual in that it has a stand collar which was not officially introduced until 1943. Cavalry and horse artillery had blue breeches as long as they were available. The sword is the 1928-pattern shaska, *which was issued to all cavalrymen including cossacks.*

184 Major-General, Red Army, 1941
The cap and tunic (called a 'French' after the British general of that name who wore a khaki tunic which was avidly copied by Tsarist officers during World War I) were the pattern introduced in 1935, whereas the blue trousers with generals' lampassen *were introduced only in July 1940. The distinctive colour for generals was scarlet, but the collar patches were in the arm-of-service colour for all but Generals of the Army and Marshals who had scarlet collar patches.*

185 Trooper, Red Army, 1941
This cavalryman is wearing the special wading gear which was intended to enable troops to cross the many rivers of the Soviet Union. Suspended from his wrists are the paddles and in his right hand he holds a rod for measuring the depth of water. The helmet is the 1936 model which was replaced in 1940–41 by the new pattern (illustrated by figure 182). The rifle is the 7.62mm Mosin-Nagant M1891/30. This was the basic weapon of the Soviet Army, and although long (1232mm) and rather clumsy, it continued in service until the 1950s. A peculiarity was the bayonet of this model, which was a long thin spike of cruciform shape.

186 Junior Sergeant, Red Army, 1941
The sun hat of this tankman was first introduced in March 1938 for personnel serving in the Central Asian, North Caucasian and Trans Caucasian commands as well as those serving in the Crimea. The shirt with stand-and-fall collar had the same reinforcing patches on the elbows as on the knees. The collar patches are in the arm-of-service colours which were the same for artillery, hence the small tank badge in metal. The red triangle denoted the rank of junior sergeant.

realised that a coherent military doctrine was an urgent priority; a doctrine, moreover, which allowed for the crucial role of armoured formations in battle. When the *Wehrmacht* struck against the Soviet Union, however, the problems of reorganisation had still to be resolved.

Reacting swiftly to the surprise German invasion on 23 June, Stalin supervised the creation of an inter-service general headquarters (*Stavka*) and took control of it a month later, becoming in effect the guiding light of military operations. By centralising all military departments under general political control, the *Stavka* was able to supervise the deployment of the nation's resources with considerable efficiency. A major function of the *Stavka* was the co-ordination of forces throughout the Soviet Union, which entailed the transfer of the Siberian divisions to the west in time for the crucial battle for Moscow. At the same time the *Stavka* struggled to form a strategic reserve with which to mount counter-attacks as soon as the opportunity arose, although this entailed depriving front-line units of desperately-needed reinforcements.

Above: A Soviet officer in a self-propelled gun. He is wearing the standard padded helmet for armoured vehicle personnel, and the issue greatcoat.

The Soviet armed forces of 1941 were organised into armies of from two to four corps, each of two to four divisions. An average army might have 12 divisions which with auxiliary services (signals, engineer, supply, maintenance and transportations), amounted to nearly 200,000 men. Following the invasion, the *Stavka* found the rifle corps unwieldy due to the shortage of trained command and staff personnel and they were abolished for a while, the size of an army being reduced as a result to around eight divisions. The rifle corps was re-introduced in the Soviet Army, but never acquired the semi-independent function of corps in the other Allied armies.

In 1944 there were 48 infantry armies stretched out between the Baltic and the Black Sea. Varying considerably in size from 60,000 to 120,000 men they could be augmented by the temporary attachment of independent tank and artillery units so they could expand to over 200,000 men.

Spearheading the armed forces were the tank armies, of which there were six by 1944. First constituted on an official basis in 1943 they were usually formed by two tank corps and one mechanised corps with a combination of supporting units making the tank army with a total strength of around 40 to 60,000 men broadly equivalent to the German panzer corps.

185

186

The basic formation of the Red Army was the rifle division. Since the debacle of the Winter War many of the specialist units, including the light tank and anti-aircraft battalions, had been withdrawn from the division, partly because they had failed to work at divisional level, but also to provide a flexible reserve of specialised units. The confusion caused by the German invasion accentuated this tendency towards decentralisation so that the Soviet division of the first year of war was almost literally a rifle formation with few supporting arms. Needless to say these rifle divisions could not match the combined-arms divisions of the German Army.

Throughout 1942 the size of Soviet divisions decreased but this was compensated for by a steady increase in fire-power derived from an increase in mortars and regimental artillery. By the end of 1942 the new Soviet rifle division had a strength of around nine-and-a-half thousand men. These were organised into three infantry regiments of 2500 men and an artillery regiment of 1000 men, plus an anti-tank and an engineer battalion and a company each of signals and reconnaissance troops. The rifle regiment was composed of three battalions of 620 men, each supported by companies of 76mm howitzers and 45mm anti-tank guns, anti-tank rifles, mortars, signals and reconnaissance troops. Each battalion comprised three rifle companies (140 men), a mortar and a machine gun company, and a platoon each of anti-tank guns and rifles and signals. The artillery regiment was equipped with 36 anti-tank rifles, 24 × 76mm guns and 12 × 122mm howitzers. Total 'gun' strength of the division was 160 mortars, 94 guns of various calibres and 228 anti-tank rifles.

Despite improvements in both the quantity and quality of Soviet artillery, divisional artillerymen played a limited role. They confined themselves to a simple 'direct' fire role (on targets directly visible to the gun's crew as opposed to 'indirect' fire, relying on forward observers), while skilled personnel were creamed off for the specialised artillery brigades and divisions. Another feature of the Soviet Army was the widespread use of the anti-tank rifle, even towards the end of the war when improved tank armour had rendered them ineffective and infantry rocket-launchers had rendered them obsolete.

The Soviet High Command considered the division to be an expendable unit and a week's hard fighting on the Eastern Front could reduce its establishment strength by half. It was not Red Army practice to replace the losses of front-line units: they were allowed to run down to a point where they were either disbanded or pulled out of line for rebuilding. Thus a nominal division might well have the actual strength of a regiment. Similarly, not only were Soviet units 'overrated', but they were often 'underled', so that in some cases full-strength divisions were commanded by colonels.

A particular feature of the division was the increase in infantry fire-power occasioned by the widespread introduction of the sub-machine gun – over 2000 men were normally equipped with sub-machine guns. The Russians had realised the value of sub-machine guns before the war but it was not until late 1942 that the front-line troops were receiving them in sufficient quantity.

The basic late-1942 rifle division set the basic organisational pattern for infantry divisions until the end of the war. The only variant was the Guards rifle division. 'Guard' status was accorded to units and formations which performed especially well in combat, the first such distinction being awarded to four rifle divisions on 18 September 1941 for their distinguished conduct in defence. The Guards divisions were better-equipped than the standard divisions and, with superior human material, they displayed a consistently higher level of military competence which brought them up to the level of the regular German divisions.

The Soviet Army placed great reliance on the role of artillery on the battlefield. The rifle divisions were well-equipped with guns as the organisational diagram shows, but at no point in the war could

187 Private, Red Army, 1942
The uniform is the standard pattern for Red Army soldiers with the M1940 steel helmet, rolled great-coat and puttees with ankle boots. Pouches were often made of a synthetic material. The weapon is the 14.5mm PTRD 1941 Degtyarev anti-tank rifle.

188 Private, Red Army, 1944
A pilotka *and waterproof rain cape is worn over the field uniform. The Red Army ground sheet was so designed that it could be worn as a hooded-cape. The weapon is the 7.62mm M44 Moisin-Nagant carbine with folding bayonet in fixed position.*

189

190

191

189 General, Red Army, 1945
This new 'wave'-green (before the revolution this same colour was called Tsar's green) parade uniform was introduced in April 1945 in time for the victory celebrations. Marshals had heavier embroidery on the collar and cuffs than generals. The belt was also identical to the Tsarist pattern but in yellow instead of silver. Orders on the right breast are (top to bottom): the Orders of Suvorov 1st Class, Kutusov and the Red Star; and on the left the Star of a Hero of the Soviet Union, three Orders of Lenin and two of the Red Banner and, underneath, the Medal for the 20th Anniversary of the Red Army and two campaign medals.

190 Junior Lieutenant, Red Army, 1945
This infantry officer wears the tunic (mundir) *introduced in January 1943. Company officers, in addition to the shoulder boards, had a single embroidered bar on the collar patches and a single spool on each cuff, whereas field officers had two.*

191 Officer, Red Army, 1942
With the 1940 fur cap, this artillery officer wears the quilted telogreika *introduced in August 1941. The boots* (valenki) *made of thick compressed felt were the best footwear for snow as long as temperatures were below freezing. The haversack on his left side held a gas mask.*

the Soviet artillery provide the level of flexible support to the infantryman that was accepted practice in the German Army. A basic problem facing the Russians throughout the war was a shortage of technically skilled personnel and in the artillery arm this dearth was most keenly felt. The solution was to concentrate the best artillerymen into large specialised units (brigades and divisions) where their skills could be improved and put to best use. Paradoxically, the large size of these units (combined with the simplified Soviet fire control systems) prevented them from being used to best advantage, with the result that artillery fire often resembled the 'creeping barrage' of World War I. At certain times, of course, this approach could be highly effective, where the *Stavka* would concentrate its guns – up to 20,000 – to form an artillery offensive to destroy the German front line systematically.

In 1941 the vast majority of artillery pieces were distributed among the rifle divisions; less than ten per cent (not including anti-tank and anti-aircraft) were at the disposal of the Soviet High Command. After the disasters of 1941 and early 1942 when thousands of guns were lost to the Germans, Soviet industry began mass artillery production. Rather than rush reserves to the divisions at the front, however, the *Stavka* re-organised artillery into brigades and divisions. Thus, by the end of the war, nearly three-quarters of the artillery was held back from the rifle divisions and organised in centralised formations.

A typical artillery division would be divided into four brigades with a signals and a fire control unit, making a total of nearly 10,000 men. The division was organised as follows: a mortar brigade equipped with 100 anti-tank rifles and over 100 120mm heavy mortars; a light field artillery brigade with three regiments of 24 × 76mm guns each; a howitzer brigade of 48 × 122mm and 24 × 152mm howitzers and a medium field artillery brigade armed with 12 × 122mm guns and 24 × 152mm gun howitzers. Each brigade consisted of between two and three regiments with auxiliary and infantry units lavishly provided with submachine guns.

Above: A Soviet soldier with the Red Flag over the ruins of Stalingrad. His clothing is the standard winter gear – greatcoat and fur-lined cap.

The largest artillery formation was the corps, in which anything up to 25 brigades would be combined under the one authority.

A special feature of the Red Army were the rocket-launcher units, armed with multiple-barrelled rocket-launchers known as *katyushas*. Although they had a limited range they were able to deliver a massive volume of fire-power in a very short space of time and for this reason they proved popular with Soviet troops. The largest formation was the brigade divided into three 800-man regiments, each equipped with six 37mm anti-tank guns (for protection against roving German tanks) and 24 ten-barrelled 132mm rocket-launchers.

Despite the German success with the tank arm it was the Soviet Union that had more tanks than any other nation in 1941, some 15,000 armoured fighting vehicles in all. Many were lost during the first six months of the war with the brunt of the fighting being borne by the infantry. It was only in 1943 that the armoured forces were able to make a decisive contribution to the Soviet victories on the Eastern Front. In 1941 much of the tank force, especially the light and obsolete models, was scattered among the rifle divisions and was overwhelmed by the panzer formations in small penny-pocket engagements. When Soviet industry established itself on a war footing in 1942 it began to produce tanks at a massive rate, so that by mid-1943 the Red Army had 8000 tanks at the front and by 1945 at least 15,000.

Many of these tanks were new models, including the KV series and the T-34, the latter the most important tank of the war, combining mobility, fire-power and armour. Rather than redistribute these tanks among the infantry formations, they were held back to form new independent tank brigades. With a strength of 1300

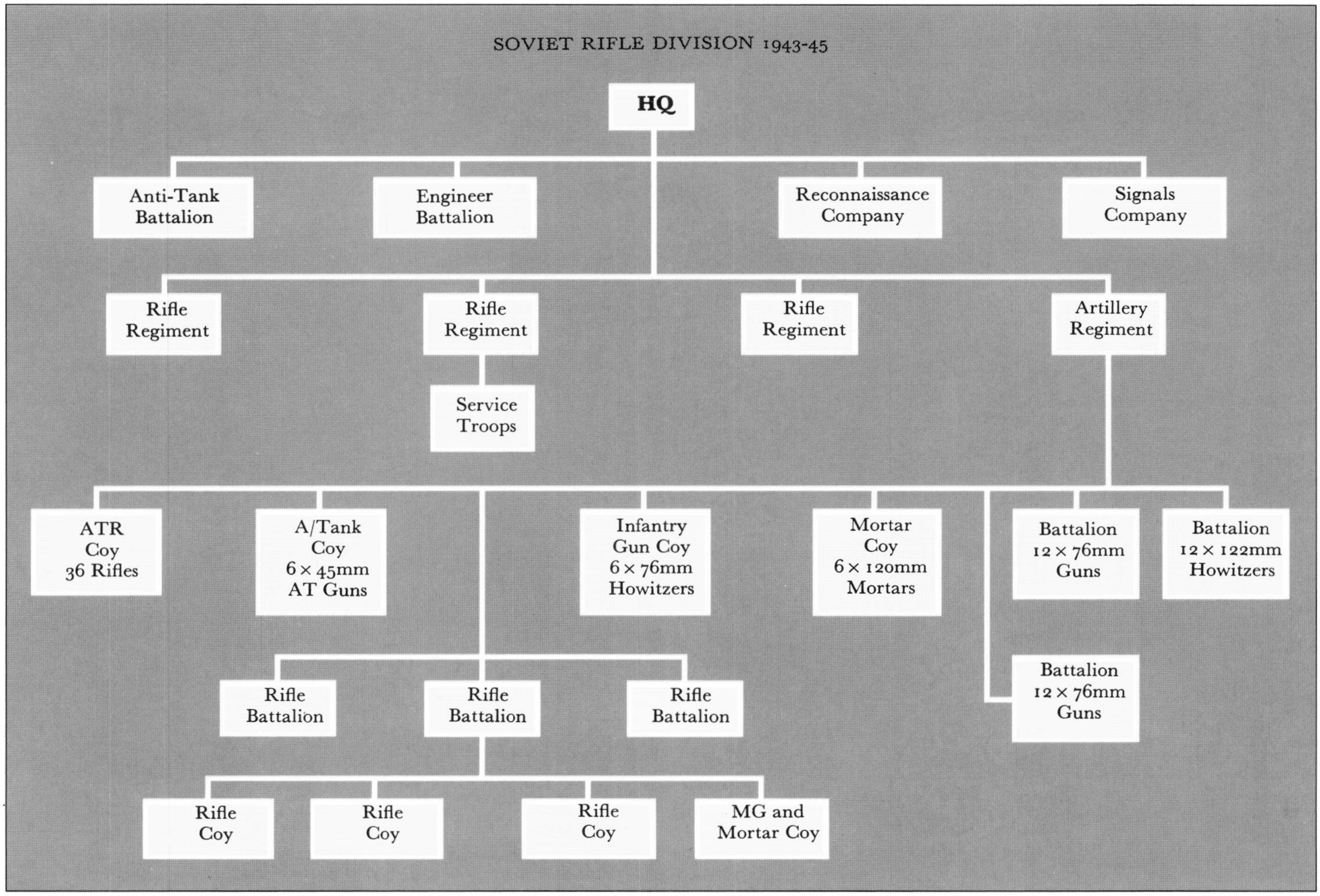

SOVIET RIFLE DIVISION 1943-45

- **HQ**
  - Anti-Tank Battalion
  - Engineer Battalion
  - Reconnaissance Company
  - Signals Company
  - Rifle Regiment
  - Rifle Regiment
    - Service Troops
    - ATR Coy 36 Rifles
    - A/Tank Coy 6 × 45mm AT Guns
    - Infantry Gun Coy 6 × 76mm Howitzers
    - Mortar Coy 6 × 120mm Mortars
    - Rifle Battalion
    - Rifle Battalion
      - Rifle Coy
      - Rifle Coy
      - Rifle Coy
      - MG and Mortar Coy
    - Rifle Battalion
  - Rifle Regiment
  - Artillery Regiment
    - Battalion 12 × 76mm Guns
    - Battalion 12 × 122mm Howitzers
    - Battalion 12 × 76mm Guns

192 Officer, Red Army, 1942
This officer wears the 1940-pattern ushanka *and the sheepskin coat* (polaschubuk) *with 1935-pattern leather equipment for officers. The sheepskin coat was usually issued to both mounted and armoured personnel.*

193 Ski Trooper, Red Army, 1942
There were no special ski troops as such in the Red Army, but in winter units sent out patrols on skis which were equipped with various kinds of snow camouflage suits. The weapon is the standard sub-machine gun of the Red Army, the PPSh, introduced in 1941. This weapon (also carried by the second lieutenant in figure 190) was easy to manufacture in large quantities, and whole divisions were armed with it rather than rifles.

194 Tankman, Red Army, 1943
The leather helmet is the pre-war model which was also worn by motorcyclists. The overall came in a number of different patterns and colours which ranged from black to grey. No insignia was usually worn on the overall until the end of the war when tank crews participating in the Moscow victory parade wore black overalls with collar patches, shoulder boards and decorations; these were similar in form to those of the old Tsarist state.

men, the brigade was broken down into three small battalions of 140 men and 21 tanks each. Unlike the old tank brigade which had a total of 80 to 90 tanks and was composed almost exclusively of tanks and its minimal support units, the new tank brigades were strengthened by a sub-machine gun battalion of 400 men and companies of anti-tank and anti-aircraft troops. The brigades were combined into tank corps which were the Soviet equivalent of the panzer division and likewise played a similar, central role. By 1943 there were 26 corps. The corps consisted of three tank brigades, a motorised rifle brigade and support units (as indicated in the diagram). The corps had about 200 armoured fighting vehicles, which compared well with the 160–180 tanks of a typical panzer division, its only weakness as an organisation being a shortage of organic artillery.

The other important motorised, mobile, divisional-size formation was the mechanised corps which, with a strength of nearly 18,000 men, was the largest and most powerful in the Soviet Army. Composed of three brigades of mechanised infantry and

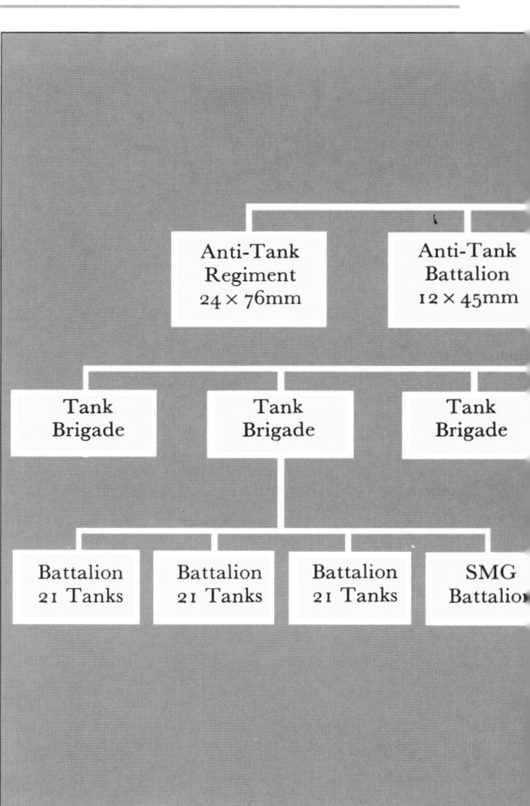

192

193

194

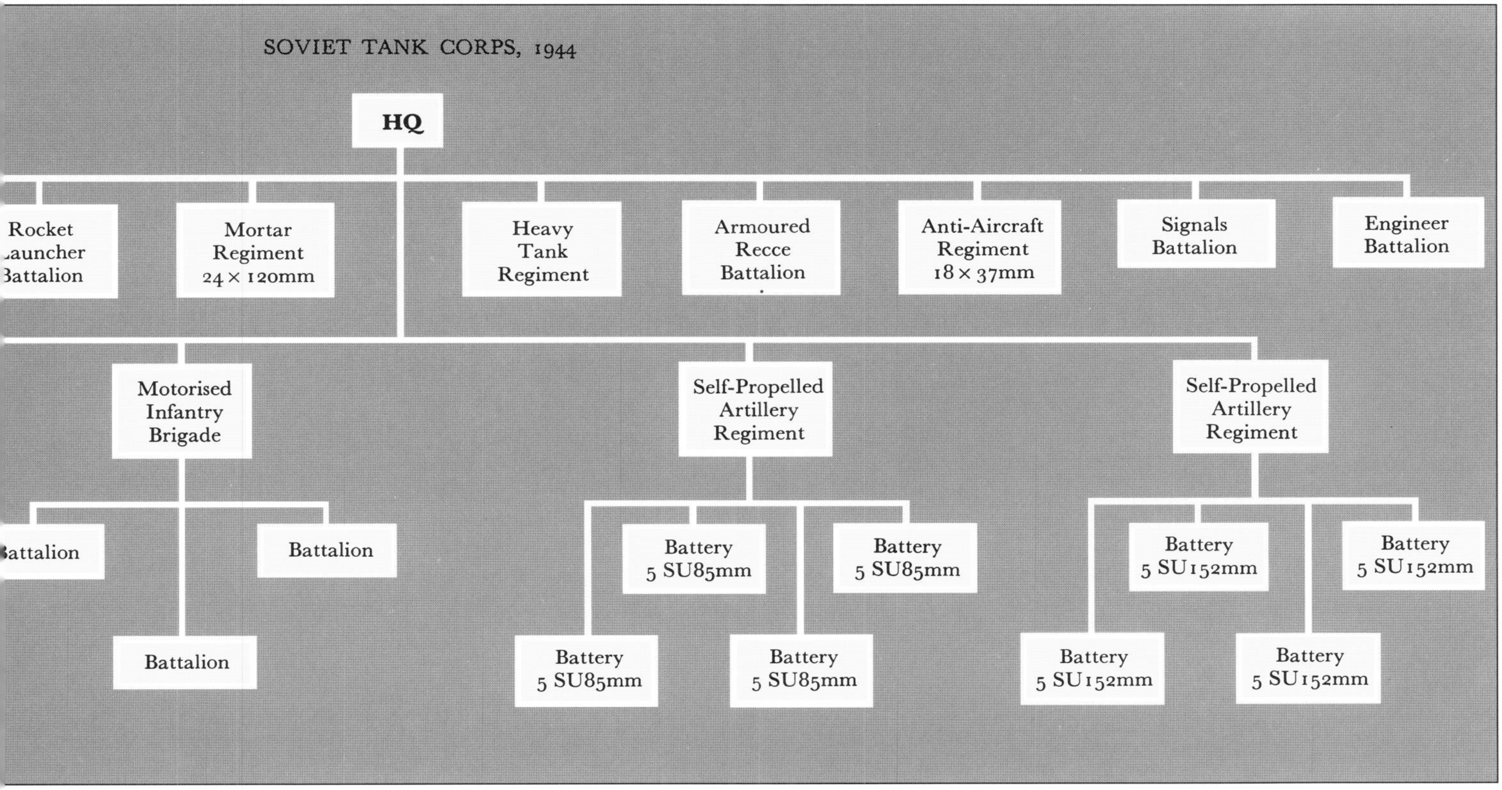

SOVIET TANK CORPS, 1944

- **HQ**
  - Rocket Launcher Battalion
  - Mortar Regiment 24 × 120mm
  - Heavy Tank Regiment
  - Armoured Recce Battalion
  - Anti-Aircraft Regiment 18 × 37mm
  - Signals Battalion
  - Engineer Battalion
  - Motorised Infantry Brigade
    - Battalion
    - Battalion
    - Battalion
  - Self-Propelled Artillery Regiment
    - Battery 5 SU85mm
    - Battery 5 SU85mm
    - Battery 5 SU85mm
    - Battery 5 SU85mm
  - Self-Propelled Artillery Regiment
    - Battery 5 SU152mm
    - Battery 5 SU152mm
    - Battery 5 SU152mm
    - Battery 5 SU152mm

a separate tank brigade with units of artillery and self-propelled artillery, the mechanised corps proved a successful combination of motorised infantry, artillery and armoured fighting vehicles. This contrasted with the Western Allies where, until the end of the war, there were too many tanks in their armoured divisions.

The mechanised infantry brigade had three battalions of motorised infantry, each of around 650 men and armed with 50 machine guns, 250 sub-machine guns, six medium (82mm) mortars and four 45mm anti-tank guns, plus a small complement of anti-tank rifles. Mobility was provided by between 40 and 50 trucks and lorries.

Support units included a small heavy mortar and an anti-tank battalion as well as companies of sub-machine guns, machine gun, engineer and reconnaissance troops. What gave the mechanised rifle brigade its punch, however, was its battalion of 31 T-34 tanks (or in some cases a regiment of 41 tanks) which, when combined with the tank brigade and self-propelled artillery, gave the corps a strength of between 200 and 230 armoured fighting vehicles.

The self-propelled artillery regiment was divided into four companies each equipped with five SU 76 or 85mm guns or, in the 'heavy' regiments, five JSU 100, 122, or 152mm guns. Although the self-propelled gun was no match for a tank, it was an effective weapon that could be produced relatively quickly and cheaply and for this reason was popular with the Soviet and German High Commands.

Like the tank corps, the mechanised corps received better equipment and personnel than did the rifle divisions and came to constitute the élite formations of the Red Army in much the same way as did the panzer divisions. The mechanised corps proved particularly adept at creating and exploiting 'breakthroughs' in the German line: it had the mobility to travel long distances quickly, the fire-power to break through defensive lines and sufficient infantry to hold a salient or bridgehead against enemy counter-attacks.

In addition to the tank and mechanised formations were the cavalry divisions, of which there were 40 in 1941. They were held in high regard in the Red Army, where the cavalry tradition had been maintained throughout the Russian Civil War and the Russo-Polish War of 1920.

During the spring thaw and late autumn before the coming of the snows, much of the Soviet Union was impassable to motor traffic, and horse-power came into its own. Horsed cavalry units added mobility to infantry, carried out reconnaissance, acted as a mobile reserve and carried out fighting patrols in depth behind the enemy lines. During the winter fighting in 1942–43 Red Army cavalrymen lived for weeks on unthreshed grain and horsemeat, while the horses munched roof thatching. The Germans were continually surprised at this ability of Russian troops to live off the land.

In 1936 five Red Army cavalry regiments, whose personnel were drawn in the main from the Cossack lands of the Terek, Kuban and Don, were redesignated Cossack cavalry regiments. By 1937 there existed a corps of Cossack cavalry, but during the purges of 1937–38 the Soviet Government back-pedalled on the controversial question of Cossack identity.

Below: Colonel-General Mikhail Katukov, commander of the 1st Tank Army in May 1945.

Cossack cavalry was again formed following the German invasion.

In April 1945 there were 34 cavalry divisions in the Red Army, and it was not until the mid-1950s that the last horsed cavalry units were finally disbanded.

The division was the basic formation, although they were normally combined into corps which would consist of three cavalry divisions, with two armoured battalions and generous artillery support. The division was divided into three cavalry regiments and an artillery regiment, plus support units. The strength of a cavalry division was about 5040 men and 5128 horses with 130 motor vehicles. Armament of the division consisted of:
447 sub-machine guns;
48 heavy machine guns;
118 light machine guns;
48 light mortars;
18 medium mortars;
8 heavy mortars;
76 anti-tank rifles;
12 × 45mm anti-tank guns;
16 × 76mm guns;
9 anti-aircraft machine guns;

Above: Battle-weary Soviet troops liberate Smolensk in 1943. This photograph captures extremely well the look of Soviet troops just after battle. The soldier on the right is wearing a quilted jacket.

195

196

6 × 37mm anti-aircraft guns;
10 T-70 light tanks.

The complement to the mobile formations was the motorised anti-tank brigade, a formation decisive in blunting the edge of the German armoured divisions. Thrown far forward in the Soviet front line, the anti-tank brigade would absorb the German attack, often being destroyed in the process, but the sacrifice was considered well worth while if the panzer division could be thrown into sufficient confusion to allow a successful Soviet tank counter-attack. The brigade was divided into three 600-man anti-tank regiments, each composed of six batteries equipped with four 76mm anti-tank guns. The battery would concentrate its fire on a single target until either it or the battery was destroyed.

The supply services in the Soviet Army were rudimentary and remained so throughout the war. Motor transport was always in short supply and much recourse had to be made to horse-drawn vehicles. The Anglo-American support programme eased the situation, however, particularly by the summer of 1943 when nearly half a million motor vehicles had been dispatched to the Soviet Union. The Soviet supply system had the disadvantage of breaking down at critical moments so that front-line troops could be starved of food and ammunition. It did have the advantage, however, of making large formations relatively self-contained, without the long straggling supply columns which were exceptionally vulnerable to the encircling thrusts of German armoured units.

Uniform One of the basic tenets of Soviet philosophy was the removal from society of the classes and privileges which had played such an important part in Tsarist Russian life. Almost immediately the infant Red Army, which was still engaged in a bitter civil war, realised that it could not exist, let alone win a war, unless it had discipline. The only way to establish discipline was to appoint commanders with the power to see that every order was carried out speedily and efficiently. The only way to achieve this was to enhance the authority of the commander by granting him special uniforms and insignia which were the outward symbols of that authority.

Stalin struggled with this problem throughout the 1920s and 1930s until he was obliged to return in stages to traditional military ways. Officers were reluctant to accept responsibilities which might ultimately lead to their deaths, especially when these dangerous appointments were unaccompanied by prestige and privileges. They fought for and gradually obtained military ranks and titles, smart new uniforms and decorations which Russian officers had traditionally enjoyed.

The typical Red Army soldier still lived a life of tedium and harshness with few comforts, poor food and even poorer clothing. Even so, the average soldier was still better-off than the industrial worker or collective farmer.

The smartening-up of Red Army uniforms really began at the end of 1935, when the uniform illustrated in figure 31 was introduced in December. In winter a silver-grey greatcoat in Tsarist cut was worn. At the same time the traditional rank titles of lieutenant, captain, major and colonel were re-introduced. New uniforms in steel grey for tank and blue for aviation officers completed the first major remodelling of Red Army uniforms.

By *ukase* (decree) of the Praesidium of the Supreme Council of the Soviet Union of 7 May 1940, the rank title of general was awarded to those general officers who had been fortunate enough to survive the purges of 1937 and 1938. In campaign dress all ranks in the Red Army wore the same uniform. In the summer it consisted of peaked cap (*fourashka*) or side cap (*pilotka*) and shirt (*rubaha*) with stand-and-fall collar which was worn outside matching breeches and high black leather boots. A shortage of leather meant that many men wore ankle boots and puttees.

Winter campaign dress was the same, but included a pointed, grey, padded cloth helmet (*shlem*) or, from 1940, a grey cloth cap with grey fleece front and neck and ear flap. The issue greatcoat was double-breasted and made from a stiff coarse greyish-brown cloth. It fastened with hooks and eyes on the right side and could be used as a blanket. Other types of winter coats were either made of sheepskin (usually worn by tankers and cavalrymen) or khaki cotton duck. The most

195 Lieutenant, Red Army Rifles, 1945
The red piping and band on the peaked cap, and the red piping on the shoulder straps identifies this officer as an infantryman. He has the 1943-pattern rubaha *and officers' equipment with pistol holster. Decorations are, on the right breast, the Orders of the Red Star and the War for the Fatherland with the Guards Badge below, and on his left two campaign medals.*

196 Private, Red Army, 1944
This rifleman wears typical Red Army summer field uniform with pilotka *with red star which was often painted khaki. The shirt or* rubaha *is in the traditional cut with shoulder boards. Boots were increasingly difficult to procure and soldiers had to make do with ankle boots and puttees. The belt is another late war economy pattern made of webbing reinforced with leather. The pouches are made from a synthetic material and were often replaced by the better-made German leather pouches.*

197 Sergeant, Red Army Medical Corps, 1945
Uniforms for women serving in the Red Army were first introduced in August 1941, but these were rapidly superseded by standard issue clothing. This sergeant wears a man's shirt with rank and arm-of-service badges on the shoulder straps. The badge on the right was worn by all personnel in Guards units and formations.

198 Captain, Red Army, 1944
This Don Cossack officer wears the pre-war coloured cap in the colours of the Don host (voisko), *the 1943-pattern tunic or* kitel *with shoulder boards piped in blue for cavalry. The trousers are the special pattern for Don cossacks with wide red stripe. The Tsarist* shaska *was worn suspended from a belt over the right shoulder.*

197

198

199 Sniper, Red Army, 1943
This woman sharpshooter wears one of the many patterns of camouflage overall which were issued to snipers, assault engineers and parachutists. One version had strips of frayed cloth sewn to the shoulder and outside sleeves, which had the effect of diffusing the outline and making a stationary figure almost invisible. The rifle is the 7.62mm Mosin-Nagant M1891/30 rifle with telescopic sight.

typical and distinctive of all Russian winter clothing was the jacket and trousers made from khaki and padded with cotton wool sewn in strips. This incredibly warm quilted outfit was known as *telogreika*. The Russian felt boots or *valenki* were ideal footwear in snow.

Two patterns of steel helmet were in general use. The first, introduced in 1936, began to be replaced in 1940 by a new model which, with minor modifications, is still in use in the Soviet Army today.

Special field uniforms were given to crews of armoured fighting vehicles, motorcyclists, parachutists, snipers and assault engineers. Armoured troops before the war had an expensively-made ribbed leather crash helmet and double-breasted black leather jacket. During the war the leather helmet was replaced by one made of grey, khaki or black cotton duck, and the most common form of protective clothing was the one-piece overall in khaki or black cotton duck. Parachute troops at first wore a grey cotton duck flying helmet and overall over their field uniforms, but during the war they wore standard field uniform and head-dress and were issued with the one-piece camouflage overall which was also worn by snipers (figure 199) and assault engineers.

Cavalry and horse artillerymen wore standard army uniform, but at the beginning of the war had blue breeches (officers' breeches were piped red). Officers retained the old 1924-pattern buttonless greatcoat which fastened with hooks and eyes and was longer than the infantry pattern. There was also the *bekesha*, which was a short khaki coat lined with lambs' fleece.

Cossacks wore either standard army head-dress or the traditional fur cap (*papacha*) with a top in the host colour which also appeared on the baggy blue trousers. This was in the form of light blue or red piping or wide red stripe for Terek, Kuban and Don cossacks respectively.

INSIGNIA Since the shoulder board was considered to have been the symbol of Tsarist oppression, the Red Army developed a new system of rank badges which consisted of red enamel geometrical shapes (triangles for NCOs, squares for company, oblongs for field and lozenges for general officers) mounted on coloured collar patches. Inverted chevrons for wear on both cuffs were introduced for officers in 1935. The traditional military titles were absent in the Red Army and officers were given appointments and known by the general title of commander so that, for instance, a man could be a squad commander (NCO) or an army commander (general). With the re-introduction of general officer rank titles on 13 July 1940, five-pointed gilt metal stars became their badge of rank. On 26 July 1940 all military titles were revived and new rank badges introduced.

Finally on 6 January 1943, Stalin surprised everybody, particularly the old Bolsheviks, by re-introducing the detested symbol of Tsarist militarism, the shoulder board. Now both rank titles and rank badges were fully-restored, although they were not identical to those worn in the Tsarist army since Stalin had chosen to re-introduce the rank of major which had been abolished in 1881.

Arm-of-service colours appeared as piping on the head-dress, shirt and tunic, and on the collar patches. From January 1943 these appeared on the shoulder straps. Within the arm of service certain special functions and duties were identified by small metal badges worn first on the collar patches and then on the shoulder straps.

AIRBORNE FORCES

Development of airborne troops began as early as 1928 and in less than seven years the Red Army was able to demonstrate an impressive airborne operation involving 600 aircraft and a complete airborne brigade with its own light artillery. By 1938, the Germans who had witnessed the 1935 manoeuvres near Kiev, were alarmed at the rapid progress made by the Soviets in this novel form of warfare, and they estimated that the Soviets possessed 4 brigades of parachute troops numbering some 4000 men.

On the eve of World War II Red parachute troops were used in the seizure of Bessarabia and northern Bukovina from Romania, but the airborne operations in the rear of the Mannerheim Line during the Winter War against Finland were not a success. During World War II a number of ambitious operations were planned and some carried out, but owing to various difficulties, including the lack of sufficient transport aircraft, bad weather, and lack of air superiority, none were very successful.

ORGANISATION Responsibility for the training of parachute troops rested with the military district commander, who relied for personnel on volunteers trained by the *Osoaviakim* organisation. Transport planes were provided by the Special Purpose Air Arm (AON) and later the Long Range Bomber Force which provided converted civil airliners of Lend-Lease C-47 transport planes. In October 1941 the VDV or Airborne Troops became an independent arm.

The basic unit was a brigade of about 4000 men formed from four rifle battalions of 700 men each and various supporting units. By June 1941, the Kiev Military District had formed the III, the Belorussian the IV and the Leningrad the V Airborne Corps. Each was to consist of three brigades but apparently only the original brigade in each corps was fully equipped when, in the summer of 1942, eight airborne corps in the process of formation were converted into Guards rifle divisions and some of them found themselves fighting as infantry in the ruins of Stalingrad.

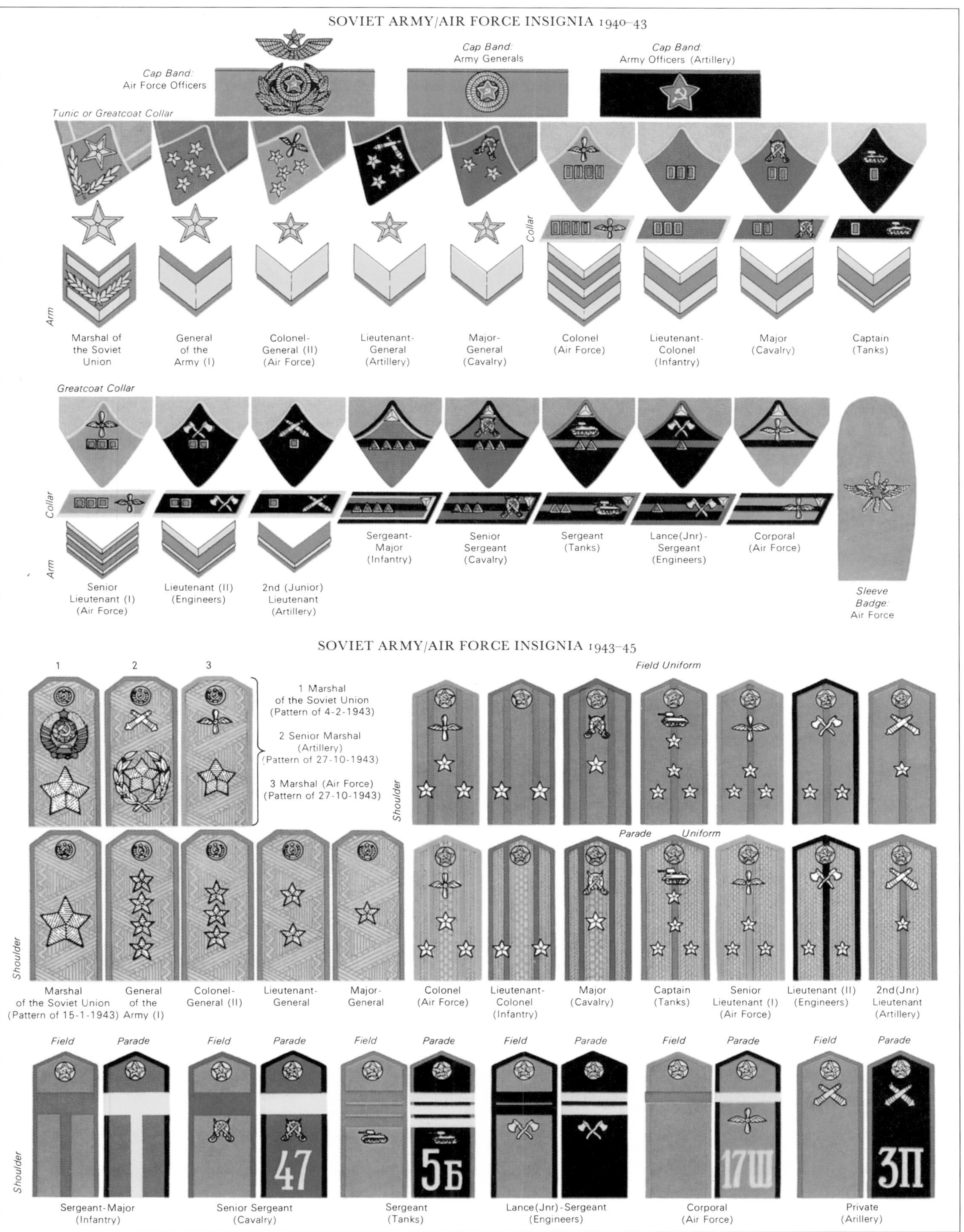
SOVIET ARMY/AIR FORCE INSIGNIA 1940–43
Cap Band: Air Force Officers
Cap Band: Army Generals
Cap Band: Army Officers (Artillery)
Tunic or Greatcoat Collar
Collar
Arm
Marshal of the Soviet Union
General of the Army (I)
Colonel-General (II) (Air Force)
Lieutenant-General (Artillery)
Major-General (Cavalry)
Colonel (Air Force)
Lieutenant-Colonel (Infantry)
Major (Cavalry)
Captain (Tanks)
Greatcoat Collar
Collar
Arm
Senior Lieutenant (I) (Air Force)
Lieutenant (II) (Engineers)
2nd (Junior) Lieutenant (Artillery)
Sergeant-Major (Infantry)
Senior Sergeant (Cavalry)
Sergeant (Tanks)
Lance(Jnr)-Sergeant (Engineers)
Corporal (Air Force)
Sleeve Badge: Air Force
SOVIET ARMY/AIR FORCE INSIGNIA 1943–45
1
2
3
1 Marshal of the Soviet Union (Pattern of 4-2-1943)
2 Senior Marshal (Artillery) (Pattern of 27-10-1943)
3 Marshal (Air Force) (Pattern of 27-10-1943)
Field Uniform
Shoulder
Parade Uniform
Shoulder
Marshal of the Soviet Union (Pattern of 15-1-1943)
General of the Army (I)
Colonel-General (II)
Lieutenant-General
Major-General
Colonel (Air Force)
Lieutenant-Colonel (Infantry)
Major (Cavalry)
Captain (Tanks)
Senior Lieutenant (I) (Air Force)
Lieutenant (II) (Engineers)
2nd(Jnr) Lieutenant (Artillery)
Field
Parade
Shoulder
47
5Б
17Ш
3П
Sergeant-Major (Infantry)
Senior Sergeant (Cavalry)
Sergeant (Tanks)
Lance(Jnr)-Sergeant (Engineers)
Corporal (Air Force)
Private (Arillery)

UNIFORM The pre-war uniform of Red Army parachute troops was that of the Red Air Force with sky blue cap bands and collar patches. The field service uniform consisted of a blue-grey padded canvas flying helmet and one-piece overall on which appeared the sky blue collar patches to which were affixed the badges of rank. The overall was worn over the standard khaki field uniform. All other items of footwear and personal equipment conformed to the standard patterns.

During the war the blue-grey overall was replaced by a khaki one with a camouflage pattern printed on it in black, as issued to snipers and assault engineers. German observers reported that although Red parachute troops 'represented the best type of Soviet infantry', they did not wear a standard uniform, but various items of army clothing, flying suits, and leather jackets. This was probably due to the fact that parachutists were drawn from both Army and Air Force units and in a time of universal shortage, continued to wear their former uniforms. Many airborne operations were mounted in support of partisans in Axis-occupied territory and a variety of clothing was useful to help disguise the arrival of regular reinforcements.

Various categories and classes of badges were worn by qualified parachutists on the left breast of the tunic, shirt and sometimes even the jump overall.

Below: Paratroops receive instruction before taking off for a combat mission in the North Caucasus in 1942. The equipment was the standard for Soviet airborne forces, and they are armed with the PPSh sub-machine gun (with magazines not fitted for safety during the drop); even at this early stage, the equipping of whole units with such weapons was a Soviet principle.

INTERIOR TROOPS

The Soviet regime relied for its internal security on a network of informers and secret agents, backed up by a totally reliable and ruthless internal security force. The subjugation of the populations of annexed territories, implementation of collectivisation and the purges of the armed forces were carried out by the special troops of the People's Commissariat for the Interior, which from July 1934 was known as the NKVD. The Soviet armies which occupied eastern Poland and parts of Finland were closely followed by NKVD troops who were responsible for security in the rear areas.

ORGANISATION The Chief Administration of Interior Troops was responsible for the recruitment, training and deployment of internal security troops, frontier guard troops and convoy troops. Internal security troops numbered about 150,000 and were trained and organised along military lines, consisting of infantry, cavalry, artillery, armoured car and flying units. Frontier guard troops were responsible for the frontier control of the Soviet Union both on land and at sea. They too were organised on military (or naval) lines and numbered some 70,000 men. Convoy troops were used to escort prisoners and guard prisons and labour camps.

UNIFORM NKVD personnel serving in military units wore Red Army uniform. The distinctive colours of the NKVD were bright blue and crimson which appeared on the peaked cap (bright blue top and crimson piping and band) and on the collar patches, which were bright blue with crimson piping.

Frontier Troops who also came under the jurisdiction of the State Ministry of the Interior were also formed in military units and equipped with infantry weapons. Their distinctive colour was bright green, which appeared on the peaked cap (green top, dark blue band and crimson piping) and on the collar patches, which were green with crimson piping.

INSIGNIA All ranks wore Army badges of rank on the collar patches, but unlike Army officers, NKVD officers did not have gold lace or gold-embroidered edging to the collar patches. Whereas Army officers wore rank chevrons on the cuffs, NKVD officers had a special badge (vertical sword within an oval wreath) on the upper left sleeve. The basic Army arm-of-service badges were worn on the collar patches.

POLITICAL COMMISSARS

At the height of their powers – between July 1941 and November 1942 – political commissars were important figures in the Red Army. No troop commander could issue an order without his commissar's approval and counter signature, but a commissar could and did issue orders independently and under his own authority. At all levels from front (army group) down to company there was a political commissar with his own staff and chain-of-command. The main tasks of the commissar were the building-up and maintenance of good political morale in the ranks and the observation and suppression of anti-party sentiments and activities. During the terrible summer of 1941, it was often necessary to resort to extraordinary measures to prevent the collapse of the front. For such tasks the political apparatus could call upon the Special Section in each regiment, division, corps and army. This section was the organ of the NKVD with special powers to suppress counter-revolution and defeatism. The staff of the Special Section attended all staff meetings and was a

200 Lieutenant, Frontier Troops, 1942
Frontier troops were part of the Ministry of the Interior, and were classified as NKVD troops. The distinctive colours which appeared on the head-dress and collar patches (and, later, shoulder boards) were green and dark blue, with crimson piping. Rank badges appeared on the collar patches only. The weapon is the ubiquitous PPSh sub-machine gun with the 71-round drum magazine.

particularly feared institution in the Red Army.

From time to time the commissar and the chief of the Special Section could, in secret, form special commandos from amongst the members of the Special Section and trusted Communists and *Komsomol* members. The task of this 'obstruction commando' was to prevent stragglers and deserters from leaving the field of battle. To maintain secrecy personnel of these commandos were changed from day to day. A similar *ad hoc* secret commando was formed at divisional level, but the 'obstruction commandos' of an army were organised on a permanent basis and were often disguised as road and bridge-building units. In this way they could control the principal routes leading to and from the front.

An average Divisional Commissar had a staff of about 50 men, organised as follows:
21 *Politruks* and their deputies;
one Propaganda instructor;
one Secretary of the Party Office;
one Secretary of the *Komsomol* office and various auxiliaries.

It is generally assumed that political commissars exercised only a negative and oppressive influence on the Red Army soldier, but like all institutions there were good and bad representatives. There is no doubt that the dedicated communist who shared all the hardships and dangers of his charges succeeded in earning their respect and even affection, especially as the conscientious commissar also carried out many of the duties traditionally undertaken by the clergy in Christian armies. The Germans recognised this fact when they issued the notorious 'Commissar Order' calling for the liquidation of every captured commissar. But apart from the illegality and inhumanity of this order, it only served to strengthen the commissars' will to resist. The Germans then changed their tack and tried to win over the commissar by offering him preferential treatment if he surrendered.

From November 1942 the commissars lost their most sweeping powers, becoming deputies for political affairs and subordinate to the troop commander.

Uniform Commissars wore the standard Red Army uniform with badges of rank on the collar, but in order to distinguish commissars from troop officers, the collar patches did not have gold or silver edging but black piping. Whereas troop officers had rank badges in the form of inverted chevrons on the cuffs, political officers wore instead a hand-embroidered, red cloth, five-pointed star. With the introduction of shoulder boards in February 1943, political officers began to wear the same badges of rank as troop officers, and the red star badge was abolished.

Air force

The Soviet Red Air Force was the largest in the world in 1941, possessing a strength of between 12,000 and 15,000 aircraft, of which about 4000 were deployed in the frontier areas. But the Red Air Force was beset by a number of serious problems.

The purges of the 1930s had destroyed the leadership of the Air Force, with many of its brightest officers being replaced by political appointees. Similarly, many of its more innovative ideas, such as long-range bombers and airborne troops, were shelved indefinitely. The Red Air Force was undergoing the turmoils of reorganisation in the summer of 1941, the Soviet Air Force commanders attempting to modernise the service in the light of the lessons of the Winter War of 1940 and the recent German successes in Europe. By the time Operation *Barbarossa* was launched, however, these reforms were far from complete.

The German invasion found the Red Air Force almost totally unprepared for action. The Soviet airfields were sited too far forward and the aircraft parked wingtip-to-wingtip were literally sitting targets for the Luftwaffe. On the first day of the offensive the Germans claimed a staggering 1811 Soviet aircraft destroyed, 1489 on the ground and 322 in the air, for the loss of only 35 aircraft. The Germans continued to wreak havoc in the months following, the Red Air Force suffering enormous casualties. Soviet airfields were systematically attacked by the German Air Force, most Soviet planes being destroyed on the ground. The Red Air Force pilots and their planes were no match for the German veterans and losses in the air mounted too. By late November the Germans claimed 16,000 Soviet aircraft (the Red Air Force admitted to only 6400, however) for the loss of 3453 destroyed and damaged.

The enforced lull in air operations during the winter period 1941–42 allowed the Red Air Force to recover from the first shocks. Training was improved and the quality of the aircrews rose generally through direct combat experience. The re-siting of industry east of the Urals began to bear fruit with military aircraft production rising rapidly: 2000 a month by mid-1942, 2500 by November 1943 and 3355 by the summer of 1944. Not only did the quantity of planes rise, but so too did the quality; 1942 saw the widespread introduction of improved models including the Ilyushin Il-2 *shturmovik* ground-attack aircraft and Yak and Lavochkin fighters.

Although the Red Air Force found itself overwhelmed by the German Luftwaffe during the summer offensive of 1942, the numbers and quality of Soviet aircraft were progressively increasing. Thus, when the counter-offensive around Stalingrad was launched, the Red Air Force was able to assume the tactical initiative. From 19 November 1942 to 2 February 1943, the Red Air Force on the southern sector flew nearly 36,000 sorties

201

202

as against 18,500 of the German Air Force.

Red Air Force strength stood at 8300 aircraft by June 1943 to pit against the 2500 aircraft of the Luftwaffe which reached peak strength during this month.

The steady increase in aircraft production and improvements in training and tactics gave the Red Air Force a decisive advantage over the Luftwaffe, whose strength on the Eastern Front was constantly being reduced by the demand for the defence of the *Reich* itself from the Anglo-American bomber offensive. By January 1944 the Soviet Air Force had approximately 11,000 military aircraft deployed against less than 2000 German planes. Aerial victory on the Eastern Front was won in the factories and on the training fields during 1942–43 and was confirmed on the battlefield in 1944–45.

The Soviet armed forces defeated the Germans through the steadfast application of numercial and material superiority. During the period 1941–45 a total of 137,271 aircraft were built which, with the 20,000 Allied Lend-Lease aircraft, gave the Red Air Force a superiority the Luftwaffe could never hope to match.

ORGANISATION The heavy losses suffered against light Finnish opposition during the Winter War led to a reorganisation of the Red Air Force. The squadron of between 20 and 30 planes was replaced by the air regiment as the basic tactical unit in the Air Force. The regiment was made up of three or four flights, making an average strength of around 60 aircraft. Three to five regiments comprised an air division (replacing the old brigade) which might operate independently by being assigned to a military district or army, or might be grouped with other divisions to form an air corps.

The aircraft of a regiment could be either of one type or mixed, the air division normally including a wide variety of different aircraft, reflecting its various tactical functions.

There were three basic roles that the Red Air Force was expected to perform; firstly, to attain tactical and strategic air superiority, secondly, to support the army in its ground operations and thirdly, to provide air reconnaissance. These objectives formed part of Soviet military doctrine that the Air Force was not an independent strategical arm (such as the USAAF and the RAF) but, as the aerial element of the land forces, its task was to facilitate Soviet ground operations on the tactical level.

In 1941 the majority of Soviet aircraft were assigned directly to ground force formations so that the Air Force could co-operate efficiently with the Army once the fighting started. This decentralisation of the Red Air Force had the major problem of scattering units amongst the armies and thereby hampering effective centralised control. This weakness was revealed during the first months of the invasion; the Soviet aerial response was confused and lacking in overall direction.

The massive losses incurred during the first months of the war entailed the reorganisation of the Red Air Force command structure. The *Stavka*, with remarkable foresight, held back air units during 1941 so that they would not be swallowed pell-mell in the fighting for the frontier area but would form part of a central reserve. By careful husbanding of resources, the *Stavka* had assembled six reserve air groups (of between three and eight air regiments), which it was able to assign to the various fronts when necessary.

The loss of planes and equipment entailed a scaling-down of Air Force organisation: the strength of the air division was reduced to two air regiments, each divided into two ten-plane squadrons.

A reorganisation of the ground services also took place during 1941. A Red Air Force Rear Services Command was established to provide overall control. The old system based on geographical areas was replaced by a centralised system of logical support organised around the air-base region which had all the necessary technical and maintenance services to keep the Soviet aerial units airborne. It was upon this supply structure that the Red Air Force was to build up a force capable of beating the Luftwaffe.

On 6 December 1941 six air regiments were accorded Guards status for their performance in the defence of Moscow and, like similar ground formations, they were allotted the best equipment and personnel. Possessing a consistently higher technical and combat proficiency than ordinary units, the Guard units – later much expanded in numbers – were considered by their German opponents to be the equal of any they had faced in other theatres of war.

201 Senior Political Officer, Red Army Air Force, 1942

This senior politruk *wears the 1935-pattern blue service dress, but is identified as a commissar by the black piping on the collar patches and the absence of rank chevrons on the cuffs. According to regulations commissars wore a red cloth five-pointed star on both cuffs, although this officer has removed these particular distinctions.*

202 Major, Red Army Air Force, 1940

This officer is identified as an airman by the cap badges, the light blue arm-of-service piping and patches and a winged propeller badge on the collar patches. The rank badges are the two red enamel rectangles on the collar patches and the inverted chevrons on the cuff.

203 Lieutenant, Red Army Air Force, 1944

The uniform is still that of the Red Army with the shirt in traditional cut with stand collar which was introduced in 1943. Badges of rank are now worn as shoulder boards, on which the air force emblem is also worn. On the right breast he wears the Guards Badge and the wound badges introduced in July 1942 (red for a light and gold for a heavy wound). On the left breast he wears the Order of the Red Star. The insignia worn by this figure contrasts with the early pattern on figures 202 and 204.

204 Lieutenant, Red Army Air Force, 1941

This fighter pilot wears the flying dress which was typical of pilots of single-seater aircraft. Over the shirt he wears a leather coat on which are the collar patches with the Air Force emblem and his badges of rank. The wearing of a gas mask by aircrew was very unusual.

203

204

The organisational changes of the first few months of the war were expanded in the reforms of spring 1942, the emphasis being on centralised control of the Red Air Force formations.

The first step was the formation of the air army, which would be assigned to a particular front under the control of an Air Force general who would act as aerial adviser to the ground forces commander. During May 1940 the first air army was brought into being and consisted of two fighter and two mixed-type air divisions, a night-fighter and a training regiment, with a squadron each of reconnaissance and communication planes. By the end of 1942 some 13 air armies had been brought into existence, removing the control of tactical aviation from the subordinate ground commanders to that of the front commander and his aerial adviser.

The recovery of the Soviet aircraft industry in 1942 made possible an increase in size of the Air Force units: fighter and ground-attack regiments were given a third squadron, giving them a total strength of 32 aircraft and 160–180 men. By 1943 most regiments had about 40 aircraft divided into three 12-plane squadrons, each of three four-plane flights, plus four command and reserve aircraft.

The size of the larger formations increased correspondingly. In 1942–43 a typical strength of an air army was just under 1000 aircraft, in 1943–44 it was about 1500 and by 1945 the average strength had risen to around 2500 to 3000 aircraft.

As well as being increased in size, the composition of Air Force units was reorganised. Mixed units of fighters, bombers and ground-attack planes were superseded by homogeneous formations, so that by mid-1942 the air division would have aircraft of one type only, the one exception being the ground-attack air division which normally consisted of two or three ground-attack regiments with one fighter regiment.

In addition to the reorganised 'Front' Air Force, there was the growing importance of reserve air groups under *Stavka* control. By November 1942 the *Stavka* reserve consisted of ten air corps which each normally comprised three air divisions of three regiments (each fighter regiment possessing 32 aircraft, and each bomber regiment 20).

These large formations gave the Soviet High Command greater operational freedom so that while the 'Front' aviation was responsible for basic tactical combat along the front line, the reserve units could either be used to plug gaps in the line or prepare for strategic offensives.

In March 1942 the Long Range Air Force (*Aviatsiia dal'nego deistviia* or ADD) was established which included medium and long-range bombers; its function was to act as a semi-independent strategic air force. Although it eventually had over 1500 aircraft under its control, the ADD was never a success as a strategic bomber force; its crews lacked sufficient long-range bombing techniques, while the Soviet emphasis on tactical aviation drained the ADD of resources – so much so that ADD units were often deployed in a battlefield role.

The reorganisation of March-May 1942 set the basic organisational pattern for the rest of the war; the period 1943–45 saw only refinements to the system.

After the first months of the war, the Red Air Force adopted a tactical organisation similar to that of the Luftwaffe. The basic fighter unit was the *para* or pair of two aircraft consisting of a leader and his defending wingman. Two pairs made up a flight (*zveno*) which, with the ten-plane squadron strength, allowed two flights plus a *para* made up of the squadron commander and his wingman.

The Soviet bomber squadrons comprised nine operational aircraft each, divided into three flights of three aircraft. The bomber formations normally flew in rigid V-formation 'wedges', as many of the crews were too inexperienced to allow the adoption of more flexible formations.

Ground-attack aircraft either operated in two *para* flights or *gruppa* (groups) which consisted of three to four *para*. The six-plane group became the standard combat formation for ground-attack planes which would be escorted to their targets by two to four fighter aircraft.

As the war progressed and Soviet pilots gained experience, less reliance was made on rigid formation flying and greater emphasis given to 'free-hunting' tactics, where small groups of planes would roam the battlefield looking for targets.

Below: Major Brekhov of the Red Air Force in August 1943. The one star on his shoulder boards denotes his rank as a major; the decorations are the Gold Star Medal (top), and below that the Order of Lenin (left) and the Order of the Red Banner. Major Brekhov had then completed 100 operational flights.

The organisation of the Red Air Force was largely determined by the military role it had to perform. Very much an adjunct of the land forces, most resources were allocated to ground-attack aircraft and light tactical bombers as well as the fighter planes needed to escort them. This fact was reflected in the numbers of sorties flown by the Red Air Force: only 6600 combat sorties were flown against strategic industrial targets out of a total of over three million for the Red Air Force as a whole during the war.

UNIFORM AND INSIGNIA The basic Air Force uniform was that of the Army, and flying clothing was as described on page 30 (see also photograph below and figure 204). Badges of rank were also as for Army personnel. The arm-of-service colours was sky blue and the emblem the winged propeller. Qualified pilots and technical personnel wore an embroidered winged badge on the upper left sleeve (for insignia see figures 202 and 203).

NAVY

While the Red Army became legendary in the West, the warships of the Red Navy provided few dramatic stories. The Commissar for the Navy, Admiral Nikolai Kuznetsov had had only two years in which to rebuild the fleet following the purges of the 1930s, which removed most experienced officers and limited the initiative of the survivors.

The Navy still lacked anti-submarine warfare vessels, minesweepers and support craft and, during the first six months of war in the Baltic, the Russians lost 25 submarines while Germany suffered the loss of only three cargo ships. In the Black Sea the Soviet Navy took on a seaport-defence role under the pressure of German airpower and, while Russian submarines later accounted for the destruction of 300,000 tons of enemy shipping, surface craft adopted a relatively defensive role.

Many Russian ships were old and the fleet lacked sophisticated underwater and anti-aircraft equipment; later on, however, asdic and radar were made available through Lend-Lease. The Navy's bases and training areas were overrun or besieged, and, although inland waterways were utilised for the movement of vessels, cruisers could not be mass-produced in factories beyond the Urals and delivered to the front line like tanks and aircraft. In 1941–42 mine warfare was the predominant feature of operations in the Baltic: Russian evacuation convoys forced their way through with heavy losses, their warships then being bottled up in besieged Leningrad. In the Black Sea most casualties sustained during withdrawals and the siege of Sevastopol were inflicted by German aircraft, although S-boats and Italian MAS-boats also played their part.

ORGANISATION The Russian Navy was organised in four geographical fleets (Baltic, Black Sea, Pacific and Arctic), a unified naval command being established on 12 August 1940. This was located in Moscow and was directly subordinate to the Commissar of Defence who, in 1941, was Marshal Timoshenko. The political and professional head of the Red Navy was the Commissar for the Navy; his Chief of Naval Staff was Rear-Admiral I. S. Isakov. Staff responsibilities included naval construction and a Naval Academy.

The People's Commissar for the Navy dispatched instructions to the local Fleet War Council, which in turn instructed the Fleet Commander. From 2 February 1945 the People's Commissar for the Navy was a member of the Staff of the Supreme Commander (Stalin's *Stavka*), and consequently there was more central direction of combined operations in the last year of the war.

The four fleets were further subdivided into area flotillas and naval defence sectors. Within these commands, warships of similar type were grouped in brigades under a seagoing rear-admiral. The brigades themselves were composed of several divisions, each consisting of between four and twenty vessels, depending on size. A brigade was commanded by a captain 1st class, a division by a captain 2nd class, both commanders proceeding in one of their ships as supernumerary 'flag' officers.

Based at Nicolaiev, Sevastopol, Novorossiysk, Poti and Batum, and commanded by Vice-Admiral F. S. Oktiabrsky, the Black Sea Fleet consisted in 1941 of:
1 battleship;
6 cruisers;
18 destroyers;
44 submarines;
84 motor torpedo-boats;
18 minesweepers;
56 escort, patrol and river craft.

The Baltic Fleet carried out the evacuation from the Baltic provinces, the amphibious advance back along the Baltic coast and assisted in the defence of Leningrad. Commanded by Admiral V. F. Tributs, it operated from bases and dockyards at Kronstadt, Tallinn and Libau and comprised:
2 battleships;
4 cruisers;
30 destroyers and torpedo-boats;
69 submarines;
48 motor torpedo-boats;
113 minesweepers;
86 escort, patrol and river craft;
50 armoured motor gunboats.

The Arctic Fleet's operations included the reception of Allied convoys and interception of German coastal traffic from Norway, the White Sea Flotilla maintaining the North-East Passage to Siberia. Based at Polyarnyy and Archangel, and commanded by Rear-Admiral Arseni Golovko, in 1941 the Arctic Fleet comprised:
11 destroyers and torpedo-boats;
15 submarines;
2 motor torpedo-boats;
3 minesweepers;
120 escort, patrol and river craft.
By 1945 the fleet included an ex-Royal Navy battleship and an ex-US Navy cruiser together with seven more submarines and numerous smaller craft.

Lastly, the Pacific Fleet, based at Vladivostok and Nicolaiev-Komsomolsk, was instrumental in the occupation of Japanese territory in 1945 under the command of Admiral I. S. Yumashev. In 1941, however, the fleet consisted of:
22 destroyers and torpedo-boats;
85 submarines;
135 motor torpedo-boats;
68 minesweepers;
3 escort and patrol craft.
By 1945 the fleet also included two cruisers and 30 additional escort and patrol boats.

The flotillas, some of which were organised under the four fleets varied greatly in size, from the Volga Flotilla comprising over 264 craft to the one escort and patrol boat operating on Lake Segozero. While the Lake Ladoga Flotilla operated under the Baltic Fleet, the Sea of Azov Flotilla formed part of the Black Sea Fleet. Other flotillas included:
Dniepr Flotilla;
Pinsk Flotilla;
Danube Flotilla;
Amur Flotilla;
Caspian Flotilla;
Lake Payazero Flotilla;
Lake Onega Flotilla;
Lake Ilmen and Volkhov River Flotillas;
Chudskoye Flotilla (Lake Peipus);
Severnaya Dvina Flotilla.

Dockyards operated under a naval commander of flag rank, but their shore and anti-aircraft defence was the responsibility of local military districts.

Early warship losses through air and mine warfare, fuel shortages, icebound seas and other operational and maintenance limitations meant that large numbers of sailors (33,000 in the Crimea and Arctic alone) were soon being landed to stem the German advance. All had some basic knowledge of shore combat, but they were not fully trained for it, while heavy casualties among technicians

205 206

205 Officer, Air Force of the Red Navy, 1941

Naval pilots wore Navy uniform with various kinds of flying clothing of which that illustrated is typical. Pilots also wore one-piece blue overalls on the cuffs of which they wore their rank distinction lace. With the re-introduction of shoulder boards, naval air force personnel wore light blue piping. The flying helmet was made of brown leather.

206 Petty Officer 2nd Class, Red Navy, 1944

The uniform is that of the Red Army with the striped vest, which was proudly retained by sailors serving on land. On his telogreika *(quilted jacket) he wears the Medal for the Defence of Sevastopol. The pouch contains a 71-round magazine for the PPSh sub-machine gun, which has in place the curved 35-round magazine.*

207

208

209

207 Seaman, Red Navy, 1942
This seaman wears the 1940-pattern steel helmet and waterproof foul weather coat. The earphones and speaker are part of the ship's gunnery control equipment. The rubber attachments on the greatcoat skirts were for hitching it to the belt.

208 Rear-Admiral, Red Navy, 1944
This kontr-admiral *of the submarine service wears the standard officer's uniform of the Red Fleet with badges of rank on both the shoulders and cuffs. The shoulder boards were introduced in 1943, and from then on only officers in the executive branch wore rank distinction lace on the cuffs. The badge on the right breast was for submariners.*

209 Petty Officer 2nd Class, Red Navy, 1943
The cap has the black and orange guard tally which was awarded to ships for distinguished service, and was worn by the whole compliment. On his blue flanelevka *he wears his badges of rank* (starshina *2nd class) on shoulder patches. On his left breast he wears a campaign medal. The blue-jean collar was called a* forminka, *while the black bell-bottomed trousers were worn outside the jumper.*

soon deprived the remaining submarines and surface warships of their specialist talents. Nevertheless, surviving personnel built up a battle-hardened nucleus of amphibious veterans. They usually landed from motor torpedo-boats and commandeered fishing vessels, although some purpose-built landing craft (including ex-US vessels) were also employed. After stopping gaps in the front line in 1941, then launching small raids, they commenced large-scale operations along the Baltic coast in 1944. It is believed that 300,000 men were put ashore in a total of 114 assaults during the Great Patriotic War.

There were about 600 men in a naval infantry battalion which was entirely composed of sailors. Two battalions sometimes formed a regiment, but usually up to ten battalions were grouped together as a brigade. Independent Naval (Marine) Rifle Brigades were established in October 1941. Eventually such units took over whole sectors of the front line and manned coastal artillery. At the end of 1941 most of the Baltic Fleet became part of the Leningrad defences – many sailors turning to infantry in defence of the Gangut peninsula and the ships' anti-aircraft guns operating in support of the artillery.

On occasions immobilised warships kept their guns firing in defence of besieged ports; in other cases the weapons were installed in fixed or railway mountings. Conversely, dockyard civilians were called upon to pass ammunition to naval guns in emergencies.

The Soviet Naval Air Service relied upon cooperation from the Red Air Force for air support and, although in 1941 2581 aircraft had been allocated for naval purposes, almost 90 per cent were obsolete. These were organised in four Naval Air Forces corresponding to the fleets. By the later stages of the conflict, the Russians had achieved aerial superiority over areas in which their ships were operating. The Naval Air Arm also had a number of specialist mining and torpedo formations equipped with landplanes and, like the rest of the Red Air Force, was

SOVIET NAVY INSIGNIA 1940–43

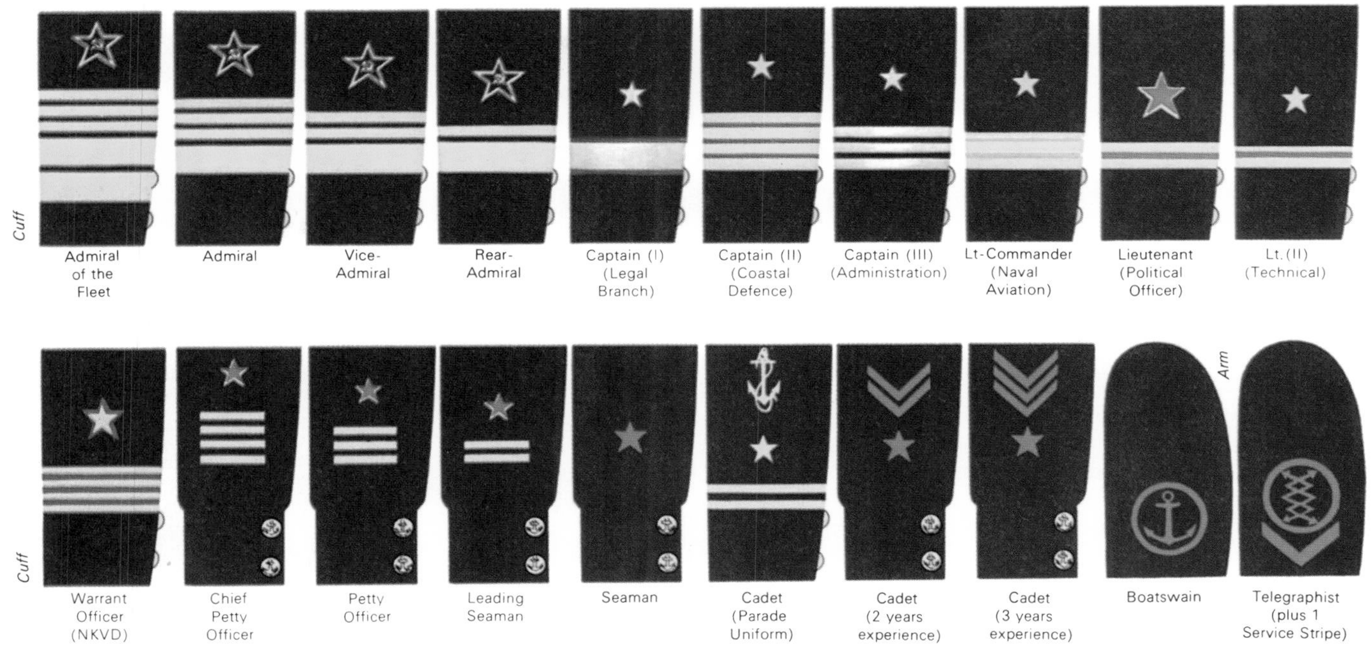

Cuff
Admiral of the Fleet
Admiral
Vice-Admiral
Rear-Admiral
Captain (I) (Legal Branch)
Captain (II) (Coastal Defence)
Captain (III) (Administration)
Lt-Commander (Naval Aviation)
Lieutenant (Political Officer)
Lt. (II) (Technical)
Cuff
Arm
Warrant Officer (NKVD)
Chief Petty Officer
Petty Officer
Leading Seaman
Seaman
Cadet (Parade Uniform)
Cadet (2 years experience)
Cadet (3 years experience)
Boatswain
Telegraphist (plus 1 Service Stripe)

SOVIET NAVY INSIGNIA 1943–45

Cap Peaks
Shoulder
Cuff
Admiral of the Fleet
Admiral
Vice-Admiral
Rear-Admiral
Captain 1st Rank
Captain 2nd Rank
Captain 3rd Rank (Engineers)
Lt.-Cmdr
Lieutenant (I)
Lieutenant (II)
Sub(Jnr)-Lieutenant
Corps Shoulder Boards
Cap Badge: Seaman to P.O. (I)
Cap Badge: C.P.O.
Shoulder
Coat
Blouse
КФ
БФ
СФ
ТФ
ЧФ
ЧФ
Warrant Officer
C.P.O. (Caspian Flotilla)
P.O. 1st Cl. (I) (Baltic Fleet)
P.O. 2nd Cl. (II) (Arctic Fleet)
Leading Seaman (Pacific Flt)
Seaman (Black Sea Fleet)
Major-General (Medical)
Lieutenant-Colonel (Aviation)
2nd(Jnr) Lieutenant (Construction)
Major (Legal Branch)
Cap Badge: Officers

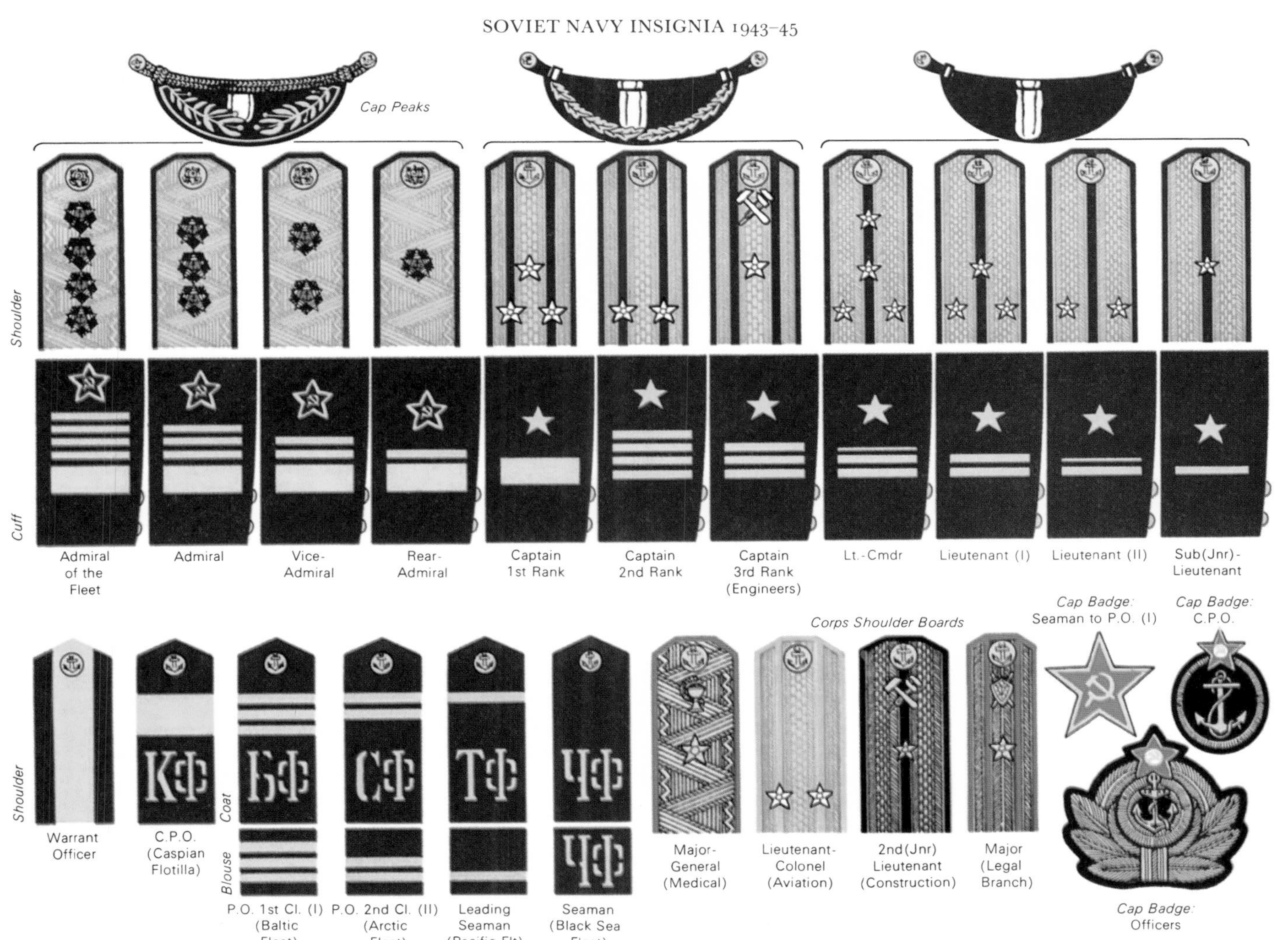

organised in divisions, brigades and regiments, particularly notable units being accorded the accolade of 'Guards Regiments'. Over 1600 flying boats (Beriev Be-2, Chetverikov MDR-6 and Consolidated Catalinas) served in maritime reconnaissance regiments.

The Soviet Merchant Navy, whose personnel included women, was state-owned. In 1939 it numbered 375 ships, totalling 1,154,000 tons. It was divided into local area services, paralleling the Navy's geographical organisation and similar to the various Fishing Boards. At the beginning of Operation *Barbarossa* they all came under naval control. A further 27 steamship services operated 10,778 powered craft and dumb barges on inland waterways. This transportation system was well-organised and made an invaluable contribution to the nation's industrial effort, in spite of river mines and aerial bombardment. These waterways also afforded a means of moving warships as big as destroyers between fleet areas.

Both inland merchantmen and sea-going vessels in landlocked waters were employed as assault transports, supply ships, harbour craft and auxiliary warships. Those still on the high seas were engaged in the delivery of Lend-Lease *matériel* to Murmansk and Archangel, to Persia (thence by rail and Caspian merchantmen) and to Siberia. Losses were heavy, but were made up by the transfer of over a hundred vessels from the United States and other sources.

Below: Seaman Fyodor Vidmira, one of the defenders of Sevastopol.

Above: Petty Officer Ziyangirov (centre) of the mine-layer Besposchadny *in the Black Sea Fleet. The other sailors are in the Soviet style of tropical square rig.*

The Sea Frontier Guard of the NKVD (People's Commissariat of Internal Affairs) operated over 350 of their own patrol craft. Most were small launches, but the largest had a full load displacement of 920 tons and mounted four-inch guns.

Overall Soviet Naval losses amounted to one battleship, three cruisers and 38 destroyers. In addition, 108 Russian submarines, 122 motor torpedo-boats and 87 minesweepers were sunk.

Uniform The uniforms of the Red Fleet followed in the Tsarist tradition. Between 1917 and 1925 cap and rank badges were improvised, until in 1925 new rank badges for wear on the cuff were introduced. In 1935 there was a thorough review of naval uniforms which resulted in new regulations.

The service dress for officers is illustrated in figure 208, and that of ratings in figure 209. Not illustrated are the double-breasted greatcoat for officers with rank distinction lace on the cuffs, and the pea-coat or *bushlat* for ratings. During the summer or in hot climates all ranks had a white uniform. For officers, warrant officers (*mishman*) and chief petty officers (*starshina*) there was a cap with white top, a single-breasted white tunic with stand collar, open patch pockets, and rank badges for officers in blue. Trousers and shoes were either black or white.

Petty officers with five or more years service would wear 'square rig' with the peaked cap, a combination not found in any other navy.

Working clothing in warm weather was made of natural undyed linen, and ratings wore their number on a patch on the left breast. During the war working clothing was often dyed blue. In winter fur caps, anoraks, rubber coats and boots and various other kinds of protective clothing were issued when needed.

There was no special uniform for sailors serving on land in naval rifle units and so they wore a combination of army and navy clothing and equipment as illustrated in figure 206.

Insignia Rank badges were originally introduced in 1925 for wear on the cuffs by all ranks. For officers these were in gold on black, or light blue on white uniforms, but for other ranks they were in yellow or red on all items of dress. When in February 1943 traditional Russian shoulder boards were re-introduced only line or executive officers and line engineering officers retained their rank distinction lace on the cuffs.

Branch of service was identified by the colour (gold or silver) of the rank lace and the colour of the backing or 'lights'. Naval aviators (officers) were identified by sky blue 'lights' and wore the same embroidered badges on the sleeve as their comrades in the Army. Ratings had red specialist badges on the upper left sleeve.

The Naval Frontier Forces which formed part of the NKVD wore naval uniform with green light's and green backing to the star worn on the cuffs.

Partisans

The rapid disintegration of the Red Army along the western frontiers of the Soviet Union as a result of the Axis invasion in June 1941 took not only the Germans, but also the Soviet Government completely by surprise. The German Army captured literally hundreds of thousands of Red Army soldiers who they could neither feed nor house, let alone guard. Thousands more avoided capture or escaped from German captivity and went into hiding.

In many areas, particularly the Ukraine, the Germans were at first welcomed as liberators. The Russian people reacted cautiously to their new masters, and remained passive as long as they were not directly threatened or maltreated. In the hinterland groups of Soviet soldiery and party officials roamed the countryside or established themselves in the vast forests of the western Soviet Union. The department responsible for organising resistance behind the German lines was part of the NKVD, and it began to parachute operatives behind the German lines in areas where large bands were known to be concentrated. The problem was that some of these bands were actively anti-Bolshevik, others anti-German, and others still were engaged in simple banditry.

While Germany was winning the war there was a definite reluctance to mount operations against the occupying forces; but as soon as stories of Axis brutality began to circulate and the Germans suffered their first defeats, there was a dramatic increase in partisan activity.

In August 1943 there were, for example, 24,500 partisans in the Ukraine alone, of whom 5000 were Communist Party members. In the whole of the Soviet Union there are estimated to have been two million partisans and resistance fighters. In response the German authorities fielded about 25 divisions (327,543 SS, security police and normal policemen and 500,000 auxiliary policemen): an immense drain on resources. Partisan losses were estimated at 85,000, 70,000 of whom were shot while 15,000 died in concentration and forced labour camps.

There was no such thing as a partisan uniform, and whatever clothing was available was gladly worn, there being an acute shortage of clothing in the Soviet Union. Ever-increasing use was made of captured clothing and equipment, particularly after the huge defeats inflicted on the Axis armies following Stalingrad.

210 Soviet Partisan, 1941–45

This partisan is wearing a typical mixture of clothing. Civilian cap and jacket are complemented by Red Army breeches and belt, and captured German boots.

211 Lieutenant, Normandie-Niemen Group, Soviet Union, 1944

The Normandie-Niemen Group was a French fighter formation which fought in the Soviet Union from 1943–45. The lieutenant has the 'Normandie' badge on his left breast. He wears French Air Force cap and tunic and Soviet breeches and boots.

210

211

Czechoslovak Armed Forces

In May 1941 a small group of Czech officers left London for Moscow where, from 22 June 1941, it became the official Czech Military Mission. Following protracted negotiations, an agreement was reached between the Czech Government-in-Exile and the Soviet Government under which a Czech military unit – the 1st Independent Czechoslovak Field Battalion – was to be formed on Soviet territory, although it was to remain under the control of the Czech Government in London.

It was organised in three infantry companies, single machine-gun, anti-tank and mortar companies and a number of independent platoons and services. By January 1943 its strength was 1500 men.

In the spring of 1943 the battalion was reinforced by a Soviet armoured brigade of 24 T34 tanks and two battalions of artillery to become the 1st Independent Czech Brigade.

The Czechoslovak formation which emerged at the end of 1944 was a complete corps with additional parachute and tank brigades. It was this formation which participated in the crossing of the Carpathian Mountains as part of the 38th Soviet Army.

The 1st Independent Czech Fighter Regiment with the Red Army was equipped with 22 Lavochkin La-5 fighter aircraft in June 1944, and in August was in action in support of the Slovak Uprising. In December 1944 this regiment formed the nucleus of the 1st Czech Mixed Air Division with both fighters and dive-bombers (*shturmoviki*), which later became the postwar Czechoslovak Air Force.

UNIFORM AND INSIGNIA The formation of the Czech Battalion came at a time of profound crisis in the Soviet Union and everything needed by this unit was in short supply. Finally it was arranged for uniforms and personal equipment to come from England via Archangelsk and later via Iran, while the Soviet Government provided arms and ammunition.

Rank badges and insignia were basically those of the former Czech Army, although in the early days these were difficult to procure and were by no means available to everyone. After the introduction of Red Army uniforms later in the war, no special insignia appears to have been worn.

POLISH ARMED FORCES

In 1941, the Soviet government began to allow the organisation of a fighting force from the Poles in labour and prisoner-of-war camps, but the bulk of the forces raised were transferred to the United Kingdom or the Middle East.

In April 1943 the Soviet Union and the Polish Government in London severed diplomatic relations. From among the thousands of Poles remaining in the Soviet Union the Soviets began to recruit an infantry division named after the Polish hero Kościuszko.

By the end of 1943, there were over 40,000 Poles in arms. In the spring of 1944, the Polish Army in the USSR consisted of the 1st Polish Army, and a formation staff for the 2nd Polish Army under General Carol Swierczewski with three infantry divisions, artillery and engineer brigades and units of a tank corps under training.

Polish forces took part in the crossing of the Vistula, the liberation of Warsaw, the breaching of the 'Pomeranian Wall' and the capture of Berlin. When the war ended on 8 May 1945 the Poles were approaching the northern suburbs of Prague. By these final offensives, there were over 200,000 Poles serving in the fight against Germany, organised in two armies, and comprising ten infantry divisions, two armoured brigades and some independent tank and artillery formations. During 1945, they suffered 32,000 casualties.

The first fighter squadron of the Polish Army in the Soviet Union was formed in 1943 and grew into the 1st 'Warsaw' Fighter Regiment. By the end of 1944 there was a mixed Polish Flying Corps attached to the 2nd Polish Army.

UNIFORM AND INSIGNIA The Polish forces in Russia went through three stages of uniformity, or more exactly dis-uniformity. The Poles who were assembled in camps in the Soviet Union wore the remains of their old Polish uniforms, tattered civilian clothing or a mixture of both. By agreement with the exiled Polish Government in London and the Soviet authorities, the British supplied large quantities of British Army clothing which was worn with Red Army equipment and weapons when these were available (see figure 212). Polish national emblems and rank badges were retained wherever possible.

After the suspension of diplomatic relations between the Soviet Union and the British-based Polish Government-in-Exile, when the Soviet Union began to raise the new Polish 'Kościuszko' Division, personnel were given Red Army uniforms on which were worn Polish rank badges and an uncrowned Polish eagle on the head-dress.

212

212 Sergeant, Polish Army in the Soviet Union, 1941
This Polish cavalryman, in the process of being transferred to the Middle East in 1941, is wearing British helmet (with Polish eagle) battledress top, leather equipment, cavalry breeches, puttees and boots, with a Soviet rifle (the Tokharev 7.62mm M1940). His rank of sergeant is shown by the chevron on the shoulder strap.

Below: The colour party of the Czech Legion in the Soviet Union. The motto on the colours reads 'we shall remain faithful': the famous phrase used by President Beneš at the funeral of his predecessor Thomas Masaryk in 1937.

Above: A Yugoslav partisan woman soldier, during a Party Congress. She has a British Sten gun, but the rest of the equipment is German and Soviet.

BALTIC STATES

Prior to the Soviet take-over in 1940, the Baltic states of Estonia, Lithuania and Latvia maintained small armed forces of their own. Only the Latvian Army with an estimated mobilised strength of 130,000 men was of any importance and was organised into four infantry divisions (each of three regiments), one cavalry regiment, an armoured car brigade and a regiment each of heavy, anti-aircraft and coastal artillery. In addition there was a brigade of border guards of five battalions of 13,000 regular troops.

Following the Soviet annexation, the armed services of the Baltic states were absorbed into the Soviet military establishment. The Estonian Army became the Soviet 22nd Territorial Rifle Corps; the Lithuanian Army became the 29th Lithuanian Rifle Corps; and the Latvian armed forces became known as the Latvian People's Army in July 1940. After a number of changes the Latvian People's Army was reorganised into the 130th Latvian Rifle Corps on 5 June 1944 comprising two 15,000-man divisions.

UNIFORM The old uniforms of Estonia and Latvia continued to be worn but with Soviet national insignia. Increasingly, however, Soviet uniforms began to replace the national patterns so that the Estonian and Latvian armed forces wore Red Army uniforms and insignia. Lithuanians serving in the 29th Rifle Corps wore Soviet uniforms with no national insignia.

YUGOSLAVIA

PARTISANS

When the Axis forces invaded Yugoslavia in April 1941, the Yugoslav Communist Party was still suffering from the effects of governmental repression, and thus its membership did not exceed 12,000. Almost as soon as the country was occupied, Communist cells and Yugoslav soldiers who had refused the order to surrender combined to form the nucleus of a partisan movement under the leadership of the General Secretary of the Communist Party Josip Broz – better known as Tito. At first Tito's partisans were almost exclusively Serbs, and it was not until 1943 that Slovenes and Croats began to join in any numbers.

Initially Tito's operations were not particularly successful, so he decided to re-organise his forces as a proper army. On 21 December 1941 Tito created the first regular unit, the 1st Proletarian Brigade, and by mid-1942 had formed a further three brigades in what was now known as the Yugoslav People's Liberation Army.

Until the arrival of the first British Military Mission to be accredited to Tito at the end of 1942, he had received no outside support. All his weapons, ammunition, supplies and uniforms were either from pre-war Yugoslav Army stocks or taken from the civilian population or occupying forces. The first Allied air-drop to Tito was made on 25 June 1943, and with his supply channel secured Tito was able to expand his army into four army corps, one for each quarter of the country, with 306,000 men and women under arms. By May 1944 the Liberation Army had grown to half a million men and there were 21 training schools for officers and NCOs. At the same time, all British personnel were withdrawn from the Chetniks and Tito was now recognised by all the Allies as the *de facto* ruler of Yugoslavia.

On 1 January 1945 Tito regrouped his 800,000-strong army into four Army Groups and, having cleared most of Yugoslavia of Axis troops and collaborators, he ordered his 4th Army Group to occupy Trieste ahead of the Western Allies. They entered Trieste on 1 May 1945 and occupied Italian territory as far as the Isonzo River.

ORGANISATION The military organisation of a partisan army must perforce be fluid, and on the whole organised in smaller units than a regular army. Establishments and weapons scales would vary from day to day, since the difficulty in supplying widely-dispersed units who chose deliberately inaccessible places for their bases presented enormous difficulties.

The smallest unit was a company with about 80 men. Nine companies formed a battalion, while three battalions formed a brigade. Three brigades, each with a mountain artillery and heavy weapons battalions, formed a division.

UNIFORM Tito's partisans wore whatever clothing they could lay their hands on. Uniformity of dress was never an important consideration, and in the type of war being waged it could be a positive disadvantage. What uniforms there were came from the former Yugoslav Army, or were taken from the German and Italian occupying forces. The usual emblem was the red five-pointed star.

From July 1941 until November 1942 an improvised system of rank badges prevailed. Badges consisted of stars, bars and chevrons cut from red cloth, and were worn on the upper left sleeve. From November 1942 a new system incorporating more ranks was devised, but on 1 May 1943 a definitive system was introduced for wear by all ranks on the cuffs. These badges were white for other ranks and yellow for officers, and were also worn by the National Liberation Navy, and by Yugoslavs serving in the National Liberation Air Force in the Middle East and in Italy.

Once Britain had transferred her help from Mihailović to Tito, increasing quantities of British uniforms, boots, arms and equipment began to be supplied to Tito's ever-expanding forces.

CHETNIKS

Having defeated the Royal Yugoslav Army and occupied Serbia, the German forces were rapidly withdrawn to prepare for the coming invasion of the Soviet Union. This meant that the mopping-up and disarming of the Yugoslav Army was hurried and incomplete.

Some 15,000 of the 300,000 men who had refused to surrender – mostly Serbs – began to organise themselves into what was officially known as the Officers' Movement, organised by the Royal Yugoslav Army general staff colonel, Dragoljub 'Draža' Mihailović. The movement was better-known as the Chetniks.

In the meantime the young King Peter had established a government-in-exile under British patronage, but the forces at his disposal in the Middle East were so insignificant that he decided to promote Mihailović to the rank of general and appoint him Minister of War. The

213 Yugoslav Partisan, 1945
By the later stages of the war, Tito's partisans were becoming a well equipped force, with supplies coming from many sources. This soldier, for example, is wearing a Yugoslav Army side-cap with the red star on the front, a captured German (or perhaps Italian) shirt, British khaki drill trousers and British anklets and ammunition boots. He has a British battledress top tied to his belt. The machine gun is a German MG 42 (with plenty of ammunition) and the grenades are the British No. 36.

214 Yugoslav Chetnik, 1944
The Chetniks wore a mixture of clothing and equipment. The side-cap here is from the Yugoslav Army, with an officer's badge on the front, and would have been the same as in the pre-war Army. The tunic is the Army model also, but with the Chetnik symbol of the skull and crossbones on the left breast. The breeches, puttees and socks were probably captured from Italian troops, and the sub-machine gun is also a captured Italian weapon, a Beretta M1938A, for which the Chetnik is holding a magazine in his right hand. The Beretta was a popular, reliable weapon and contained the unusual feature of two triggers. This Chetnik would have counted himself fortunate to have acquired it.

Above: Chetniks display some of their equipment and weapons. They are basically wearing the uniform of the former royal army, although considerable modification has taken place under the strain of the war.

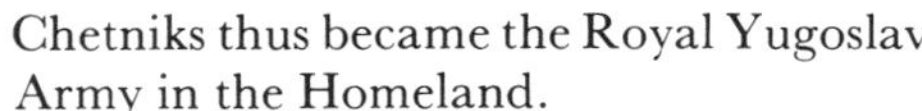

Chetniks thus became the Royal Yugoslav Army in the Homeland.

At first there were attempts to unify the Chetniks and Partisans, but such attempts failed; indeed Chetniks and partisans often displayed more hostility to each other than to the occupying forces.

Rumours of collaboration and lack of activity were to lead the British to remove their support from Mihailović in May 1944. He was shot by the communists in 1946.

ORGANISATION The Royal Yugoslav Army in the Homeland was, in theory at least, organised on standard army lines. A corps consisted of a headquarters and two to six brigades, its strength varying from 1200 to 9000 men. The brigade likewise varied in size being composed of from four to six battalions with signals, medical, engineer and supply units. Each battalion had a headquarters and three to five companies, each of which was made up of five 50-strong platoons.

The best men in the Royal Yugoslav Army were concentrated in the 'assault' brigades which were used to carry out the most hazardous operations. The honorary title, 'assault' was awarded to the best brigades in recognition of particularly brave and successful conduct.

The territorial troops consisted of older men and women who were not called upon to operate outside their home district. They were responsible for the security of their villages and represented the military and administrative authority. It also included members of the former frontier guards and police. In case of attack the garrison battalions would defend prepared positions, while mobile units would endeavour to attack the enemy forces in the rear or on the flanks.

213

214

GERMANY

ARMY

At 3.15 am on 22 June 1941 Operation *'Barbarossa'* was launched – the greatest invasion in military history. For the invasion of Russia the German Army assembled 120 infantry, 14 motorised and 19 panzer divisions plus supporting elements, totalling in all 3680 tanks and 2.5 million men. The German forces were divided into three Army Groups which were to operate in a broad front, their objectives being the destruction of the Red Army and the conquest of all territory west of the Volga-Archangel line. After a short but intense artillery barrage the German Army crossed the border and overran the Soviet forward positions. Taken by surprise the Red Army almost collapsed, sustaining enormous casualties as the German panzer columns drove deep into Russian territory. Within six months the German Army had captured over three million Soviet troops and its forward units were at the gates of Moscow.

Despite the seeming success of the first phase of the war the German Army had failed to achieve its objectives and the Red Army, which had suffered enormous losses, was still a force in being. The Germans had suffered heavily too, losing 173,722 men during 1941.

In 1942 the emphasis of the German attacks switched south. Hitler's plan was the capture of the industrial centre of Stalingrad and the Caucasus area, so giving the Germans access to the rich mineral deposits of the southern Soviet Union. The offensive went well at first but got bogged down and met intense Soviet resistance around Stalingrad.

On 19 November 1942 a massive Soviet offensive was launched, which trapped the German 6th Army in Stalingrad. Rather than allow the encircled army to break out, Hitler insisted that it fight on in Stalingrad; this it duly did until forced to surrender on 2 February 1943. Stalingrad was a terrible blow to German prestige; a complete army had been destroyed with the loss of over 200,000 men.

During the spring of 1943 the German Army rested and regrouped, so that by the summer the size of the Army on the Eastern Front was nearly three million men strong. The lull in German offensive operations was in preparation for Operation *'Zitadelle'*, the reduction of the Kursk Salient. The new offensive was not a success, however, and the Germans suffered heavy casualties for only small territorial gains. The battle wrecked the panzer divisions; 1000 tanks were destroyed.

After the failure at Kursk the Germans lost the strategic initiative and were forced permanently on the defensive. The growing strength of the Soviet armed forces, both in terms of quantity and quality, ensured the defeat of the German Army. The Soviet summer offensive of 1944 all but destroyed the German Army Group Centre; the Balkans were lost and the German Army forced back to its own borders.

Desperate measures were taken to stave-off defeat on the Eastern Front, but Soviet material superiority (around 15 to 1 in the spring of 1945) was overwhelming. On 7 May 1945 the Soviet Army was master of the German capital and fighting ceased with the surrender of all German armed forces.

The war on the Eastern Front absorbed most of Germany's military manpower (over three-quarters of the German Army was in the East in early 1943) and ultimately destroyed it. The Army lost two million men killed.

215 Soldier, German Army, 1943

This German taken prisoner at Stalingrad presents a pitiable picture. Under the greatcoat is stuffed old newspapers or straw to improve insulation while over his leather boots he has a pair of straw overboots which were normally issued to sentries who remained mostly stationary, since it was almost impossible to move rapidly when wearing them. The blankets were a luxury in wartorn Russia and it is doubtful if he would have kept them long. In his left hand he carries a clothing bag.

216 Colonel-General, German Army, 1941

Generaloberst *Hoth wears the new pattern field cap for officers introduced in 1938, obsolete* Reichswehr-*pattern tunic with slash side pockets, and breeches with red* Lampassen. *He wears the Knight's Cross of the Iron Cross at his collar. The rank class of general officer is shown by the collar embroidery, while the rank itself is shown by the three pips on the shoulder straps. Hoth was one of Germany's leading tank commanders, and during 1941 commanded the 3rd Panzer Group in the invasion of Russia. During 1942 he led frantic efforts to relieve Stalingrad, and in 1943 took control of the largest German armoured force of the war at the battle of Kursk.*

215

216

ORGANISATION When the German Army invaded the Soviet Union in 1941 the organisation of its units and formations were much the same as they had been during the war in France in 1940 with the exception of the armoured divisions. The rigours of the Russian campaign forced changes on the German Army, however, as it took into account the military reality of fighting on the Eastern Front.

The largest formation in the German Army was the Army Group, the size of which varied considerably according to circumstances. Immediately prior to the invasion of the Soviet Union, von Rundstedt's Army Group South consisted of three German armies, a panzer group and two allied Romanian armies.

The Army was a more tightly knit formation than the army group, and normally consisted of three army corps with substantial numbers of support troops. An army in a hard sector would be considerably reinforced and its size could reach a quarter of a million men. The 17th Army in September 1943, for instance, comprised three corps consisting of 11 infantry divisions. The corps was a flexible formation, containing various types of division – as shown in the corps breakdown for 1941 on page 111.

The largest organisation of armoured troops was the Panzer Group which was to become the Panzer Army, which was broken down into corps and divisions. Von Kleist's 1st Panzer Army consisted of three panzer corps made up of five panzer, two motorised and two SS motorised divisions.

The infantry division was still the basic combat formation. In June 1941 there were 175 infantry divisions available to the German Army; by January 1943 this figure had been expanded to 226 and at the end of the war there were about 240 divisions. Although the overall numbers of infantrymen increased, the front-line division of 1945 probably had half the actual manpower of a 1941 division.

In 1943 the shortage of available men for the Army began to be apparent, and so the establishment strength of the division was reduced and a new organisation introduced. Known as the 1944 division, this new formation had a strength of 12,772 men as opposed to the 17,734 soldiers of the 1939 division, although its fire-power was in fact greater.

The division consisted of three infantry regiments (approximately 2000 men in each), an artillery regiment (2000 men) and the usual divisional services as illustrated in the organisational diagram. In most 1944 divisions the old triangular organisation of three-battalion regiments was abandoned in favour of the two-battalion regiment plus supporting companies of infantry and anti-tank guns. The battalion had a strength of just over 700 men and was normally divided into three rifle companies (140 men each), a heavy weapons company (200 men) and a supply unit. The support armament of the infantry regiment included:

24 heavy machine guns
107 light machine guns
334 sub-machine guns
4 × 12cm mortars
6 × 8.1cm mortars
2 × 15cm infantry howitzers
6 × 7.5cm infantry howitzers
3 × 7.5cm anti-tank guns
36 light anti-tank weapons
(eg *Panzerfaust*, *Panzerschreck*).

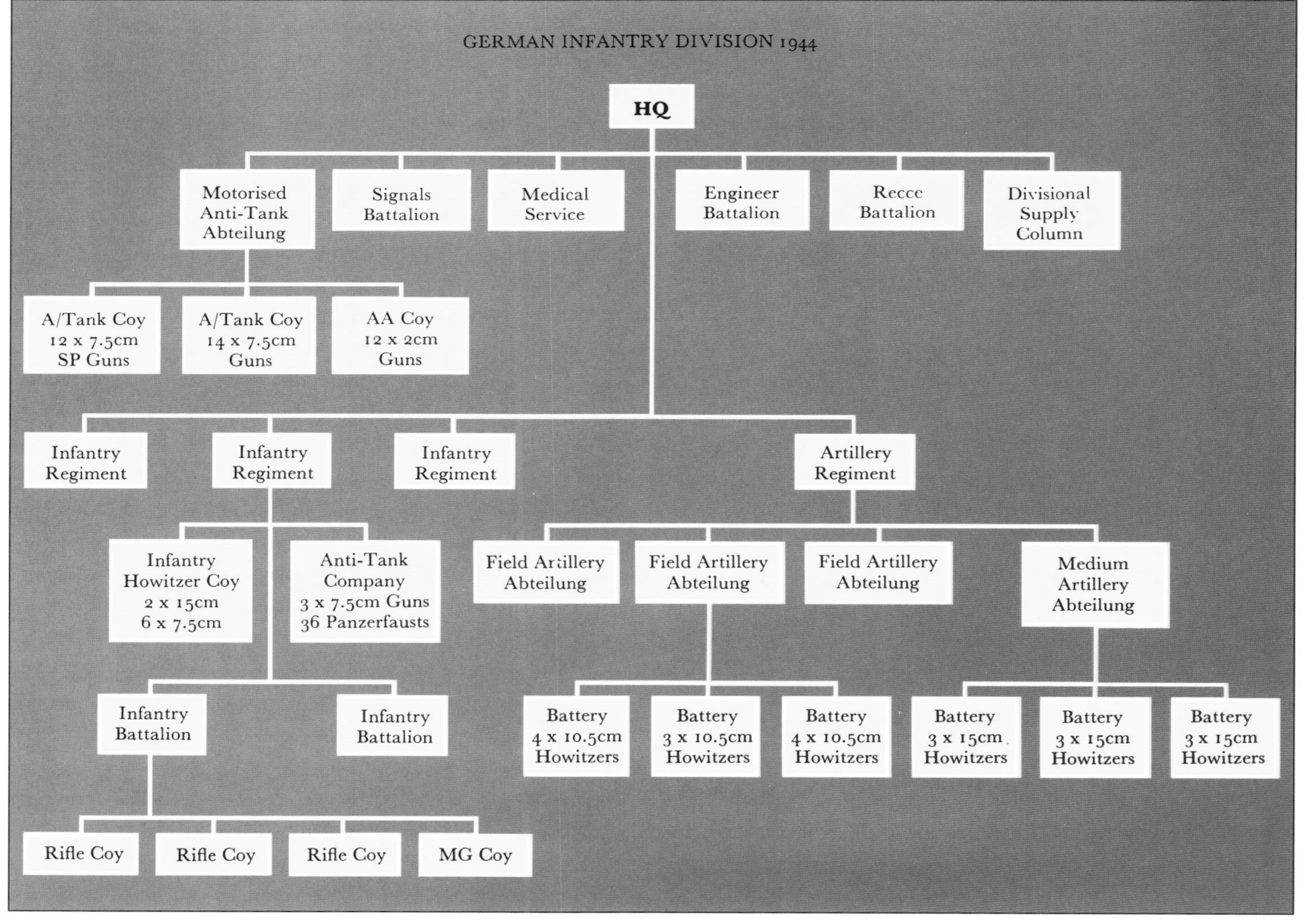

217 Lance-Corporal, German Army, 1941
This is the typical field service uniform of the first two years of war. Camouflage material is attached to the helmet by means of a piece of rubber cut from an inner tube. He is armed with a Bergmann MP34 sub-machine gun and has an 08 pistol (Luger) stuffed into his left boot.

218 Private, German Army, 1944
Some of the newly-formed panzer grenadier divisions formed towards the end of the war received the special field-grey clothing for all their personnel, since in theory all were supposed to be mounted in armoured or semi-armoured vehicles. Arm of service was identified by the colour of the piping on the collar patches and shoulder straps. He carries an unusual selection of weapons including two 98K rifles, and a metal container for a spare MG42 barrel.

During the first months of the war with the Soviet Union the motorised (or panzer grenadier) division consisted of two infantry regiments of three battalions, one artillery regiment, and battalions of reconnaissance, signals, engineer, anti-tank and anti-aircraft troops plus the usual divisional services. The motorised divisions' strength was set at 16,400 men with 2800 motor vehicles. In 1942 a tank battalion was added to the division, although later in the war this would normally be a battalion of self-propelled guns. In 1944 the various minor changes that had taken place since 1941 were officially confirmed, so that the division's numerical strength was reduced to 14,738 men and its fire-power slightly increased.

The cutting edge of the German Army was the panzer division, which played the key role in the fighting on the Eastern Front. The number of panzer formations rose from 10 divisions in 1940 to 25 in the spring of 1942 and to 35 understrength divisions in 1945 (including one Luftwaffe and seven SS). The organisation and equipment of the division changed considerably during the war to take into account developments in armoured warfare and the growing shortage of men and materials.

The panzer division of 1941–42 with an establishment strength of 15,600 men and 150–200 armoured fighting vehicles, consisted of one tank regiment of two or three battalions (each with three companies), a panzer grenadier brigade of two – or occasionally three – regiments, an artillery regiment and the standard divisional support units including strong battalions of anti-tank and reconnaissance troops.

The anti-tank unit was always an integral part of the offensive element of the panzer division and its importance increased as the war developed. Originally the battalion comprised three motorised companies of light 3.7cm or 5cm guns mounted on obsolete tank chassis, and an anti-aircraft company of twelve 2cm guns. As Soviet tanks' defensive capability improved and new weapons became available the battalion was upgunned with specialised 7.5cm anti-tank guns and with heavily armoured *Jagdpanzer* (tank destroyers).

The reconnaissance battalion was a fighting as well as a purely reconnaissance unit, the Germans attaching great importance to battlefield information, and with a strength of 1140 men, was highly mobile and heavily-armed. Although organisation was flexible, the battalion could comprise three ordinary squadrons and one heavy squadron equipped with armoured cars and self-propelled guns.

In 1944 a new panzer division organisation was introduced which reduced establishment strength to 14,727 men and rationalised the tank regiment to two four-company battalions, each with 48 tanks. One battalion would be equipped with the now ageing, though upgunned, Mark IV tanks and the other with the new Mark V Panther tanks. The artillery regiment could consist of an *Abteilung* of 12 *Wespe* (10.5cm) and 6 *Hummel* (15cm) self-propelled guns, an *Abteilung* of two batteries of six 10.5cm Howitzers and a

219 Lance-Corporal, German Army, 1941

Gefreiter *Friedhelm Ollenschläger wears the war-time walking out dress for panzer troops. Before the war the black uniform was only worn on duty with the vehicle and field-grey uniform was worn walking-out. On duty only non-commissioned officers were allowed to wear gloves.*

220 Lieutenant, German Army, 1941

This panzer officer, veteran of the Spanish Civil War, weats the special black clothing for crews of enclosed armoured vehicles. In the button-hole is the ribbon of the Iron Cross 2nd Class, and next to it the Condor Legion Tank Badge, Iron Cross 1st Class and Wound Badge.

221 Sergeant, German Army, 1942

The field-grey version of the special panzer uniform was introduced in 1940 for crews of self-propelled guns, but later in the war personnel in newly formed, and newly equipped panzer grenadier divisions were all given this uniform (see figure 217). This uniform was worn with a number of different types of collar patch depending on the unit. Decorations are the Knight's Cross, Iron Cross 1st and 2nd Class, General Assault Badge and Wound Badge.

third *Abteilung* of three batteries of four 15cm howitzers. The panzer grenadier element consisted of two regiments, one of which was well-equipped with armoured vehicles (including at least twelve 7.5cm self-propelled guns); the first battalion was mounted in half-tracks and the second in lorries. Each regiment had a company of six 15cm self-propelled infantry guns and a pioneer company.

A company of Mark VI Tiger tanks was included in some panzer divisions to give the division more hitting power, but the formation of separate Tiger tank battalions under the direct control of the battlefield commander was more usual. The battalion was divided into four tank companies with support units including twelve 2cm anti-aircraft guns, and had a numerical strength of 650 men, as well as 45 Tiger tanks. Although lacking in manoeuvrability, the Tiger was an exceptionally good defensive tank and so were used to plug gaps in the line and cover tactical withdrawals.

The last organisational change took place in March 1945 with the introduction of the 1945 panzer division, which saw a drastic reduction in the strength of the tank regiment to 50 vehicles – a cut reflected in the overall reduction of manpower to 11,400 men. As the new order was promulgated only six weeks before the final surrender, it is unlikely that the 1945 division ever saw much action.

In keeping with the German policy of decentralising armament and equipment, most artillery was divided up amongst the division, but the large Soviet artillery formations encountered on the Eastern Front led the German Army to imitate their opponents with the introduction of the artillery division in late 1943. The division was able to bring vast amounts of firepower to bear on specific targets, an ability of great importance in blunting massed Soviet attacks.

The weakness of the German Army's artillery organisation was the failure to develop sophisticated fire control systems (standard practice in the British and American armies) which could combine all artillery units within a formation under a flexible and centralised control. The German tendency was to displace their guns among the infantry units, which certainly strengthened them enormously but at the same time made artillery commanders too concerned with localised tactical action and not the battlefield as a whole. The artillery division was designed to rectify this shortcoming but lack of equipment during the later stages of the war prevented it from being as effective as it might have been.

The artillery division comprised three mixed artillery regiments (each of three *Abteilungen*) with supporting infantry and anti-tank units.

Prior to the introduction of the artillery division, many artillery units were kept back from the divisional system. Normally these would be heavy artillery units which were organised into *Abteilungen* of 12 guns and were under the control of the corps or army. Perhaps the most important form of non-divisional artillery was the *Nebelwerfer Abteilung* equipped with multi-barrelled 15cm mortars and widely used on the Eastern Front.

From late 1942 onwards the Army was faced with an increasingly serious shortage of manpower. Various solutions were implemented to attempt to solve this problem including the introduction of Luftwaffe field divisions from surplus Air Force troops but the most desperate was the formation of *Volksgrenadier* infantry divisions in late 1944. Many of these divisions were raised from the remnants of ordinary infantry divisions destroyed in combat, and their quality varied considerably depending on the number of experienced men in the division and the allocation of sufficient equipment and armament. Altogether some 50 such divisions were formed or rebuilt before the final German collapse.

The *Volksgrenadier* division consisted of three two-battalion regiments, and an artillery regiment (24 × 10.5cm howitzers, 12 × 15cm howitzers, 18 × 7.5cm guns), an anti-tank, an engineer and a signals battalion. With rudimentary divisional services it amounted to about 10,000 men.

Although not divisional organisations as such, the period 1942–45 saw the introduction of battle-groups (*Kampfgruppen*) which were *ad hoc* formations usually brought into being from disparate units in situations of dire emergency. Size could vary considerably from a battle-group of one to two hundred men to divisional-sized formations of eight or nine thousand men, with supporting arms. Their existence was usually fairly short, either being wasted away in sustained combat or re-allocated once the emergency was past. An example of this formation was the Battle Group Fretter Pico (named after its commander), formed from the remains of two infantry divisions in order to hold the German line following the collapse of the Axis allied armies during the Soviet counter-offensive at Stalingrad.

Similar to the battle-group was the army detachment which was numerically larger and usually contained complete formations: thus, Army Detachment Hollidt, formed in late 1942, had three panzer and four worn-down infantry divisions as well as two Luftwaffe field divisions.

The German Army lost World War II on the Eastern Front. This was not because it lacked basic tactical and organisational skills but because they gravely underestimated the strength of the Soviet Union; the German Army just did not have enough men and material to take on an opponent who lacked neither and at the same time could sustain massive losses without breaking.

The failure of the German High Command to mechanise the Army ensured that the panzer and motorised divisions were overstretched and the infantry divisions

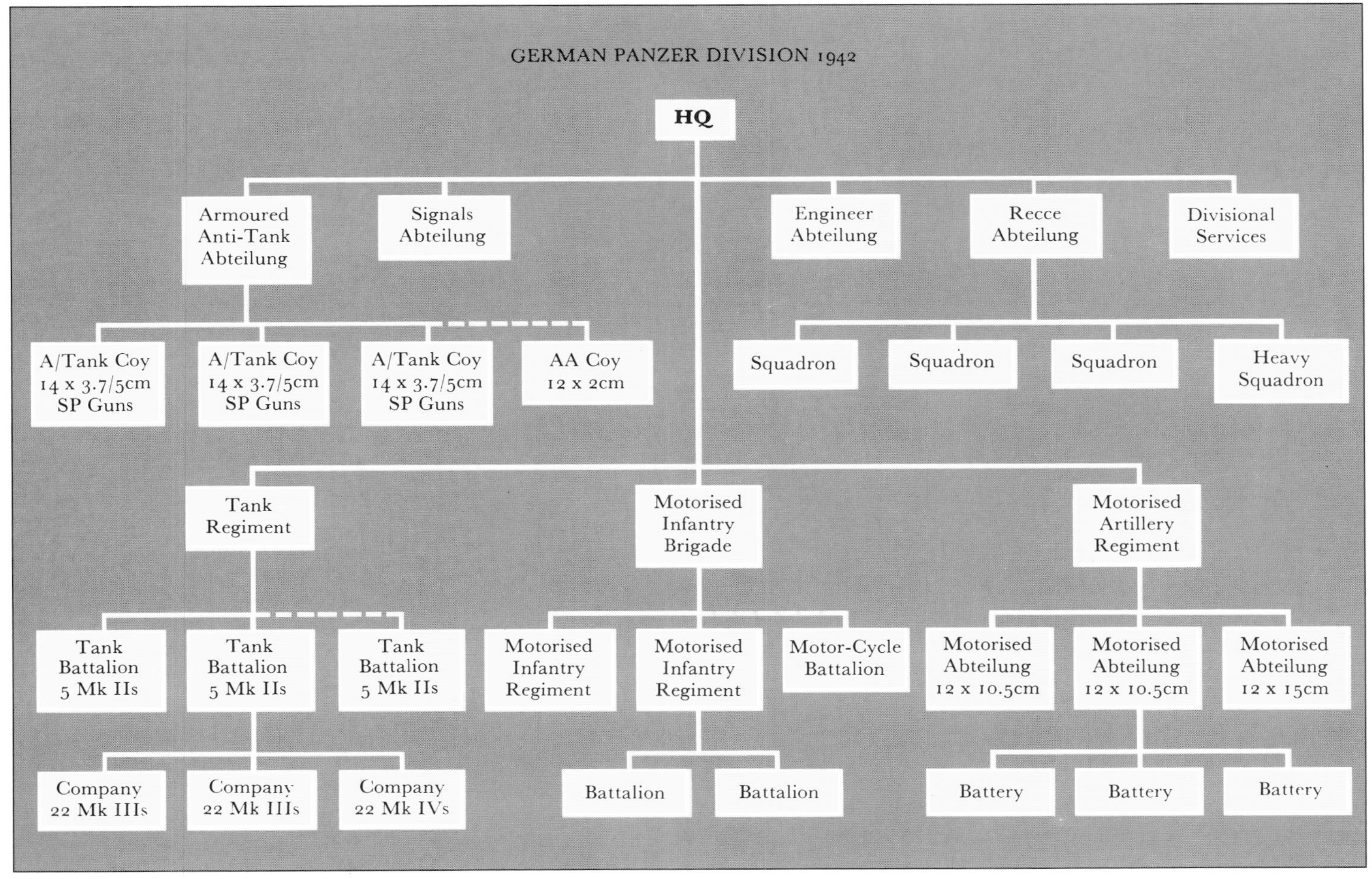

often reduced to the role of footsloggers. Although Germany lacked sufficient vehicles and fuel to mechanise the Army completely, more could have been done to increase the overall mobility of the Army. Human legs and horse transport had obvious limitations over the vast distances of the Russian steppes.

UNIFORM At the beginning of the invasion of the Soviet Union, German uniform was basically the same as that worn at the beginning of the war, although some of the economy measures introduced on mobilisation were beginning to reach the troops in the field. The most important changes were that the Army uniform began to loose the dark bluish-green badge cloth which had appeared on field blouse and greatcoat collar, on the shoulder straps, and on the rank badges worn on the sleeve. Instead, field-grey was now used as badge cloth. The grey trousers were becoming rarer, as the new patterns were made in field-grey material, and the white or silver thread used in the manufacture of insignia and rank distinction lace was being replaced by a colour called mouse-grey.

The extremes of climate encountered by the German troops in the Soviet Union, the lack of facilities for the cleaning and repairing of uniforms, and the difficulties in transporting to the front replacement clothing meant a marked and rapid deterioration in the general appearance of the German soldier. Officers were equally affected as they began to wear issue uniforms and leave their tailor-made field blouses, grey breeches and high boots with the baggage.

The first winter was a disaster that found German soldiers out in the open in temperatures as low as 35 degrees below freezing, with little more than their basic field uniforms. There was no issue of special winter clothing and men were reduced to stuffing newspaper into their tunics and filling their boots with straw.

The winter uniform developed in time for the second winter was a masterpiece of rapid development and mass production. With its special underclothing, weather-resistant properties and both white and drab camouflaged sides, this uniform was the first of the modern combat clothing which is now to be found the world over. Its one disadvantage was its weight, which would be unacceptable by present-day standards. For some reason Waffen-SS personnel only began to receive the version with SS camouflage in time for the last winter of the war.

In the summer on the Eastern Front officers had lightweight field blouses made from linen or captured Red Army groundsheets, while other ranks wore various kinds of working clothing. Gradually even the conservative German Army accepted the wearing of a shirt with open collar as a valid summer uniform. The various kinds of shirt in use in the German Army were all replaced by a standard model in field grey in 1943.

Another development was the increase in the types of protective clothing such as the one-piece overalls issued to tank crews and artillerymen. Then camouflage

222 223

222 2nd Lieutenant, German Army, 1942
This Leutnant *is dressed typically for a front line officer. Instead of a tailor-made uniform he wears an issue one, but with the M1938 officers' side cap. The decoration is the German Cross in Gold, instituted for distinguished leadership in battle as an intermediary award between the Iron Cross 1st Class and the Knight's Cross.*

223 Private, German Army, 1943
The special winter combat uniform was made of a number of different materials. One side was always white while the reverse was in two different patterns of camouflage or plain field-grey. Over-boots were made of felt and leather. Equipment was standard but often painted with whitewash as were the weapons.

224 Corporal, Waffen-SS, 1943
A typical panzer grenadier NCO in the latter stages of the war he wears the peaked service dress cap which differed from the officers' model in that it had a leather chin strap. The field-blouse is a late war model with plain patch pockets omitting the pleats, while the marching boots have shortened shafts. Rank badges appear on the shoulder straps and left collar patch. The two lace rings around the cuffs identified him as a 'Spiess' *or acting sergeant major* (Stabsscharführerdiensttuer).

225 Private, Waffen-SS, 1944
At the beginning of the war in Russia extensive use was made by tank crews of various kinds of overalls, often from captured stocks of clothing. In September 1941 a one-piece overall was introduced in SS camouflage material but this was found impractical, and in January 1944 the two-piece drill uniform began to be issued in camouflage material. On the shoulder straps which are piped in pink (the panzer troop colour), he wears his formation's cypher 'LAH' (Leibstandarte Adolf Hitler) *which was first a regimental and then a divisional badge.*

helmet covers and smocks, following in the footsteps of the Waffen-SS, began to reach Army personnel but never in such numbers that everyone could get them.

INSIGNIA There was an increase in the amount of special insignia for élite units. Special metal badges were given to a number of grenadier regiments for wear on the shoulder straps, cuff-titles in various colours were worn on the right sleeve, and finally, late in the war, small metal badges were awarded to a number of formations for wear on the head-dress. The only new insignia developed for the whole Army were the special rank badges for uniforms without shoulder straps (see rank insignia chart on page 7). These badges were, with the exception of two ranks (*SS-Oberführer* and Army field-marshal), identical for the Army and Waffen-SS.

Waffen-SS

Before Germany went to war the term Waffen-SS had not been coined. The small units which at the beginning of the war had a strength of 18,000 men were to grow into a formidable army of nearly one million which had earned a reputation for ruthlessness and the grudging respect of not only the German Army, to which it was subordinated, but also the armies against which it fought.

As soon as Hitler came to power he entrusted the Reich Leader of the SS, Heinrich Himmler, with the task of forming an armed SS guard unit for his personal protection, and as an instrument for special tasks. The original unit was the *SS-Stabswache* (Staff Guard) which in September 1933 became the Bodyguard Regiment Adolf Hitler (*Leibstandarte SS Adolf Hitler*). Under its energetic commander Sepp Dietrich and with the help of Army and Police instructors, the LAH grew rapidly. Then a further two regiments – *Deutschland* in Munich and *Germania* in Hamburg – were formed. When conscription was re-introduced in Germany on 16 March 1935 the combined strength of the three regiments was 8459 men. While the men were hand-picked, equipment was often obsolete and motor transport vitually non-existent, but already there were plans to expand these scattered units into a division, which could be used by Himmler in case of internal unrest or subordinated to the Army High Command in time of war.

The theoretical strength and organisation of the *SS-Verfügungstruppe* on the eve of war was a divisional staff, the *Leibstandarte* and three infantry regiments – all of which were motorised – a regimental staff controlling two motorcycle battalions, a motorised engineer and signals battalion and a medical unit.

Although small and inexperienced, the SS units were a welcome addition to the Army's fighting strength because they were all fully-motorised at a time when the bulk of the Army still travelled on foot or was horse-drawn.

The *SS-Verfügungstruppe* (Waffen-SS from April 1940) took part in the Polish, French and Balkans campaigns not as an integral formation, but split up in Army formations. Often in the van and always eager for the fray, the Waffen-SS was to show an aggressiveness which sometimes bordered on the reckless.

The pre-war expansion of the *SS-Verfügungstruppe* had exhausted Himmler's supply of manpower allowed him by the Army Recruiting Office, but in one year he was able to raise the strength of the Waffen-SS to 150,000. First he removed the hand-picked and well-disciplined concentration camp guard regiments (*SS-Totenkopfstandarten*) and formed them into a division under the command of the former Inspector of Concentration Camps Theodor Eicke. Then he formed another division from policemen. The difficulty in finding recruits was to prevent more rapid expansion, and it was in order to overcome this problem that Himmler's recruiters began to look to the men in the countries recently defeated and occupied by Germany who had expressed an interest in joining the Waffen-SS.

In June 1941, when Germany invaded the Soviet Union, the Waffen-SS field formations were as follows: SS divisions *Das Reich*, *Totenkopf*, *Polizei* and *Wiking*; Battle Group *Nord*, *Leibstandarte Adolf Hitler Brigade*, and an infantry regiment, with a strength of 36,517 men. Total Waffen-SS strength including staffs, establishments and schools was 160,405 men. However, the fighting on the Eastern Front was to be tougher than anything previously encountered and by November the Waffen-SS had already suffered 30,000 casualties.

By mid-1942 the four crack divisions

224

225

226

227

228

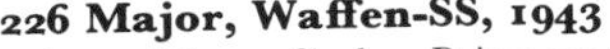

226 Major, Waffen-SS, 1943
SS-Sturmbannführer *Jochen Peiper wears one of many types of winter cap with the special reversible winter tank combination introduced in January 1943. On his shoulder straps he wears the 'LAH' cypher in bronzed metal.*

227 Lieutenant Colonel, Waffen-SS, 1944
SS-Obersturmbannführer *Schmidhuber serving with the 7th SS Volunteer Mountain Division* 'Prinz Eugen' *wears standard Waffen-SS mountain troop uniform with ski cap (later replaced by the M1943 standard field cap), field blouse, mountain trousers tucked into mountain boots, and short elasticated puttees. His badges of rank appear on the shoulder straps and on the left collar patch. As an SS member serving in a formation not entitled to wear the SS runes on the right collar patch, he wears them on the left breast pocket under the Iron Cross 1st Class.*

228 Private, Waffen-SS, 1942
This grenadier wears the M1940 side cap, knitted toque and the special fur-lined anorak and overalls which had been specially developed and manufactured by the SS. In snowy weather a special white smock was worn over the anorak as it was not reversible.

of the Waffen-SS *Leibstandarte*, *Das Reich*, *Totenkopf* and *Wiking* had all been withdrawn from the front for badly-needed rest and refit, and the addition of a component of Mark IV tanks, so that they could then be classified as panzer grenadier divisions. At this time the organisation of a panzer grenadier division was two grenadier regiments, an artillery regiment and a tank regiment and ancillary units.

The replacement of heavy battle-casualties and the need for increased manpower for the strengthened divisions led to the Army lifting some of its recruiting restrictions. SS strength, which in September 1942 was 187,638, had reached 350,000 by the autumn of 1943.

During the last two years of the war the well-equipped German Waffen-SS panzer divisions were used as a fire-brigade to plug gaps in the German line wherever they occurred. At the end of the war the Waffen-SS had 38 divisions on paper and a strength nearing one million men, half of whom were Germans, one quarter 'ethnic' Germans and one quarter foreigners.

UNIFORM The pre-war uniform of the SS was black, but in 1935 a grey uniform began to be worn on active service. At first Himmler attempted to develop an SS field uniform, but the more the SS came to rely upon the Army for training and equipment, the more the SS men wanted to look like soldiers.

On the field-grey uniform Waffen-SS men retained the SS cap badges (a national emblem above a death's head), SS rank badges on the left collar patch and Army rank badges on the shoulder straps. On the right collar patch they wore a unit emblem (either SS runes or death's head), while on the left cuff they had a narrow black band with silver edging on which was embroidered the name of the unit, formation or establishment. Another distinctive feature of Waffen-SS uniform was the wearing of the field-blouse open at the neck with brown (later field-grey) shirt and black tie.

Before the war the SS began to develop new lightweight equipment suitable for wear by their shock troops, and camouflage clothing. After initial difficulties in printing suitable quantities of camouflage cloth, helmet covers and smocks began to be issued in limited quantities. During the war this spotted camouflage was widely issued and became a distinguishing feature of Waffen-SS troops.

INSIGNIA Badges of rank were worn on the left collar patch by all ranks up to and including lieutenant-colonel (*Obersturmbannführer*). Officers with the rank of colonel and above had rank badges on both collar patches. On the shoulder straps they wore Army rank badges. On uniforms without shoulder straps they wore a new Army/Waffen-SS pattern rank badge on both sleeves. According to SS regulations all officers had white piping on their head-dress (including side cap) while general officers had silver. SS generals had grey lapels on the greatcoat.

Arm-of-service colours (*Waffenfarbe*) were worn as piping on the shoulder straps and as a chevron on the front of the side cap at the beginning of the war. Unofficially some officers and men wore coloured piping on the peaked cap, but according to regulations piping on the peaked cap and long trousers was always white and not in the arm-of-service colour. Specialists wore a diamond-shaped badge on the left cuff.

Below: SS cavalrymen towards the end of the war. The camouflage clothing is clearly shown. The rifle is the MP 43, a weapon of very advanced design as one of the first automatic assault rifles.

Foreign troops in the SS

Men from many nations fought with the SS, especially as Nazi ideals of racial hierarchy began to bend under the pressing need to recruit any troops to stave off impending defeat.

Norwegians

In June 1941 the SS began the formation of a Norwegian volunteer force of two battalions which formed the Norwegian Volunteer Legion.

At the beginning of 1943 it was decided to build-up a new 'Germanic' division to be called *Nordland*, in which it was intended that Danes and Norwegians would serve alongside Dutchmen.

In all some 2000 Norwegians served in *Nordland*, which was a small part of the estimated 50,000 Norwegians who served in military and para-military formations under German auspices during World War II.

UNIFORM Initially, early Norwegian volunteers in the Waffen-SS wore the standard field-grey uniform with the Norwegian flag on the left sleeve. Later the Norwegian lion appeared on the right collar patch, although the SS runes were also widely worn. The flag was replaced on the sleeve by a shield-shaped badge in the Norwegian colours, and on the left sleeve, members of the Legion (but not its companies formed from Norwegian policemen) wore the cuff-band *'Frw. Legion Norwegen'* (Volunteer Legion Norway). When the Legion was disbanded and a regiment formed in the *'Nordland'* division, its regimental cuff-band was *'Norge'*.

Danes

Military collaboration began with the Danish volunteers serving in the SS Regiments *Nordwest* and *Nordland*. By February 1941 it was estimated that there were 200 Danes serving in or with the Waffen-SS. In June 1941 recruiting began for a Danish Volunteer Legion which, following training, was dispatched to the northern sector of the Eastern Front. The Danish Free Corps, as it was called, fought with distinction and suffered heavy losses. In March 1943 the battered *Freikorps* returned to Germany where it was disbanded on 6 May 1943. Many Danes joined a new Danish regiment which formed part of the new *Nordland* Division. They fought in Yugoslavia and on the Eastern Front.

UNIFORM On Waffen-SS uniform Danes wore SS insignia with a shield in the national colours on the left sleeve, or in the form of a *Danebrøg* on the right collar patch. On the left cuff they wore a black cuff-band with *Freikorps Danmark* in silver lettering.

Dutch

Recruitment to the SS began with the establishment of the *Niederlande* foreign legion. This was reorganised and expanded into two regiments, which were brigaded together and, as a force 5500 strong, served in Croatia from late 1943. In December 1944 they were moved to the Eastern Front proper, and became the *Nederland* Division.

UNIFORM Dutch volunteers in the Waffen-SS wore Waffen-SS uniform with national insignia on the collar, sleeve and on the left cuff. The first insignia was Dutch-made and included a right collar patch with the emblem of the Dutch National Party, the 'wolf hook', a shield-shaped or rectangular badge in the Dutch colours on the left sleeve and a cuff-band with *'Legioen Nederland'* in white lettering.

Later these Dutch-made badges were replaced by the regulation Waffen-SS pattern. The *Wolfsangel* on the collar patch was horizontal instead of vertical as formerly, the shield conformed to the standard SS pattern, and the cuff-band bore the inscription *'Frw.Legion Niederlande'*.

Belgians

On 8 August 1941 the first draft of Belgian (Walloon) volunteers left Brussels for training in Poland. The thousand-strong Belgian contingent was eventually designated Infantry Battalion 373. On the Eastern Front it served first alongside the Romanians and then the German 100th Rifle (*Jäger*) Division.

In June 1943 the Walloon Legion was transferred to the Waffen-SS as SS Assault Brigade *Wallonien*. Thereafter it continued to serve on the Eastern Front as part of the *Wiking* Division. The Belgians fought in several desperate, losing actions, notably at Cherkassy in 1943 and Narva in 1944.

Uniform On German Army uniform Belgian nationals wore a shield-shaped badge in the Belgian national colours.

On Waffen-SS uniform these three Army badges were retained and since the Belgians wore the SS runes on the right collar patch, the only item of Belgian SS insignia was the cuff-band *Wallonie* which was worn on the left cuff.

French

Beginning in 1943, Frenchmen of pure Aryan descent between the ages of 20 and 25 were admitted to the Waffen-SS, and recruiting began for a French SS regiment. In July 1944 the Regiment with a full complement of 1688 men was redesignated the French SS Volunteer Assault Brigade and was sent to the Eastern Front, which was now in Galicia. It sustained heavy losses in bitter fighting and was withdrawn from the front and sent to Danzig.

In Danzig the survivors were joined by volunteers from the disbanded LVF and formed into the *Waffen-Grenadier-Brigade der SS Charlemagne*. The Brigade then moved to Wildflecken and when enough Frenchmen had volunteered or been coerced into joining the Brigade, it was decided to call it a Division.

Uniform The Frenchmen serving in the Waffen-SS wore standard Waffen-SS uniform with a *Tricolor* shield on the lower left sleeve. Although special *Charlemagne* collar patches and cuff-bands were under consideration, they were never introduced.

Baltic States

Beginning in the summer of 1942, the Waffen-SS began the formation of an Estonian Legion which by March 1943 had a strength of 37 officers, 175 NCOs and 757 men.

In May 1943 the Legion was expanded into a Brigade, and in January 1944 into a Division. From February until September 1944 the Division fought on the northern sector of the Eastern Front.

In August 1941 the Germans began to recruit Latvians into the auxiliary police battalions which by 1944 numbered over 40. These battalions were called *Schutzmannschaften* (literally, protection teams).

On 10 February 1943 Hitler ordered the formation of a Latvian Volunteer Legion and almost simultaneously two Waffen-SS divisions (later designated 15th and 19th Waffen-SS Grenadier Divisions) began formation. Both comprised three grenadier and one artillery regiment plus supporting units with a strength of about 15,000 men each. From October 1943 the divisions and a grenadier regiment formed VI SS Corps.

UNIFORM Estonians in the Waffen-SS wore standard field-grey uniform with the Estonian colours in the form of a shield-shaped badge on the left sleeve.

Latvians serving in the German auxiliary police battalions at first wore Latvian uniforms with a green armlet, but these were gradually replaced by German police uniforms on which Latvian and then German police rank insignia was worn. On the left or right sleeve Latvians wore a shield-shaped badge in the Latvian colours.

The Latvian Legion (which had become the generic term for all Latvians serving with the Germans) wore Waffen-SS uniforms with the Latvian shield on the sleeve. Members of the 15th Division wore the Latvian Army sunburst and stars emblem, and the 19th a swastika on the right collar patch.

CROATIANS

On 1 March 1943 Hitler ordered the formation of the 13th Waffen-SS Volunteer Division; this was to be raised from the Moslem population of Croatia, which was known to have a traditional hatred for the Christian Serbs, a group which made up a large percentage of Tito's partisans.

This was also the first SS division to be recruited from non-Aryans. At first there were many volunteers, but it eventually became necessary to introduce conscription.

The division was in action during 1944 against Tito's partisans as part of the V SS Mountain Corps, alongside the SS division *Prinz Eugen*.

In June 1944 a second Moslem division, *23 Waffen-Gebirgs-Division der SS (Kroat Nr 2) Kama* was formed from some eight to nine thousand Moslems and *Volksdeutsche*. But the division was found unreliable and in the autumn of 1944 it was disbanded.

AIR FORCE

On 22 June 1941 nearly 2800 aircraft of the German Air Force were committed to the invasion of the Soviet Union. The first day of action was a brilliant German success, the Luftwaffe destroying 1811 planes and securing the skies for the German Army. The Luftwaffe was deployed in four air fleets (*Luftflotten*) for Operation *'Barbarossa'*.

As the German Army advanced so too did the Luftwaffe, setting up forward airfields to continue its support of ground operations. Towards the end of 1941 things became more difficult: stiffening Soviet resistance and shortage of airworthy planes and spare parts began to wear down the Air Force. By early December the Luftwaffe had lost 2092 aircraft with a further 1361 damaged; unacceptable losses to a service that had few reserves to draw on.

During the winter months aerial activity was greatly reduced on account of the severe weather conditions, the Air Force preparing itself for the coming spring offensive. The Luftwaffe was engaged in the reduction of the fortress city of Sevastopol during the June of 1942 and in the assault upon Stalingrad. The great test for the Luftwaffe came in the winter of 1942–43, when it was called upon to supply the trapped 6th Army by air. It was an impossible task – despite Göring's boast to the contrary – and only about a third of the minimum necessary was supplied, for the loss of nearly 500 sorely needed aircraft.

By the end of 1942 the German Air Force was in a serious position. There were only 375 single-seat fighter aircraft to combat the mass Soviet assaults on the German front line. Germany was not producing enough planes, and attempts

229

230

229 Senior Sergeant, Waffen-SS Military Police, 1944
This German SS-Scharführer *serving with the 13th Armed Mountain Division of the SS* 'Handschar' *wears the division's distinctive head-dress. The divisional emblem appears on the right collar patch and the Croatian national colours on the left sleeve. The metal gorget was identical to the Army pattern and was worn as a duty badge. On the left sleeve is worn the police national emblem and the cuff-band* SS-Feldgendarmerie, *while on the right sleeve is the badge of the SS mountain troops. He wears special snow gaiters over the issue mountain boots. Decorations include the Iron Cross First and Second Class and wound badges.*

230 Captain, German Air Force, 1942
Hauptmann *Hans Phillipp wears the* Fliegermütze, Fliegerbluse, *breeches and boots to which he has strapped extra cartridges for a flare pistol. Phillipp was awarded the Swords to the Knight's Cross of the Iron Cross with Oak Leaves on 12 March 1942 with 82 victories to his credit. Rank is shown by the two pips on the shoulder straps and the three wings on the collar patch. The arm-of-service colour is yellow (for a flyer) and the flying badge is on the left breast. The boots are the service dress issue, not flying dress pattern.*

231 Major, German Air Force, 1941
Werner Mölders was one of Germany's leading fighter aces and by September 1940 had already been awarded the Oak Leaves to the Knight's Cross of the Iron Cross. As Commodore of Jagdgeschwader *51 he wore the* Fliegermütze *and instead of his tunic or flying blouse, a non-issue black leather flying jacket. The life jacket is the self-inflating type issued to crews of single-seat aircraft.*

232 Lieutenant, German Air Force, 1944
Oberleutnant *Erich Hartmann serving with* Jagdgeschwader *52 wears the peaked cap with* 'Jagdfliegerknicke' *(literally fighter pilot's nick) which was achieved by removing the wire stiffener from the cap and squashing it flat. He wears a leather jacket with rank badges and national emblem on the right breast. The boots are the standard Luftwaffe suede pattern.*

233 Private, German Air Force, 1944
The uniform of the Luftwaffe field divisions was basically that of the other Luftwaffe branches, although collar patches were often absent from the tunic and flying jacket collars. The most distinctive item of clothing was the camouflage jacket.

were made to increase aircraft production which until 1943 had only been increasing at a moderate pace.

The Luftwaffe's last great military effort was in preparation for the Kursk offensive when some 1800 aircraft (70 per cent of all German planes on the Eastern Front) were thrown in to destroy Soviet prepared positions. Kursk was a failure for the Luftwaffe, however, as the Red Air Force proved too powerful, blunting the effect of the German assaults.

The demands of the Western Front were a further drain on resources and only the skill of the German pilots staved off complete disaster. By the early summer of 1944, thanks to vastly increased production, the Air Force was able to deploy 2085 aircraft on the Eastern Front (just under 50 per cent of the Air Force total) but this was still insufficient against Soviet numerical superiority.

During the last months of the war the Luftwaffe, desperately short of aviation fuel, was only able to provide a token defence against the overpowering East-West Allied offensive. Total casualties are hard to assess although the Soviet Union claimed 77,000 German aircraft destroyed or captured during the course of the war.

ORGANISATION The German Air Force maintained the same basic organisational structure on the Eastern Front as it had during the aerial battles of 1940 (see page 9). The war over the Russian skies only confirmed German tactical configurations. The *Schwarm* of two *Rotten* (pairs), each of a leader and wingman, formed the standard fighting unit of the Air Force.

The Luftwaffe was a tactical weapon which consisted of fighters to gain air superiority so that the ground-attack planes – such as the famed Junkers Ju 87 Stuka dive-bomber – could destroy enemy communications and strongpoints. The larger bombers would also be used tactically to add more 'weight' to the German assault. Some attempts were made to employ the Luftwaffe in a strategic role, namely the bombing of

231

232

233

Above: A Luftwaffe lieutenant shows auxiliaries the intricate skills of anti-aircraft range-finding. Anti-aircraft defence had always been one of the most important tasks of the Luftwaffe. The Luftwaffe eagle (a design distinct from the Army eagle) is clearly visible above the national cockade on the lieutenant's peaked cap and on the side caps.

Moscow and industrial targets well behind the lines, but Germany lacked the right planes for such a task and there was little interest amongst most German aerial commanders for this form of warfare.

The German Air Force was a vast institution and when, in late 1942, the Army began to demand more men, it was decided to transfer surplus personnel to the Army from the Luftwaffe. Fearing a reduction in his power, Goring protested that he would supply sufficient men organised as 'Luftwaffe Field Divisions' under Air Force control. This was a grave error, as the officers and men had no background of infantry fighting and many of these formations disintegrated at their first experience of combat. Altogether some 20 divisions were formed, although some of the most badly-shattered units were absorbed into the Army.

The Luftwaffe Field Divisions comprised two regiments, each of three battalions. They were broadly similar to the 1944 infantry divisions but support units were organised on a reduced scale and their strength was only 9800 men each.

The most effective elements in the Luftwaffe ground forces – besides the paratroop divisions – were the flak units. Most non-divisional anti-aircraft weapons came under Air Force control and those units deployed in the field had a dual-purpose role as anti-aircraft artillery and as field and especially anti-tank artillery.

When the Anglo-American strategic air offensive against Germany began to be felt in 1943 many of the heavy flak units were withdrawn from the Eastern Front to defend the *Reich*. This had an unfortunate effect on the hard-pressed infantry units who lost the benefit of the excellent 8.8cm guns.

The flak units were organised from corp level (there being one flak corps on the Eastern Front) down through to the battalion. There were various types of battalion: the light battalion could consist of three batteries of twelve 2cm guns plus, sometimes, a battery of nine 3.7cm guns; the mixed battalion would have two or three batteries of four 8.8 or 10.5cm guns and two light batteries of twelve 2cm guns, and the heavy battalion might have three batteries of nine 15cm guns with searchlights. Two or three battalions would form a flak regiment, which in turn would be combined with two or more other regiments to form a flak division. There were seven such divisions on the Eastern Front in 1943, rising to eleven by 1944.

UNIFORM In previous pages the standard temperate uniform of the Luftwaffe has been both described and illustrated. These temperate service uniforms and flying clothing were also worn on the Eastern Front. During the very hot summers tropical uniform was also widely worn, although the most typical item of dress was a shirt worn with breeches and boots. On the shirt officers wore their badges of rank and sometimes the Luftwaffe national emblem on the right breast. Luftwaffe ground crew wore their old white drill uniforms or the black overalls, or simply swimming trunks. Air Force uniform on the Eastern Front was not noted for its formality or smartness.

In the bitter winter weather, when the temperature dropped many degrees below freezing, aircrew were reasonably fortunate since they could eat, sleep and fly in their warm, fur-lined, flying clothing. It was the ground crew who suffered the most because they could not obtain warm flying clothing but had to rely on makeshift modifications to their normal uniforms like their comrades in the Army.

The Luftwaffe solution to the problem of winter clothing was to issue its personnel with various kinds of underclothing and fur waist-coats for wear under their uniforms, and a sheepskin cap with peak and earflaps and a sheepskin coat for wear on top. The white sheepskin blended well with the snow, and the fleece provided good insulation. On the front of the cap was attached either a metal or cloth national emblem above a circular cockade in the national colours. No insignia was usually worn on the coat.

During the last winter of the war Luftwaffe personnel also received the two-piece reversible Army winter uniform.

NAVY

The role of the *Kriegsmarine* on the Eastern Front was relatively slight in classical naval terms. Large surface vessels found little active employment in the Baltic because of extensive minefields and the importance of air power, and in the Black Sea only small craft and submarines were employed. The main tasks of the Navy early on were the laying of minefields, the harassment of Russian supply routes, and the protection of German convoys, notably those to Sweden. Later on, however, during the evacuation of German troops from southern Russia in 1943–44 and from the Baltic coast in 1944–45, the Navy proved invaluable and came into its own.

ORGANISATION Based at Kiel, Admiral Albrecht was C-in-C Group East, responsible for the Baltic. Subordinate to Albrecht was a flag officer commanding the seagoing ships which were further organised according to type. There were also naval districts and regional coast defence units which included shore-based naval artillery and infantry.

The fleet, squadron or flotilla, was either permanently allocated to a particular C-in-C or district or, alternatively, Raeder dispatched selected warships on an operation. In the latter case, area commanders merely transmitted orders and cooperated with the force at sea.

In the Baltic, the *Kriegsmarine* usually maintained a fleet comprising:
2 pre-dreadnought battleships;
3 destroyers;
9 large torpedo-boats;
2 light cruisers;
8 large minelayers.
In addition to this force there were normally several dozen minesweepers and E-boats in operation. But the number of German vessels in the Baltic varied frequently because of traffic through the Kiel Canal, and the fact that most training of all types of warship took place in the southern Baltic.

When, on 22 June 1941, the war with Russia commenced, the Germans took the offensive in the Baltic with mine warfare

234

235

236

and, in the opening days of the campaign, Germany and Finland laid over 5000 mines. Heavy losses were inflicted by German mines, E-boats and aircraft, and command of the Baltic was secured without committing a single large warship to action.

When, in September 1944, Finland was lost to the Axis cause and Sweden closed her ports to German shipping, naval operations in the Baltic became the evacuation of troops and refugees.

In the Black Sea the German Navy played a useful if limited role. Its duties included minelaying and sweeping and the maritime transportation of the Army. A total of 428 small vessels were brought along the Danube to this theatre.

UNIFORM The uniform of Navy personnel serving in the Baltic Sea or along the Soviet Russian coastline in support of land operations was standard German Navy uniform.

In the summer and particularly in the Black Sea, sailors wore their summer whites, vests, shorts, or even swimming trunks until in 1943 a sand-coloured tropical uniform began to be issued. It consisted of a cap with matching peak for all those entitled to wear a peaked cap and a peaked field cap (similar to that issued to Africa Corps personnel) for ratings. The tunic was the standard four-pocket pattern and it could be worn over either a long or short-sleeved shirt. With shirt sleeve order the shirt could be worn on its own with a black tie for more formal occasions. Trousers were both long or short and were worn with khaki socks and black shoes. Insignia was woven in yellow including the rank distinction lace which, however, was also manufactured in blue. Badges of rank were worn on the shoulder straps.

In the winter typical Navy foul-weather clothing was worn, as illustrated by figure 234, but could also include a black leather cap with fur earflaps, a heavy lined watchcoat with leather shoulder pads, special sea boots and lined water-proof mittens.

234 Petty Officer, German Navy, 1944
The foul-weather suit, pea-coat and sou'wester of this figure were typical of the winter clothing necessary for operations in the Baltic. Rank is shown by the lace on the collar and the foul-anchor on the sleeve of his coat.

235 Sergeant, Estonian Frontier Regiment, 1944
The field cap is the new standardised pattern introduced in 1943 for all troops including those in mountain regiments. Over his Army field blouse he wears the German Army reversible camouflage to white winter combat jacket. The leather equipment is Estonian, but the holster is for the German O8 pistol or P38.

236 Auxiliary, German Air Force, 1944
This Latvian Flakhelfer *wears the uniform originally introduced for German Hitler Youth anti-aircraft artillery auxiliaries. Instead of the Hitler Youth insignia this Latvian wears the Latvian national emblem and colours on the cap and armlet. Badges of rank were worn on the shoulder straps. At the end of the war all Flak auxiliaries were taken over by the SS and called* SS-Zoglinge, *although this did not always mean that SS insignia was adopted.*

FOREIGN TROOPS WITH THE GERMAN ARMED FORCES

Quite apart from the foreign personnel serving with the Waffen-SS, the Germans recruited troops from occupied nations to perform a variety of tasks. These troops often played a subordinate role, mainly being employed behind the front line on police duties, but nevertheless well over a million men were so recruited.

BALTIC STATES

The inhabitants of Estonia, Latvia and Lithuania were used by the Germans in various ways. A large number of Estonians, for example, were recruited by the German 18th Army to carry out security duties in the rear areas.

The first contribution of the Lithuanian nation to the German war effort was the formation in April 1943 of Lithuanian companies attached to German Army construction battalions.

Twenty battalions with a total of 12,000 Lithuanians also served with the German police in the so-called *Schutzmannschaften.*

In September 1943 the Luftwaffe began to form Latvian units which in August 1944 were brought together to form the Latvian Aviation Legion.

The Legion was composed of three night bomber squadrons, an aviation school and an anti-aircraft battalion, and various supporting units. Total personnel strength was about 628 men.

In August 1944, 5500 conscripts who had been found unsuitable for front duty were transferred to the Luftwaffe as war auxiliaries (*Luftwaffen-Kampfhelfer*) and were taken to Germany and distributed amongst various Luftwaffe units. In the same month the Latvian Youth Organisation was ordered to call up youths born in 1928 and eventually about 4000 youths, and later 1000 girls became another category of Luftwaffe auxiliaries.

UNIFORM Members of Frontier Protection units wore German Army uniform on which they sometimes wore a shield-shaped badge in the Estonian national colours, while Estonians serving in the German Police wore German Police uniforms with a shield-shaped badge on the upper right sleeve in the Estonian national colours.

On German Army and Police uniforms Lithuanians sometimes wore a shield-shaped badge in the Lithuanian colours – yellow, green and red.

Latvian personnel wore Luftwaffe uniform with the shield-shaped badge in the Latvian colours on the right sleeve. Male youths wore the uniform illustrated in figure 236, while girls wore Latvian Youth uniform and insignia.

SOVIET UNION

The continuous drain of German military personnel brought about by the bitter fighting on the Eastern Front, together with increasing partisan activity in the German rear, brought about a gradual process which began with the employment of the vast numbers of Red Army prisoners of war held by the Germans.

These selected Red Army men were given German uniforms stripped of insignia, and were often entered on the strength returns of the German unit. These *'Ivans'* or *'Hiwis'* (short for *Hilfswillige* or volunteer helper) meant that German units could use all German personnel in the fighting units and rely on *Hiwis* to carry out all the supply, construction and other non-combattant tasks.

237

238

237 Cossack Artilleryman, 1944

This Gefreiter *of the Artillery Battalion of the 1st Cossack Cavalry Division during the period when they were serving in Yugoslavia wears standard German Army uniform for mounted personnel with the Cossack fur cap* (papakha). *Badges of rank are worn on the shoulder straps, while on his right sleeve he has the early pattern shield for Don Cossacks with the red stripe which indicates the artillery* Abteilung. *The rifle is the German 98K.*

238 Cossack, Caucasian Cossack Cavalry, 1942

Terek Cossacks and those of the mountainous regions of Caucasus wore the traditional national costume consisting of fur cap (papakha), *coat* (cherkesska) *with cartridges* (gaziri) *on the chest, and hood* (bashlyk). *German insignia was often worn on the fur cap and* cherkesska *and this dress also became a sort of full-dress which was worn by other cossacks and some of the more Russophile German officers. The wearing of spurs by cossacks was most unusual since they always carried a whip. Weapons are the Soviet Simonov Model 1936 semi-automatic rifle and the cossack sword* (shashka) *– the latter being rarely used in action.*

It is estimated that about 1,500,000 Soviet citizens served in the German forces.

The next phase was to employ *Hiwis* in a more active role, either as interpreters, scouts or sentries, and finally as fighting soldiers. At the same time the commanders of the vast rear areas began to recruit units, usually of battalion strength, from Red Army prisoners, who were then employed on security duties protecting the German rear and particularly the vital railway network which was the prime target of Soviet partisans. At first these men wore Red Army uniforms stripped of Soviet emblems and with an armlet identifying them as being '*Im Dienst der deutschen Wehrmacht*' (In the Service of the German Armed Forces'). By August 1942 these uniforms had been replaced by German ones on which was worn newly-introduced insignia. On the head-dress they wore an oval cockade, rank badges were worn first on the collar patches and later on the shoulder straps, and on the sleeve appeared a shield-shaped badge in national colours. The colour of the cockades and the design of the sleeve badge for cossacks was in the colours of the host (*voisko*). However, the chronic difficulties in supplying the armed forces meant that uniforms never became very standardised, and the general level of uniformity was never high.

Don, Kuban and Siberian cossack wore the fur *papakha* and when available blue breeches with piping or stripes in the host colours, while Terek and Caucasian cossacks wore the fur cap with black *cherkesska* (figure 238), and carried the curved cossack *shashka*. German cadre personnel in these units either affected the cossack look, or retained their German uniforms and rank badges.

SERBIA

Under the premiership of General Milan Nedić, the Serbian area of Yugoslavia was treated as an occupied country but allowed to raise a limited number of armed troops for internal security duties.

Gendarmerie-type units which existed during the war were the Serbian City Guard with a total strength of 15,000, the Serbian State Guard (*Srpska Državna Straža*), successor to the Royal Yugoslav Gendarmerie with *Danube* and *Dvina* regiments, and the Serbian Frontier Guard (*Srpska Granična Straža*).

The most overtly collaborationist was the Serbian Volunteer Corps (*Srpska Dobrovoljački Korpus*) formed in the spring of 1943. At the end of 1944 the Corps and its German liaison staff were transferred to the Waffen-SS as the Serbian SS Corps and comprised a staff, four regiments each with three battalions and a training battalion.

UNIFORM Members of the Serbian Volunteer Corps received Yugoslav or Italian uniforms on which they wore black cloth collar patches, rank badges on the shoulder straps, and corps badge in metal on the right breast. Helmets were Italian.

FRANCE

In October 1941 a French infantry regiment, 2452 men strong, crossed the Soviet frontier as part of the foreign contingent of the German invasion force.

During the spring of 1942, the *Légion Volontaire Française* was reorganised with only the 1st and 3rd battalions and spent the rest of its tour of duty on the Eastern Front fighting partisans in the rear areas. In June 1943 the two independent battalions were again united as a single regiment and continued fighting the partisans in the Ukraine. On 1 September 1944 the *Légion Volontaire Française* was officially disbanded.

UNIFORM French volunteers wore German uniform but, like other foreign volunteers, the French were allowed to wear their national colours (the French *tricolor*) on the right sleeve of their German uniform and on the German steel helmet. Both German and French decorations were worn.

SPAIN

In return for German help in the Spanish Civil War, Franco agreed to the formation of a Spanish Volunteer Division of 18,000 men, most of whom were regular soldiers, to participate in the 'crusade' against Bolshevism on the Eastern Front.

On 25 July 1941 the Spanish 'Blue' (*Azul*) Division became the 250th Infantry Division of the German Army. The usual four infantry regiments in a Spanish division were reduced to three (262nd, 263rd, and 269th) with the 250th Artillery Battalion and divisional units. Personnel strength was 641 officers, 2272 non-commissioned officers and 15,780 men.

After sustaining 12,776 casualties, the Division was withdrawn from the front in October 1943.

From November 1943 a Spanish 'Blue' Legion with two infantry *banderas* (battalions) and a mixed *bandera* with artillery, anti-tank and combined companies was engaged in fighting partisans in the northern sector of the Eastern Front. Following the general retreat into Estonia the Legion began to leave for Spain in April 1944.

239 Infantryman, French Volunteer Legion, 1942

This soldier is a member of the Légion Volontaire Française, *the French contingent of the 'Crusade against Bolshevism'. A German uniform is worn, but the medals are French: from left to right, the Military Medal (for distinguished conduct by non-commissioned officers), the Combattants' Cross (for those called up in 1940) and the Colonial Medal with bars for two campaigns. On the left side of the M1935 steel helmet and on the right sleeve of the standard greatcoat the French* tricolor *appears in the form of a shield-shaped badge. The rifle is the German 98K which is carried in the French manner.*

239

Five Spanish Air Force squadrons, trained and equipped by the Germans served with Army Group Centre. Only one squadron at a time served at the front. The squadrons served mainly as bomber escorts and accounted for 156 Soviet aircraft on the Eastern Front.

UNIFORM Spanish volunteers arrived in Germany wearing Spanish Army and Falangist uniforms, which were then exchanged for German ones, although the blue shirt of the Falangist Party continued to be worn under the field-blouse with the collar showing; hence the name 'Blue' Division. On the right sleeve of the field blouse and greatcoat, and on the right side of the steel helmet Spanish volunteers wore a shield-shaped badge in the national colours. The Yoke and Arrows emblem of the Falange and other Falangist insignia appeared in various places on some items of head-dress and on the field-blouse. Spanish and German medals were often worn in the Spanish manner.

Spaniards with the Luftwaffe at first wore the blue-grey uniform of the Spanish Air Force, which in Germany was replaced by the standard Luftwaffe uniform with the Spanish national colours in the shape of a shield on the upper right sleeve. Spanish 'wings' and other insignia as well as Spanish medals and decorations were worn on Luftwaffe uniform.

CROATIA

Even before the German victory over Yugoslavia was complete, the country was already in the process of dismemberment and on 10 April 1941 the Independent State of Croatia was proclaimed.

The new Croat State began raising its own armed forces by conscription. This new army was known as the *Hrvatsko Domobranstvo* (which literally means Home Army), and by the end of 1941 it comprised four army corps, six divisions and 46 battalions. Two types of Croat formation came into existence; these were the rifle brigades (*Jägerbrigaden*) and the mountain rifle brigades (*Gebirgsjägerbrigaden*). The mountain rifle brigades were composed of two rifle regiments and two battalions of artillery. In 1944 the personnel strength of the four rifle brigades was 35,000 men.

The Croat para-military organisation which fought against both the partisans and the *Chetniks* was the *Ustashi* which had both a military and police role. In addition to some of the better organised and disciplined units, there were a number of 'wild' bands – mere bandits.

By the end of 1941 there were 15 *Ustashi* battalions, which were combined with Army units to form 16 combined *Domobranen-Ustachi* divisions and another 30 brigades with a total strength of some 114,000 men with another 38,000 in territorial units. At the end of the war the remnants of these units were gathered together to form one battle-worthy division, the 1st Croatian Storm Division.

UNIFORM The uniform of the Croat Army was khaki. Officers wore a service dress tunic with stand-and-fall collar and either matching breeches or long trousers. Head-dress was either the peaked cap or peaked field cap. The cap band and tunic collar wre dark brown. Buttons and badges were gold for generals, silver for officers and bronze for other ranks. Badges of rank were worn on the collar patches which were in the arm-of-service colour. On Croat uniforms the five-pointed stars which indicated the rank were replaced by metal trefoils.

Initially the Croatian Air Force was equipped with aircraft from the former Yugoslav Air Force or machines supplied by Italy. In October 1941 a Croatian Air

240 Infantryman, Spanish Blue Division, 1942

The Spanish volunteer wears standard German field uniform as simplified in 1940. The helmet is no longer shiny but painted with a matt grey paint with rough finish. The field blouse no longer has a dark bluish green collar, but like the shoulder straps it is made from field-grey cloth. All badges are woven in mouse-grey yarn on field-grey backing. The marching boots have been replaced by ankle boots and anklets. Like his French comrade in arms the nationality of the Spanish volunteer was declared by the Spanish national colours on his helmet and sleeve. As a section commander he is armed with an MP40. The MP40 was a simplified version of the MP38 and was extremely popular. Not only were German soldiers and the troops of the German satellites impressed by it, but Allied soldiers often used captured models.

241 Captain, Croat Air Force, 1942

This officer wears the grey-blue service dress as worn by the former Royal Yugoslav Air Force, but with Croatian cap badges, and collar patches which were based on the Luftwaffe model. Later German-pattern shoulder straps were also introduced. The uppermost of the two cap badges bore the letters 'NDH' which stood for Nezavisna Drźava Hrvatska *or Independent State of Croatia.*

240

241

Force Legion was formed consisting of one fighter squadron (Messerschmitt Bf 109s) and one bomber squadron.

UNIFORM Air Force officers wore the grey-blue service dress of the former Yugoslav Air Force with new insignia. On the collar patches and shoulder straps they wore Croatian versions of the Luftwaffe rank badges. On the shoulder straps the German star was replaced by a metal trefoil. There were no rank badges for wear on the sleeve by other ranks; instead they wore white metal trefoils on grey cloth shoulder straps.

The Croatian Air Force Legion which served on the eastern front was issued with Luftwaffe uniforms, but continued to wear Croatian flying badges. On the right sleeve of the tunic and greatcoat they wore the winged badge of the Croatian Air Force.

The Italians did not allow the Croats to form a Navy, but the Germans recruited a small Naval Legion to serve with the German Navy in the Black Sea and the Sea of Azov. It had a strength of about 900 men who manned 12 mine-sweepers and coastal artillery.

UNIFORM Members of the Croatian Naval Legion wore either the uniforms of the former Yugoslav Navy or German naval uniforms with Croatian insignia. On German naval uniform Croatians wore a shield-shaped badge on the sleeve in the Croatian national colours, while members of the Legion wore an oval white metal breast badge on the left breast.

In 1944 new uniform regulations were published for the Croatian Navy but it is not known to what extent they were implemented.

SLOVAKIA

In March 1939 Hitler summoned the leaders of the Slovak populist party to Berlin and told them that unless they broke away from Czechoslovakia, he would allow the Hungarians to invade their country. Slovakia declared itself independent on the next day, 14 March 1939. An Army of six divisions was recruited from the remains of the Czech Army under German supervision.

For the German invasion of the Soviet Union the Slovaks placed at the disposal of the Germans a light brigade of 3500 men which was partially motorised and included a battalion of Czech light tanks, and an army corps of two infantry divisions and divisional troops. The total strength of the Slovak commitment in July 1941 was 40,393 men, 1346 officers, 2011 motor vehicles and 695 lorries.

These Slovak units fighting on the Eastern Front suffered heavy casualties and in 1943 were withdrawn to carry out security duties.

UNIFORM The Slovak Army continued to wear the khaki uniform of the former Czechoslovak Army, but with rank badges on the collar patches instead of on the shoulder straps. The collar patches were in the arm-of-service colour.

In the autumn of 1939 a German Luftwaffe mission arrived in Slovakia to undertake the modernisation and reorganisation of the Slovak Air Force. The Light Division was accompanied by a small air detachment consisting of two fighter squadrons equipped with Czech Avia B-534s and a reconnaissance group with Letov Š 328s.

UNIFORM The uniform worn by officers in the Slovak Air Force was grey-blue with open collar and grey shirt and black tie. Rank badges were worn on the sky-blue collar patches, while flying badges were worn on the right breast pocket. Air Force other ranks wore Army uniform.

ITALY

Mussolini ordered the formation of an Italian Expeditionary Corps in Russia (*Corpo di Spedizione Italiano in Russia* or CSIR) in 1941.

Under the command of General Zingales, the Corps was to consist of three 'motor-transportable' divisions – *Pasubio*, *Torino* and the 3rd *Celere* (rapid) Division, *Principe Amedeo d'Aosta* – 3rd Artillery Group and a special *Superintendenza Est* (Supply Service East) with two motor groups, one for personnel and the other for supplies. The corps had a strength of 3000 officers and 59,000 men and 4600 horses and mules. Two cavalry regiments, the *Savoia* and *Lancieri di Novara* formed part of the *Celere* division.

After the first winter of the Russian Campaign, General Messe, the Italian commander, requested that the Corps be sent home, since it was on the brink of paralysis due to the state of the troops and shortages of spare parts and supplies. On 9 July 1942, however, the CSIR was reinforced by the *Sforzesca* Division to become the 35th Italian Army Corps attached to the German 17th Army. The new Italian Army in Russia (*Armata Italiana in Russia* or Arm IR) came into being under the command of General Italo Garibaldi and consisted of the 2nd Army Corps (*Cosseria* and *Ravena* Divisions), the *Alpini* Army Corps (*Giulia, Tridentina* and *Cunense* Divisions) and lines-of-communication troops (*Vicenza* Division).

242 Sergeant, Slovak Army, 1942
This is the uniform of the former Czechoslovak Army but with the special helmet markings of the Slovak Light Division. Rank badges were worn on the collar patches which were in the arm-of-service colour. The rifle is the Czech version of the German Mauser. It was designated VZ (short rifle) 24.

The Soviet breakthrough on the Don on 19 November 1942 signalled the end of Italian aspirations in Russia. The Italian line was shattered and the frozen soldiers had to retreat up to 40 kilometres a day. The *Alpini* division *Giulia* set out for Russia with 16,000 men and 4000 mules, and returned to Italy with only 3200 men and 40 mules. In 18 months on the Eastern Front 85,000 Italians were listed dead or missing and a further 30,000 wounded.

UNIFORM The uniform and insignia of the Italian forces were as already described in the section on the Mediterranean.

ROMANIA

ARMY

In 1939 Romania was faced with territorial demands from Hungary, Bulgaria and the Soviet Union. Britain and France stepped in to guarantee her territorial integrity in May 1939, but this was renounced by Romania in June 1940, when the Soviet Union annexed Bessarabia and northern Bukovina. German forces began to infiltrate the country to safeguard oil supplies and under Axis pressure Romania was forced to satisfy the demands of Hungary and Bulgaria. In November 1940 Romania's status as a German satellite was confirmed when her dictator Antonescu signed the Axis Pact.

ORGANISATION In September 1940 Germany was asked to re-organise the Romanian Army and soon military missions numbering some 18,000 German 'instructors' began by reducing the large, and basically obsolete, Army into one of a million men with modern arms and equipment. Many of the divisions had a second cadre, which in case of mobilisation, could provide the framework for a second division.

Below: The colour party of a Romanian infantry regiment is pictured at a march-past in 1941. Visible here are the distinctively-shaped Romanian helmets and the difference between the uniforms of the officers (in the leading rank) and non-commissioned soldiers. As in all armies, the regimental colours – carried here by a junior officer – were held in high regard.

In 1940, the Romanian Army was divided into three armies, consisting of 11 corps. These comprised:
21 infantry divisions;
6 reserve infantry divisions;
1 guards division;
1 frontier division;
2 armoured divisions;
1 guards infantry brigade;
3 infantry brigades;
4 mountain infantry brigades;
1 armoured brigade;
9 cavalry brigades.

The army and corps support troops included seven heavy artillery regiments. There was also a corps of frontier troops.

An infantry division was composed of three infantry regiments, one field artillery regiment and a reconnaissance battalion; the armoured divisions consisted of two motorised rifle regiments, one armoured regiment and one motorised artillery regiment.

The cavalry was a large, prestigious arm; the brigades (six of which were redesignated divisions in March 1942) were composed of three mounted regiments, one mounted artillery regiment, and engineer, signals and anti-aircraft companies. Three of the brigades were partly motorised in that one of the mounted regiments received Skoda half-tracks.

Since the modernisation programme had not been completed by the time Germany invaded the Soviet Union, the Romanian Army was not assigned independent tasks. Three fully-motorised divisions, part of the 3rd and 4th Romanian Armies, joined the German 11th Army to form Army Group Antonescu, with the Ukrainian capital, Kiev, as its first objective. The bulk of the Romanian Army (15 divisions) was assigned occupation duties in conquered territories.

243

243 Infantryman, Romanian Army, 1942
This infantryman in Odessa wears the Dutch-pattern steel helmet with stamped badge bearing the Romanian coat of arms on the front. The uniform is the standard pattern, while the equipment is a mixture of German and Romanian. The folding entrenching tool is of German manufacture. The rifle is the Mauser M1924.

By the autumn of 1941 the Romanians had advanced – mostly on foot or on horseback – across the Ukraine and Bessarabia to the Black Sea, had taken Odessa after a two-month siege and were entering the Crimea. Losses, however, had been huge with over 130,000 men (including 5400 officers) killed or wounded. The survivors were in poor shape, often going barefoot, and one of

244 Infantryman, Romanian Army, 1944
This Romanian soldier fighting alongside the Red Army in the last summer of the war wears the peaked field cap, and has a rolled greatcoat slung over his left shoulder. The German metal ammunition box has an offset handle which enabled a soldier to carry two boxes in one hand. The rifle is the Mauser M1924.

245 Lieutenant, Romanian Army, 1942
A cavalry officer, Lieutenant I. V. Emilian of the 2nd Calarasci *Regiment, wears standard officers' service dress with rank badges on the shoulder straps, and arm-of-service colour appearing on the collar patches and cap band. On his shoulder straps and boots are the special cavalry-pattern buttons. Apart from the Romanian medal ribbon worn above the left breast pocket the ribbon for the German Iron Cross 2nd Class is also visible by the Sam Browne belt.*

246 Major-General, Romanian Army, 1944
This general officer wears the later pattern field cap and service dress made from serge. The collar patches are the special pattern for generals while badges of rank are worn on the shoulder straps. This soldier wears a field cap in preference to the more usual General officers' peaked cap.

the main forms of transport seems to have been gaily-painted peasant carts.

The Germans noted the rigid hierarchical system in their royal ally's Army. Officers still retained their servants and received special rations, and as the regular officers were killed, their replacements from the reserve lacked the necessary quality of leadership. During the bitter winter of 1941–42 the temperature east of Feodosia often fell to minus 30 degrees, and Romanian troops, even more poorly clad than the Germans, struggled to hold the line. Reinforcements were withdrawn from occupation duties and sent to the front despite the fact that they were inadequately armed for front line fighting.

On 2 July 1942 Romanian formations forming part of the German 11th Army took Sevastopol, and then moved to the Don region. In the summer of 1942, the Romanian Army on the Eastern Front consisted of the 3rd and 4th Armies (13 infantry, one armoured and two cavalry divisions), two divisions in the Crimea, and six divisions in the Caucasus. Also on active duty were a further 26 divisions on security duties behind the front, but these were below strength and badly equipped. But in November 1942, and despite heavy losses (20,000 in the Crimea), the Romanian Army was still the largest Axis allied contingent with some 267,727 men. However, the Romanians were still desperately ill-equipped, particularly with anti-tank weapons, and all the divisions were under strength. A typical division in 1942 comprised:

3 infantry regiments of 2 instead of 3 battalions each (no lorries);
1 reconnaissance battalion (bicycles, horses and a few VW jeeps);
2 artillery regiments with a total of 6 horse-drawn batteries;
1 pioneer battalion (horsedrawn);
1 cavalry squadron (for reconnaissance);
anti-tank platoon (6 medium guns);
signals platoon (obsolete equipment);
supply service (horsedrawn).

The Germans were aware of the lack of anti-tank guns, and from October 1942 began to supply each division with six horsedrawn 7.5cm anti-tank guns.

When the Soviet Army launched its offensive against the Romanians on 19 November 1942, it outnumbered them nine to one. The Romanians put up a bitter resistance but were thrown back in total confusion. When the front stabilised six weeks later 18 Romanian divisions had been swept away, and 173,000 Romanians had been reported killed, wounded or missing. The evacuation of the Crimea in May 1944 cost another 25,800 lives.

In July 1944 the remaining Romanian formations were grouped together with the Germans into Army Group South Ukraine with 24 German and 27 Romanian divisions (in name only) totalling some 900,000 men. The Army Group was sub-divided into Group Dumitrescu (3rd Romanian and 6th German Armies) in the south, and Group Wöhler (8th German and 4th Romanian Armies) for the defence of Romania.

On 20 August 1944 the Soviet Army struck the German 6th Army and the situation deteriorated so rapidly that Romania had no option but to end her alliance with Hitler, and place herself at the mercy of the Soviets. King Michael overthrew the Antonescu regime and declared war on Germany on 25 August. On 31 August the Soviet Army occupied Bucharest. At first Romanian soldiers were rounded up and treated as prisoners of war, but gradually two Romanian armies with over 28 divisions and 540,000 men joined the Soviet Army in operations in the Danube region. Under Soviet command, they engaged in the fighting in Hungary, Slovakia, Austria and Moravia. This last period of fighting cost the Romanians a further 170,000 men killed, wounded and missing.

UNIFORM The Romanian Army adopted khaki uniforms during World War I, but it was only in 1931 that an English-style service dress was introduced for officers (figure 245).

Other ranks had the khaki field uniform illustrated in figures 243 and 244. Wartime changes were the introduction of a tunic with closed stand-and-fall collar for officers (figure 246), and the side cap began to be manufactured with a peak. Mountain troops wore a green beret and tank crews a black one. The steel helmet was the Dutch M1928 manufactured under licence both with and without the Romanian coat of arms on the front.

The summer field uniform consisted of various patterns of lightweight tunic which became bleached almost white by the sun, and these were worn with khaki cloth pantaloons with puttees or long trousers with ankle boots and leather anklets.

During the winter on the Eastern Front Romanians suffered through lack of proper winter clothing and the average soldier had little more than a lambswool cap, short unlined greatcoat, unpadded trousers, and short lace-up boots.

INSIGNIA Badges of rank were worn on the front or side of the side and field cap and on the shoulder straps. Generals had two rows of gold embroidery on their cap peak, and special collar patches in red with gold embroidery.

Arm-of-service colours appeared on the cap band and on the collar patches.

AIR FORCE

When Romania joined in Germany's attack on the Soviet Union in June 1941, her air force was operating a miscellany of aircraft types, which reflected the shifts in her pre-war diplomacy. Twelve fighter squadrons flew Polish PZL P.11s (148) and P.24s (56), together with British Hurricanes (12) and German Heinkel He 112Bs (24). Twenty bomber squadrons were equipped with French Bloch 210s (24) and Potez 633 (20), Polish P.37s (39), British Blenheims (34), Italian SM-79Bs

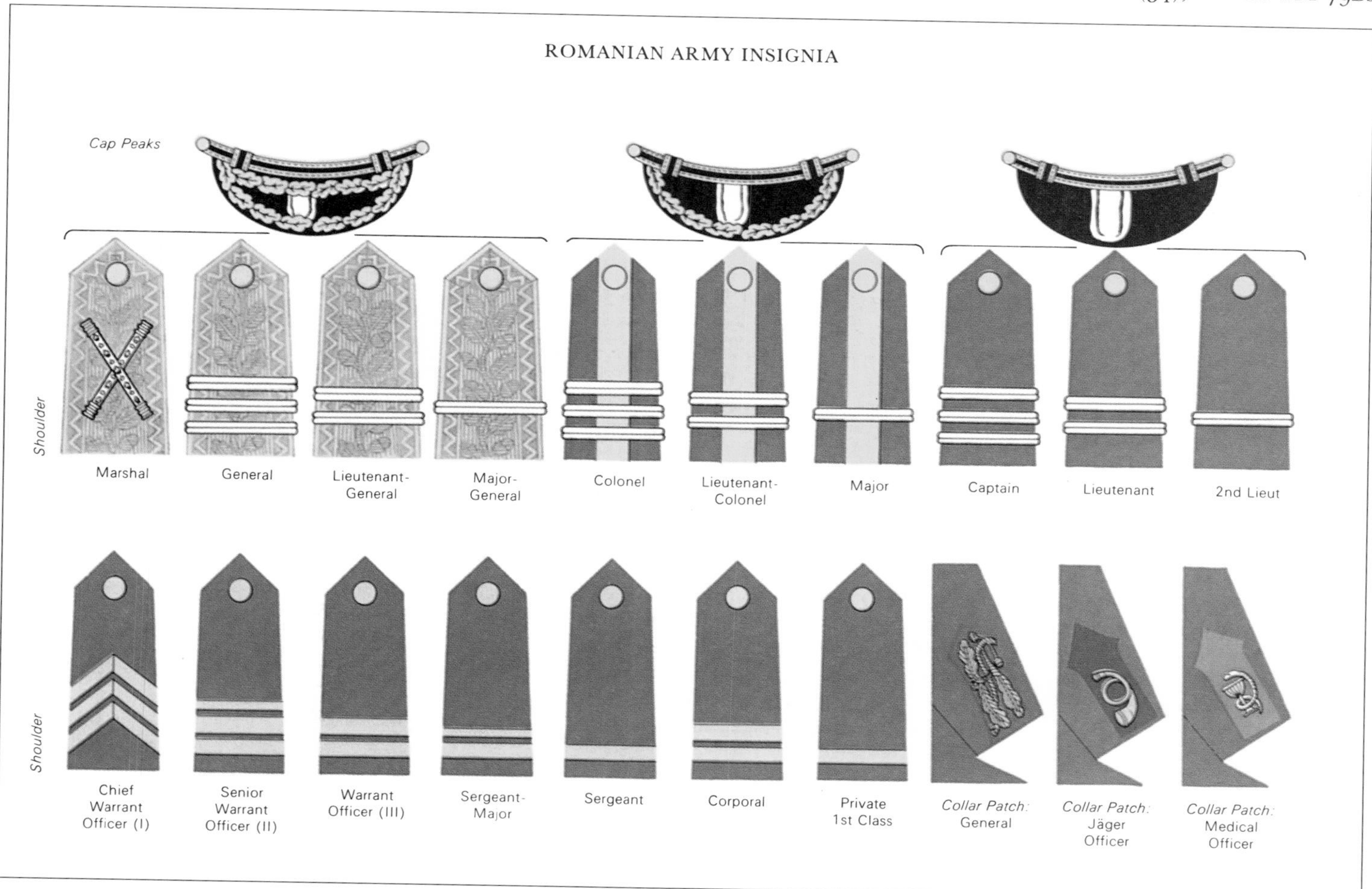

Above: A Romanian airman is helped into the cockpit of his Messerschmitt Bf 109 by a groundcrewman. He wears a fighter pilot's seat-type parachute and carries flare cartridges in a bandolier strapped to the left leg of his flying overalls. A flare pistol is visible in the top of his German-made suede leather boots. The Bf 109 equipped four squadrons of the 1st Air Corps in 1942.

(24) and German He 111Hs (35) and Ju 87Bs (50). Eighteen reconnaissance squadrons flew Polish P.23s (30) and indigenous IAR 37s, 38s and 39s (325). One naval squadron was equipped with Cant Z-501s and a second flew He 114Bs.

The Romanian Air Force was attached to the Luftwaffe's *Luftflotte* 4 and operated in support of the Romanian Army during the advance on Odessa. Attrition was high, due to the difficulties of maintaining a diversity of aircraft types, rather than to Soviet opposition. At the end of the year the Romanian air units withdrew to reorganise for the spring offensive. A modest infusion of German equipment at this time included nearly 70 Bf 109E and 12 He 112 fighters and some 20 Ju 88A bombers.

In support of the advance on Stalingrad, the Romanian 1st Air Corps comprised in July 1942 four Bf 109E fighter squadrons, six bomber squadrons with the He 111H and SM-79B and two Ju 87B dive-bomber squadrons, supported by light bomber and reconnaissance units. The Soviet counter-offensive in November hit the Romanians hard and made re-equipment of the 1st Air Corps a matter of urgency. The fighter squadrons received the Bf 109G (150 of which were eventually taken on charge) and Ju 87Ds and Hs 129s were introduced for close-support work. Three bomber and one reconnaissance squadron converted to the Ju 88 and the Romanian IAR 80 and 81 equipped four squadrons in the fighter-bomber and tactical reconnaissance roles.

In the summer of 1943 the Romanian Air Force had 350 warplanes on the Eastern Front, but by this time the air defence of the homeland (and especially the oilfields) had become the Service's top priority task. Although the USAAF Ploeşti raiders had been badly mauled during the raid of August 1943, the oil refineries were extensively damaged. Consequently all but one of the Romanian Bf 109 squadrons in Russia were pulled back to boost the home defence force.

In the early months of 1944 the situation on the Eastern Front further deteriorated and by August the Soviet armies were on Romania's border. The Air Force was still numerically impressive, with a front-line aircraft strength of 500 machines in 58 squadrons and 37,000 men. Yet relations with Germany had reached crisis point. Antonescu was overthrown by King Michael and on 24 August the new government declared war on Germany. The Romanian Air Force commenced operations against the Germans in September, but as its aircraft were mostly of German manufacture front-line strength dwindled to 174 machines in 15 squadrons by October. Repair and manufacture in Romanian factories raised the strength to 20 squadrons in January. At the end of the war, however, after 4500 sorties had been flown against the Germans, attrition had reduced the force to only ten squadrons.

UNIFORM AND INSIGNIA A blue-grey service dress was introduced for officers in 1931. This uniform illustrated by figure 248 was also worn by regular NCOs. Both the overcoat and raincoat were double-breasted and badges of rank were sometimes worn on the upper sleeves rather than on the cuffs of these garments.

Other ranks wore the uniform illustrated by figure 247, although the most common form of working head-dress was a black beret either with or without the Air Force badge on the front.

On both flying suits and overalls rank badges were worn in metal on the shoulder straps or above the left breast pocket under the flying badge.

Badges of rank and arm-of-service colours are shown in the rank badge table.

NAVY

Subordinate to the Romanian Minister of National Defence, General Pantazi, was the Under-Secretary of the Naval and Air Department. The Chief of Naval Staff in 1944 was Rear-Admiral I. Georgescu. The Royal Romanian Navy itself was organised into the Black Sea Division (whose commanding officer in 1944 was Rear-Admiral Marcellariu), and the Danube Flotilla.

Based at Galatz and Constança the Royal Romanian Navy was 4980 men strong in 1939 and consisted of:
7 destroyers and torpedo-boats (two of which were modern);
3 motor torpedo-boats of British Royal Navy design;
1 submarine;
1 minesweeper;
4 escort and patrol craft;
7 rivercraft;
35 merchant ships.

Most of the warships of the Royal Romanian Navy had been designed or built in Britain or Italy.

After the alliance with Germany, the Navy was slightly expanded (although priority was in general being given to the Army). Two further submarines were assembled under German supervision and several more motor torpedo-boats were

Below: Members of the crew of a Romanian destroyer are seen during a Black Sea voyage. The sailor on the right wears a lifejacket over the Romanian Navy greatcoat.

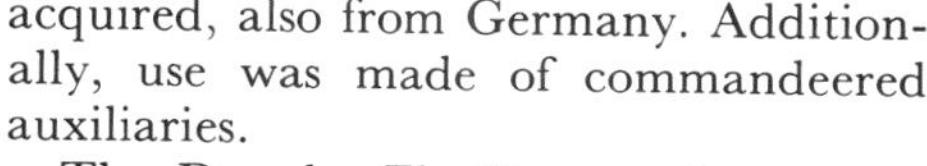

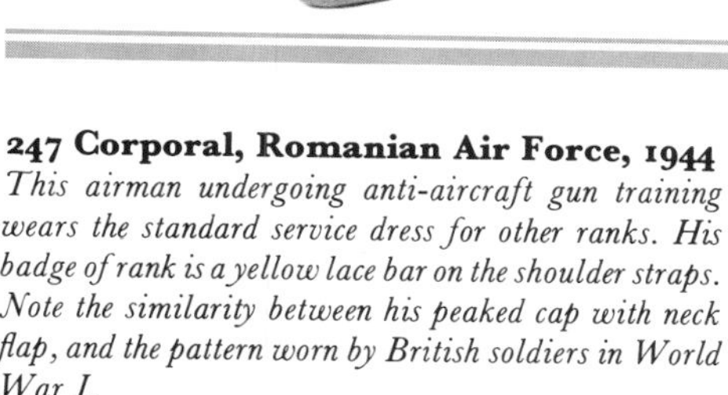

247 Corporal, Romanian Air Force, 1944
This airman undergoing anti-aircraft gun training wears the standard service dress for other ranks. His badge of rank is a yellow lace bar on the shoulder straps. Note the similarity between his peaked cap with neck flap, and the pattern worn by British soldiers in World War I.

248 Officer, Romanian Air Force, 1942
This officer wears the standard service dress with the arm-of-service colour appearing on the collar patches. The badge on the left breast was made of white metal and was worn by aircrew. The Air Force Officers' cap badge is clearly visible although rank lace is not being worn on the cuffs of this uniform. On flying uniform, badges of rank were worn in a number of places including the shoulder straps, the side cap or on the left breast pocket. In summer a white tunic would be worn with a white cap cover. Rank on the summer uniform was displayed not on the cuffs but on grey shoulder straps.

249 Rating, Romanian Navy, 1941
This sailor on guard duty on the Black Sea wears the cap with tally on which 'Marina Regala' appeared in gold letters, and greatcoat which was issued instead of the more usual pea-coat in cold weather.

acquired, also from Germany. Additionally, use was made of commandeered auxiliaries.

The Danube Flotilla was first to see action, while the seagoing warships of the Black Sea Division were soon harassing Russian supply and evacuation routes. The motor torpedo-boats did not prove to be as successful as had been hoped. The destroyers were engaged in screening minelayers, which were putting down defensive fields, and minesweepers, which were clearing coastal channels, and in protecting supply and evacuation convoys and tankers proceeding to and from the Aegean via the Bosphorus.

After the arrival of German naval forces on the Danube, the Romanian ships operated under the command of the German Admiral-Black Sea, Vice-Admiral Brinkmann, and later, in August 1943, five midget submarines, formerly in Italian service in the Black Sea, were handed over to the Romanian Navy.

By the time of the Soviet invasion in 1944, five pre-war vessels had been lost, all survivors being seized by the Russians.

UNIFORM AND INSIGNIA Wartime Romanian naval uniforms conformed to the international pattern. The ratings' cap was similar to the German model, while the officers' peaked cap was like that worn by British naval officers, having an embroidered badge and embroidery on the peak.

The jumper was worn outside the trousers and had a blue denim collar with three white lines, black silk and white lanyard. Petty officers wore a single-breasted tunic with stand collar and peaked cap.

Officers wore the peaked cap, reefer jacket with white shirt and black matching long trousers; but on the double-breasted greatcoat, rather unusually, Romanian officers wore rank distinction lace on the cuffs rather than on the shoulder straps.

In June 1943 metal battle badges, based on the German model, were introduced for crews of submarines, torpedo-boats and minelayers.

Badges of rank are illustrated in the rank insignia chart.

ROMANIAN AIR FORCE INSIGNIA

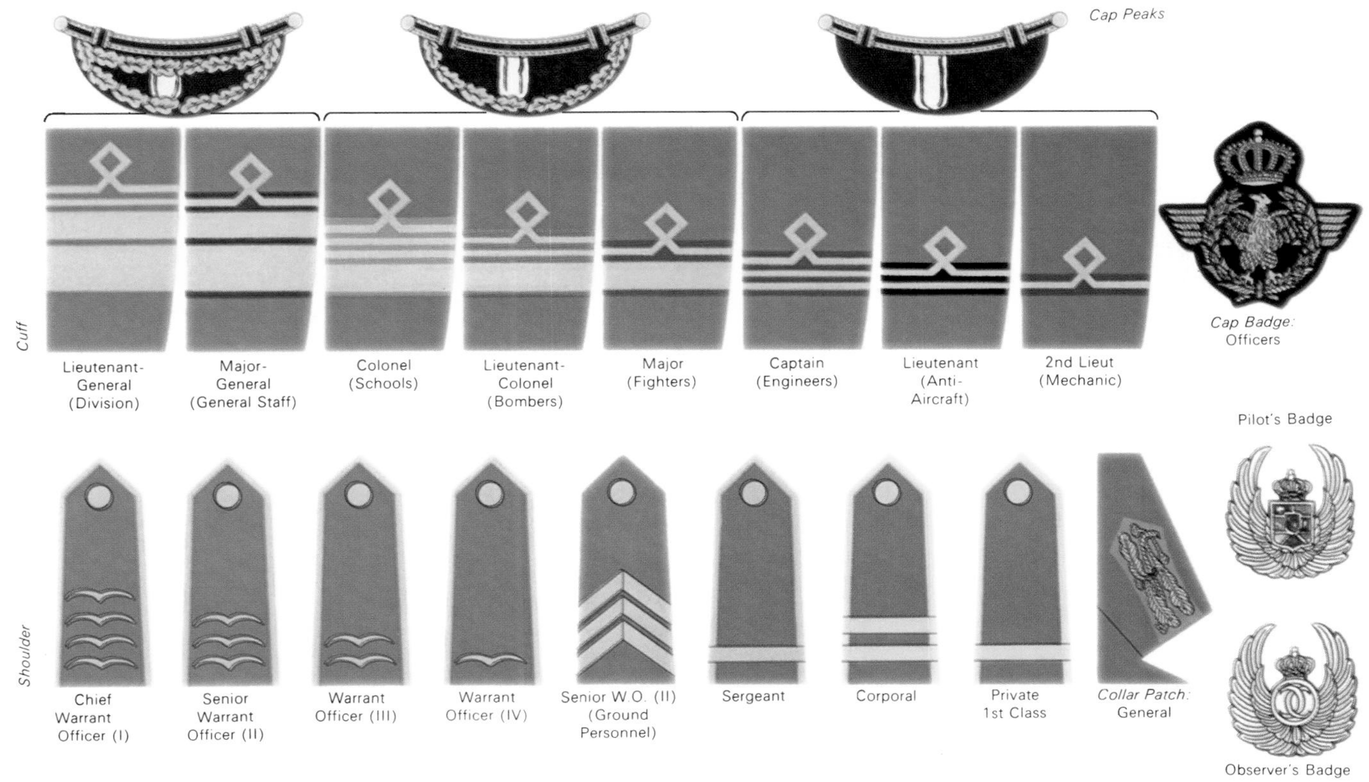

Cap Peaks
Cuff
Lieutenant-General (Division)
Major-General (General Staff)
Colonel (Schools)
Lieutenant-Colonel (Bombers)
Major (Fighters)
Captain (Engineers)
Lieutenant (Anti-Aircraft)
2nd Lieut (Mechanic)
Cap Badge: Officers
Pilot's Badge
Shoulder
Chief Warrant Officer (I)
Senior Warrant Officer (II)
Warrant Officer (III)
Warrant Officer (IV)
Senior W.O. (II) (Ground Personnel)
Sergeant
Corporal
Private 1st Class
Collar Patch: General
Observer's Badge

ROMANIAN NAVY INSIGNIA

Cap Peaks
Cuff
Admiral of the Fleet
Admiral
Vice-Admiral
Rear-Admiral
Captain (Engineers)
Commander (Administration)
Lieutenant-Commander (Medical)
Senior Lieutenant (Construction)
Lieutenant (Pharmacy)
Sub-Lieut (Music)
Shoulder
Arm
Cuff
Midshipman
Warrant Officer (I)
Warrant Officer (II)
Sergeant Major
Sergeant (Navigation)
Corporal (Gunner)
Private 1st Class (Torpedoes)
Collar: Marine Flyer Off.
Greatcoat Collar: Seaman
Cap Badge: Officers

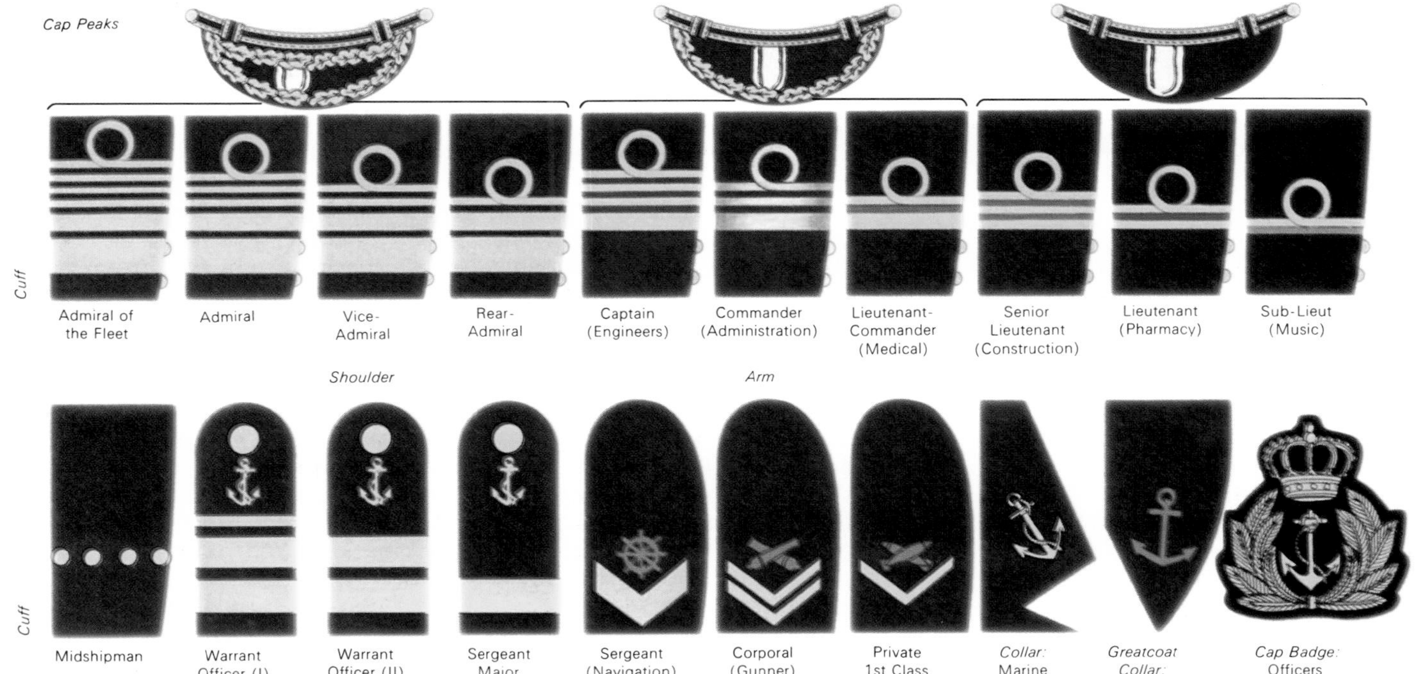

250 Infantryman, Hungarian Army, 1942
This infantryman marching in a field review wears winter field service uniform with German-pattern steel helmet, greatcoat, special trousers with integral cloth anklets, and ankle boots. The cow hide pack, rolled blanket and mess tin were similar to the Imperial Austrian pattern.

251 2nd Lieutenant, Hungarian Infantry, 1941
On the front of the side cap is worn the cockade in national colours and the braid chevron according to rank. On the left side of the cap is a triangle in the arm-of-service colour to which was sewn three pieces of khaki braid. Collar patches are also in arm-of-service colour.

HUNGARY

ARMY

Before the outbreak of World War II, Hungary was engaged in a number of military operations in the acquisition of territories which had been granted to her as a result of the Vienna Awards. In October 1939 Hungarian troops occupied parts of Ruthenia and southern Slovakia, and in 1940 half of Transylvania was ceded by Romania. Having allied herself with Germany, Hungarian troops participated in the invasion of Yugoslavia in April 1941, and occupied the Bács-Kiskun region, home of 500,000 Hungarians.

ORGANISATION The peacetime strength of the Army was about 80,000 men. The country was divided into seven corps commands; each army corps consisted of three infantry divisions (each of three infantry regiments and an artillery regiment of 24 horse-drawn guns), two cavalry brigades, two motorised brigades, an anti-aircraft battery, a signals company and a cavalry reconnaissance troop.

The most effective fighting forces were organised as the 9th Army, which comprised:
3 light divisions (each with two infantry and one artillery regiment);
1 'Rapid' Corps;
2 motorised rifle brigades;
2 cavalry brigades;
2 mountain brigades;
3 frontier rifle brigades.

Hungary's first and major contribution to the Axis war effort was the deployment of her élite Rapid Corps (two motorised and one armoured brigade with about 40,000 men) on the Eastern Front. Although designated 'rapid' the corps still relied on horses and bicycles, while its 'armour' consisted of 65 Italian Ansaldo and 95 Hungarian Toldi (Swedish but made under licence in Hungary) light tanks. In July 1941 the Rapid Corps joined the German 17th Army and advanced as far as the Donets where it took part in the Battle of Uman which resulted in the capture of 103,000 Red Army soldiers. But having advanced over 1000 kilometres the corps had suffered 26,000 casualties, lost 90 per cent of its armour, and over 1000 precious motor vehicles. On 6 December 1941 the Corps returned to Budapest.

This left on the Eastern Front a bicycle battalion and four infantry brigades (about 63,000 men) which were ill-equipped to cope with the vast distances and appalling conditions. Only the cavalry were able to make a useful contribution.

Germany now demanded a maximum effort and the Hungarians despatched to the front the 2nd Hungarian Army, consisting of nine light infantry divisions (two instead of three infantry regiments each), and the pride of the *Honvéd*, the 1st Armoured Division with 83 LT-38 (Czech) tanks, two Toldi tanks and 22 German Panzer Mk I tanks. Unfortunately, none were a match for the Soviet T34s. Although the cadre was made up of regular personnel, the rest had only undergone eight weeks' training, and their only tactical experience had been the manoeuvres held just prior to their departure for the front.

By now the rank-and-file of the *Honvéd* was made up of Hungarians, Romanians

252 2nd Lieutenant, Hungarian Infantry, 1944
The steel helmet is the German M1935 with camouflage net. The uniform is the standard pattern with rank badges appearing on the collar patches which were in arm-of-service colour.

253 2nd Lieutenant, Hungarian Army, 1943
At the beginning of the war tank crews wore the Italian pattern leather helmet and coat, but during the war the most typical outfit was a one-piece overall and side cap. The uniform illustrated was made of khaki cotton and leather and was worn concurrently with another pattern of khaki uniform which closely resembled the special field-grey uniform for German self-propelled gun crews. Rank badges are on the collar and cap.

254 Sergeant, Hungarian Gendarmerie, 1941
As a member of an élite corps this sergeant wears the distinctive cockerel feather plume and green woollen whistle lanyard. Rank badges were worn on the collar patches which are in the arm colour. Since all members of the Gendarmerie were regulars he does not wear the triangular badge on the left sleeve which in other units indicated regular status.

from Transylvania, Slovakians from southern Slovakia, Ukrainians from Ruthenia and Serbs from Bács-Kiskun, and this did not contribute to the homogeneity or morale of the Hungarian Army.

In the rear areas labour and construction work was carried out by Labour Service Companies which had been formed from those liable for military service, but considered unreliable on ethnic or political grounds.

The end of 1942 found the Hungarian 2nd Army holding a line which ran for 150 kilometres southwards from Voronezh. This meant that a division had a frontage of 21 kilometres, a regiment 10.5 and a battalion 3.5 kilometres. All the heavy weapons were in the front line with none in reserve, nor were there any stocks of ammunition. Between the 12 and 14 January 1943 a massive Soviet offensive pierced the line in a number of places and the Hungarians retreated westwards in temperatures of minus 30 degrees, leaving behind them most of their equipment and 147,971 comrades. Following this disaster the remains of the 2nd Army returned to Budapest, or served as security troops in the Ukraine.

Hungarian troops continued to serve under German operational command in rear areas, (although it was the desire of the Hungarian authorities that her troops should only serve in the defence of the homeland) but Hungarian units refused to help in the suppression of the Warsaw Uprising in August 1944. As the Soviet Army approached the Carpathians negotiations began between the Hungarian and Soviet governments which led to a provisional cease-fire on 15 October 1944. But on the very same day German troops occupied Budapest and a new installed 'Arrow Cross' government under Ferenc Szálasi undertook to continue the war against the Soviet Union.

In December 1944 Budapest was encircled by the Soviet Army. Of the three Hungarian armies only two remained and one of these was in Slovakia. Other Hungarian units were under German command or undergoing training in Germany and Austria. On 2 February 1945 the strength of the Hungarian Army was 214,463 men, but 50,000 of these had been formed into unarmed labour battalions. During the very last phase of the war Hungarians fought in Vienna, Breslau, Küstrin and on the Oder River. The final cost to Hungary was over 136,000 soldiers killed.

Above: Hungarian troops, in camouflage capes, greatcoats and German M1915 helmets.

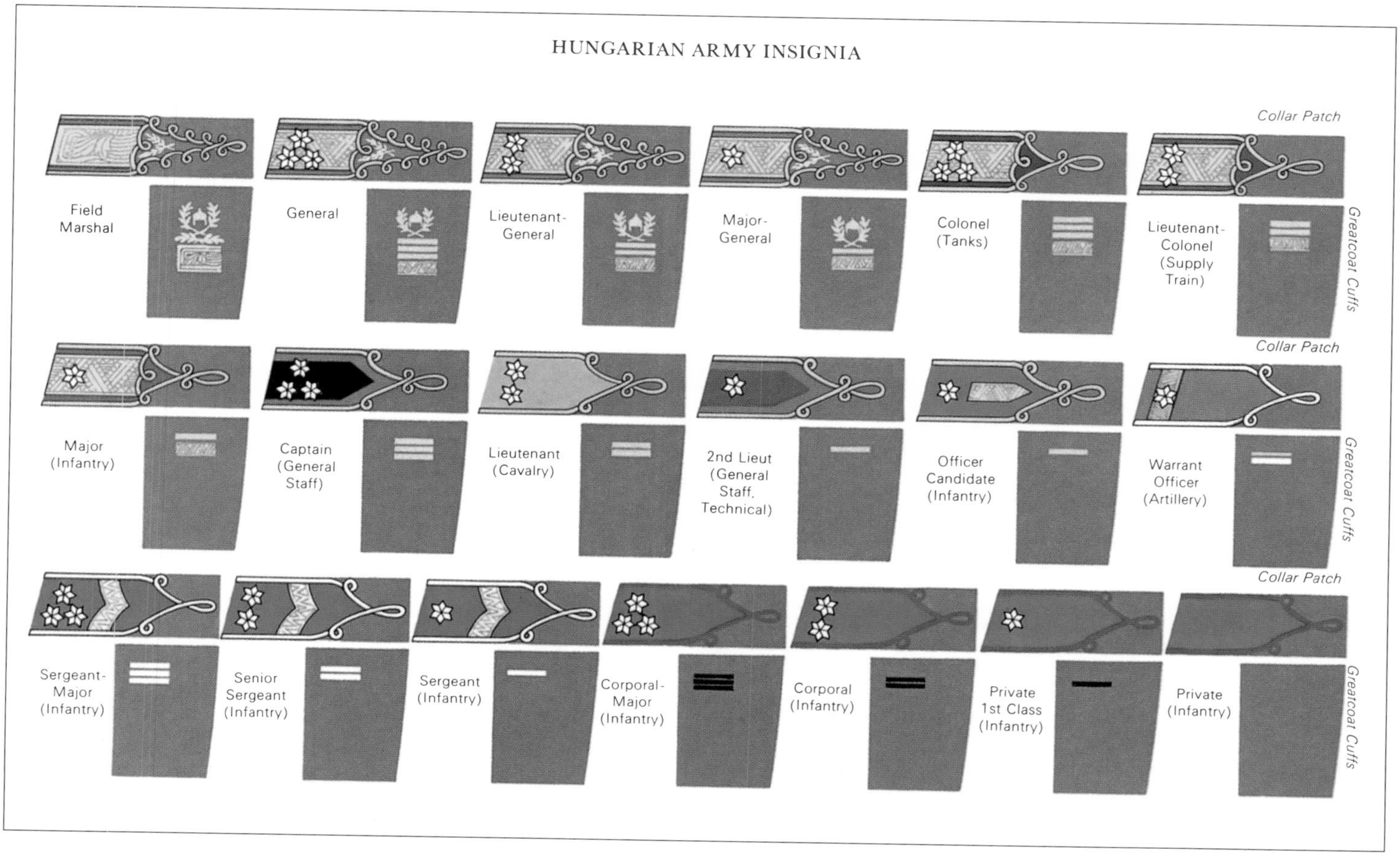

UNIFORM The khaki uniform of the Royal Hungarian Army was introduced in 1922. Unusual features of the uniform were a side cap, with high pointed crown, and special pantaloons, which were fastened tightly at the calf with buttons and incorporated a cloth anklet for wear with ankle boots. Mounted personnel wore breeches and boots.

The standard service dress for officers is illustrated in figures 251 and 252 and that of other ranks in figure 250. The tunic, which was in the same cut for all ranks, was single-breasted with stand-and-fall collar, five buttons in front, and breast and side pleated patch pockets. Head-dress consisted of the side cap and, in the latter stages of the war, field cap with cloth-covered peak. The German-pattern steel helmet (both 1915 and 1935 models) was also worn.

Tank crews at the beginning of the war wore overalls, a double-breasted leather coat and the Italian black-leather tank helmet with neck flap. During the war, khaki overalls and a side cap were the most typical garments, but with the shortage of leather a new jacket as illustrated in figure 253 was introduced for wear by tank crews.

The élite Royal Hungarian Gendarmerie (figure 254) wore a black felt hat with cockerel feather plume, but this fell into disuse in the Soviet Union and was replaced by the side cap with the same plume on the left side. This mark of distinction was not always recognised by their allies on the Eastern Front, and so it became necessary to introduce a German-type metal gorget as a duty badge.

INSIGNIA Badges of rank were worn on the tunic collar patches. Just before the war rank badges were worn as

HUNGARIAN ARMY INSIGNIA

Collar Patch

Field Marshal

General

Lieutenant-General

Major-General

Colonel (Tanks)

Lieutenant-Colonel (Supply Train)

Greatcoat Cuffs

Collar Patch

Major (Infantry)

Captain (General Staff)

Lieutenant (Cavalry)

2nd Lieut (General Staff, Technical)

Officer Candidate (Infantry)

Warrant Officer (Artillery)

Greatcoat Cuffs

Collar Patch

Sergeant-Major (Infantry)

Senior Sergeant (Infantry)

Sergeant (Infantry)

Corporal-Major (Infantry)

Corporal (Infantry)

Private 1st Class (Infantry)

Private (Infantry)

Greatcoat Cuffs

Above: This soldier wears the standard Hungarian Army greatcoat with a camouflaged cape affixed. This cape could be used to form part of a bivouac.

Below: A collection of Hungarian troops are shown with an assortment of Hungarian and German equipment. In the far distance is a Czech-designed LT-35 light tank, which was built in Hungary under licence as the 40M Turan 1. *Armed with a 40mm gun, it was no match for Soviet armour.*

shoulder straps on the greatcoat, but these were abolished in favour of badges of rank on the cuffs. Regular NCOs were distinguished by a triangular badge worn on the upper left sleeve. All ranks wore lace and braid chevrons on the front of the side cap and field cap according to rank.

Arm-of-service colours appeared on the collar patches and on the left side of the side and field cap in the form of a triangle. Some units had a distinctive metal badge on the left side of the head-dress. Parachutists wore embroidered or metal 'wings' on the right breast.

Air force

All forms of aviation were prohibited in Hungary by the Treaty of Trianon (1920), but the lifting of restrictions on civil flying in 1922 opened the way for clandestine military air activity. Hostility towards the 'Little Entente' powers of Czechoslovakia, Yugoslavia and Romania, to whom Hungary had lost territory at the end of World War I, provided the impetus for Hungarian rearmament. Italy supplied her with modern warplanes in the mid-1930s, including 70 Caproni Ca 135bis bombers and the same quantity each of Fiat CR-42 and Reggiane Re 2000 fighters, together with a licence to manufacture the latter type. There were 3300 personnel.

In 1938 Germany offered help in modernising and expanding the Hungarian Air Force and a Luftwaffe mission and training aircraft were dispatched. On 26 June 1941 a purported Soviet air raid on Košice, a Slovak town annexed in 1938, brought Hungary into the war against Russia. At this time her Air Force was well-trained and morale was high, yet by international standards her aircraft were outdated and her Air Force under strength. There were eight fighter squadrons (96 aircraft), ten bomber squadrons (120 aircraft), ten battlefield reconnaissance squadrons (80 aircraft), one long-range reconnaissance squadron (18 aircraft) and one transport squadron (6 aircraft). The main fighter types were the Italian Fiat CR-42 and Reggiane Re 2000, bombers were Junkers Ju 86Ks and Caproni Ca 135bis, while reconnaissance was undertaken by long-range

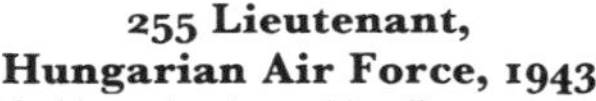

255 Lieutenant, Hungarian Air Force, 1943

Over his khaki service dress this officer wears a German sheepskin flying jacket with rank badges on the cuffs, and German black suede flying boots. On the left side of the field cap he wears the Air Force cap badge.

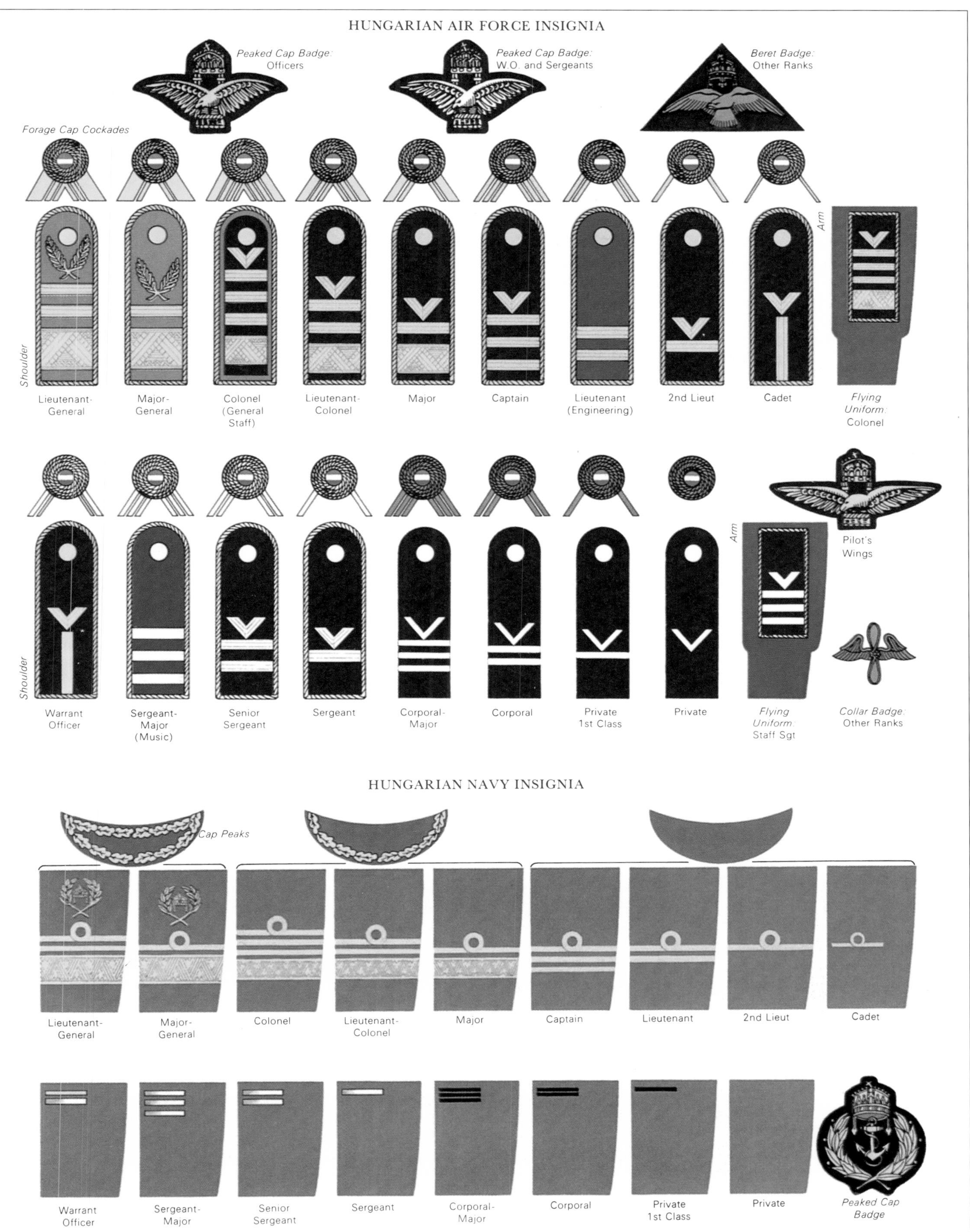
HUNGARIAN AIR FORCE INSIGNIA
Peaked Cap Badge: Officers
Peaked Cap Badge: W.O. and Sergeants
Beret Badge: Other Ranks
Forage Cap Cockades
Shoulder
Arm
Lieutenant-General
Major-General
Colonel (General Staff)
Lieutenant-Colonel
Major
Captain
Lieutenant (Engineering)
2nd Lieut
Cadet
Flying Uniform: Colonel
Pilot's Wings
Warrant Officer
Sergeant-Major (Music)
Senior Sergeant
Sergeant
Corporal-Major
Corporal
Private 1st Class
Private
Flying Uniform: Staff Sgt
Collar Badge: Other Ranks
HUNGARIAN NAVY INSIGNIA
Cap Peaks
Lieutenant-General
Major-General
Colonel
Lieutenant-Colonel
Major
Captain
Lieutenant
2nd Lieut
Cadet
Warrant Officer
Sergeant-Major
Senior Sergeant
Sergeant
Corporal-Major
Corporal
Private 1st Class
Private
Peaked Cap Badge

Heinkel He 170s and short-range He 46s and Hungarian WM 21s.

The Hungarian air brigade, dispatched to the Eastern Front in July 1941, encountered little opposition, yet attrition was high because much of its equipment was obsolescent. The brigade was recalled in December 1941 and plans were made for the licence production of German Messerschmitt Bf 109G and Me 210 warplanes. However, deliveries of these did not start until 1943 (1200 warplanes being built in Hungary in 1943–44) and so some 200 warplanes were supplied from Germany.

A new air brigade left for Russia in June 1942, but it was still poorly equipped. It comprised an independent fighter group equipped with Re 2000s, 4/II Bomber Group with Ca 135bis bombers, a long range reconnaissance group of He 111s and the 3/2 Short Range Reconnaissance Squadron with He 46s: a total of some 100 aircraft. Not until the Soviet breakthrough on the Don in early 1943 revealed the Air Force's weakness did substantial supplies of modern aircraft arrive. During 1943–44 some 300 Bf 109Gs reached Hungarian units, Ju 87 squadrons were re-equipped with the Focke Wulf Fw 190F and reconnaissance units converted to the Fw 189.

Below: This Hungarian pilot is fully-equipped for action and sports a brand-new German parachute harness. His oxygen mask is also clearly visible, with facemask hanging by the left arm, and the rank badges attached to this arm show him to be a 2nd lieutenant. This airman is of the later period of the war, when Allied pressure forced an expansion of the Air Force.

As with all of Germany's allies in Eastern Europe, Hungary relied on modern German aircraft to provide the backbone of the Air Force. Although Germany made great efforts to supply her allies with aircraft and instructors – in order to guarantee their military survival – there were never enough aeroplanes to go round. The shortage of aircraft became particularly acute during the last two years of the war as Germany herself came under increasing pressure from the Allied bomber offensive.

In the spring of 1944 Hungary came under attack from USAAF strategic bombers based in Italy, and a rapid expansion of air defence units took place. In May 1944 there were only three fighter squadrons for home defence, but this force was doubled within two months. The Romanian defection in August 1944 forced the Luftwaffe's *Fliegerkorps* I to withdraw into Hungary and all combat units of the Hungarian Air Force, except the air defence squadrons, were absorbed by this formation.

Soviet forces advanced into Hungary in the autumn of 1944 and early the following year a Hungarian puppet government signed an armistice with them. Yet the Hungarian Air Force fought on alongside the Luftwaffe, retreating into Austria when all Hungary was occupied in March 1945. By May only two units still had airworthy aircraft and these were destroyed before surrendering to the Americans.

UNIFORM As a branch of the Army, Air Force personnel wore khaki uniforms which differed only in detail from those worn by the rest of the Army. Officers and senior non-commissioned officers had a peaked cap with brown leather peak and open khaki service dress jacket, which was worn with a white or (off duty) khaki shirt and khaki tie, matching long trousers and brown shoes.

Other ranks had a special head-dress, not unlike that worn by sailors, or the side cap and the same tunic as that worn in the rest of the Army. During the war, however, other ranks also received an open tunic for wear with khaki shirt and black tie.

Flying clothing was varied and included an unlined leather one-piece overall with numerous zip-fastened pockets, or a lightweight khaki overall with knee pockets. Flying helmets were either linen or leather. Parachutes were supplied by Italy, as were many of the aircraft. Later in the war German aircraft and flying clothing began to be used in greater quantities.

INSIGNIA Badges of rank were worn on the front of the side and field caps, on the shoulder straps on the tunic and on the cuffs of the flying gear (figure 255). Arm-of-service colours appeared on the shoulder straps and cuff patches for generals (scarlet straps), general staff (scarlet piping) and technical officials (cherry velvet).

NAVY

Although for most of the war, Hungary was ruled by the pro-German Admiral Miklós Horthy, the country had no coastline and no Navy. The Ministry of the Interior did, however, maintain the ten old rivercraft of the Danube Flotilla of the Royal Hungarian *Honvéd* River Force at Budapest for police work. The Flotilla was taken over by the Ministry of Defence when war broke out.

With the beginning of the Allied air offensive the Flotilla became responsible for keeping the river free of mines. Other units were based on Újvidék (now Novi Sad) in northern Yugoslavia from where they carried out important occupation duties.

During the Battle of Budapest the Danube bridges were defended by riverboats mounting anti-aircraft guns and artillery pieces.

UNIFORM AND INSIGNIA The colour of the uniform of the Royal Hungarian River Forces was khaki. Officers and senior non-commissioned officers had a khaki peaked cap, single-breasted open service dress tunic – worn with either khaki or white shirt and khaki tie – matching long trousers and black shoes. The greatcoat was double-breasted, with two rows of six metal buttons in front and a brown velvet collar.

Ratings wore a khaki cap with black silk tally bearing the words '*M.Kir.Honvéd Folyami erok*' in silver letters. The khaki tunic could be worn open at the neck with matching trousers and black marching boots. Equipment was standard infantry pattern in brown leather. The greatcoat for other ranks was double-breasted, with two rows of five buttons.

Badges of rank were worn on the cuffs by all ranks. On the service dress tunic rank distinction lace went round the cuff, whereas on the greatcoat it appeared in a shortened form. The three rank groups were identified by the colour of the buttons, badges and lace: ratings and junior NCOs had bronze, senior NCOs silver and officers gold.

256

257

256 Private, Bulgarian Army, 1941
Russian influence upon Bulgarian uniform is evident in this illustration, especially the single-breasted tunic with stand collar. During the course of the war, however, the Bulgarian Army began to adopt features from German uniform, Germany being the predominant military influence in the Balkans at this time. The helmet is similar in shape to the German pattern and has the Bulgarian national colours on the soldier's right-hand side and a red shield with rampant golden lion on the other. The leather equipment is of Russian origin, while over the pack is strapped a grey bedding-roll. The rifle is the Bulgarian version of the Italian Mannlicher Carcano M1891. The Mannlicher Carcano, which had first seen service in 1891, was becoming increasingly outdated by the 1940s and its small calibre of 6.5mm was out of line with the ammunition of most other countries.

257 Major, Bulgarian Army
This figure wears the standard Bulgarian Army officer's greatcoat with two rows of gilt buttons. The arm of service, indicated by the piping on the collar and cuffs, is that of the cavalry. Rank is shown by the one pip and two stripes on the shoulder boards. Instead of riding boots which were commonly worn by officers, this major has marching boots and puttees.

Bulgaria

Army

Throughout World War II Tsarist Bulgaria was only officially at war with England and America. Her alliance with Germany was due in part to their common experiences during World War I, the hope of territorial gains, and her distrust of Soviet intentions. Following the Balkan Campaign during which German troops were allowed to traverse Bulgaria, she was allowed to occupy Greek Macedonia, Thrace and Salonika, a huge territory of some 50,000 square kilometres.

The principal task of the Bulgarian Army between 1941 and 1944 was the garrisoning of the new territories, where often side-by-side with other Axis forces it waged a relentless war on partisans. In the summer of 1944, the Bulgarian Army disposed of over 21 infantry and two cavalry divisions as well as two frontier brigades. Seven divisions in two army corps were under German operational control in Western Macedonia and Serbia for the protection of the main German supply arteries between Belgrade and Greece. All but 10 of the divisions were basically obsolete, horse-drawn and lacking in both modern armoured fighting vehicles and anti-tank guns. The armoured brigade was equipped with German armoured fighting vehicles, while in the whole Bulgarian Army there were only 121 tanks.

At the end of August 1944, as a Soviet army group was approaching the Bulgarian frontier, the Tsar, Boris III, died. On 9 September a *coup d'état* took place, and the new Government of the Fatherland Front made peace with the Allies and changed sides. The armed forces were purged of their most reactionary officers, political officers (commissars) were appointed, and overnight Royal Guard Regiments became People's Liberation Brigades. In October 1944, the Bulgarian Army was organised into the 1st, 2nd and 4th Armies and a strategic reserve of:
10 infantry divisions;
1 guards division;
2 cavalry divisions;
1 armoured brigade;
1 independent brigade.

Now the task of the 1st, 2nd and 4th Bulgarian Armies with Soviet air support and under Soviet operational control, was to prevent the Germans from retreating from Greece and the Aegean. The fighting was by no means over and the fighting was hard. Relations between former enemies were often strained, while the changing of sides and uncertainty about the future affected morale. May 1945 found the Bulgarian Army on Austrian soil, where on 13 May they linked up with British troops. Between September 1944 and May 1945 the Bulgarians lost 31,910 killed, wounded and missing.

Uniform and insignia The predominantly Tsarist Russian influence in the uniforms of the Bulgarian Army remained until the end of the war, despite the introduction of a number of German features such as collar patches.

The officer illustrated in figure 257 wears wartime service dress with the greatcoat, which for general officers had scarlet lapels and scarlet piping around the collar, cuffs, down the front and on the half belt, and pocket flaps at the back. The tunic worn under the greatcoat had either a stand and fall collar or an open collar worn with shirt and tie. Badges of rank appeared in the form of Russian shoulder boards but were much narrower. Both the breeches and long undress trousers had either the red double stripe (*Lampassen*) for generals or piping in arm-of-service colour for other officers.

There were three basic kinds of headdress. The steel helmet which was made in Czechoslovakia resembled the German pattern. The side cap had a shield on the right side in the national colours, white, green and red, and a gilt metal or brass Bulgarian lion on the front. On the left side officers wore rank distinction lace. The peaked cap was khaki with coloured band and piping and black peak and chin strap. On the front was an oval metal cockade in the national colours.

An infantryman is illustrated in figure 256, wearing summer uniform. The cloth tunic was single-breasted with stand and fall collar, six buttons in front and breast and side pockets with Austrian-pattern three-pointed pocket flaps. Arm of service was identified by the colour of the shoulder straps and collar patches. The greatcoat was made of coarse greyish-brown cloth and was double-breasted but with a single central row of six metal buttons down the front and vertical slash side pockets.

Tank crews wore standard Army uniform with either a khaki overall or leather jacket and Italian leather tank helmet.

Badges of rank were worn on the shoulder straps by all ranks, and on the left side of the side cap. Arm-of-service colours appeared on the peaked cap, as piping or underlay on the shoulder boards. The buttons, badges and lace were either gold or silver, depending on the arm of service.

Air force

After World War I the treaty of Neuilly (1919) banned military aviation in Bulgaria, but this prohibition was circumvented. In the mid-1930s the Bulgarian Air Force was built up with Italian and German aid and the provisions of the 1919 treaty were openly repudiated in 1938. In the following year Poland supplied fighter and attack aircraft to Bulgaria and by September 1939 her Air Force comprised eight air regiments.

The outbreak of war cut off Polish supplies and, as the Italians had been ousted by their Axis partners, the way was open for German penetration of the Bulgarian Air Force. A Bulgarian mission to German-occupied Czechoslovakia bought a substantial number of former Czech Air Force warplanes, including 72 Avia B-534 biplane fighters and 32 Avia B-71 bombers (Czech-built Tupolev SB-2s).

Luftwaffe advisors were dispatched to Bulgaria in 1940 and German training and liaison aircraft were supplied, together with 10 Messerschmitt Bf 109E fighters and 11 Dornier Do 17M bombers. Despite this infusion of new equipment, morale in the Air Force was low. The presence of German advisors was resented and the mass of the population was pro-Russian, only the Royalist party favouring friendship with Germany. Nevertheless, in March 1941 Bulgaria signed the Axis Pact and Luftwaffe units moved into the country in preparation for the assault on Yugoslavia and Greece.

The Luftwaffe mission in Sofia aimed to bring the Bulgarian Air Force into line with German operational standards, so that it could be entrusted with its own national air defence. However, the Bulgarians firmly resisted all attempts to involve them in the war with Russia and as a result few German warplanes were supplied to her in 1941–42.

The threat to the Romanian oilfields from American strategic bombers changed the picture and in 1943 German supplies resumed. Yet the first large-scale USAAF raid on Ploeşti (1 August 1943) found the

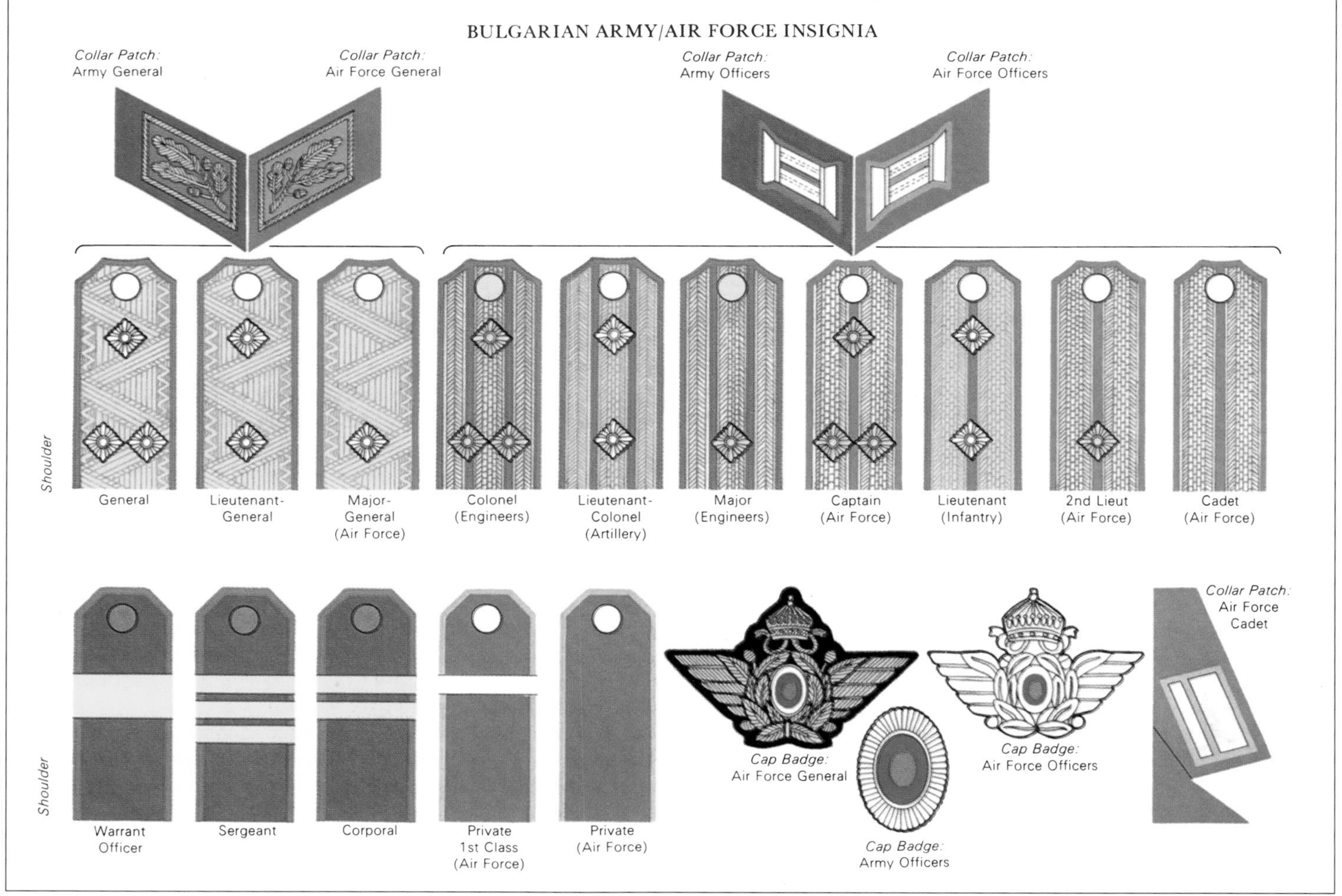

BULGARIAN NAVY INSIGNIA

Cuff

Admiral

Vice-Admiral

Rear-Admiral

Captain

Commander

Lieutenant-Commander

Lieutenant

Sub-Lieut

Midshipman

Shoulder

Shldr Strap: Adml Rank (here Adml)

Shldr Strap: Snr Officers (here Capt.)

Shldr Strap: Jnr Officers (here Lieut)

Chief Petty Officer

Petty Officer (I)

Petty Officer (II)

Leading Seaman

Cap Badge: Other Ranks

Cap Badge: Officers

Bulgarians woefully unprepared. Only three B-24s fell to their guns, out of a total of 54 American bombers lost. The Bulgarian Air Force was further strengthened by the supply of 100 French Dewoitine D 520 fighters and 48 Bf 109Gs were promised by Germany. Even so, the Bulgarians had little success against escorted American raids between November 1943 and January 1944.

By September of the latter year, the hostile Soviet forces were on Bulgarian soil. Many Bulgarians surrendered or joined the partisans and on 9 September Bulgaria declared war on Germany. Thereafter, her Air Force fought alongside Soviet air regiments.

UNIFORM AND INSIGNIA During the war Air Force personnel wore either the Army khaki or Air Force grey uniform concurrently. The blue-grey uniform was in the same cut as the Army uniform, and officers and senior NCOs had both a closed tunic with stand and fall collar or an open tunic which was worn with shirt and tie. On the collar officers wore German-pattern collar patches (*Litzen*) embroidered in silver wire. NCOs had rectangular light blue collar patches with silver grey bars of differing thickness. Pilots wore embroidered wings on the right breast.

Head-dress was either the side cap or peaked cap with black leather peak and chin strap. The blue-grey peaked cap had a dark grey band, light blue piping and silver cap badge with national cockade.

Badges of rank were worn on the shoulder boards by all ranks, and also on the left side of the side cap. Arm-of-service colour (light blue) appeared as piping on the peaked cap, on the collar patches and shoulder straps, and as piping on the trousers, breeches and greatcoat.

NAVY

Based at Varna on the Black Sea, in 1939 the Bulgarian Navy comprised four ageing destroyers and torpedo boats, five motor torpedo-boats of S-boat design and six rivercraft. In addition, she possessed 14 merchant ships; naval air support was supplied by Army seaplanes.

After declaring for the Axis in 1941, Bulgaria is thought to have purchased six more motor torpedo-boats from Germany. These had been captured when incomplete near Rotterdam, and moved across Europe. Their service and fate is uncertain: some may have remained in German service in the Adriatic, while others may have been repossessed after Bulgaria's enforced change of sides.

UNIFORM AND INSIGNIA The uniform of the Royal Bulgarian Navy was very similar to that which had been worn by the Tsarist Russian Navy prior to 1917. Officers and chief petty officers wore a black peaked cap with white piping, embroidered cap badge and black leather peak and chin strap. The black reefer was double-breasted with two rows of buttons in front and was worn with white shirt, black tie and matching long trousers. The greatcoat was double-breasted. In hot weather officers and chief petty officers wore a white cap cover and white tunic with stand collar.

Ratings had a Russian-style cap on the front of which was an oval metal cockade in the national colours. The inscription on the tally was in cyrillic letters. The blue jumper was worn inside the trousers, as was the blue linen working jumper which had an open patch pocket on the left breast. The vest was striped in light blue and white and the blue denim collar had three white lines. In winter ratings wore the pea-coat.

Badges of rank were worn on the shoulder boards or patches. Executive officers had an embroidered crown above the rank distinction lace on the reefer cuffs. On the white tunic rank distinction lace was worn on the outside of the cuffs only.

Arm of service was indicated by the colour of the underlay and stripes on the shoulder boards, and the 'lights' on the rank distinction lace. Only officers in the executive or line branch were allowed to wear rank distinction lace on the cuffs and all their badges, buttons and lace were in gold. Officers in the administrative branches did not wear rank distinction lace, and all badges, buttons and shoulder-board lace were in silver.

Finland

Army

Although the signing of the Moscow Treaty in March 1940 guaranteed Finland her borders with the Soviet Union, the Finnish Government remained uncertain of Soviet intentions towards the independence of Finland. So when Hitler informed the Finns of his impending invasion of the Soviet Union they readily cooperated with Germany to secure the contested Karelian region and the strategically important centre of Murmansk.

On 10 July 1941 the Finnish Army attacked Soviet troops deployed around Lake Ladoga for the protection of Leningrad. But when they had fulfilled their objective of recovery of territories lost in 1939–40, the Finns halted their advance. On 12 December Mannerheim ordered his men to go over to the defensive, and the Finnish Army played little part in the fighting until the Soviet offensive of 1944. Finnish casualties in this phase of the war amounted to 25,000 killed and more than 50,000 wounded.

On 9 June 1944 the Soviet Army launched its attack on Finland deploying five armies totalling 450,000 men and 10,000 guns. The Finnish Army was caught by surprise, largely because of the complacency of the Finnish High Command which had failed to take the necessary defensive precautions during the preceding years. Indeed, the long period of static positional warfare had undermined the morale of the troops and made the Red Army's attack all the more successful. The powerful Russian onslaught caused some units to panic and the Finnish Army withdrew towards its own territorial boundaries. After a month's hard fighting the Soviet advance was held and the front stabilised, but Mannerheim realised that his small forces had no chance against the five armies facing him: on 5 September there was a cease-fire. Casualties during the whole of World War II were 90,000 killed. German troops evacuated Finland peacefully, apart from an unsuccessful attempt to take the island of Sur Sari.

Organisation The period following the Winter War saw a rapid expansion of the Finnish armed forces: by 1941 the Army fielded 16 divisions plus three crack brigades (two *Jäger* – rifle – and one cavalry). The inadequate Finnish artillery had been overhauled so that the Army was supported by modern field pieces adequately supplied with munitions. Armoured vehicles were formed into regular units for the first time, some equipped with captured Soviet tanks from the Winter War. Despite these improvements, however, the Finnish Army was still basically an infantry army and was woefully lacking in the support services (especially radio communications) that were commonplace in most modern armies. The Army compensated for these deficiencies by the overall quality of its officers and men, although the war was to prove that Finns fought better when defending their homeland than in initiating offensive operations.

The basic divisional organisation had changed little since the Winter War (see page 23) and consisted, on average, of three infantry regiments and one field artillery regiment plus a limited number of support troops. A typical division was the 2nd, which was made up as follows:
Karjala Guards Regiment;
Tampere Infantry Regiment;
Central Finland Infantry Regiment;
2nd Field Artillery Regiment.

In addition to the regular troops

258 Captain, Finnish Army, 1943
This is the typical wartime field service uniform of the Finnish Army, in which simplicity was combined with a deterioration of quality. Many of the frills had been dropped and so the stars instead of being fixed to coloured collar patches are pinned directly onto the tunic collar. The breeches are patched with leather. Every Finnish soldier carried a personal knife which did not conform to any regulation pattern, but came in useful for such tasks as skinning animals.

259 Lieutenant, Finnish Army, 1944
The field uniform worn by this figure differs in a number of ways from the normal service dress uniform: the tunic is shorter; the breast pocket is fastened by an ordinary button and the cut and quality of the uniform is generally inferior. The helmet is the old German M1915 which had largely been replaced in 1944 by the standard M35 model as worn by figure 261. Over the shoulder a map case is carried and tucked into his left boot a spoon is just visible. This lieutenant is armed with a captured Soviet PPD 1940G sub-machine gun, a well made weapon which was a useful supplement to the home manufactured Suomi sub-machine gun.

260 Private, Finnish Army, 1944
This infantryman wears the usual field cap and light-weight linen tunic-cum-shirt which was worn outside the trousers in the Russian manner. Under his ruck-sack is an entrenching tool. The rifle is the Finnish Moisin-Nagant M1928.

261 Sergeant, Finnish Army, 1944
This sergeant wears the M1935 German steel helmet and lightweight summer tunic. The collar patches are in arm-of-service colour and also show his badges of rank. He is armed with a Suomi model 1931 sub-machine gun and a German Panzerfaust *which was a one-shot rocket-propelled anti-tank weapon.*

organised either on the divisional basis outlined above or as non-divisional units such as the Heavy Artillery Regiment and Coast Artillery, there was the Civil Guard which consisted of those Finns not already in the armed forces but capable of bearing arms. The Civil Guard was organised on a regional basis and included female troops.

As part of Operation '*Barbarossa*' Finland was militarily divided in two. The northern half of the country came under German control (AOK *Norwegen*) and consisted of General Dietl's Mountain Corps, the XXXVI Corps (including the Finnish 6th Division) and the Finnish III Corps of only one division. The area south of Oulu came under direct Finnish control, its forces being deployed on the Karelian front comprising 13 divisions and three brigades organised as follows:

IV Corps: four infantry divisions;
II Corps: three infantry divisions;
VII Corps: two divisions;
VI Corps: two divisions and one *Jäger* brigade;
Gruppe Oinonen: one cavalry and one *Jäger* brigade;
14th Division;
Army Reserve: one division.

In addition to these forces there was one Finnish division blockading the Soviet outpost of Hanko on the Finnish coast and from the end of June 1941 the German 163rd Division was engaged in support of the Karelian Army. In all, the Finns had managed to mobilise 400,000 men.

During the period leading up to the Soviet invasion of 1944 there were no major changes in the organisation of the Finnish Army. German aid helped to give a more modern face to the armed forces but the disasters on the Eastern Front ensured that this help was necessarily limited. By May 1944 the front-line strength of the Army stood at 270,000 soldiers, 1900 guns and 800 tanks now organised into a full armoured division. The Army still suffered from two critical shortages: too few aircraft to protect the ground forces and inadequate anti-tank weapons to use against the well-armoured Russian T-34 and KV tanks. The Army of 1944 was much as it had been in 1941 – well-trained and led but lacking in sufficient modern equipment.

UNIFORM AND INSIGNIA The uniform and insignia of the Finnish Army had changed little since 1940, although the greater use of German uniforms had led to rather more standardisation.

ESTONIAN VOLUNTEERS

Estonian volunteers served in the Finnish Army during both the Winter War and the so-called Continuation War. By 1944 there were over 3000 Estonians and it was from these men that Infantry Regiment 200 was formed. Under its Finnish commander the Regiment fought with distinction on the Eastern Front, until August 1944, when 2600 Estonians returned to defend their homeland from the Red

Army. The remaining Estonians remained in Finnish service until the capitulation when they escaped across the frontier into Sweden.

UNIFORM Estonian volunteers wore Finnish uniforms with a shield-shaped badge in the Estonian national colours on the sleeve.

AIR FORCE

The Finnish Air Force had put up a stiff resistance to the numerically stronger Red Air Force during the Winter War (November 1939–March 1940) and in so doing had gained invaluable experience. Although small, with about 222 front line aircraft in June 1941, the Finnish Air Force was a useful addition to German air strength on the northern sector of the Eastern Front.

The Air Force was part of the Army but commanded by the Chief of Flying Troops. It was organised in five flying regiments and a number of independent units. Anti-aircraft artillery which in 1939 had been about 192 anti-aircraft guns of various calibres, had increased to nearly 700 by June 1941.

During the Continuation War the Finns split their units into smaller flights of about ten aircraft which could be deployed nearer the front and in the vicinity of the sector where they were required.

By spring 1944, the Air Force had about 223 fighters and 106 bombers of various types, many old-fashioned, but at least four flights flew Bf 109Gs.

Following the September 1944 armistice with the Allies the Finnish Air Force was used against its former ally in Finland and northern Norway. During the Continuation War the Finnish Air Force and anti-aircraft artillery claimed 2674 enemy aircraft destroyed. Losses were 366 combat aircraft and 361 men.

UNIFORM AND INSIGNIA The uniform remained the same throughout the war, and is described in the chapter dealing with the Winter War. As an ally of Germany and in receipt of German aircraft, equipment and training, Finnish airmen began to wear German flying clothing and parachutes, and received German badges and German decorations.

NAVY

During the Continuation War the Finnish Navy was reactivated and equipped with vessels left by the retreating Red Army. Finland possessed a Minister of Defence and a C-in-C Naval Forces, Major-General V.L.R. Valve. The Coastal Fleet, which was organised in flotillas and divisions, was commanded by a seagoing flag officer, Commodore E. A. Rahola; personnel totalled 4500.

From June 1941 onwards, when Finland fought alongside Germany, Finnish naval forces contributed one large coastal defence vessel and around 30 gun-boats, minesweepers and motor torpedo-boats to the Axis naval force in the Baltic. There were also an additional 432 vessels comprising the Finnish Mercantile Marine.

Throughout the Continuation War the tiny Finnish Navy operated in conjunction with German and Finnish land forces, rather than as an independent sea-going force. Its principal tasks were minelaying, transportation and evacuation of friendly troops, and attempts to cut enemy coastal lines of communication and supply.

The Lake Ladoga Flotilla was also reactivated in 1941 and equipped with 41 craft seized from the Red forces. Other inland flotillas were formed on Lake Segozero (one tug), Payazero (two tugs and motor boats) and Onega (130 vessels). All were later abandoned during the subsequent retreat.

Above: This picture contrasts the various styles of Finnish Air Force combat and service dress. A Messerschmitt Bf 109 stands behind.

Finnish losses in the Continuation War were two minelayers, 16 minesweepers, one yacht, two motor torpedo-boats and various other small vessels. At the end of the war the Soviet government seized the one remaining armoured coastal defence ship and five submarines.

UNIFORM AND INSIGNIA The Finnish Navy wore the same uniforms as it had during the Winter War.

NORTH-WEST EUROPE
1941-45

The war in north-west Europe and the Atlantic from 1941 onwards fell into three connected but quite distinct areas: the Battle of the Atlantic; the bombing offensive against Germany; and the Allied invasion of France which culminated in the defeat of the German armies in the West. On the Allied side, these three aspects of the war were marked by increasingly practical and sophisticated organisations and uniforms, while the Germans were forced to make the most effective use of whatever resources they could find. By the end of the war, uniform had often acquired a very modern look, as the experience of war had made the battle clothing of both sides extremely functional.

Great Britain

Army

After the defeat in western Europe of 1940, the British Army's primary task changed from the provision of an expeditionary force for Continental service to the formation of a field force capable of resisting an invasion of the United Kingdom. In June 1940 the Army's manpower stood at 2,221,000 plus 42,800 members of the ATS. Between June and August a further 275,000 men were conscripted and 120 new infantry battalions were formed, but although an eventual target of 55 British and Empire divisions had been accepted by the Government, the losses in weapons and transport occasioned by the evacuation from Dunkirk meant that a considerable period would elapse before anywhere near this number could be fully equipped.

Above: British troops move forward on the back of a Sherman tank in September 1944. They are wearing standard battledress.

Organisation For the immediate anti-invasion role the resources of the Army and the civil defence organisations were co-ordinated by the Home Defence Executive, initially under the chairmanship of the Commander-in-Chief, Home Forces. This latter post was held by General Sir Edmund Ironside until July 1940 when he was succeeded by General Sir Alan Brooke. The C-in-C, Home Forces commanded all military formations in the United Kingdom with the exception of the anti-aircraft divisions which were subordinated to Fighter Command, and the Free French. The troops at his disposal fell into three main categories: the Home Guard, Home Defence units, and the formations of the Field Force. By the autumn of 1941 there were 27 British, Canadian, and Polish motorised infantry divisions available for the Field Force, each containing a front line strength of approximately 15,500 men. To support these divisions there were 10 corps organisations with 61,000 corps troops. For beach defence eight county divisions had been formed each with a strength of 10,000 officers and men but equipped with only minimal artillery and transport. In addition to the divisional forces there were seven infantry brigades, four motorised brigade groups incorporating artillery, 12 independent battalions, and eight airfield defence battalions. The need to provide flank protection for the Atlantic sea lanes meant that garrisons had also to be maintained in the Faroes, Iceland (24,000 British troops by October 1941), the Azores, St. Helena, the Falkland Islands, and the West Indies.

After the fall of France Britain's armoured forces reached a very low ebb. The surviving units of the 1st Armoured Division and the 1st Army Tank Brigade returned from the Continent with few of the tanks and vehicles with which they had set out. In the United Kingdom an armoured division and four army tank brigades were in the process of formation but they also were short of weapons and vehicles. Despite these weaknesses it was decided to rebuild on the basis of the two existing types of armoured formations; the armoured division for mobile offensive operations on the battlefield, and the army tank brigade for close range fighting and infantry co-operation.

By the end of 1940 the armoured forces stationed in Britain consisted on paper of five armoured divisions (1st, 6th, 8th, 9th and 11th) and three army tank brigades, (21st, 25th and 31st), all of which had reached varying degrees of completeness and training. The planned expansion during 1941 was carried out by converting existing infantry units into Royal Armoured Corps formations, beginning with the establishment of the Guards armoured division and continuing with the conversion of the 42nd Infantry Division. A major change in the organisation of the armoured division occurred in May 1942 when one of the armoured brigades in each division was replaced by an infantry brigade. The HQ Support Group was replaced by an HQ Divisional Royal Artillery and the number of horse or field artillery regiments was doubled. The resulting organisation was as in the chart on page 121.

Each armoured regiment could deploy 55 cruiser, six close support cruiser, and eight anti-aircraft tanks, which when added to the HQ tanks gave the division a total strength of 201 cruisers and 26 anti-aircraft tanks. Although there were to be further modifications to the organisation of the armoured division – the introduction of an armoured reconnaissance regiment in place of the armoured car regiment for example – its basic structure was to remain the same until the conclusion of hostilities. The division's tank strength however, did increase, to 244 tanks plus 34 AA tanks in April 1943, and to 310 tanks with 25 AA tanks and eight OP tanks in March 1944.

The army tank brigades were henceforth normally assigned to infantry divisions replacing one infantry brigade in each division. The fighting complement of a tank brigade was approximately 1950 officers and men with 178 tanks of which at least 135 were infantry tanks. The 1st, 3rd, 4th, 43rd and 53rd Infantry Divisions each received an army tank brigade during 1942. From 1943 onwards the Army's specialised armour in the form of flail, amphibious, and flame-throwing tanks was grouped in one formation, the 79th Armoured Division.

The successful use of German paratroops during the campaign in the low countries in 1940 led Britain to form her own airborne forces. The first training parachute drop was made on 13 July 1940 and volunteers were quickly raised to form the units which were to become known as the Parachute Regiment. The enthusiasm and professionalism which could be seen in the Army's airborne troops was also reflected in the British talent for raising specialised 'irregular' units. These 'private armies' were trained to fulfil particular tactical requirements, such as amphibious raiding, and to deal with abnormal climatic and terrain conditions such as desert reconnaissance. As there was a surplus of volunteer recruits the units could be highly selective. The Army's principal special forces in Europe were the Commandos and the Special Air Service.

The Home Army's role as the defender of the United Kingdom against invasion was retained during 1943 but with the additional commitment of being able to mount large-scale offensive operations on the mainland of Europe. In terms of manpower the Army continued to grow slowly deploying 2,720,000 officers and men (plus 199,000 ATS) in June 1944 and reaching its peak strength of 2,920,000 (plus 190,800 ATS) in June 1945.

The Army's examination of the problems of a return in strength to France had begun in the summer of 1940 and the amphibious raid on Dieppe in August 1942 had been the logical outcome of that programme of study and assessment. In June 1944 the Army returned to the continent, and it was to the commander of the British forces, Field-Marshal Montgomery, that the Germans offered to surrender their forces in May 1945.

ORGANISATION As the planning for D-Day was finalised the British and Canadian formations assigned to the invasion comprised: 10 infantry divisions; 2 airborne divisions; 5 armoured divisions; (plus a Polish armoured division); 9 independent armoured brigades; 2 special service commando brigades; GHQ, Army and Corps troops.

The units, both British and American,

262 Corporal, British Army, 1944
As a dispatch rider this corporal in the Royal Corps of Signals wears a motorcyclist's crash helmet, leather jerkin over his battledress blouse, reinforced cord breeches, and special motorcycle boots. Insignia on the sleeve is the corps shoulder flash, arm-of-service strip, corporal's chevrons and Royal Signals armlet. The sub-machine gun is the 9mm Sten gun Mk II.

263 Private, British Commandos, 1942
This is the 'light raiding order' worn by British commandos on the Boulogne raid in April 1942. He wears a woollen cap comforter, battledress, 1937-pattern web equipment, inflatable life-belt, toggle rope for scaling cliffs, and instead of 'ammunition' boots wears plimsolls. The weapon is the US M1928 A1 'Thompson' sub-machine gun.

264 Private, British Commandos, 1944
The critical moment for troops taking part in assault landings was when, heavily laden, they had to jump into water of unknown depth. If the water was too deep a soldier could easily drown if the equipment could not be quickly jettisoned, and for this reason 'quick release' equipment was often issued and lifebelts worn, as here. This soldier wears the green beret, the combined-operations flash, and the machine gun proficiency badge on the left cuff.

262 263 264

in the initial landing were assembled as the 21st Army Group under the command of General Montgomery, to whom the responsibility for the assault and opening stages of the campaign had been delegated. The British and Commonwealth elements in the assault waves were formed into the 2nd British Army.

The 6th Airborne Division with a strength of approximately 12,000 all ranks and comprising two parachute brigades (3rd and 5th) and one airlanding brigade (6th) was dropped in advance of the beach landings to secure canal and river bridges and eliminate coastal batteries. The infantry divisions attacked with their brigades strengthened by the addition of artillery, armoured fighting vehicles, and combat engineers, and the resulting brigade groups had an average strength of 5500 all ranks, of whom approximately 40 per cent were infantry.

On D-Day itself 59,900 troops and 8900 vehicles were landed and by D+50 these figures had risen to 631,000 and 153,000 respectively. The expansion of the Second Army took place on the basis of four corps (1st, 8th, 12th and 30th) with additional formations allocated to the Army Group.

Throughout the campaign the corps organisation remained relatively fluid and units were transferred between corps or attached from the Army Group as occasion demanded. Prominent amongst the GHQ and Army troops were a number of independent armoured and tank brigades which, although still intended primarily for co-operation with infantry, were also expected to be able to slot into armoured divisions as required. Their average strength was 3400 officers and men with a normal complement of 190 medium or infantry tanks (plus 33 light tanks) depending upon the type of brigade. An HQ Army Group Royal Artillery (AGRA) was usually assigned to each Corps and they comprised three medium and one heavy regiment with a total strength of 4400 personnel. The British 1st and 6th Airborne Divisions forming 1 British Airborne Corps were part, along with American airborne units, of the First Allied Airborne Army.

Although the British casualty figures fell short of the level anticipated during planning, the customary shortage of infantry, despite reinforcements of 38,900 from the UK, had led to the disbandment of the one infantry division (the 59th) and one brigade of the 49th Infantry Division on 16 August. The 50th Infantry Division was also subsequently disbanded.

During the campaign in Europe the establishment of a British infantry division was 18,347 all ranks, but the fighting strength of the divisions in 21st Army Group rarely exceeded 16,000 officers and men. A further 25,000 personnel were required to support front line troops so that the total strength of an infantry division – or, as it was known to the Army, the 'divisional slice' – amounted to 41,000 men and 8000 vehicles. Thus the 18 divisions serving in the British order of battle on 30 November 1944 had under their immediate command a total of 287,000 fighting troops out of 21st Army Group's gross strength of 805,000. The remainder comprised GHQ, Army, Corps, administrative, service, and line of communication troops.

During its eleven month battle across France, Belgium, Holland, and Northern Germany the 21st Army Group sustained 141,646 British casualties of which 30,276 were killed, 96,672 wounded, and 14,698 listed as missing or taken prisoner.

Uniform and insignia The uniform of the British 'tommy' remained basically the same throughout the war, but there were certain changes. In 1940 the battledress blouse was simplified by doing

265

266

265 Lieutenant, British Glider Pilot Regiment, 1944

Lieutenant J. F. Hubble of the 1st Glider Pilot Regiment wears parachutist uniform with Denison smock and ordinary battledress trousers. Under his fibre protective helmet he wears a Type C flying helmet with Type F oxygen mask. The wings on the left breast were worn by all qualified glider pilots until after the battle of Arnhem, when so many were lost that trainee pilots had their courses cut short and were made into second pilots, with smaller wings, and a gold 'G' set in a gold ring. The red beret is the type issued to all airborne forces in the British Army; and this mark of distinction rapidly became famous.

266 Trooper, British Army, 1945

The one-piece tank suit shown here was made from water-repellent canvas with khaki cloth lining and had a hood. The black beret was the distinctive head-dress of the Royal Tank Regiment, although many cavalry regiments converted to armour, such as the 11th Hussars, wore their own distinctive head-dress. The British Enfield .38 pistol is in its web holster; the small pouch above it carries spare ammunition. It was not until a late stage in the war that British tank crews were issued with this uniform; previous to this Royal Tank Regiment overalls were worn.

away with the pocket pleats and having all buttons, which were made of vegetable compound, exposed; the field service cap was unpopular and was gradually replaced by the beret, or the 'general service' cap, which looked like a beret but was made from a number of pieces of khaki cloth, and a new steel helmet made its appearance in 1944.

In addition, crews of armoured fighting vehicles, parachute troops and commandos all required special clothing and equipment, and British troops fighting globally in extremes of climate required special clothing to suit the environment.

Despite a number of experimental helmets an ideal head-dress for tank crews was not found. In training crews were issued with a fibre miner's helmet but since this afforded no protection against bullets or splinters it was not worn in action. During the latter stages of the war tank commanders began to wear the rimless steel helmet as issued to parachutists but with a webbing chin strap. Over the battledress tank crew usually wore either a black or khaki overall or denims, and it was only in the last year of the war that crews received a special tank suit (figure 266).

Airborne troops presented another problem which was partially solved when examples of German parachutists clothing and equipment were captured in Holland and in Crete. By October 1941 British parachute troops were receiving a padded rubber training helmet, a smock for wear over the equipment, battledress trousers with a large thigh pocket and ankle boots with rubber soles. In action 'paras' wore a rimless steel helmet with leather chin strap and chin cup, and over the battledress but under the equipment a camouflage 'Denison' smock (figure 265), on the right sleeve of which were the para wings and rank chevrons.

Badges of rank and arm-of-service strips remained constant throughout the war, although new insignia was introduced for airborne forces and commandos. Coloured berets replaced the old field service caps and new colours (maroon for airborne and green for commandos for example) were introduced as new formations and corps came into existence.

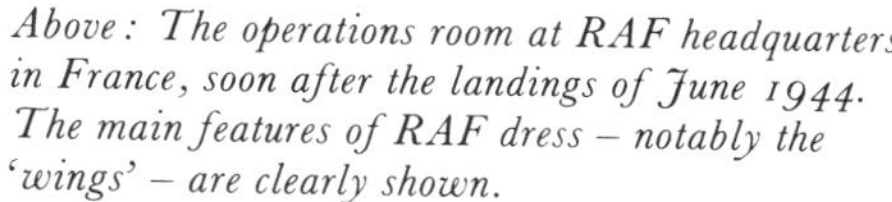

Above: The operations room at RAF headquarters in France, soon after the landings of June 1944. The main features of RAF dress – notably the 'wings' – are clearly shown.

Below: Infantrymen of the King's Own Scottish Borderers using a captured Hotchkiss machine gun in Caen in 1944. They are wearing the new-pattern British helmet.

ROYAL AIR FORCE

Having successfully repulsed the Luftwaffe's immediate aerial threat to the United Kingdom in the Battle of Britain, the Royal Air Force took the offensive as Hitler turned his attention towards the Middle East and the Russian Front. It was the turn of Bomber Command to come into its own and operating almost exclusively by night, and aided by H2S and Oboe bombing radar, the Command pressed home its attacks.

Bomber Command's role in World War II was a controversial one. A sizable proportion of Britain's industrial and military resources were devoted to the strategic bomber offensive and heavy casualties were incurred by the squadrons of Bomber Command for only limited military gains.

By July 1941 the strength of Bomber Command stood at 45 squadrons with a theoretical deployment of 1000 aircraft. In practice, only 37 squadrons could be considered for active operations and not all of these were fully-trained. As a result the tally of sorties over Germany in the last five months of 1941 seldom averaged more than 60 per night. 38 squadrons were operationally effective by the spring of 1942, but of these only 14 were equipped with the new heavy bombers (Stirling, Halifax, and Manchester). The dispatch of reinforcements to the Far East and the demands of

Coastal Command further delayed the growth of Bomber Command, and by March 1943 only 50 squadrons with some 800 first-line aircraft were in commission instead of the planned total of 4000 operational aircraft.

The introduction to large-scale service in early 1942 of the four-engined heavy bombers – such as the Avrc Lancaster and Handley Page Halifax – posed a double problem for Bomber Command, in addition to posing one for the German defences. Due to their increased size, the new types required both a mid-upper gunner and a flight engineer in addition to the usual pilot, navigator, wireless operator and gunners. This meant an extra stage in the conversion process, as training aircraft such as the Vickers Wellington were too small to accommodate these personnel. Thus came into being the Heavy Conversion Units or HCUs, which were established alongside the Operational Conversion Units. Runways had also to be lengthened from 1400 to 2000 feet.

Meanwhile, Fighter Command had begun the counter-offensive. While their poorly-equipped night fighters were making halting progress towards stemming the German bombers by night, many 'Rhubarb' intruder sorties were being flown by day over occupied Europe. By 13 June 1941, 104 such missions had been flown, together with 11 'circuses' involving larger numbers of fighters. The RAF intruder force came under the jurisdiction of No. Eleven Group until August 1942, when it passed to Fighter Command HQ. The Dieppe Raid on 19 August, however, was a disaster both on the ground and in the air; the Allies lost about 4000 or the 7500 troops engaged, while the loss of over 100 aircraft compared unfavourably with the Luftwaffe's 50.

A major development in the Royal Air Force's operations over France was the advent of the Hawker Typhoon rocket-armed fighter. These were employed with some success against rail targets, river bridges and airfields, and – importantly – against launching sites then in preparation for the V-1 flying bomb. Some 98,000

Below: Ground crew bomb-up a Lancaster with a 12,000 lb 'Tallboy' bomb. They are wearing the standard working dress (similar to Army battledress) with side-caps. The bombs on the side of the Lancaster indicate missions flown.

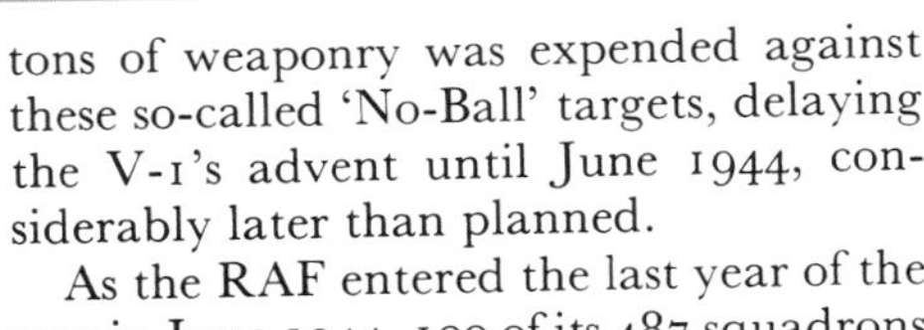

tons of weaponry was expended against these so-called 'No-Ball' targets, delaying the V-1's advent until June 1944, considerably later than planned.

As the RAF entered the last year of the war in June 1944, 100 of its 487 squadrons were manned by personnel from the Dominions. Canada furnished 42 squadrons, South Africa 27, Australia 16, India 9 and New Zealand 6. In addition 51 Allied squadrons from Poland, France, Czechoslovakia, Norway, Belgium, Holland, Greece and Yugoslavia were serving in the major theatres of war.

At the end of April 1945 460,000 RAF personnel were serving in the European campaign, the overall strength of the RAF having reached its peak of 1,011,427 officers and men and 174,406 women in July 1944. Between April 1944 and May 1945 the RAF suffered casualties of 23,649 in Western Europe; its total war casualties amounted to 112,296 of which 69,606 were killed, 22,839 wounded, 6736 listed as missing and 13,115 as prisoners of war. In Europe and the Middle East the RAF lost a total of 22,120 aircraft, of which Bomber Command lost 9163 and Fighter Command 3558.

The most spectacular show of strength mounted by Bomber Command was seen on the night of 30/31 May 1942, when 1046 bombers were dispatched to bomb Cologne. Although some 30 per cent of the aircraft on this raid had been culled from training units and thus rendered the raid untypical, the 'Thousand Bomber Raid' was a considerable propaganda triumph and cost only 39 aircraft. Under the leadership of Air Marshal A. T. Harris, the Command progressed to the Ruhr, Hamburg and, in the autumn of 1943, Berlin.

RAF Coastal Command reacted to the threat of the U-Boat in the North Atlantic with the meagre means at its disposal: of the 196 aircraft based in the United Kingdom for maritime reconnaissance, only 12 Lockheed Hudsons and 18 Short Sunderland flying boats could operate further than 300 miles from home base. Despite their lamentable lack of training, the crews registered some success, such as the first aircraft-assisted kill claimed by a Short Sunderland on 30 January 1940 when *U-55* was sunk off Ushant. Although conventional bombs proved ineffective, aircraft still proved a deterrent for the U-Boats, and the advent of Air-to-Surface Vessel radar (ASV) in February 1940 proved valuable. It was augmented later that year by the Leigh Light, which illuminated the U-Boat at close range where radar was ineffective.

From August 1942, the increased escort strength of the convoys had driven the

267

268

269

U-Boats into the mid-Atlantic, where they were tackled by the very-long-range Consolidated Liberator, which entered service with No. 120 Squadron Coastal Command in September 1941. Nos. 59 and 86 Squadrons later joined this lone unit, driving the U-Boats into the Bay of Biscay and within range of the RAF's other types. At the peak of Coastal Command's operations in 1944, 52,183 sorties were flown in that year, during which 355 aircraft were lost.

ORGANISATION Bomber Command was organised, like Fighter and Coastal Command, in Groups of varying squadron strength. By March 1943 there were seven Groups (Nos. 1, 2, 3, 4, 5, 6 and 8), of which No. 6 Group was formed of Royal Canadian Air Force squadrons. The expansion of the heavy bomber force during 1943 led to the introduction of a new level of command between the group and the squadron. This was known as a base and it controlled six heavy bomber squadrons or three heavy conversion units, under the command of an Air Commodore. By April 1944 Bomber Command had a personnel strength of 155,510 and in January 1945 its squadron deployment stood at 95. The total casualties suffered by the Command during the war numbered 79,147, of which 64,780 were battle casualties.

Bomber Command's total of 955,040 tons of bombs dropped during the whole of World War II included 196,335 tons of incendiaries and was delivered in 389,809 sorties. Total aircraft losses sustained numbered 10,688.

Coastal Command was organised in four groups – Nos. 15, 16, 18 and 19 – with No. 17 being designated a training group at Dundee. They corresponded in geographical location to the four naval commands with which they closely worked. The air officer commanding the RAF group would hold the rank of Air Vice-Marshal, while his opposite number in the corresponding Royal Navy command would be a Vice-Admiral or, in some cases, a full Admiral.

For the invasion of Europe the RAF's tactical air strength was deployed as part of the Allied Expeditionary Air Force under two main commands, the Air

267 Flying Officer, Royal Air Force, 1944
This Boston III crew member wears RAF battledress under a US 'flak' vest. Over the British Type C flying helmet he wears a special protective helmet which was lined with strips of manganese steel (its US designation was USM-4). The flying boots are the British 1943-pattern which were so designed that the shafts could be easily removed, leaving a simple black walking shoe which could be worn by pilots shot down in enemy-occupied territory.

268 Flight Lieutenant, Royal Australian Air Force, 1941
Flight Lieutenant Truscott DFC wears the dark blue service dress of the RAAF which continued to be worn throughout Word War II. During the war dark blue battledress was also issued to RAAF personnel on which they wore the usual RAF rank distinction lace on the shoulder straps.

269 Head Officer, Royal Observer Corps, 1944
The ROC was originally formed in 1918 and by 1941 was 30,000 strong with both men and women in its ranks. The RAF-type battledress was introduced in June 1941. The ROC badge was worn on the beret and left breast, while the Spitfire badge was the mark of a master spotter from January 1944.

270

271

270 Squadron Leader, Royal Air Force, 1941–42

Squadron Leader A. H. Rook commanded No. 81 Squadron, 151 Wing, in north Russia during 1941–42. The units in Russia were intended to familiarise the Russians with aeroplanes they would soon be using (No. 81 Squadron flew Hurricanes), and to cover the Arctic convoys on the last part of their journey; Rook's aeroplanes were based in Murmansk. He is wearing the RAF blue peaked service cap with officers' cap badge, and the M1940 flying suit with fur collar. The web equipment is the 1937-pattern. The life-jacket is the 1932-pattern; this was originally produced in a grey-green colour but was often painted yellow, which produced the buff effect.

271 Sergeant, Royal Air Force, 1943

Sergeant Harold Oliver of RAF Coastal Command here wears flying clothing typical of that of the crews of the aircraft used on the long sweeps over the Atlantic and Arctic. Flights of up to 12 hours were common in the Liberators of which Sergeant Oliver was a pilot, and so the accent was on comfort and practicality. Oliver wears a side cap (with the yellow badge of RAF other ranks) a polo-neck sweater (called the Frock White sweater) and an Irvin sheepskin jacket over a pre-war flying suit.

Defence of Great Britain (formerly Fighter Command) and the Second Tactical Air Force. The main elements of the former comprised four groups (Nos. 10–13) and in the latter four groups (Nos. 2, 83, 84 and 85), one wing (No. 34) and an Air Spotting Pool. The Groups of the Second Tactical Air Force were organised as Wings, each usually of three squadrons. On 16 October 1944 Headquarters Allied Expeditionary Force was absorbed into Supreme Headquarters Allied Expeditionary Force and the units of the Air Defence of Great Britain reverted to the control of the British Air Ministry and were redesignated as Fighter Command. The group composition of the Second Tactical Air Force remained unchanged except for the addition of two RAF special groups, No. 38 (airborne forces) and No. 46 (transport).

Uniform The uniform of the RAF conformed to the pattern established by 1940 (see page 69) and remained in service throughout the war. The various styles of dress are illustrated.

Royal navy

The German conquests in Europe during 1940 placed the Royal Navy in an extremely difficult position. The acquisition of Norway provided the German Navy with deep-water bases for its surface ships which by their very presence, astride Britain's sea-route to the Soviet Union, tied down many Royal Navy vessels. Even more dangerous was the German occupation of naval bases on the French Atlantic coast providing perfect havens for the U-boat packs. This easy German access to the Atlantic was to stretch British resources to the limit.

The Royal Navy had two essential tasks during the early years of the war, firstly the naval blockade of Germany and secondly, the protection of the sea lanes to and from Britain that were vital to the nation's survival. The German threat to Britain's supply routes came from the surface warships and the U-boats.

The surface raiders were less of a problem than the U-boats; after the sinking of the *Bismarck* on 26 May 1941 Hitler was reluctant to risk his remaining battleships in direct confrontation with the Navy and for the rest of the war they spent most of their time bottled-up in safe harbours. Occasionally they were sent out in hunting forrays but with little success: the *Scharnhorst* was sunk in December 1943 and the *Tirpitz* was sunk at anchorage by the RAF in November 1944.

The great threat to Britain's ability to continue to wage the war came from Germany's submarine arm. Prior to the outbreak of war the value of the convoy system was not highly regarded by many Navy experts although it had proved itself during World War I. Only the heavy losses during the early months of the war convinced the Admiralty to reinstitute convoys. Unfortunately lack of pre-war development meant that there were insufficient vessels to escort the convoys and that most of these ships – old destroyers and corvettes – lacked sufficient range to provide a continuous escort. It was only by the end of 1941 that coast-to-coast Atlantic convoys were achieved.

The British convoy system was centred around the three operational bases of the Western Approaches: Liverpool, Greenwich and Londonderry, controlling some 25 escort groups which totalled around 70 destroyers and 95 smaller ships. An escort group was formed of about eight ships (although in practice there were rarely more than six at sea at one time) and, once formed, every effort was made to prevent the group from being broken-up, so that the constituent vessels could operate as a well-oiled machine.

272

273

274

Despite the acceptance of the convoy as the best protection against the U-boat, losses rose throughout 1941 (300,000 tons of Allied shipping was sunk in June alone) and continued into the next year. The Battle of the Atlantic was nearly lost by the Allies and it was only won through the massive allocation of Allied resources in developing new anti-submarine techniques, increasing the numbers and quality of escort vessels and introducing escort carriers whose aircraft both inhibited U-boat activity on the surface and destroyed them when submerged. By October 1943 the Battle of the Atlantic was won; U-boat successes were few and in March 1944 they were withdrawn from the North Atlantic.

In addition to its North Atlantic commitments the Royal Navy was heavily engaged in convoy duties in the Arctic Ocean, escorting Allied supplies to the Soviet Union. At first these Arctic convoys met with little opposition: the six convoys which sailed during the autumn of 1941 landed 120,000 tons of supplies for only small losses. But during 1942 casualties mounted as a consequence of sustained German aerial and submarine attacks, culminating in the P.Q.17 convoy in which, of the 156,000 tons loaded, nearly 100,000 tons were sunk. Despite heavy losses the convoys continued, the Germans suffering high casualties themselves and through their poor performance in the battles of the North Cape and Barents Sea the initiative passed to the British.

Having defeated both the surface raiders and the U-boats, the Royal Navy was called upon to transport the D-Day invasion fleet across the English channel and then to support the landings with battleship artillery barrages. The naval operations for D-Day were a triumph of planning, the British and American troops being put ashore with no interference from the German Navy or Air Force. Altogether some 7000 vessels were involved, which included 1200 warships of all sizes.

Following the invasion of Europe the Royal Navy played a more limited role; the supply of the Allied troops in Europe

272 Petty Officer, Royal Navy, 1941
This petty officer serving in a 4.7 inch gun crew wears the special cap badge for petty officers. The rest of the uniform, consisting of Balaclava helmet, duffle coat and sea socks and boots was drawn from ships' stores when required according to the weather.

273 Gunlayer 2nd Class, Royal Navy, 1942
This is a typical action rig worn by naval gun crews during World War II. Over his clean underwear (dirty underclothing could cause infection in wounds) he wears a one-piece blue overall with a canvas money belt round his waist. His non-substantive badge is worn on the upper right sleeve. The steel helmet is perched on top of an anti-flash hood.

274 Lieutenant-Commander, Royal Navy, 1941
Commander Kimmins, on his return from a combined operation in Norway, wears naval service dress under an Army steel helmet and leather jerkin. The web equipment is the 1937-pattern and the binoculars are marked with the broad white arrow which indicates that they are War Department property. The white lanyard is attached to a folding jack knife. Above the rank distinction lace on the left cuff are the pilot's 'wings' of the Fleet Air Arm.

275 2nd Officer, Women's Royal Naval Service, 1942

This is the standard women's version of the naval service dress with three cornered hat, reefer and matching skirt. Rank distinction lace in blue on the cuffs had white lights for those in the paymaster branch. Instead of a gold-embroidered cap badge worn by male officers, women had blue laurel leaves.

and the opening up of the Belgian and Dutch ports were its main tasks.

During the period 1939–45 the Royal Navy lost 119 warships in home waters and 84 in the North Atlantic.

UNIFORM As in the RAF, Royal Navy uniform followed the basic pattern discussed in the previous sections. Operations in the extreme temperatures and conditions of the North Atlantic and Arctic required warm, effective clothing. Individuals frequently combined elements of uniform (see figure 272, for example) to combat the hostile climate. Balaclava helmets, oilskins, wellington boots and duffle coats were among the items employed in this respect.

CZECHOSLOVAK ARMED FORCES

When the fighting in North Africa came to an end, the Czech troops in the Middle East returned to England where, in 1943, they began to be formed into the 1st Independent Armoured Brigade Group. Its 4500 men were organised in:

1st, 2nd and 3rd Czech Armoured Regiments;
Czech Field Artillery Regiment;
Czech Motor Battalion.

In June 1944 the Czech Brigade landed in Normandy where it took over from the 154th Infantry Brigade (British 51st Division) and on 9 October 1944 invested the German position in and around Dunkirk. The Czech Brigade fought with the Canadian 1st Army for a time as part of the 21st Army Group.

A detachment of Cromwell tanks manned by Czech crews was sent as a token force to participate in the liberation and final entry into Prague.

UNIFORM Members of the Independent Czechoslovakian Armoured Brigade wore British battledress with Czech rank badges. The nationality flash, 'Czechoslovakia' was worn on the upper arm.

Above: The submarine Seraph *returning to harbour. The ratings are wearing long sweaters and 'bell-bottoms' – a sharp contrast to the officers' clothing.*

Below: D-Day casualties are brought on board HMS Frobisher. *The sailors in the foreground are wearing the anti-flash hoods and gauntlets (also shown in figure 273), and various overgarments.*

CANADA

ARMY

In direct contrast to the experience of World War I, the Canadian Army which was assembled in Britain during 1939–45 was offered few opportunities for combat during its first three-and-a-half years in Europe. Its role, save for one or two minor expeditions and the single day's fighting at Dieppe, was that of a garrison force.

The initial convoy carrying 7400 troops of the 1st Division arrived in the Clyde on 17 December 1939, and by the end of February 1940 the Canadian Active Service Force in Britain numbered 1066 officers and 22,238 other ranks. The troops were not fully trained for modern warfare, they lacked essential items of equipment such as steel helmets, and nearly all their heavy weapons were obsolescent. The division worked through a crash training course at Aldershot in order to be ready for deployment in France as part of the 4th British Corps. The pace of events was such that the Canadians played only a limited covering role in France and were evacuated soon after landing in June 1940.

In July 1940 the 1st Canadian Division combined with the 1st British Armoured Division and the majority of the 2nd New Zealand Division to form the 7th Corps. Since May 1940, units of the 2nd Canadian Division had begun to arrive in Britain but the divisions' concentration was not achieved until 25 December 1940. From late October the units that had arrived in the United Kingdom joined the 1st Division guarding the beaches of Sussex between Worthing and Newhaven, and on Christmas Day 1940 the 7th Corps was disbanded and the Canadian Corps (later 1st Canadian Corps) was created with nearly 57,000 Canadians serving in Britain.

During 1941 the flow of Canadian units to the European theatre continued, and by the beginning of 1942 the Canadian Force in Britain consisted of four divisions, an army tank brigade and supporting troops, and it had obviously outgrown the bounds of a normal army corps. Accordingly, Headquarters 1st Canadian Army was established on 6 April 1942. In September and October a further armoured force came under its command with the arrival of the 4th Canadian Armoured Division which had been formed by converting the 4th Infantry Division. The armoured divisions adopted the British organisation of one armoured and one infantry brigade and thereby created a number of surplus armoured regiments, three of which temporarily became the 3rd Army Tank Brigade until, in the summer of 1943, they assumed the designation 2nd Canadian Armoured Brigade. At the end of 1942 the Canadian Army Overseas totalled 177,000.

Canadian training for combined operations began in September 1941 and in April 1942 a contingent took part in an abortive commando raid to the south of Boulogne. The failure of this raid only served to add fuel to the frustration felt by the Canadians after two-and-a-half years without close contact with the enemy.

When in April 1942 Combined Operations Headquarters authorised the plan to raid the port of Dieppe, General Montgomery suggested that the Canadians were the troops most suited to the enterprise. The 1st Canadian Army commander General A. G. L. McNaughton agreed to this proposal and the 2nd Canadian Division was chosen for the operation. The selected units were the 4th and 6th Infantry Brigades and the 14th Canadian Army Tank Regiment (Calgary Regiment) of the 1st Army Tank Brigade. They were supported by engineers and artillery detachments from the 2nd Division, by the British No. 3 and 4 Commando, and by 50 rangers of the 1st US Ranger Battalion.

When the expedition set sail on the night of 18 August its military force numbered 6100 officers and men, of whom 1075 were British and 4963 Canadian. The attack, launched at dawn the next day, tragically miscarried and in nine hours of bitter fighting the Canadians suffered 3369 casualties of whom 907 were killed in action or died later in captivity. Only 2211 returned to England and 1944 were taken prisoner.

In October 1943 the 'Canloan' scheme was proposed with the object of meeting the British Army's need for junior officers for the forthcoming campaign in North-West Europe. In all, 673 Canadian officers were provided for British units under this scheme and they saw extensive service in Europe and later South-East Asia. They were paid by the Canadian Government, wore the badges of their British units on their battledress along with a 'Canada' badge and, by the end of the war, had suffered 465 casualties.

On the morning of 6 June 1944 the 3rd Canadian Infantry Division landed on the beaches of Normandy supported by the tanks of the 2nd Canadian Armoured Brigade. As part of the 1st British Corps their role after the initial landing was to advance between Bayeux and Caen, cutting the communications between the two towns. Almost 14,000 Canadians went ashore on D-Day of whom 335 were killed in the landing or subsequent advance. The Canadian objectives were reached on 7 June.

The 1st Canadian Parachute Battalion dropped as a unit of the 6th British Airborne Division on D-day and took part in the battle for the bridgehead. In the first week of July the 2nd Canadian Division arrived in Normandy to form, together with the 3rd Division and the 2nd Armoured Brigade, the 2nd Canadian Corps. The 4th Canadian Armoured Division landed in France at the end of the month to relieve the 3rd Division.

276

276 Lieutenant, Royal Canadian Women's Naval Service, 1943

This lightweight uniform was worn by all ranks in the Royal Canadian Women's Naval Service. Officers had the three cornered hat instead of the round sailor's hat worn by women of non-commissioned rank. Ratings had black plastic instead of gilt brass buttons. The regulation bag was also called a 'pochette'. The white lights between the rank distinction lace on the shoulder straps identifies this officer as being in the paymaster branch.

277

278

277 Lieutenant, Canadian Army, 1942
This private of the Royal Winnipeg Rifle Regiment taking part in the Normandy landings wears the new 1944-pattern British steel helmet and battledress. Canadian battledress was popular because it tended to be made of better quality cloth than its British counterpart, and in a slightly greener shade. The light blue rectangle was the formation sign of the 3rd Canadian Division. The arrangement of personal equipment varied from soldier to soldier. This one carries additional pouches for Bren gun magazines on his back, a shovel, blanket roll and late-war No. 4, Mark 1 or Mark 1 .303. Troops in the first wave of landings had to be sufficiently equipped to maintain a fire-fight with German defences until support weapons or naval fire could be brought in to assist them.*

278 Private, Canadian Army, 1944
The greatcoat is the standard pattern for British Army officers, but with the 'Canada' nationality title. The cap, however, is the Canadian pattern with earflaps and regimental badge (Le Regiment de Levis) *on the front. There was a winter version of this head-dress with fur earflaps which was called a Yukon helmet. These items of uniform were the most distinctive worn by the Canadian Army, although they soon fell into disuse.*

The 4th Canadian Armoured Division was soon heavily involved in Normandy; the Canadian troops played a leading part in the offensive operations around Caen, and they then joined the Allied pursuit of the retiring enemy, pushing north and east towards Belgium and the channel coast. By November 1944 the 1st Canadian Army was rapidly becoming a cosmopolitan fighting force with the following divisions and brigades:

Canadian 2nd, 3rd and 4th (Armoured) Divisions;
British 49th and 52nd Divisions;
American 104th Division (also briefly 82nd and 101st Airborne);
Polish 1st (Armoured) Division;
Dutch Royal Netherlands Brigade;
Czechoslovakian 1st Independent Armoured Brigade Group.

From November 1944 to February 1945 the Canadians stood on the defensive, holding a perimeter which ran for 200 miles from the German frontier through Holland to Dunkirk. On 8 February the 1st Army began its attack against the *Reichswald* meeting German resistance which stiffened considerably as the Canadian and British troops advanced.

With the arrival of the formations from Italy there were now two Canadian Corps available for the final offensive against Germany and on 24 March Canadian troops began to cross the Rhine. On 28 April German resistance in western Holland came to an end, but for the 2nd Canadian Corps deployed in northern Holland and Germany to protect the 2nd Army's left flank, bitter fighting continued until 4 May. The eleven-month campaign since 6 June 1944 had cost the 1st Canadian Army 3680 officers and 44,272 men in casualties, of whom 12,579 had been killed.

Newfoundland

In the inter-war years Newfoundland maintained no military force of any kind but on the outbreak of hostilities in 1939 her citizens quickly demonstrated their willingness to serve. It was agreed with the War Office that Newfoundlanders should be enlisted for the Royal Artillery and the first draft of 403 volunteers left for Britain in April 1940. By September the number of men had reached 1373. Together with British officers and NCOs these drafts formed the 57th and 59th (Newfoundland) Heavy Regiments Royal Artillery.

The 59th Regiment landed in Normandy on 5 July 1944 under the British 1st Corps and it was soon in action. It supported the 2nd Canadian Division in its advance towards Falaise and covered the crossing of the Seine. Its batteries fought at Flushing, in south-west Holland and in the operations to clear the Scheldt. Early in 1945 half the regiment was in the Ardennes and half on the Venlo-Roermond sector, and in February the whole regiment moved to Grave for Operation 'Veritable'. In March the 59th supported the crossing of the Rhine and from then until the end of the war fought in the British operations around Bremen and at the crossing of the Elbe. Altogether 2327 Newfoundlanders served overseas during World War II and of this number 72 were killed.

Uniform Canadian Army uniform was basically the same as that worn by the British Army, and although the pattern was usually identical, clothing and equipment manufactured in Canada did vary slightly in colour and quality. For example Canadian battledress was very popular with British soldiers because the material was not so rough and the colour was a smarter shade of khaki. The winter cap worn by the first contingents of Canadians soon fell into disuse. Badges of rank were the same as the British.

FRANCE

ARMY

The formation and organisation of a French Army to fight alongside the Allies in the liberation of its homeland was an extremely difficult and complicated task. France was still occupied by Germany, equipment and supplies were difficult to find, despite generous American assistance. The legacy of distrust and enmity between those who had sided with de Gaulle and those who supported Vichy still lingered on, and this occasionally tended to create difficulties.

French troops were withdrawn from Italy to take part in Operation 'Dragoon', the Allied invasion of southern France. Known as Army B the French came under the command of General de Lattre de Tassigny as part of the US 7th Army. Operating on the flanks of the Americans the French were hotly engaged against the Germans, following the landings on 15 August 1944. Army B liberated Toulon on the 25 August and played a major role in securing Marseille, France's second city. French casualties during this period were 1444 killed and 4346 wounded.

On 15 September, Army B became the French 1st Army, comprising two corps which included the 1st Free French, 1st Armoured, 2nd Moroccan, 3rd Algerian and 9th Colonial Divisions. During the course of the subsequent fighting the 1st Army received numerous reinforcements so that by 1945 it had a strength of 200,000 men organised into 12 divisions.

One of these divisions was the 2nd Armoured Division which had fought its way through Normandy, inflicting heavy losses on the Germans (13,000 killed or taken prisoner, and 800 vehicles destroyed) while loosing only 800 men and 57 armoured fighting vehicles in the process. Its organisation at this time consisted of a motorised infantry regiment of three battalions, three groups of artillery, one group of anti-aircraft artillery, one reconnaissance regiment, three tank regiments, one regiment of tank destroyers, a battalion of engineers and supporting services.

The infantry divisions were based around the organisation of three or four infantry regiments with a strong reconnaissance regiment and an artillery regiment plus units of engineers, signals and service troops.

The French 1st Army fought on the southern flank of the Allied line of battle and contributed significantly to the liberation of Alsace and in the invasion of southern Germany. At the end of hostilities on 7 May 1945 the French Army had lost 250,000 men killed during the entire period of World War II.

UNIFORM As the French Army was gradually re-organised and received its American equipment, the heterogeneous uniforms from the former Vichy Army, the French Colonial Army and North African units, and those of the Free French, were replaced by the American uniform (see figure 279).

As and when available (or for as long as they lasted) the various forms of French head-dress continued to be worn with American uniform. These were mainly the *Adrian* steel helmet and the motorised troop helmet, but also included some of the more exotic and brightly coloured head-dresses of the French North African forces. One of the most unusual combinations was worn by members of the Naval Infantry Tank Regiment who wore naval head-dress and insignia.

Badges of rank were worn in the usual French manner on the head-dress, on the shoulder straps or on a patch on the front of combat clothing.

On the upper left sleeve personnel wore a cloth badge shaped like the patch worn on the collar of French tunics. The colour of the badge, the chevrons and the regimental number or emblem conformed to the old collar patches, but in order to distinguish themselves from metropolitan troops, personnel in units formed in North Africa had three chevrons instead of two.

Below: Tunisian troops of the French Army soon after their entry into Germany.

279

279 Private, French Army, 1944
This private of the 2nd Moroccan Division serving in the French 1st Army wears predominantly US uniform and equipment. Above the US khaki wool trousers is the American winter combat jacket with vertical slit pockets favoured by the crews of armoured vehicles. Footgear consists of the French M1917 boots, and he is armed with a British Lee Enfield .303 rifle.

UNITED STATES ARMY

American troops had been arriving in England since 1942 as part of the preparation for the invasion of German occupied Europe and by the summer of 1944 over two million Allied soldiers had been amassed for Operation 'Overlord'.

The US 1st Army under General Bradley was responsible for the two western beaches of the Normandy landings and his initial forces consisted of seven infantry and two airborne divisions. Despite heavy casualties on Omaha Beach the American landings on the 6 June were successful and the beachhead was consolidated in order to bring up reinforcements for the breakout from Normandy – Operation 'Cobra'.

During July American troops flooded into Normandy so that Bradley had 21 divisions under his command by 1 August. This entailed a reorganisation of American forces: the US 12th Army Group was created consisting of the 1st Army (V, VII and XIX Corps) and the newly-formed 3rd Army (XII, XV, XX and VIII Corps). Operation 'Cobra' was an American triumph and the rapid exploitation of the breakthrough by armoured elements of Patton's 3rd Army turned the tactical advantage into a major strategic victory. Out-numbered and out-manoeuvered, the Germans were forced back across France towards the Rhine.

Allied progress slowed-up in the late autumn of 1944 as a result of stiffening German resistance and a growing shortage of supplies and manpower. The front-line stabilised along the Franco-German border during the winter of 1944–45. American forces on 1 January 1945 consisted of 31 infantry, 11 armoured and 3 airborne divisions. These formations were organised into the 12th Army Group (1st and 3rd Armies) and the newly formed 6th Army Group which consisted of the US 7th Army and the French 1st Army (these two armies had invaded southern France as part of Operation 'Dragoon' and had joined up with the main invasion force in September). During 1945 a further 15 US divisions (including four armoured)

280 2nd Lieutenant, US Army, 1942

On their arrival in Northern Ireland the first US soldiers wore this uniform. The helmet is the M1918, while the coat is the short version of the officers' greatcoat with rank badges on the shoulder straps. OD trousers are worn inside canvas leggings with russet ankle boots. The equipment consists of woven cartridge belt, braces and gas mask. The rifle is the US Cal.30 M1903 AI Springfield.

281 2nd Lieutenant, US Army, 1944

Equipped for the D-Day landings, this officer wears the special waistcoat with sewn-in pockets for carrying extra ammunition. The basic uniform consists of the M1941 combat jacket and olive drab fatigue trousers. A flotation bag – half inflated – is strapped to the chest and below that is an officer's dispatch case. Rank is indicated by the single bar on the M1 steel helmet. An M1 carbine is carried with an M1911 A1 .45 automatic pistol.

282 Private, US Army, 1942

This GI arriving in England wears the overseas cap with light blue piping and OD greatcoat over the Class A uniform. OD trousers are tucked into canvas leggings and worn with russet leather ankle boots over which he has put rubber overboots. The rifle is the US Cal.30 Model 1903 Springfield.

280 281 282

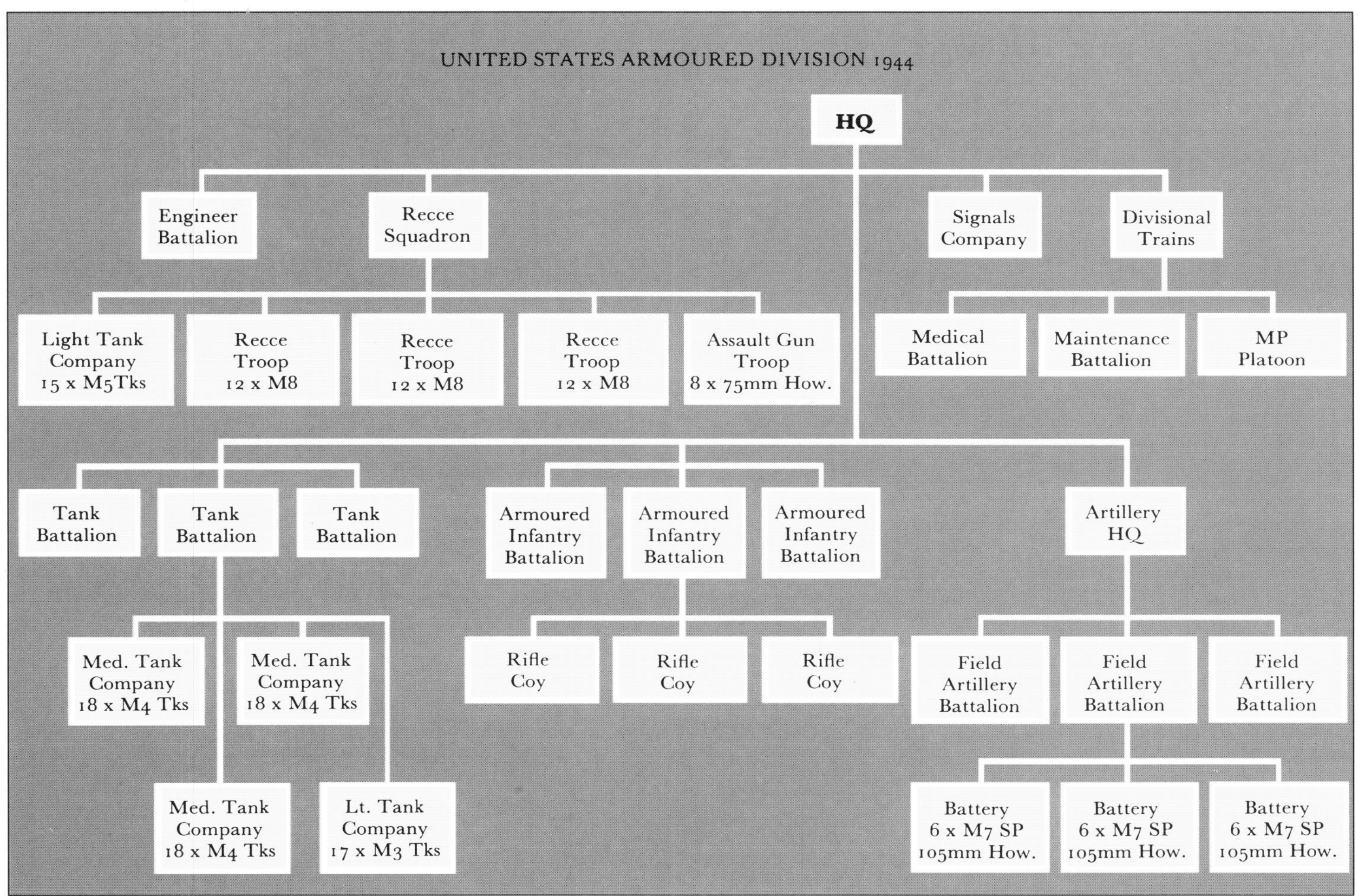

arrived in Europe bringing the American total up to 60.

Having countered the German Ardennes offensive, the American forces prepared to cross the Rhine and invade Germany itself. The Rhine barrier was breached during March and the 12th Army Group advanced into Germany. In conjunction with the Anglo-Canadian 21st Army Group over 300,000 Germans were taken prisoner in the Ruhr pocket by the US 1st Army. On 25 April contact was made with the advancing Soviet forces and by the first week of May all organised German resistance had ended.

During the eleven month campaign in Western Europe the US armed forces had borne the brunt of the fighting and suffered 591,802 casualties.

Organisation The basic formation in the United States Army was the infantry division. The triangular organisation of three infantry regiments, each of three battalions (see page 151), continued in use throughout the war in western Europe. There were few changes except a general increase in the number and the calibre-size of the division's weapons. The infantry regiment of 1944 consisted of an HQ company; an infantry gun company (six 105mm infantry howitzers); and anti-tank company (12×57mm anti-tank guns); a service company and the usual three infantry battalions (each 860 men strong).

The division's artillery regiment had one medium artillery battalion and three light artillery battalions. The combat element of each battalion comprised three batteries of four towed howitzers; 155mm for the medium and 105mm for the light battalion.

The infantry division of 1944, once in combat, often had its establishment strength of 14,253 men augmented by units of tanks, tank destroyers, anti-aircraft, mechanised cavalry and field artillery.

Besides the artillery units within the divisional system, a considerable number of artillery units were organised outside the division into battalions of medium (4.5-inch guns and 155mm howitzers) and heavy artillery (155mm, 8-inch and 240mm guns). By the end of the war there were 111 heavy battalions with 81 medium battalions authorised. The Army also controlled anti-aircraft units which amounted to 575 battalions in October 1943 but this figure was reduced to 460 in 1944.

During the period June 1944 to May 1945, some 15 American armoured divisions served in western Europe and made a vital contribution towards the Allied victory. The US armoured division was based on the pattern of September 1943 which had three tank, three armoured infantry and three self-propelled artillery battalions with an establishment strength of 10,937 men (see organisation chart). The division was divided into two Combat Commands, 'A' and 'B', each of which could control a varying number of units at the discretion of the divisional commander. An additional Command was introduced which was responsible for reserve elements of the division, being known as Combat Command 'C' or Reserve.

A considerable number of American tank units were formed separately from the armoured divisions as semi-independent tank battalions. During the winter of 1944 there were 65 tank battalions under arms. The organisation of the battalion was that of the armoured division tank battalion, consisting of three medium and one light tank company with a combined strength of 729 men and 68 tanks. Initially the non-divisional tank battalions acted as close support for the infantry, but in the fighting in France they were given a more mobile role, often being combined into groups of five (later three) battalions. When brigaded with armoured infantry units they were termed 'armoured groups'.

A further type of non-divisional armoured organisation was the tank destroyer battalion which had been formed in 1942 as a means of providing a highly mobile anti-tank weapon to blunt the effect of the German panzer divisions. With a strength of about 100,000 men, the tank destroyer force consisted of 80 battalions each with 36 self-propelled or towed guns. The backbone of the battalion were the M10 and M18 self-propelled tank destroyers, lightly armed but equipped with a high-velocity anti-tank gun.

The United States had a long cavalry tradition that continued well into the 20th Century but the outbreak of war signalled the end of the horsed cavalry when regulations for the mechanisation of this arm were issued in 1942. Some cavalry regiments formed the basis of the new tank divisions, while the remainder were broken up to form mechanised reconnaissance units at squadron and group level. Two cavalry divisions remained within the American military establishment; one fought as dismounted infantry in the Pacific, while the other was sent to the Mediterranean theatre. Once there it was disbanded, its constituent units being transferred to other formations.

In 1941 the US Army had only one parachute battalion but, impressed by the success of the German paratroopers, a rapid expansion of airborne troops was instigated. By 1944 the 82nd and 101st Airborne Divisions were ready to support the D-Day landings, while the 13th and 17th were still in formation but were subsequently to be involved in the fighting in Europe.

The airborne division was conceived as a small, highly mobile air-transportable formation comprising one parachute infantry regiment and two glider infantry regiments, which with the usual divisional support units came to a strength of 8505 men.

Above: US troops of the 89th Division crossing the Rhine in March 1945.

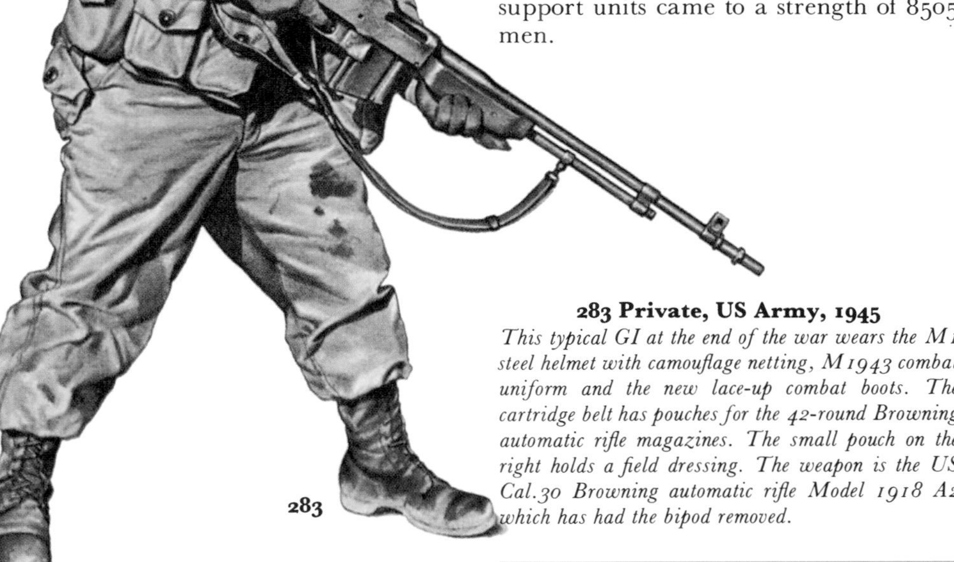

283 Private, US Army, 1945

This typical GI at the end of the war wears the M1 steel helmet with camouflage netting, M1943 combat uniform and the new lace-up combat boots. The cartridge belt has pouches for the 42-round Browning automatic rifle magazines. The small pouch on the right holds a field dressing. The weapon is the US Cal.30 Browning automatic rifle Model 1918 A2 which has had the bipod removed.

In September 1944 the size of the division was increased so that its strength totalled 12,979 personnel. Similarly, the organisation was modified on the following basis:

two infantry parachute regiments, each of 2364 men consisting of three battalions with a regimental HQ and a service company;

one infantry glider regiment of 2978 men divided into three battalions and a regimental HQ, a service and an anti-tank company;

one anti-aircraft/anti-tank battalion of three machine gun batteries (each of 12 × .50 machine guns) and three gun batteries (each with 8 × 57mm anti-tank guns);

divisional artillery consisting of three batteries of 75mm pack howitzers.

Additionally there were companies of maintenance, engineer and signals troops and a reconnaissance platoon.

A number of other divisional patterns were organised including motorised and light divisions but they played little or no part in the operations in western Europe.

A particular feature of the United States Army was its logistical support services which backed up the man at the front. As in other technically sophisticated armies, the majority of the US Army's soldiers were not engaged in combat but were part of the technical services, namely: engineers, signals, chemical warfare, ordnance, medical and transportation. Thus, although infantry division might have an establishment strength of 15,000 men, with all the necessary supply and back-up troops (including assigned Air Force Units) there might be as many as 50,000 men. All these troops were known as the divisional 'slice' and on average needed 1600 tons of supplies a day.

To meet the complex logistical requirements of the US Army in Europe, the 'Red Ball Highway' was introduced, which consisted of a one-way road system reserved exclusively for the transportation of supplies to the front-line. Although the system was a success, the Army was often short of supplies, especially fuel, during the rapid advances of the autumn of 1944. By early 1945, however, the strength of the American logistical system proved itself and the GI was probably the best equipped soldier of any of the armed forces of World War II.

UNIFORM The American troops who landed in Normandy in June 1944 wore the M1 steel helmet and liner, the M1941 field jacket, olive drab (OD) trousers, canvas gaiters and russet leather ankle boots. Equipment was the standard American woven pattern.

But experience in North Africa and Italy had already exposed serious shortcomings in the practicality of much of the Army's clothing, and a number of new items, particularly for wear in winter, were developed during 1943. Despite the American reputation for lavishly providing every luxury for its soldiers, the average GI suffered as much as his allies and his enemies from the cold and wet.

In time for the last winter of the war American troops received the M1943 combat uniform, which consisted of a single-breasted tunic with four patch pockets and matching trousers all made from an olive drab water-repellant and windproof cotton. It was issued with a detachable pile fabric liner. The canvas gaiters and ankle boots were gradually replaced by high lace-up brown leather combat boots (see figure 283).

In 1944 the Americans began to wear a wool field jacket (actually a blouse) which was similar in cut to the British battledress blouse. The pattern for other ranks was standardised, but officers wore many different models with different pocket arrangements, and some with concealed and others with exposed buttons. The blouse was worn with either matching trousers or 'pinks'.

284 Private, US Army, 1944
Some US troops were issued with this two-piece camouflage suit for the campaign in Normandy in June 1944, but it was soon withdrawn because soldiers wearing it were mistaken for Waffen-SS men who also wore camouflage uniforms. On his right hip he carries a captured German Walther automatic pistol in its holster. The weapon is the US Cal.30 M1 (Garand) semi-automatic rifle.

285 Major-General, US Army Airborne Forces, 1944
This major-general wears the overseas cap with gold piping and infantry para-glider badge. Artillery para-gliders had the same badge with red edging. The M1944 'Ike' field jacket came in a number of different patterns, while the OD trousers are worn tucked into lace-up para boots. Rank badges are worn on the side of the overseas cap and on the shoulder straps. On the right breast is the unit citation badge and on the left the Army paratrooper badge above an infantry combat badge.

286 NCO, US Army Military Police, 1942
American military policemen dressed like this were to be seen patrolling London's black-out streets during the war and were known locally as 'snow drops' because of their white helmets and accoutrements. The rest of the uniform is the standard (Class A) service uniform.

284

285

286

287

287 Sergeant Grade 4, US Army Airborne Forces, 1944

The special two-piece combat uniform, M1 steel helmet and high lace-up para boots were all developed for wear by airborne troops. Unlike German and British parachutists who wore a smock over their equipment, American paratroopers strapped everything which might become entangled with the rigging lines to their body with lengths of webbing strap. On his upper right sleeve he wears an American flag as an identification for the benefit of the local population, and on both sleeves his rank chevrons. On the upper left sleeve is the badge of the 101st Airborne Division. The carbine is a folding-stock US Cal.30 M1A1.

Americans began to form parachute troops in June 1940 and the first jump dress consisted of a Riddle helmet, a one-piece OD sateen overall, and high lace-up jump boots with rubber soles. Unlike German and British paratroopers Americans did not wear a smock over their equipment; instead, every item that could become entangled with the rigging lines of the parachute was strapped to the body with lengths of webbing. They also wore two parachutes, the main one on the back and a reserve strapped horizontally to the front of the body.

Most of the other additions to the American soldier's wardrobe during the war were connected with improving the weatherproof qualities of his uniform by providing additional warmth, and waterproof footwear for wear over leather boots.

Badges of rank were as illustrated in the insignia chart (page 239) but the two grades of warrant officer were only introduced in January 1942, and it was not until December 1944 that the grade of General of the Army, with five stars as his rank badge, was created.

During the war there was a rapid increase in the number and variety of 'shoulder sleeve insignia' worn, which corresponded to the increase in size and complexity of the United States Army.

Air force

In June 1941 the United States Army Air Corps became the Army Air Force and was commanded by Major-General Henry H. Arnold. At that time its strength was only a small force of 9078 officers and 143,563 enlisted men. Within six months its strength had risen to 22,524 officers (including cadets) and 274,579 men. The numbers of aircraft had risen from 6102 to 10,329 in the same period. Eight Air Forces were constituted. Four were based within the continental United States and one each was based in the Philippines, Hawaii, Alaska and the Caribbean. Between 1943–44 the AAF doubled in size and reached a peak strength in March 1944 of 2,411,294 men, of which 38 per cent served overseas. By April 1945 52 per cent of its personnel served overseas. Supplying this sizeable force was a considerable constraint on the number of infantry divisions the US could ship abroad.

Formed on 28 January 1942, the United States 8th Army Air Force was established at Savannah, Georgia, as the air component of the projected invasion of North-West Africa. With the escalation of war in the Pacific, this was cancelled and, re-numbered from its original title of the 5th AF, the 8th was diverted to Britain; an advance party landed in February under the command of Brigadier General Ira Eaker. Initial plans called for a total of 60 combat groups – 33 of bombers, 12 of fighters and 15 of transport and observation aircraft, with a proposed strength of 3500 machines.

April and May 1942 saw the first personnel arrive on British soil. The first raid of major proportions was mounted on 17 August by 12 Boeing B-17 Fortresses, the giant four-engined bombers which, with the Consolidated B-24 Liberator, bore the brunt of the US bombing effort. This raid on Rouen, mounted in daylight, sustained no losses, but this

Below: The crew of a Marauder bomber, having returned from their mission on D-Day, are questioned by the base intelligence officer.

288

289

290

was not to be the case in the majority of its successors.

Despite the unfavourable weather encountered over Europe, which hindered accurate day bombing, and the inability of escorting fighters to shadow their charges to the extent of the bombers' range, the Eighth continued its campaign. The objectives were, at first, limited to military targets in occupied France, but when the Casablanca directive of January 1943 demanded the strategic bombing of Germany's industrial system, the pattern of operations was changed.

In 107,001 sorties flown by the US 8th and 9th Air Forces from then until 1 March 1944, some 1509 aircraft were lost. On the credit side, however, 92,468 tons of bombs were dropped and 5304 enemy aircraft destroyed. At peak strength, the 8th numbered 40½ heavy bombardment, 15 fighter and two photo-reconnaissance groups. It claimed 20,419 enemy aircraft in a total of 1,034,052 flights, and lost 11,687 planes.

The B-17 carried a crew of ten, consisting of pilot and co-pilot, navigator, bomb-aimer, flight engineer, wireless operator and four gunners; two at the waist guns, one in a ventral turret and one at the tail. The navigator was entrusted with two window guns, the bomb-aimer with forward-firing armament and the flight engineer with two dorsal weapons. With each aircraft thus armed with some 15 machine guns of varying calibres, a 'box' or formation of Fortresses was not to be taken lightly. Not until the arrival of the North American P-51 Mustang in early 1944, however, could the 8th Army Air Force bombers be assured of a fighter escort at all stages of their mission.

This vulnerability which belied the USAAF's apparent strength in numbers was vividly exhibited at Schweinfurt on 14 October 1943, when 60 B-17s fell victim to the Luftwaffe and 133 were damaged out of a total of 291. This was the 8th Air Force's infamous 'Black Thursday', after which the Mustang's introduction was hastened. The target, a complex of five plants producing bearings vital to Germany industry, was significantly affected, three of the factories receiving considerable damage. Nevertheless, the heavy losses sustained caused

288 Aircrewman, USAAF, 1944
This aircrewman with the 8th Army Air Force wears olive-green flying overalls, brown leather boots and the standard peaked cap. His flak-suit (of which he is holding the abdominal protector) was devised in October 1942 by Brigadier-General Grow, in conjunction with the Wilkinson Sword Company, to cut down aircrew casualties. Its manganese steel plates could stop a .45 calibre bullet at close range. The suit weighed 20lb, but soon became popular, and by 1944 13,500 were in service with the 8th Army Air Force.

289 Major-General, US Army Air Force, 1944
This was the typical service dress of American Army airmen in the ETO (European Theatre of Operations). Badges of rank appear on the shoulder straps and on the left side of the overseas cap. The silver wings were worn by command airmen, and the patch on the left sleeve identified the wearer as being a member of the 9th Air Force.

290 Captain, US Army Air Force, 1944
This pilot of a Mustang (P-51B) wears the overseas cap with rank badges on the left side. Over his leather flying jacket is a life preserving vest. The OD trousers are tucked into A-6 type flying boots, the standard pattern.

Right: Army Air Force men crowd around one of the first Liberators to arrive in Great Britain.

a reappraisal of the 8th Air Force's daylight bombing policy.

The 9th Air Force had commenced operations in the Middle East in mid-1942, disrupting Axis supply lines in the eastern Mediterranean and co-operating with the British 8th Army in driving the enemy westwards. Established on 16 October 1943 as the tactical arm of the US Army Air Force in Europe, the 9th provided its 'big brother' with escort and medium bombing support, as well as being engaged in the Overlord invasion offensive on its own account. The 9th was responsible for a total of 659,513 missions, dropping 582,701 tons of bombs and destroying 9,497 enemy aircraft for the loss of 6,731 of its own.

291 Bomber Crewman, US Army Air Force, 1945

This crewman of the 8th Air Force wears the intermediate wool-and-alpaca-lined flying suit with A-11 helmet, B-8 goggles and A-10 oxygen mask. His flying boots were fur-lined for added warmth.

292 Technical Sergeant Grade 2, US Army Air Force, 1945

Over an OD pullover this ground crewman of the 9th Air Force in the United Kingdom in 1945 wears the one-piece herringbone twill fatigue suit and baseball cap. The rank badges are worn on the sleeves.

Organisation The structure of the AAF in each theatre of operations differed with the climatic, geographical conditions and tactical requirements pertaining there. The smallest administrative unit was the group of two to four squadrons. If a group was stationed at a permanent base the various squadrons usually pooled their administrative services; but wherever the squadrons were stationed the group trained together. The air group was the Air Force equivalent of the Army regiment.

The various groups were differentiated by the type of aircraft they flew. For example, a very heavy bombardment group, flying B-29s would comprise 462 officers and 1616 men. But the number of men and aircraft in each group varied. Above this was the wing of two groups which was a non-administrative unit and only concerned with tactical plans and operations.

Two or more wings were usually brigaded together with auxiliary units to form a command – an organization of one kind of air strength, fighters or bombers. If these forces were too large for one man to control, then they would be split into air divisions which rested between wing and command levels. The air force was the largest single unit in the AAF and consisted of three or more commands. If, however, the tactical demands of a theatre required a particular type of air support then an air force would be created within a theatre air force.

Uniform United States Army Air Force personnel wore Army uniform with the modifications discussed on page 154. The artwork captions examine the many variations worn in the European theatre of operations.

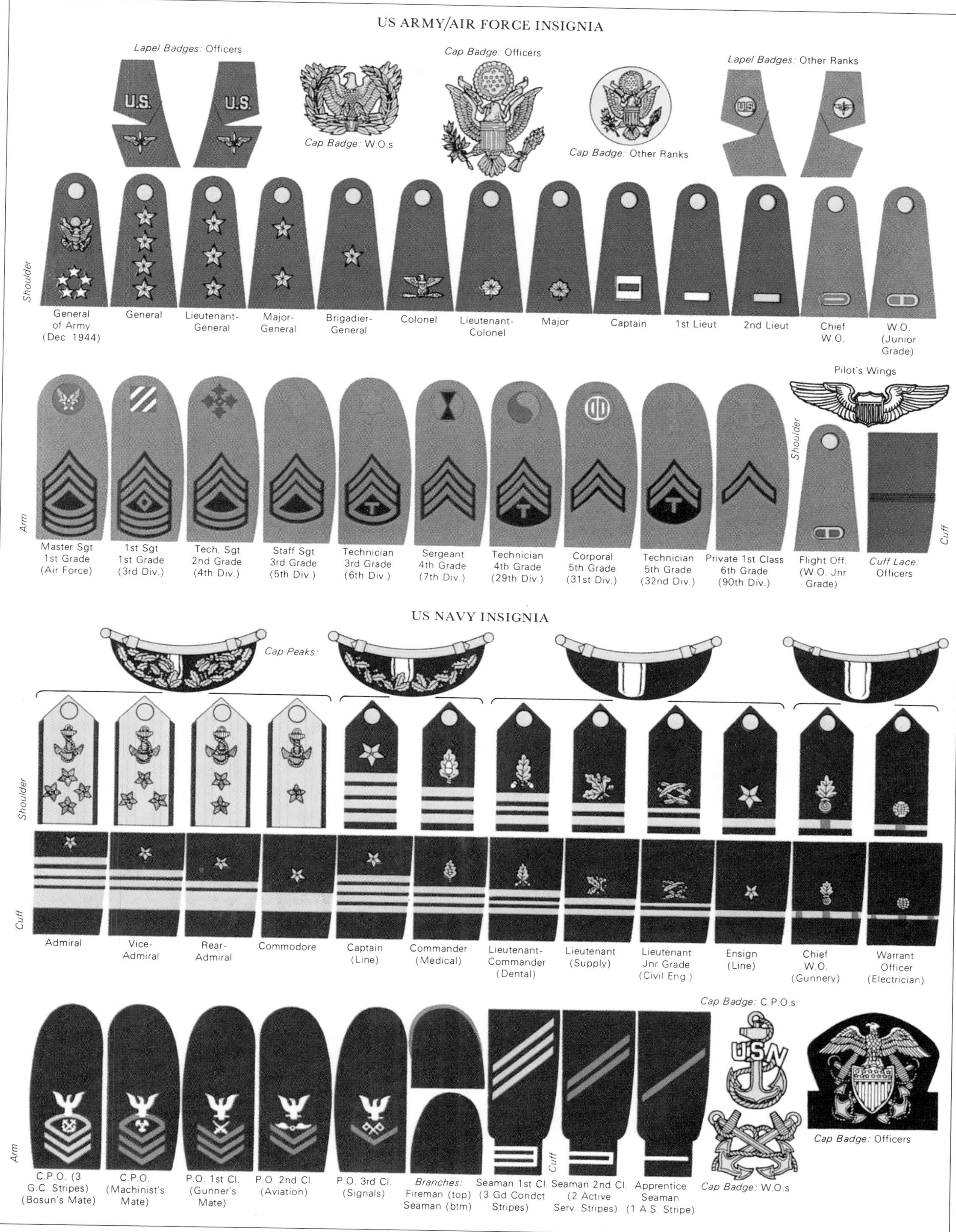
US ARMY/AIR FORCE INSIGNIA
Lapel Badges: Officers
U.S.
U.S.
Cap Badge: W.O.s
Cap Badge: Officers
Cap Badge: Other Ranks
Lapel Badges: Other Ranks
Shoulder
General of Army (Dec. 1944)
General
Lieutenant-General
Major-General
Brigadier-General
Colonel
Lieutenant-Colonel
Major
Captain
1st Lieut
2nd Lieut
Chief W.O.
W.O. (Junior Grade)
Pilot's Wings
Arm
Master Sgt 1st Grade (Air Force)
1st Sgt 1st Grade (3rd Div.)
Tech. Sgt 2nd Grade (4th Div.)
Staff Sgt 3rd Grade (5th Div.)
Technician 3rd Grade (6th Div.)
Sergeant 4th Grade (7th Div.)
Technician 4th Grade (29th Div.)
Corporal 5th Grade (31st Div.)
Technician 5th Grade (32nd Div.)
Private 1st Class 6th Grade (90th Div.)
Shoulder
Flight Off. (W.O. Jnr Grade)
Cuff
Cuff Lace: Officers
US NAVY INSIGNIA
Cap Peaks:
Shoulder
Cuff
Admiral
Vice-Admiral
Rear-Admiral
Commodore
Captain (Line)
Commander (Medical)
Lieutenant-Commander (Dental)
Lieutenant (Supply)
Lieutenant Jnr Grade (Civil Eng.)
Ensign (Line)
Chief W.O. (Gunnery)
Warrant Officer (Electrician)
Cap Badge: C.P.O.s
USN
Arm
C.P.O. (3 G.C. Stripes) (Bosun's Mate)
C.P.O. (Machinist's Mate)
P.O. 1st Cl. (Gunner's Mate)
P.O. 2nd Cl. (Aviation)
P.O. 3rd Cl. (Signals)
Branches: Fireman (top) Seaman (btm)
Cuff
Seaman 1st Cl. (3 Gd Condct Stripes)
Seaman 2nd Cl. (2 Active Serv. Stripes)
Apprentice Seaman (1 A.S. Stripe)
Cap Badge: W.O.s
Cap Badge: Officers

NAVY

The US Navy was in many ways unprepared for war when the Japanese brought America into World War II with their attack on Pearl Harbor. Too great an emphasis was placed upon the battleship to the exclusion of anti-submarine warfare, which was essential to success in the Battle of the Atlantic. It was to the great credit of the US Navy that in a remarkably short space of time it was able to re-organise its forces and, in conjunction with the Royal Navy, defeat the U-boat menace.

Even before America's entry into the war, the pro-British Roosevelt government had provided aid to the British which included the 100 destroyers of the 'lend-lease' agreement and the escort of convoys by US Navy vessels.

Above: A depth charge explodes off the stern of an American destroyer on escort duty in the Atlantic.

293 Ensign, US Navy, 1944

Ensign Roosevelt wears standard officers' service dress with white cap cover. Rank distinction lace and the five-pointed star of a line officer appear on the cuffs. The aiguillette was worn by presidential aides.

293

As early as February 1941 a Support Force had been set up from the Atlantic Fleet, consisting of three destroyer squadrons and four patrol squadrons of 12 Catalina or Mariner aircraft each. By the end of the following month this force was 27 destroyers strong and was concentrated on the Argenta to Iceland sector of the transatlantic convoy route. In 1942 the United States Atlantic Fleet consisted of seven battleships, one fleet and seven escort carriers, three heavy and nine light cruisers, and 76 destroyers.

A major problem facing the Navy planners was the allocation of resources: to many Americans the Pacific was the most important area of operations and although the Atlantic was not stinted of supplies, the main effort was justifiably devoted to the Pacific Command. Nevertheless, by 1944 seven escort carrier groups had been formed with 7 carriers and 97 destroyers.

In spite of the British example the American Navy, under the direction of Admiral King, was reluctant to develop the convoys system and suffered very heavy losses. During the spring and summer of 1942 the German U-boats decimated shipping off the Atlantic seaboard: during May alone, over 450,000 tons of Allied shipping was sunk off the American coast. Like the Royal Navy the US Navy gained the upper hand over the U-boats by adopting the convoy system, increasing the numbers of escort vessels and introducing new anti-submarine devices such as Asdic and 'Huff-Duff'.

The organisation of the US Atlantic Fleet was initially a hurriedly improvised affair but once was was declared efforts were made to rationalise the Fleet's organisation. Originally, the US Atlantic coast was divided into a number of coastal naval districts, and there were seven of these guarding the vast area of the eastern seaboard stretching from Canada to Florida. These were abolished and replaced by sea frontiers on 1 July 1942. A sea frontier was an area of ocean extending out to sea from a definite section of the coast to a distance of over 200 miles. In all there were four sea frontiers, three of which were relevant to the fight against the U-boat: the Canadian Coastal Zone, the Panama Sea Frontier, and most important of all, the Eastern Sea Frontier. The commanders of each of these areas controlled all the vessels inside them for the duration of their voyage within the sea frontier.

Although the idea of appointing one officer responsible for conducting the U-boat war was discarded, Admiral King set up the 10th Fleet in May 1942 under his own command 'to exercise unity of control over US anti-submarine operations in that part of the Atlantic under its strategic control'. This was a further step in the process of ironing out the series of hasty improvisations created to meet the needs of the moment. The basic function of this force was to destroy U-boats, protect allied and neutral shipping and also to supervise training in anti-submarine methods.

By early 1944 the US Navy switched most of its resources to the Pacific, although convoy duties continued and valuable support was given to the Army during the Normandy landings in June 1944.

UNIFORM In the Atlantic theatre of operations US Navy uniforms kept to the basic pattern discussed on page 155.

294

295

294 Soldier, German Army, 1944
This infantryman is equipped with flamethrowing gear consisting of a main cylinder mounted on his back, a flamethrower gun and a protective suit made of a rubberised material which was worn over the standard uniform. The flamethrower worked on the principle of squirting out a liquid or semi-liquid stream of fire at the target. The weapon had four basic elements: a fuel storage system, a compressed gas system, a flame gun and an igniter. The gun element had two triggers, one to release the fuel from the cylinder and the other to ignite the fuel/gas mixture at the nozzle. The flamethrower was not widely used by the Germans, however, being more common in the armouries of Britain and the USA.

295 Private, German Army, 1944
This Panzergrenadier *has fitted wire mesh to his steel helmet to hold foliage, and over his field blouse wears an Army camouflage smock, which was reversible to white and was originally issued only to snipers. The field blouse is the 1943 model with plain, unpleated, patch pockets. In his belt he carries a* Stielgranate *24 and the rifle is the Mauser 98K.*

Below: This crewman of a Panzer Mark IV wears the unofficial dress of the 12th SS 'Hitler Jugend' *Panzer Division which consisted of a black leather jacket and the trousers worn by U-boat crews. The* 'Hitler Jugend', *under the command of* Oberführer *Fritz Witt, was one of the crack armoured formations of the German Army on the Western Front and sustained heavy casualties in the attempt to drive the Allies into the sea. The tank has been coated with Zimmerrit paste, a special anti-magnetic mine solution that had been applied to the external surfaces of most German tanks by 1944. The Mark IV was armed with two 7.92mm machine guns (one visible here) and a long-barrelled 7.5cm high-velocity gun.*

GERMANY

ARMY

Following the defeat of France in the summer of 1940 and the abandonment of plans to invade Great Britain, the German Army found itself allotted a defensive role as the occupying force in western Europe. At first France was little more than a retraining and reorganising ground for the battered divisions withdrawn from the Eastern Front but by the autumn of 1943 it had become obvious to the German High Command that an Allied invasion of western Europe was certain. The only questions in doubt were when and where and how the invasion should be countered. Many German commanders thought that the Allied invasion would be directed against the Pas de Calais region and not Normandy, the actual site of the landings.

Although the German soldiers fought fiercely against the Allied invasion forces in 1944, Hitler's refusal to allow a steady withdrawal led to the disaster of Falaise, and the headlong retreat through France during the autumn of 1944.

The retreat cost the German Army heavy casualties but by the end of 1944 the front line had stabilised near the frontiers of Germany itself. Manpower shortages and logistic problems held up the Allied advance, so allowing the Germans a breathing space to mount their last major offensive in the west – the Battle of the Bulge.

Despite some initial success this last gamble ended in failure with the German Army using up its remaining forces.

After the failure of the Ardennes offensive the Germans were forced back to the Rhine and by February 1945 the forces available in the west consisted of 73 understrength divisions. The Army was nearing collapse: the absence of air support and shortages of all necessary war materials made defeat inevitable. On 30 April Hitler committed suicide and the German Army began to lay down its arms, the final surrender being signed on 7 May 1945.

296

297

296 Corporal, German Army, 1944
This Unteroffizier *wears the final version of the World War II German field uniform which was very similar in cut to the British battledress. All insignia was now woven in mouse-grey on field-grey backing. The breeches lined with leather and high riding boots were issued to personnel in horse-drawn units, of which there were still a number in 1944–5. Above the left breast pocket he wears the ribbon for the Winter Campaign on the Eastern Front (often called the 'frozen meat medal'), and on the pocket he wears a wound badge in black.*

297 2nd Lieutenant, German Security Police, 1943
This SS-Untersturmführer *wears the field-grey service dress of the Waffen-SS. Badges of rank appear on the shoulder straps and on his left collar patch. Security service (SD) and security police* (Sipo) *personnel wore a plain right-hand collar patch and police green piping on the shoulder straps. Those entitled wore the SD badge on the left cuff. The chevron on his right sleeve is not a rank badge but indicated that the wearer had fulfilled certain conditions, such as having been a member of the Nazi Party prior to 1933.*

Organisation Not only did the Army have insufficient men to guard Hitler's 'Fortress Europe', the quality of many of the available divisions was only second rate. A further problem was the fragmented command structure of the German Army in western Europe. Field Marshal von Rundstedt was Commander-in-Chief West but had only nominal authority while Rommel as commander of Army Group B fought with the other Army generals for control of the western defences. This failure to unify German Army command, coupled with inter-service rivalries with the Air Force and Navy, was a fatal organisational error, for when the Allies struck on 6 June 1944 the German response was sluggish and uncoordinated.

Of the 58 divisions available to Rundstedt 43 were under the command of Army Group B (Rommel) which covered northern France and the Low Countries, while the remainder were under the control of Army Group G (Blaskowitz) which was responsible for central and southern France. Although Rommel had influence with Hitler he had no authority over the armoured divisions which came under direct OKW control and were commanded by Geyr von Schweppenburg (commander, Panzer Group West) an opponent of Rommel's tactical ideas.

Panzer Group West – the German armoured reserve – consisted of four panzer and two SS-panzer divisions, five of them deployed in France with the sixth stationed in Belgium. Allied air power ensured that these formations had less effect than they might have; exposed to aerial rocket attacks, tank units were forced to travel by night and hide by day.

Many divisions were destroyed in the battle for Normandy but by the winter of 1944 there were sufficient troops to consider a further offensive. For the Battle of the Bulge the German Army deployed three armies:
7th Army (one paratroop and three *Volksgrenadier* divisions);
5th Panzer Army (two panzer and four *Volksgrenadier* divisions);
6th SS Panzer Army (four SS panzer, four *Volksgrenadier* and one parachute division).

The composition of these three armies reflected the state of the Army towards the end of the war: the infantry component consisted mainly of the *Volksgrenadier* divisions (examined in detail on page 187) while Army tank strength was greatly reduced compared to that of the Waffen-SS (the 6th SS Panzer Army with 640 tanks had about twice the number of the 5th Panzer Army). Despite the fact that the SS formations had better equipment and armament than their Army counterparts, it was the 5th Panzer Army that had the greatest success during the Ardennes offensive.

By the spring of 1945 the size of the German Army units and formations had been greatly reduced: the infantry divisions averaged around 7000 men each and the eight armoured divisions were desperately short of equipment and fuel. The *Volkssturm* (the German equivalent of the British Home Guard) was called out but, consisting of adolescents and middle-aged men lacking in weapons and training, its influence was minimal. By the end of April 1945 the German Army ceased to exist as a coherent force.

The Army had been at war for nearly six years and had fought throughout Europe and in North Africa. Although the Army had won many great victories during these years the political ambitions of Germany's leaders made victory impossible: the combined numerical advantage of the Allied forces wore the German Army

Above: Taken in Normandy in the summer of 1944, this picture shows part of the crew of a 7.5cm German anti-tank gun. The personnel, who are in an SS division, wear the regulation SS camouflage smocks and helmet covers. The 7.5cm gun was the German Army's standard anti-tank weapon towards the end of the war but its size made it difficult for infantry to handle.

Below: Two soldiers of the Volkssturm *– the German equivalent of the British Home Guard – are pictured in a typical variety of civilian and army clothing. The* Volkssturm *arm-band or brassard is visible on their left arms. The organisation was mainly composed of middle-aged men or youths and, with few weapons and little equipment, was clearly unsuited to play a significant part in modern warfare.*

down in a battle of attrition it could never hope to win. The final casualty figure for the German Army during World War II was 3,250,000 men killed.

UNIFORM The German soldier in Normandy in 1944 had an appearance rather different from the typical *Landser* (German Tommy) of 1940. First of all, the various kinds of side and mountain caps had been replaced by the standard M1943 field cap. The steel helmet was no longer shiny and adorned with national emblem and national colours; instead, it now displayed a matt, gritty, field-grey finish or was sprayed in a camouflage pattern, or was worn with camouflage cover or netting. The colour of the field uniform was no longer as green as it had been formerly. It was now becoming increasingly grey, and as the quality of the material was getting poorer so uniforms tended to be baggier. Most insignia were now manufactured in mouse-grey yarn, and *Waffenfarbe* only appeared on the shoulder straps. The expensive marching boot was now a comparative rarity and most soldiers wore ankle boots with canvas anklets, which were disparagingly called 'retreat gaiters'.

A standard field-grey shirt had been introduced to replace the former varieties and colours of shirt; this could be worn without a tunic. New trousers with built-in cloth belt were also produced.

The special black and field-grey clothing for crews of enclosed armoured fighting vehicles and self-propelled artillery were also simplified, while the field-grey uniform began to be issued to all personnel in newly-formed panzer grenadier divisions.

To protect what were becoming increasingly precious uniforms and to improve the protective colouring, various types of overalls, some of which were camouflaged, began to be issued (see figure 295). These were not, however, standardised or as widely issued as those of the Waffen-SS.

Officers were finding it very difficult to obtain uniforms and accessories on the open market because of the widespread shortage of textiles, so they began to wear issue uniforms. Their tailor-made service dress was kept for formal occasions. The rather rigid orders of dress were relaxed to take into account all these difficulties. Some officers, finding the stiff closed collar uncomfortable, began to wear their field blouse open at the neck with shirt and tie, while others had tailor-made blouses which were designed to be worn open at the neck.

During the last winter of the war the typical German soldier was wearing either the reversible camouflage combat uniform or the standard issue field-grey greatcoat with large matching collar and built-in hood. The coat came in a lined and unlined version.

Since it was impractical to wear shoulder straps on many of the camouflage uniforms (and the various kinds of protective clothing), a new system of rank badges for wear on both sleeves was introduced in August 1942 (see rank insignia chart, page 7).

AIR FORCE

One of the major lessons of the Battle of Britain was the realisation of the vulnerability of the bomber to a well organised fighter defence. The German solution was to turn to night bombing as a means of escaping the fighter menace. Throughout the winter and spring of 1940–41, Britain's major cities were subjected to the Luftwaffe's bomber arm which although causing widespread damage and heavy casualties (50,000 people were killed during the 'Blitz') did not seriously affect war production or civilian morale, as had been hoped. This attempt to bring Britain to her knees petered out in the spring of 1941 as the German Air Force was redeployed in eastern Europe.

The Luftwaffe moved over to the defensive during the summer of 1941 mainly because the strategic focus had been transferred towards Russia and resources transferred accordingly but also because of the development of a small but growing British bomber offensive against Germany which necessitated a response from the Air Force. The British and later American aerial offensive against Germany was to engage the Luftwaffe in a massive operation to save the *Reich* from destruction.

Below: German soldiers are marched into captivity under Allied guard in September 1944. Their uniform displays the characteristics of late-war German issue, with jackboots having been replaced by marching boots and gaiters in the British style. The soldier to the right wears the chevron of a lance-corporal on his left sleeve, while the leading figure carries the regulation German canteen.

Besides its main function from 1942 onwards as the cutting edge of the Luftwaffe's defensive screen the German fighter arm scored a number of notable successes on the Western Front; these included the intricate fighter umbrella erected to defend the *Scharnhorst* and *Gneisenau* during the 'Channel Dash' and the disruption of the Allied fighter screen over Dieppe in July 1942.

During 1943 the intensity of the Allied bomber offensive increased and the German Air Force was engaged in a desperate struggle against the RAF by night and USAAF by day. Success in this war depended on the application of material resources and technical developments; sometimes the German defenders were in the ascendant and Allied casualties rose and at other the Allies gained the upper hand and Germany's cities were destroyed.

A major turning point was the firestorm raids on Hamburg during July 1943 in which the German air defence was blinded through the jamming of the radar system by 'window' (thin aluminium strips dropped through the air simulating

298 Officer, German Air Force
This figure wears the standard Luftwaffe officers' leather greatcoat. An anachronistic touch is the brown leather Sam Browne belt which is still being worn even though it had officially been discontinued after the Polish campaign in 1939. The officer's rank is not visible from this illustration although the Luftwaffe version of the German eagle can be seen on the peaked cap. Since 1941 the German Air Force had taken on a defensive role on the Western Front as the strategic initiative passed over to the Air Forces of the Allies.

299 Reich Marshal
As the one and only Marshal of the Reich, Göring designed his own uniform, which, since he was also Commander-in-Chief of the Luftwaffe, had a certain Air Force flavour about it. Badges of rank appeared on the shoulder straps and collar patches (see insignia chart). Decorations include the highest Prussian award for bravery, the Pour le Mérite, *which is almost totally overshadowed by the highest class of the Order of the Iron Cross, the Grand Cross, of which he was the only recipient. In his right hand he carries an* Interimstab *which was the everyday version of the field marshal's baton.*

300 Corporal, German Air Force, 1944
As a paratrooper, this Oberjäger *has the yellow (flying) arm-of-service colour while his rank is displayed on the collar patches and the shoulder straps. The popular flying blouse or* Fliegerbluse *is the later pattern with pockets and is worn with the field-grey paratroop trousers. Deprived of an airborne role the German paratroops were employed as ground forces and acquitted themselves with distinction in the bitter fighting in the Normandy bocage and against the British paratroops during the battle of Arnhem.*

aircraft on German radar screens). Hamburg was virtually razed to the ground: 50,000 people were estimated to have been killed and nearly 1,000,000 made homeless.

New tactics were evolved in this crisis period for the Air Force and during late 1943 British losses rose as did those of the USAAF whose unescorted bombers were appallingly vulnerable to fighter attack. During 1943 the German Air Force tactically defeated the American 8th Army Air Force, which for a time was forced to bomb easier targets in France. But the tables turned to the Allies' advantage in 1944 as the Americans made massive use of Mustang long-range escort fighters which not only protected their own bombers but began to wear down the Luftwaffe's own fighters.

By the summer of 1944 the strain on Germany's industrial and military capacity was beginning to show. Only 419 serviceable German aircraft were able to oppose the enormous Allied deployment of over 10,000 planes to support the Normandy landings.

Although German aircraft production reached its peak in 1944 the Luftwaffe's trained pilots were being destroyed in the daily and nightly running battles over Germany. As serious as the loss of trained aircrew was the growing shortage of aviation fuel in 1944 due to the destruction of oil refineries in Eastern Europe and the systematic attacks on the synthetic fuel industry. In January 1944 Germany was producing 159,000 tons of synthetic fuel a month; by December of that year production was down to 26,000 tons.

During the last year of the war overwhelming Allied superiority destroyed the Luftwaffe which was now unable to either support Army operations or defend German cities from Allied attacks. Despite

Right: A groundcrewman hands night glasses to the pilot of a German aircraft prior to take-off on an operational sortie. Both wear the standard German Air Force overalls. The Luftwaffe conducted both offensive and defensive campaigns by night; in the latter case, 'Wild Sow' and 'Tame Sow' tactics were employed to effect in the defence of the Reich, *claiming many Allied bombers.*

298

299

300

301

desperate efforts by the German air crews and the introduction of technically superior aircraft – such as the jet propelled Me 262 – there was little that could be done and only the signing of the peace treaty on 7 May 1945 saved the Luftwaffe from complete destruction.

Organisation The Allied bomber offensive forced the German Air Force to adopt new tactics and organisations to counter this aerial threat. A new and constantly developing system of defence evolved that integrated the various elements of air defence – radar, searchlights, anti-aircraft artillery and interceptors – into a whole.

Originally the defence of Germany was left to the powerful anti-aircraft arm which with its searchlight batteries and later radar controlled height/range finders and predictors was the most numerous element within the Luftwaffe – out of a total of 1,500,000 men in 1939, two-thirds were involved in anti-aircraft duties. And during the course of the war their role increased in importance.

By 1942 it had become clear to the German Air Force planners that an early-warning radar system was necessary to identify enemy planes soon after leaving England so that they could be intercepted before reaching the target. A series of linked radar stations stretching from France to the north of Denmark was built during 1942. Known as the Kammhuber line (after its guiding light, General Josef Kammhuber) this, through a combination of wide and narrow beam radar sets, was able to guide night-fighters on to the bomber streams, often to deadly effect.

The introduction of 'window' in 1943 forced new developments on the German Air Force: *Wilde Sau* ('Wild Sow') and *Zahme Sau* ('Tame Sow') tactics. The 'Wild Sow' method concentrated the German fighters over the target itself where they would search for their prey semi-independently of the radar controller, relying mainly on visual contact. The 'Tame Sow' tactics kept to the basis of the old method: the fighters were directed to where the 'window' interference was the thickest in the hope of picking up the bomber stream and then engaging the enemy in a long running battle over Germany. Improvements in

301 Captain, German Air Force, 1944
This Hauptmann *wears flying clothing typical of the end of the war. The field cap is the standard model introduced in 1943, and the flying suit is a two-piece model consisting of zip-fastened jacket and the so-called* 'Kanalhosen' *(Channel trousers) which had large pockets containing survival kit. Badges of rank are worn on the shoulder straps.*

Below: Crewed by Luftwaffe personnel, this is one of Germany's many 2cm light flak guns employed for anti-aircraft defence. The arm-of-service eagle is visible on the uniform of the soldier to the left, whose rank is that of senior lance-corporal.

the interceptors' own radar sets, culminating in the 'SN-2' radar, allowed the airborne operators to work on frequencies not so disturbed by 'window' as the old Lichtenstein radar sets had been. The successful use of this new system led to heavy British casualties: during the period 18 November 1943 to the end of March 1944 over 1000 planes were lost and a further 1682 damaged during a series of 35 major raids over Germany.

Against the US day bombers the Air Force attacked in groups of up to 40 aircraft usually concentrating on a certain section of the massed American bomber formation. The lead planes which commanded the formations were a frequent target. Rockets fired from the fighters themselves were highly effective and in certain instances small bombs would be dropped directly onto the enemy plane from the fighters above. The advent of the long range fighter-escort prevented the German interceptors from closing with the US bombers so cutting down their success rate. By late 1944 the German fighter units often found themselves outnumbered and out-fought by the American escort fighters.

The air war in Western Europe was a steady drain on Luftwaffe resources. Hundreds of thousands of men were employed in anti-aircraft duties and in post-bombardment construction work and planes were withdrawn from other fronts, where they were desperately needed, to shore up the German defensive system in the West. Although beaten by the combined Allied Air Forces the Luftwaffe did not waver in its defence of Germany while the physical means to do so remained.

Above: Officers and men of a German U-boat cluster in the conning tower. Facing the camera to the right is a lieutenant, identifiable as such by the single pip on his shoulder strap. His rank group is indicated by the gold lace on the cap peak.

UNIFORM Luftwaffe uniform changed little during the war despite the German realisation that much could be done towards standardising cut if not the colour of the uniforms of the three branches of the Armed Forces.

From 1943 some officers began to wear their tunic and flying blouse closed at the collar, rather than open with shirt and tie. The side cap was changed for the standard peaked field cap, but the greatest uniform changes took place in the Luftwaffe field formations.

The Luftwaffe uniform had not really been designed for ground combat and both the colour and cut were most unsuitable. The first thing to be done was to remove the brightly coloured collar patches since these were far too conspicuous. Tunics, greatcoats and flying blouses were worn without collar patches until the new rifle-green pattern could be issued. These were piped for other ranks in arm-of-service colour, but the difficulty in manufacturing these collar patches and getting them to the right units at this stage in the war meant that plain green collar patches were eventually issued and the *Waffenfarbe* appeared as piping on the shoulder straps (figure 233 on page 194).

Those units in Luftwaffe field formations which were equipped with armoured fighting vehicles also received the special black tank uniform on which Luftwaffe insignia was worn. A blue-grey and later field-grey version was issued to crews of self-propelled assault guns. Finally the Luftwaffe began to produce field-grey uniforms for members of the field formations. The field blouse had plain patch pockets and was worn with blue-grey shoulder straps piped in *Waffenfarbe*, no collar patches and the Luftwaffe national emblem on the right breast.

NAVY

The German Navy, although in the end thoroughly defeated during operations in Atlantic and Arctic waters from 1941 to 1945, threatened to win the war against Great Britain during the Battle of the Atlantic, and its surface vessels posed a threat to convoys until 1945.

In 1940 Admiral Karl Dönitz, head of the German U-boat Arm, stated that, 'the U-boat alone can win this war', and the submarine was, indeed, the greatest obstacle to Allied success. For the second time in 25 years, Germany almost succeeded in severing Allied sea communications. The German U-boat arm, banned under the Treaty of Versailles, was reactivated after the signing of the Anglo-German Naval Treaty in 1935.

The U-boat arm of the *Kriegsmarine* was organised under the *Führer der Unterseeboote* (Senior Officer Submarines) Admiral Karl Dönitz. In 1939 a total of 55 submarines were organised in flotillas of between five and eight boats each, some of the flotillas being named after U-boat heroes of World War I.

With the introduction of wolf pack tactics in 1941, tonnage sunk rose steadily and the following year proved to be the most successful: U-boats sunk 1160 ships totalling 6,266,215 tons. Gradually, however, the Allies' improved tactics and the use of long-range aircraft and aircraft carriers and radar-equipped escorts began to yield results. Between April and May 1943, tonnage sunk by U-boats began to decline as their losses rose, soaring from 13 to 30 per cent during May, and the remaining 16 or so U-boats were withdrawn from the North Atlantic.

Mid-1943 marked a turning-point in the Battle of the Atlantic; the Allied offensive was beginning to gain momentum and the German attempt to redress the balance had come too late. Nevertheless, German U-boats accounted for the loss of 175 Allied warships and a total of 14 millions tons of Allied shipping throughout the war. Of 1162 U-boats built, 785 were destroyed, 156 surrendered and the rest were scuttled.

Typical German submarines serving in the Atlantic – Types IXC and IXC/40 – had four bow and two stern torpedo tubes and an armament of 41 torpedoes and three anti-aircraft guns. In all, 141 of these types were commissioned with a complement of 48.

Unrelated to the main stream of research were the midget submarines, manned by a crew of up to seven, and deployed to attack shipping in harbours.

In 1941 *Rudeltaktik* (pack tactics) or 'wolf packs' as they were known to the

302

303

Allies, were initiated under the direction of Admiral Dönitz. Groups of 15 to 20 U-boats patrolled the sealanes approaching Britain: when a convoy was sighted it was tracked by the U-boat which radioed its position, course and composition to Dönitz' headquarters, keeping in touch until other U-boats had received their orders and made contact. The boats then attacked simultaneously, but independently, later reporting their success, or lack of it, to Dönitz who issued the orders for a further attack, or a new patrol line. Admiral Dönitz was thus able to make best use of his forces. However, so much radio traffic had its disadvantages: Royal Navy vessels carrying high-frequency direction-finders were able to pinpoint the transmitting U-boats, enabling escorts to run them down. The efficiency of the wolf pack tactics was further reduced when Allied long-range aerial searches intensified and autumn 1943 saw the final defeat of this strategy.

Far left: A petty officer (with binoculars) interviews captured British sailors aboard the German heavy cruiser Admiral Hipper. *Displacing 10,000 tons and armed with 8-inch guns, the vessel operated with the* Tirpitz *against the convoy PQ-17 in July 1942. For most of the war the* Admiral Hipper *was based in Norway and operated against British arctic convoys, but with only limited success.*

Left: Commander Gysae looks through the periscope of his U-boat. He wears the white cap cover adopted almost universally by U-boat commanders. His shoulder straps indicate the rank of Korvettenkapitän. *The success of Germany's U-boat fleet owed much to the bravery of their commanders, who considered themselves the élite of the German Navy.*

Despite appalling losses, the morale of the U-boat arm was high and it fought with unrelenting discipline and efficiency. Over 39,000 officers and men served in German submarines and 32,000 were killed in action, the highest proportion of any other force, Allied or Axis, in World War II.

The final defeat of the U-boats reflected not on the ability and courage of the men who served in them, but on the intensive Allied anti-submarine measures and outstanding technical advances which the Germans were unable to match.

Since in September 1939 there were not enough warships in the *Kriegsmarine* to drive the Royal Navy from the seas, or even to escort any of the merchantmen outside German waters, the best that could be hoped for was to distract or damage part of the British Home Fleet long enough to enable a few blockade-runners to evade its patrols. Meanwhile a handful of surface and submarine raiders were to conduct a campaign against the merchant navies of the British Empire.

Following the declaration of war, the German surface raiders which were already at sea – *Deutschland* in the North Atlantic and *Graf Spee* south of the equator – began to attack commerce. The *Graf Spee* destroyed a total of nine ships during her cruise through the South Atlantic and Indian Ocean, but was herself scuttled following the Battle of River Plate in December 1939.

After the fall of Norway and France, the Atlantic became more accessible to the German Navy. Converted merchantmen

304

302 Petty Officer, German Navy, 1942

As an Obersteuermann *or chief coxswain, this petty officer wears the cap with plain leather peak and lifejacket over his reefer. The latter carries badges of rank on the shoulder straps. He wears leather trousers outside his sea boots.*

303 Petty Officer, German Navy, 1943

The black leather jacket and trousers worn here by a petty officer were issued to personnel working in machine rooms, since grease stains were not easily visible against the black. The uniform was worn without insignia, save for the badges of rank on the shoulder straps of the jacket. A cap with plain leather peak is also worn. Regulation uniforms such as this, however, were to become difficult to obtain as the war continued and Germany's position grew ever more parlous.

304 Commander, German Navy, 1943

This officer wears the double-breasted leather jacket which was issued with matching trousers for wear in bad weather. Badges of rank could be worn on the shoulder straps, but often (as in this illustration) no badge of rank were worn. Various kinds of working trousers were worn in preference to the blue service dress trousers.

305 Lieutenant, German Navy, 1942

This Leutnant zur See *and U-boat commander wears the peaked cap with obligatory white cover, battered reefer, working trousers and sea boots. Unofficially, crews of submarines began to wear flotilla badges on their head-dresses. He has just been awarded the Knight's Cross of the Iron Cross, while the Iron Cross 1st Class is worn on the left breast of his reefer jacket.*

305

306

put to sea: with disguised armament (which equalled that of a cruiser), they were able to approach enemy vessels without attracting undue attention. Between 1940 and 1942 vessels such as *Thor*, *Atlantis* and *Pinguin*, which were engaged in attacking Arctic whaling fleets, accounted for vast amounts of Allied tonnage sunk.

On 18 May 1941 the battleship *Bismarck* departed for the Atlantic on her first and only cruise accompanied by the heavy cruiser *Prinz Eugen*. Although the *Prinz Eugen* escaped the *Bismarck*'s fate, she was put out of action by the RAF in Brest harbour in July, as were the *Scharnhorst* and *Gneisenau*.

In order to prevent further attacks by the RAF, Hitler decided to move the three ships east, where they would be better able to protect Norway. The 'Channel Dash' of February 1942 was one of the most daring German naval operations of World War II in which combined air-sea operations played an important part.

Although the large German warships now turned their attention to raiding the Arctic convoys, they had little initial success, and after the sinking of the *Scharnhorst* in December 1943, surface craft left the convoys alone. The *Tirpitz*, which had almost suffered the same fate as her sister ship *Bismarck* was also damaged and immobilised. She had only once fired her guns in combat when she bombarded a gun emplacement at Spitzbergen.

By May 1945 only three cruisers and a dozen destroyers remained of the surface fleet of the *Kriegsmarine*.

Throughout the war the German Navy was divided between those who wanted a large surface fleet and those who wanted priority given to U-boat production. Fortunately for the Allies, the U-boat arm never received the resources which might have tipped the scales.

Uniform There was little change to the blue uniforms of the German Navy after 1940, although the increasing difficulties in replacing worn out clothing led to a lowering of uniformity amongst Navy personnel. At the end of the war it was not uncommon to see an officer wearing a blue reefer with checked or coloured shirt and black tie, simply because it was impossible to obtain the correct white shirts.

Land-based sailors continued to wear field-grey (figure 306). In June 1943 even admirals began to appear dressed in field-grey with blue stripes on their breeches and Army generals' collar patches embroidered in gold or yellow on blue.

Insignia In 1944 Naval officers serving on the Atlantic Wall began to wear shoulder straps which identified their rank on the reefer in addition to the rank distinction lace on the cuffs. This was probably to facilitate inter-service rank identification in a situation where soldiers and sailors were working together.

306 Seaman, German Naval Artillery, 1944

The field-grey uniform of the German Navy was similar to that worn by the Army, but had different pockets on the field blouse as well as buttons with an anchor on them. Trousers were often worn with ankle boots and canvas anklets (or 'retreat gaiters' as they were known) which began to replace the costly marching boot from 1941 on. Certain field-grey-clad branches of the Navy had emblems on their shoulder straps, such as the exploding shell as illustrated. The rifle is the Mauser 98K.

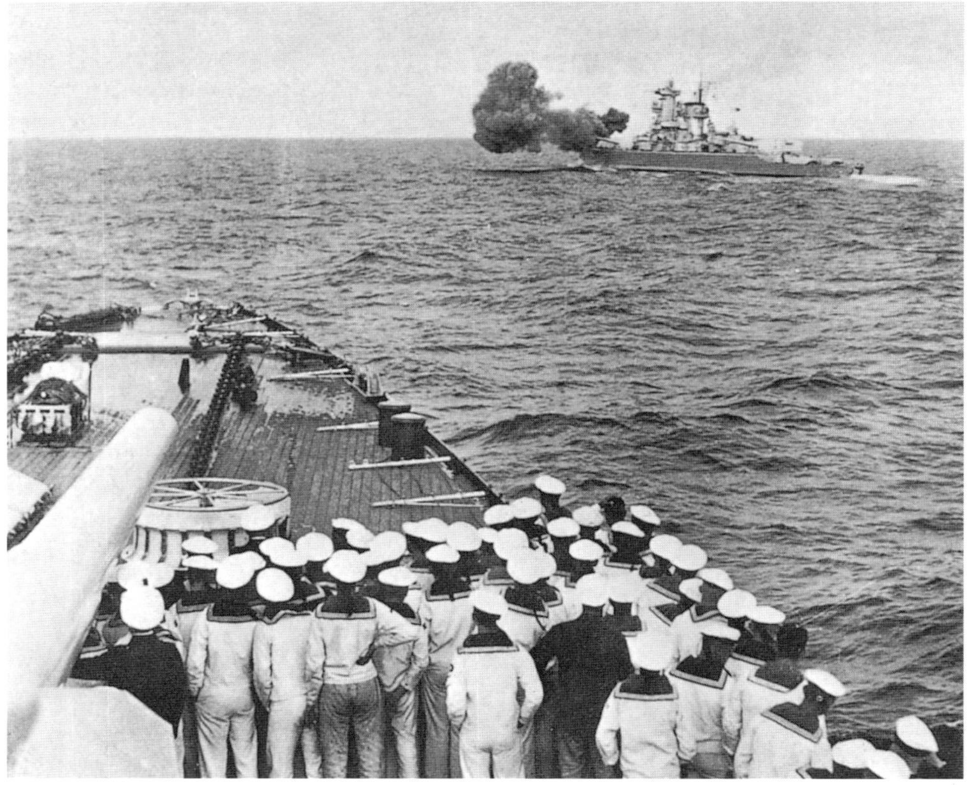

Right: A group of ratings and petty officers watches a salvo fired from the Admiral Scheer *during a training exercise. The* Admiral Scheer *was one of Germany's pocket battleships and with a gross tonnage of 12,000 tons was armed with six 11-inch guns. The most successful ship in this class, the* Scheer *began the war as a commerce raider in a 161-day cruise which took the ship to the Indian Ocean. Evading capture, the* Admiral Scheer *returned to Germany in 1941 and was dispatched to the Baltic Sea in 1942 to operate against Soviet convoys. In this photograph the sailors are wearing the square rig uniform with white-topped caps, an unusual order of dress for the later period of the war.*

THE PACIFIC WAR

Japanese forces had been engaged in China since 1937 and, after the Japanese attack on Pearl Harbor in December 1941, the war was extended world-wide. Japanese, Chinese, US, British and Empire and Commonwealth troops were all engaged in a struggle marked by the vast distances involved, often fighting in conditions of extreme humidity.

The results were the creation of many distinctive organisations (especially in the campaigns in the Pacific islands) and the adoption of uniforms which were serviceable during weather such as the Burmese monsoon or in terrain such as the jungle of Guadalcanal.

JAPAN
ARMY

The Japanese Army was a mirror of Japanese society before 1945. It contained a peculiar amalgam of medieval attitudes and modern *matériel*, for the Army still followed the code of *Bushido* which upheld the virtues of man-to-man combat in a machine age, and demanded that the Japanese soldier die rather than surrender.

The political influence of the Japanese Army had substantially increased in the years between the two world wars. The Army saw Japan's salvation in China: Japan should secure the vast resources of the Asian mainland by carving out for herself a continental empire. The Army consequently viewed the Soviet Union as Japan's most dangerous enemy – a power which had traditional interests in North China. The Navy looked to the Pacific Ocean, and particularly to the South West Pacific, with the rich prize of Malaya and the Dutch East Indies as the means by which the resources vital to the maintenance of Japan as a great power could be seized. The Navy, therefore, regarded the world's two greatest naval powers, Great Britain and the United States, as Japan's most deadly enemies. It was no coincidence that the two services shaped Japan's strategy to suit the exclusive capacity of either the Army or the Navy. Before 1941 the Army had most of its own way.

Japan seized Manchuria in 1931 and the province of Jehol in 1934. Three years later the Japanese Army embarked on a full-scale undeclared war against China. The Japanese aimed to destroy the Chinese Army in the field and thus bring the country to its knees quickly; this would avoid the colossal task of trying to conquer and hold the vast spaces of China. The Japanese generals failed. The Chinese Army was more elusive and remained intact, and Japan's need to keep large forces on the Chinese mainland was a limiting factor on her strategy throughout World War II.

The peacetime strength of the Japanese army was 17 divisions. By 1940 it had 2 divisions in Japan and Korea, 12 in Manchuria and 27 in China. Even in 1943 the commitment in China still amounted to 25 infantry divisions, 1 armoured division, 11 mixed brigades, 1 cavalry brigade and 1 flying division – a total of 620,000 men and 14,000 vehicles. This force, known as the Kwantung Army, was called upon to provide a constant stream of reinforcements for the Pacific War, and by 1945 its units were understrength and too weak to pose any real threat.

307

307 Private 2nd Class, Japanese Army, 1937
The peaked cap with coloured band and piping of this infantryman was replaced by the peaked field cap on active service. The greatcoat is the standard pattern with detachable hood. Rank badges are worn on the shoulders. Equipment includes the waistbelt with ammunition pouches, bayonet for M38 rifle, water bottle and gas mask on right hip. The 6.5mm M38 Arisaka rifle was adapted from the German Mauser and, by 1937, was considered outdated.

308 Lieutenant, Japanese Army, 1937
This artillery officer wears the old-style service dress with stand collar and coloured collar patches with rank badges on the shoulders. The field cap with yellow cloth star on the front was standard issue, but the goggles suggest that his unit was motorised, or that he at least travelled in a car. A pistol is carried in the leather holster on the right hip, and field glasses in a case on the left.

309 Private, Japanese Army, 1941
This infantryman wears the standard M98 field service uniform with full equipment. On the waist belt are two 30-round pouches and at the back one 60-round ammunition pouch. On the left is the gas mask in canvas bag, and bayonet for the M38 rifle. On his back he carries a canvas pack with rolled greatcoat or ground sheet and entrenching tool and mess tin strapped to it.

Below: Heavily-laden Japanese soldiers are pictured while crossing a pontoon bridge in China. They wear M98 field service uniforms and carry bolt-action 6.5mm Arisaka rifles. The enormous distances which warfare in China necessitated were hard to cover, especially for an Army as unmechanised as the Japanese. Logistics were a constant problem for them.

308

309

The focus of the war moved away from China to the Pacific when Japan attacked American and British bases in the Far East in December 1941. The Army was involved in a number of amphibious operations in the Pacific Island chains although this area was the Navy's prime responsibility. The Army's greatest success was probably the capture of Singapore and the expulsion of the British from Malaya and Burma. Outnumbered by the British forces the spirit of the Japanese soldiers and the ability of their commanders proved unbeatable: by March 1942 the Japanese Army stood on the frontiers of India. The Army grew to a maximum strength of five million men, in 140 divisions and numerous small independent units.

The summer of 1942 marked the high-water mark of the Japanese advance, however, and when America's vast industrial and military strength was brought to bear the Japanese Army was forced over to the defensive. In the Pacific, US troops waged a bitter island-hopping war and in Burma the British eventually managed to get the upper hand against the extended Japanese Army.

Although the war was clearly lost for Japan by 1944 the Army fought on as resolutely as ever and continued to do so until ordered to lay down its arms following the surrender on 2 September 1945. The armed forces of Japan suffered 1,700,000 casualties during World War II.

ORGANISATION The figurehead presiding over the Japanese war machine was the Emperor, the titular Commander-in-Chief, who had the power to declare war and make peace. His power was actually merely formal. He was advised by two councils, the Board of Marshals and Admirals and the Supreme Military Council. The real power was vested in the Imperial Headquarters, however. This comprised the Army and Navy Chiefs of Staff, the Army and Navy Ministers and their service advisors. Responsible to these officers were the General Staff, the War Ministry and the two Inspectorates of Military Training and Aviation. The General Staff was composed of five main bureaux: general affairs, operations, intelligence, transport and historical. They prepared for war, trained the troops and researched Japan's strategical requirements. The Chief of the General Staff was officially appointed by the Emperor. The War Ministry – the focus of the Army's political power, for the War Minister sat in the Cabinet and was always a soldier – provided liaison with the Chief-of-Staff and in theory the *Diet* (or Parliament) and handled the administrative, logistical and mobilisation plans. The two Inspectorates undertook the training of the troops.

Once in the field, the Japanese army was divided into army groups, area armies, armies, divisions, and forces with special missions which were not commanded by any particular army or division. Groups of armies represented an entire theatre of war: the Japanese Defence Army, the Kwantung Army and the Southern Army. An area army like the 23rd in Burma was the equivalent of a British or an American field army. The Japanese army was much smaller than its British equivalent, mustering only a strong British corps strength. There were no army corps in the Japanese Army. A Japanese army would vary in size from 50,000–150,000 men. The 18th Army in the south-west Pacific in April 1943, for example, had a nominal strength of 130,000 men, though its actual strength was much lower. This force comprised three divisions and an independent mixed brigade. The artillery component consisted of four independent field artillery companies, two field machine gun companies, one independent anti-tank battalion, six field artillery battalions, six field searchlight companies, and support units, which included engineer, transport and airfield defence troops.

The dominant Japanese organisational weakness, throughout the war, was the splintering of formations. Men were taken from one unit, thrown together with men from another and given a special mission; once this had been undertaken, the unit was either split up again to form another or sent back to its parent formation. There was little continuity and consequently a profusion of independent units.

The typical Japanese infantry division of December 1941 consisted of three infantry regiments, an artillery regiment, a cavalry or reconnaissance regiment and a regiment of engineers. Along with the divisional staff and the signals unit, the division was supported by a transport regiment, a medical unit and field hospital staff, water purification unit, an ordnance unit and a veterinary unit. As the war progressed 'comfort battalions' of prostitutes were attached to the divisions. There was, however, a great variation in the organisation and strength of Japanese forces depending on their location and the terrain encountered.

Under the strain of war the Japanese categorised their forces under three headings: 'A' the strongest; 'B' representing the standard; and 'C' the special. Not all Japanese divisions were composed of the same category of men. A standard 'B' division might include 'A' category artillery. Further, there might also have been a variation in strength within the divisional units themselves. In an 'A' class infantry regiment, the regimental gun unit could be either one company of four guns or two companies of four guns under a small battalion HQ. Despite these variations there were generally four kinds of Japanese infantry division. First was the standard division of 'B' troops, the type most frequently encountered by Allied forces. Second was the strengthened division, composed of 'A' type units which might also include an additional artillery group, consisting of a group HQ and a field or a mountain artillery regiment and possibly a tank unit. Third was the modified strengthened division which included the additional artillery but not the armoured elements. The rifle company strength of this formation dropped from 265 to 205. Finally there was the special division. This was a lighter type of division composed mainly of 'C' troops with two brigades, each of four independent infantry battalions with supporting elements of small units of auxiliary troops (mainly of category 'A'). These divisions were frequently used for garrisoning Japan's small island bases and, in China, for combating guerrillas.

Left: Japanese paratroops prepare for action. Note the special helmets with which they were issued. Paratroops were not used in great numbers in their airborne role, although like their German counterparts they were employed as élite ground troops.

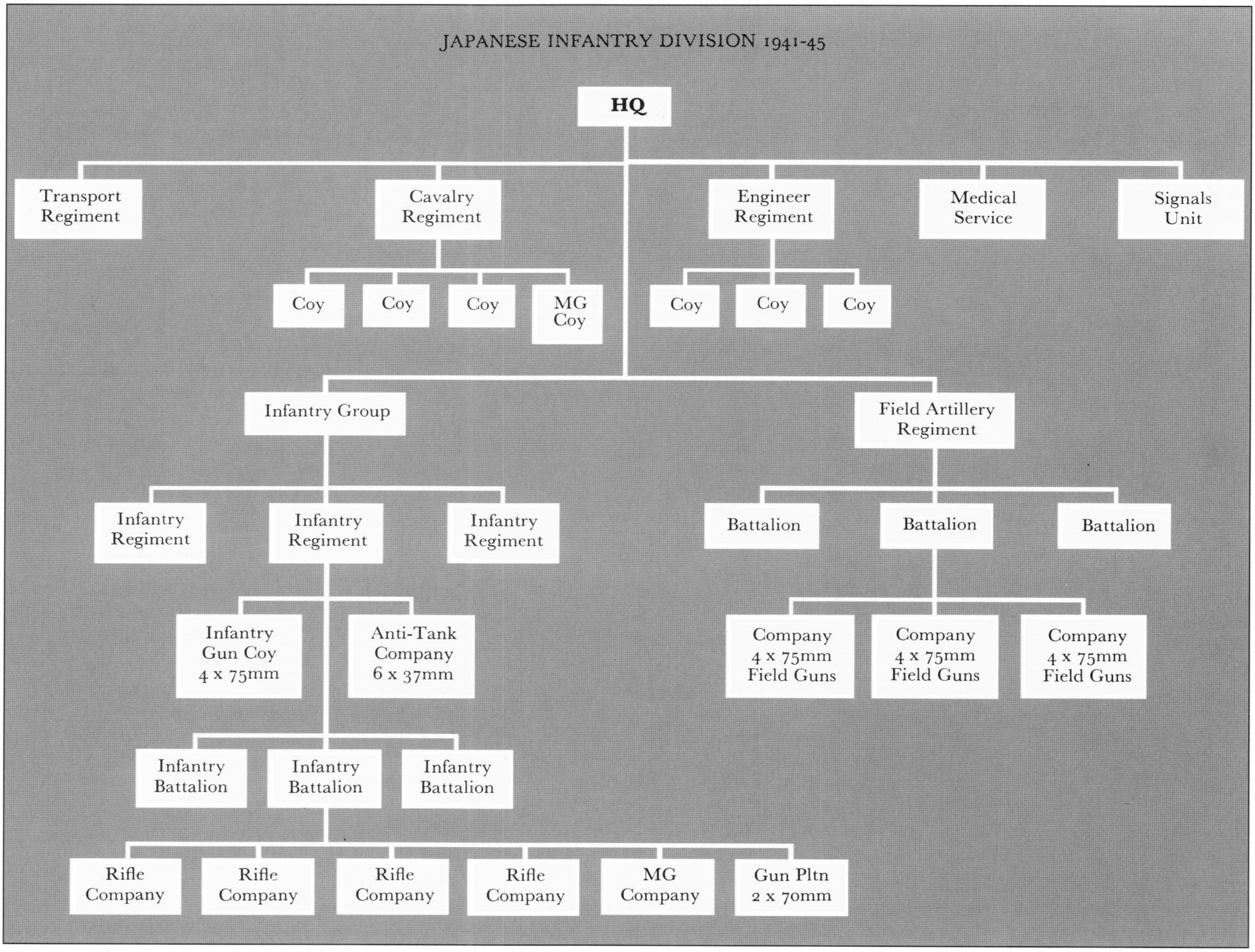

JAPANESE INFANTRY DIVISION 1941-45

- **HQ**
  - Transport Regiment
  - Cavalry Regiment
    - Coy
    - Coy
    - Coy
    - MG Coy
  - Engineer Regiment
    - Coy
    - Coy
    - Coy
  - Medical Service
  - Signals Unit
  - Infantry Group
    - Infantry Regiment
    - Infantry Regiment
      - Infantry Gun Coy 4 x 75mm
      - Anti-Tank Company 6 x 37mm
      - Infantry Battalion
      - Infantry Battalion
        - Rifle Company
        - Rifle Company
        - Rifle Company
        - Rifle Company
        - MG Company
        - Gun Pltn 2 x 70mm
      - Infantry Battalion
    - Infantry Regiment
  - Field Artillery Regiment
    - Battalion
    - Battalion
      - Company 4 x 75mm Field Guns
      - Company 4 x 75mm Field Guns
      - Company 4 x 75mm Field Guns
    - Battalion

Japanese divisions were commanded by lieutenant-generals, following the German rather than the British model. Each lieutenant-general had a colonel as his chief-of-staff. The divisional staff was divided into two sections: the general staff section and the administrative section. Added to these were five departmental sections and an ordnance, a signal and a veterinary detachment including about 300 officers and men; the division would also have at its disposal 32 telephones and 30 miles of insulated telephone wire, two ground to air radios and eight other radios. It also had pigeons, dogs, helio lamps and semaphores to aid communication. The infantry component of the division – the infantry group – was commanded by a major-general who co-ordinated the three regiments. He had his own HQ and staff of 70–100 officers and men. He might also be allocated tankette companies of 80–120 men with 10–17 tankettes. The group tankette companies were organised into three or four platoons and a company train. Their main purpose was reconnaissance and they were usually sent to divisions which lacked a cavalry or reconnaissance regiment.

The infantry regiment, commanded by a colonel, was formed of the regimental HQ and train, signal company, the regimental infantry gun train and anti-tank company and three infantry battalions with the possible addition of pioneer units. The regimental HQ was composed of 55 officers and men. They were mainly concerned with the tasks of administration, ordnance, and codes and intelligence, with a small detachment reserved for the anti-aircraft section, the headquarters guard and the colour guard. The pioneer or labour units were arranged in seven sections with a strength of 100–200 men. Men from the category 'B' units might find themselves arbitrarily used to build airfields or beach defences. The regimental artillery element consisted of a small HQ staff of 24 officers and men. While one company consisted of two platoons each with two low-velocity infantry guns, the other had three platoons, each with two 37mm and, later in the war, two 47mm anti-tank guns. The machine-gun companies were armed with 12, 8 or 4 machine guns and depending on this number would have a strength of 174, 144, or 73 officers and men.

The forces supporting the division were independent of the infantry group. The divisional artillery usually consisted of a regiment of field or mountain artillery. The guns might be motorised, horse-drawn or pack. There were three battalions with 12 × 75mm guns each, and three gun companies (each with four 75mm guns) and a regimental train, giving a total strength of 2300 men. The divisional cavalry regiment had three rifle and sabre companies and a machine-gun company, with a total strength of 950 officers and men. The medical units were of poor quality as Japanese soldiers were expected to stand, fight and die and would, therefore, not require an elaborate medical service. A Japanese division might have three field hospitals. Each medical unit consisted of three collecting companies of three stretcher platoons and one ambulance platoon each. In all it would have 180 litters and 45 ambulances. The headquarters train might also include additional carts for carrying the wounded and medical supplies. But these aspects of war were invariably neglected by the Japanese; indeed it was not unknown for their medical personnel to be armed and used as ordinary fighting troops.

Above: Japanese infantry are pictured in action in south China. This photograph clearly shows the shape of the standard Japanese helmet. The machine gun is the 6.5mm Type 96, which incorporated features of the Czechoslovak ZB.

310 Private 1st Class, Japanese Army, 1942

This infantryman wears typical jungle fighting uniform and equipment. The steel helmet is worn over the field cap with neckflaps. Badges of rank appear on the collar patches. Equipment is the standard infantry pattern, with water bottle, gas mask, waist belt with ammunition pouches and bayonet. Footgear consists of the canvas tabi.

310

311

The Japanese armoured division usually consisted of three tank regiments, and a motorised infantry brigade of 3800 men. The tank regiment would have a headquarters, three or four tank companies and a regimental ammunition train. The strength of the regiment was about 90 light and medium tanks and 800–850 men. In addition, there would be an artillery regiment of eight 105mm guns, and four 155mm howitzers; an anti-tank unit with 18 × 47mm anti-tank guns and an anti-aircraft unit of four 75mm guns and 16 × 20mm guns. There were also supporting engineers, transport and medical units. The whole division totalled 10,500 men and 1850 vehicles. Japanese armoured divisions had some success against poorly equipped Chinese forces, but were in no sense the equal of the tank forces of the other great powers.

The Japanese Army also had a large number of independent units and it was easy to organise special forces for specific missions. Rather than give all of these units heavy elements of anti-tank guns and artillery, these weapons were formed into independent units so that they could be used when needed. This trend reinforced the tendency towards fragmentation. In the first days of the war such combat teams spearheaded the Japanese advance into Malaya, the Dutch East Indies and the Solomons. The heavy losses sustained in 1943 were often due to a careless and haphazard combination of small independent units with little coordination and training. For example, one unit, the

312

311 Private, Japanese Army, 1941
The helmet of this tankman is the summer pattern made from cork covered in cotton drill with leather chin strap. On the lightweight tank troops' overall rank badges were usually worn on the collar. He carries a bayonet on his left and slung over his shoulders are a haversack, water bottle and gas mask. The Japanese soldier was frequently able to survive in extreme conditions – a trait the Allies found difficult to counter.

312 Captain, Japanese Army, 1939
The uniform of this tank officer is the standard M90 service dress for officers worn here with a tank helmet. This padded helmet came in both summer and winter versions, and later a model with a steel shell was introduced. Equipment is the standard pattern for officers. A pistol is carried in a holster which was worn suspended from a strap over the right shoulder. Other equipment such as binoculars, map case and water bottle was worn over the shoulders.

Right: Cadets at a Japanese military academy are taught how to identify different types of tanks, in this case Soviet models. Officer training in the Japanese Army was thorough and stressed the primacy of the offensive.

313 Superior Private, Japanese Army, 1937
This infantryman wears the special winter clothing for extreme climates with fur cap, double-breasted lined greatcoat, mittens and special felt boots with brown-leather uppers. Badges of rank are worn on the shoulders. The rifle is the 7.7mm M38 long rifle with bayonet.

314 Colonel, Japanese Army, 1944
This officer wears typical service dress as worn during the campaigns in Burma, Malaya and the Pacific. The cork sun helmet came in either white or light khaki. The shirt collar is worn outside the tunic collar, so the rank badges are pinned to the lapels of the tunic. Officers were also allowed to wear shirt sleeve order on active service or on informal occasions. The sword is the tachi *style and was worn suspended from a fabric belt worn under the tunic, or from the leather waistbelt.*

315 Lieutenant-General, Japanese Army, 1944
This soldier wears the standard general officers' uniform with rank insignia displayed on the collar patches and cuffs. Swords were a common feature in the Japanese Army.

6th Independent Anti-Aircraft Battalion, was rushed from Manchuria to Guadalcanal in 23 days to reinforce the task force thrown together in a hasty attempt to retake the island.

After about 1943 the Japanese also began to use raiding forces (*teishintai*). These were chosen from the infantry, and trained with a particular mission in mind; they were quite independent of larger forces. A typical role was the attempt by Japanese special forces in Burma to destroy British artillery by commando-style operations. The strength of these forces varied with the size of their objectives. A typical example included:
HQ group (officer, NCO and orderly);
demolition and assault section (15 men);
support section (12 men);
reserve section (12 men).

There were in addition small groups organised for raids into enemy territory to destroy bridges and lines of communication; to attack pillboxes, and fortified positions; demolition forces and tank fighting units; and also there were suicide squads which would be used to defend a vital point to the last man.

Within the more traditional army structure, special provision was made for amphibious operations. After 1941, amphibious brigades were created of three battalions with a total strength of 3200 men. Each battalion was 1035 strong and had three rifle companies of 195 men each, divided into three platoons of four sections each and a trench mortar platoon. The 1st Amphibious Brigade had supporting artillery, engineer, machine gun, signal and tank units operating under the brigade HQ which boosted its strength to about 4000 men. During the advance through Malaya each Japanese division was equipped with 50 small motorboats and 100 collapsible launches for the assault on Singapore. All of these were carried on the shoulders of the troops themselves. A first wave of 4000 men and 440 guns (with 20 rounds of ammunition for each) were ferried across in this way.

UNIFORM Japanese uniform developed both together and separately in its two principal theatres of war in China and

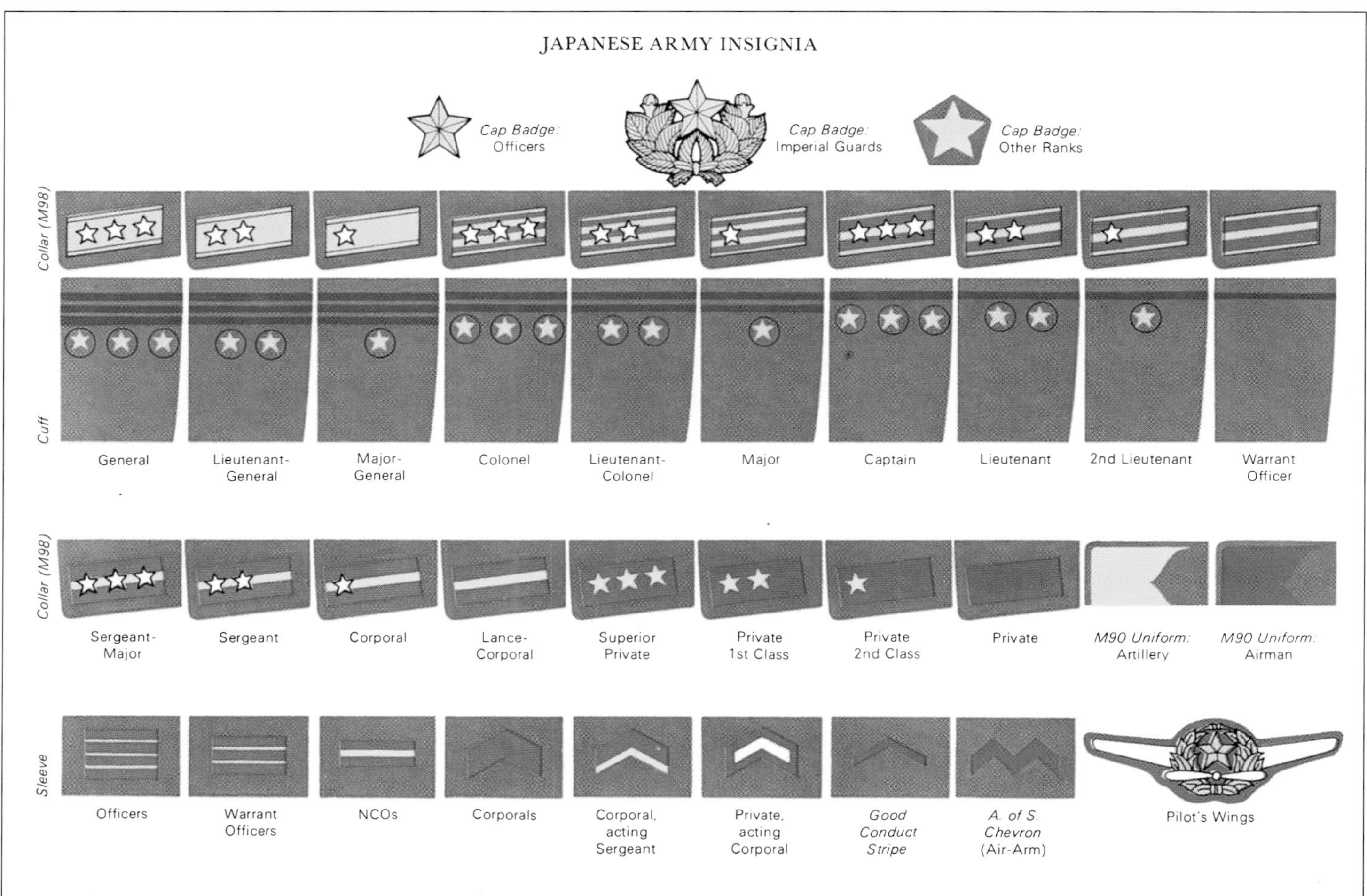

the Pacific. The beginning of the Sino-Japanese War in 1937 saw the Japanese Army dressed in uniforms introduced in 1930 which were designated Model 90. Two versions existed in either a yellowish khaki wool for wear in temperate climates, or in khaki drill for summer and tropical wear.

The basic service dress for officers is illustrated by figures 312 and 315. The wool tunic for other ranks was the same as the officers' model and was worn with matching pantaloons, puttees and leather ankle boots. The standard head-dress (a peaked cap) and greatcoat are illustrated by figure 307. Typical winter clothing worn in China is illustrated by figure 313.

On the M90 uniform badges of rank were worn on red passants on the shoulders while the colour of the collar patches on the tunic identified the arm of service.

Two types of steel helmet were in use at the beginning of the war in China. The first model was already on the way out, and was being replaced by the pattern worn throughout World War II which had a metal five-pointed star on the front.

The standard tunic for officers is worn by figure 315. Badges of rank were either on the tunic collar or lapels, or sometimes fixed to the shirt collar which was worn outside the tunic collar. Breeches and long trousers matched the tunic and were worn with either high boots, ankle boots and leather leggings or simply brown shoes with long trousers. Other ranks wore matching pantaloons with puttees tied in a distinctive criss-cross manner, with either leather ankle boots or black canvas *tabi* (a form of footwear with separate big toe). Special uniforms were introduced for crews of armoured fighting vehicles and parachute troops. Figure 312 is a tank officer wearing standard service dress with the padded tank helmet, while figure 311 shows a typical tank man in helmet and overall. There was also a two-piece winter tank suit with short lined jacket with synthetic fur collar and pocket on the left breast. The trousers were cut in the form of a bib and brace overall, like the American tank man's overalls. On the winter jacket badges of rank were worn on the left breast, while on the summer version they were worn on the collar.

Japanese Army parachute troops were first used in Palembang Sumatra in February 1942 and later in Leyte. They wore the uniform illustrated by figure 322. A whole range of infantry weapons had been developed for airborne use, and on Leyte the typical Japanese paratrooper carried the following weapons and equipment: Model 89 (1929) 50mm grenade discharger and four grenades, two small M94 (1934) smoke candles, two anti-tank grenades and a pick and mattock in a specially designed canvas bag strapped to the leg. Strapped to the other leg was another bag containing an M2 (1942) 7.7mm paratroop rifle, a bayonet, four more grenades for the M89 discharger two M97 (1937) hand grenades and 30 rounds of 7.7mm rifle ammunition. A third bag contained demolition material comprising three M99 (1939) magnetic mines and six blocks of demolition explosive. A fourth bag held a variety of canned and concentrated rations, extra socks, an extra shirt, first aid pouch and a length of rope.

INSIGNIA Badges of rank were worn on the shoulders, on the collar of tunics and shirts, and on the front or sleeve of various kinds of special clothing. The rank badges, which were small red rectangles with horizontal yellow or gold stripes and five-pointed stars, were detachable (see rank insignia chart). On the cuffs of the greatcoat officers wore khaki rank distinction lace (one for company, two for field and three for general officers). In 1944 this system was extended to the tunic cuffs (see figure 315).

Arm-of-service colours appeared on the collar patches on the M90 tunic, but in 1938 rank badges were moved to the collar patches, and from this date arm of service was identified by small yellow metal badges worn on the collar behind the collar patches, or by a zigzag strip of cloth in the arm-of-service colour which was worn on the right (sometimes also on the left) breast. The basic colours were scarlet for infantry, and tanks until 1940, green for cavalry, yellow for artillery and dark brown for engineers.

Air force

There was no independent Japanese air force. The Army and the Navy each had their own air service. Each was nominally controlled by the Emperor. Actual control was vested in the General Staff, the Army and Navy Ministries and the Inspector General of Aviation.

The function of the Japanese Army Air Service was to provide support for the ground troops and to conduct counter-air force operations. It was not expected to initiate strategic operations on its own behalf, as was the case with the RAF for instance.

The Air Service was relatively small at the outbreak of war and Japan's highly-trained pilots were soon casualties. Their replacements lacked the necessary flying ability to take on the growing technical and numerical superiority of the Americans. Partly as a response to this shortage *kamikaze* aircraft were introduced. The *kamikaze* aircraft was simply an aimed bomb in which the pilot sat over an explosive charge and aimed the aircraft at the target. First used at Leyte Gulf, these planes caused some consternation to the American forces; but overall their effect was negligible to the final outcome of the conflict.

The Japanese Army Air Service was organised into five air armies with clear areas of operations. Coordination was achieved between the Army and the Air Service by placing the air forces in each theatre under the command of the theatre commander. The largest Japanese tactical organisation was the air division, two or more of which would form an air army. Beneath this was the air brigade; two air brigades formed an air division. The composition of the brigade was flexible. Its HQ was small and concerned primarily with tactical planning. It was usually composed of three or four air regiments; each regiment was equipped with the same type of aircraft (fighters, or light or medium bombers) divided into three or four companies. The company was the most important operational unit; it was normally of nine aircraft, divided into three sections, each of three aircraft.

The total strength of the Japanese Army Air Service in 1940 was 36 fighter, 28 light and 22 medium bomber and 29 reconnaissance companies, with a personnel total of 33,000 officers and men.

Uniform As a branch of the Army, Japanese Air Service personnel wore Army uniforms with sky-blue arm-of-service colour which appeared on the zigzag breast badge, and on the collar patches, tunic and shoulder strap piping of Air Force cadets. Qualified pilots wore embroidered 'wings' on the right breast in the traditional manner.

The winter flying suit is worn by figure 316. The two-piece summer version was unlined. The only insignia worn on flying clothing were the badges of rank which were worn either on the breast or sleeve of the winter jacket, or on the collar of the summer jacket. Pilots' wings were also worn on the flying jacket.

Below: Japanese bomber crews are lined up on an airfield in northern China in preparation for a raid on the city of Chungking. They are wearing the regulation issue summer flying uniform with rank insignia displayed on the left breast.

316

316 Captain, Japanese Air Force, 1943
This fighter pilot wears the lined winter flying suit with rank badge on the left sleeve. He carries a short version of the tachi *sword, which was symbolically carried in the aircraft. The parachute harness is the standard pattern. He is also armed with an 8mm M94 automatic pistol.*

317

318

317 Commander, Japanese Navy, 1941
This officer wears the regulation peaked cap with embroidered cap badge and fur-lined watchcoat with badges of rank on the shoulder straps. The binoculars had a strap in different colours according to the rank group of the wearer: flag officers had gold, commanders white and lieutenants blue.

318 Seaman 1st Class, Japanese Navy, 1939
This rating in landing rig wears the Navy pattern steel helmet with the anchor badge on the front which was replaced during the war by the standard Army pattern. With the basic square rig he wears infantry equipment and white canvas gaiters. Badges of rank are worn on the sleeve. The rifle is the 7.7mm M38 long rifle.

NAVY

By mid-1941 the Japanese Navy was finalising its plans for the Pacific war. Firstly, the US Pacific Fleet was to be knocked out and, at the same time, warships would support the Army's southwards drive to gain the oil and raw materials necessary for Japan's existence and military success in China. A defensive perimeter was to be established through the islands of South-East Asia and the Pacific; it was thought that the Americans would grow weary of battering at this impregnable screen.

When war was declared on the United States in December 1941 Japan had made several serious miscalculations. She had underestimated the will of the American people to fight a long, drawn-out war and had, perhaps, been overconfident of her own fighting ability, together with her wartime ship-building capacity. Although the Japanese Command had recognised that fast carrier strikes were the best strategic weapon for the Pacific war (shipboard and land-based aviation had seen extensive service during the China campaign), her success at Pearl Harbor was somewhat lessened by her failure to destroy even one aircraft carrier.

During the initial run of Japanese victories, however, Allied forces in the Pacific had been building up and in April 1942 there were six American and three British aircraft carriers in the theatre against a Japanese total of ten. The Japanese attempt to isolate Australia in May 1942 in the battle of the Coral Sea was a failure and resulted in heavy losses among aircrew. The following month saw the battle of Midway and further disaster for the Japanese Fleet, which was severely mauled by carrier-based planes: four of her carriers were sunk for the loss of only one US Navy carrier.

The Japanese had lost superiority and naval operations now became concentrated in the South Pacific. After the heavy losses at Coral Sea, Midway and Guadalcanal the Navy began to run short of experienced pilots; squadrons were not rotated so that trainees did not learn from the experience of front-line pilots. An extensive carrier construction programme was instigated, but Japanese industrial capability was not sufficient for this to change the course of the war. In April 1943 the Navy failed to regain air superiority in the South-West Pacific after launching a concerted offensive, a defeat which indicated the significance of better-trained American pilots flying new aeroplanes from the recently-introduced Essex-class carriers.

In June 1944 the Japanese launched an unsuccessful attack on US naval forces in the battle of the Philippine Sea; this resulted in the loss of around 300 aircraft and the sinking of three Japanese aircraft carriers. Shortly thereafter (in October) the Japanese Fleet finally ceased to exist as an important force in the war when, with the loss of four carriers, three battleships and ten cruisers in the Battle of Leyte Gulf, her surface fleet was destroyed.

Unable to accept the idea of defeat and with no proper defensive strategy, the Japanese Navy now wasted surviving aircrew in *kamikaze* attacks, achieving only a limited measure of success.

ORGANISATION As Prime Minister, General Hideki Tojo presided over Imperial General Headquarters (GHQ) which was split in two sections – Army and Navy. Holding positions at Imperial GHQ were the Navy Minister, Admiral Shigetaro, and the Chief of the Navy General Staff, Admiral Osami Nagano. Other officers and departments handled the responsibilities of staff and ministry.

Executing the naval instructions emanating from Imperial GHQ was the C-in-C of all seagoing warships. In 1941, this was Admiral Isoroku Yamamoto, and following his death in April 1943, his successors were Admiral Mineichi Koga, Admiral Soemu Toyoda (from March 1944) and Admiral Jisaburo Ozawa (from May 1945 to the end of the war).

In addition to the responsibility for implementing strategic moves generally, they were also expected to take tactical command of the most important operation in progress. Admiral Yamamoto flew his flag in the battleship *Nagato* until the superbattleship *Yamato* was commissioned on 16 December 1941. There was a constant restriction on radio communication whenever she put to sea, and at such crucial times, the C-in-C was out of touch with all but the immediate situation. From May to September 1944, the C-in-C's flagship was the *Oyodo*, a command cruiser for combined striking forces of submarines and aircraft. Although permanently anchored first in Tokyo and then in Hiroshima Bay, her communications facilities proved inadequate. The HQ of C-in-C Combined Fleet was finally located at Keio University in the Tokyo suburb of Hiyodashi.

As its name implies, the Combined Fleet (*Rengo Kantai*) was just that – the whole Navy. All other units, regardless of function or size, were designated as *tai* or *butai*, both of which could be translated as corps, force or body. The intelligence sections of other navies assigned the terms fleet, squadron and division for the purpose of description as appropriate.

It was customary for groups of smaller warships to be led by a bigger one. Thus four destroyers made up a division, four divisions a destroyer squadron, plus a cruiser as flagship. A somewhat similar organisation existed for submarines.

For administrative purposes, the Combined Fleet was divided into lesser fleets according to function. At the time of Pearl Harbor in December 1941, its approximate composition was as follows:

1st Fleet (the Battle Fleet) based at Hiroshima – 10 battleships, 3 seaplane carriers, 10 cruisers, 30 destroyers;
2nd Fleet (Scouting Fleet) based at Hainan – 13 cruisers, 32 destroyers;
3rd Fleet (Blockade and Transport) based at Formosa – 5 cruisers, 12 destroyers, 6 minelayers, 1 escort;
4th Fleet (the Pacific Mandated Islands) based at Truk – 4 cruisers, 1 seaplane carrier, 12 destroyers, 2 minelayers;
5th Fleet (Northern Waters) based at Maizuru/Ominato – 2 cruisers;
6th Fleet (Submarines) based at Kwajalein – 3 cruisers, 63 submarines;
Carrier Fleet based at Kure – 10 carriers.

In addition there were base forces located on the islands of Formosa, Truk, Palau, Saipan, Kwajalein, Maizuru and Ominato, and in Indo-China. These and other support units totalled 89 armed merchant cruisers, sub-chasers and patrol vessels, 6 minelayers, 42 minesweepers, 46 auxiliaries and 87 transports. All those which had started life as merchantmen retained their '*maru*' suffix, some being manned by civilian crews. Repair ships and transports had their own special flag.

Vessels did not all operate in these administrative groupings, but were allocated to whatever formation required their presence. Thus the Pearl Harbor strike force consisted of six vessels from the Carrier Fleet, and two battleships, two cruisers and a destroyer squadron from the Battle Fleet. The Southern Force, heading towards South-East Asia and the Philippines, comprised the whole of the 2nd and 3rd Fleets, plus battleships, cruisers and destroyers from the 1st Fleet, as well as submarines, some of which had been allocated to, and then detached from the 1st Fleet.

319 Rating, Japanese Navy, 1942
This rating is wearing the white rig which was worn for clean work, such as clerical and office duties. Note the single blue band around the cap, whereas all commissioned ranks had two blue bands.

320 Lieutenant, Japanese Navy, 1943
This officer wears the cap with white cover and regulation whites. Badges of rank were worn on the shoulder straps. On his left hip he carries an undress dirk which was suspended from a fabric belt worn under the tunic.

319 320

Every force had a scouting and a main body, which was quite separate from the 2nd or Scouting Fleet and from the Combined Fleet main body which concentrated at sea around the C-in-C's flagship. Sometimes these groupings were assembled before departure, sometimes they rendezvoused at sea, and sometimes their routes were so planned that the first time they sighted each other after crossing the ocean, the enemy would be in view.

Such detailed and complicated plans worked well when operating from the centre, as in the first six months of the war, but they could also go seriously awry as they did in the triple Coral Sea-Midway-Aleutians thrust.

Japanese Navy personnel totalled 291,359 in December 1941, rising to 1,663,223 in July 1945. Officers were trained at the Eta Jima Naval Academy. There was further training at various specialist schools, in particular at the main base area around Yokosuka, but it was the cadet's graduation position after three years at the Academy which determined his future career. Those with a first class grade were destined for Staff College and headquarters appointments; second grade – battleships and cruisers; third – destroyers; fourth – submarines; fifth – naval aviation. The sixth grade were regarded as virtual failures, given no further training and consigned to duties in auxiliary patrol and depot ships.

Probably the Japanese Navy's worst mistake was to ignore the merchant marine which in 1939 numbered 2337 vessels, totalling 5,629,845 tons. As indicated by the Eta Jima graduations, commerce protection was uninteresting, and fit only for the unintelligent. Admittedly, in 1939–40 there had been courses for training mercantile masters in Navy procedures, but they had not amounted to much. There was no preparation for a DEMS (defensively equipped merchant ships) organisation, nor was much attention paid to combating undersea warfare, whether in the form of mines or submarines. There was not even any convoy system, although the Japanese Navy had assisted in escorting convoys during World War I.

A further 4,250,000 tons of merchant shipping was built or acquired during World War II, but it still could not keep pace with the losses inflicted by American submarines. Convoys were begun in November 1943, and escort vessels laid down, but they were introduced too late and were still vulnerable to attack from submarines.

A total of 2346 merchant ships were sunk during the war, and most of the survivors were disabled or too small for practical traffic, or were lying idle as Army or Navy transports.

321

322

Built to cooperate with the surface fleet, the Submarine Fleet was employed principally in scouting for the Battle Fleet, also deploying seaplanes and midget submarines against coastal targets from Madagascar to Oregon. There were a few notable occasions when submarines successfully interfered in the set-piece air-sea battles, but generally they did little to disrupt Allied supply lines.

Parallel with the warship organisation was the Directorate of Naval Aviation which, in 1941, was organised under Vice-Admiral Katagiri. The General Affairs Department was responsible for both shore-based and ship-borne units, while the Training Department arranged for nearly all training to be done in Japan by the Combined Air Training Command, principally at Kasumigara. The Technical Department prepared designs for new aircraft and equipment, and undertook their storage and repair at Navy air arsenals, including Yokosuka, Kasumigara, Hiro, Sasebo, Kanoya and

321 Officer, Japanese Navy, 1945
Like their counterparts in the US Navy, Japanese Navy personnel adopted khaki during the war. The Navy emblem appears on the front of the field cap and the two blue stripes denoted an officer.

322 Paratrooper, Japanese Navy Parachute Troops, 1942
The helmet is the steel pattern covered with canvas; this replaced the old fibre helmet which afforded no ballistic protection for the head. The overall was sometimes worn over the olive-drab naval khaki uniform. Clipped to the parachute harness is a special weapons container which held either firearms or a light mortar.

323 Sub-Lieutenant, Japanese Navy Air Service, 1945
This pilot wears the two-piece summer flying suit which was worn both by Army and Navy pilots. The form of rank badge illustrated was unusual, since most pilots either wore naval collar patches or one 'collar' patch on the breast or on the left sleeve. The Japanese Navy Air Service played a crucial role in the sea battles of the Pacific theatre which decided the course of the war. By 1945 the Air Service had few experienced pilots left.

323

alongside other Navy installations.

Apart from 370 training and reserve machines, the Japanese Naval Air Force totalled 1750 aircraft in 1941. There were 660 fighters (mainly the legendary Mitsubishi A6M Zero), 330 carrier-borne strike aircraft, 240 twin-engined shore-based torpedo-bombers specifically intended for fleet cooperation, and 520 flying boats and seaplanes. It was standard procedure for floatplanes to be catapulted from cruisers for fleet reconnaissance, thus allowing the strike carriers to be freed from that task.

All these aircraft were organised in the Combined Air Fleet, based at Kanoya, and were subdivided into the 1st Air Fleet (the Carrier Fleet) and the 11th Air Fleet (under Vice-Admiral Nishizo Tsukuhura) shore-based in Formosa and Indo-China. The fleets were further divided into air flotillas (each commanded by a rear-admiral), which were themselves composed of two or more air groups. Each air group comprised a base unit and 12 to 36 aircraft with 4 to 12 in reserve, depending on size. The combat formation was the air division of about nine aeroplanes.

Navy land forces

There were no such thing as 'marines' in the Japanese armed forces until after the First World War. Under the *ad hoc* tradition of the Japanese Army, if amphibious operations were imminent, naval landing groups were improvised for individual missions. Every Navy recruit received training in land as well as naval warfare. If a recruit showed any aptitude for this and showed any special skills, such as proficiency with a machine gun or the ability to drive, they were noted on his file for future reference. The fleet commander would nominate several ships to provide troops for amphibious operations and from these crews assault groups were organised. Needless to say, the military training of these sailors was scanty and their casualties heavy. In the 1920s the Japanese Navy began to experiment with special naval landing forces in an attempt to overcome these heavy losses of highly trained naval personnel. These were permanent units and were first used in China in 1932. During World War II they became increasingly involved in the defence of Japan's island bases. To further this defence, the Japanese Navy developed several other land formations: the base force, the ground force, the pioneers and the engineering and construction units. These formations never matched the excellence of US engineers, however.

The special naval landing forces usually stayed in the areas they seized as garrisons. When unopposed their efficiency was high, but their tactical skills were mediocre

Below left: The colour party of a Japanese naval detachment marches through the streets of Osaka before embarkation to the Front in China.

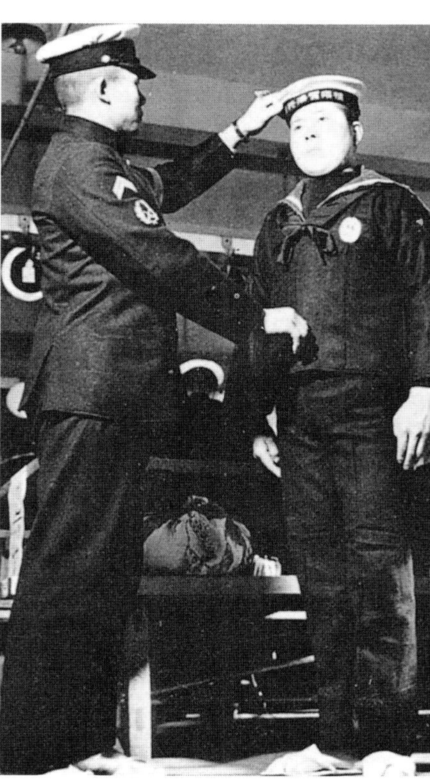

Below centre: A Japanese naval recruit is issued with his uniform.

Below right: A Navy pilot, complete with life-jacket, helps prepare a Kawanishi E7K2 floatplane.

324

324 Leading Seaman, Japanese Navy, 1942

Japanese Marines took a very active part in the combined operations during the Japanese offensive in the Pacific. Marines were distinguished by the olive-green colour of their khaki uniforms and by black leather footwear, and other minor differences in clothing and equipment. Rank badges are worn on the right sleeve. This Marine is protected by a bullet-proof vest and is armed with a Swiss 7.63mm sub-machine gun which was modified by the Japanese. The rank badges conform to the old style (as compared to the new style on page 265).

when opposed. At first they were organised into battalions of about 2000 men of four companies. The first three companies were divided into six rifle platoons and one heavy machine gun platoon. The last company, the fourth, was composed of three rifle platoons and a heavy weapons platoon which was equipped with four 3-inch naval guns and two 75mm regimental guns and two 70mm battalion guns. Depending on circumstances they might be supported with tank or armoured car units. On the outbreak of war they were used to seize small islands like Wake, and were used as spearheads by the Army against Java and Rabaul. In these operations they might be used as mobile striking forces. They would be employed with two rifle companies (each with its own machine-gun platoon) and one or two companies of heavy weapons in formations of 1200–1500 men. They might also include special supporting troops, engineers, ordnance and signals. Once Japan lost the initiative in the Pacific these forces had to adapt to defensive warfare, particularly when the Army refused to defend some islands, claiming that they were a Navy responsibility. Consequently, formations were adapted to meet this change. A typical example was the Yokosaka 7th Special Naval Landing Force. When first used at the beginning of the war, this formation had no infantry for defensive purposes and no heavy defensive weapons. By 1943 the platoon

Right: Japanese Marines watch the bombardment of the city of Manila in the spring of 1942. The fall of Manila was one of the stepping-stones of Japan's conquest of the Philippines. This reconnaissance detachment is wearing the regulation Marine uniform of olive-drab with cloth covers over their helmets. The bugler in the centre of the picture is armed with the M98 Arisaka rifle, as are most of the other Marines. In contrast to the Marine illustrated above (figure 324) these soldiers are wearing puttees (and not the black leather boots and leggings).

JAPANESE NAVY INSIGNIA

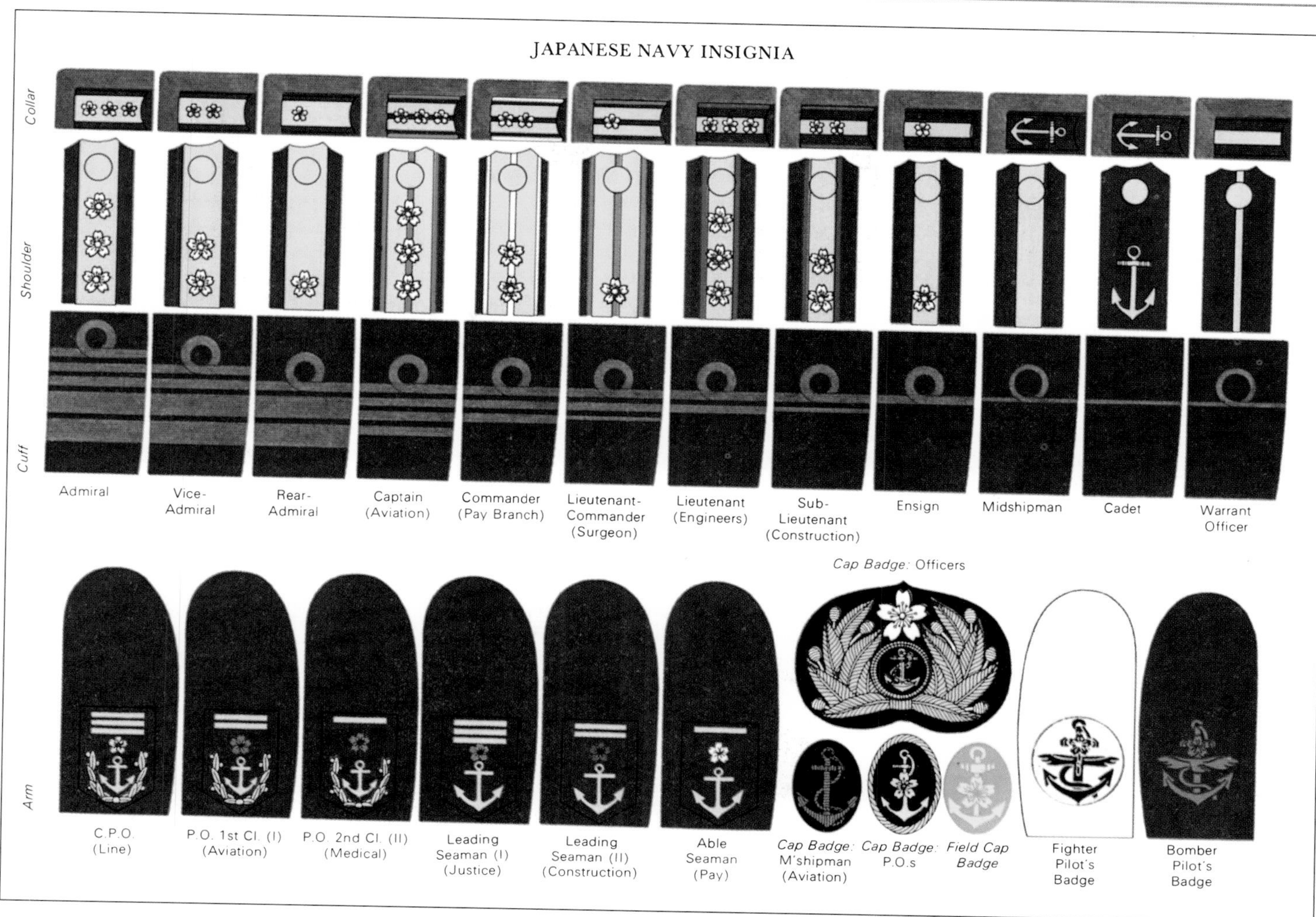

rather than the company had become the basic tactical unit and its artillery component had been greatly increased.

UNIFORM Of all the navies of the great powers, Japan's was the youngest and the uniforms worn by its personnel were basically the same as those introduced when the Navy was first formed at the end of the last century. To the pre-war navy blue and white uniforms were added those in various shades of khaki.

Officers wore the peaked cap with embroidered cap badge and undress tunic with stand collar which was trimmed with black lace. On the cuffs rank distinction lace was in black. This tunic was worn with matching trousers and black shoes and socks. In winter officers wore various kinds of double-breasted watch and greatcoats (figure 317). In summer or in tropical waters officers wore the white uniform illustrated by figure 320, which much resembled that of other navies.

Chief petty officers wore the peaked cap with special badge, single-breasted tunic in navy blue or white with five gilt metal buttons in front. It was worn with matching long trousers and black shoes and socks.

Ratings wore the square rig illustrated by figure 318. The basic head-dress was the round sailor's cap with silk tally on which appeared Japanese characters. The matching trousers were worn with either black leather footwear or white socks and sandals. The white version of the square rig was identical in cut to the navy blue one. The dress version was worn with the blue denim collar and was trimmed with blue denim. The working whites were plain, but ratings also received a one-piece white overall.

During the war the Japanese Navy received a peaked field cap in navy blue, white or khaki, which was identical in shape to the Army pattern. The anchor badge on the front was in yellow on the navy blue and khaki caps, and light blue on the white cap.

Sailors serving on land during the war wore a field uniform made of olive-drab cotton drill. The colour was more similar to that worn by American Marines than to the uniform of the Japanese Army. A typical Japanese Marine in service dress is illustrated by figure 324. Officers wore brown leather equipment and short black leather boots. Navy parachute troops wore the uniform illustrated by figure 322.

A khaki drill uniform consisting of field cap, short sleeve shirt with left breast pocket, open necked single-breasted tunic with patch breast and side pockets, and either short or long trousers was introduced during the war for Navy personnel.

INSIGNIA Officers wore their rank badges on the collar and sometimes on the tunic lapels. Shoulder straps were only worn on the white tunic and various kinds of greatcoat. They were occasionally worn on the khaki tunic.

On the peaked field cap officers had one or two stripes (yellow on blue and blue on white and khaki caps) according to rank. Originally ratings had one stripe and officers two, but this was changed so that ratings had no stripes, lieutenants one, and captains two stripes. From January 1944 officers began to wear one to three narrow lace rings above one to three cherry blossoms on the cuffs of both the blue and khaki tunics.

Ratings wore rate badges on the sleeves. The first pattern was in red on the blue uniform, and light blue on the white uniform. These were replaced by a new pattern (see rank insignia chart) in yellow on blue backing, worn on all uniforms.

The branch was indicated by the emblem which appeared in red on a circular blue badge on the right sleeve. On white uniforms the emblem was in light blue. On the new pattern rate badge the colour of the cherry blossom indicated the branch of the wearer. Officers in certain branches had coloured piping on the collar patches, shoulder straps, and possibly also on the bottom of the peaked cap band.

JAPANESE ALLIES

With the exception of the Indian National Army, the Japanese were not very enthusiastic about recruiting non-Japanese to do their fighting for them, and although Japan occupied vast territories she never really attempted to raise coherent military units from amongst the subject peoples. Most units raised from foreigners were employed in construction work, or, as in the case of the White Russians from Harbin in Manchuria, were formed into small units for clandestine operations behind enemy lines. The intense martial code of the Japanese was ill-suited to other nationalities.

Below: Supplies are handed out to troops of the Indian National Army who have just deserted from the Japanese. The reliability of the INA was always questionable and during the course of the war they proved more a liability than an asset to the Japanese. The soldiers here are shown wearing their old regular Indian Army uniforms and equipment.

INDIAN NATIONAL ARMY

The Indian National Army (INA), inspired by the goal of achieving independence for India from British rule, was raised in January 1942 at Kuala Lumpur. Its recruits were Indian prisoners of war, some only hours out of battle, enlisted by Captain (later General) Mohan Singh, previously of the 14th Punjab Regiment. With the fall of Singapore in February 1942 there were approximately 55,000 Indian POWs available to Mohan Singh and about 20,000 joined the INA in its first months of existence. A further 20,000 POWs enlisted in the summer of 1942 largely as a means of escaping the deprivations of prison-camp life and the brutal treatment handed out to those who stood firm in their allegiance to the British. Some Indian and Gurkha troops joined simply in order to return to a battlefront from which they could regain the British lines, while others joined to sabotage the INA from within. In general very few recruits were pro-Japanese.

In September 1942 one poorly equipped division was formed with three guerrilla units – the Gandhi, Nehru, and Azad Regiments – and three infantry battalions, the No. 1 Hindi Field Force Group. Supporting units included artillery, motorised, engineer, signal, and transport companies, a reinforcement group, and a medical unit with hospital. A second division was planned but in December disagreements with the Japanese led to an

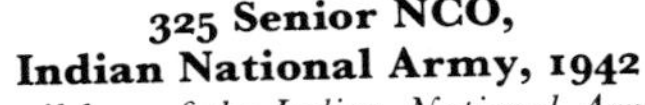

325 Senior NCO, Indian National Army, 1942
This havildar *of the Indian National Army wears the old Indian Army khaki drill uniform with a khaki turban. The rank of this soldier is identified by the cloth coloured stripes on the shoulder straps. No arms are being carried except for the regulation British bayonet.*

326 1st Sergeant, Chinese Army, 1942
The sergeant shown here is unusually well equipped for the Chinese Army, whose members were normally badly supplied. This NCO is part of the presidential guard. He wears a German helmet, and his rank is indicated by the three gold triangles on the blue stripe. The khaki uniform is the regulation woollen field service dress with a stand and fall collar and patch pockets on the tunic. Above the left breast pocket is an identification patch bordered in red arm-of-service colour for the infantry. Well equipped, this soldier is armed with the 7.63mm Mauser semi-automatic pistol complete with wooden holster acting here as a butt extension (just visible below his left hand). Used by the German Army in World War I, the Mauser was modified post-war to take a 20-round magazine and a wooden stock and it was this version that proved popular with the Chinese warlords.

326

80 per cent reduction in the strength of the INA as many of its personnel requested that they should be allowed to revert to the status of POWs. Only with the arrival from Germany of Subhas Chandra Bose, the head of the Provisional Government of Free India, did the appeal of the INA begin to achieve any enduring foundation. Bose had already formed the Free India Legion in Germany from 2500 POWs in Annaburg Camp near Dresden.

Bose persuaded the Japanese to bring the INA's second division to a state of operational readiness and he secured permission for the establishment of a third division. The 1st Division was deployed between January–June 1944 in support of the Japanese offensives in the Arakan and against Kohima and Imphal. Of the 7000 men who joined the operations in the Imphal plain only 2600 survived the fighting and subsequent retreat.

UNIFORM The INA wore either Indian Army khaki drill uniforms with puggree or field service side cap in khaki cloth. Japanese uniforms were also issued. On the left side of the side cap was worn a brass cap badge in the shape of a map of India with the letters INA.

INSIGNIA Badges of rank were worn on the shoulder straps which were usually in khaki cloth. NCOs had one to three stripes across the shoulder strap, company officers one to three stripes above the letters INA, field officers one to three stripes surmounted by an eight-pointed star above the letters INA (all in metallic thread embroidery), and general officers one to three bars surmounted by crossed sabres with an eight-pointed star above, once again all in metallic thread embroidery.

BURMESE NATIONAL ARMY

The Minaimi Organisation in Burma was founded in February 1940. Its 50 members carried out clandestine operations in aid of the Burma Independence Movement. With the beginning of the war in the Far East these men provided the cadre for the Burma Independence Army which, by the time Burma had been overrun by the Japanese, had a strength of 50,000 men which rose to about 200,000. But Japanese occupation policies so disillusioned the BIA that it became a centre for opposition to the Japanese and was disbanded.

The Japanese then formed the Burma Defence Army which was organised in seven infantry battalions, and artillery and miscellaneous units. By April 1943 its strength was about 55,000 men.

On 15 September 1943 the BDA was renamed the Burma National Army (*Bama Tatmadaw*), but it was still only used for garrison duties. By the autumn of 1944 a resistance movement had developed and in March 1945 first the BNA in Mandalay and then the rest of the Army changed sides. On 30 April 1945 the BNA was reorganised by the British as the Patriotic Burmese Forces.

UNIFORM AND INSIGNIA The Burmese forces fighting for the Japanese never found a standardised pattern of uniform and insignia, but wore a variety of British, Japanese and native dress, depending on what was available.

From 1938 Koreans were allowed to enlist for military service, but were mainly used as labourers in Army and Navy constructions corps. In 1944 Koreans were subject to conscription by the Japanese.

In May 1939 the Japanese recruited a number of Mongolian cavalrymen who served alongside Japanese cavalry units under Japanese officers. The Manchurian Army proper in 1939 had a strength of some 75,000 men in infantry and cavalry units. The Mongolian Navy was stationed on the Amur and Sungari rivers which it patrolled with eight large and six small river gunboats.

The puppet government established at Nanking in China was allowed to raise its own forces; these were of dubious reliability and fluctuated in size. Although local disputes often took precedence over national issues, few Chinese fought for the Japanese.

In Sumatra, a force of about five to six thousand men was formed for coastal defence. Many of the men had previously served in the Netherlands East India Army, and seventeen Indonesians were trained in the Imperial Japanese Military Academy.

The Japanese allowed the Malays to form a volunteer force of some 2000 men in early 1944. Some personnel had uniforms and captured British firearms. By March 1944 this so-called Volunteer Corps had a strength of about 5000 men and was used for coastal defence and the maintenance of public order. One Malay graduated from the Imperial Japanese Military Academy.

On 8 December 1943 'General' Artemio Ricarte formed the Patriotic League of Filipinos with about 4000 members who were used on guard and construction duties. Both qualified instructors and arms were in short supply. This was followed by a security force of 300 men, also under Ricarte's command, which provided the personnel for his Guard.

In the other occupied territories various forces were raised: a force of some 1300 Dyaks was formed in 1944 for security duties in North Borneo, for example, and in March 1944 the Japanese formed an Indo-Chinese *Giyutai* of about 3000 men.

The Java Defence Volunteer Army was formed on Java, since the Japanese had only very limited forces there with which to resist an expected invasion. By November 1944, there were 66 battalions with about 33,000 men on Java and three battalions with about 1500 men on Bali, although the Japanese did not recruit in the Christian areas from where the Netherlands East India Army had traditionally acquired its indigenous troops.

Another 50,000 men were formed into a Moslem para-military training organisation (*Hizbullah*), but its weaponry was seldom more sophisticated than sharpened bamboos. There were a number of other para-military organisations and groups with a total membership in the region of one and a half million men, but they did not play any significant role in the war.

CHINA
ARMY

The seizure of Mukden on 19 September 1931 marked the beginning of overt Japanese aggression against China, and from 1937 there was open war. The disorganised Chinese forces were no match on the battlefield for the Japanese armies, but determined resistance prevented a complete collapse. The very size of China precluded a total Japanese victory, and although the Chinese Nationalist government was forced to abandon the major industrial areas and set up a new capital at Chunking, it maintained the struggle, and, in alliance with the communist forces of Mao Tse-tung, tied down enormous numbers of Japanese troops.

Left: A light field gun (a US 75mm howitzer) is brought into action at an engagement late in the war. Short of arms and equipment the generals of the Chinese Nationalist Army placed great value upon artillery, not so much for military reasons but for the prestige it bestowed.

327 Private, Chinese Nationalist Army, 1942

This soldier wears blue quilted winter uniform, with white stockings and plimsoll-type shoes secured with string or tapes. His personal equipment was made largely of cotton or canvas and secured with ribbons or string. He carries small-arms ammunition in a cotton bandolier round his shoulders and waist, stick-type German grenades in canvas pockets round his neck and a captured Japanese gas mask and helmet.

327

328

328 Colonel, Chinese Nationalist Army, 1942

The ski-type khaki peaked cap of this Nationalist infantry officer carries the Chinese cockade. The collar patches in the red arm-of-service colour bear the three triangles of a colonel, while his service dress is completed by the ubiquitous Sam Browne belt. The uniform of this colonel, like that of figure 326, has a distinctly German feel reflecting the German involvement in the building-up of the Chinese Army in the 1920s and early '30s. Footwear is European in style and consists of brown leather ankle boots and knee-length leggings.

329 Private, Chinese Nationalist Army, 1944

Re-equipped and re-clothed by the Allies in Northern Burma, this Chinese infantryman wears British khaki drill uniform, woollen knitted sweater and 1937 webbing equipment. Woollen puttees are worn in typically Chinese fashion, rolled up to the knee, with light plimsoll-type footwear. He carries a water bottle in a Japanese-type web holder and wears an American M1 steel helmet. His rifle is an American 'Enfield' Cal.30 M1917. The 'Enfield' rifle was first issued to United States troops during World War I but was replaced by the Garand M1 before World War II: surplus stock was sent to arm America's allies including the British (see figure 69) and the Chinese Army.

ORGANISATION Central power was represented by the Generalissimo, Chiang Kai-shek, who presided over the National Military Council, but a unified control proved elusive. Chiang's forces were commanded by men who had distinguished themselves by loyalty to the Generalissimo – and not by feats on the field of battle. Obsequiousness, and not valour, was the secret of a successful military career in Nationalist China. There were 12 war areas and these received their instructions from Chiang and his Council through a chief of staff, General Ho Yin-chin. Such military operations as were undertaken were concentrated on one war area at a time.

The prospect of action was not greeted with any enthusiasm locally because the war lords often doubled as provincial governors as well as military commanders and the expenditure of military force detracted from their local political power *vis-à-vis* neighbouring war lords. Military operations received little support from central authority in Chungking because if a provincial governor fought a successful campaign, he might feel sufficiently powerful to challenge the power of the Generalissimo. To prevent this from happening, Chiang kept loyal divisions in the rear of the war areas to ensure the continued co-operation of the provincial governors. Consequently, there was no central strategic reserve, and the scattered distribution of military power contributed to the growth of petty satrapies of provincial power which, in turn, contributed to the spiral of inefficiency which reacted on any effort to drive the Japanese back and restore the power of central government. Each area commander recruited, trained, and (in so far as it was possible) equipped his own men. If the Japanese attacked one area, then the National Military Council would try to coordinate its defence.

A Chinese Nationalist Division was a heterogeneous organisation with considerable potential; but as an American report

Below: Chinese- and American-crewed M3A3 Stuart light tanks advance down the Ledo road against Japanese-held positions.

329

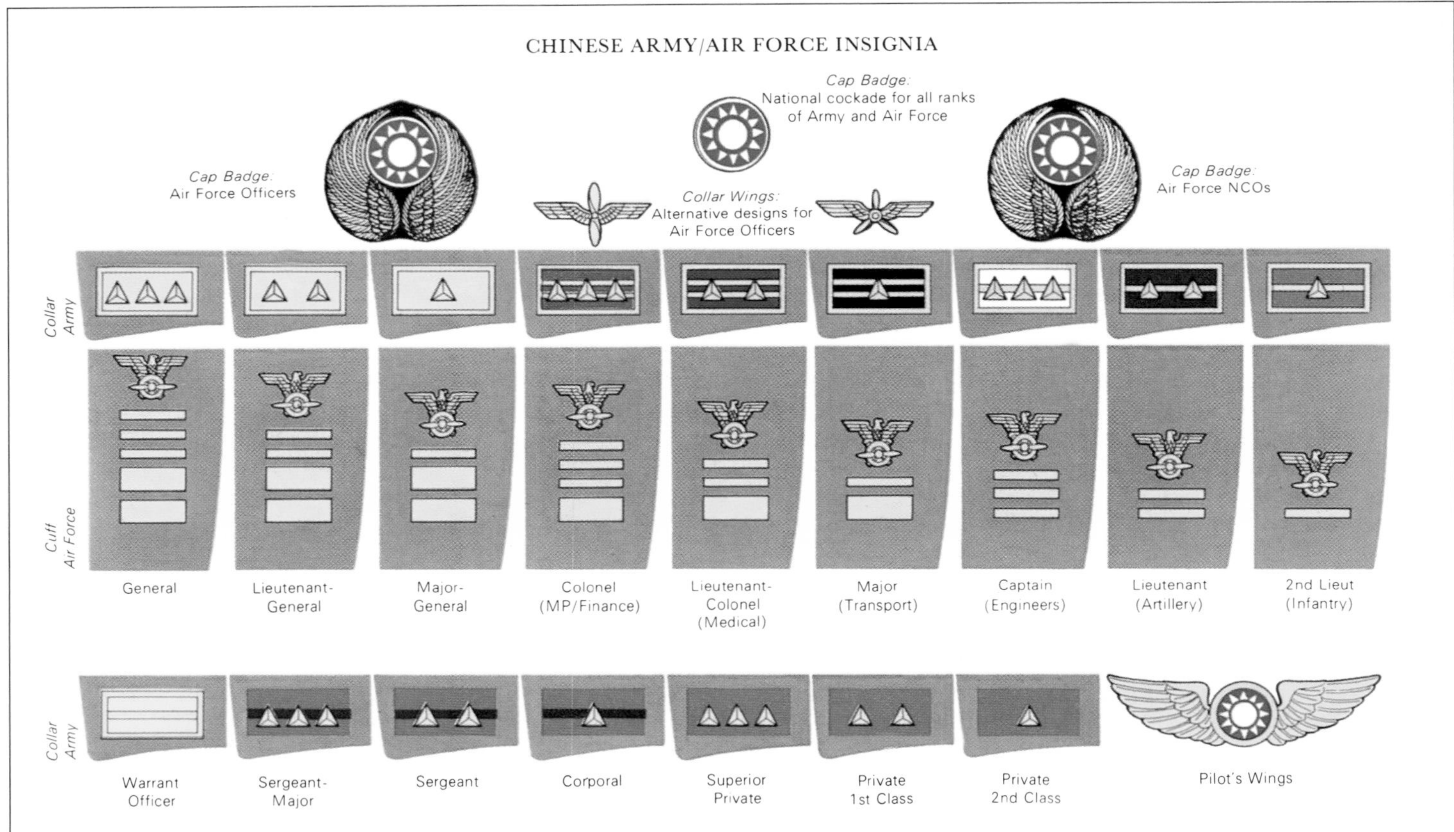

on the Chinese Army in 1941 observed it was ill-equipped, poorly trained and quite inefficient. The nominal strength of such a division was 9529 officers and men. Most divisions averaged only 6000–7000 men, and others were even weaker. They lacked heavy equipment and an efficient supply system was conspicuous by its absence. It had no artillery or heavy weapons because Chiang hoarded the 800 pieces of Chinese artillery so that he could allot a well-behaved war lord some pieces for continued loyalty; thus they were never used effectively in large numbers.

Chinese divisions normally relied upon trench mortars for artillery support, and a reasonably equipped division would field anything from 18 to 30 of these weapons. Firepower was supplemented on paper by 324 light and heavy machine guns (7.92 mm) – though the average number was 200 light and 36 heavy machine guns per division. Because Chinese divisional commanders looked upon their formations as their private property, American aid had little impact on relative inefficiency because once new weapons arrived, they were immediately impounded by the commanding officer and hoarded.

It is an indication of the level of corruption in China that she received between March 1941 and October 1945 $631,509,000 worth of aid, but nothing like an efficient force was ever permanently established.

In nomenclature Chinese divisions resembled the Japanese (and, therefore, the German) system rather than the American. Chinese divisions were arranged in a triangular structure. There were three regiments to a division, but there was no army corps. This was replaced by a land army of three divisions and three of these armies formed a group army – a force which resembled a Western army. On average, each war lord had three group armies at his disposal. Chiang had a total of 3,819,000 men under arms by the end of 1942. 2,919,000 of these were formed into 246 divisions, employed as 'front line' troops, plus 44 brigades (a loose term applied to miscellaneous military formations). In the rear areas there were another 70 divisions and three brigades with a total strength of approximately 900,000 men. In addition, Chiang had another 30 divisions under his personal command to ensure the loyalty of his war area commanders and to keep a watchful eye on the activities of the communists. Against the Japanese he fielded something like 300 divisions. This alignment was only theoretical, however, because serious fighting was not contemplated.

In October 1942 Lieutenant-General Joseph W. Stilwell was appointed Chiang's co-Chief of Staff. In trying to create an efficient fighting force he was faced with insuperable difficulties that would have taxed the talents of a more tactful and patient man than he. Political and social factors determined which troops fought in which theatres.

Stilwell enthusiastically supported the so-called 'Thirty Division Plan' which attempted to circumvent the usual restraints on Chinese efficiency by allotting 30 divisions for re-training at American training schools and giving these troops the best American equipment; Stilwell planned to use these troops in Burma. Chiang at first seemed to favour the plan and 20 divisions were initially made available to take part in the scheme. The 5th and 6th Armies were also placed under Stilwell's command in Burma. But Chiang gradually turned against the idea because of the dangers of placing such an efficient force under Chinese officers.

Stilwell was ordered not to use his forces offensively, and when he received copies of the orders being sent out from Chungking, he discovered that all the Chinese commanders from Siam to Indo-China were being instructed to stay on the defensive and await an American victory in the Pacific War – the basis of Chiang's strategy throughout World War II.

UNIFORM Between 1937 and 1945 Chinese uniforms underwent a number of changes. Both the Nationalist and communist armies suffered great shortages of clothing and equipment and had to make do with home or locally made items, so that uniformity was never very extensive and uniforms could vary considerably from region to region, army to army, and year to year.

Initially Germany had been instrumental in organising, training and equipping the Chinese Army, and this fact becomes obvious when one looks at figure 326. However, this shows a member of an élite guard unit, and more typical are figures 327 and 328. Uniforms in khaki drill and blue, which faded to grey, were worn concurrently, and during the bitter winters in central and northern China, it was the blue padded uniform which became the most typical form of uniform.

INSIGNIA Badges of rank were worn on the collar (see rank insignia chart). The collar patches were originally made of cloth, but during the war metal and plastic patches were most common. The colour of the collar patches differed according to the arm of service. On the left breast soldiers wore a cotton label on which was printed in black characters the soldier's name and unit. Some labels had a border in the arm-of-service colour.

AIR FORCE

During the 1930s, the Chinese Air Force was composed largely of foreign volunteers, at first Americans but later Italians.

330 1st Lieutenant, Chinese Nationalist Air Force, 1943
The gilt badge on the left breast of this Chinese officer identifies him as a pilot. His officer's peaked service cap with light khaki band bears a winged badge which, in other ranks, was white. The cuff markings are those of a 1st lieutenant. Non-flyers wore blossoms instead of eagle badges.

331 Pilot, American Volunteer Group, 1941
Enrolled in the Chinese Air Force as civilians, US personnel wore an amalgam of American and Chinese uniform. The US peaked service cap with light khaki crown bears the Chinese Air Force officers' cap badge. The zip-fronted flying jacket is very similar to the US Army tankman's windcheater, with the Nationalist emblem on the left breast. The patch (inset left) was sewn onto the back of the jacket and instructed any Chinese to safeguard the pilot should he force land or bale out. The pistol in his shoulder holster is the US Cal.45 Model 1911A1, a very powerful military pistol.

Right: Chinese ground crew work on a US-supplied Curtiss P-40 of the 76th Fighter Group at Kunming. Clothing is a mixture of native Chinese and American government issue.

By 1937 the strength of the Air Force stood at 500 aircraft, but few of these were serviceable, and the remainder were destroyed by the Japanese in the air battles of 1937.

Chiang Kai-shek and his wife Madame Chiang called for further foreign aid to form an international force to fight the Japanese. At first an international squadron was established of mixed membership, mainly British, American and Dutch pilots. It only had 36 aircraft and had been destroyed by 1938. The international squadron was replaced by six Russian squadrons, two of bombers and four of fighters provided under a clause of the Sino-Soviet Non-Aggression Pact of 1937. The Russian force was totally self-contained and provided all its own supplies and ground crew. It allowed the Chinese Air Force to regroup in the north around Kunming and the Russians sent it 400 aircraft, and a number of new and more efficient flying schools were set up. The kernel of the postwar Chinese Air Force was very largely Russian-trained.

Although efficient, this Russian contribution was too small to provide an overall air defence of China, and in January 1939 after extensive Japanese raids on Chungking, Madame Chiang searched for reinforcements. The American Volunteer Group (AVG) filled the breach. In October 1940 Major-General Mao Pang-tzo, the Director of the Operations Branch of the Chinese Air Force, was sent to the United States to buy aircraft. Though the Chinese wanted 650, they eventually got 100 P-40s discarded by the British. The recruitment of pilots was much more difficult. Chennault enthusiastically agreed to head the AVG. To get round the Neutrality Acts two corporations were set up as go-betweens, the Central Aircraft Manufacturing Company (CAMCO) and China Defence Supplies. All AVG recruits were considered as 'employees' of CAMCO, and General Chennault was named as their 'supervisor'.

In June 1941 the AVG consisted of 100 pilots and 150 mechanics. The following month the AVG was allotted 269 new fighters and 66 bombers and a scheme was considered to extend the AVG to a second group equipped with Hudson bombers, though the entry of the US into the war after Pearl Harbor pre-empted this.

The opening of the official war against Japan found the AVG in the midst of its worst crisis. The cumulative strain of countless missions, a sense of isolation and lack of adequate equipment – the neglect and incompetence of Chinese ground crews ruined most of their aircraft – led to a catastrophic drop in the morale of AVG pilots and 24 resigned. Chennault persuaded all but four of these to withdraw their resignations or face charges of desertion. But this kind of disagreement poisoned the atmosphere of the AVG and when it was absorbed into the China-America Task Force, commanded by Chennault in July 1942, only a handful volunteered to join the USAAF. The CATF inherited 57 fighters from the AVG. In turn the CATF was absorbed into the 14th US Air Force in 1943 as China's main air defence.

Uniform Since they formed part of the Army, Air Force personnel wore khaki uniforms. Those officers undergoing training abroad, or forming part of a military mission wore the uniform illustrated by figure 330, but the majority of officers wore whatever items of Army uniform they could find, and in general were not as well-dressed.

Other ranks wore Army uniforms. In hot weather all ranks wore the field cap with khaki shirt and shorts, or overalls.

Aircrew and ground crew wore various kinds of flying suits and overalls either of Chinese manufacture, purchased from the United States, or taken from the Japanese. Americans serving with the Chinese Air Force wore the uniform illustrated by figure 331.

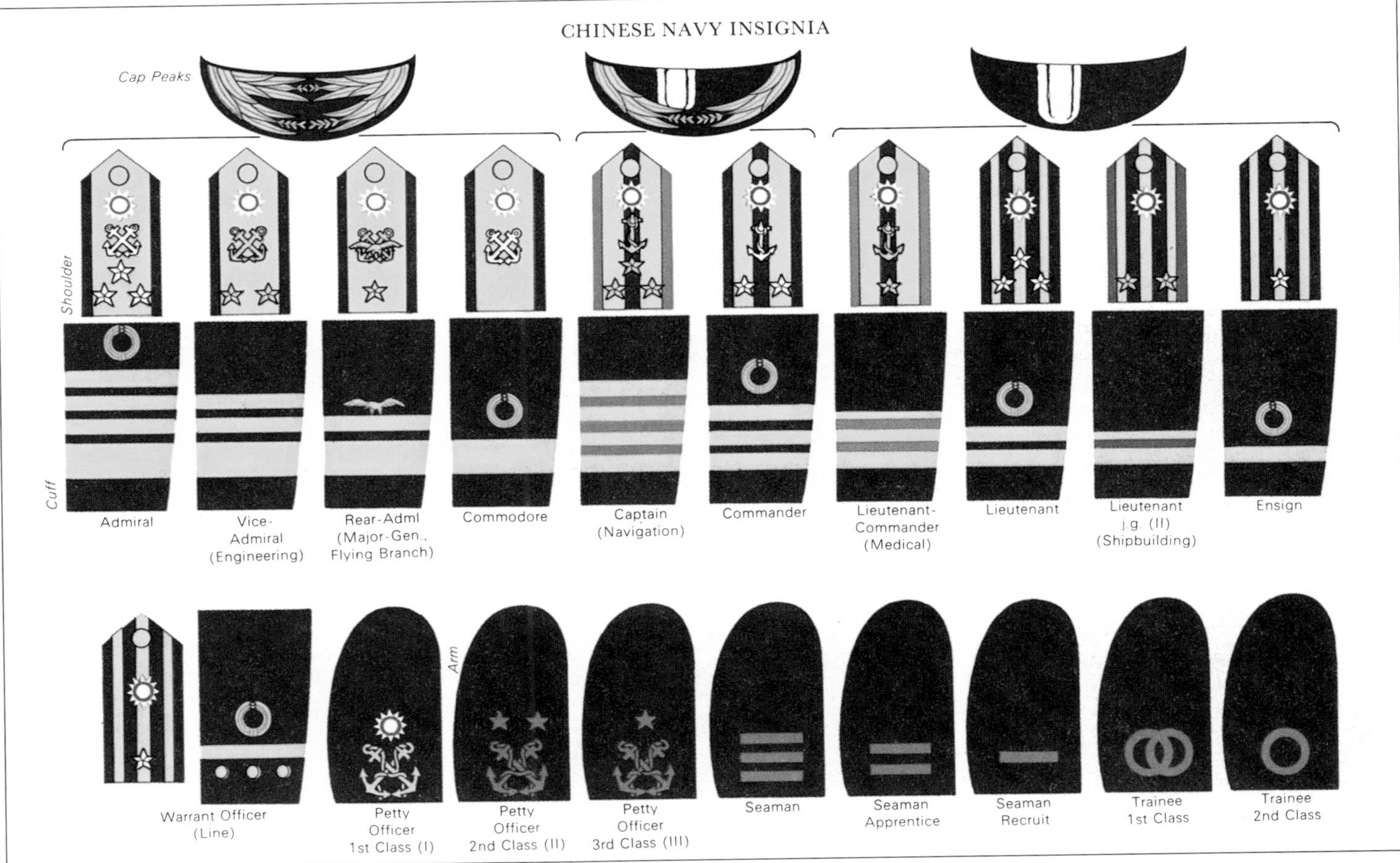

INSIGNIA Air Force personnel wore the sunburst badge on their head-dress, and sometimes the same badge was worn on the service dress or flying jacket. Rank badges were worn on the sleeves by officers and on the collar patches by other ranks.

NAVY

In 1937 the Chinese Navy was very small by Western standards and totalled 59 vessels. The largest vessels were six light cruisers, none of which exceeded 3600 tons. Supporting these were 30 gunboats and a miscellaneous collection of 23 gunboats, sloops and transport vessels. Most of these were sunk in the Yangtze, at Shanghai, Tsingtao and Canton during the Japanese attacks of 1937 and fell easy victim to Japanese bombing and artillery fire. Some vessels that were beached were salvaged and repaired by the Japanese, but for all intents and purposes the Chinese Navy had ceased to exist. The great stream of Lend-Lease aid was diverted (when it did not find its way into the pockets of the generals) into military rather than naval uses. In 1945 it was discovered that one torpedo boat and 13 river gunboats were still operating. Five of these gunboats were former British, American and French craft, transferred when their Western crews had crossed overland from Burma.

Below: Two high-ranking Chinese Navy officers confer with their British counterparts. Their rank insignia is clearly visible in this picture.

UNIFORM The Navy of the Chinese Republic received a standardised Naval uniform in 1913, which followed closely the European pattern.

The uniform for officers is illustrated by figure 332. The greatcoat was double-breasted and was worn with shoulder straps. Summer whites were in the same cut as the Navy blue uniform.

Ratings wore the traditional square rig with British-style cap. The white version of the jumper had blue denim cuffs.

Badges of rank are illustrated in the rank badge chart.

332 Commander, Chinese Nationalist Navy, 1943

Based in London as Chinese Naval Attaché, Commander Chow Ying-tsung wears a single-breasted tunic with concealed fly fastening, trimmed at the edges and collar with black lace.

332

333

COMMUNIST FORCES

In north China, the communist forces of Mao Tse-tung were the main opponents of the Japanese. Like the Nationalists, however, they preferred to maintain a low level of operations, saving themselves for the coming struggle for the control of China. After Pearl Harbor, they decided that Japanese defeat was inevitable, and in any case the major communist offensive of the war up to 1941 (the 'Hundred Regiments' Campaign' of 1940) had been very costly.

ORGANISATION After the losses of the Long March, communist forces had begun operations against the Nationalists from their new base in Yenan in 1936, but in 1937 a truce was patched up to meet the Japanese menace, and the three communist Front Armies under Chu Teh were designated the 8th Route Army; this had an official strength of 45,000 men but was probably 80,000-strong, including guerrillas. After the losses of the 'Hundred Regiments' Campaign', the communists set about expanding their forces and creating a tightly knit army. By the end of 1943, the 8th Route Army was probably 325,000 men strong, of whom two-thirds were guerrillas, but the core was the regular force, which had a very precise structure. The basic organisation was quite standard: three squads (each of 10 to 16 men) made up a platoon; three platoons a company (with its administrative troops about 120 men strong); three companies a battalion; three battalions a regiment; three regiments a division and three divisions an army. Support weapons were whatever was available, and the communist forces were woefully lacking in machine guns and artillery until the Japanese surrender.

The cohension of this ill-equipped army was enormous, however. The basic squad of 10 to 16 men was composed of three small teams, and the team leaders were often either members or aspirant members of the Communist Party. The platoon leader was invariably a member of the Party. This arrangement cemented loyalty at a very basic level, and was to give the communists a priceless advantage.

In April 1945, Chu Teh, the communist commander, addressing the 7th Party Congress, claimed a total of 910,000 regulars, organised in the 8th Route Army, the New 4th Army, the South China Anti-Japanese Column and the Anti-Japanese Allied Forces. He estimated that two and a half million communist guerrillas were operational.

UNIFORM Chinese communist troops wore the same khaki uniforms as the Nationalists, and, while they were united against the Japanese, they wore the same 'white sun and blue sky' emblem and rank badges. Once civil war broke out again, however, the communists began to replace the army field cap by either a round peaked cloth cap or the so-called 'Mao cap', on the front of which was sometimes worn the five-pointed red star.

333 Guerrilla, Communist Chinese Forces, 1944
This representative Chinese guerrilla wears a rudimentary bandolier fashioned from cotton or canvas, in which is stored the small-arms calibre ammunition for his Chinese-made 'Chiang Kai-shek' rifle. Also of note are the two easily-accessible stick-type grenades slung over the shoulders of his blue jacket. Communist guerrillas often wore a red star on the front of their caps, but this was by no means invariable. Diversity rather than uniformity was the order of the day amongst the Chinese communist armies of World War II.

Right: Chinese communist regular troops stand on guard over captured Japanese Type 97 medium tanks. The Type 97 with a top speed of 25 mph and a 57mm gun was the mainstay of Japan's tank force and although not comparable with the armoured vehicles of the European theatre, was a considerable bonus for the Chinese communist forces. Often short of equipment and heavy armament, the communists made up for this with the discipline of their organisations. The soldiers depicted here with padded jackets and trousers are well equipped for the cold Chinese winter which could bring military operations to a virtual halt.

GREAT BRITAIN

ARMY

The troops fighting in Burma considered themselves to be the 'Forgotten Army' of the Allied war effort, and theirs was arguably the toughest campaign, certainly in terms of terrain and climate, in which British units were engaged in the whole of the war. Supply and medical problems assumed an importance which at times relegated actual battle to a secondary consideration, while the enemy they fought made up for an inadequate logistical system with a ferocity and tenacity of purpose seldom equalled.

The campaign in the Far East fell into three main phases: first the loss of Hong Kong and Malaya and the retreat from Burma; secondly a period of defensive consolidation with minor offensive operations in the Arakan and the deployment of Chindit columns, and thirdly a victorious advance through Burma. The initial period of defeat owed much to the deployment of inadequate forces, to an underestimation of the enemy and of the problems of jungle warfare, and to the process of milking units of their experienced officers and NCOs in order to provide a cadre for new formations.

When the Japanese attacked, the long argument between the three British services over the strategic deployment of their forces still rumbled in the background. Despite the creation of a new appointment of Commander-in-Chief, Far East in November 1940, the defence was still far from adequately coordinated. There were two commanders-in-chief in Singapore; General Officers Commanding in Burma, Malaya, and Hong Kong who reported to the War Office, and the Governors of Hong Kong, Burma, and the Straits Settlements who were responsible to the Colonial Office. The forces in India were controlled by their own commander-in-chief who was not made responsible for the defence of Burma until 12 December 1941. The sphere of command was further complicated by the creation of the ABDA (American-British-Dutch-Australian) theatre command spanning the South-West Pacific area on 4 January 1942.

ORGANISATION The main deployments of British troops in the Far East, outside India, were in Malaya, Singapore, Ceylon, Burma, and Hong Kong. The two battalions forming the North China garrison at Shanghai had been withdrawn in August 1940. The forces in Malaya included three British infantry battalions in Singapore Fortress and one battalion in each of three Indian infantry brigades (6th, 12th and 15th). There were two infantry battalions in the garrison of Hong Kong serving with the Mainland and Island Infantry Brigades under Headquarters China Command. The two British battalions in Burma could muster only two companies each in December 1941 and they were deployed in 1st Burma Brigade and the Rangoon Garrison.

Reinforcements of British troops did arrive in Malaya and Burma, notably the 18th Infantry Division and the 7th Armoured Brigade (with only two of its three regiments). Of the 38 battalions defending Singapore until its surrender, 13 were wholly British. The forces which retreated nearly 1000 miles across the length of Burma were organised as Burcorps, comprising two divisions – 1st Burma and 17th Indian Infantry and in April 1942 they included approximately 13,700 British troops, with detachments from the Empire and the Dominions.

334

335

334 Lance-Corporal, British Army, 1945
With his new boots round his neck, this infantryman stands in jungle-green twill shirt and felt bush hat with light khaki puggree. The hat also bears the formation sign of the 19th Indian ('Dagger') Division – divisional signs were only worn when out of the line. His rifle is the British .303 SMLE Rifle No. 4 Mk. I. The No. 4 was the standard British infantry rifle of the war and with a 10-round magazine and a muzzle velocity of 2400 feet per second was one of the best bolt-action rifles of its day. A lighter and shorter version, the No. 5, was introduced for use in the jungle but the violent recoil of the weapon made it unpopular with the front-line troops.

335 Brigadier, Indian Army, 1945
Brigadier Denham-Young of the 5th Indian Division, 14th Army, wears the divisional sign press-studded to the sleeve of his bush jacket. His felt bush hat carries the badge of a brigadier, while the gorget (collar) patches were also worn by colonels. He carries British-pattern web equipment and a leather bandolier with small-arms ammunition. The rough terrain and atrocious climate encountered by the British Army in Burma encouraged a more informal approach to uniform which was facilitated by the introduction of the jungle-green uniform worn by this officer.

Above top: A group of Chindits awaiting transportation to 'Broadway', the invasion airfield behind Japanese lines. British, West African and Indian troops formed the backbone of the Chindits who paid little attention to parade ground 'spit and polish' and instead emphasised battle and field craft skills. The transport planes in the background are Douglas C-47s, better known to the British as the Douglas Dakota.

Above: A section of British soldiers of the 14th Army in Burma are briefed by their company commander. A wide variety of weapons can be seen, including the Sten sub-machine gun, the Bren light machine gun and the SMLE rifle. The soldier (left background) carries ammunition pouches for Bren gun magazines. The dishevelled appearance of the troops reflects the harshness of the Burmese terrain.

The defence of India and Ceylon and particularly the need to maintain internal security tied down a large proportion of the troops available in the Far East; in August 1942, for example, 57 battalions were involved in containing civil disturbances. The threat of political unrest was the more alarming since after the outbreak of war in Europe many of the British regular units stationed in India had been transferred to the United Kingdom and the Middle East, their place being taken by Territorial units who were obviously unfamiliar with the sub-continent and its peoples. The Army in India was divided into three commands, Northern, Eastern, and Southern, until 21 April 1942 when India Command was re-organised as a Central Command, containing the majority of training depots and establishments, and three armies: Southern, Eastern, and North-Western. The major operational command was Eastern Army with responsibility for the defence of Assam, Bengal, Bihar, and Orrissa, and it was largely from the formations of this command that the 14th Army was formed in October 1943.

The direction of operations which were based on India and Ceylon was transferred from the C-in-C India (General Sir C. Auchinleck) to a new appointment, filled by Acting-Admiral Lord Louis Mountbatten, of Supreme Allied Commander, South-East Asia (SEAC). The land forces in SEAC, consisting of 14th Army and the Ceylon Army Command, were brought under the new Headquarters, 11th Army Group. 14th Army was composed of XV Corps (5th, 7th Indian Divisions and 81st West African Division) and IV Corps (17th, 20th, 23rd and 26th Indian Infantry Divisions and 254th Indian Tank Brigade). The XXXIII Corps (2nd British and 36th Indian Infantry Divisions) was allocated to South-East Asia Command but remained for the time being with India Command, as did the 19th and 25th Indian Divisions and the 50th Tank Brigade. The major formations within Ceylon Army Command were the 11th East African Division and the 99th Indian Infantry Brigade.

A number of special force units were attached to SEAC, among them 44 Royal Marine Commando, 5 Commando, and 3 Special Service (SS) Brigade. The largest special force was the '3rd Indian Division' which provided the Long Range Penetration Groups (Chindits) commanded by Major General Orde Wingate. The initial LRP groups had been formed as the 77th Indian Infantry Brigade in July 1942, but these were expanded to a strength of six infantry brigades (14th, 16th, 23rd, 77th, 111th and 3rd West African) by breaking up the 70th British Division and appropriating a brigade of the 81st West African Division. Each Special Force brigade consisted of a number of columns, either British or Gurkha in composition, the former with a strength of 306 all ranks and the latter a strength of 369. Each column had an RAF section, a medical section, signallers, sabotage group, a Burma Rifles platoon, an infantry company, and a support group. At full strength and including divisional and attached troops, the Chindits amounted to the equivalent of almost two divisions.

In the spring of 1945 Allied Land Forces South-East Asia comprised one command HQ, one army HQ, three corps HQs, a combat area command incorporating two Chinese armies, two British, two West African, one East African, and seven Indian divisions. In addition 14th Army had three independent brigades. The successful occupation of southern Burma and the requirements of the proposed amphibious operation against Malaya necessitated a command reorganisation in May and June. The headquarters of 14th Army was brought back from Burma to supervise the Malayan operations, its place being taken by a new formation, 12th Army, which became operational on 28 May 1945. The 14th Army which, with nearly 1,000,000 men serving in 1944 and early 1945, had been the largest single army of the war, finally stood down on 1st December 1945. At various periods it had controlled four corps (IV, XV, XXXIII and XXXIV) and 13 divisions had served with it (2nd, 36th British; 5th, 7th, 17th, 19th, 20th, 23rd, 25th, 26th Indian; 11th East African; 81st, 82nd West African). British casualties in Burma between 11 December 1941 and 15 September 1945 amounted to 25,170 officers and other ranks, of which 6921 were killed, 15,585 wounded, and 2664 listed as missing or prisoners of war.

In World War II as a whole the British Army suffered 569,501 casualties consisting of 144,079 killed, 239,575 wounded, 33,771 missing, and 152,076 taken prisoner.

UNIFORM At the beginning of the war in the Far East, British soldiers wore the same khaki drill uniform which was worn in the Middle East, but sandy yellow was found an unsuitable colour for jungle warfare, and the uniform was both uncomfortable and impractical.

In 1942 a new jungle-green uniform (figure 334) began to be introduced and by the time of the 1943–1944 campaigns it had become universal.

The basic uniform was made of a jungle-green cellular material and consisted of a bush jacket and shirt with both long and short sleeves, and long and short trousers. Various kinds of regimental head-dresses were worn when out of action, while on active service the most common headgear was the steel helmet or the slouch hat.

Web equipment was often painted a dark green or black to improve its protective colouring and to make it more impervious to moisture. Much of what is written about the Australian jungle fighter applies equally to the other British and Dominion forces (see page 284).

INSIGNIA Badges of rank were the same as worn on the temperate uniform except for the fact that metal rank badges were often painted black, and the chevrons for NCOs were made of a plain tape.

Regimental and formations signs were sometimes worn as illustrated in figures 334 and 335.

ROYAL AIR FORCE

By 1941 the prime responsibility for the defence of Britain's possessions in the Far East lay with the Royal Air Force. But the RAF was beset with problems, not the least of which was the difficulty of constructing and operating airfields amidst a terrain which gave scant consideration to the need for flat, open, and defensible spaces. In October 1940 it was estimated that the Far Eastern Theatre would require 566 aircraft. When hostilities began, however, there were 362 aircraft available of which only 233 were operational. Moreover, the demands made by the air defence of Britain and the Middle East meant that modern bomber and fighter aircraft were dispatched to South-East Asia in woefully inadequate numbers. The Brewster Buffalo fighter and the Vildebeest torpedo-bomber could

336 Pilot Officer, Royal Air Force, 1945

Pilot officer Alasdair Campbell, Unit Adjutant of the RAF Mobile Repair and Salvage Unit in Burma, wears a jungle-green tropical shirt, on which rank is indicated by slip-on khaki tags on the shoulder. The bush hat was of British, rather than Australian origin, while the overall trousers and anklets were standard RAF issue. The role of maintenance and back-up troops was never more vital than in Burma where vast numbers of men were needed to keep the fighting man supplied. In the case of the Royal Air Force this was especially true as airfields had to be hacked out from the jungle.

337 Squadron Leader, Royal Air Force, 1941

This officer of the Royal Air Force Volunteer Reserve displays the service's tropical dress, but has retained the cap from his blue-grey service uniform. Squadron leader rank badges are worn on the shoulder straps, while his reserve status is indicated by the letters 'VR' on the collar. He wears the observers' 'half wing' qualification badge on the left breast. This smart khaki drill service dress typical of the early period of the Pacific War contrasts markedly with the generally relaxed appearance of the British armed forces by 1945.

336

337

not match the speed and manoeuvrability of the Japanese Zero. The transfer of Hurricanes to the Far East did little to redress the balance and it was not until the arrival of the Spitfire and the Thunderbolt that air superiority began to be firmly established in the 1943–44 campaigning season. Thereafter RAF squadrons aided by the Royal Indian Air Force and by Dominion squadrons, provided every form of aerial support to the forces on the ground, from strategic bombing and air supply, to reconnaissance and casualty evacuation.

ORGANISATION Headquarters Royal Air Force, Far East, directly controlled the stations and squadrons in Malaya, Burma, Ceylon, and Hong Kong from its formation in 1933 until the establishment of the first group (221 Group) in 1941 to command the units in Burma. In the same year additional groups were formed in Ceylon (222 Group) and for the air defence of Singapore (224 Group). By December 1941 22 airfields with either concrete or grass runways had been constructed in Malaya with a further four airfields on Singapore. The RAF, RAAF, and RNZAF units operating from these bases comprised four Blenheim, two Hudson, two Vildebeest, one Catalina, and four Buffalo squadrons. During the retreat from Burma three bomber, three fighter, and two army co-operation squadrons supported the campaign waged by the land forces. The Royal Indian Air Force (RIAF), which had been formed in 1933, was entirely Indian in composition and it began the war with one army co-operation unit and 285 officers and airmen.

In September 1942 the RAF and RIAF squadron strength stood at 31, of which 25 were operational, and by June 1943 the total had grown to 52 squadrons with 34 operational. The number of airfields available in India had increased to 285, of which 140 were fully operational, and the RAF Regiment deployed five field squadrons and 50 anti-aircraft flights in their defence. India Command comprised one bomber group (No. 221), a tactical group (No. 224), a reconnaissance group (No. 222), two training groups (Nos. 225 and 227), one composite group (No. 223), and a maintenance group (No. 226). With the creation of South-East Asia Command the operational RAF squadrons in north-east India were integrated with the United States 10th Army Air Force as Eastern Air Command, forming a Tactical Air Force, a Strategic Air Force, and a Troop Carrier Command. By May 1944 the Combined Air Forces could call upon 64 RAF and 28 USAAF squadrons.

The personnel strength of the RAF and RIAF in the Far East had risen by July 1945 to 207,632 officers and men, of which 13,225 were RAF officers and 118,582 British other ranks. The Royal Indian Air Force strength in August stood at 29,201 officers and airmen and nine squadrons.

UNIFORM AND INSIGNIA The Royal Air Force also made use of the jungle-green clothing, as well as the tropical dress as described in the section on the Mediterranean. The normal head-dress was worn with the jungle-green uniform, together with the appropriate badges and other insignia.

ROYAL NAVY

The fall of the British naval base at Singapore effectively prevented the Royal Navy from participating in the Pacific war until the closing stages of World War II. With the loss of the *Repulse* and the *Prince of Wales*, the Royal Navy was in danger of being driven from its bases in the Indian Ocean. Nevertheless, British leaders were determined to play some part in the war in the Pacific, not only to avenge a catastrophic blow dealt to the prestige of British arms, but to ensure that they would be in a position to protect their colonial possessions that had fallen into Japanese

Below: Admiral Sir Tom Phillips in naval whites. He went down with his ship, the Prince of Wales *on 10 December 1941.*

338

338 Groundcrew, Royal Air Force, 1945
Designed to provide the wearer with the maximum possible protection from the heat and flames generated by burning kerosene, this asbestos suiting was issued both to RAF aerodrome fire-fighting units and to Royal Navy ships carrying aircraft. Vision was provided by the tinted reinforced glass plate; otherwise the fire-fighter was totally enclosed in his asbestos suit. Fire aboard ships had always been a hazard of naval warfare but was especially so in the Pacific due to the Japanese kamikaze attacks on the decks of the Allied aircraft carriers.

339 Sub-Lieutenant, Royal Navy, 1945
An officer of the Royal Naval Volunteer Reserve, Sub-Lieutenant A. Lloyd Morgan served aboard HM Submarine Shakespeare *of the East Indies Fleet. He wears khaki drill shirt and shorts, with rank badges on shoulder strap slides. The Royal Navy officers' peaked cap is worn with a white cover. The Royal Naval Volunteer Reserve, instituted in 1903, was distinguished by the square curl of the rank lace which can be seen on the shoulder strap slide of this figure. The Royal Naval Reserve, in contrast, had a star-shaped curl and 'wavy' rank lace. Both types of insignia are illustrated in the rank insignia chart on page 130.*

339

340

341

340 Marine, Royal Marines, 1941
Stationed in Singapore, this Marine wears RM tropical kit of khaki shorts and shirt with full-length khaki puttees, M1908 web equipment and marine service cap with white cover. He carries a British .303 SMLE rifle No. 1 Mk. III with bayonet. The old 1908-pattern webbing reflects the out-dated look of this Marine at the outset of the war. British forces in the Far East were starved of the latest equipment until towards the end of the war and many troops considered themselves to be part of the 'Forgotten Army'. The Mark III rifle was of World War I vintage and although highly-considered by those who used it, was a costly weapon to manufacture and so was replaced by the cheaper No. 4 Mk. 1 rifle. In conditions of active service the distinctive marine cap would be replaced by the steel helmet.

341 Officer, Royal Navy, 1943
Depicted in working garb, this engineer wears the Royal Navy officers' peaked cap with white cover, white overalls and strong gloves. An interesting feature is the absence of shoe laces, which may have been due to the custom of wearing lace-less shoes and boots by those crew members working in confined spaces under the water-line, so that they could be quickly kicked off if the vessel was sinking.

hands. The Japanese had presented themselves as the champions of oppressed colonial peoples; the United States was not sympathetic towards British imperial aspirations and thus British leaders were anxious to preserve British power in the Far East by military and naval action.

At the First Quebec Conference Churchill offered the Chief of US Naval Staff, Admiral Ernest J. King, a British fleet, but this offer was not enthusiastically received. At the second Quebec Conference Churchill repeated his offer of a British fleet. Thanking the United States for its aid during the dark days of the struggle against Germany, he added, 'It was only to be expected that the British Empire in return should wish to give the United States all the help in their power towards defeating Japan'. Roosevelt returned these fulsome sentiments and concluded that 'the British fleet was no sooner offered than accepted'. At last Churchill's dream of a British fleet operating in the Pacific Ocean moved a step nearer reality when it was agreed that it would be based in Australia.

At the beginning of the war against Japan, Admiral Sir James Somerville commanded a sizeable fleet of five battleships, three light aircraft carriers, seven cruisers, and sixteen destroyers. Although fairly strong in numbers, the quality of this fleet was indifferent. The battleships were old and slow, aircraft carriers were no match for the Japanese, and the Royal Navy was inexperienced in the technique of launching large numbers of aircraft from fleet carriers and co-ordinating attacks against a distant enemy. Nevertheless, although Somerville lost one aircraft carrier in his evasive tactics against the Japanese, at least he was successful in keeping the British fleet in being in the Indian Ocean.

Following the defeat of Italy a 'British Pacific Ocean Force' was formed of three battleships, one or two fleet carriers and a number of cruisers and destroyers. This force was broken up because of a decision to re-start Arctic convoys to Murmansk, but by the summer of 1944 Somerville had received two aircraft carriers, HMS *Victorious* and *Illustrious*. He was not,

Above: Royal Marine commandos land on Akyab beach in the Arakan. The Marine in the right foreground wears regulation Royal Marine denims and is armed with a short Lee Enfield rifle. The Marines had an important role to play in spearheading the Army's amphibious operations along the Burmese coast.

however, to command this force, and in August 1944 was relieved by Admiral Sir Bruce Fraser, ex-C-in-C Home Fleet.

In January 1945 the British Pacific Fleet now comprised one battleship, four aircraft carriers, three cruisers and ten destroyers, and was based at Sydney, Australia. One argument that the Americans employed to dissuade the British from employing a fleet in the Pacific Ocean was the difficulties that the British would have in forming a 'Fleet Train' to support the warships over vast expanses of ocean and, indeed, the Royal Navy did have considerable difficulty in acquiring sufficient merchantmen to carry out this duty. Tankers from the Royal Fleet Auxiliaries were employed, and merchant ships were lent from European navies. Eventually it reached a strength of 60 ships, but the mixed origins of many of the ships did not facilitate easy co-operation.

In December 1944 the United States Navy reluctantly agreed that the British Pacific Fleet should use Manus in the Admiralty Islands as an intermediate base before moving to a more advanced base in the Philippines. By March 1945 it consisted of one battleship, the *King George V*, the fleet carriers, *Indomitable*, *Victorious*, *Indefatigable*, and *Illustrious*, five cruisers and eleven destroyers in addition to 218 bombers and fighters. Fine though this force was, by American standards it was very small, and was only one component in Admiral Spruance's Fifth Fleet of over 1200 vessels. After action off Okinawa in July 1945, the British Pacific Fleet was switched to the US Third Fleet as an additional group of the US Fast Carrier Task Force, initially taking part in attacks on the Japanese mainland.

The Royal Marines were active in the Far East theatre as commandos, quite apart from their normal role as part of the complement of Royal Navy vessels. Their special qualities as élite soldiers were put to good use in Burma where 42(RM) and 44(RM) Commando formed part of No. 3 Commando Brigade.

A typical Marine commando detachment in the later stages of the war would be 100 men strong and consist of a small HQ and three troops of about 30 officers and men, each divided into three sections. Generally, however, the organisation of these units varied according to the operation and to the resources available.

UNIFORM AND INSIGNIA Royal Navy uniform was basically the tropical issue described in the section on the Mediterranean, although the jungle-green clothing was often worn. As with the Air Force, normal head-dress and insignia were worn with the jungle-green uniform. Royal Marine insignia is illustrated in the accompanying chart.

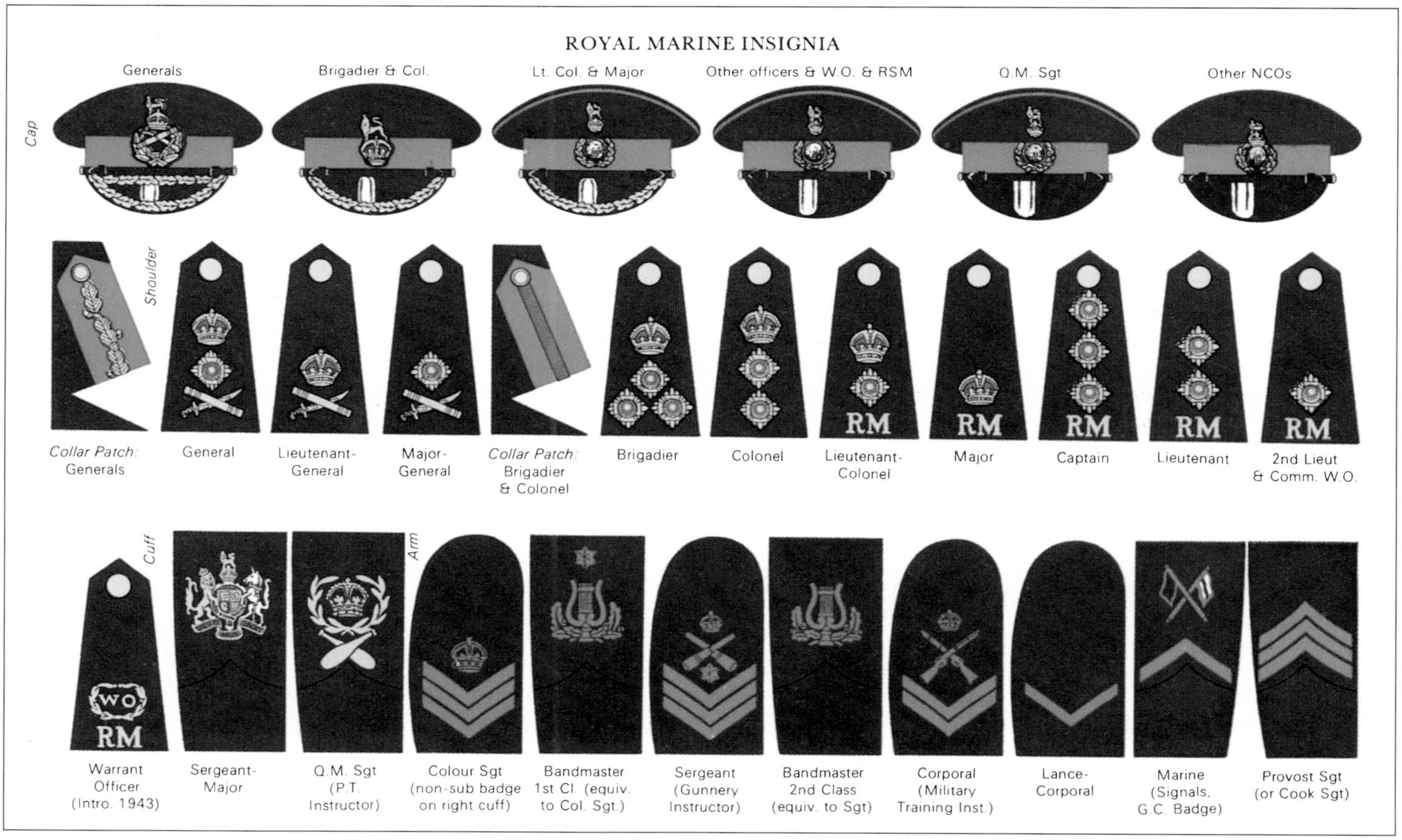

ROYAL MARINE INSIGNIA

Cap

Generals

Brigadier & Col.

Lt. Col. & Major

Other officers & W.O. & RSM

Q.M. Sgt

Other NCOs

Shoulder

Collar Patch: Generals

General

Lieutenant-General

Major-General

Collar Patch: Brigadier & Colonel

Brigadier

Colonel

Lieutenant-Colonel

Major

Captain

Lieutenant

2nd Lieut & Comm. W.O.

Cuff

Warrant Officer (Intro. 1943)

Arm

Sergeant-Major

Q.M. Sgt (P.T. Instructor)

Colour Sgt (non-sub badge on right cuff)

Bandmaster 1st Cl. (equiv. to Col. Sgt.)

Sergeant (Gunnery Instructor)

Bandmaster 2nd Class (equiv. to Sgt)

Corporal (Military Training Inst.)

Lance-Corporal

Marine (Signals, G.C. Badge)

Provost Sgt (or Cook Sgt)

EMPIRE FORCES

As in the Mediterranean, the forces of the British Empire made a full contribution to victory in the Far East, in conditions which were often extremely difficult and against a redoubtable foe.

INDIAN ARMY

By December 1941 the Indian Army had approximately 900,000 men under arms, of whom almost 300,000 were serving overseas in the Middle East and Malaya. Of the remainder, about 150,000 were deployed in the area of the North-West Frontier and on internal security duty, and a further 300,000 were undergoing training. When the Japanese offensive began, the preponderance of trained and experienced Indian units were in the Middle East, but three divisions were in Malaya and one understrength division was in Burma. This dispersal of strength overseas and the orientation of training towards conditions in the Middle East seriously affected the battleworthiness of the Indian units remaining in the Far East. The rapid expansion of the recruiting programme during 1940–41 compounded these difficulties and led to modifications in the composition of the Indian Army. The martial classes drawn from Moslems and Sikhs of the Punjab and NW Frontier, who traditionally supplied the recruits needed by the army, could no longer provide a large enough reservoir of manpower. In their place new sections of the population were recruited and by the beginning of 1943 the percentage figures of the provincial composition of the Army were as follows: Punjab 50, United Provinces 15, Madras 10, Bombay 10, NW Frontier Province 5, Ajmere and Merwara 3, Bengal 2 and Central Provinces 5. The two largest religious groupings were Hindus who accounted for 50 per cent and Moslems with 34 per cent.

The Indian Army played a major role in the fighting in Malaya and Burma and at one point Indian units amounted to three-quarters of the strength of the 14th Army. After being driven out of Burma by the Japanese in 1942 the Indian Army was able to make a stand against Japan virtually on the frontiers of India itself. The last Japanese attempt to invade India was repulsed at the two battles of Imphal and Kohima in the spring of 1944.

Following these battles, troops of the Indian Army went over on the offensive and successfully cleared the Japanese from Burma in 1945. Casualties in the campaign were high: in the Malayan débâcle the Indian Army suffered 62,175 casualties (59,000 POWs), and in the fighting in Burma 40,458 men were lost.

ORGANISATION On the outbreak of war in 1939 the Army in India was composed not only of Indian troops but also of British units which formed an integral part of the subcontinent's military forces. The Regular Indian Army consisted of units of native troops commanded by British and Indian officers, but a complete hierarchy of Indian officers was being introduced into a small number of units with the aim of eventually providing a complete Indian division. When sent out to India, British units were transferred from the Home to the Indian establishment.

In the first years of the war, infantry brigades normally contained one British battalion and two Indian (or Gurkha) battalions, although all-Indian brigades and divisions were later introduced in the 14th Army. The British and Indian regulars were supported by a number of irregular and auxiliary formations including the Indian States' Forces, the Indian

342

343

342 Sepoy, Indian Army, 1944

Wearing standard issue khaki drill shirt and shorts, this sepoy also displays 1908 webbing belt and equipment. Short puttees are worn over khaki socks. The two large leather ammunition pouches are probably specially-made, and are intended to carry magazines for the Vickers-Berthier Indian Mark III machine gun he holds in his right hand. This was adopted by the Indian Army while the British Army carried out comparative trials between this weapon and the externally-similar Bren gun. Although the British Army eventually adopted the latter weapon as its standard light machine gun, the Indian Army continued to utilise the Vickers-Berthier.

343 Subedar-Major, Burma Rifles, 1942

This subedar of the Burma Rifles is wearing the light khaki service dress with Sam Browne belt; battledress was drill shirt and shorts and 1908 web equipment. The infantry officer's sword had a steel hilt, and the scabbard was of black leather with steel fittings. The two silver badges on the collar were each fashioned in the shape of a peacock. Wool puttees and ammunition boots were also worn. His rank is indicated by the three pips on each shoulder strap. The 20th Burma Rifles had their origin in units formed in World War I.

Territorial Force, and the North-West Frontier Province Irregulars.

Many of the problems experienced by the Indian Army in the first two years of the war in the Far East stemmed from the contradictions inherent in an ambitious expansion programme, and a lack of trained manpower, particularly in the fields of artillery and communications. The 1940 expansion programme, for example, was framed for an armoured division, five infantry divisions, and supporting troops; that for 1941 had a similar target of five infantry divisions. The divisional 'slice' in the Far East at 56,000 men was larger than in any other theatre, despite the fact that divisional fighting strengths tended to be lower – largely of course due to casualties caused by disease and to tactical and logistical problems which restricted frontline deployment. In June 1944 the fighting strength of the 7th Indian Division was 10,014 officers and men including 819 British other ranks. Of the Indian Army's strength of 2,000,000 men almost 1,200,000 were ancillary troops.

The original preparation of the Indian Army for service in the Middle East meant that even as late as 1943 divisions tended to be equipped and organised for warfare in that theatre, even though they were due to be dispatched to Assam and Burma. By 1944 there were four types of Indian division plus the British divisions serving in the Far East. The Indian light divisions had a reduced establishment of men and vehicles, the Indian A & MT (animal and motor transport) divisions had a high or low scale of transport, while the 36th Indian Division was organised for amphibious operations and had two brigades each with four battalions. In August 1944 it was decided that the organisation of all

344

344 Corporal, Indian Army, 1941
This naik of the 9th Gurkha Rifles is serving with the 11th Indian Division in Malaya. He wears the khaki drill shirt and shorts (the latter nicknamed 'Bombay Bloomers') with short puttees, 1937-pattern web equipment, special web pouches to carry the magazines for his Thompson sub-machine gun and a web binocular case. His kukri *and felt hat (with rifle green patch on the puggree) make him unmistakably a Gurkha. Renowned as fierce hand-to-hand fighters, the Gurkhas were a martial race originating from the poverty-striken country of Nepal. They had formed a recognised part of the British Army since the 19th Century and had seen action on many fronts. Their most famous exploits were in the Western Desert, in the Italian campaign (especially at the battle of Monte Cassino) and with the Chindits in Burma.*

Right: Indian troops on a training exercise near Singapore. They are wearing the side cap and also the 'Bombay Bloomers' shown in figure 344. The Indian Army provided the bulk of the garrison of Singapore, and the surrender of this great naval base left 32,000 Indian troops in Japanese hands, as compared to the 15,000 British and 13,000 Australians who were taken prisoner at the same time, in this short and (for the British Empire) disastrous episode.

infantry divisions should be standardised on an organisation of three (later four) brigades of three battalions each, a machine-gun battalion, a reconnaissance battalion, and a headquarters battalion. Artillery support would be provided by two field regiments (each of 24 × 25-pdrs), an anti-tank regiment (36 × 6-pdrs), and a mountain regiment (12 × 3.7-inch howitzers). The large establishment of vehicular transport would be reduced and each division would have three animal transport companies.

It had been decided in 1941 that the Indian Army should have its own armoured corps consisting of three armoured divisions. The raising of the 31st Indian Armoured Division had been part of the 1940 expansion programme, the 32nd Indian Armoured Division was included in the 1941 programme, and the 43rd Armoured Division in the programme for 1942. The headquarters and a brigade of the 31st Division were soon dispatched to Iraq but their loss was balanced by the arrival of the 50th Indian Tank Brigade consisting of three Royal Armoured Corps regiments. The Indian armoured divisions were initially formed with two armoured brigades each but in the summer of 1942 their organisation was altered to conform to the British system of one armoured and one motorised infantry brigade per division. The two surplus armoured brigades were thereafter employed as independent tank brigades.

In August 1943 the 32nd and 43rd Armoured Divisions were amalgamated to form the 44th Indian Armoured Division, and this division, together with three tank brigades (50th, 251st, 254th), comprised the Indian armoured strength in the Far East. The artillery element of armoured divisions had been established in October 1942 at two field regiments, one anti-tank regiment, and one light anti-aircraft regiment.

In the autumn of 1943 consideration was given to the question of raising an Indian airborne division and as there was no longer an urgent need for an armoured division in SEAC the 44th Armoured Division was disbanded in March 1944 and its headquarters and divisional personnel used to form the nucleus of the 44th Indian Airborne Division. The establishment of the division was laid down as one air-landing brigade and two Indian parachute brigades each of one British, one Gurkha, and one Indian battalion. The formation of the Indian Parachute Regiment was authorised on 18 December 1944.

In August 1945 the strength of the Indian Army stood at 2,065,554 officers and men, and its major units comprised 19 cavalry and armoured regiments, 268 battalions of infantry, 207 artillery batteries, and 107 engineer companies.

Above: Subedar-Major Multon Singh of the Frontier Force Rifles raises the Union Jack at Prome. Lieutenant-Colonel Marks is on the left.

UNIFORM At the beginning of the campaign in the Far East, Indian troops wore the same puggrees, grey shirts and khaki drill clothing as worn by Indian troops in the Middle East. This uniform was also worn by troops serving in India including those guarding the India/Burma border.

During the war the various kinds of head-dress such as the peaked and field service caps worn by British officers, and the saffa, puggree or slouch hat worn by Indians and Gurkhas gradually gave way to the ubiquitous beret. The puggree was still occasionally worn on ceremonial occasions, or if worn in action was dyed various shades of olive green.

In 1942 jungle-green clothing in various shades began to be issued to Indian troops. On active service it was worn without insignia, except possibly a strip of cloth in a regimental colour on the shoulder straps, or a coloured lanyard. Out of the line formation flashes were worn on the upper sleeves, and a cloth with a regimental designation (for example 6L for 6th Duke of Connaught's Own Lancers – Watson's Horse) embroidered in black. The Indian Army also pioneered the use of knitted cardigans in various colours such as black for Skinner's Horse and brown for the Gurkha Rifles.

INSIGNIA In the Indian Army there were both British and Indian officers. British officers and those Indians holding a King's Commission ranked equally and wore the same badges of rank which were exactly the same as those worn in the British Army. There were also Indian officers holding a Viceroy's Commission who were known as Viceroy's Commissioned Officers or VCOs. These subordinate ranks were jemadar, subedar or rissaldar in cavalry, and subedar major or rissaldar major in cavalry. The jemadar and subedar were usually platoon commanders or in some cases company second in command. The subedar major was the senior subordinate officer and advised the British commanding officer in all matters concerning the Indian rank and file. An important Indian appointment was the jemadar adjutant or 'woordie' major in cavalry. These officers acted as assistants to the British adjutants.

In October 1942 details of rank badges for VCOs were laid down. On khaki cloth shoulder straps VCOs wore one (jemadar), two (rissaldar and subedar) or three (rissaldar major and subedar major) miniature silver pips mounted on transverse bars made up of three strands of braid – red, yellow and red.

MALAYAN FORCES

The Government of Malaya could call upon one regular infantry battalion composed of British and Malay officers and Malay other ranks and a cadre of a second battalion which started to form in December 1941. There were also four volunteer infantry battalions, an armoured car company, and a light artillery battery maintained by the Federated Malay States with a further four battalions raised as the Straits Settlements Volunteer Force. Local flying clubs formed the basis of the Malay Volunteer Air Force which was manned by British residents.

BURMESE FORCES

Until 1937 Burma was part of India Command but with the political separation of the two countries in April of that year the Government of Burma became responsible for internal security, and control of the armed forces passed to the Governor. The Burma Rifles were transferred from the Indian Army and the country's auxiliary and territorial forces became the Burma Auxiliary Force and the Burma Territorial Force. The former comprised the Rangoon Field Brigade RA and four rifle battalions with a combined strength of 11 companies and one armoured car section. The Territorial Force consisted of a Burma Rifles battalion and the Rangoon University Training Corps. On Separation, six of the nine battalions of the Burma Military Police were formed as the Burma Frontier Force.

The outbreak of the war in Europe saw the introduction of an expansion programme for the local forces in Burma. The strength of the Burma Rifles was doubled with the formation of six new battalions and two extra territorial battalions were also embodied; an observer corps was formed, all British subjects resident in Burma became eligible for service in the Auxiliary Force, and four mobile units were raised from the Frontier Force for outpost duty. Several major drawbacks reduced the effectiveness of the expansion programme, among them an acute shortage of transport and equipment, a lack of trained regimental officers and general reserves, and the failure to expand the Army Headquarters staff in keeping with the force they administered.

After the withdrawal of the Allied forces from Burma the Japanese raised the Burma National Army (BNA) in August 1943, but in January 1945 this force informed the Allies of its intention of rising in revolt against the Japanese occupying army. The BNA, with a strength of approximately 8000 men, carried out guerrilla attacks against the Japanese from 27 March 1945.

DOMINION FORCES

The Dominions of Australia and New Zealand were naturally involved in the Pacific War, but whereas the Australian government saw the Far East as its main concern, the bulk of the New Zealand Army remained in the Middle East.

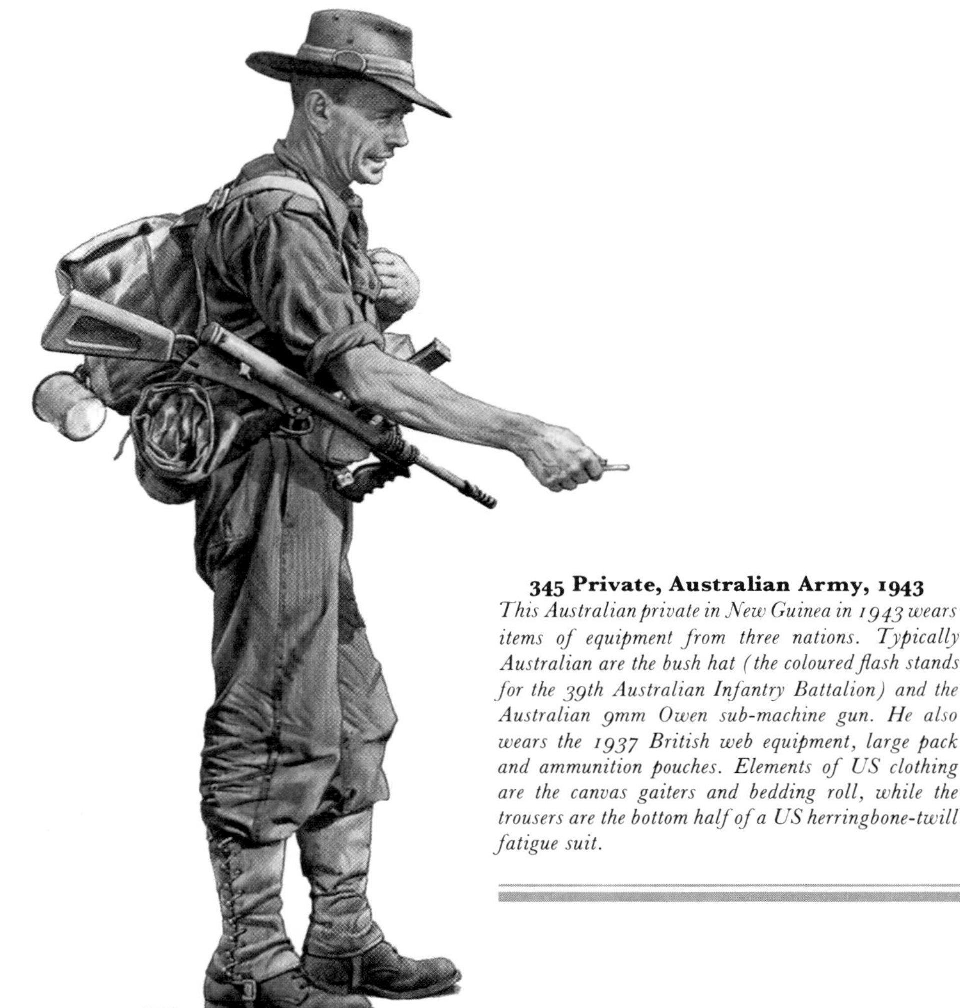

345 Private, Australian Army, 1943
This Australian private in New Guinea in 1943 wears items of equipment from three nations. Typically Australian are the bush hat (the coloured flash stands for the 39th Australian Infantry Battalion) and the Australian 9mm Owen sub-machine gun. He also wears the 1937 British web equipment, large pack and ammunition pouches. Elements of US clothing are the canvas gaiters and bedding roll, while the trousers are the bottom half of a US herringbone-twill fatigue suit.

AUSTRALIAN ARMY

As soon as Japan began hostilities the Australian Government decided that a corps of two divisions should be transferred from the Middle to the Far East, and from the end of January 1942 units of the 6th and 7th Divisions began to withdraw from North Africa. Altogether 64,151 troops were to be transferred. The 6th Division was 18,465 strong, the 7th 18,620, with an additional 17,866 corps troops and 9200 base and line of communication personnel. To support this veteran corps there were seven divisions of militia which had been mobilised in December 1941 and the Volunteer Defence Corps which consisted largely of men who had served in World War I.

General Blamey had been appointed Commander-in-Chief of the Australian Military Forces, and in April 1942 he grouped his forces for the defence of Australia as follows:
1st Army in Queensland and NS Wales;
2nd Army in Victoria, South Australia and Tasmania;
III Corps in Western Australia;
one division in Northern Territory.

In troop strengths this organisation embodied about 46,000 experienced combat troops, approximately 63,000 AIF volunteers in various stages of training, 280,000 militia soldiers, and 33,000 Americans with little or no combat experience.

The Australian 8th Division had been engaged in Malaya and Indonesia; its 22nd and 27th Brigades had lost 1789 killed, 1306 wounded and 15,000 prisoners at Singapore. The main Australian effort in the Pacific War, however, was to be in the South-West Pacific. In July 1942, a mainly Australian force had defeated the first Japanese assault on Port Moresby in Papua, and Australian forces bore the brunt of the savage fighting along the Kokoda trail.

By March 1943 the major units of the Australian Army in Australia were grouped as follows:
1st Army – 3rd Armoured Division, 4th Division;
II Corps – 6th (16 and 30 Brigades), 7th and 9th Divisions;
2nd Army – 1st Division, 3rd Army Tank Brigade;
III Corps – 1st Armoured Division, 2nd Division;

Northern Territory Force – 12th Division;
Reserve – 3rd Brigade, 4th Armoured Brigade.
Based in Papua-New Guinea were 3rd Division (17 Brigade), 11th Division (7 and 15 Brigades) and 5th Division (4 and 29 Brigades).

Both of the armoured divisions, whose original establishment had been two armoured brigades and a support group, had by this time been reduced in strength by an armoured brigade each, but the independent tank brigades were retained by the Army. For most of 1943 the Australian forces in the combined South-West and South Pacific armies were larger than those deployed by the Americans, and in October 1943, for example, there were 492,000 Australian land forces in the South-West Pacific and 198,000 United States troops.

During the early months of 1944, Australian troops continued to advance along the east coast of New Guinea, and in April 1944 the Australian troops in the South-West Pacific theatre were grouped as two corps. I Corps consisted of the 6th, 7th and 9th AIF Divisions in Queensland (the 9th Division had returned from the Middle East after El Alamein) and II Corps of the 3rd, 5th and 11th Militia Divisions which now formed New Guinea Force.

Since the end of 1943 it had been envisaged that US Army forces would progressively take over the operational role of the Australian troops in New Guinea. As the American task forces leap-frogged from island to island their bases were still threatened by Japanese troops who had retreated into the hinterland after losing the battles for the beach-heads. Although the Japanese were largely cut off from their sources of supply their very presence could seriously disrupt American strategy since the momentum of the advance would be lost if American forces had to be constantly detached to hold the base perimeters. MacArthur decided that this was a task for the Australians. Twelve Australian brigades were to be distributed amongst the bases in Bougainville, New Guinea, New Britain, and the smaller islands, thereby freeing six American divisions. To carry out this deployment the 6th Division was transferred to II Corps and together with the Militia divisions it was to see considerable action against the surviving Japanese garrisons.

In April 1945 the remaining divisions of I Corps were given a role in the northern advance, the 7th Division being allocated to the conquest of Balikpapau in Dutch Borneo and the 9th Division to that of Tarakan in Dutch Borneo and Brunei Bay in British Borneo. In May and July the landings were successfully accomplished and Australian forces continued mopping-up operations until the Japanese surrender in August.

The gross strength of the Australian Army during World War II was 727,703, and of this figure 396,661 had served overseas. Its total battle casualties amounted to 61,575 including 18,713 dead. When Japan surrendered, the Army's strength stood at 385,000 with 167,000 serving beyond the mainland.

UNIFORM During the long hard and humid campaign in New Guinea, the Australians found that their tropical clothing simply rotted and fell apart, uniforms and equipment were gnawed by rats and metal fittings rusted.

The Australians began to develop a new jungle-green battledress which would stand up to the ravages of jungle warfare. Buttons had to be made of a material which did not rust and shirts and trousers had to be both rat and mosquito-proof. The felt slouch hat, although popular was expensive, and had to be replaced by a much cheaper and more practical jungle beret.

Footwear was a great problem, and a new jungle boot which gripped in mud and slime, and non-shrinking socks replaced the leather ammunition boot.

During the final stages of the war, Australian troops began to receive increasing amounts of American clothing and equipment.

At the beginning of the New Guinea campaign the average Australian infantryman carried 80 lb of equipment, but this was found to be far too heavy, so much thought was given to reducing the soldier's load to a bare minimum of 35 lb or maximum of 40 lb. It was also found

Below: Australian infantrymen of the 42nd Battalion advancing through swamps on Bougainville, January 1945.

more practical to wear the personal equipment as high up the body as possible (see figure 345) since this prevented items of equipment swinging and making a noise. The Australian jungle veteran carried his personal possessions in a waterproof wallet and his ammunition and extra rations in special large pouches, while the haversack had an extra pocket for clothing. The blanket roll was made up of a special lightweight blanket, half shelter tent, and either a gas cape or light waterproof poncho which was termed the 'Brown Special'.

Australian Air Force

Australia provided four units to help defend Malaya; these were Nos. 1 and 8 Squadrons with Lockheed Hudson bombers and Nos. 21 and 453 Squadrons with Brewster Buffalo fighters. The latter suffered badly, however, at the hands of superior Japanese fighters.

As the war in the Pacific brought hostilities closer to home, two further Hudson units were established on the islands of Timor and Ambon. After the all-but-unopposed attack on Darwin, Nos. 75 and 76 Squadrons formed for home defence, while Nos. 452 and 457 were recalled, with No. 54 Squadron RAF, in January 1943 for the same purpose.

By mid-1943, nearly 144,000 personnel were serving in the RAAF, of whom over 127,000 were in Australia or the Pacific Islands. No. 9 Group was to play a vital role in the American attack on Rabaul, New Britain, with its amphibious aircraft and bombers. No. 10 Group, now known as 1st Tactical Air Force, forged north to the Philippines.

The RAAF's total wartime enlistment had numbered 189,700 men and 27,200 women. Its losses in Europe were 5397 killed and 947 injured, in the Middle East 1135 and 413 respectively, and the totals in all theatres 10,562 and 3192.

Uniform Uniform and insignia were basically similar to those of the British forces, although later in the war American items of clothing became more common.

Australian Navy

In 1939 the Royal Australian Navy comprised seven cruisers, 17 destroyers and 74 escort and minesweeping vessels. Up to 1941 it had supplied vessels to the Allied war effort in the Mediterranean (where the cruiser HMAS *Sydney* had sunk the Italian cruiser *Bartolomeo Colleoni* before being herself sunk with all hands by a German raider) and to convoy escort.

The main thrust of Australian naval effort after 1941 was naturally in the Pacific, however, and the Navy's vessels were heavily engaged from the battle of the Java Sea onwards, and participated in the landings in the Solomons and at Guadalcanal. Task Force 44 (the Anzac Squadron) was part of the Allied drive back to the Philippines, and its units played their part in the battle of Leyte Gulf. Vessels also served in the Burma campaign, and as part of the British Pacific Fleet late in the war.

Uniform Uniform was basically as for the British Royal Navy.

346 Leading Seaman, Royal Australian Navy, 1943

Depicted in an off-duty moment, this Australian seaman wears a white tropical version of the serge temperate uniform. His badge of rank, an anchor on the left arm, surmounts a chevron denoting at least three years' good conduct. The non-substantive badge on the right arm is that of a leading torpedoman.

346

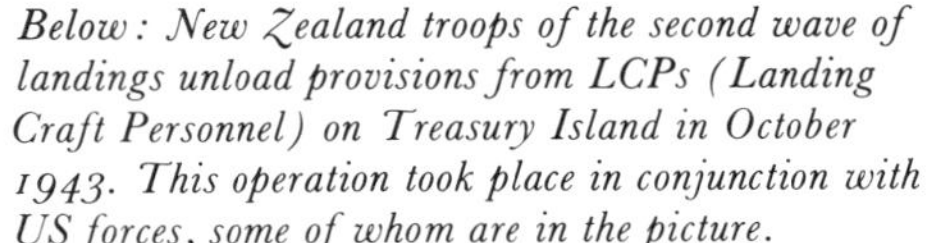

Below: New Zealand troops of the second wave of landings unload provisions from LCPs (Landing Craft Personnel) on Treasury Island in October 1943. This operation took place in conjunction with US forces, some of whom are in the picture.

New Zealand army

The 8th New Zealand Brigade Group arrived on the island of Fiji on 1 November 1940. Its units were brigaded with those of the Fiji Defence Force (one full battalion of Fijian troops plus a number of cadres) and in addition a number of guerrilla groups were formed consisting of 30 New Zealand officers and NCOs and 200 native Fijians.

By the end of November 1940 the 8th Brigade Group totalling 3053 all ranks was established on Viti Levu, the most important island of the Fiji group, in two defence zones 150 miles apart. The 8th Brigade was then joined by the 14th Brigade and eventually became the 3rd New Zealand Division. In July 1942 the division was relieved by American troops.

In November 1942 the division moved to New Caledonia as part of training for the Solomons campaign. A third brigade was formed with two battalions but saw only a short period of service, being disbanded before the division moved up to the Solomons. Nevertheless by the spring the strength of the formation had reached 17,800 officers and men. In August 1943 the division moved to the New Hebrides where final planning and battle training was carried out before it sailed for Guadalcanal. The New Zealanders served in a support capacity for the rest of the war.

Uniform and insignia New Zealand forces wore uniform based on the British pattern (see figure 347), although later in the war the vast influx of US material meant that American clothing became much more common (for example see the pilot in figure 348). Badges of rank were as for the British armed forces, with formation signs on the upper arm.

New Zealand air force

On the outbreak of war, the Royal New Zealand Air Force numbered some 756 regulars and 404 territorials. It had, however, supplied over 100 fully-trained pilots to the Royal Air Force. The New Zealand Government waived its claim to 30 Vickers Wellington bombers, the first six of which became the 'New Zealand Flight, RAF'. By April 1940, this had expanded to form No. 75 (NZ) Squadron.

The RNZAF in the Pacific was well-supplied with American equipment, and eight bomber, eleven fighter, two transport and two flying boat squadrons were mustered. Final casualty figures were 338 dead, and 58 seriously wounded.

For uniform see under Army.

347

348

New Zealand navy

The New Zealand Division of the Royal Navy was renamed the Royal New Zealand Navy in 1941. At this time, its order of battle comprised: two light cruisers, one minesweeping trawler and one training ship.

The RNZN was dependent to a large degree on assistance from Royal Navy personnel on secondment. The total of 1339 serving men at the outbreak of war included 615 RN, while reserve strength numbered 732. By the cessation of hostilities, the RNZN numbered 5794 persons, of whom only 562 were from the Royal Navy. Additionally, 1086 officers and 2397 ratings of New Zealand origin had joined the Royal Navy.

The two light cruisers *Leander* and *Achilles* were active in support of the American Task Force in the Pacific before the former was holed by a torpedo in mid-1943 and later retired. By this time, four minesweeping trawlers, corvettes and many smaller vessels had been added to the line. A corvette and a cruiser were launched in 1945.

Uniform was as for the Royal Navy.

347 Lieutenant, New Zealand Army, 1944

This New Zealand officer serving with the 1st Battalion of the Fiji Infantry in the central Solomons wears a British steel helmet with string netting, 1937-pattern web anklets and ammunition boots, with khaki drill uniform and wool puttees. His lieutenant's stars are carried alongside the Fiji Infantry formation sign at the shoulder. His belt, pistol magazine pouch and dispatch case are US Army issue, while he is armed with a US Cal.45 M1911A1 automatic pistol in a russet leather holster. A field dressing pouch is also visible on the belt.

348 Officer, Royal New Zealand Air Force, 1944

This aircrewman has British ankle boots, but his lightweight flying overalls, cap and knife are American. By this stage of the war, the immense output of US industry meant that US equipment was used by nations such as New Zealand which were traditionally supplied by Great Britain. The 'New Zealand' shoulder insignia in red on light khaki remained, however, a distinctive recognition feature. The pictured officer was one of the crew of a twin-engined Lockheed Ventura patrol bomber, a type widely used by the Allies in the Pacific where maritime surveillance was of paramount importance. Normal crew complement of the American-built Ventura was four or five.

349

Netherlands

The original Dutch East Indies Army had been formed in 1830, but when war broke out in the Far East, Dutch forces numbered about 1000 officers and 34,000 men, of whom 28,000 were natives.

The island of Curaçao was defended by a reasonably well-trained and armed local militia, while the East Indies had only weak territorial guard units. The Royal Netherlands Indian Army comprised one division and several independent units.

In December 1941 there were 400 marines in the Dutch East Indies. At Surabaia and at the marine barracks at Goebeng there were two companies of 125 men, a motorised anti-parachute brigade and a guard detachment.

On 21 January 1942 a group of Dutch marines left for training in the United States, where it was planned to form an armoured battalion of 1200 marines with 74 tanks to serve in the USMC in the Pacific. With the liberation of Holland in 1944–45 the brigade was able to recruit additional personnel.

The Air Force in December 1941 was controlled by a commandant with an operational headquarters, inspectorate, and services department which dealt with administration and supply.

The flying forces were formed into a regiment with three bomber groups, two fighter groups, and one reconnaissance group. In December 1941 the aircraft strength was 389 planes of all types.

Uniform The grey-green colonial uniform, originally introduced in 1916, was worn by both Army and Air Force personnel. The uniform was the same as that worn by figure 349 except that the Army straw hat was worn with the flap turned up on the left and fastened with a circular cockade in a reddish-orange, white and blue. There was also a peaked cap with black band, peak and chinstrap and circular cockade. All ranks wore their badges of rank on detachable collar patches. In 1939 a khaki drill uniform was introduced for Air Force personnel, but it is not known how widely it was worn.

Marines wore the uniform illustrated by figure 349, although the steel helmet was usually worn in action. Officers wore their badges of rank on detachable shoulder straps. Marines trained and equipped in America wore the USMC uniform with either American Marine rank badges or miniature Dutch marine rank badges in metal on the collar.

350

349 Sergeant-Major, Royal Netherlands Marines, 1942
This marine NCO wears a lightweight version of the standard Dutch grey-green uniform. His straw hat with tally would have been replaced by the distinctive Dutch steel helmet before going into action. The equipment is natural leather, and the gas mask was the Dutch pattern. His rank is shown by the collar patches.

350 Aircrewman, Royal Netherlands Indian Army Air Service, 1942
Serving in Singapore during the preparations to withstand the Japanese assault, this airman has been issued with a Dutch 6.5mm M95 rifle. He wears the lightweight grey-green uniform and padded cap with black band and national cockade. The badge on his left breast (a bomb on a winged wreath) is for bomber aircrew.

Left: A captain (recognisable as such by the three stars on his collar patch) checks the equipment of a Dutch bugler. As with the British colonial forces, the Dutch units in the East Indies were noted for their smartness; but they were far too few to resist the Japanese onslaught.

UNITED STATES
ARMY

The rapid Japanese advance across South-East Asia and the Pacific following the attack on Pearl Harbor on 7 December 1941 caught the US Army by surprise. Outnumbered and isolated, America's Pacific island garrisons fell to the Japanese armed forces, although the beleaguered US troops put up a fierce struggle.

By the spring of 1942, the Japanese had achieved their initial war aims and looked to extend their conquests further south; New Guinea and Guadalcanal were the targets. It was here that the Japanese met their first check on land, as combined US Army and Marine forces, with the aid of the Australian Army, repulsed the Japanese offensive.

The battles of 1942 exhausted the Japanese and put them on the defensive, thereby giving the US forces the initiative which they kept throughout the remainder of the war. Given the amphibious nature of much of the fighting, the Army worked in close co-operation with the Navy and the Marine Corps. There was considerable debate within the services as to the conduct of the Pacific War – inter-service rivalries centring on the primacy of their respective roles and allocation of resources – but these conflicts did little to impair the overall American effort.

American strategy in the Pacific involved a two-pronged assault: the one under General MacArthur (mainly the responsibility of the Army) and the other under the command of Admiral Nimitz to capture the Central Pacific islands, this second offensive coming under the control of the Navy but involving Army and Marine troops as the land fighting force.

Although the Japanese held on to their island bastions with a remarkable tenacity, they were unable to stem the American advance. By the end of 1944 the US Army had returned to the Philippines, where the US 6th Army, with the 8th in support, set about the destruction of the 250,000-strong Japanese 14th Army. Parallel with the fighting in the Philippines, the newly-formed US 10th Army undertook the assault on Okinawa, which fell to the American forces on 22 June 1945.

During the summer of 1945, preparations were being made for the assault on the Japanese home islands, but this potentially bloody conflict was prevented by the Japanese surrender following the atomic bomb attacks.

Army casualties were relatively light in the Pacific theatre of operations: 160,454 casualties were sustained, of whom 28,880

Above: The land fighting in Leyte in October 1944. These soldiers, heavily laden with communications equipment, have managed to fight their way off the beach, but are still targets for small arms fire from isolated Japanese strongpoints or snipers who put up a brave defence against the Americans.

Below: While a phosphorous charge explodes on a Japanese fortification on the island of Corregidor in February 1945, soldiers of the 34th Regiment prepare to shoot any Japanese who emerge. The characteristic water bottle pouch of the American infantryman is clearly shown.

351 Major-General, US Army, 1944
Major-General Innis P. Swift, commander of the 1st Cavalry Division, is here shown at Los Negros in the Admiralty Islands in 1944. He wears the light khaki trousers and shirt, with canvas leggings and russet brown leather boots. The two stars on the helmet denote the rank of major-general. The corresponding service dress of a major-general is depicted in figure 354.

352 Officer, US Women's Army Corps, 1944
This officer wears the dark olive-drab cap and tunic with light khaki shirt. Her cap badge is the standard officers' late-war pattern of an unadorned eagle, while the collar badges are the head of Pallas Athene in gold (a winged propeller was used for USAAF women officers). Women other ranks wore circular gold badges on the collar with a similar design thereupon. The olive braid on tunic cuffs denoted the wearer's officer status.

353 Private, US Army, 1944
This infantryman in northern Burma wears waterproofed laced boots, two-piece jungle suit and M1 helmet. Apart from water bottle and ammunition pouches, he carries wire cutters on his belt. His weapon is the M1903 A4 sniper's rifle, with the M73 B1 (Weaver 330c) telescopic sight.

354 Major-General, US Army, 1944
This officer wears the light khaki service dress worn from 1943 onwards. The half-inch olive-drab band on the cuffs were borne by all officers, while those of general rank wore the letters 'US' in gold on the collar and had gold piping on the cap. This cap, the light khaki version of the garrison cap, was known as the 'chino'.

351

352

were killed in action. A further 4458 casualties were incurred by US forces in the China-Burma-India theatre.

ORGANISATION In 1941 the US Army was scattered in small outposts across the Pacific with the exception of the Philippines, where a substantial American presence was maintained to support the US-trained Philippine forces. American ground troops were formed into the Philippine Division, which was destroyed by the Japanese at Bataan, the whole formation either being killed or taken prisoner.

Activated in January 1943, the US 6th Army was the Army's spearhead in the Pacific island-hopping campaigns. Its first battle was the capture of Kiriwina in the Woodlark Islands in July 1943 which marked the opening stage in a 2700-mile advance to the Philippines. For the assault on the Philippines, the 6th was joined by the 8th Army which played a major role in the recapture of these islands.

By the end of the war, the 6th Army was organised into three corps of 10 divisions and the 8th Army consisted of two corps of eight divisions.

The 10th Army originally had been formed in June 1944 for the proposed invasion of Formosa, but its target was later changed to Okinawa. For the assault on Okinawa, the 10th Army comprised one infantry corps of four divisions and an amphibious corps of three US Marine divisions, a force of some 154,000 men. Although only activated for one battle during World War II, the 10th Army lost nearly 50,000 men on Okinawa.

The infantry divisions which formed the backbone of the three US armies in the Pacific were organised on the same basis as those in Europe (examined on page 150). What was required for fighting small last-ditch groups of Japanese in difficult conditions was a cohesive structure at the section and platoon level and the Army gave much thought to the selection of individuals able to lead small groups of men.

The United States possessed two cavalry divisions at the outbreak of war, but only the 1st Cavalry Division saw action as part of the 6th Army. The division was organised on the old 'square' (as opposed to 'triangular') basis of two cavalry brigades, each of two regiments. In addition there were two field artillery battalions which, with the standard auxiliary divisional services brought the formation's strength to 12,724 men.

One airborne division was allocated to the Pacific theatre, the 11th, which fought in an infantry as well as an airborne role in the Philippines. The 11th Airborne Division was organised as the European theatre divisions, but on the old, smaller pattern (see page 234), with an overall strength of only 8505 men. No large independent tank forces were formed in the Pacific theatre; only in the Philippines and on Okinawa were tanks used extensively.

As well as the main Pacific theatres of operation, US Army troops were actively engaged in the fighting in China and Burma. The most famous US unit involved in the Burmese campaign was 'Merrill's Marauders' which, under the command of General Stilwell, became the 'Mars' Task Force and consisted of the

353

354

a new M1942 one-piece olive drab overall began to be issued, but it too was found impractical for wear during a campaign in which dysentery was common.

In the meantime the Office of the Quarter-Master General (OQMG) had been modifying the one-piece overall and developing other items of clothing for wear in jungle operations. Towards the end of July 1942 the OQMG received an urgent request from General MacArthur for 150,000 sets of special jungle equipment, and although development was not complete twelve items had to be standardised for immediate procurement and issue. The resulting one-piece camouflage jungle uniform was found satisfactory in the jungles of Panama, but in New Guinea the 'frog skin', as it was known, was found too heavy, too hot and too uncomfortable.

These criticisms led to the development of new materials which, unlike the herringbone twill, did not become so heavy when wet. In this new material a two-piece jungle suit was developed and manufactured and became standard issue in May 1943.

Below: American soldiers examine the damage done by a Japanese air attack on Paranaque in the Philippines on 13 December 1941. These Japanese raids were very successful and crippled the American air defences. General Douglas MacArthur commanded a force of almost 100,000 men in the islands; but of these, only 15,000 were American regulars. The men here are wearing a mixture of uniforms, including British helmets.

US 475th Infantry and 124th Cavalry Regiments, the Chinese 1st Regiment and the US 612th Field Artillery Regiment.

Uniform At the start of the war in the Pacific, American soldiers wore khaki drill uniforms which were officially known as Class C uniforms or 'chinos'. The basic service dress for enlisted men consisted of a sun helmet, worn officially until 1942, a side or overseas cap, long-sleeved shirt either worn open or with matching tie and long matching trousers with black shoes and socks. Officers wore the same uniform but in addition had a khaki drill service dress tunic. Both officers and men had a drill version of the peaked service cap with brown leather peak and chin strap.

Combat dress was also the Class C 'chino' worn with either the British pattern steel helmet or the new M1 helmet and canvas leggings with brown leather laced ankle boots. Equipment was the standard woven pattern.

This uniform was immediately found to be uncomfortable and impractical, and far too conspicuous for jungle warfare, so

355

355 Captain, US Army Air Force, 1944
Captain Benjamin Oliver Davis Jnr. wears the Shearling flying suit with B-3 jacket and A-3 trousers. The B-2 flying cap was fleece lined and had earflaps. Normal dress under the flying suit was either a beige or OD shirt and beige tie, and beige trousers or 'pinks'.

356 Pilot, USAAF, 1944
This pilot with the 1st US Air Commando Force in Burma wears the standard peaked cap, olive-drab shirt and airborne forces' trousers. His weapons are a fighting knife and a M1911 A1 automatic pistol.

356

Another problem was one of colour. Reports from the South-West Pacific indicated that the camouflage uniform was fine for stationary snipers, but made men on the move easy to spot. Early in 1944, 400 sets of a new jungle uniform in both poplin and cotton drill were issued for field testing. After various modifications suggested by those who had worn the suit in action, the new two-piece jungle uniform made of 5-ounce olive green poplin was standardised on 11 July 1945.

INSIGNIA Generally speaking no insignia or badges of rank were worn in combat, but various units devised systems of markings which were painted on the helmet or back so that they were only visible from the rear. The 27th Infantry Division painted their steel helmets in dark green with black splodges and a parallelogram. Within the parallelogram was a regimental emblem, on the left was a number which corresponded to a rank, and on the right the company letter. On all other uniforms the same badges of rank and other insignia were worn as on the temperate uniform.

AIR FORCE

In the war against Germany the United States Air Force had a virtual monopoly of aerial operations but in the Pacific theatre the Air Force worked in conjunction with the aviation branches of the Navy and the Marine Corps. Despite this the Air Force's own contribution to the defeat of Japan was far from negligible, some seven air forces being deployed in the Pacific and Far East.

Many American bases in the Pacific were lost to the Japanese in the first few months of the war, a period which revealed the superiority of Japanese aircraft against America's slow and outdated planes. The American recovery was rapid, however, and by the end of 1942 an organisational network had been established in which to deploy the United States' vast industrial resources. The Doolittle raid on Japan on 18 April 1942 was a foretaste of things to come; although the raid did little material damage it was a considerable source of humiliation to the Japanese and a morale-booster to the Americans.

Throughout 1942–43 the Air Force acted in a largely tactical role in support of naval and land forces operations. The Air Force provided transportation and reconnaissance duties as well as carrying out massive bombardments on Japanese island strongholds. By 1944 the air war against Japan was taking on an increasingly strategic aspect as long range bombers attacked Japanese supply centres in China and Indo-China as well as instigating an all-out offensive against the major cities of the Japanese homeland.

During the last months of the war the US Air Force was almost unopposed over Japan and inflicted massive damage on the Japanese urban centres and huge casualties on the civilian population. Tokyo, for instance, had an urban area of 110 square miles, over half of which was destroyed in a series of raids by the USAAF. The war was brought to a conclusion with the dropping of atomic bombs on Hiroshima and Nagasaki.

In the Pacific war the US Air Force flew a total of 669,235 sorties, dropped 502,781 tons of bombs, lost 4530 aircraft and claimed 10,343 enemy aircraft.

Total United States Army Air Force casualties for World War II were 116,501, of whom 32,170 were killed in action.

Organisation The vast distances of the Pacific and the Far East entailed the division of the USAAF into a number of separate air forces stationed in India, China, Australia and the Pacific Islands. Each air force was responsible for a certain geographical area and certain tasks within that area. The seven US air forces were as follows:

5th Air Force – based in Australia, covered the South-West Pacific and was later engaged in the bombing of Japan from bases in Okinawa;
7th Air Force – operated from Hawaii against Japanese targets in the central Pacific and the Japanese homeland;
10th Air Force – responsible for transport and reconnaissance duties as well as combat operations in Burma and Thailand including support for the Chindits and 'Merrill's Marauders';
11th Air Force – a defence and reconnaissance air force based in Alaska, although it carried out attacks on the Kurile Islands;
13th Air Force – conducted independent strategic bombing as well as tactical support for the land forces in the Solomons;
14th Air Force – originated from the 'Flying Tigers' and worked with the Chinese Army against Japanese targets in China;

Above: Groundcrewmen in casual working clothing arm an American fighter-bomber with rockets. Rockets were a useful weapon against enemy communications, and they were highly effective against tanks.

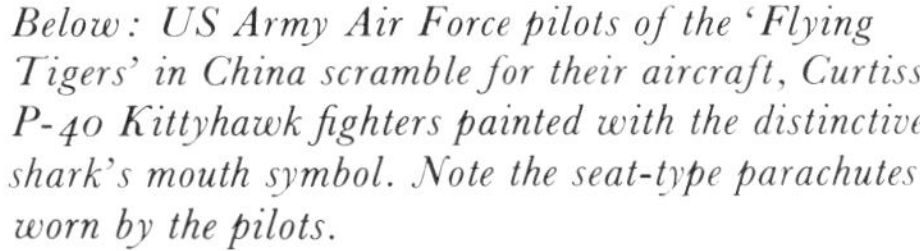

Below: US Army Air Force pilots of the 'Flying Tigers' in China scramble for their aircraft, Curtiss P-40 Kittyhawk fighters painted with the distinctive shark's mouth symbol. Note the seat-type parachutes worn by the pilots.

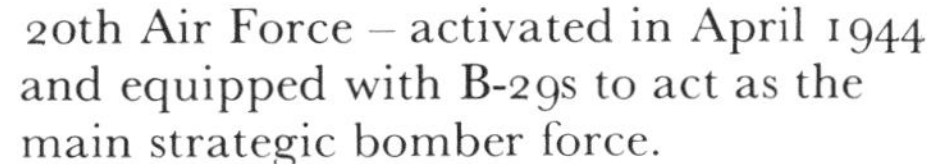

20th Air Force – activated in April 1944 and equipped with B-29s to act as the main strategic bomber force.

The war in the Pacific demonstrated American organisational flexibility with each air force carrying out its various tasks with considerable success. The Japanese in contrast lacked this flexibility and paid the price accordingly; their failure to adapt to changing circumstances ensured that their meagre resources were wasted and their homeland left unprotected against US bombers.

Uniform Air Force personnel wore the same Class C uniforms as the rest of the Army. Officers wore the khaki drill service dress consisting of peaked cap, shirt, tunic, long trousers and brown shoes.

The Air Force winged-propeller emblem in metal appeared on the left side of the overseas cap worn by enlisted men and on the left side of the shirt collar. Officers wore the same emblem on the tunic lapels.

On Class C uniforms rank chevrons were in khaki on blue backing.

Above: The 201st Mexican Fighter Squadron assembles in front of a P-47 Thunderbolt on Porac strip, Clark Field, Luzon.

357 Petty Officer 3rd Class, US Navy, 1943
This Samoan fita-fita *was a cook with the US Navy (he wears his speciality badge on his* lava-lava*). He has a ribbon of the Purple Heart on a standard Navy undershirt. Note the red turban, waist sash and four – sometimes three – red bands below the badge. The US armed forces were obliged to employ numerous foreign auxiliaries to maintain their long lines of supply. This was particularly necessary in the Pacific island chains.*

358 Lieutenant, US Navy, 1941
This naval airman wears the green service dress. The black lace stripes and star on the cuffs and the silver bars on the shirt collar denote the rank of lieutenant. The wings on his left breast are the naval aviation badge.

359 Lieutenant Junior Grade, Women's Auxiliary Volunteer Service, 1942
This lieutenant's rank is shown by the sleeve stripes in reserve blue, and the silver bars on the shirt. Her head-dress is the standard summer cap with Navy officers' cap badge. The collar badges represented a white anchor on a blue propeller.

MEXICAN AIR FORCE

The first Mexican military unit ever to fight outside Mexico was the 201st Mexican Fighter Squadron (*Escadrilla Aguilas Aztecas*) which arrived in Manila on 1 May 1945.

After a short period of acclimatisation and intensive training in American fighter command tactics its 52 officers and 244 men joined in group support missions against Japanese ground forces in central and north Luzon. Nine Mexican airmen lost their lives before the unit was finally disbanded on 1 December 1945.

UNIFORM Mexican Expeditionary Air Force personnel wore Mexican uniforms off duty but American Army Air Force clothing and equipment on active service. Some pilots continued to wear the olive green Mexican Army peaked and side caps. Mexican rank badges were worn on flying clothing and overalls.

NAVY

The weight of American naval effort was directed to the Pacific and, in this theatre of war, naval power, usually expressed in terms of carrier-based aircraft, was to be absolutely crucial. The great influence of American manufacturing capacity was nowhere more clearly shown than in the Pacific naval battles, where the US superiority in building aircraft carriers quickly became the decisive factor.

In late 1941, the US Navy consisted of:
16 battleships;
7 aircraft carriers;
18 heavy cruisers;
19 light cruisers;
6 anti-aircraft cruisers;
171 destroyers;
114 submarines.

At the beginning of the Pacific War, the United States Pacific Fleet based at Pearl Harbor consisted of eight battleships and three aircraft carriers. After the attack on 7 December the Japanese sunk four battleships, severely damaged three others, and one was beached. In all, 2403 Americans were killed and 1176 wounded. Fortunately, the three fleet carriers, *Enterprise*, *Lexington* and *Saratoga* were absent from Pearl Harbor and survived unscathed along with five cruisers and twenty-nine destroyers to form the nucleus of the new expanded Pacific Fleet.

Naval building had been increasing in tempo since the 'Two Ocean' Act of 1940, but the Navy was hard-put to match the Japanese forces in the aftermath of Pearl Harbor. The immediate reaction of the United States was to construct, with great speed, four fast carriers of the Essex class (which carried 90 aircraft each) and five carriers carrying 40 aircraft each.

After the stalemate of the Coral Sea and the victory of Midway in the summer of 1942, the initiative lay with the US Navy, and it rapidly brought into service

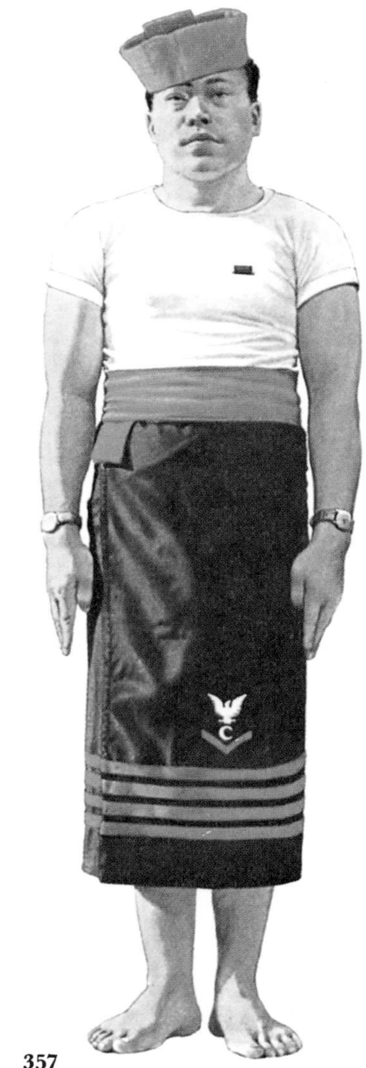

357

an enormous tonnage of new warships. The defeat of Japan then became inevitable. The attempts of the Japanese fleet to inflict a large-scale defeat on the American Navy at the battle of the Philippine Sea in June 1944 and the battle of Leyte Gulf later that year, were both disasters and hastened American victory.

There were three basic layers to the US Navy's success in the Pacific. The first was its carrier fleet, and the creation of such organisations as the Fast Carrier Task Forces based upon this strength. A total of 27 new carriers was completed before the end of hostilities, and over 75,000 aircraft were delivered to the Navy as a whole between 1940 and 1945. Naval aviation personnel strength went from 10,923 (2,695 of whom were pilots) in 1940 to 437,524 (with 60,747 pilots) by August 1945.

The second layer was the development of techniques of amphibious landing. Over 66,000 landing craft were built during the war, and the vast majority were used in the Pacific.

Thirdly, there was the submarine war.

Above: During the invasion of Mindoro in December 1944, anti-aircraft gunners on a US Navy cruiser anxiously watch a plane overhead.

358

359

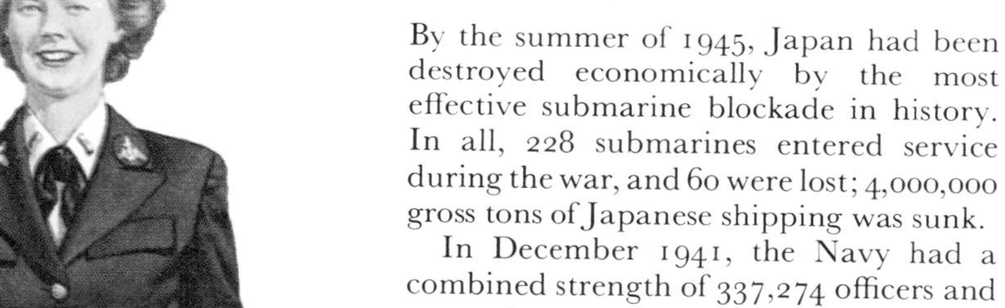

By the summer of 1945, Japan had been destroyed economically by the most effective submarine blockade in history. In all, 228 submarines entered service during the war, and 60 were lost; 4,000,000 gross tons of Japanese shipping was sunk.

In December 1941, the Navy had a combined strength of 337,274 officers and men; by 1945, there were 3,383,196 personnel of whom 1,574,614 served afloat.

Organisation Within the Pacific theatre, two commands were set up: the Pacific Ocean Area under the command of Admiral Chester W. Nimitz and the South West Pacific Area commanded by General Douglas MacArthur. The former advocated an advance across the expanse of the Pacific Ocean via the Gilbert, Marshall and Marianas Islands towards Formosa; the latter rejected this in favour of an 'island hopping' manoeuvre based on Australia towards the Philippines. Both strategies would have the effect of isolating the Japanese home islands from the oil resources of the Dutch East Indies. The means differed, however, reflecting the interests of the two services: Nimitz's thrust would give maximum scope for the use of naval power, whilst MacArthur's would relegate the Navy to a supporting role. In the event, such were the resources of the United States that she could sustain both these axes of advance.

Right: Ordnancemen load 500lb demolition bombs onto a Douglas SBD Dauntless bomber on board the USS Enterprise *on 7 August 1942. This was the first day of the attacks on Guadalcanal – Tulagi, the opening of the campaign which wrested the initiative in the Pacific away from the Japanese. The US Navy, fighting hard in the 'Slot' to keep the US ground forces supplied and to isolate the Japanese, suffered severe casualties; and the* Enterprise *herself was so severely damaged on the night of 24 August that she had to withdraw from the battle.*

Far right: Marine Corps artillerymen operate a field howitzer lashed to a cliff edge on Tinian in the Marianas.

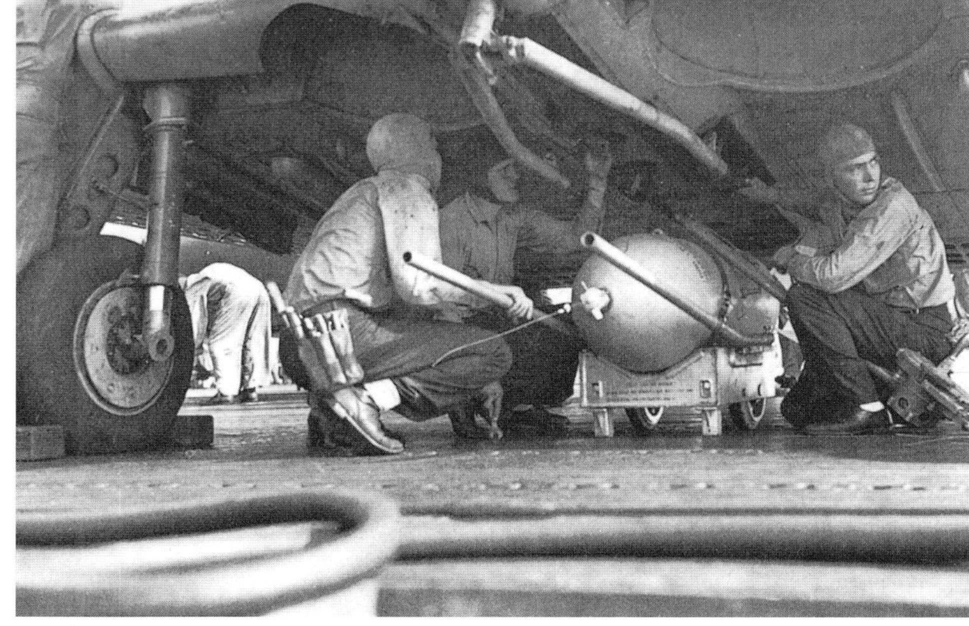

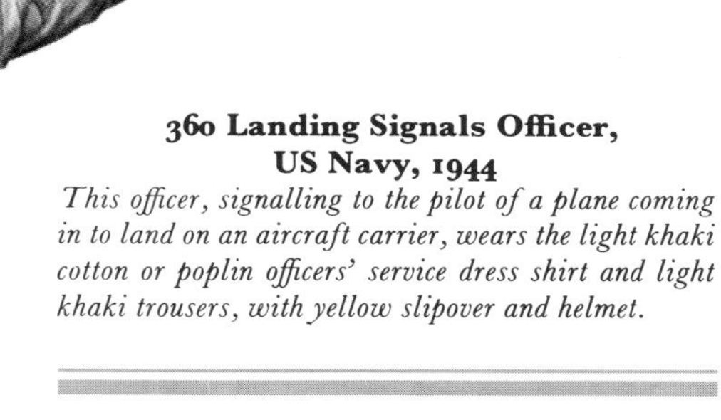

360 Landing Signals Officer, US Navy, 1944

This officer, signalling to the pilot of a plane coming in to land on an aircraft carrier, wears the light khaki cotton or poplin officers' service dress shirt and light khaki trousers, with yellow slipover and helmet.

360

In March 1943 the Central Pacific Force was created as part of Nimitz's Pacific Fleet and commanded by Admiral Raymond Spruance. By the summer of 1943 it had been built up into the largest fleet the world had ever seen and was designated the 5th Fleet in April 1944. There were three task forces: TF50, a fast carrier force with eleven aircraft carriers, six battleships and six heavy cruisers; TF54 which included the amphibious assault force; and TF57 which combined control of all the shore-based naval aircraft, plus the Mobile Service Squadron of repair ships, destroyer tenders and tugs. The whole force totalled 19 aircraft carriers and 900 aircraft.

The fleet was naturally subdivided to suit the operation in hand. For example, the attacks on the Gilbert and Marshall Islands served as models for later amphibious operations. TF52 and 53 formed the attack forces North and South. Each task force was a separate, self-contained force of three escort carriers, a squadron of battleships and a squadron of cruisers with 14 destroyers for bombardment and close escort of the transport ships. The Fast Carrier Force, now redesignated TF58, organised into four task groups sharing six large and five light carriers, each group protected by its own screen of fast battleships, cruisers and destroyers, provided the aerial assault force. TF57 provided land-based air cover (which included over 100 Liberator heavy bombers) under Navy command – an innovation borrowed from Japanese organisation. This vast armada totalled

over 200 ships and 1000 aircraft. During the attack on the Marianas, Task Force 58 was divided into self-contained task groups of even greater size and fighting power. TF58.1 comprised the aircraft carriers *Hornet, Yorktown, Bellau Wood,* and *Bataan*; TF58.2 *Bunker Hill, Wasp, Monterey* and *Cabot;* TF58.3 *Enterprise, Lexington, Princeton* and *San Jacinto;* TF58.4 *Essex, Langley* and *Cowpens.* In all, there were 15 aircraft carriers, seven battleships, 13 cruisers and 58 destroyers.

Meanwhile, MacArthur's drive in the South-West Pacific was supported by the South Pacific Force under Admiral Halsey (formed in 1942) which was redesignated the 3rd Fleet in March 1943. MacArthur did not, however, have total control over Halsey's forces. The naval units most closely connected to MacArthur's advance were the Naval Forces South-West Pacific, redesignated the 7th Fleet under the command of Vice-Admiral Carpender in March 1943; Carpender was succeeded by Vice-Admiral Kinkaid in November 1943.

In 1944, as the Americans gradually closed in on the Japanese, the decision was taken to combine the 5th Fleet with the 3rd Fleet and to alternate the command of this vast force between Spruance and Admiral Halsey. When the one Admiral commanded the other would retire with his staff to Pearl Harbor to plan his next operation. When Halsey commanded it became the 3rd Fleet, and when Spruance returned it reverted to the 5th; thus the task forces became 38 and not 58; the ships' names, however, remained the same.

This arrangement worked very well; it was one of the most novel solutions to the organisation problems of this vast theatre.

UNIFORM During the war the service dress of US Navy officers and chief petty officers was the khaki drill Army uniform. It consisted of peaked cap with khaki cover, open single-breasted khaki tunic, shirt which could be worn open or closed with black tie, matching long trousers and black shoes. Other forms of head-dress were the khaki drill overseas cap and a drill baseball cap with peak. The pre-war white uniform continued as a dress uniform.

The khaki drill uniform was not totally satisfactory, however, and its colour was found to be conspicuous, so it was sometimes dyed grey, or officers acquired a grey working dress on which black rank distinction lace was worn on the shoulder straps.

The Navy blue and white square rigs were retained for dress or undress occasions, and the most typical form of everyday wear in wartime was the white fatigue cap, white T-shirt, blue denim shirt and blue jeans. In action all ranks wore the grey-painted M1 steel helmet, and a blue canvas lifejacket. In many ships during the war helmets were painted in bright colours which indicated special duties, so that, for example, fire control men wore red-painted steel helmets.

INSIGNIA Rank badges not only identified rank but also whether the wearer was a member of the executive (or line branch) or one of the other Navy corps. Officers and warrant officers wore rank distinction lace in gold on the sleeves of the navy blue reefer and on the shoulder straps of the khaki tunic. On the shirt they wore Army rank badges on the collar (both sides for executive officers and on the right side only for other officers), as well as on the left front of the side cap. Petty officers had a special cap badge and wore their rank badges on the sleeve. Ratings only wore rank badges on the cuffs of the blue dress jumper.

MARINE CORPS

During World War II the US Marine Corps built up a reputation as one of America's toughest combat services; they were continuously engaged in the Pacific War from Wake Island in 1941 to Okinawa in 1945.

The Marines' first major campaign began with the assault on Guadalcanal in the Solomon Islands on 7 August 1942. With little naval and air support the Marines fought a desperate battle against the Japanese who launched a series of fanatical, but ultimately unsuccessful, attacks in an attempt to dislodge the Americans. After their victory on Guadalcanal the Marines were involved in the fighting in the central Pacific, most notably on Tarawa. The Marines' war continued with the capture of the Marianas Islands, and Iwo Jima and Okinawa.

361 Gunnery Sergeant, US Marine Corps, 1941

This sergeant is in full dress uniform. His rank is shown by the chevrons on the upper sleeve; the stripes on the lower sleeve are service stripes, one for each four years of service. The three medal ribbons are (left to right) that for service in Nicaragua (at some time between 1926 and 1933), the Marine Corps expeditionary badge and a Purple Heart. Below these he has two proficiency badges; the expert rifleman's badge (with four requalification bars) and the pistol competency badge.

361

Marine Corps casualties for World War II were 91,718 men of whom 15,161 were killed in action with a further 4322 dead through other causes.

Organisation The Marine Corps performed two basic military functions, firstly, to act as land combat troops for the Navy and, secondly, to carry out autonomous amphibious operations of their own. It was this latter function that expanded enormously during World War II within the branch known as the Fleet Marine Force.

In 1939 the strength of the Marine Corps stood at just under 20,000 men; by the outbreak of war in 1941 this had grown to 65,881 and by the end of the war there were more than 450,000 officers and men in the Marines. To some extent the Marine Corps was an army within an army, possessing its own aviation units.

In February 1941 the USMC was organised as two brigades which were then redesignated as the 1st and 2nd Marine Divisions. The process of bringing the new divisions up to strength was a slow one and it was not until the middle of 1942 that the formations were ready for action.

The Marine division was organised as a reinforced infantry division with three infantry regiments each of three battalions, and artillery, engineer and pioneer regiments. The size of the division was a little under 20,000 men and was often strengthened further for particular operations. Specialising in amphibious landings against fortified Japanese strongholds the Marine division had a large compliment of pioneers to clear the way for assault troops.

The two Marine divisions were combined into the First Marine Amphibious Corps (or IMAC), although because of the dispersed nature of the fighting in the Pacific this was more an administrative than a tactical grouping.

During 1943 a further three Marine divisions were raised followed by the activation of the 6th Marine Division in September 1944. A new corps was formed in 1943 and was called V Amphibious Corps (or VAC). This corps was engaged in the struggle for the Gilberts and the Marshalls and later the Marianas Islands. The 4th and 5th Marine Divisions led the assault on Iwo Jima, supported by the 3rd Marine Division, and suffered 23,303 casualties in the bitter struggle for the island.

The III Amphibious Corps, which had replaced IMAC, supported Army operations on Okinawa and consisted of the 1st, 2nd and 6th Marine Divisions. Some 15,000 Marine casualties were sustained out of a combined American total of nearly 50,000 men.

The Marine Corps aviation consisted of two air groups and 10 squadrons at the outbreak of war. Once at war the aviation branch underwent an exceptionally rapid expansion, however, so that by January 1945 there were five aircraft wings made up of 132 squadrons plus other auxiliary units. Personnel strength rose from a figure of 11,000 men in 1941 to 135,000 by 1945. The function of the Marine Corps aviation was to provide tactical air support for Marine land operations.

362

362 Lieutenant, US Marine Corps, 1945
Equipped for action in the Pacific theatre, this Marine officer carries two water bottles, a pistol in the leather holster, an M4 knife bayonet and pouches for field dressings and ammunition. He has a camouflage poncho strapped to his pack. Rank is denoted by the silver bars on the collar.

363 Lieutenant-Colonel, US Marine Corps, 1942
Lieutenant-Colonel Harold W. Bauer (shown here during the Guadalcanal campaign) was one of the first aces of the Marine air service. When he died in action in November 1942, he had scored eleven victories. He wears the one-piece herringbone-twill olive-drab overall (rather than the lightweight flying overalls) and a lightweight flying helmet. His parachute is the seat type for pilots of single-engined aircraft.

363

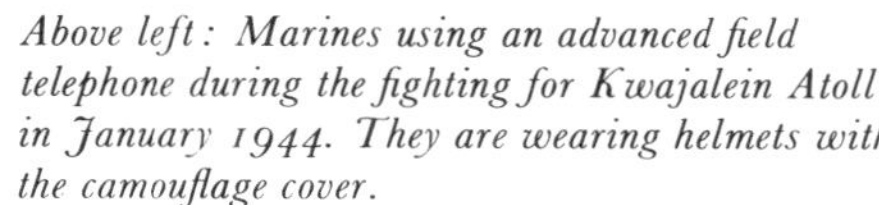

Above left: Marines using an advanced field telephone during the fighting for Kwajalein Atoll in January 1944. They are wearing helmets with the camouflage cover.

Above: A wounded Marine is brought off Iwo Jima by Coast Guardsmen. The landing craft which went in at Iwo Jima came back with the wounded, who were transferred to hospital ships. The speedy evacuation of wounded personnel was considered essential to maintain morale.

364

364 Private, US Marine Corps, 1943
This private in the New Guinea campaign has the M1 steel helmet with webbing cover. The two-piece herringbone-twill fatigue suit was introduced in 1942. The woven belt was normally worn only by officers, but is here seen with magazine and field dressing pouches affixed. The latter were very necessary in the hot and humid climate of New Guinea, where even minor wounds could quickly become infected without immediate attention. The herring-bone-twill suit was later discarded, as it became very heavy when wet.

365 Private, US Marine Corps, 1943
The basic clothing of this Marine is the two-piece USMC 'dungaree' uniform, which differed from the Army pattern in having a flapless pocket on the left breast. His M1 helmet has the 'beach' design of camouflage cover, and above the russet brown boots his gaiters are worn under the trousers. He has two captured Japanese trophies (sword and water bottle) hanging from the woven belt. His standard US-issue water bottle has been relegated to his left hip, while the badge is the USMC 'globe and anchor' design stencilled onto his uniform; the cherished symbol of this famous corps.

365

Left: Marines move forward on Saipan in June 1944. They are heavily armed to flush out Japanese strongpoints: the man on the left is carrying a bazooka.

UNIFORM The peacetime tropical uniform for American Marines was the Class C 'chinos' which were to all intents and purposes identical to those worn by American soldiers. The three basic items of head-dress were the side or overseas cap, the peaked service cap with black leather peak and chin strap, and the pith helmet. The Marine Corps cap badge in bronzed metal was worn on the front of the peaked cap and sun helmet, and on the left front of the side cap. The long sleeve shirt, tie and trousers were all made of matching khaki drill.

The fatigue dress consisted of an overseas cap, single-breasted jacket with patch pockets (on the left breast of which was printed in black the Marine Corps emblem surmounted by the letters USMC) and matching trousers. This uniform was also worn with woven equipment and steel helmet in combat.

At the beginning of the campaign in Guadalcanal in August 1942, most Marines wore the herringbone-twill fatigue suit, but camouflage clothing began to be introduced in stages. The first item was the helmet cover followed by a camouflage poncho, and then a one-piece camouflage jungle uniform.

A typical wartime Marine outfit was the sloppy peaked field cap, olive-drab T-shirt, long trousers tucked into lace-up gaiters, or into buckled combat boots.

INSIGNIA The Marine Corps emblem was worn on the left front of the overseas cap by enlisted men, while officers wore their badge of rank in metal. NCOs' chevrons on khaki drill were in dark green. Officers wore their badges of rank on the shirt collar.

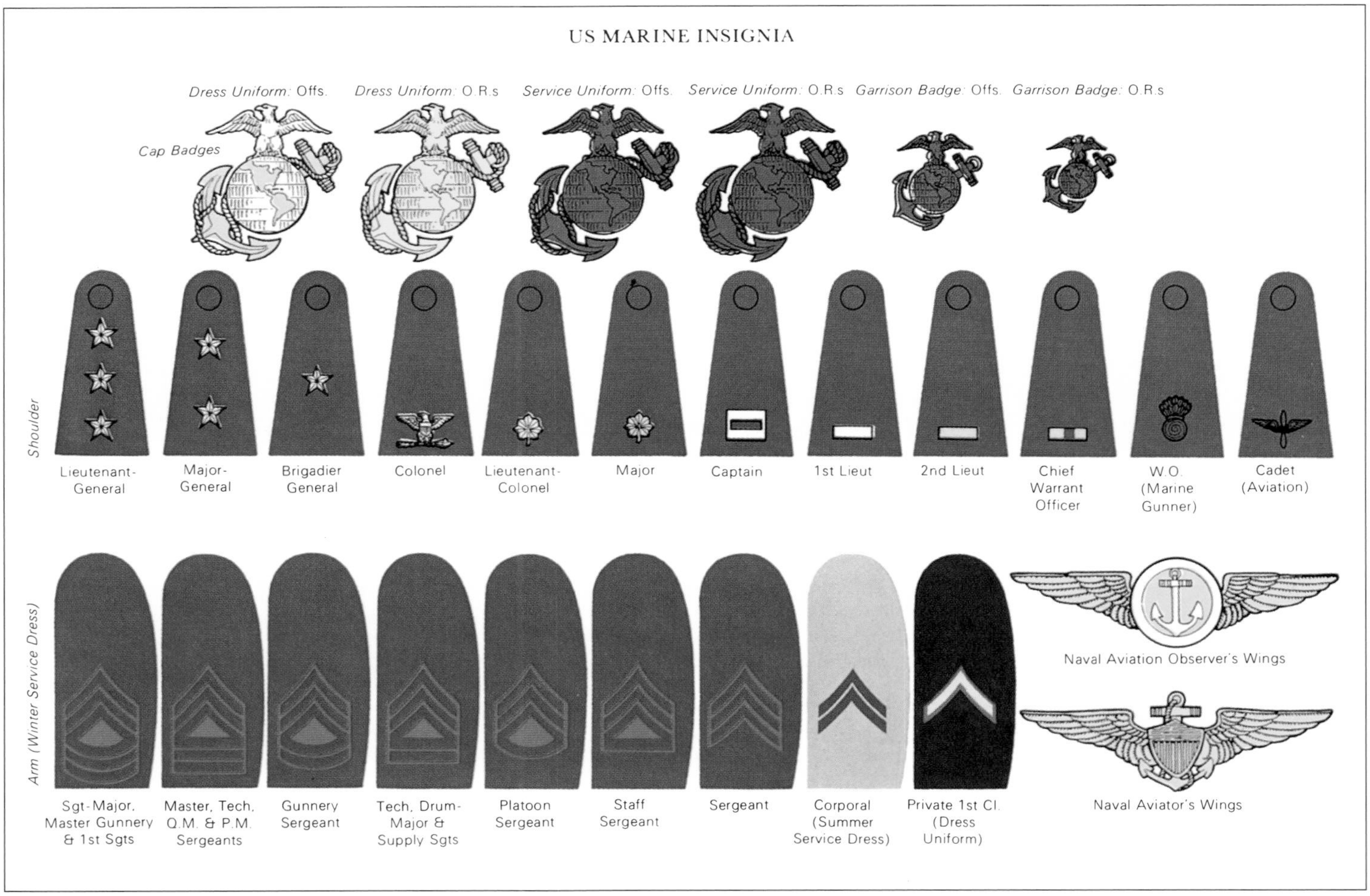

US MARINE INSIGNIA

Cap Badges

Dress Uniform: Offs. · *Dress Uniform:* O.R.s · *Service Uniform:* Offs. · *Service Uniform:* O.R.s · *Garrison Badge:* Offs. · *Garrison Badge:* O.R.s

Shoulder

Lieutenant-General · Major-General · Brigadier General · Colonel · Lieutenant-Colonel · Major · Captain · 1st Lieut · 2nd Lieut · Chief Warrant Officer · W.O. (Marine Gunner) · Cadet (Aviation)

Arm (Winter Service Dress)

Sgt-Major, Master Gunnery & 1st Sgts · Master, Tech. Q.M. & P.M. Sergeants · Gunnery Sergeant · Tech. Drum-Major & Supply Sgts · Platoon Sergeant · Staff Sergeant · Sergeant · Corporal (Summer Service Dress) · Private 1st Cl. (Dress Uniform)

Naval Aviation Observer's Wings

Naval Aviator's Wings

TABLE OF RANKS

The table of ranks which follows has been produced by the editors of the book, Ashley Brown and Adrian Gilbert, as a companion to Malcolm McGregor's insignia charts. It is the most comprehensive list available of the ranks of the Armies, Air Forces and Navies of World War II, and gives the original language versions of the translations we have used in the rank insignia plates. It is, of course, impossible to find completely accurate translations of all titles; and the problem of rank equivalents is compounded by the fact that similar sounding titles may involve different functions in different armies. We have, therefore, produced a comprehensive list of ranks in English, which we have used to translate the ranks of non-English speaking nations. Strictly speaking, each nations' ranks should be treated in isolation, but this list allows us to place most ranks within a broad rank grouping (in the Armies from marshals through generals, field officers, company officers, WOs and NCOs to private ranks), and in many cases to demonstrate accurate equivalents – for example in almost all cases, the rank translated as captain in the Army table will command a company. There is, however, no possibility of absolute equivalence for all ranks. This is most marked for the marshals, NCOs, petty officers in the Navy and senior versions of the basic rank of private or rating. In these cases we have been forced to provide what can at best be an approximate equivalent. The British and US armed forces' ranks are listed separately, to avoid confusion with the main rank list in English; any problems are dealt with in footnotes.

		ARMY/AIR FORCE RANKS IN ENGLISH	BELGIUM ARMY/AIR FORCE	BULGARIA ARMY/AIR FORCE	CHINA ARMY/AIR FORCE	DENMARK ARMY/AIR FORCE
GENERAL OFFs	1	1st Marshal				
	2	Senior Marshal				
	3	(Field) Marshal			T'e chih shang chiang	
	4	General (I)		General	I chi shang chiang	General
	5	General (II)			Erh chi shang chiang	
	6	General (III)				
	7	Lieutenant-General	Lieutenant-Géneral/Luitenant-Generaal	General-leytenant	Chung chiang	Generalløjtnant
	8	Major-General	Géneral-Major/Generaal-Majoor	General-major	Shao chiang	Generalmajor
FLD OFFs	9	Brigadier				
	10	Colonel	Colonel/Kolonel	Polkovnik	Shang hsiao	Oberst
	11	Lieutenant-Colonel	Lieutenant-Colonel/Luitenant-Kolonel	Podpolkovnik	Chung hsiao	Oberstløjtnant
	12	Major	Major/Majoor	Major	Shao hsiao	
COY OFFs	13	Captain (I)	Capitaine-Commandant/Kapitein-Kommandant	Kapitan	Shang wei	Kaptajn
	14	Captain (II)	Capitaine/Kapitein			Kaptajnløjtnant
	15	Lieutenant (I)	Lieutenant/Luitenant	Poruchik	Chung wei	Premierløjtnant
	16	Lieutenant (II)				Løjtnant af reserven
	17	2nd Lieutenant	Sous-Lieutenant/Onder-Luitenant	Podporuchik	Shao wei	Sekundløjtnant
	18	Ensign				
WOs	19	Warrant Officer (I)	Adjudant de 1ère Classe/Adjutant 1e Vilos[1]	Feldfebel	Chun wei	Korpsofficiant
	20	Warrant Officer (II)	Adjudant/Adjutant			Stabsofficiant
	21	Warrant Officer (III)				Overofficiant
	22	Warrant Officer (IV)				Officiant
NCOs	23	Staff Sergeant				
	24	Sergeant-Major	1er Sergent-Major/1e Sergeant-Majoor		Shang shih	Oversergent
	25	Senior Sergeant	Premier Sergent/1e Sergeant			
	26	Sergeant	Sergent/Sergeant	Podofitser	Chung shih	Sergent
	27	Lance-Sergeant				
	28	Staff Corporal				
	29	Corporal-Major				
	30	Corporal	Caporal/Korporaal	Kandidat podofitser	Hsia shih	Korporal
OTHER RANKS	31	Staff Lance-Corporal				
	32	Lance-Corporal-Major				
	33	Senior Lance-Corporal				
	34	Lance-Corporal				Underkorporal
	35	Superior Private			Shang teng ping	
	36	Private 1st Class	Soldat d'élite/Soldaat 1e Klasse	Efreytor	I teng ping	
	37	Private 2nd Class			Erh teng ping	
	38	Private	Soldat/Soldaat	Rednik		Menig
	39	Cadet		Ofitserski kandidat		

		NAVY RANKS IN ENGLISH	NAVY	NAVY	NAVY	NAVY
ADMIRALS	1	Admiral of the Fleet	Officers			
	2	Admiral (Fleet Commander)	as Army ranks			
	3	Admiral		Admiral	Hai-tziun shan-tzian	Admiral
	4	Vice-Admiral (I)		Vitse-admiral	Hai-tziun chzhun-tzian	Vice-Admiral
	5	Vice-Admiral (II)				
	6	Rear-Admiral		Kontr-admiral	Hai-tziun shaotzian	Kontreadmiral
OFFICERS	7	Commodore			Hai-tziun tai chiang	Kommandør
	8	Captain (I)		Kapitan I rang	Hai-tziun shan-tzo	Kommandørkaptajn
	9	Captain (II)				
	10	Captain (III)				
	11	Commander		Kapitan II rang	Hai-tziun chzhun-tzo	Orlogskaptajn
	12	Lieutenant-Commander		Kapitanleitenant	Hai-tziun shao-tzo	Kaptajn-løjtnant
	13	Lieutenant (I)		Mitschman I rang		Søløjtnant af 1'grad[1]
	14	Lieutenant (II)				
	15	Sub-Lieutenant		Mitschman II rang		Søløjtnant af 2'grad
	16	Ensign			Hai-tziun shao-wei	
	17	Midshipman		Ofitserski kandidat		Kadet
POs & RATINGS	18	Chief Warrant Officer				
	19	Warrant Officer	Premiere Maître	Konduktor	Hai-tziun shih	
	20	Chief Petty Officer (I)		Korabnik		Kvartermester I'grad
	21	Chief Petty Officer (II)				Kvartermester 2'grad
	22	Chief Petty Officer (III)				Kvartermester 3'grad
	23	Petty Officer (I)	Maître de 1ère classe	Podofitser	Hai-tziun chong shih	Underkvartermester 1'grac
	24	Petty Officer (II)	Maître de 2ème classe	Kandidat podofitser	Hai-tziun hsiao shih	Underkvartermester 2'grac
	25	Petty Officer (III)	Second Maître			
	26	Petty Officer (IV)				
	27	Boatswain				
	28	Leading Seaman (I)	Quartier Maître	Efreitor	Ye ding ping	
	29	Leading Seaman (II)			Erh deng ping	
	30	Leading Seaman (III)			San deng ping	
	31	Leading Seaman (IV)				
	32	Able Seaman	Matelot breveté		Yi deng lien ping	
	33	Ordinary Seaman				
	34	Seaman	Matelot	Morjak	Erh deng lien ping	Orlogsgast
	35	Cadet				

1 The silver bar on the cuffs and collars of Warrant Officers 1st Class was worn only by those acting as platoon commanders.

1 Between the ranks of Søløjtnant af I'grad and af 2'grad were two grades of engineering officer known as Junior Machine Masters 1st and 2nd Class.

	FINLAND ARMY/AIR FORCE	FRANCE ARMY/AIR FORCE	GERMANY ARMY	GERMANY AIR FORCE
1	Sotamarsalkka			Reichsmarschall
2		Maréchal de France		
3			Generalfeldmarschall	Generalfeldmarschall
4	Kenraali	Général d'Armée	Generaloberst	Generaloberst
5		Général de Corps d'Armée[1]	General der Infanterie etc.[1]	General der Flieger
6				
7	Kenraaliluutnantti	Général de Division	Generalleutnant	Generalleutnant
8	Kenraalimajuri	Général de Brigade	Generalmajor	Generalmajor
9				
10	Eversti	Colonel	Oberst	Oberst
11	Everstiluutnantti	Lieutenant-Colonel	Oberstleutnant	Oberstleutnant
12	Majuri	Chef de Bataillon	Major	Major
13	Kapteeni	Capitaine	Hauptmann/Rittmeister[2]	Hauptmann
14				
15	Luutnantti	Lieutenant	Oberleutnant	Oberleutnant
16				
17	Vänrikki	Sous-Lieutenant	Leutnant	Leutnant
18				
19	Sotilasmestari	Adjudant-Chef		
20		Adjudant		
21				
22				Stabsfeldwebel/Wachtmeister
23			Stabsfeldwebel/Wachtmeister[3]	
24	Vääpeli	Sergent-Chef	Oberfeldwebel/Wachtmeister	Oberfeldwebel/Wachtmeister
25	Ylikersantti		Feldwebel/Wachtmeister	Feldwebel/Wachtmeister
26	Kersantti	Sergent	Unterfeldwebel/Wachtmeister	Unterfeldwebel/Wachtmeister
27	Alikersantti			
28				
29		Caporal-Chef		
30	Korpraali	Caporal	Unteroffizier/Oberjäger[4]	Unteroffizier/Oberjäger
31				Stabsgefreiter[7]
32			Stabsgefreiter	Hauptgefreiter
33			Obergefreiter	Obergefreiter
34			Gefreiter	Gefreiter
35				
36		Soldat de 1ère Classe	Oberschütze	
37				
38	Sotamies	Soldat de 2ème Classe	Schütze	Soldat/Flieger etc.
39		Aspirant		

	NAVY	NAVY	NAVY
1		Amiral de la Flotte[2]	Grossadmiral
2			Generaladmiral[5]
3	Amiraali	Vice-Amiral (chef d'état major)	Admiral
4	Vara-amiraali	Vice-Amiral (commandant en chef)	Vizeadmiral
5		Vice-Amiral	
6	Kontra-amiraali	Contre-Amiral	Konteradmiral
7			Kommodore
8	Kommodori	Capitaine de Vaisseau	Kapitän zur See
9			
10			
11	Komentaja	Capitaine de Frégate	Fregattenkapitän[6]
12	Komentajakapteeni	Capitaine de Corvette	Korvettenkapitän
13	Kapteeniluutnantti	Lieutenant de Vaisseau	Kapitänleutnant
14		Enseigne de Vaisseau de 1ère Classe	Oberleutnant zur See
15	Luutnantti	Enseigne de Vaisseau de 2ème Classe	Leutnant zur See
16	Aliluutnantti		
17			
18		Maître-Principal	
19	Erikoismestari (I, II/III, IV Cl.)	Premier-Maître	
20	Pursimies	Maître	Stabsoberfeldwebel
21			Oberfeldwebel
22			
23	Ylikersantti	Second-Maître[3]	Stabsfeldwebel
24	Kersantti	Second-Maître	Feldwebel etc.
25	Alikersantti		Obermaat
26			Maat
27			
28	Ylimatrussi	Quartier-Maître de 1ère Classe	Matrosenoberstabsgefreiter
29		Quartier-Maître de 2ème Classe	Matrosenstabsgefreiter
30			Matrosenhauptgefreiter
31			Matrosenobergefreiter
32		Matelot breveté	Matrosengefreiter
33			Matrose
34	Matrussi	Matelot	
35			

1 Air Force designation: General Commandant un Région.
2 Officers of admiral rank wore five-pointed stars on the peaked cap according to rank.
3 Following two years' service new rank badges issued but rank title remained Second-Maître.

1 Other arms were artillery, cavalry and panzer troops.
2 Hauptmann redesignated as Rittmeister in transport and cavalry.
3 Feldwebel ranks redesignated Wachtmeister in cavalry, artillery, Flak, mounted signals and transport.
4 Unteroffizier redesignated Oberjäger in mountain rifle units.
5 A Generaladmiral serving as Navy C-in-C wore four cuff rings.
6 A Fregattenkapitän had four cuff rings until 1-8-1940, thereafter three medium rings. On 1-4-1944, regulations prescribed three medium and one narrow ring.
7 A new rank of Stabsgefreiter introduced on 4-2-1944, while the rank of Hauptgefreiter was abolished on 12-5-1944.

		ARMY/AIR FORCE RANKS IN ENGLISH	GERMANY WAFFEN-SS	GREECE ARMY	GREECE AIRFORCE	HUNGARY ARMY/AIR FORCE
GENERAL OFFs	1	1st Marshal				
	2	Senior Marshal				
	3	(Field) Marshal		Stratigos[1]		Tábornagy
	4	General (I)	SS-Oberstgruppenfuhrer u.Gen.Obst.d.W-SS[1]	Archistratigos	Pterarchos	Vezérezredes
	5	General (II)	SS-Obergruppenführer u.Gen.d.W-SS			
	6	General (III)				
	7	Lieutenant-General	SS-Gruppenführer u.Gen.Lt.d.W-SS	Antistratigos	Antipterarchos	Altábornagy
	8	Major-General	SS-Brigadeführer u.Gen.Maj.d.W-SS	Ypostratigos	Ypopterarchos	Vezérőrnagy
FLD OFFs	9	Brigadier	SS-Oberführer		Taxiarchos Aeroporias	
	10	Colonel	SS-Standartenführer	Syntagmatarchis	Sminarchos	Ezredes
	11	Lieutenant-Colonel	SS-Obersturmbannführer	Antisyntagmatarchis	Antisminarchos	Alezredes
	12	Major	SS-Sturmbannführer	Tagmatarchis	Episminagos	Őrnagy
COY OFFs	13	Captain (I)	SS-Hauptsturmführer	Lochagos	Sminagos	Százados
	14	Captain (II)				
	15	Lieutenant (I)	SS-Obertsturmführer	Ypolochagos	Yposminagos	Főhadnagy
	16	Lieutenant (II)				
	17	2nd Lieutenant	SS-Untersturmführer	Anthypolochagos	Anthyposminarchos	Hadnagy
	18	Ensign				
WOs	19	Warrant Officer (I)		Monimos Anthypaspistis	Archisminias	Alhadnagy
	20	Warrant Officer (II)				
	21	Warrant Officer (III)				
	22	Warrant Officer (IV)				
NCOs	23	Staff Sergeant	SS-Sturmscharführer			Főtörsőrmester
	24	Sergeant-Major	SS-Hauptscharführer	Monimos Epilochias	Episminias	Törzsőrmester
	25	Senior Sergeant	SS-Oberscharführer			
	26	Sergeant	SS-Scharführer	Monimos Lochias	Sminias	Őrmester
	27	Lance-Sergeant				
	28	Staff Corporal				
	29	Corporal-Major				Szakaszvezető
	30	Corporal	SS-Unterscharführer	Monimos Dekaneus	Yposminias A	Tizedes
OTHER RANKS	31	Staff Lance-Corporal				
	32	Lance-Corporal-Major				
	33	Senior Lance-Corporal	SS-Rottenführer			
	34	Lance-Corporal	SS-Sturmmann	Efredos Dekaneus	Yposminias B	
	35	Superior Private				
	36	Private 1st Class	SS-Oberschütze			Őrvezető
	37	Private 2nd Class				
	38	Private	SS-Schütze	Stratiotis	Sminitis	Honvéd
	39	Cadet				Zászlós

		NAVY RANKS IN ENGLISH		NAVY		NAVY
ADMIRALS	1	Admiral of the Fleet		Archinávarchos[2]		
	2	Admiral (Fleet Commander)				
	3	Admiral		Návarchos		
	4	Vice-Admiral (I)		Antinávarchos		Vezérfőkapitány
	5	Vice-Admiral (II)				
	6	Rear-Admiral		Yponávarchos		Vezérkapitany
OFFICERS	7	Commodore				
	8	Captain (I)		Pluiarchos		Főtörzskapitány
	9	Captain (II)		Antipluiarchos		
	10	Captain (III)				
	11	Commander		Plutatarchos		Törzskapitány
	12	Lieutenant-Commander		Ypopliarchos		Törzsalkapitány
	13	Lieutenant (I)		Antiplupliarchos		Kapitány
	14	Lieutenant (II)				Főhajónagy
	15	Sub-Lieutenant		Semaiuphóros		Hajónagy
	16	Ensign				Folyami zászlós
	17	Midshipman				
POs & RATINGS	18	Chief Warrant Officer		Archikeleustes A		Alhajónagy
	19	Warrant Officer		Archikeleustes B		Főtörzshajómester
	20	Chief Petty Officer (I)		Keleustes		Törzshajómester
	21	Chief Petty Officer (II)				
	22	Chief Petty Officer (III)				
	23	Petty Officer (I)		Ypokeleustes A		Hajómester
	24	Petty Officer (II)		Ypokeleustes B		Szakaszvezető
	25	Petty Officer (III)		Dókimos ypokeleustes		Tizedes
	26	Petty Officer (IV)				
	27	Boatswain				
	28	Leading Seaman (I)		Diopos[3]		
	29	Leading Seaman (II)				
	30	Leading Seaman (III)				
	31	Leading Seaman (IV)				
	32	Able Seaman		Náftis A		Őrvezető
	33	Ordinary Seaman		Náftis B		
	34	Seaman				Honvéd
	35	Cadet				

1 General officers in the Waffen-SS used both SS and military rank titles.

1 The Marshal's shoulder strap was that of the monarch with the royal cypher worn under the crossed batons.
2 The shoulder strap for Admiral of the Fleet was worn by the King with the royal cypher.
3 Red chevrons of Leading and Able Seaman were for conscripts; regulars had gold chevrons.

	ITALY ARMY	ITALY AIR FORCE	JAPAN ARMY/AIR FORCE	NETHERLANDS ARMY/AIR FORCE
1	1° Marescillo dell'Impero			
2	Maresciallo d'Italia	Maresciallo dell Avia		
3			Gen-sui	
4	Generale d'armata	Generale d'armata Aerea	Tai-shō	Generaal
5	Generale di C.A.designato d'armata	Generale di Corpo d'armata Aerea		
6	Generale di Corpo d'armata	Generale di Squadra Aerea		
7	Generale di Divisione	Generale di Divisione Aerea	Chū-jō	Luitenant-generaal
8	Generale di Brigata	Generale di Brigata Aerea	Shō-shō	Generaal-majoor
9				
10	Colonnello	Colonnello	Tai-sa	Kolonel
11	Tenente Colonnello	Tenente Colonnello	Chū-sa	Luitenant-kolonel
12	Maggiore	Maggiore	Shō-sa	Majoor
13	1° Capitano	1° Capitano	Tai-i	Kapitein
14	Capitano	Capitano		
15	1° Tenente	1° Tenente	Chū-i	Eerste-luitenant
16	Tenente	Tenente		
17	Sottotenente	Sottotenente	Shō-i	Tweede-luitenant
18				
19	Aiutante di Battaglia[1]	Aiutante di Battaglia[1]	Tokumo sō-chō	Adjudant-onder-officier
20	Maresciallo Maggiore	Maresciallo Maggiore		
21	Maresciallo Capo	Maresciallo Capo		
22	Maresciallo ordinario	Maresciallo ordinario		
23				
24	Sergente Maggiore	Sergente Maggiore	Sō-chō	Sergeant-majoor[1]
25				Sergeant ter 1e klasse
26	Sergente	Sergente	Gun-sō	Sergeant
27				
28				
29	Corporale Maggiore	Primo Aviere		
30	Corporale	Aviere scelto	Go-chō	Korporaal
31				
32				
33				
34			Go-chō kimmu jōtō hei	
35			Jōtō hei	
36	Appuntato[2]		Ittō hei	Soldaat ter 1e klasse
37			Nitō hei	
38	Soldato	Aviere		Soldaat
39				

	NAVY	NAVY	NAVY/MARINES
1	Grande Ammiraglio		Admiraal
2			
3	Ammiraglio d'armata	Taishō	Luitenant-admiraal
4	Ammiraglio designato d'armata	Chujō	Vice-admiraal
5	Ammiraglio di Squadra		
6	Ammiraglio di Divisione	Chōshō	Schout-bij-nacht
7	Contrammiraglio		
8	Capitano di Vascello	Taisa	Kapitein ter zee
9			
10			
11	Capitano di Fregata	Chūsa	Kapitein-luitenant ter zee
12	Capitano di Corvetta	Shōsa	Luitenant ter zee 1e klasse
13	1° Tenente	Dai-i	Luitenant ter zee 2e klasse
14	Tenente di Vascello		
15	Sottotenente di Vascello	Chū-i	Luitenant ter zee 3e klasse
16		Shō-i	
17		Shō-i Kōhosei	
18			
19	Cap di 1a, 2a, 3a classe	Seito	Opper schipper/Adjudant-onder-officier
20		Jōtō heisō	Schipper/Sergeant-majoor
21			
22			
23	Secondo capo	Ittō heisō	Bootsman/Sergeant
24	Sottocapo	Nitō heisō	
25			
26			
27			
28	Marinaio comune di 1a classe	Heichō	Kwartiermeester/Korporaal
29	Marinaio comune di 2a classe	Jotō hei	
30			
31			
32	Marinaio comune di 3a classe	Ittō hei	Matroos 1e klasse
33			Matroos 2e klasse
34			Matroos 3e klasse
35			

1 In September 1917 the rank of Auitante di Battaglia was introduced and other ranks could be promoted to this rank for exceptional acts of bravery.
2 Appuntato was a cavalry rank, indicated on the uniform by a single red stripe.

1 The silver crown worn on the cuff by the Sergeant-Major was not a badge of rank, but signified that the wearer was an instructor.

		ARMY/AIR FORCE RANKS IN ENGLISH	NORWAY ARMY/AIR FORCE	POLAND ARMY/AIR FORCE	ROMANIA ARMY	ROMANIA AIR FORCE[1]
GENERAL OFFs	1	1st Marshal				
	2	Senior Marshal		Marszałek Polski	Maresal al Romînia	
	3	(Field) Marshal				
	4	General (I)	General	Generał Broni	General de armată	
	5	General (II)			General de corp de armată	
	6	General (III)				
	7	Lieutenant-General	Generalløytnant	Generał Dywizji	General de divizie	General comandant
	8	Major-General	Generalmajor	Generał Brygady	General de brigadă	General de escadră
FLD OFFs	9	Brigadier				
	10	Colonel	Oberst	Pułkownik	Colonel	Comandor
	11	Lieutenant-Colonel	Oberstløytnant	Podpułkownik	Locotenent-colonel	Capitan-comandor
	12	Major	Major	Major	Maior	Locotenent-comandor
COY OFFs	13	Captain (I)	Kaptein	Kapitan	Căpitan	Căpitan
	14	Captain (II)				
	15	Lieutenant (I)	Løytnant	Porucznik	Locotenent	Locotenent
	16	Lieutenant (II)				
	17	2nd Lieutenant	Fenrik	Podporucznik	Sublocotenent	Sublocotenent
	18	Ensign				
WOs	19	Warrant Officer (I)		Chorąży	Plutonier adjutant	Adjutant şef aviator
	20	Warrant Officer (II)			Plutonier maior	Adjutant maior aviator
	21	Warrant Officer (III)			Plutonier	Adjutant aviator
	22	Warrant Officer (IV)				Adjutant stagiar aviator
NCOs	23	Staff Sergeant	Stabsersjant[1]			
	24	Sergeant-Major		Starszy Sierżant	Sergent maior	
	25	Senior Sergeant				
	26	Sergeant	Sersjant	Sierżant	Sergent	Sergent
	27	Lance-Sergeant		Plutonowy		
	28	Staff Corporal				
	29	Corporal-Major				
	30	Corporal	Korporal	Kapral	Caporal	Caporal
OTHER RANKS	31	Staff Lance-Corporal				
	32	Lance-Corporal-Major				
	33	Senior Lance-Corporal				
	34	Lance-Corporal	Visekorporal	Starszy Szeregowiec	Fruntas	Fruntaş
	35	Superior Private				
	36	Private 1st Class				
	37	Private 2nd Class				
	38	Private	Menig	Szeregowiec	Soldat	Soldat
	39	Cadet		Aspirant[1]		

		NAVY RANKS IN ENGLISH	NAVY	NAVY	NAVY
ADMIRALS	1	Admiral of the Fleet		Admirał	
	2	Admiral (Fleet Commander)			
	3	Admiral	Admiral		Amiral
	4	Vice-Admiral (I)	Viseadmiral	Wiceadmirał	Vice-amiral
	5	Vice-Admiral (II)			
	6	Rear-Admiral	Kontreadmiral	Kontradmirał	Contraamiral
OFFICERS	7	Commodore	Kommandør		
	8	Captain (I)	Kommandørkaptein	Komandor	Comandor
	9	Captain (II)			
	10	Captain (III)			
	11	Commander	Orlogskaptein	Komandor Podporucznik	Căpitan-comandor
	12	Lieutenant-Commander	Kapteinløytnant	Kapitan Marynarki	Locotenent-comandor
	13	Lieutenant (I)	Løytnant	Porucznik Marynarki	Căpitan de marină
	14	Lieutenant (II)			Locotenent de marină
	15	Sub-Lieutenant	Fenrik	Podporucznik Marynarki	
	16	Ensign			
	17	Midshipman			Aspirent de marină
POs & RATINGS	18	Chief Warrant Officer			Plutonier maior
	19	Warrant Officer		Chorąży	Plutonier
	20	Chief Petty Officer (I)	Flaggkvartermester	Starszy Bosman	Sergent maior
	21	Chief Petty Officer (II)		Bosman	
	22	Chief Petty Officer (III)			
	23	Petty Officer (I)	Kvartermester 1 kl[2]	Bosmanmat	Sergent
	24	Petty Officer (II)	Kvartermester 2 kl		
	25	Petty Officer (III)	Kvartermester 3 kl		
	26	Petty Officer (IV)			
	27	Boatswain			
	28	Leading Seaman (I)	Konstabel 1 kl	Mat	Caporal
	29	Leading Seaman (II)	Konstabel 2 kl		
	30	Leading Seaman (III)	Konstabel 3 kl		
	31	Leading Seaman (IV)			
	32	Able Seaman	Ledende dekksmann	Starszy Marynarz	Marinar frinklas
	33	Ordinary Seaman	Dekksmann		
	34	Seaman	Menig	Marynarz	Marinar
	35	Cadet	Kadet		

Norway: *1 At the beginning of the war there were only two grades of NCO: Sersjant and Korporal, as illustrated in the insignia chart.*
2 Conscripted Petty Officers wore red chevrons on the cuffs whereas regular Petty Officers wore gold.

Poland: *1 The rank of Aspirant was only used in the Polish Army in France and Great Britain.*

Romania: *1 A special rank of General of the Air Force was instituted for King Michael of Romania which was distinguished by one broad, one medium and three narrow gold lace rings worn on the cuffs.*

	SOVIET UNION ARMY/AIR FORCE 1939–40[1]	SOVIET UNION ARMY/AIR FORCE 1940–1945	YUGOSLAVIA ARMY/AIR FORCE
1	Marshal Sovetskogo Soyuza	Marshal Sovetskogo Soyuza	
2		Glavnyy marshal (artilleriyi, etc.)	
3		Marshal (aviatsiyi, etc.)	Vojvoda
4	Komandarm pervogo ranga	General armiyi	Armijski djeneral
5	Komandarm vtorogo ranga	General polkovnik	
6	Komandir korpusa		
7	Komandir diviziyi	General leytenant	Divizijski djeneral
8	Komandir brigady	General major	Brigadni djeneral
9			
10	Polkovnik	Polkovnik	Pukovnik
11		Podpolkovnik	Potpukovnik
12	Major	Major	Major
13	Kapitan	Kapitan	Kapetan I klase
14			Kapetan II klase
15	Starshiy leytenant	Starshiy leytenant	Poručnik
16	Leytenant	Leytenant	
17	Mladshiy leytenant	Mladshiy leytenant	Podporučnik
18			
19			
20			
21			
22			
23			
24	Starshina	Starshina	Narednik vodnik I, II, III klase
25	Starshiy serzhant	Starshiy serzhant	Narednik
26	Serzhant	Serzhant	Podnarednik
27	Mladshiy serzhant	Mladshiy serzhant	
28			
29			
30	Yefreytor	Yefreytor	Kaplar
31			
32			
33			
34			
35			
36			
37			
38	Krasnoarmeyets	Krasnoarmeyets	Redov
39			

	NAVY 1940–43	NAVY 1943–45[2]	NAVY
1	Flagman flota pervogo ranga	Admiral flota	
2			
3	Flagman flota vtorogo ranga	Admiral	Admiral
4	Flagman pervogo ranga	Vitse-admiral	Vice-admiral
5			
6	Flagman vtorogo ranga	Kontr-admiral	Kontra-admiral
7			
8	Kapitan pervogo ranga	Kapitan pervogo ranga	Kapetan bojnog broda
9	Kapitan vtorogo ranga	Kapitan vtorogo ranga	
10	Kapitan tret'yego ranga	Kapitan tret'yego ranga	
11			Kapetan fregate
12	Kapitan-leytenant	Kapitan-leytenant	Kapetan korvete
13	Starshiy-leytenant	Starshiy-leytenant	Poručnik bojnog broda I klase
14	Leytenant	Leytenant	Poručnik bojnog broda II klase
15	Mladshiy-leytenant	Mladshiy-leytenant	Poručnik fregate/korvete
16			Poručnik
17		Michmann	
18			
19	Starshina		
20	Starshiy komandir zvod	Glavnyy starshina	Narednik vodnik I klase
21			Narednik vodnik II klase
22			Narednik vodnik III klase
23	Komandir otdeleniya	Starshina pervoy stat'i	Narednik
24		Starshina vtoroy stat'i	Podnarednik
25			
26			
27			
28		Starshiy krasnoflotets	Kaplar
29			
30			
31			
32			
33			
34	Krasnoflotets	Krasnoflotets	Mornar
35			

1 The infantry arm-of-service badge (crossed rifles over a white enamel target) was rarely worn and was abolished for all but units of NKVD infantry with the re-introduction of shoulder boards.
2 Following the re-introduction of shoulder boards rank distinction lace was worn only by line officers while officers serving in non-line branches wore shoulder boards and used Army rank titles.

GREAT BRITAIN

ARMY	AIR FORCE	NAVY	MARINES
Field-Marshal	Marshal of the R.A.F.	Admiral of the Fleet	General
General	Air Chief Marshal	Admiral	Lieutenant-General
Lieutenant-General	Air Marshal	Vice-Admiral	Major-General
Major-General	Air Vice Marshal	Rear-Admiral	Brigadier
Brigadier	Air Commodore	Commodore 1st Class	Colonel
Colonel	Group Captain	Commodore 2nd Class	Lieutenant-Colonel
Lieutenant-Colonel	Wing Commander	Captain	Major
Major	Squadron Leader	Commander	Captain
Captain	Flight Lieutenant	Lieutenant Commander	Lieutenant
Lieutenant	Flying Officer	Lieutenant	2nd Lieutenant/Commissioned W.O.
2nd Lieutenant	Pilot Officer	Sub-Lieutenant	Warrant Officer
Warrant Officer 1	Warrant Officer[1]	Commissioned Warrant Officer	Quartermaster-Sergeant
Staff Sergeant-Major etc.	Flight Sergeant	Warrant Officer	Colour-Sergeant
Regimental Sergeant-Major	Sergeant	Chief Petty Officer	Sergeant
Warrant Officer 2	Corporal	Petty Officer	Corporal
Regtl. Quartermaster Sgt.	Leading Aircraftman	Leading Rating	Lance-Corporal
Company Sergeant-Major	Aircraftman 1st class	Able Seaman	Marine
Warrant Officer 3	Aircraftman 2nd class	Ordinary Seamen	
Platoon Sergeant-Major			
Colour Sergeant etc.			
Sergeant			
Corporal/Lance-Sergeant			
Corporal/Bombardier			
Private/Lance-Corporal etc.			
Private etc.			

UNITED STATES

ARMY/AIR FORCE 1941	ARMY/AIR FORCE 1945	NAVY	MARINE CORPS 1945
General of the Armies of the United States	General of the Army	Admiral of the Fleet[3]	General
General	General	Admiral	Lieutenant-General
Lieutenant-General	Lieutenant-General	Vice-Admiral	Major-General
Major-General	Major-General	Rear-Admiral	Brigadier-General
Brigadier-General	Brigadier-General	Commodore	Colonel
Colonel	Colonel	Captain	Lieutenant-Colonel
Lieutenant-Colonel	Lieutenant-Colonel	Commander	Major
Major	Major	Lieutenant-Commander	Captain
Captain	Captain	Lieutenant	First Lieutenant
First Lieutenant	First Lieutenant	Lieutenant junior grade	Second Lieutenant
Second Lieutenant	Second Lieutenant	Ensign	Commissioned Warrant Officer
Chief Warrant Officer	Chief Warrant Officer	Midshipman	Warrant Officer
Warrant Officer junior grade	Warrant Officer junior grade	Warrant Officer	Sergeant Major etc.
Master Sergeant	Master Sergeant	Chief Petty Officer	First Sergeant
First Sergeant	First Sergeant	Petty Officer 1st class	Technical Sergeant
Technical Sergeant	Technical Sergeant	Petty Officer 2nd class	Staff Sergeant
Staff Sergeant	Staff Sergeant	Petty Officer 3rd class	Sergeant
Sergeant	Sergeant	Seaman 1st class	Corporal
Corporal	Corporal	Seaman 2nd class	Private first class
Private first class	Private first class	Seaman 3rd class	Private
Private	Private		

1 Warrant Officers wore a metal version of the officers' rank badge on the peaked cap. The rank of Warrant Officer 2nd Class only existed in the Royal Canadian Air Force.

3 The rank of Admiral of the Fleet (with five stars) was introduced on 14-12-1944.

GLOSSARY OF TERMS USED

AIGUILLETTE metallic plaited cords worn over the shoulder by general staff officers, aide-de-camps and adjutants; see figure 293.

ANKLETS covering for the ankle, buckled or buttoned at the side; see figures 336, 347.

BATTLEDRESS standard British field uniform introduced in 1937; see page 63 and figure 66.

BUSTINA Italian side cap; see figure 88.

CAP COMFORTER small woollen item of head-dress; see figure 263.

CELLULAR CLOTH fabric with a very open weave, i.e. aertex, especially suitable for humid conditions.

CHECHIA cylindrical felt head-gear, worn by colonial troops; see figure 165.

CHINO items of US Class C uniform, in a light-khaki cotton twill cloth; see figures 176, 354.

COTTON DUCK heavy, durable cotton fabric of plain close weave.

CURL loop on the uppermost row of lace on the cuffs or shoulder straps of naval uniforms; see figure 79.

DJELLABAH loose gown, often with hood, worn by North African troops; see figures 160, 168.

DOGS small metal badge worn on the collar.

EXECUTIVE BRANCH see line branch.

FASCIO lictor's symbol in ancient Rome (axes contained in a tight bundle of bound twigs) adopted by Mussolini's regime.

FATIGUES clothing worn to carry out duties involving manual work; see figure 172.

FEZ form of felt head-dress worn by colonial troops; see figure 159.

FIELD BLOUSE (*feldbluse*) basic tunic of German Army introduced in 1936; see figures 3, 5.

FIELD CAP soft head-dress worn on active service instead of the steel helmet; see figure 301.

FIELD UNIFORM order of dress worn on active service.

FLYING BLOUSE (*fliegerbluse*) short jacket designed to be worn by the Luftwaffe under the flying suit; see figure 10.

FOURRAGÈRE, plaited cord worn on the shoulder; see figure 56.

FROG device for attaching a bayonet or sword to a belt; see figure 80.

GAITERS covering for the ankle (and sometimes lower leg up to the knee), usually buttoned or laced and often strapped under the instep; see figures 53, 170, 177.

GLADIO symbol of a sword through a wreath, used as emblem by the Italian Social Republic; see figures 106, 107.

GORGET small metal shield worn around the neck as a mark of duty; see figure 124.

HERRINGBONE TWILL fabric used by the US armed forces but found unsuitable for humid conditions; see figures 345, 365.

HORIZON BLUE (*horizon bleu*) standard colour of French Army uniform before 1935.

KEPI soft peaked cap, usually cylindrical in shape; see figures 52, 167.

KHAKI DRILL strong khaki-coloured linen or cotton cloth; see figures 146, 347.

LAMPASSEN double stripe with piping between on the breeches or trousers of certain uniforms; see figures 1, 6.

LANYARD cord worn round the neck, usually to hold a whistle, knife or pistol; see figures 144, 254.

LIGHTS colours between the lace rings on the cuffs and shoulder straps of naval uniforms denoting branch; see figure 79.

LINE BRANCH or EXECUTIVE BRANCH that branch of the Navy responsible for the actual sailing and running of the ship as opposed to the technical and administrative branch.

LITZEN lace worn on the collar patches of German uniforms; see figure 1.

LOUISE BLUE very dark blue uniform colour adopted by the French Air Force in 1934; see figure 55.

MACKINAW short, lined coat used by US Army; see figure 171.

PASSANTS small strips of cloth decorated with lace or embroidery, worn across the shoulder, and holding the full-dress epaulette in place; see figures 58, 101.

PEA-COAT short overcoat worn by naval personnel.

PUGGREE Indian word for a turban; see figure 147. The Puggree was later adopted by Europeans for wear on the sun helmet and bush hat; see figures 155, 156.

PUTTEES protection for the ankle and lower leg, consisting of a strip of cloth wound around the leg; see figures 62, 63, 326.

REEFER JACKET standard double-breasted open jacket worn by officers and petty officers of most navies; see figure 101.

SAHARIANA practical, comfortable khaki drill jacket, part of Italian tropical uniform; see figure 87.

SERVICE DRESS order of dress worn when carrying out official duties other than on active service.

SIDE CAP soft head-dress without peak designed to be folded flat when not worn; in Great Britain also known as Field-Service cap; see figures 69, 70.

SIRICAL TROUSERS baggy trousers, usually gathered at the ankle; see figure 94.

SLIDES removable cloth slide worn on the shoulder strap on which badges of rank and other insignia were mounted; see figure 339.

SQUARE RIG standard sailors' dress for wear by ratings in most navies; see figures 24, 43, 78. The phrase originates from the basic arrangement of sails on warships before the age of steam.

STAND COLLAR, STAND-AND-FALL COLLAR two main types of collar. Compare the collars of figures 202 and 203.

SUBSTANTIVE, NON-SUBSTANTIVE substantive badges were for a permanent rank, whereas non-substantive badges denoted a trade or qualification; see figure 78.

TALLY a black ribbon with lettering worn around the cap of a naval rating; see figures 39, 43.

TARBUSH also known as a fez, felt head-dress worn by colonial troops; see figure 159.

TOPEE head-gear worn as part of the tropical uniform of some nations; see figures 156, 162, 164.

WAFFENFARBE arm-of-service colours in the German armed forces.

WALKING-OUT DRESS order of dress worn off duty.

WEBBING strong fabric of cotton, jute or other fibres woven into strips; used instead of leather to carry basic personal equipment; see figure 340.

WHITES white clothing worn by navies as tropical uniform; see figures 145, 320.

INDEX

Pages numbers in italics refer to illustrations